S0-DFK-379

The Heritage of World Civilizations

VOLUME B: FROM 1300 TO 1800

SIXTH EDITION

Albert M. Craig
Harvard University
William A. Graham
Harvard University
Donald Kagan
Yale University
Steven Ozment
Harvard University
Frank M. Turner
Yale University

Prentice Hall

UPPER SADDLE RIVER, NJ 07458

Library of Congress Cataloging–in–Publication Data

The heritage of world civilizations/ Albert M. Craig... [et al.].—
Combined ed., 6th ed.
p. cm.
Includes bibliographical references and index.
ISBN 0-13-098796-4
1. Civilization—History. I. Craig, Albert M.
CB69.H45 2002b
909—dc21 20022018790

Editorial Director: Charlyce Jones Owen
Senior Acquisitions Editor: Charles Cavaliere
Associate Editor: Emsal Hasan
Editor-in-Chief, Development: Susanna Lesan
AVP, Director of Production
and Manufacturing: Barbara Kittle
Production Editor: Louise Rothman
Manufacturing Manager: Nick Sklitsis
Prepress and Manufacturing Buyer: Sherry Lewis
Director of Marketing: Beth Mejia
Marketing Manager: Claire Bitting
Creative Design Director: Leslie Osher
Art Director, Interior,
and Cover Designer: Ximena P. Tamvakopoulos
Cover Art: Buddha Head/Ric Ergenbright/CORBIS
Interior Image Specialist: Beth Boyd-Brenzel
Cover Image Specialist: Karen Sanatar
Photo Research: Elaine Soares
Image Permission Coordinator: Michelina Viscusi
Manager, Production, Formatting, and Art: Guy Ruggiero
Electronic Page Layout: Wanda España
and Scott Garrison
Cartographers: GEOSYSTEMS, Mirella Signoretto
Editorial Assistant: Adrienne Paul

This book was set in 10/12.5 Caslon 540 by the HSS in-house formatting and production services group and was printed and bound by Quebecor World. The cover was printed by Phoenix Color Corp.

Prentice Hall

© 2003, 2000, 1997, 1994, 1990, 1986 by Pearson Education
Upper Saddle River, New Jersey 07458

All rights reserved. No part of this book may be reproduced, in any form or by any means, without permission in writing from the publisher.

Printed in the United States of America
10 9 8 7 6 5 4 3 2 1

ISBN 0-13-098809-X

Pearson Education Ltd., London
Pearson Education Australia Pty., Limited, Sydney
Pearson Education Singapore, Pte., Ltd.
Pearson Education North Asia Ltd., Hong Kong
Pearson Education Canada, Ltd., Toronto
Pearson Educación de Mexico, S.A. de C.V.
Pearson Education—Tokyo, Japan
Pearson Education Malaysia, Pte., Ltd.
Pearson Eudcation, Upper Saddle River, New Jersey

The Heritage of World Civilizations

Brief Contents

13 The Islamic Heartlands and India (ca. 1000–1500) 336

ART AND THE WORLD: THE ALHAMBRA 344

14 Ancient Civilizations of the Americas 358

ART AND THE WORLD: MESOAMERICAN ART 376

15 Europe to the Early 1500s: Revival, Decline, and Renaissance 384

ART AND THE WORLD: IMAGES OF DEATH IN THE LATE MIDDLE AGES 402

PART IV — THE WORLD IN TRANSITION 416

16 The Age of Reformation and Religious Wars 420

ART AND THE WORLD: WARRING ARCHITECTURAL STYLES: BAROQUE VERSUS PLAIN CHURCHES 448

RELIGIONS OF THE WORLD: CHRISTIANITY 458

17 Africa (ca. 1000–1800) 460

ART AND THE WORLD: BENIN AND IFE "BRONZES" 472

18 Conquest and Exploitation: The Development of the Transatlantic Economy 484

ART AND THE WORLD: A DRAMATIC MOMENT IN THE TRANSATLANTIC WORLD: COPLEY'S "WATSON AND THE SHARK" 502

19 East Asia in the Late Traditional Era 512

ART AND THE WORLD: UTAMARO WOODBLOCK PRINT 540

20 European State-Building and Worldwide Conflict 554

ART AND THE WORLD: RACHEL RUYSCH, "FLOWER STILL LIFE": FLOWERS, COMMERCE, AND MORALITY 558

21 European Society Under the Old Regime 580

ART AND THE WORLD: "THE BREAKFAST" AND "THE RETURN FROM MARKET": TWO SCENES OF DOMESTIC LIFE 590

22 The Last Great Islamic Empires (1500–1800) 604

ART AND THE WORLD: SHAH-NAMEH, BOOK OF KINGS 618

PART V — ENLIGHTENMENT AND REVOLUTION IN THE WEST 624

23 The Age of European Enlightenment 628

ART AND THE WORLD: JOSEPH WRIGHT, "AN EXPERIMENT ON A BIRD IN THE AIR-PUMP": SCIENCE IN THE DRAWING ROOM 636

24 Revolutions in the Transatlantic World 654

ART AND THE WORLD: FRANCISCO GOYA MEMORIALIZES A NIGHT OF EXECUTIONS: "THE THIRD OF MAY, 1808" 670

Contents

Preface xxi

13 The Islamic Heartlands and India (ca. 1000–1500) 336

Religion and Society 337
- Consolidation of Sunni Orthopraxy 337
- Sufi Piety and Organization 338
- Consolidation of Shi'ite Traditions 339

Regional Developments 340
- The Islamic West: Spain and North Africa 340
- The Islamic West: Egypt and the Eastern Mediterranean World 341

ART AND THE WORLD: THE ALHAMBRA 344

- The Islamic East: Before the Mongol Conquests 346
- The Islamic East: The Mongol Age 347

The Spread of Islam Beyond the Heartlands 348
The Spread of Islam to India 349
Muslim-Hindu Encounter 349
Islamic States and Dynasties 350
Religious and Cultural Accomodation 351
Hindu and Other Indian Traditions 352
In World Perspective: The Islamic Heartlands and India, 1000—1500 356
Review Questions 356
Suggested Readings 356

14 Ancient Civilizations of the Americas 358

Problems in Reconstructing the History of Native American Civilization 359
Mesoamerica 360
The Formative Period and the Emergence of Mesoamerican Civilization 361
- The Olmec 361
- The Valley of Oaxaca and the Rise of Monte Alban 363

The Classic Period in Mesoamerica 363
- Teotihuacán 363
- The Maya 365

The Post-Classic Period 368
- The Toltecs 368
- The Aztecs 368

Andean South America 373
The Preceramic and the Initial Period 374
Chavín de Huantar and the Early Horizon 375
The Early Intermediate Period 375
- Nazca 375
- Moche 375

ART AND THE WORLD: MESOAMERICAN ART 376

The Middle Horizon Through the Late Intermediate Period 378
- Tiwanaku and Huari 378
- The Chimu Empire 378

The Inca Empire 379
In World Perspective: Ancient Civilizations of the Americas 381
Review Questions 381
Suggested Readings 382

15 Europe to the Early 1500s: Revival, Decline, and Renaissance 384

Revival of Empire, Church, and Towns 385

Otto I and the Revival of the Empire 385
The Reviving Catholic Church 386
The First Crusade 387
Towns and Townspeople 388
Society 391
The Order of Life 391
Medieval Women 394
Growth of National Monarchies 395
England and France: Hastings (1066) to Bouvines (1214) 395
France in the Thirteenth Century: Reign of Louis IX 395
The Hohenstaufen Empire (1152–1272) 397
Political and Social Breakdown 397
Hundred Years' War 397
The Black Death 397
Ecclesiastical Breakdown and Revival: The Late Medieval Church 400
Boniface VIII and Philip the Fair 400
The Great Schism (1378–1417) and the Conciliar Movement to 1449 400
The Renaissance in Italy (1375–1527) 401
The Italian City-State: Social Conflict and Despotism 401
ART AND THE WORLD: IMAGES OF DEATH IN THE LATE MIDDLE AGES 402
Humanism 404
Renaissance Art 405
Italy's Political Decline: The French Invasions (1494–1527) 407
Charles VIII's March Through Italy 407
Niccolò Machiavelli 408
Revival of Monarchy: Nation Building in the Fifteenth Century 409
Medieval Russia 410
France 410
Spain 411
England 411
In World Perspective: The High Middle Ages 412
Review Questions 413
Suggested Readings 413

PART IV — THE WORLD IN TRANSITION 416

16 The Age of Reformation and Religious Wars 420

On the Eve of the Reformation 422
The Discovery of a New World 422
Religion and Society 424
The Northern Renaissance 425
The Reformation 426
Martin Luther and the German Reformation to 1525 426
Zwingli and the Swiss Reformation 428
Anabaptists and Radical Protestants 429
John Calvin and the Genevan Reformation 431
Political Consolidation of the Lutheran Reformation 432
The English Reformation to 1553 432
Catholic Reform and Counter-Reformation 435
The Reformation'a Achievements 437
The Revolution in Religious Practices and Institutions 437
The Reformation and the Changing Role of Women 437
The Wars of Religion 439
French Wars of Religion (1562–1598) 440
Imperial Spain and the Reign of Philip II (1556–1598) 441
England and Spain (1558–1603) 443

The Thirty Years' War (1618–1648) 446
Superstition and Enlightenment: The Battle Within 446
Witch Hunts and Panic 447

ART AND THE WORLD: WARRING ARCHITECTURAL STYLES: BAROQUE VERSUS PLAIN CHURCHES 448

Writers and Philosophers 450
In World Perspective: The Renaissance and Reformation 453
Review Questions 455
Suggested Readings 455

RELIGIONS OF THE WORLD: CHRISTIANITY 458

17 Africa (ca. 1000–1800) 460

North Africa and Egypt 461
The Spread of Islam South of the Sahara 462
Sahelian Empires of the Western and Central Sudan 463
Ghana 463
Mali 464
Songhai 466
Kanem and Kanem-Bornu 468
The Eastern Sudan 470
The Forestlands—Coastal West and Central Africa 470
West African Forest Kingdoms: The Example of Benin 470
European Arrivals on the Coastlands 471

ART AND THE WORLD: BENIN AND IFE "BRONZES" 472

Central Africa 474
East Africa 475
Swahili Culture and Commerce 475
The Portuguese and the Omanis of Zanzibar 476
Southern Africa 478
Southeastern Africa: "Great Zimbabwe" 478
The Portuguese in Southeastern Africa 480
South Africa: The Cape Colony 480
In World Perspective: Africa, 1000–1800 481
Review Questions 482
Suggested Readings 482

18 Conquest and Exploitation: The Development of the Transatlantic Economy 484

Periods of European Overseas Expansion 485
Mercantilist Theory of Economic Exploitation 486
Establishment of the Spanish Empire in America 488
Conquest of the Aztecs and the Incas 488
The Roman Catholic Church in Spanish America 489
Economies of Exploitation in the Spanish Empire 491
Varieties of Economic Activity 491
The Decline of the Native American Population 492
Commercial Regulation and the Flota System 492
Colonial Brazil and Slavery 495
French and British Colonies in North America 497
Slavery in the Americas 498
Establishment of Slavery 498
The Plantation Economy and Transatlantic Trade 498
Slavery on the Plantations 499
Africa and the Transatlantic Slave Trade 500
The Background of Slavery 501
Slavery and Slaving in Africa 501

ART AND THE WORLD: A DRAMATIC MOMENT IN THE TRANSATLANTIC WORLD: COPLEY'S "WATSON AND THE SHARK" 502
The African Side of the Transatlantic Trade 505
The Extent of the Slave Trade 506
Consequences of the Slave Trade for Africa 506
In World Perspective: The Transatlantic Economy 509
Review Questions 509
Suggested Readings 510

19 East Asia in the Late Traditional Era 512

LATE IMPERIAL CHINA 514
Ming (1368–1644) and Ch'ing (1644–1911) Dynasties 514
Land and People 514
China's Third Commercial Revolution 514
Political System 517
Ming-Ch'ing Foreign Relations 521
Ming-Ch'ing Culture 524
JAPAN 527
Warring States Era (1467–1600) 527
War of All Against All 527
Foot Soldier Revolution 528
Foreign Relations and Trade 529
Tokugawa Era (1600–1868) 531
Political Engineering and Economic Growth During the Seventeenth Century 531
Eighteenth and Early Nineteenth Centuries 535
Tokugawa Culture 538
ART AND THE WORLD: UTAMARO WOODBLOCK PRINT 540
KOREA AND VIETNAM 545
Korea 545
Early History 545
The Choson Era: Late Traditional Korea 546
Vietnam 547
Southeast Asia 547
Early Vietnam 548
The Second Millenium: Politics and Society 549
In World Perspective: Late Traditional East Asia 550
Review Questions 551
Suggested Readings 552

20 European State-Building and Worldwide Conflict 554

The Netherlands: Golden Age to Decline 555
Urban Prosperity 556
Economic Decline 556
Two Models of European Political Development 556
Constitutional Crisis and Settlement in Stuart England 557
James I 557
ART AND THE WORLD: RACHEL RUYSCH, "FLOWER STILL LIFE": FLOWERS, COMMERCE, AND MORALITY 558
Charles I 560
The Long Parliament and Civil War 560
Oliver Cromwell and the Puritan Republic 561
Charles II and the Restoration of the Monarchy 562
James II and Renewed Fears of a Catholic England 562
The "Glorious Revolution" 563
The Age of Walpole 563
Rise of Absolute Monarchy in France: The World of Louis XIV 565

Years of Personal Rule 565
Versailles 565
King by Divine Right 566
Louis's Early Wars 566
Revocation of the Edict of Nantes 568
Louis's Later Wars 568
Russia Enters the European Political Arena 569
Years of Turmoil 570
Peter the Great 570
Central and Eastern Europe 572
The Habsburg Empire and the Pragmatic Sanction 572
Prussia and the Hohenzollerns 574
The First Worldwide Wars 575
The Colonial Arena and the War of Jenkins's Ear 575
The War of the Austrian Succession (1740–1748) 576
The Seven Years' War (1756–1763) 576
In World Perspective: Eighteenth-Century European States and Warfare 577
Review Questions 578
Suggested Readings 578

21 European Society Under the Old Regime 580

Major Features of Life in the Old Regime 581
Maintenance of Tradition 582
Hierarchy and Privilege 582
Aristocracy 582
Great Britain 582
France 582
Eastern Europe 583
Russia 583
The Land and Its Tillers 584
Peasants and Serfs 584
Family Structures and the Family Economy 585
Households 585
The Family Economy 586
Women and the Family Economy 586
Children and the World of the Family Economy 588
ART AND THE WORLD: "THE BREAKFAST" AND "THE RETURN FROM MARKET": TWO SCENES OF DOMESTIC LIFE 590
Growth of Agriculture and Population 592
The Revolution in Agriculture 592
Population Expansion 594
The Eighteenth-Century Industrial Revolution 594
An Event in World History 594
Industrial Leadership of Great Britain 595
Cities 597
Patterns of Preindustrial Urbanization 597
Urban Classes 597
The Jewish Population: Age of the Ghetto 599
In World Perspective: The European Old Regime 600
Review Questions 601
Suggested Readings 602

22 The Last Great Islamic Empires (1500–1800) 604

ISLAMIC EMPIRES 605
The Ottoman Empire 605
Origins and Development of the Ottoman State before 1600 605
The "Classical" Ottoman Order 607
After Süleyman: Challenges and Change 608
The Decline of Ottoman Military and Political Power 610
The Safavid Shi'ite Empire 610
Origins 610

Shah Abbas I 611
Safavid Decline 611
Culture and Learning 612
The Empire of the Indian Timurids, or "Mughals" 613
Origins 613
Akbar's Reign 613
The Last Great Mughals 614
Sikhs and Marathas 614
Political Decline 614
Religious Developments 615
ISLAMIC ASIA 616
Central Asia: Islamization and Isolation 616
Uzbeks and Chaghatays 616
Consequences of the Shi'ite Rift 616
ART AND THE WORLD: SHAH-NAMEH, BOOK OF KINGS 618
Power Shifts in the Southern Seas 620
Southern-Seas Trade 620
Control of the Southern Seas 620
The Indies: Acheh 621
In World Perspective: The Last Islamic Empires 621
Review Questions 622
Suggested Readings 622

PART V — ENLIGHTENMENT AND REVOLUTION IN THE WEST 624

23 The Age of European Enlightenment 628

The Scientific Revolution 629
Nicolaus Copernicus Rejects an Earth-Centered Universe 630
Tycho Brahe and Johannes Kepler 631
Galileo Galilei 632
Francis Bacon: The Empirical Method 633
Isaac Newton Discovers the Laws of Gravitation 634
Women in the World of the Scientific Revolution 634
John Locke 635
ART AND THE WORLD: JOSEPH WRIGHT, "AN EXPERIMENT ON A BIRD IN THE AIR-PUMP": SCIENCE IN THE DRAWING ROOM 636
The Enlightenment 638
Voltaire 638
The Encyclopedia 639
The Enlightenment and Religion 639
Deism 640
Toleration 641
The Enlightenment and Society 641
Montesquieu and "The Spirit of the Laws" 641
Adam Smith on Economic Growth and Social Progress 642
Rousseau 643
Women in the Thought and Practice of the Enlightenment 644
Enlightened Absolutism 646
Joseph II of Austria 647
Catherine the Great of Russia 649
The Partition of Poland 651
In World Perspective: The Enlightenment Heritage 651
Review Questions 652
Suggested Readings 652

24 Revolutions in the Transatlantic World 654

Revolution in the British Colonies in North America 655
- Resistance to the Imperial Search for Revenue 655
- American Political Ideas 656
- Crisis and Independence 656

Revolution in France 658
- Revolutions of 1789 659
- Reconstruction of France 662
- A Second Revolution 663
- The Reign of Terror and Its Aftermath 665
- The Napoleonic Era 668

ART AND THE WORLD: FRANCISCO GOYA MEMORIALIZES A NIGHT OF EXECUTIONS: "THE THIRD OF MAY, 1808" 670

- The Congress of Vienna and the European Settlement 675

Wars of Independence in Latin America 678
- Eighteenth-Century Developments 678
- First Movements Toward Independence 678
- San Martín in Río de la Plata 679
- Simón Bolívar's Liberation of Venezuela 679
- Independence in New Spain 681
- Brazilian Independence 681

Toward the Abolition of Slavery in the Transatlantic Economy 682

In World Perspective: The Transatlantic Revolutions 684

Review Questions 685

Suggested Readings 685

Index 689

Documents

CHAPTER 13

Jalaluddin Rumi: Who is the Sufi? 340
A Muslim Biographer's Account of Maimonides 343
Quatrains (Ruba'iyat) from the Pen of Umar Khayyam (d. 1123) 348
The Mongol Catastrophe 349
How the Hindus Differ from the Muslims 354

CHAPTER 14

A Maya Myth of Creation 366
A Spaniard Describes the Glory of the Aztec Capital 369
Nezahualcoyotl of Texcoco Sings of the Giver of Life 372
The Incas Organize Their Empire 379

CHAPTER 15

Pope Urban II (1088–1099) Preaches the First Crusade 388
The Services of a Serf 393
The English Nobility Imposes Restraints on King John 396
Pico Della Mirandola States the Renaissance Image of Man 407
Machiavelli Discusses the Most Important Trait for a Ruler 409

CHAPTER 16

German Peasants Protest Rising Feudal Exactions 430
Ignatius of Loyola's "Rules for Thinking with the Church" 434
A German Mother Advises Her Fifteen-Year-Old Son, Who Is away from Home at School for the First Time (1578) 436

CHAPTER 17

Ghana and Its People in the Mid-Eleventh Century 465
Muslim Reform in Songhai 469
Affonso I of Kongo Writes to the King of Portugal 475
Visiting Mogadishu and Kilwa (1331) 477

CHAPTER 18

Buccaneers Prowl the High Seas 487
A Contemporary Describes Forced Indian Labor at Potosí 490
Visitors Describe the Portobello Fair 495
A Slave Trader Describes the Atlantic Passage 505

CHAPTER 19

The Thin Horse Market 516
The Seven Transformations of an Examination Candidate 519
Ch'ien Lung's Edict to King George III of England 524
A Star in Heaven 526
The Virtuous Wife 539
A Tokugawa Skeptic 544
On Husband Sharing 549

CHAPTER 20

Parliament Presents Charles I with the Petition of Right 561
Lady Mary Wortley Montagu Advises Her Husband on Election to Parliament 564

CHAPTER 21

Priscilla Wakefield Demands More Occupations be Opened to Women 588
An Edinburgh Physician Describes the Dangers of Childbirth 589

CHAPTER 22

The Distinctiveness of Ottoman Identity and Culture 609
A Safavid Historian Praises Shah Abbas I 613
Guru Arjun's Faith 616

CHAPTER 23

Galileo Discusses the Relationship of Science to the Bible 632
Rousseau Argues for Separate Spheres for Men and Women 644
Mary Wollstonecraft Criticizes Rousseau's View of Women 646
Maria Theresa and Joseph II of Austria Debate Toleration 648

CHAPTER 24

The Stamp Act Congress Addresses George III 657
French Women Petition to Bear Arms 661
A Pamphleteer Describes a Sans-Culotte 664
Napoleon Describes Conditions Leading to the Consulate 669
A Commander Recalls an Incident in Spain 673
Bolívar Denounces Spanish Rule in Latin America 680

Maps

13–1 The Islamic heartlands, 1000–1500 338
13–2 Islamic political sovereignty in 1500 351
13–3 The Indian subcontinent, 1000–1500 353
14–1 Pre-Aztec Mesoamerican sites discussed in this chapter 362
14–2 The Aztec and Inca Empires on the eve of the Spanish conquest 370
14–3 Pre-Inca sites discussed in this chapter 374
15–1 Medieval trade routes and regional products 390
15–2 Germany and Italy in the Middle Ages 398
15–3 Spread of the Black Death 399
15–4 Renaissance Italy 401
16–1 European voyages of discovery and the colonial claims of Spain and Portugal in the fifteenth and sixteenth centuries 422
16–2 The empire of Charles V 427
16–3 The Swiss confederation 429
16–4 The Netherlands during the Reformation 442
16–5 Religious division ca. 1600 444
16–6 The Holy Roman Empire ca. 1618 445
17–1 Africa ca. 900–1500 464
17–2 Africa ca. 1500–1800 467
18–1 Viceroyalties in Latin America in 1780 494
19–1 Ming Empire and the voyages of Cheng Ho 521
19–2 The Ch'ing Empire at its peak 523
19–3 Tokugawa Japan and the Korean peninsula 533
20–1 The early wars of Louis XIV 567
20–2 Europe in 1714 569
20–3 The Austrian Habsburg Empire, 1521–1772 572
20–4 Expansion of Brandenburg-Prussia 574
22–1 Sixteenth-century Islamic empires 606
23–1 Expansion of Russia, 1689–1796 650
23–2 Partitions of Poland, 1772, 1793, and 1795 650
24–1 North America in 1763 656
24–2 Napoleonic Europe in late 1812 674
24–3 Europe 1815, after the Congress of Vienna 677
24–4 The Independence Campaigns of San Martín and Bolívar 679

Art and the World

Chapter 13 The Alhambra 344

Chapter 14 Mesoamerican Art 376

Chapter 15 Images of Death in the Late Middle Ages 402

Chapter 16 Warring Architectural Styles: Baroque versus Plain Churches 448

Chapter 17 Benin and Ife "Bronzes" 472

Chapter 18 A Dramatic Moment in the Transatlantic World: Copley's "Watson and the Shark" 502

Chapter 19 Utamaro Woodblock Print 540

Chapter 20 Rachel Ruysch, "Flower Still Life": Flowers, Commerce, and Morality 558

Chapter 21 "The Breakfast" and "The Return from Market": Two Scenes of Domestic Life 590

Chapter 22 Shah-nameh, Book of Kings 618

Chapter 23 Joseph Wright, "An Experiment on a Bird in the Air-Pump": Science in the Drawing Room 636

Chapter 24 Francisco Goya Memorializes a Night of Executions: "The Third of May, 1808" 670

Preface

The events of September 11, 2002, as nothing in the immediate past, have brought upon the world a new awareness of human history in a global context. Prior to that day North American readers generally understood world history and globalism as academic concepts; they now understand them as realities shaping their daily lives and experience. The new, immediate pressures of the present draw us to seek a more certain and extensive understanding of the past.

The idea of globalization is now a pressing reality on the life of nations, affecting the domestic security of their citizens, their standard of living, and the environment. Whether, as Samuel Huntington, the distinguished Harvard political scientist, contends, we are witnessing a clash of civilizations, we have certainly entered a new era in which no active citizen or educated person can escape the necessity of understanding the past in global terms. Both the historical experience and the moral and political values of the different world civilizations now demand our attention and our understanding. It is our hope that in these new, challenging times *The Heritage of World Civilizations* will provide one path to such knowledge.

The Roots of Globalization

Globalization—that is, the increasing interaction and interdependency of the various regions of the world—has resulted from two major historical developments: the closing of the European era of world history and the rise of technology.

From approximately 1500 to the middle of the twentieth century, Europeans gradually came to dominate the world through colonization (most particularly in North and South America), state-building, economic productivity, and military power. That era of European dominance ended during the third quarter of the twentieth century after Europe had brought unprecedented destruction on itself during World War II and as the nations of Asia, the Near East, and Africa achieved new positions on the world scene. Their new political independence, their control over strategic natural resources, and the expansion of their economies (especially those of the nations of the Pacific rim of Asia), and in some cases their access to nuclear weapons have changed the shape of world affairs.

Further changing the world political and social situation has been a growing discrepancy in the economic development of different regions that is often portrayed as a problem between the northern and southern hemispheres. Beyond the emergence of this economic disparity has been the remarkable advance of political Islam during the past forty years. In the midst of all these developments, as a result of the political collapse of the former Soviet Union, the United States has emerged as the single major world power.

The second historical development that continues to fuel the pace of globalization is the advance of technology, associated most importantly with transportation, military weapons, and electron communication. The advances in transportation over the past two centuries including ships, railways, and airplanes have made more parts of the world and its resources accessible to more people in ever shorter spans of time. Military weapons of increasingly destructive power over the past century and a half enabled Europeans and then later the United States to dominate other regions of the globe. Now, the spread of these weapons means that any nation with sophisticated military technology can threaten other nations, no matter how far away. Furthermore, technologies that originated in the West from the early twentieth century to the present have been turned against the West. More recently, the electronic revolution associated with computer technology has sparked unprecedented speed and complexity in global communications. It is astonishing to recall that personal computers have been generally available for less than twenty-five years and the rapid personal communication associated with them has existed for less than fifteen years.

Why not, then, focus only on new factors in the modern world, such as the impact of technology and the end of the European era? To do so would ignore the very deep roots that these developments have in the past. More important, the events of recent months and the response to them demonstrate, as the authors of this book have long contended, that the major religious traditions continue to shape and drive the modern world as well as the world of the past. The religious traditions link today's civilizations to their most ancient roots. We believe this emphasis on the great religious traditions recognizes not only a factor that has shaped the past, but one that is profoundly and dynamically alive in our world today.

Strengths of the Text

Balanced and Flexible Presentation
In this edition, as in past editions, we have sought to present world history fairly, accurately, and in a way that does justice to its great variety. History has many facets, no one of which can account for the others. Any attempt to tell the story of civilization from a single perspective, no matter how timely, is bound to neglect or suppress some important part of that story.

Historians have recently brought a vast array of new tools and concepts to bear on the study of history. Our coverage introduces students to various aspects of social and intellectual history as well as to the more traditional political, diplomatic, and military coverage. We firmly believe that only through an appreciation of all pathways to understanding of the past can the real heritage of world civilizations be claimed.

The Heritage of World Civilizations, Sixth Edition, is designed to accommodate a variety of approaches to a course in world civilization, allowing teachers to stress what is most important to them. Some teachers will ask students to read all the chapters. Others will select among them to reinforce assigned readings and lectures.

Clarity and Accessibility Good narrative history requires clear, vigorous prose. Our goal has been to make our presentation fully accessible to students without compromising on vocabulary or conceptual level. We hope this effort will benefit both teachers and students.

Recent Scholarship As in previous editions, changes in this edition reflect our determination to incorporate the most recent developments in historical scholarship and the expanding concerns of professional historians.

The Sixth Edition includes greater discussion of the origins of humankind in Chapter 1, incorporation of new scholarship on Islam and East Asia, updated coverage of developments in Africa and Latin America, and analysis of globalization, terrorism, women's rights, and recent events in the Middle East.

Pedagogical Features This edition retains the pedagogical features of the last edition, helping to make the text accessible to students, reinforcing key concepts, and providing a global, comparative perspective.

- Part Essays open each of the seven major sections of the book. These serve to preview the coverage in the subsequent chapters and highlight major trends and movements.
- Part Timelines show the major events in five regions—Europe, the Near East and India, East Asia, Africa, and the Americas—side by side. Appropriate photographs enrich each timeline.
- Chapter Topics introduce each chapter.
- Chronologies within each chapter help students organize a time sequence for key events.
- Primary Source Documents, including selections from sacred books, poems, philosophy, political manifestos, letters, and travel accounts, introduce students to the raw material of history, providing an intimate contact with the people of the past and their concerns.
- Questions accompanying the source documents direct students toward important, thought-provoking issues and help them relate the documents to the material in the text. They can be used to stimulate class discussion or as topics for essays and study groups.
- Map Explorations, new to the Sixth Edition, prompt students to engage with at least one map per chapter in an interactive fashion. Each *Map Exploration* is found on the Companion Website for the text.
- In World Perspective sections conclude most chapters. These brief essays place important developments in the chapter into a world context. An all-new "In World Perspective" on democratization, globalization, and political terrorism ends the final chapter.
- Chapter review questions help students focus on and interpret the broad themes of a chapter. These questions can be used for class discussion and essay topics.
- Religions of the World essays introduce students to the five major world religious traditions—Judaism, Hinduism, Buddhism, Christianity, and Islam.
- Comparative Perspectives essays, located on the *Companion Website* for *The Heritage of World Civilizations,* examine technology and civilizations from a cross-cultural perspective.

New in the Sixth Edition

This edition of *The Heritage of World Civilizations* includes new pedagogical features, many content revisions, and a new feature, Art and the World essays, described below.

Content and Organization The many changes in content and organization in this edition of *The Heritage of World Civilizations* reflect our ongoing effort to present a truly global survey of world civilization that at the same time gives a rich picture of the history of individual regions.

To better accomplish this, several significant changes to the book's organization have been carried out in this revision. Coverage of events during the European High Middle Ages and the Renaissance, which was formerly treated in two chapters, has been reconceived into a single chapter (Chapter 15) entitled, "Europe to the Early 1500s: Revival, Decline, and Renaissance." Coverage of Europe and North America in the nineteenth century, which formerly was addressed in four chapters, has been streamlined so that it is discussed in two new chapters (Chapters 25 and 26) that integrate discussion of the ideas, politics, society, and culture of the period. This consolidation of material on Europe provides for an even more balanced treatment of world history, a smoother narrative line, and a reduction of the total number of chapters from thirty-eight to thirty-five.

To provide instructors with more flexible teaching options, *The Heritage of World Civilizations* is available in both two volumes (Volume One: To 1700; Volume Two: Since 1500), and three volumes (Volume A: To 1500; Volume B: From 1300 to 1800; Volume C: Since 1700).

ART AND THE WORLD ESSAYS A beautiful and important new feature enhances students' understanding of the artistic heritage of world civilizations. In every chapter we highlight a work of art or architecture and discuss how the work illuminates and reflects the period in which it was created. In chapter 6, for example, Nok sculpture is examined for what it can tell us about West African society in antiquity. In chapter 11, the magnificence and antiquity of medieval Islamic civilization is discussed through the prism of the Alhambra. In chapter 16, Baroque church architecture is looked at as a commentary on the religious clashes of the Reformation. And in chapter 35, Latin-American painters Jacobo Borges and Fernando Botero are interpreted for their ability to vividly critique ruling regimes.

WORLD AND THE WEB To help students effectively use the vast resources of the Internet for research related to world history, each chapter in the text concludes with an annotated listing of stable and notable sites pertinent to the topics at hand.

A NOTE ON DATES AND TRANSLITERATIONS
We have used B.C.E. (before the common era) and C.E. (common era) instead of B.C. (before Christ) and A.D. (*anno domini*, the year of our Lord) to designate dates.

Until recently, most scholarship on China used the Wade-Giles system of romanization for Chinese names and terms. In order that students may move easily from the present text to the existing body of advanced scholarship on Chinese history, we have used the Wade-Giles system throughout. China today, however, uses another system known as *pinyin*. Virtually all Western newspapers have adopted it. Therefore, for Chinese history since 1949 we have included the *pinyin* spellings in parentheses after the Wade-Giles.

Also, we have followed the currently accepted English transliterations of Arabic words. For example, today *Koran* is being replaced by the more accurate *Qur'an*; similarly *Muhammad* is preferable to *Mohammed* and *Muslim* to *Moslem*. We have not tried to distinguish the letters *'ayn* and *hamza*; both are rendered by a simple apostrophe (') as in *shi'ite*.

With regard to Sanskritic transliteration, we have not distinguished linguals and dentals, and both palatal and lingual *s* are rendered *sh*, as in *Shiva* and *Upanishad*.

ANCILLARY INSTRUCTIONAL MATERIALS

The Heritage of World Civilizations, Sixth Edition, comes with an extensive package of ancillary materials.

- An **Instructor's Manual** provides summary and multiple choice questions for each part essay, as well as chapter summaries, outlines of key points and concepts, identification questions, and multiple choice and essay questions to be used for tests, and a suggested list of relevant films and videos for each chapter.

- A **Study Guide** includes chapter summaries, key concepts, identification questions, short-answer exercises, and essay questions.
- **Documents in World History** (Volumes 1 and 2) is a collection of additional primary source documents that underscore the themes in the text. Includes review questions for each document.
- A **Test Item File** provides more than 1,000 test questions.
- **Test Manager** Prentice Hall's new testing software program permits instructors to edit any or all items in the Test Item File and add their own questions. Other special features of this program, which is available as a dual-platform CD, include random generation of an item set, creation of alternative versions of the same test, scrambling of questions, and test previews before printing.
- **Color Transparencies** of maps, charts, and graphs from the text provide strong visual support for lectures.
- A **Map Workbook** helps students develop geographical knowledge. This workbook is free to students using new copies of this text.
- ***Understanding and Answering Essay Questions.*** This brief guide suggests helpful study techniques as well as specific analytical tools for understanding different types of essay questions and provides precise guidelines for preparing well-crafted essay answers. The guide is available free to students when packaged with *The Heritage of World Civilizations.*
- ***Reading Critically About History.*** This brief guide provides students with helpful strategies for reading a history textbook. It is available free when packaged with *The Heritage of World Civilizations.*

Prentice Hall and Penguin Bundle Program. Prentice Hall and Penguin are pleased to provide adopters of *The Heritage of World Civilizations* with an opportunity to receive significant discounts when orders for *The Heritage of World Civilizations* are bundled together with Penguin titles in world history. Contact your local Prentice Hall representative for details.

The ancillary package also includes an extensive array of multimedia supplements:

The Prentice Hall Guide to Evaluating Online Sources takes students from Web surfers to critical researchers. This guide helps students to search and locate appropriate research articles, critically evaluate them, and cite them properly. In addition, it contains a unique access code that gives students entry into ***Content Select***, a powerful online research database. A multitude of articles from both history journals and popular periodicals are accessible to students from wherever they are doing research: at home, in their dorm, in a lab, or at work. ***The Prentice Hall Guide to Evaluating Online Resources*** is available free when wrapped with copies of *The Heritage of World Civilizations.*

Documents CD-ROM. Packaged free with each new copy of *The Heritage of World Civilizations*, the brand-new *Documents CD-ROM* features all of the source documents from *The Heritage of World Civilizations Documents Set* ($16.00 net value per volume) as easily navigable PDF files, viewable in *Adobe Acrobat Reader*™. Additionally, document-study questions are linked to the *Companion Website*™ that accompanies the text, allowing students to submit answers directly to their instructor via e-mail for grading.

The ***Companion Website*** **(http://www.prenhall.com/craig)** works in tandem with the text to help students use the online resources to enrich their understanding of world history. Featuring chapter objectives and study questions organized by the main subtopics of each chapter, document-based essay questions, map labeling exercises, and map explorations, it links the text with related material available on the Internet. For instructors, the *Companion Website* offers maps, charts, and graphs in PDF format for classroom presentations, as well as an online version of the instructor's manual.

Instructor CD-ROM for The Heritage of World Civilizations. This new multimedia ancillary contains a PowerPoint™ presentation directly linked to the organization of the text, as well as maps and graphs from *The Heritage of World Civilizations*, lecture outlines, and digitized images from the "Art and the World" essays.

Course Management Systems. Prentice Hall provides a variety of course management solutions for teachers of world history. Contact your local Prentice Hall representative for details, or visit www.prenhall.com.

Acknowledgments

We are grateful to the many scholars and teachers whose thoughtful and often detailed comments helped shape this as well as previous editions of *The Heritage of World Civilizations*:

Wayne Ackerson, *Salisbury State University*
Jack Martin Balcer, *Ohio State University*
Charmarie J. Blaisdell, *Northeastern University*
Deborah Buffton, *University of Wisconsin at La Crosse*
Loretta Burns, *Mankato State University*
Chun-shu Chang, *University of Michigan, Ann Arbor*
Mark Chavalas, *University of Wisconsin at La Crosse*
Anthony Cheeseboro, *Southern Illinois University at Edwardsville*
William J. Courteney, *University of Wisconsin*
Samuel Willard Crompton, *Holyoke Community College*
James B. Crowley, *Yale University*
Bruce Cummings, *The University of Chicago*
Stephen F. Dale, *Ohio State University, Columbus*
Clarence B. Davis, *Marian College*
Raymond Van Dam, *University of Michigan, Ann Arbor*
Bill Donovan, *Loyola University of Maryland*
Wayne Farris, *University of Tennessee*
Suzanne Gay, *Oberlin College*
Robert Gerlich, *Loyola University*
Samuel Robert Goldberger, *Capital Community-Technical College*
Andrew Gow, *University of Alberta*
Katheryn L. Green, *University of Wisconsin, Madison*
David Griffiths, *University of North Carolina, Chapel Hill*
Louis Haas, *Duquesne University*
Joseph T. Hapak, *Moraine Valley Community College*
Hue-Tam Ho Tai, *Harvard University*
David Kieft, *University of Minnesota*
Frederick Krome, *Northern Kentucky University*
Lisa M. Lane, *Mira Costa College*
Richard Law, *Washington State University*
David Lelyveld, *Columbia University*
Jan Lewis, *Rutgers University, Newark*
James C. Livingston, *College of William and Mary*
Richard L. Moore Jr., *St. Augustine's College*
Beth Nachison, *Southern Connecticut State University*
Robin S. Oggins, *Binghamton University*
Louis A. Perez Jr., *University of South Florida*

Cora Ann Presley, *Tulane University*
Norman Raiford, *Greenville Technical College*
Norman Ravitch, *University of California, Riverside*
Philip F. Riley, *James Madison University*
Thomas Robisheaux, *Duke University*
David Ruffley, *United States Air Force Academy*
Dankwart A. Rustow, *The City University of New York*
James J. Sack, *University of Illinois at Chicago*
William Schell, *Murray State University*
Marvin Slind, *Washington State University*
Daniel Scavone, *University of Southern Indiana*
Charles C. Stewart, *University of Illinois*
Carson Tavenner, *United States Air Force Academy*
Truong-buu Lam, *University of Hawaii*
Harry L. Watson, *Loyola College of Maryland*
Paul Varley, *Columbia University*

Finally, we would like to thank the dedicated people who helped produce this revision: our acquisitions editor, Charles Cavaliere; our development editor, Gerald Lombardi; our photo researchers, Barbara Salz, Francelle Carapetyan and Elaine Soares; Ximena Tamvakopoulos, who created the handsome new design for this edition; Louise Rothman, our production editor; Sherry Lewis, our manufacturing buyer; and Ariel Blumenthal and Alexandra Bonfante-Warren, who helped us research and write several of the Art and the World essays.

A.M.C.
W.A.G.
D.K.
S.O.
F.M.T.

About the Authors

ALBERT M. CRAIG is the Harvard-Yenching Research Professor of History at Harvard University, where he has taught since 1959. A graduate of Northwestern University, he took his Ph.D. at Harvard University. He has studied at Strasbourg University and at Kyoto, Keio, and Tokyo universities in Japan. He is the author of *Choshu in the Meiji Restoration* (1961), *The Heritage of Chinese Civilization* (2001), and, with others, of *East Asia, Tradition and Transformation* (1989). He is the editor of *Japan, A Comparative View* (1973) and co-editor of *Personality in Japanese History* (1970). At present he is engaged in research on the thought of Fukuzawa Yukichi. For eleven years (1976–1987) he was the director of the Harvard-Yenching Institute. He has also been a visiting professor at Kyoto and Tokyo Universities. He has received Guggenheim, Fulbright, and Japan Foundation Fellowships. In 1988 he was awarded the Order of the Rising Sun by the Japanese government.

WILLIAM A. GRAHAM is Albertson Professor of Middle Eastern Studies and Professor of the History of Religion at Harvard University, and Master of Currier House at Harvard University. From 1990–1996 he directed Harvard's Center for Middle Eastern Studies. He has taught for twenty-six years at Harvard, where he received the A.M. and Ph.D. degrees. He also studied in Göttingen, Tübingen, and Lebanon. He is the author of *Divine World and Prophetic World in Early Islam* (1977), awarded the American Council of Learned Societies History of Religions book prize in 1978, and of *Beyond the Written Word: Oral Aspects of Scripture in the History of Religion* (1987). He has published a variety of articles in both Islamic studies and the general history of religion and is one of the editors of the *Encyclopedia of the Qur'an*. He serves currently on the editorial board of several journals and has held John Simon Guggenheim and Alexander von Humboldt research fellowships. *Three Faiths, One God*, co-authored with Jacob Neusner and Bruce Chilton, will be published in January 2003.

DONALD KAGAN is Hillhouse Professor of History and Classics at Yale University, where he has taught since 1969. He received the A.B. degree in history from Brooklyn College, the M.A. in classics from Brown University, and the Ph.D. in history from Ohio State University. During 1958–1959 he studied at the American School of Classical Studies as a Fulbright Scholar. He has received four awards for undergraduate teaching at Cornell and Yale. He is the author of a history of Greek political thought, *The Great Dialogue* (1965), a four-volume history of the Peloponnesian War, *The Origins of the Peloponnesian War* (1969), *The Archidamian War* (1974), *The Peace of Nicias and the Sicilian Expedition* (1981), and *The Fall of the Athenian Empire* (1987), a biography of Pericles, *Pericles of Athens and the Birth of Democracy* (1991), *On the Origins of War* (1995), and *While America Sleeps* (with Frederick W. Kagan) (2000). With Brian Tierney and L. Pearce Williams, he is the editor of *Great Issues in Western Civilization*, a collection of readings.

STEVEN OZMENT is McLean Professor of Ancient and Modern History at Harvard University. He has taught Western Civilization at Yale, Stanford, and Harvard. He is the author of nine books. *The Age of Reform, 1250–1550* (1980) won the Schaff Prize and was nominated for the 1981 National Book Award. Four of his books: *Magdalena and Balthasar: An Intimate Portrait of Life in Sixteenth Century Europe* (1986), *Three Behaim Boys: Growing Up in Early Modern Germany* (1990), *Protestants: The Birth of a Revolution* (1992), and *The Bürgermeister's Daughter: Scandal in a Sixteenth Century German Town* (1996) were selections of the History Book Club. His most recent books are *Flesh and Spirit: Private Life in Early Modern Germany* (1999), and *Ancestors: The Loving Family of Old Europe* (2001).

FRANK M. TURNER is John Hay Whitney Professor of History at Yale University, where he served as University Provost from 1988 to 1992. He received his B.A. degree at the College of William and Mary and his Ph.D. from Yale. He has received the Yale College Award for Distinguished Undergraduate Teaching. He has directed a National Endowment for the Humanities Summer Institute. His scholarly research has received the support of fellowships from the National Endowment for the Humanities and the Guggenheim Foundation. He is the author of *Between Science and Religion: The Reaction to Scientific Naturalism in Late Victorian England* (1974), *The Greek Heritage in Victorian Britain* (1981), which received the British Council Prize of the Conference on British Studies and the Yale Press Governors Award, and *Contesting Cultural Authority: Essays in Victorian Intellectual Life* (1993). He has also contributed numerous articles to journals and has served on the editorial advisory boards of *The Journal of Modern History*, *Isis*, and *Victorian Studies*. He edited *John Henry Newman, The Idea of a University* (1996). Since 1996 he has served as a Trustee of Connecticut College.

The Heritage of World Civilizations

13 The Islamic Heartlands and India

ca. 1000–1500

A miniature painting of the Army of Tamerlane storming the walls of the Rajput city of Bhatnair in the year 1398. Bhatnair was one of the many north Indian cities and fortresses that fell to the relentless onslaught of Tamerlane's armies. Bildarchiv Preussischer Kulturbesitz

Chapter topics

THE ISLAMIC HEARTLANDS

- Religion and Society
- Regional Developments
- The Spread of Islam Beyond the Heartlands

INDIA

- The Spread of Islam to India
- Muslim-Hindu Encounter
- Islamic States and Dynasties
- Religious and Cultural Accommodation
- Hindu and Other Indian Traditions

IN WORLD PERSPECTIVE
The Islamic Heartlands and India, 1000–1500

CENTRALIZED CALIPHAL POWER IN THE ISLAMIC world had broken down by the mid–tenth century. Regional Islamic states with distinctive political and cultural identities now dominated—a pattern that would endure to modern times (see Map 13–1). Yet the diverse Islamic lands remained part of a larger civilization. Muslims from Córdoba in Spain could (and did) travel to Bukhara in Transoxiana or Zanzibar on the East African coast and feel, at home. Regionalism and cosmopolitanism, diversity and unity, have characterized Islamic civilization ever since.

The next 500 years saw the growth of a truly international Islamic community, united by shared norms of communal order represented and maintained by the Muslim religious scholars (*ulama*). Sufism, the strand of Islam that stressed piety and allegiance to a spiritual master, gained popularity, especially after 1200. The growth of Sufi affiliations or brotherhoods influenced Muslim life everywhere, often countering the more limiting aspects of *ulama* conformity. Shi'ite ideas offered another alternative vision of society. Movements loyal to Ali and his heirs challenged but failed to reverse centrist, Sunni predominance in most of the Islamic world, even though Shi'ite dynasties ruled much of the Islamic heartlands in the tenth and eleventh centuries.

A cultural renaissance fueled the spread of Persian as the major language of Islam alongside Arabic. The Persian-dominated Iranian and Indian Islamic world became more distinct from the western Islamic lands.

Two Asian steppe peoples, the Mongols and the Turks, came to rule much of the Islamic world in these centuries, but with different results. The spread of the Turks added a substantial Turkish element, especially where they became rulers, as happened with the Saljuqs in Iran and Anatolia, the Mamluks in Egypt, and the "slave-kings" in Delhi. The Mongols conquered much of the Islamic heartlands in the thirteenth century, but their culture and religion did not become dominant. In this age, Islam became the major new influence in the Indian subcontinent, Southeast Asia, and sub-Saharan Africa.

The Islamic Heartlands

RELIGION AND SOCIETY

In this period Islamic society was shaped by the consolidation and institutionalization of Sunni legal and religious norms, Sufi traditions and personal piety, and Shi'ite legal and religious norms.

CONSOLIDATION OF SUNNI ORTHOPRAXY

The *ulama* (both Sunni and Shi'ite) gradually became entrenched religious, social, and political elites throughout the Islamic world, especially after the breakdown of centralized power in the tenth century. Their integration into local merchant, landowning, and bureaucratic classes led to stronger identification of these groups with Islam.

From the eleventh century onward the *ulama*'s power and fixity as a class were expressed in the institution of the *madrasa*, or college of higher learning. On the one hand, the *madrasa* had grown up naturally as individual experts frequented a given mosque or private house and attracted students seeking to learn the Qur'an, the *Hadith* ("Tradition"), jurisprudence, Arabic grammar, and the like. On the other hand, rulers endowed the

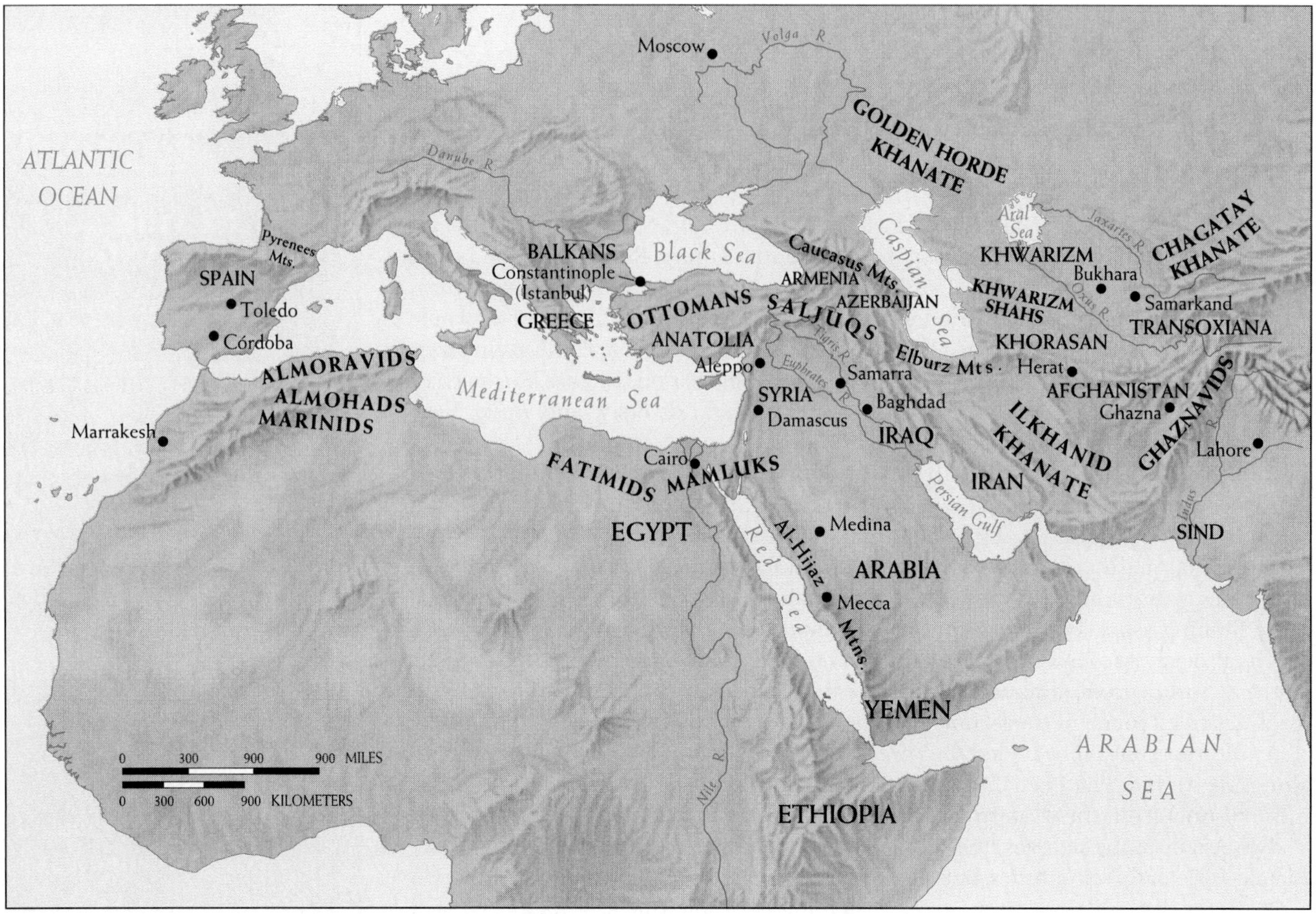

Map 13–1 The Islamic heartlands, 1000–1500. Shown are the major ruling dynasties.

madrasas with buildings, scholarships, and salaried chairs, so that they could control the *ulama* by appointing teachers and influencing the curriculum. In theory, such control might combat unwelcome sectarianism. Unlike the university, with its corporate organization and institutional degrees, the *madrasa* was a support institution for individual teachers, who personally certified students' mastery of particular subjects. It gave an institutional base to Islam's long-developed system of students seeking out the best teachers and studying texts with them until they received the teachers' formal certification, or "permission" to transmit and teach those same texts themselves.

Largely outside *ulama* control, popular "unofficial" piety flourished in local pilgrimages to saints' tombs, in folk celebrations of Muhammad's birthday, in veneration of him in poetry, and in ecstatic chant and dance among Sufi groups. But the shared traditions that directed family and civil law, the daily worship rituals, fasting in the month of Ramadan, and the yearly Meccan pilgrimage united almost all Muslims, even most Kharijites or Shi'ites. In the Christian world, theological dogmas determined sectarian identity. In contrast, Muslims tended to define Islam in terms of what Muslims do—by practice rather than by beliefs. The chief arbiters of "normative" Sunni and Shi'i Islam among the *ulama* were the *faqihs*, or legal scholars, not the theologians.

Basic Sunni orthopraxy discouraging religious or social innovations, was well established by the year 1000 as the dominant tradition, even though Shi'ite aspirations often made themselves felt either politically or theologically. The emergence of a conservative theological orientation tied to one of the four main Sunni legal schools, the Hanbalites (after Ibn Hanbal, d. 969), narrowed the scope, for creative doctrinal change. The Hanbalites relied on a literalist reading of the Qur'an and the *Hadith.* The *ulama* also became more socially conservative regional as they became integrated into social aristocracies. The *ulama* were often as committed to the status quo as the rulers.

SUFI PIETY AND ORGANIZATION

Sufi piety stresses the spiritual and mystical dimensions of Islam. The term *Sufi* apparently came from the Arabic *suf* ("wool"), based on the old ascetic practice of wearing only a coarse woolen garment. Sufi simplicity and humility had roots with the Prophet and the companions but developed as a distinctive tendency when, after about 700 C.E., male and female pietists emphasized a godly life over and above mere observance of Muslim duties. Some stressed ascetic avoidance of temptations, others loving devotion to God. Sufi piety bridged the abyss between the human and the Divine that the exalted Muslim concept of the omnipotent God of creation implies. Socially, Sufi piety merged with folk piety in such popular practices as saint veneration, shrine pilgrimage, ecstatic worship, and seasonal festivals. Sufi writers collected stories of saints, wrote treatises on the Sufi path, and composed some of the world's finest mystical poetry.

Some Sufis were revered as spiritual masters and saints. Their disciples formed brotherhoods with their own distinctive mystical teaching, Qur'anic interpretation, and devotional practice. These fraternal orders became the chief instruments of the spread of Muslim faith, as well as a locus of popular piety in almost all Islamic societies. Organized Sufism has always attracted members from the populace at large (in this, it differs from monasticism), as well as those dedicated to poverty or other radical disciplines. Indeed, Sufi orders became in this age one of the typical social institutions of everyday Muslim life. Whether Sunni or Shi'ite, many Muslims have ever since identified in some degree with a Sufi order.

CONSOLIDATION OF SHI'ITE TRADITIONS

Shi'ite traditions crystallized between the tenth and twelfth centuries. Many states now came under Shi'ite rulers, but only the Fatimids in Egypt established an important empire. A substantial Shi'ite populace developed only in Iran, Iraq, and the lower Indus (Sind).

Two Shi'ite groups emerged as the most influential. The first were the "Seveners," or "Isma'ilis," who recognized Isma'il (d. ca. 760), first son of the sixth Alid *imam*, as the seventh *imam*. Their thought drew on Gnostic and Neo-Platonic philosophy, knowledge of which they reserved for a spiritual elite. Isma'ili groups were often revolutionary.

By the eleventh century, however, most Shi'ites accepted a line of twelve *imams*, the last of whom is said to have disappeared in Samarra (Iraq) in 873 into a cosmic concealment from which he will eventually emerge as the Mahdi, or "Guided One," to usher in the messianic age and final judgment. The "Twelvers," the Shi'ite majority, still focus on the martyrdom of the twelve *imams* and look for their intercession on the Day of Judgment. They have flourished best in Iran, the home of most Shi'ite thought. The Buyids

The Sultan Hasan Madrasa and Tomb-Mosque. This imposing Mamluk building (1356–1363) was built to house teachers and students studying all four of the major traditions or "schools" of Islamic law. Living and teaching spaces are combined here in a building with a mosque and the Sultan's tomb enclosure. SuperStock, Inc.

DOCUMENT JALALUDDIN RUMI: WHO IS THE SUFI?

Rumi (d. 1273) was one of the greatest and most influential mystics of Islamic history. Born in Mazar-e-Sharif (in a region that was once part of Khorasan), his family moved westward just before the Mongol invasion of Iran to settle finally in Seljuq Konya, in central Anatolia. Rumi succeeded his father as a madrasa professor and studied in Syria. The Mevlevi Sufi brotherhood considers him its founder. The following two selections come from Rumi's two longest works of mystical poetry.

What qualities or attributes does the Sufi seem to have, or to seek to develop? What seems to be the Sufi's goal? What might be the aim of the remarks about the "patched mantle" (a common mark of Sufi initiation) and "lust perverse"? What does "Beauty" seem to refer to in the first poem?

What makes the sufi? Purity of heart;
Not the patched mantle and the lust perverse
Of those vile earth-bound men who steal his name.
He in all dregs discerns the essence pure:
In hardship ease, in tribulation joy.
The phantom sentries, who with batons drawn
Guard Beauty's palace gate and curtained bower,
Give way before him, unafraid he passes,
And showing the King's arrow, enters in.

Mathnawi, p. 54

What to do, Muslims? For I do not recognize myself;
not a Christian I nor Jew, Zoroastrian nor Muslim.. . .
Not of India am I nor China, not Bulgar-land nor Turkistan;
not the Kingdom of Both Iraqs nor the Land of Khurasan.
Not of this World am I nor the next, not of heaven or hell;
not of Adam nor of Eve, not of Paradise nor Ridwan.
My place is no place, my trace has no trace; not body nor soul, for I belong to the soul of Love.
Duality have I put aside, I have seen both worlds as one.
One I seek, One I know, One I see, One I call.
He is the first, He the last; he the Outward, He the inward.

Diwan-i Shams-i Tabriz

The first poem is from *Rumi: Poet and Mystic* by R. A. Nicholson. Copyright © 1950 by George Allen and Unwin Ltd., an imprint of Harper-Collins Publishers Limited. The second poem translated from the Arabic by John Alden Williams, reprinted from *The World of Islam* edited by John Alden Williams, Copyright © 1994. By permission of the author and the University of Texas Press.

who took control of the Abbasid caliphate in 945 were Twelvers. The Safavids of Iran made Twelver doctrine the "state religion" in the sixteenth century (see Chapter 23).

REGIONAL DEVELOPMENTS

The western half of the Islamic world after the tenth century developed two regional foci: (1) Spain, Moroccan North Africa, and to a lesser extent, west Africa; and (2) Egypt, Syria-Palestine, Anatolia, along with Arabia and Libyan North Africa. The history of the eastern half of the Islamic world in the period between 1000 and 1500 was marked by the violent Mongol incursions of the thirteenth century.

THE ISLAMIC WEST: SPAIN AND NORTH AFRICA

The grandeur of Spanish Islamic ("Moorish") culture is visible still in Córdoba's Great Mosque and the remnants of the Alhambra castle. In European tradition, the *Chanson de Roland* preserves the echo of Charlemagne's retreat through the Pyrenees Mountains after failing to check the first Spanish Umayyad's growing power. That ruler, Abd al-Rahman I (r. 756–788), was the founder of the cosmopolitan tradition of Umayyad Spanish culture at Córdoba, which was the cultural center of the Western world for the next two centuries. Renowned for its medicine, science, literature, intellectual life, commercial activity, public baths and gardens, and courtly elegance, Córdoba reached its zenith under Abd al-Rahman III (r. 912–961), who took the title of caliph in 929. His absolutist but benevolent rule saw a largely unified, peaceful Islamic Spain. The mosque-university of Córdoba that he founded attracted students from Europe as well as the Islamic world.

A sad irony of this cosmopolitan world was recurring religious exclusivism and conflict among Muslims and Christians alike. Abroad, Abd al-Rahman III checked both the new Fatimid power in North Africa and the Christian kingdoms in northern Spain, making possible a golden era of Moorish power and culture. But after his death fragmentation into warring Muslim principalities allowed a resurgence of Spain's Christian states between about 1000 and 1085, when the city of Toledo fell permanently into Christian hands.

Brief Islamic revivals in Spain and North Africa came under the African reform movements of the Almoravids and Almohads. The Almoravids originated as a religious-warrior brotherhood among Berber nomads in West Africa. Having subdued northwestern Africa, in 1086 they carried their zealotry from their new capital of Marrakesh into

The Alhambra, Muqarnas dome in the Hall of the Abencerrahes, Palace of the Lions. Built largely in the 14th century by the Nasrid dynasty, the magnificent, sprawling palace buildings of the Alhambra marked the twilight of Islamic culture in Spain. Art Resource, N.Y.

Spain and reunited its Islamic kingdoms. Under their rule, arabized Christians (Mozarabs) were persecuted as were some Moorish Jews. The subsequent wars began the last major phase of the Spanish "Reconquest" (*Reconquista*). These conflicts, in which Christian rulers sought to regain and Christianize the peninsula, are best known in the West for the exploits of El Cid (d. 1099), the mercenary adventurer who became the Spanish national hero.

The Almohads ended Almoravid rule in Morocco in 1147 and then conquered much of southern Spain. Before their demise (1225 in Spain; 1275 in Africa), they stimulated a brilliant revival of Moorish culture. During this era, paper manufacture reached Spain and then the rest of western Europe. The long westward odyssey of Indian fable literature through Iran and the Arab world ended with Spanish and Latin translations in thirteenth-century Spain. The greatest lights of this Spanish Islamic intellectual world were the major philosopher and physician Ibn Rushd (Averroës, d. 1198); the great Muslim mystical thinker Ibn al-Arabi (d. 1240); and the famous Arab-Jewish philosopher Ibn Maymun, or Maimonides (d. 1204)

The Islamic West: Egypt and the Eastern Mediterranean World

The Fatimids The major Islamic presence in the Mediterranean from the tenth to the twelfth century was that of the Shi'ite Fatimids, who claimed descent from Muhammad's daughter, Fatima. They began as a Tunisian dynasty, then conquered Morocco, Sicily, and Egypt (969), where they built their new capital, Cairo (*al-Qahira*, "the Victorious"). Their rule as Shi'ite caliphs meant that, for a time, there were three "caliphates"—in Baghdad, Córdoba, and Cairo. The Fatimids were Isma'ilis (see above). Content to rule a Sunni majority in Egypt, they sought recognition as true imams by other Isma'ili groups and were able, for a time, to take western Arabia and most of Syria from the Buyid "guardians" of the Abbasid caliphate (see Chapter 11).

Fatimid rule spawned two splinter groups that have played visible, if minor, roles in history. The Druze of modern Lebanon and Syria originated around 1020 with a few members of the Fatimid court who professed belief in the divinity of one of the Fatimid caliphs. The tradition they founded is too far from Islam to be considered a Muslim sect. The Isma'ili Assassins, on the other hand, were a radical Muslim movement founded by a Fatimid defector in the Elburz mountains of Iran around 1100. The name "Assassins" comes not from the political assassinations that made them infamous but from a European corruption of the Arabic *Hashishiyyin* ("users of hashish"). It was possibly connected with the story that their assassins were manipulated with drugs to undertake their usually suicidal missions. The Assassins were destroyed by the Mongols in the thirteenth century.

The Fatimids built the Azhar mosque in Cairo as a center of learning, a role it maintains today, although for Sunni, not (as then) Shi'ite, scholarship. Fatimid rulers treated Egypt's Coptic Christians generally as well as they did their Sunni majority and many Copts held high offices. Jews, also usually fared well under the Fatimids.

After 1100 the Fatimids weakened, falling in 1171 to Salah al-Din (Saladin, 1137–1193), a field general and administrator under the Turkish ruler of Syria, Nur al-Din (1118–1174). Saladin, a Sunni Kurd, is well known in the West for his battles (including the retaking of Jerusalem in 1187) with the Crusaders. After Nur al-Din's death, Saladin added Syria-Palestine and Mesopotamia to his Egyptian dominions and founded the Ayyubid dynasty that, under his successors, controlled all three areas until Egypt fell to the Mamluks in 1250 and most of Syria and Mesopotamia to the Mongols by 1260.

Like Nur al-Din, and on the model of the Saljuqs (see Chapter 11), Saladin founded *madrasas* to teach and promote Sunni law. His and his Ayyubid successors' reigns in Egypt saw the entrenchment of a self-conscious Sunnism under a program of mutual recognition and teaching of all four Sunni schools of law. Henceforward Shi'ite Islam disappeared from Egypt.

Banner of Las Navas de Tolosa, made of silk tapestry with gold parchment (3.3 × 2.2 m) in southern Spain in the early 13th century, reflects the emphasis on architectural designs that emerged at this time among Spanish weavers. The central section of the banner, bordered with Qur'anic inscriptions, resembles a Spanish courtyard garden. The banner was captured in battle by Christians not long after it was made.
Arxiu Mas/Museo de Telas Medievales, Monasterio de Santa Maria la Real de Las Hueglas, Burgos, Spain, Patrimonio Nacional.

CHRONOLOGY

WESTERN ISLAMIC LANDS

756–1021	Spanish Umayyad dynasty
912–961	Rule of Abd al-Rahman III; height of Umayyad power and civilization
969–1171	Fatimid Shi'ite dynasty in Egypt
ca. 1020	Origin of Druze community (Egypt/Syria)
1171	Fatimids fall to Salah al-Din (Saladin), Ayyubid lieutenant of the ruler of Aleppo
1056–1275	Almoravid and Almohad dynasties in North Africa, West Africa, and Spain
1096–1291	Major European Christian crusades into Islamic lands; some European presence in Syria-Palestine
1189	Death of Ibn Rushd (Averroës), philosopher
1204	Death of Musa ibn Maymun (Maimonides), philosopher and Jewish savant
1240	Death of Ibn al-Arabi, theosophical mystic
1250–1517	Mamluk sultanate in Egypt and (from late 1200s) Syria; claim laid to Abbasid caliphate
1260	Mamluk victory at Ain Jalut halts Mongol advance into Syria
ca. 1300	Rise of Ottoman state in western Anatolia
1406	Death of Ibn Khaldun, historian and social philosopher

DOCUMENT: A MUSLIM BIOGRAPHER'S ACCOUNT OF MAIMONIDES

The following are excerpts from the entry on Maimonides (Arabic: Musa ibn Maymun) in the biographical dictionary of learned men by Ibn al-Qifti (d. 1248). In one section (omitted here), Ibn al-Qifti describes how this most famous Spanish Jewish savant at first feigned conversion to Islam when a new Berber ruler demanded the expulsion of Christians and Jews from Spain in about 1133. He tells how Maimonides moved his family to the more tolerant Islamic world of Cairo, where he became the court physician. (Jews or Christians held high office under Muslim rulers.)

Which Islamic dynasty forced Maimonides to leave Spain for Cairo? Why were the Fatimids in Cairo tolerant of Christians and Jews when their Berber co-religionists were not? From the Muslim biographer's treatment of his subject, what can you infer about Islamic societies and the intellectual atmosphere of the time?

. . . This man was one of the people of Andalus, a Jew by religion. He studied philosophy in Andalus, was expert in mathematics, and devoted attention to some of the logical sciences. He studied medicine there and excelled in it.. . .

. . . After assembling his possessions in the time that was needed for this, he left Andalus and went to Egypt, accompanied by his family. He settled in the town of Fustāt [part of greater Cairo], among its Jews, and practiced his religion openly. He lived in a district called al-Masīsa and made a living by trading in jewels and suchlike. Some people studied philosophy under him.. . .

He married in Cairo the sister of a Jewish scribe called Abu'l-Ma'ālī, the secretary of the mother of Nūr al-Dīn 'Alī, known as al-Afdal, the son of Salāh al-Dīn Yūsuf ibn Ayyūb, and he had a son by her who today is a physician in Cairo after his father.. . .

Mūsā, ibn Maymūn died in Cairo in the year 605 [1208-9].[1] He ordered his heirs to carry his body, when the smell had ceased, to Lake Tiberias and bury him there, seeking to be among the graves of the ancient Israelites and their great jurists, which are there. This was done.

He was learned in the law and secrets of the Jews and compiled a commentary on the Talmud, which is a commentary and explanation of the Torah; some of the Jews approve of it. Philosophic doctrines overcame him, and he compiled a treatise denying the canonical resurrection. The leaders of the Jews held this against him, so he concealed it except from those who shared his opinion in this.. . .

Reading the Torah in a Spanish synagogue. A picture from a Hebrew Haggada, Spain, 14th century. Until their expulsion by Christian rulers at the end of the 15th century, Jews formed a significant minority in Spain. By permission of The British Library

In the latter part of his life he was troubled by a man from Andalus, a jurist called Abu'l-'Arab ibn Ma'īsha, who came to Fustāt and met him. He charged him with having been a Muslim in Andalus, accused him [of apostasy] and wanted to have him punished.[2] 'Abd al-Rahīm ibn 'Alī al-Fādil prevented this, and said to him, "If a man is converted by force, his Islam is not legally valid."

[1] In fact, he died in 1204.

[2] The penalty for apostasy was death.

Excerpt from *Islam from the Prophet Muhammad to the Capture of Constantinople*, Vol. 2 by Bernard Lewis, ed. and trans. Copyright © 1974 by Bernard Lewis. Reprinted by permission of HarperCollins Publishers, Inc.

THE MAMLUKS The heirs of the Fatimids and Saladin in the eastern Mediterranean were the redoubtable sultans ("[those with] authority") of the Mamluk dynasty. The Mamluks were the only Islamic dynasty to withstand the Mongol invasions. Their victory at Ain Jalut in Palestine in 1260 marked the end of the Mongols' westward movement. The first Mamluk sultan, Aybak (r. 1250–1257), and his successors were elite Turkish and Mongol slave officers drawn originally from the bodyguard of Saladin's dynasty. Whereas the early Mamluks were often succeeded by sons or brothers,

Art and the World

THE ALHAMBRA

"The Sabikah is a crown on Granada's brow . . . and the Alhambra (may God watch over it) is the ruby that surmounts that crown."

Abu 'Abd Allah ibn Zamraq

The fabled Alhambra—one of the greatest examples of Islamic architecture and decoration and one of the most beautiful of all surviving medieval buildings—rises within its curtain walls above Granada, the last of the great Moorish cities of Andalusia.

A spur of the Sierra Nevada, the Sabikah, as the Alhambra's hill is called in medieval sources, overlooks the Genil River and its fertile valleys. The hilltop itself, however, has no sources of water—the water that flowed into the baths and gardens of the Alhambra was brought by aqueducts, which were very vulnerable to attack. (Cisterns, which gathered rainwater, were subject to the vagaries of weather.) Thus, the palace could only have been built during an extended period of relative peace.

According to tradition, in the ninth century C.E. there was a fortress on the Sabikah called al-Hamra ("the red"), whose name lives on in "Alhambra," though the meaning has not been satisfactorily explained. The site's history is better documented in the eleventh century, when Yusuf ibn Naghrallah, the Jewish vizier of the reigning Zirids, built a castle there. The vizier's residence was lavish enough to inspire the accusation that he had wished to outshine the king's own palace. (Yusuf was murdered in 1066; whether for this or another reason is unknown.)

In 1238, Muhammad ibn Yusuf ibn Nasr, a descendant of the Companions of the Prophet and a shrewd diplomat, accepted the suzerainty of the Christian kings of Castile, thereby becoming sovereign of prosperous Granada; the Nasrid dynasty would reign until the triumph of the Reconquista, in 1492. Most of the Alhambra was built between 1338 and 1390, first under Yusuf I (r. 1333–1354) then under the enlightened Muhammad V (r. 1354–1359 and 1362–1391), a

The Alhambra's serene, almost severe aspect belies the wealth of interior ornamentation, which consists of expressions of faith, but also praise of the ruler. The Alhambra's interior and architectural design, like many traditional Islamic artistic expressions, represents at least one metaphor: that what is—literally—essential is the adoration of Allah within oneself.
Robert Frerck/Getty Images, Inc.

patron of science, art, and poetry and a victorious military leader. (Christian rulers added to the complex in the sixteenth century, and again in the eighteenth.)

The Alhambra holds its ancient secrets, but its builders' faith is one of the keys to its mysteries—along with their secular pride. Recurring quotations from the Qur'an unite the hilltop complex, emphasizing the fundamental Muslim belief that God, manifest in the words of the Qur'an, is in all places. At the same time, poetry throughout the palace praises the king's victories, while the decoration of the throne room placed him at the center of the revolving heavens. The palace is composed of a series of serenely geometric courtyards, between which are labyrinthine passages that may represent the human inability to—literally—see the big picture, a privilege reserved for God.

It is paradoxical that the Alhambra was at its most magnificent as Muslim sovereignty was declining in Spain, but paradox, ambiguity, and contrast characterize it as they do so much Islamic architecture. Here, as elsewhere, the handsome, austere exterior gives no hint of the elaborately opulent decorations within; inside, slender columns support upper walls and ceilings that appear heavy with muqarnas. Water is everywhere—another recurring theme—in its two states: static, as in serene pools, and dynamic, leaping from fountains. And no fountain is more charming than the Fountain of the Lions, in the courtyard of the same name, Muhammad V's masterpiece, shown here. The lions date to the eleventh or twelfth century, perhaps to the palace of the vizier Yusuf. But perhaps not: they are twelve, which may be a reference to the Twelve Imams. The exquisite Courtyard of the Lions itself is quadripartite, like Christian gardens of the same period; the four cultivated quadrants may, like their Christian counterparts, represent the seasons, and so the universe. In one respect, however, the courtyard embodies a purely Islamic aesthetic: the relationship between the square pavilions at either end and the rectangular space of the court transforms and inverts the definitions of positive and negative space. This ambiguity characterizes all the arts that originated in Andalusia, from rugs to tilework to calligraphy. It is a delightful conceit—and, perhaps, an invitation to intellectual humility. In the Islamic tradition, courtyards are the most resonant of architectural metaphors, representing both the sensual pleasures of earthly life and portents of paradise. And nowhere is this more true than in the Alhambra, the last effulgence of a brilliant civilization.

The regal beauty of the Court of the Lions lies in its proportions, symmetry, and the rhythm of its elegant colonnades. The precious water that flowed through the palace—like the courtyards, a reminder of Paradise—also cooled the complex. The significance of these handsome lions is lost with the passing of those who planned the courtyard's decorative and symbolic programs. All we know is that, for the inhabitants of Al Andalus, as for most of the world, everything here below mirrors a higher reality. Art Resource, N. Y.

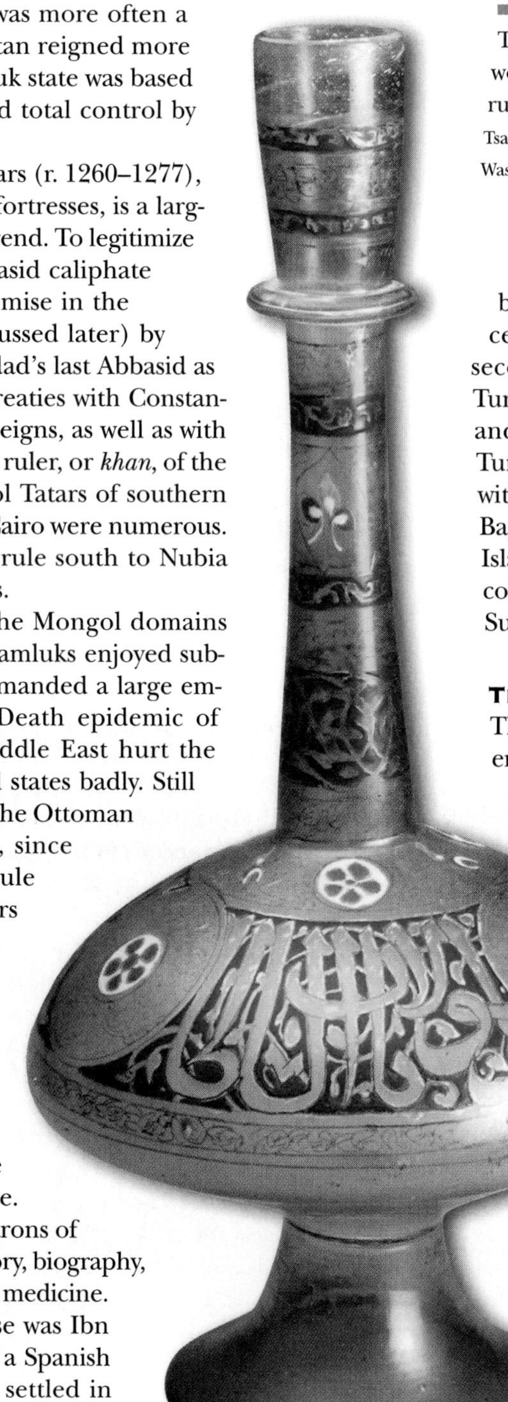

This elegant glass bottle was made in Mamluk workshops in Syria in the mid–14th century for the rulers of the Yemen in southern Arabia. John Tsantes/Courtesy of the Freer Gallery of Art, Smithsonian Institution, Washington, D.C.

succession after the 1390s was more often a survival of the fittest; no sultan reigned more than a few years. The Mamluk state was based on a military fief system and total control by the slave-officer elite.

The Mamluk sultan Baybars (r. 1260–1277), who took the last Crusader fortresses, is a larger-than-life figure in Arab legend. To legitimize his rule he revived the Abbasid caliphate at least in name after its demise in the fall of Baghdad (1258; discussed later) by installing an uncle of Baghdad's last Abbasid as Caliph at Cairo. He made treaties with Constantinople and European sovereigns, as well as with the newly converted Muslim ruler, or *khan*, of the Golden Horde—the Mongol Tatars of southern Russia. His public works in Cairo were numerous. He also extended Mamluk rule south to Nubia and west among the Berbers.

As trade relations with the Mongol domains improved after 1300, the Mamluks enjoyed substantial prosperity and commanded a large empire. However, the Black Death epidemic of 1347–1348 in the Arab Middle East hurt the Mamluk and other regional states badly. Still the Mamluks survived even the Ottoman conquest of Egypt in 1517, since Mamluks continued to rule there as Ottoman governors into the nineteenth century.

Architecture, much of which still graces Cairo, remains the most magnificent Mamluk bequest to posterity. In addition, mosaics, calligraphy, and metalwork were among the arts and crafts of special note. The Mamluks were great patrons of scholars who excelled in history, biography, astronomy, mathematics, and medicine. The most important of these was Ibn Khaldun (d. 1406). Born of a Spanish Muslim family in Tunis, he settled in Cairo as an adult. He is still recognized as the greatest Muslim social historian and philosopher of history.

The Islamic East: Before the Mongol Conquests

The Iranian dynasties of the Samanids at Bukhara (875–999) and the Buyids at Baghdad (945–1055) were the major usurpers of eastern Abbasid dominions. Their successes epitomized the rise of regional states that had begun to undermine the caliphate by the ninth century. Similarly, their demises reflected a second emerging pattern: the ascendancy of Turkish slave-rulers (like the Mamluks in the west) and of Oghuz Turkish peoples, known as Turkomans. With the Saljuqs, the process begun with use of Turkish slave troops in ninth-century Baghdad ended in the permanent presence in the Islamic world of Turkish ruling dynasties. As late converts, they became typically the most zealous of Sunni Muslims.

The Ghaznavids

The rule of the Samanids in Transoxiana was finally ended by a Turkoman group in 999. But they had already lost all of eastern Iran south of the Oxus in 994 to one of their own slave governors, Subuktigin (r. 976–997). He set up his own state in modern Afghanistan, at Ghazna, whence he and his son and successor, Mahmud of Ghazna (r. 998–1030), launched successful campaigns against his former masters. The Ghaznavids are notable for their patronage of Persian literature and culture and for their conquests in northwestern India, which began a lasting Muslim presence in India. Mahmud was their greatest ruler. He is still remembered for his booty raids and destruction of temples in western India. At its peak, his empire stretched from western Iran to the Oxus and to the Indus.

Mahmud attracted to Ghazna numerous scholars and artists, notably the great scientist and mathematician al-Biruni (d. 1048) and the epic poet Firdawsi (d. ca. 1020). Firdawsi's *Shahnama* ("The Book of Kings") is the masterpiece of Persian literature, an epic of sixty thousand verses that helped fix the New Persian language and revive the pre-Islamic Iranian cultural tradition. After Mahmud the empire began to break up, although Ghaznavids ruled at Lahore until 1186.

THE SALJUQS The Saljuqs were the first major Turkish dynasty of Islam. They were a steppe clan who settled in Transoxiana, became avid Sunnis, and extended their sway over Khorasan in the 1030s. In 1055 they took Baghdad. As the new guardian of the caliphate and master of an Islamic empire, the Saljuq leader Tughril Beg (r. 1037–1063) took the title of *sultan* to signify his temporal power and control. He and his early successors made various Iranian cities their capitals instead of Baghdad.

As new Turkish tribes joined their ranks, the Saljuqs extended Islamic rule for the first time into the central Anatolian plateau at Byzantine expense, even capturing the Byzantine emperor in a victory in Armenia in 1071. They also conquered much of Syria and wrested Mecca and Medina from the Shi'ite Fatimids. The first Turkish rule in Anatolia dates from 1077, when the Saljuq governor there formed a separate sultanate. Known as the Saljuqs of Rum ("Rome," i.e., Byzantium), these latter Saljuqs were only displaced after 1300 by the Ottomans, another Turkish dynasty, who would eventually conquer all of Anatolia and southeastern Europe (see Chapter 23).

The most notable figure of Saljuq rule was the vizier Nizam al-Mulk, the real power behind two sultans from 1063 to 1092. In his time new roads and inns (caravanserais) for trade and pilgrimage were built, canals were dug, mosques and other public buildings were founded (including the first great Sunni *madrasas,* and science and culture were patronized. He supported an accurate calendar reform and authored a major work on the art of governing, the *Siyasatnamah.* Before his murder by an Isma'ili assassin in 1092, he appointed as professor in his Baghdad *madrasa* Muhammad al-Ghazzali (d. 1111), probably the greatest Muslim religious thinker ever. He also patronized the mathematician and astronomer Umar Khayyam (d. 1123), whose Western fame rests on the poetry of his "Quatrains," or *Ruba'iyat.*

After declining fortunes in the early twelfth century, Iranian Saljuq rule crumbled and by 1194 was wholly wiped away by another Turkish slave dynasty from Khwarizm in the lower Oxus basin. By 1200 these Khwarizm Shahs had built a large if shaky empire and sphere of influence covering Iran and Transoxiana. In the same era the Abbasid caliph at Baghdad, al-Nasir (r. 1180–1225), established an independent caliphal state in Iraq. But neither his heirs nor the Khwarizm Shahs were long to survive.

THE ISLAMIC EAST: THE MONGOL AGE

MONGOLS AND ILKHANIDS The building of a vast Mongol empire spanning Asia from China to Poland in the thirteenth century proved momentous not only for eastern Europe and China (see Chapter 8), but also for Islamic Eurasia and India. A Khwarizm Shah massacre of Mongol ambassadors brought down the full wrath of the Great Khan, Genghis (ca. 1162–1227), on the Islamic east. He razed entire cities (1219–1222) from Transoxiana and Khorasan to the Indus. After his death, a division of his empire into four khanates under his four sons gave the Islamic world respite. Then in 1255 Hulagu Khan (r. 1256–1265), a grandson of Genghis, led a massive army again across the Oxus. Adding Turkish troops to his forces (Mongol armies typically included many Turks), he went from victory to victory, destroying every Iranian state. In 1258, when the Abbasid caliph refused to surrender, Hulagu's troops plundered Baghdad, killing at least 80,000 inhabitants, including the caliph and his sons.

Under the influence of his wife and many Nestorian Christians and Buddhists in his inner circle, Hulagu spared the Christians of Baghdad. He followed this policy in his other conquests, including the sack of Aleppo—which, like Baghdad, resisted. When Damascus surrendered, Western Christians had hopes of the impending fall of Mamluk Cairo and Islamic power. But Hulagu's drive west was slowed by rivalry with his kinsman Berke. A Muslim convert, Berke ruled the khanate of the Golden Horde, the Mongol state centered in southern Russia north of the Caucasus. He was in contact with the Mamluks, and some of his Mongol troops even helped them defeat Hulagu in Palestine (1260), which prevented a Mongol advance into Egypt. A treaty in 1261 between the Mamluk sultan and Berke established a formal alliance that confirmed the breakup of Mongol unity and the autonomy of the four khanates: in China (the Yuan dynasty), in Iran (the Ilkhans), in Russia (the Golden Horde), and in Transoxiana (the Chagatays).

Hulagu and his heirs ruled the old Persian Empire from Azerbaijan for some seventy-five years as the Great Khan of China's viceroys (*Il-Khans*). Here, as elsewhere, the Mongols did not eradicate the society they inherited. Their native paganism and Buddhist and Christian leanings yielded to Muslim faith and practice, although they practiced religious tolerance. After 1335 Ilkhanid rule fell prey to the familiar pattern of a gradual breaking away of provinces, and for fifty years, Iran was again fragmented.

TIMURIDS AND TURKOMANS This situation prepared the way for a new Turko-Mongol conquest from Transoxiana, under Timur-i Lang ("Timur the Lame," or "Tamerlane," 1336–1405). Even Genghis Khan's invasions could not match Timur's savage campaigns between 1379 and his death in 1405. These raids were not aimed at building a new empire but at sheer conquest. In successive campaigns he swept everything before him in a wave of devastation: eastern Iran (1379–1385); western Iran, Armenia, the Caucasus, and upper Mesopotamia (1385–1387); southwestern Iran, Mesopotamia, and Syria (1391–1393); Central Asia from Transoxiana to the Volga and as far as Moscow (1391–1395); North India (1398); and northern Syria and Anatolia (1400–1402). Timur's sole

DOCUMENT — QUATRAINS (RUBA'IYAT) FROM THE PEN OF UMAR KHAYYAM (D. 1123)

Although Edward Fitzgerald's beautiful free translation of Khayyam's Persian Ruba'iyat is famous, the following more literal translation of three quatrains by the famous astronomer-poet conveys the pessimistic and cynical but wry, pensive reflection of many of the Ruba'iyat.

On the basis of these three quatrains, can you account for the popularity of Umar Khayyam among Western readers? How does the view of life expressed here compare with that of other Islamic writers, such as that of al-Jahiz in Chapter 11?

Since all a man gets in this place of two doors
Is only a heart of sorrow and the giving up of life,
He who never lived a moment is happy—
That man is at peace whose mother never bore him.

Drink wine, you will lie long enough under the ground,
Without companion, friend or comrade.
Take care you tell no one this hidden secret,
"No lily that withers well will bloom again."

Rise up my love and solve our problem by your beauty,
Bring a jug of wine to clear our heart
So that we may drink together
Before wine-jugs are made of our clay.

From *The Ruba'iyat of Omar Khayyam* trans. by Peter Avery and John Heath-Stubbs (Penguin Classics, 1979). 1979 Translation copyright © Peter Avery and John Heath-Stubbs.

Genghis Khan holding an audience. This Persian miniature shows the great conqueror and founder of the Mongol Empire with members of his army and entourage as well as an apparent

positive contributions seem to have been the buildings he sponsored at Samarkand, his capital. He left behind him ruins, death, disease, and political chaos across the entire eastern Islamic world, which did not soon recover. His was, however, the last great steppe invasion, for firearms soon destroyed the steppe horsemen's advantage.

Timur's sons ruled after him with varying results in Transoxiana and Iran (1405–1494). The most successful Timurid was Shahrukh (r. 1405–1447), who ruled a united Iran for a time. His capital, Herat, became an important center of Persian Islamic culture and Sunni piety. He patronized the famous Herat school of miniature painting as well as Persian literature and philosophy. The Timurids had to share Iran itself with Turkoman dynasties in western Iran, once even losing Herat to one of them. They and the Turkomans were the last Sunnis to rule Iran. Both were eclipsed at the end of the fifteenth century by the militant Shi'ite dynasty of the Safavids, who ushered in a new, Shi'ite era in the Iranian world (see Chapter 23).

THE SPREAD OF ISLAM BEYOND THE HEARTLANDS

The period from roughly 1000 to 1500 saw the spread of Islam as a lasting religious, cultural, and political force into new areas (see Map 13–2). Not only Eurasia from the Caspian and Black Seas north to Moscow (under the Golden Horde), but also Greece and the Balkans, through the Ottoman Turks, came under the control of Islamic rulers (see Chapter 23). India, Malaysia, Indonesia, inland West Africa, and

DOCUMENT THE MONGOL CATASTROPHE

For the Muslim East, the sudden eruption of the Mongol hordes was an indescribable calamity. The shock and despair can be seen in the history of Ibn al-Athir (d. 1233). He writes here about the year 1220–1221, when the Mongols ("Tartars") burst in on the eastern lands.

Is this a positive, negative, or neutral description of the Mongols? Why might the Mongols be compared to Alexander rather than, say, the Huns (see Chapter 5)?

I say, therefore, that this thing involves the description of the greatest catastrophe and the most dire calamity (of the like of which days and nights are innocent) which befell all men generally, and the Muslims in particular; so that, should one say that the world, since God Almighty created Adam until now, hath not been afflicted with the like thereof, he would but speak the truth. For indeed history doth not contain aught which approaches or comes nigh unto it.. . .

Now this is a thing the like of which ear hath not heard; for Alexander, concerning whom historians agree that he conquered the world, did not do so with such swiftness, but only in the space of about ten years; neither did he slay, but was satisfied that men should be subject to him. But these Tartars conquered most of the habitable globe and the best, the most flourishing and most populous part thereof, and that whereof the inhabitants were the most advanced in character and conduct, in about [a] year; nor did any country escape their devastations which did not fearfully expect them and dread their arrival.

Moreover they need no commissariat, nor the conveyance of supplies, for they have with them sheep, cows, horses, and the like quadrupeds, the flesh of which they eat, [needing] naught else. As for their beasts which they ride, these dig into the earth with their hoofs and eat the roots of plants, knowing naught of barley. And so, when they alight anywhere, they have need of nothing from without. As for their religion, they worship the sun when it arises, and regard nothing as unlawful, for they eat all beasts, even dogs, pigs, and the like; nor do they recognise the marriage-tie, for several men are in marital relations with one woman, and if a child is born, it knows not who is its father.

Therefore Islâm and the Muslims have been afflicted during this period with calamities wherewith no people hath been visited. These Tartars (may God confound them!) came from the East, and wrought deeds which horrify all who hear of them, and which thou shalt, please God, see set forth in full detail in their proper connection.. . .

From Edward C. Sachau, *Alberuni's Indian*, Vol. I (London: Kegan Paul, Trench, Truebner, 1910). pp. 17, 19, 20.

coastal East Africa all became major spheres of Islamic political or commercial power. In all these regions Sufi orders were most often responsible for converting people and spreading Islamic cultural influences. Merchants, too, were major agents of Islamization in these regions.

Conquest was a third (but demographically less important) means of conversion to Islam in these regions. Sometimes only ruling elites, sometimes wider circles, became Muslim, but in India, Southeast Asia, and sub-Saharan Africa much, often most, of the populace retained their inherited religious traditions. Nonetheless, in the most important of these regions, India, the coming of Islam signaled epochal changes.

India

Islamic civilization in India (like earlier Indian civilization) was formed by creative interaction between invading foreigners and indigenous peoples. The early Arab and Turkish invaders were a foreign Muslim minority; their heirs were truly "Indian" as well as Muslim, adding a new dimension both to Indian and Islamic civilization. From then on, Indian civilization would both include and enrich Islamic traditions.

THE SPREAD OF ISLAM TO INDIA

Well before the Ghaznavids came to the Punjab, Muslims were to be found even outside the original Arab conquest areas in Sind (see Map 13–3). Muslim merchants had settled in the port cities of Gujarat and southern India to profit from internal Indian trade as well as from trade with the Indies and China. Wherever Muslim traders went, converts to Islam were attracted by business advantages as well as by the straightforward ideology and practice of Islam and its officially egalitarian, "classless" ethic. Sufi orders had also gained a foothold in the south, giving today's South Indian Muslims old roots. Sufi piety also drew converts in the north, especially when the Mongol devastation of Iran in the thirteenth century sent refugees into North India. These Muslim refugees strengthened Muslim life in the subcontinent.

MUSLIM-HINDU ENCOUNTER

From the outset Muslim leaders had to rule a country dominated by utterly different cultural and religious

The Gur-i-mir, the tomb of Timur in Samarkand. Built from 1490 to 1501 by Timur's grandson, this tile-covered structure houses the tombs of Shahrukh, Ulug Beg, and other Timurid

traditions. Much as early Muslim rulers in Iran had given Zoroastrians legal status as 'people of Scripture' (like Christians and Jews; see Chapter 11), the first Arab conquerors in Sind (711) had treated Hindus similarly as "protected peoples" under Muslim sovereignty. These precedents gave Indian Muslim rulers a legal basis for coexistence with their Hindu subjects, but did not remove Hindu resistance to Muslim rule.

The chief obstacle to Islamic expansion in India was the military prowess of the Hindu warrior class that emerged after the Hun and other Asian invasions of the fifth and sixth centuries. Apparently descended from such invaders and the native warrior (Kshatriya) class of Hindus, this class was known from about the mid–seventh century as *Rajputs.* The Rajputs were a large group of north-Indian clans bound together by a fierce warrior ethic and strong Hindu cultural and religious traditionalism. They fought the Muslims with great tenacity, but their inability to unite brought them eventually under Muslim domination in the sixteenth century (see Chapter 23).

Islamic States and Dynasties

A series of Turkish-Afghan rulers known as the "Slave Sultans of Delhi" extended and maintained Islamic power over North India for nearly a century (1206–1290). Such slaves, or *mamluks,* figured prominently in the leadership and elites of the new regime. Five descendants of Iltutmish ruled after him until 1266. The most vigorous of these was his daughter Raziyya, who ruled as sultana from 1237 to 1241.

Four later Muslim dynasties—the Khaljis, Tughluqs, Sayyids, and Lodis—continued the Delhi sultanate through the fifteenth century. This run of Muslim dynasties was interrupted by the Mongol-Turkish invasion and sack of Delhi by Timur in 1398, from which the city took decades to recover. Even before this devastation, however—roughly from the mid-1300s, the sultanate's central authority began to dwindle. In the two centuries before the advent of the Mughals in the mid–sixteenth century, many regions became partially or wholly independent, smaller sultanates, Rajput kingdoms,

Chronology

Eastern Islamic Lands

875–999	Samanid dynasty, centered at Bukhara
945–1055	Buyid Shi'ite dynasty in Baghdad, controls caliphs
994–1186	Ghaznavid dynasty in Ghazna (modern Afghanistan) and Lahore (modern Pakistan), founded by Subuktigin (r. 976–997) and his son, Mahmud of Ghazna (r. 998–1030)
1020	Death of Firdawsi, compiler of *Shahnama*
ca. 1050	Death of al-Biruni, scientist and polyglot
1055–1194	Saljuq rule in Baghdad
1063–1092	Viziership of Nizam al-Mulk
1111	Death of al-Ghazzali, theologian and scholar
1219–1222	Genghis Khan plunders eastern Iran to Indus region
1258	Hulegu Khan conquers Baghdad
1261	Mamluk-Mongol treaty halts westward Mongol movement
1260–1335	Hulegu and his Il-Khanid successors rule Iran
1379–1405	Campaigns of Timur-i Lang (Tamerlane) devastate entire Islamic East
1405–1494	Timurids, successors of Tamerlane, rule in Transoxiana and Iran
1405–1447	Shahrukh, Timurid ruler at Herat; great patronage of the arts and philosophy

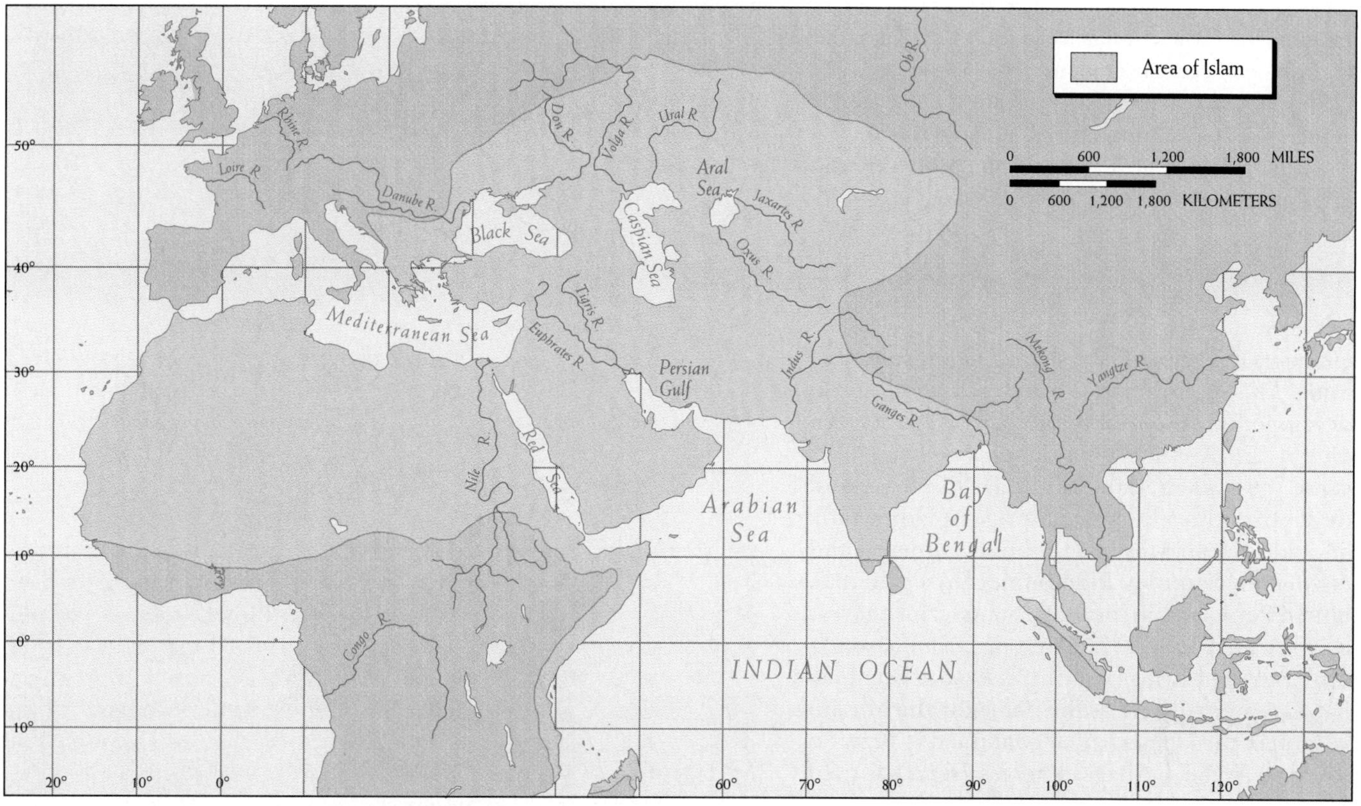

Map 13–2 Islamic political sovereignty in 1500. Areas with either Islamic political control or majority Muslim populations. Southern Spain had been under Islamic control until 1492.

or tiny Hindu or Muslim principalities. The sultanate was often only the most prominent among various kingdoms. Regional rule predominated across the subcontinent.

The most important independent Islamic state was that of the Bahmanids in the Deccan (1347–1527). These rulers were famous for their architecture and the intellectual life of their court, as well as for their role in containing the powerful South Indian Hindu state of Vijayanagar (1336–1565). (The first documented use of firearms in the subcontinent was in a Bahmani battle with the raja of Vijayanagar in 1366.) Most regional capitals fostered a rich cultural life. Jaunpur, to the north of Benares (Varanasi), for example, became an asylum for artists and intellectuals after Timur's sack of Delhi and boasted an impressive tradition of Islamic architecture. Kashmir, an independent sultanate from 1346 to 1589 was a center of literary activity where many Indian texts were translated into Persian.

Religious and Cultural Accommodation

Despite the enduring division of the subcontinent into multiple political and administrative units, the five centuries after Mahmud of Ghazna saw Islam become an enduring and influential element of Indian culture—especially in the north and the Deccan. The Delhi sultans were able, except for Timur's invasion, to fend off the Mongol danger, much as the Mamluks had in Egypt. They thereby provided a basic political and social framework within which Islam could take root. Although the ruling class remained a Muslim minority of Persianized Turks and Afghans ruling a Hindu majority, conversion went on at various levels of society. Some Hindu converts came from the ruling classes who served the Muslim overlords. Sufi orders converted many Hindus among the lower classes across the North. The Muslim aristocracy, at first mostly foreigners, was usually treated in Indian society as a separate caste group or groups. Lower-class or other Hindu converts were assimilated into lower "Muslim castes," often identified by occupation.

Sanskrit had long been the Indian scholarly and common language, but in this period regional languages, such as Tamil in the south, gained status as literary and administrative languages, and Persian became the language of intellectual and cultural life for the ruling elites of North India. However, the coming of substantial numbers of Muslims to the subcontinent led to the emergence of a new language, Urdu-Hindi, with both Perso-Arabic and indigenous Indian

Building the castle of Khawarnaq, ca. 1494. This is one of the magnificent illustrations of the *Khamsa*, or "Five Poems," of Nizami, painted by the head of the great art academy of Herat, Bihzad (d. ca. 1515). It was Shahrukh's patronage that led to this flourishing school of painting. By permission of The British Library

elements. It began to take shape not long after the initial Muslim influx in the eleventh century and developed in response to the increasing need of Hindus and Muslims for a shared language. It became the spoken idiom of the Delhi region and developed into a literary language of North Indian and Deccan Muslims in the seventeenth and eighteenth centuries. Indo-European in grammar, it used Perso-Arabic vocabulary and script and was at first called *Hindi* ("Indian") or *Dakani* ("southern"), then in British times *Hindustani*. Eventually *Urdu* came to serve as the name for the Muslim version of the language that continued to draw on its Perso-Arabic heritage, whereas *Hindi* was used for the version associated with Hindu culture and oriented in its further development toward its Hindu and Sanskritic heritage. Each became an official national language: Urdu for modern Pakistan and Hindi for modern India.

Indian Muslims were always susceptible to Hindu influence (in language, marriage customs, and caste consciousness). However, unlike earlier invaders, they were never utterly absorbed into the predominant Hindu culture, but remained in some measure a group apart, conscious of their uniqueness in the Hindu world and proud to be distinct. The Muslim ruling classes saw themselves as the protectors and propagators of Islam in India, and most of the sultans of Delhi sought formal recognition for their rule from the nominal Abbasid caliphs in Baghdad or, in Mamluk times, in Cairo.

Nevertheless, reciprocal influence of Muslims and Hindus was inevitable, especially in popular piety. Sufi devotion had an appeal similar to that of Hindu devotional, or *bhakti* movements (see Chapter 10), and each influenced the other. Some of India's most revered Sufi and *bhakti* saints date from the fourteenth and fifteenth centuries. During this period, various theistic mystics strove to transcend the mutual antagonism and exclusivism of Muslims and Hindus. They typically preached devotion to a God who saves his worshipers without regard either to Hindu caste obligations or to legalistic Muslim observance. The poet-saints Ramananda (d. after 1400) and Kabir (d. ca. 1518) were the two most famous such reformers.

Hindu and Other Indian Traditions

The history of India from 1000 to 1500 was also important for the other religious and cultural communities of India that as a whole vastly outnumbered the Muslims. The Jain tradition flourished, notably in Gujarat, Rajputana, and Karnataka. In the north the Muslim conquests effectively ended Indian Buddhism by the eleventh century. However, Buddhism had already been waning in Indian culture long before Islam arrived.

Hindu religion and culture flourished even under Muslim control, as the continuing social and religious importance of the Brahmans and the popularity of *bhakti* movements throughout India attest. This was an age of Brahmanic scholasticism that produced many commentaries and manuals but few seminal works. *Bhakti* creativity was much greater. The great Hindu Vaishnava Brahman Ramanuja (d. 1137) reconciled *bhakti* ideas with the classical Upanishadic Hindu worldview in the Vedantin tradition. *Bhakti* piety underlies the

MAP EXPLORATION

Interactive map: To explore this map further, go to http://www.prenhall.com/craig_map13.3

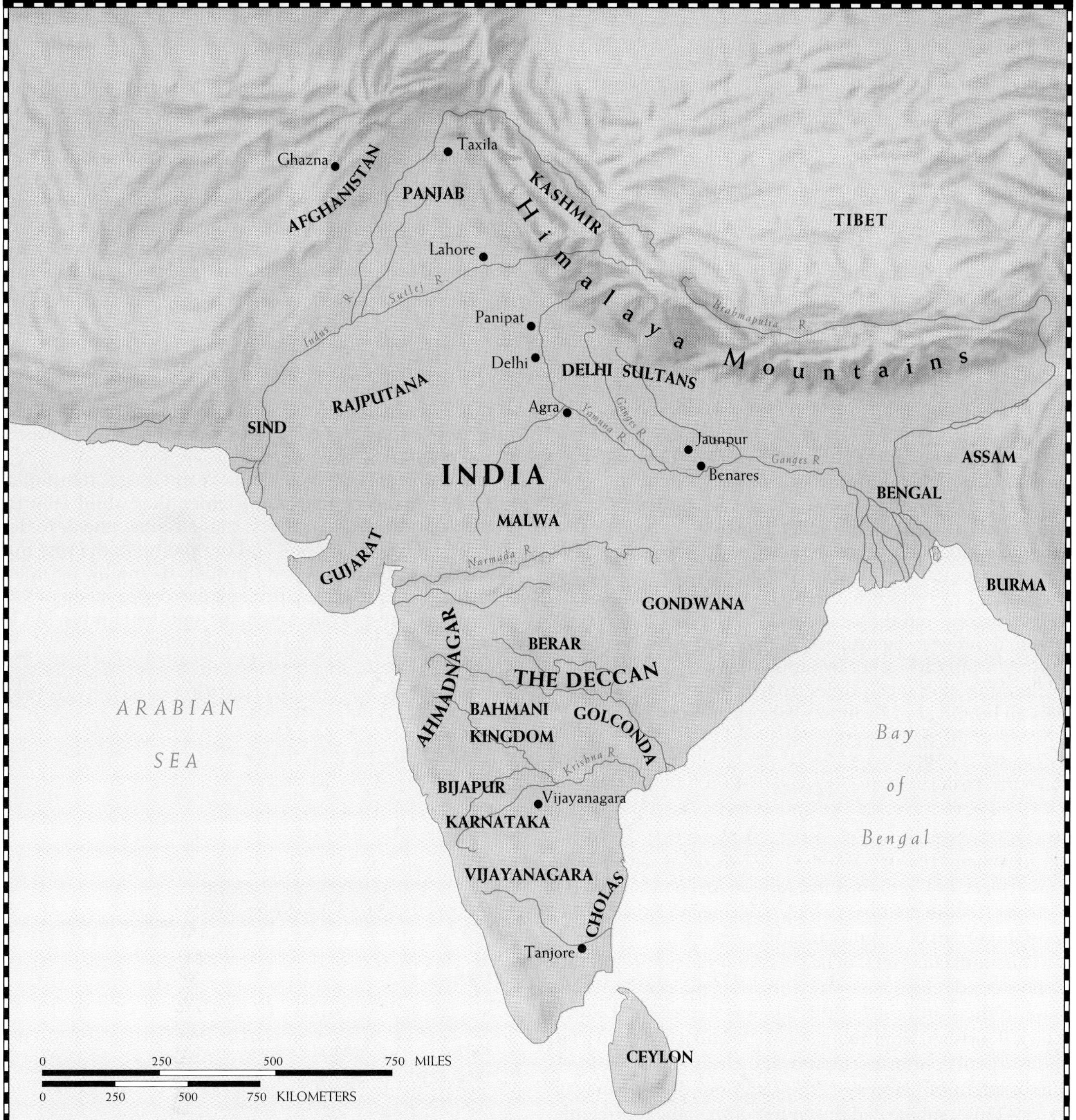

Map 13–3 The Indian subcontinent, 1000–1500. Shown are major kingdoms and regions.

DOCUMENT HOW THE HINDUS DIFFER FROM THE MUSLIMS

Al-Biruni (d. ca. 1050), the greatest scholar-scientist of medieval Islam, was born in northeastern Iran. He spent much of his life at the court of Mahmud of Ghazna, whom he accompanied on expeditions into northwestern India. Alongside his scientific work, he learned Sanskrit, studied India and the Hindus, and wrote a "History of India." The following selections from this work illustrate the reach and sophistication of his mind.

How does the emphasis on purity and the impurity of foreigners that Biruni imputes to the Hindus compare with the attitudes of Islam and other religions? Does this passage suggest why the Hindu tradition has remained largely an Indian one, while Islam became an international religion? At what might Biruni's comments about the relative absence of religous controversy among Hindus be aimed?

. . . The barriers which separate Muslims and Hindus rest on different causes.

First, they differ from us in everything which other nations have in common. And here we first mention the language, although the difference of language also exists between other nations. If you want to conquer this difficulty (i.e., to learn Sanskrit), you will not find it easy, because the language is of an enormous range, both in words and inflections, something like the Arabic, calling one and the same thing by various names, both original and derived, and using one and the same word for a variety of subjects, which, in order to be properly understood, must be distinguished from each other by various qualifying epithets.. . .

Secondly, they totally differ from us in religion, as we believe in nothing in which they believe, and vice versá.

On the whole, there is very little disputing about theological topics among themselves; at the utmost, they fight with words, but they will never stake their soul or body or their property on religious controversy. On the contrary, all their fanaticism is directed against those who do not belong to them—against all foreigners. They call them *mleecha*, i.e., impure, and forbid having any connection with them, be it by intermarriage or any other kind of relationship, or by sitting, eating, and drinking with them, because thereby, they think, they would be polluted. They consider as impure anything which touches the fire and the water of a foreigner; and no household can exist without these two elements. Besides, they never desire that a thing which once has been polluted should be purified and thus recovered, as, under ordinary circumstances, if anybody or anything has become unclean, he or it would strive to regain the state of purity. They are not allowed to receive anybody who does not belong to them, even if he wished it, or was inclined to their religion. This, too, renders any connection with them quite impossible, and constitutes the widest gulf between us and them.

In the third place, in all manners and usages they differ from us to such a degree as to frighten their children with us, with our dress, and our ways and customs, and as to declare us to be devil's breed, and our doings as the very opposite of all that is good and proper. By the by, we must confess, in order to be just, that a similar depreciation of foreigners not only prevails among us and the Hindus, but is common to all nations towards each other.

From Edward C. Sachau, *Alberuni's India*, Vol. 1 (London: Kegan Paul. Trench, Truebner, 1910), pp. 17, 19, 20.

masterpiece of Hindu mystical love poetry, Jayadeva's *Gita Govinda* (twelfth century), which is devoted to Krishna, the most important of Vishnu's incarnations.

The south continued to be the center of Hindu cultural, political, and religious activity. The most important dynastic state in the south during this age was that of the Cholas which flourished from about 900–1300 and patronized a famous school of bronze sculpture at their capital of Tanjore. Their mightiest successor, the kingdom of Vijayanagar (1336–1565), subjugated the entire south in the fourteenth century and resisted its Muslim foes longer than any other kingdom. Vijayanagar itself was one of India's most lavishly developed cities and a center of the cult of Shiva before its destruction by the Bahmanid sultan of the Deccan.

CHRONOLOGY

INDIA

ca. 900-1300	Chola dynasty in southern India
1137	Death of Ramanuja
1206-1290	Slave-kings of Delhi
1290-1320	Khalji sultans of Delhi
1320-1413	Tughluqid sultans of Delhi
1414-1526	Sayyid sultans of Delhi
1336-1565	Hindu dynasty of Vijayanagar
1347-1527	Muslim Bahmanid dynasty in the Deccan
1398	Timur's sack of Delhi

South Indian bronze figure of Krishna dancing on the head of the serpent Kaliya, from Vijayana-gar, ca. 15th century. Kaliya, according to a legend, was infesting the waters of the Jumna River until Krishna leaped in and emerged dancing on the vanquished snake. Asian Art Museum of San Francisco. The Avery Brundage Collection B65B72

In World Perspective

THE ISLAMIC HEARTLANDS AND INDIA, 1000–1500

This period in both Islamic and other Asian territories is difficult to characterize simply. The spread of Islam to new peoples or their ruling elites has been taken as a theme of this chapter. However, the history of Islam in India is hardly the history of India as a whole. The vast conquests and movements of the Mongols and Central Asian Turks across inner Asia were among the most striking developments in world history in this period; they often had cataclysmic effects, whether on Chinese, south Asian, west Asian, or eastern European societies. These conquests and migrations wiped out existing orders and forced many to flee to new areas. They contributed, even if unintentionally, new and often significant human resources to existing civilizations such as those of China and the Islamic heartlands.

In this age Islam became a truly international tradition of religious, political, and social values and institutions. It did so by being highly adaptable and open to "indigenization" in the seemingly hostile contexts of polytheistic Hindu and African societies. Also in this period, distinct traditions of art, language, and literature, for all their local or regional diversity, became part of a larger Muslim whole. Islamic civilization had none of the territorial contiguity or linguistic and cultural homogeneity of either Chinese or Japanese civilization. Nevertheless, the Islamic world was an international reality in which a Muslim could travel and meet other Muslims of radically diverse backgrounds and have much in common with them.

Indian traditional culture was not bound up with an expanding missionary religious tradition like that of Islam. Yet in this age Hindu kingdoms flourished in Indonesia. Buddhism was expanding across much of Central and eastern Asia, thereby solidifying its place as an international missionary tradition.

Christianity, by contrast, was not rapidly expanding in Africa, Asia, or Europe; but by 1500 its western European branch was poised on the brink of internal revolution and international expansion following the recently launched, fateful "voyages of discovery." In the year 1000 Europe was almost a backwater of culture and power by comparison with major Islamic or Hindu states, let alone that of China. By 1500, however, European civilization was riding the crest of a cultural renaissance, enjoying economic and political growth, and starting the global exploration that would turn into a flood of imperial expansion and affect most of the rest of the globe. Neither Islamic, Indian, African, Chinese, nor Japanese culture and society were so radically changed or changing in their basic ideas and institutions as were

REVIEW QUESTIONS

1. In 1000–1500, why did no Muslim leader build a large-scale Islamic empire of the extent of the early Abbasids?
2. How were the *ulama* educated? What was their relationship to political leadership? What social roles did they play?
3. What was the role and impact of religious sectarianism in this period? Of the institutionalization of Sufi piety and thought?
4. Discuss the cultural developments in Spain before 1500. Why was Córdoba such a model of civilized culture?
5. Why might Islam have been able to survive the successive invasions by steppe peoples (Turks and Mongols) from 945 on? What were the lasting results of these "invasions" for the Islamic world?
6. What were the primary obstacles to stable rule for India's Muslim invaders and immigrants? How did they deal with them?

SUGGESTED READINGS

The Islamic Heartlands

C. E. BOSWORTH, *The Islamic Dynasties: A Chronological and Genealogical Handbook* (1967). A handy reference work for dynasties and families important to Islamic history in all periods and places.

J. A. BOYLE, ED., *The Cambridge History of Iran*, Vol. 5, *The Saljuq and Mongol Periods* (1968). Useful and reasonably detailed articles on political, social, religious, and cultural developments.

P. K. HITTI, *History of the Arabs*, 8th ed. (1964). Still a useful English resource, largely for factual detail. See especially Part IV, "The Arabs in Europe: Spain and Sicily."

M. G. S. HODGSON, *The Expansion of Islam in the Middle Periods*, Vol. 2 of *The Venture of Islam*. 3 vols. (1964). The strongest of Hodgson's monumental three-volume survey of Islamic civilization and the only English work of its kind to give the period 945–1500 such broad and unified coverage.

A. HOURANI, *A History of the Arab Peoples* (1991). The newest survey history and the best, at least for the Arab Islamic world.

S. K. JAYYUSI, ED., *The Legacy of Muslim Spain*, 2 vols. (1994). A comprehensive survey of the arts, politics, literature, and society by experts in various fields.

B. LEWIS, ED., *Islam and the Arab World* (1976). A large-format, heavily illustrated volume with many excellent articles on diverse aspects of Islamic (not simply Arab, as the misleading title indicates) civilization through the premodern period.

D. MORGAN, *The Mongols* (1986). A recent and readable survey history.

J. J. SAUNDERS, *A History of Medieval Islam* (1965). A brief and simple, if sketchy, introductory survey of Islamic history to the Mongol invasions.

D. SOURDEL, *Medieval Islam*, trans. by W. M. Watt (1983). The synthetic, interpretive chapters on Islam and the political and social orders (4, 5) and on towns and art (6) are especially helpful.

B. SPULER, *The Muslim World: A Historical Survey*, trans. by F. R. C. Bagley (1960). 3 vols. Volumes I and II are handy references offering a highly condensed chronicle of Islamic history from Muhammad through the fifteenth century.

B. SPULER, *The Mongols in History*, trans. by Geoffrey Wheeler (1971). A short introductory survey of Mongol history, of which Chapters 2–5 are most relevant.

India

W. T. DE BARY ET AL., COMP., *Sources of Indian Tradition*, 2nd ed. (1958). Vol. I, *From the Beginning to 1800*, ed. and rev. by Ainslie T. Embree (1988). Excellent selections from a wide variety of Indian texts, with good introductions to chapters and individual selections.

S. M. IKRAM, *Muslim Civilization in India* (1964). The best short survey history, covering the period 711 to 1857.

R. C. MAJUMDAR, GEN. ED., *The History and Culture of the Indian People*, Vol. VI, *The Delhi Sultanate*, 3rd ed. (1980). A comprehensive political and cultural account of the period in India.

M. MUJEEB, *The Indian Muslims* (1967). The best cultural study of Islamic civilization in India as a whole, from its origins onward.

F. ROBINSON, ED., *The Cambridge History of India, Pakistan, Bangladesh, Sri Lanka, Nepal, Bhutan, and the Maldives* (1989). A very helpful quick reference source with brief but well-done survey essays on a wide range of topics relevant to South Asian history down to the present.

A. WINK, *Al-Hind: The Making of the Indo-Islamic World*, Vol. 1 (1991). The first of five promising volumes to be devoted to the Indo-Islamic world's history. This volume treats the seventh to eleventh centuries.

DOCUMENTS CD-ROM

1. William of Rubruck: Impressions of the medieval Mongols
2. Farid al-Din Attari: The Conference of Birds
3. The Thousand and One Nights
4. Two Bhakti Poets: Ravidas and Mirabai

WORLD AND THE WEB

A Shi'ite Encyclopedia (Version 2.0)

http://www.al-islam.org/encyclopedia/

A collection of information that addresses Shia/Sunni inter-school-related issues. This encyclopedia covers the most important lines of thought of the Shia.

The Baobob Project Narratives: Islam and Indigenous African Cultures

http://web-dubois.fas.harvard.edu/dubois/baobab/narratives/narrative.html

This narrative consists of interwoven media (text, images, video, and audio clips) cross-referenced through hypertext to give the user full independence to explore a topic.

The Indian History Sourcebook

http://www.fordham.edu/halsall/india/indiasbook.html

The Indian History Sourcebook, created by Paul Halsall of Fordham University, contains hundred of local files as well as links to source texts throughout the net that pertain to India's vast history including the formation of religious traditions, Medieval India, and Muslim Era India

Sanskrit Documents

http://sanskrit.gde.to/

This site contains a compilation of Sanskrit documents and e-texts in Devanagari display and transliteration format, as well as various tools for learning Sanskrit, such as the Online Sanskrit Dictionary, Sanskrit Tutorials, and software for learning Sanskrit.

Encyclopædia Iranica

http://www.iranica.com/

An extensive compendium that covers the wide range of precise and reliable reference work on the lands, life, culture, and history of all Iranian peoples and their interaction with other societies.

14 Ancient Civilizations of the Americas

This magnificent earspool of gold, turquoise, quartz, and shell was found in the tomb of the Warrior Priest in the Moche site of Sipan, Peru, 300 C.E. Courtesy of UCLA Fowler Museum of Cultural History/Susan Einstein

Chapter topics

- Problems in Reconstructing the History of Native American Civilization
- Mesoamerica
- The Formative Period and the Emergence of Mesoamerican Civilization
- The Classic Period in Mesoamerica
- The Post-Classic Period
- Andean South America
- The Preceramic and the Initial Period
- Chavín de Huantar and the Early Horizon
- The Early Intermediate Period
- The Middle Horizon Through the Late Intermediate Period
- The Inca Empire

In World Perspective
Ancient Civilizations of the Americas

HUMANS FIRST SETTLED THE AMERICAN CONTINENTS between 12,000 and 40,000 years ago. At that time glaciers locked up much of the world's water, lowering the sea level and opening a bridge of dry land between Siberia and Alaska. The earliest undisputed evidence of humans in Tierra del Fuego, at the southern tip of South America, dates to 11,000 years ago, indicating that at least by then the immigrants and their descendants had spread over all of both North and South America. When the glaciers receded the oceans rose, flooding the Bering Straits and severing Asia from America. Despite some continued contact in the Arctic and perhaps sporadic contacts elsewhere, the inhabitants of the Americas were now isolated from the inhabitants of Africa and Eurasia, and would remain so until overwhelmed by European invaders after 1492.

Although isolated from one another, the peoples of the Americas and the peoples of Africa and Eurasia experienced similar cultural changes at the end of the Paleolithic. In the Americas, as in the Eastern Hemisphere, people in some regions gradually shifted from hunting and gathering to a settled, agricultural way of life. And in some places civilization emerged as society grew increasingly stratified, villages coalesced into urban centers, monumental architecture appeared, and craft specialists developed sophisticated artistic traditions.

The two most prominent centers of civilization—and the focus of this chapter—were Mesoamerica, in what is today Mexico and Central America, and the Andean region of South America. Both regions have a long, rich history of civilization that reaches back thousands of years. At the time of the European conquest of the Americas in the sixteenth century both regions were dominated by powerful expansionist empires—the Aztecs, or Mexica, in Mesoamerica, and the Inca in the Andes. In both regions Spanish conquerors obliterated the native empires and nearly succeeded in obliterating native culture. But in both, Native American traditions have endured, overlaid and combined in complex ways with Hispanic culture, to provide clues to the pre-Hispanic past.

Problems in Reconstructing the History of Native American Civilization

Several difficulties confront scholars trying to understand the ancient civilizations of the Americas. One is simply the nature of the evidence. Andean civilizations never developed writing, and in Mesoamerica much of the written record was destroyed by time and conquest, and what remained was until recently undeciphered. The primary source of information has thus been archaeology, the study of the physical remains left by past cultures. Archaeologists have been successful at teasing out many details of the American past. Turning from the study of monumental remains in great urban centers to the study of the remains left by ordinary people in their everyday lives, they have been able to create an increasingly rich picture of the economic and social organization of ancient American civilizations. But archaeology alone cannot produce the kind of narrative history that thousands of years of written records have made possible for Eurasian civilization. For at least one ancient Mesoamerican people, however—the Maya—this situation is changing. Scholars have recently been able to decipher their writing and attach specific names, dates, and events to heretofore silent ruins.

We also have accounts of the history and culture of the Aztecs and Inca, the last great native American civilizations, that were related to Spanish missionaries and officials in the wake of the conquest. Although these accounts are invaluable sources of information, it is almost impossible to know how much they are colored by the conquest and the needs and expectations of the conquerors. This dilemma raises another. The long physical separation of the peoples of the Americas from the peoples of Asia and Europe created a great cultural separation as well. Since the conquest, however, European culture has predominated. Both the Spanish conquerors seeking to make sense of the wonders they encountered and later scholars seeking to understand preconquest Native American civilization and reconstruct its history have had to rely on the language and categories of European thought to describe and analyze peoples and cultural experiences that had nothing to do with Europe. Cultural blinders and arrogance—the Spaniards, for example, sought to eradicate Native American religion and replace it with Christianity—have exacerbated this gap.

Again and again, European words, categories, and values have been used to describe the experience of America before it was America. Columbus and other early explorers (see Chapter 17), believing they had reached the East Indies, called the people they met in the Caribbean "Indians." This misnomer stuck, extending to all Native American peoples who, of course, have other names for themselves. The name *America* itself is European, taken from Amerigo Vespucci (1451–1512), a Florentine who explored the coast of Brazil in 1501 and 1502.

MESOAMERICA

Mesoamerica (the name means "middle America") extends from central Mexico into Central America. This is a region of great physical diversity, ranging from lowland tropical rain forests to temperate highlands with fertile basins and valleys. Lowland regions include the Yucatán Peninsula and the Gulf and Pacific coasts. Highland regions include Mexico's central plateau, with the Valley of Mexico and the Oaxaca region, and the mountainous areas of Guatemala. Most of Mesoamerica's mineral resources are found in the highlands. The lowlands were the source of many important trading goods, including hardwoods, plant dyes, and the prized feathers of exotic birds.

Mesoamerica also designates a distinctive and enduring cultural tradition that emerged in this region between 1000 and 2000 B.C.E., manifested itself in a succession of impressive and powerful states until the coming of European conquerors in the sixteenth century, and continues to express itself in the lives of the region's Native American peoples. This is not to say that Mesoamerica was or is culturally homogeneous. The peoples of Mesoamerica were and are ethnically and linguistically diverse. There was no single Mesoamerican civilization, nor was there a single linear development of civilization in the region. Nonetheless, Mesoamerican civilizations shared many traits, including writing, a sophisticated calendrical system, many gods and religious ideas, a ritual ball game, and urban centers with religious and administrative buildings symmetrically arranged around large plazas.

Throughout its history the peoples of the region were linked by long-distance trade. Unlike the Andean region, where sophisticated metallurgy developed early, metallurgy came late to Mesoamerica. When it did come, it was used primarily for ceremonial objects rather than for weapons and tools. Instead, Mesoamericans made weapons and other tools from obsidian, a volcanic glass capable of holding a razor-sharp edge, and for that reason a valued trade commodity.

Mesoamerican history before the Spanish conquest is conventionally divided into four major periods: The term *Classic*, with its associations to ancient Greece and its connotations of "best" or "highest," derives from European historical frameworks. It reflects the view of many early Mesoamericanists that the Classic period, which corresponds more or less to the time during which the Maya civilizations of the southern Yucatán erected dated stone monuments, was the high point of Mesoamerican civilization. That view is no longer so prevalent, but the terminology has endured. The chronology continues to provide a useful framework for understanding Mesoamerican history.

The transition from hunting and gathering to settled village life occurred gradually in Mesoamerica during the Archaic period. The cornerstone of the process was the domestication of maize (corn) and other staple crops, including beans and squash. Other plants native to the Americas that were domesticated in this period include tomatoes, chili peppers, and avocado. Maize and beans were particularly important because together they provide a rich source of protein compared to the grains that were the basis of the Neolithic revolution in the ancient Near East and China. In those regions domesticated animals supplied the protein settled agriculturalists needed in their diet. Mesoamerica, however, was poor in sources of animal protein. It had only a few domesticated animals—among them dogs and turkeys—and no large herd animals like the cattle, sheep, and goats of the Old World.

The domestication of maize, beans, and other plants secured the people of Mesoamerica an adequate and dependable diet. Over time they devised myriad ways to prepare and store these staples. Maize has also been one of Mesoamerica's major contributions to the world. Since the conquest, maize cultivation has spread to many other parts of the world. Corn is now one of North America's most important crops, and it is used to feed livestock in both North and South America.

Probably because they had no large draft animals—no horses or oxen—the people of the Americas, including Mesoamerica, never developed the wheel, although they made wheeled toys. In Mesoamerica humans did all the carrying. And because there were no horses and chariots, warfare in Mesoamerica (and in Andean South America) was always between armies of foot soldiers.

Between 5000 and 2500 B.C.E. villages began to appear in both highland and lowland regions of Mesoamerica. By about 2000 B.C.E. settled agricultural life had taken hold in much of the region. As in the Old World when this happened, people began to make fired clay vessels, and ceramic technology appeared. Nomadic hunter-gatherers have little need of storage, but farmers do, and clay vessels filled that need. Pottery is also a medium for artistic expression, and it played a role in religion and ritual observance throughout Mesoamerican history.

The Formative Period and the Emergence of Mesoamerican Civilization

By about 1500 B.C.E. Mesoamerica's agricultural villages were beginning to coalesce into more complicated societies, with towns and monumental architecture, the division of society into elite and commoner classes, long-distance trade among regions, and the emergence of sophisticated artistic traditions.

The Olmec

The most prominent of the Early Formative period cultures is that of the Olmec, centered on the lowlands of Mexico's Gulf coast. This is a densely vegetated region with slow, meandering streams bordered by areas of rich, alluvial soil. The Olmec were once thought of as Mesoamerica's "mother culture," but evidence is accumulating that similarly complex societies were emerging at about the same time throughout Mesoamerica.

Most of what is known about the Olmecs comes from the archaeological sites of San Lorenzo and La Venta (see Map 14–1). Other Olmec centers have not been as intensively studied. San Lorenzo was first occupied about 1500 B.C.E. and had developed into a prominent center by about 1200 B.C.E. It included public buildings, a drainage system linked to artificial ponds, and what was probably the earliest court for the Mesoamerican ball game. The center flourished until about 900 B.C.E. but then went into decline and had been abandoned by about 400 B.C.E. As San Lorenzo declined, La Venta rose to prominence, flourishing from about 900 to 400 B.C.E. La Venta's most conspicuous feature is a 110-foot, scalloped pyramid, known as the Great Pyramid, which stands at one end of a group of platforms and plazas aligned along a north–south axis. Archaeologists have recovered many caches of carved jade, serpentine, and granite artifacts that had been buried along the center line of this axis. Like San Lorenzo, La Venta also had an elaborate drainage system.

Probably the best-known Olmec works of art are the massive stone heads, some weighing more than twenty tons, that have been found at both San Lorenzo and La Venta. Thought to be portraits of Olmec rulers, these were carved from basalt from quarries as much as sixty five miles distant and transported, probably by raft, to the centers. The Olmec also carved other large basalt monuments, including altars and seated figures.

The population of San Lorenzo and La Venta was never great, probably less than 1,000 people. The monumental architecture and sculpture at these sites nonetheless suggests that Olmec society was dominated by an elite class of ruler-priests able to command the labor of the rest of the population. The elite probably lived in the centers, supported by farmers who lived in villages of pole-and-thatch houses.

Among the most pervasive images in Olmec art is that of the were-jaguar, a half-human, half-feline creature. The were-jaguar may have been a divine ancestor figure, perhaps providing the elite with the justification for their authority. Similarities between the were-jaguar iconography and that of later Mesoamerican deities suggests some of the underlying continuities linking Mesoamerican societies over time.

The raw material for many Olmec artifacts, such as jade and obsidian, comes from other regions of Mesoamerica. Likewise, Olmec goods and Olmec iconography like the were-jaguar are found in other regions, all suggesting that from an early time the parts of Mesoamerica were linked in a web of trade. These contacts would have fostered the spread of ideas, contributing to the formation of common Mesoamerican traditions. Control of trade in high-status

Chronology

Major Periods in Ancient Mesoamerican Civilization

8000–2000 B.C.E.	Archaic
2000 B.C.E.–150 C.E.	Formative (or Pre-Classic)
150–900 C.E.	Classic
900–1521 C.E.	Post-Classic

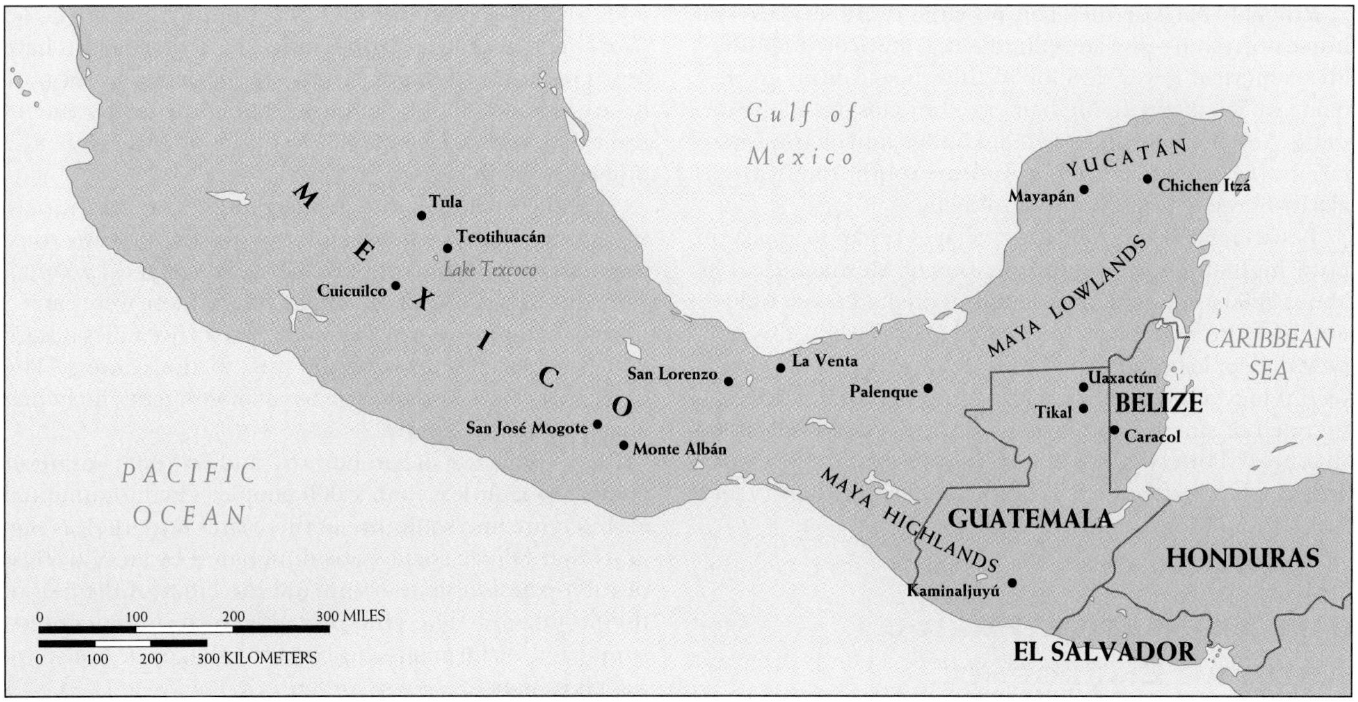

Map 14-1 Pre-Aztec Mesoamerican sites discussed in this chapter.

A large carved monument from the Olmec site of La Venta with a naturalistically rendered human figure. Robert and Linda Mitchell Photography materials like jade and obsidian by the Olmec elite would also have contributed to their prestige and authority.

THE VALLEY OF OAXACA AND THE RISE OF MONTE ALBAN

Olmec civilization faded after about 400 B.C.E. and had disappeared by about 200 B.C.E. Other regions, however, were rising to prominence. Some of the most significant developments in the Late Formative period occurred in the Valley of Oaxaca. The site of San José Mogote, located in one branch of the valley, had arisen at about the same time as San Lorenzo. By about 600 B.C.E. San José Mogote was a thriving center of perhaps 1,000 people. Around 500 B.C.E. a new center, Monte Alban, was built on a hill where three branches of the valley meet. Monte Alban's population soon grew to about 5,000, and it emerged as the capital of a state that dominated the Oaxaca region. Carved images of bound prisoners at Monte Alban suggest that warfare played a role in establishing its authority. They also suggest an early origin for the practice of ritual human sacrifice that characterized most Mesoamerican cultures. Monte Alban retained its authority in Oaxaca into the Classic period, maintaining its independence against the growing power of the greatest Classic city, Teotihuacán.

THE EMERGENCE OF WRITING AND THE MESOAMERICAN CALENDAR The earliest evidence of writing and the Mesoamerican calendar have been found in the Valley of Oaxaca at San José Mogote and Monte Alban. The Mesoamerican calendar is based on two interlocking cycles, each with its own day and month names. One cycle, tied to the solar year, was of 365 days; the other was of 260 days. Combining the two cycles produced a "century" of fifty-two years, the amount of time required before a particular combination of days in each cycle would repeat itself. The hieroglyphs found in Oaxaca relate to the 260-day cycle.

At the time of the Spanish conquest, all the peoples of Mesoamerica used this fifty two-year calendrical system. As we will see, only the Maya developed a calendar based on a longer time period, anchored—like the Jewish, Christian, or Muslim calendars—to a fixed starting point in the past.

THE CLASSIC PERIOD IN MESOAMERICA

The Classic period was a time of cultural florescence in Mesoamerica. In Central Mexico, it saw the rise of Teotihuacán, a great city that rivaled the largest cities of the world at the time. The Maya, who built densely populated cities in the seemingly inhospitable rain forests of the southern Yucatán, developed a sophisticated system of mathematics and Mesoamerica's most advanced hieroglyphic writing. Indeed, Classic-urban life in Mesoamerica was richer and on a larger scale than in Europe north of the Alps at the same time.

Archaeologists and art historians have recently made enormous strides in understanding Classic-civilization. Progress in deciphering Maya hieroglyphics has opened a window on the politics and statecraft of the Maya elite. Archaeological studies have broadened our understanding of Teotihuacán and Maya cities, revealing their extent and structure and providing clues to the lives of the people who lived in them.

Classic cities, with their many temples, plazas, and administrative buildings, were religious and administrative centers whose rulers combined secular and religious authority. It was once thought that Classic society was composed of peaceful theocracies, without the chronic warfare characterizing Mesoamerica at the time of the Spanish conquest. It is now clear, however, that warfare was common during the Classic period and that Classic rulers did not hesitate to use force to expand their influence and maintain their authority. The ritual sacrifice of captive enemies was also a feature of Classic societies.

TEOTIHUACÁN

In the Late Formative period two centers competed for dominance over the rapidly growing population of the Valley of Mexico. One of these, Cuicuilco, was located at the southern end of the valley. The other, Teotihuacán, was located about thirty miles northeast of Mexico City. When a volcano destroyed Cuicuilco in the first century C.E., Teotihuacán was left unopposed and grew explosively into a great city, perhaps Mesoamerica's first true city-state, dominating central Mexico for many centuries and strongly influencing the rest of Mesoamerica.

Several natural advantages contributed to Teotihuacán's rise. The original source of its prestige may have been a network of caves recently discovered under its most prominent monument, the Pyramid of the Sun (the name by which the Aztecs knew it). These caves may have been considered an entrance to the underworld. Recent studies indicate that stone quarried from them was used to construct the city, creating a direct symbolic link between the city's buildings and its sacred origins. Teotihuacán is also located near an important source of obsidian, straddling a trade route to the Gulf coast and southern Mesoamerica. The quarrying of obsidian and the manufacture and trade of obsidian goods were apparently major sources of the city's wealth and influence. Finally, Teotihuacán is surrounded by fertile farmland susceptible to intensive cultivation with terracing and irrigation.

At its height in about 500 C.E. this remarkable city extended over almost nine square miles and had a population of more than 150,000, making it one of the largest cities in the world at the time. Its size and organization suggest that it was ruled by a powerful, centralized authority. It is laid out on a rigid grid plan dominated by a broad, three-mile-long thoroughfare known as the Avenue of the Dead. Religious and administrative structures and a market occupy the center of the city. At one end of the Avenue of the Dead is the so-called Pyramid of the Moon, and near it, to one side, is the 210-foot-high Pyramid of the Sun. More than 2,000 residential structures surround the city center. The most lavish of these, the homes of the city's elite, lie nearest the center. Most of the city's residents lived in walled apartment compounds farther from the center. These compounds were also centers of craft manufacture, with neighborhoods devoted to pottery, obsidian work, and other specialties. Some parts of the city were reserved for foreign traders. One neighborhood, for example, was home to people from Monte Alban and the Oaxaca region. Paintings and murals adorned the interiors of many buildings, including those of the common people as well as the elite. The humble dwellings of poor farmers occupied the city's periphery. As the city grew, local farmers had apparently been forced to abandon their villages and move to Teotihuacán, another indication of the power of the city's rulers.

Teotihuacán's influence extended throughout Mesoamerica. In the central highlands, dispersed settlements were consolidated into larger centers laid out similarly to Teotihuacán, suggesting conquest and direct control—a Teotihuacán empire. The city's influence in other, more distant regions may have reflected close trading ties rather than conquest. Buildings in Teotihuacán's distinctive architectural style at the site of Kaminaljuyu in the highlands of modern Guatemala, for example, may have been residences for Teotihuacano merchants. The city's obsidian and pottery were exchanged widely for items like the green feathers of the quetzal bird and jaguar skins, valued for ritual garments.

Many of the buildings in Teotihuacán were decorated with striking, skillfully made sculptures and murals of the city's gods and ritual practices. Among the deities of Teotihuacán are a storm god and his goddess counterpart, whose representation suggests a link to the Aztec's rain god, Tlaloc, and his consort, Chalchiuhtlicue. The people of Teotihuacán also worshiped a feathered serpent who is recog-

The Pyramid of the Sun stands near the southern end of Teotihuacán's great central thoroughfare, the Avenue of the Dead. Kal Muller/Woodfin Camp & Associates nizably antecedent to the god the Aztecs worshiped as Quetzalcoatl and the Maya as Kukulcan. Murals also suggest that the Teotihuacán elite, like the Maya and later Mesoamerican peoples, drew their own blood as a form of sacrifice to the gods. A mass burial under one of the city's principal temples indicates that they also practiced human sacrifice.

After 500 C.E. Teotihuacán's influence began to wane, and some time in the eighth century, for reasons that are still poorly understood, its authority collapsed. A fire swept through the city, destroying the ritual center and the residences of the elite and hinting at an internal revolt. Although a substantial population lived on in the city, it never regained its former status. It retained its hold on the imagination of succeeding generations of Mesoamericans, however, much like the ruins of ancient Greece and Rome on the imaginations of later Europeans. The name by which we know it, Teotihuacán, is an Aztec word meaning "City of the Gods," and it was still a revered pilgrimage site at the time of the Spanish conquest.

THE MAYA

Maya civilization arose in southern Mesoamerica, which includes modern Guatemala, the Yucatán Peninsula, Belize, and parts of Honduras and El Salvador. Village life established itself in this region during the first millennium B.C.E., and thereafter the population began to rise steadily. The earliest distinctively Maya urban sites date to around 300 B.C.E. in the Late Formative period. During the Classic period, Maya civilization experienced a remarkable florescence in the lowland jungles of the southern Yucatán.

All the pre-Spanish societies of Mesoamerica were literate, recording historical and religious information on scrolled or screenfold books made with deerhide or bark paper. Only a handful of these books, four of them Mayan, have survived the ravages of time and the Spanish conquest. (Spanish priests, who viewed native religious texts as idolatrous, burned almost all of them.) The Maya of the Classic period, who developed Mesoamerica's most advanced writing system, were unique in the extent to which they inscribed writing and calendrical symbols in stone, pottery, and other imperishable materials.

Thanks to rapid advances in the decipherment of Maya writing and to intensive archaeological work at Maya cities, our understanding of the nature of Classic Maya civilization has changed radically in recent decades. According to earlier views, Maya cities were not really cities but empty ceremonial centers inhabited by scholar-priests. The inscriptions were thought to be concerned entirely with astronomical and calendrical observations tied to Maya ritual. Scattered farming communities were thought to have surrounded the centers, supporting the priestly elite. Relations between centers were thought to be peaceful. Contributing to this view was the belief that intensive agriculture capable of supporting dense populations was impossible in the tropical forests of the southern Yucatán where Classic Maya civilization developed.

Archaeologists have shown that Maya centers were indeed cities, and that the largest of them, Tikal, probably had a population of between 50,000 and 70,000 at its height. They have also found evidence of terracing, irrigation systems, and other agricultural technologies that would have increased yields enough to support dense populations. Powerful ruling families and their elite retainers dominated these cities, supported by a far larger class of farmer-commoners. The inscriptions are almost entirely devoted to recounting important events in the lives of these rulers. Cities competed for dominance, and warfare between them was chronic. As murals and sculptures show, captured prisoners were sacrificed to appease the gods and glorify the victorious ruler.

Religion deeply informed the social and political realm of the Maya. They believed that the world had gone through several cycles of creation before the present one. They recognized no clear distinction between a natural and a supernatural world. As was probably true also of Teotihuacán, rulers and the elite combined religious and political authority, mediating between humans and gods through elaborate rituals in the temples and plazas of their cities. Rulers claimed association with the gods to justify their authority. They wore special regalia that symbolized their power, and they performed rituals to sustain the gods and the cosmic order. These rituals included bloodletting ceremonies, the sacrifice of captives, and ball games.

This reproduction of one of the remarkable murals found at the Maya site of Bonampak shows the presentation of captives to the city's ruler, Chan Muan. Copyright © President and Fellows of Harvard College 1998. All rights reserved Peabody Museum, Harvard University. Photograph by Hillel Burger.

DOCUMENT A MAYA MYTH OF CREATION

This segment of the Maya creation myth is from the Popol Vuh, a compendium of Maya mythology and history transcribed into European script by a Quiche Maya noble in the sixteenth century.

How does this myth describe the world before creation? Who are the beings that exist before creation and decide how it is to be carried out? What did they do to create the earth?

There was not yet one person, one animal, bird, fish, crab, tree, rock, hollow, canyon, meadow, forest. Only the sky alone is there; the face of the earth is not clear. Only the sea alone is pooled under all the sky; there is nothing whatever gathered together. It is at rest; not a single thing stirs. It is held back; kept at rest under the sky.

Whatever might be is simply not there; only murmurs, ripples, in the dark, in the night. Only the Maker, Modeler alone, Sovereign Plumed Serpent, the Bearers, Begetters are in the water, a glittering light. . . .

So there were three of them, as Heart of Sky, who came to the Sovereign Plumed Serpent, when the dawn of life was conceived:

"How should it be sown, how should it dawn? Who is to be the provider, nurturer?"

"Let it be this way, think about it: this water should be removed, emptied out for the formation of the earth's own plate and platform, then comes the sowing, the dawning of the sky-earth. But there will be no high days and no bright praise for our work, our design, until the rise of the human work, the human design," they said.

And then the earth rose because of them; it was simply their word that brought it forth. For the forming of the earth, they said, "Earth." It arose suddenly, just like a cloud, like a mist, now forming, unfolding. Then the mountains were separated from the water, all at once the great mountains came forth. By their genius alone, by their cutting edge alone they carried out the conception of the mountain-plain, whose face grew instant groves of cypress and pine.

Reprinted with the permission of Simon & Schuster from *Popol Vuh* by Dennis Tedlock. Copyright © 1985 by Dennis Tedlock.

The significance of sacrifice and the ball game in Maya ideology is reflected in a Maya creation myth recorded in the *Popol Vuh*, a Maya book transcribed into European script by a Maya noble in the sixteenth century. Imagery in Classic Maya art has been linked to this myth, which tells how the Hero Twins defeated the gods of the underworld in the ball game and returned to life after being sacrificed. One became the sun and the other Venus, and in their regular rising and setting reenact their descent into the underworld and their subsequent rebirth. All Maya cities had ball courts. The games played there were a symbolic reenactment of the confrontation between the Hero Twins and the lords of the underworld, and the losing team was sometimes sacrificed.[1]

The Classic Maya developed a sophisticated mathematics and were among the first peoples in the world to invent the concept of zero. In addition to the fifty two-year calendar round based on interlocking 260- and 365-day cycles they shared with other Mesoamerican societies, the Maya developed an absolute calendar, known as the Long Count, tied to a fixed point in the past. The calendar had great religious as well as practical significance for the Maya. They viewed the movements of the celestial bodies to which the calendar was tied—including the sun, moon, and Venus—as deities. The complexity and accuracy of their calendar reflect Maya skills in astronomical observation. They adjusted their lunar calendar for the actual length of the lunar cycle (29.53 days) and may have had provisions like our leap years for the actual length of the solar year. They also made accurate observations of Venus and recognized before other peoples that it is both the morning and the evening star. The importance of the calendar, its association with divine forces, and the esoteric knowledge required to master it must have been an important source of prestige and power for its elite guardians.

Scholars have been able to correlate the Long Count calendar with the European calendar, and so can date Maya monuments with a precision unknown for other ancient Mesoamerican societies. The commemorative monuments erected by Classic Maya rulers to record their accomplishments almost always have Long Count dates. As a result, it is now possible to reconstruct the dynastic histories of many Maya cities in detail, keeping in mind, of course, that Maya rulers—like rulers everywhere throughout history—may have exaggerated their accomplishments to put themselves in a favorable light.

During the Classic period no single center dominated the Maya region. Rather, many independent units, each composed of a capital city and smaller subject towns and villages, alternately vied and cooperated with each other, rising and falling in relative prominence. Tikal, at its height the largest Classic Maya city, is also one of the most thoroughly studied. The residential center covers more than fourteen square miles and has more than 3,000 structures. The city follows the uneven terrain of the rain forest and is not, like Teotihuacán, laid out on a grid. Monumental causeways link the major structures of the site.

[1] Robert J. Sharer, *The Ancient Maya*, 5th ed. (Stanford: Stanford University Press, 1994), p. 522.

Ruins of Tikal. The structure on the right, towering above the jungle canopy, is known as Temple I or the Temple of the Giant Jaguar. It housed the tomb of Ah Cacao, who ruled Tikal from 682 to about 723.
Robert Frerk/Odyssey Productions

Tikal emerged as an important center in the Late Formative, benefiting from its strategic position. The city is located near a source of flint, valued as a raw material for stone tools. It is also located near swamps that, with modification, might have been agriculturally productive. And it has access to river systems that lead both to the Gulf and the Caribbean coasts, giving it control of the trade between those regions.

A single dynasty of thirty-nine rulers reigned in Tikal from the Early Classic until the eighth century. The early rulers in this Jaguar Paw line were buried in a structure known as the North Acropolis, and the inscriptions associated with their tombs provide us with details about them, including in many cases their names, the dates of their rule, and the dates of major military victories. Monuments associated with the ruler Great Jaguar Paw, for example, suggests that in 378 C.E. he conquered the city of Uaxactún and installed a relative on its throne.

Late in the fourth century links developed between Tikal and Teotihuacán. One ruler, Curl Nose, who ascended to the throne in 379, may have married into the ruling family from the Teotihuacán-dominated city of Kaminaljuyu in the southern highlands.

For about 100 years beginning in the mid–sixth century, Tikal and most other lowland Maya sites experienced a hiatus during which there was little new construction. The city lost much of its influence and may have suffered a serious defeat at the hands of the city of Caracol. Then in 682 the ruler Ah Cacau (r. 682–723?) ascended the throne and initiated a new period of vigor and prosperity for Tikal, again expanding its influence through conquest and strategic marriage alliances. He and his two immediate successors, Yax Kin (r. 734–?) and Chitam (r. 769–?), began an ambitious building program, creating most of Tikal's surviving monumental structures, including the dramatic, soaring temples that dominate the site. Chitam was the last ruler in the Jaguar Paw dynasty. After he died Tikal again declined and, like other sites in the southern lowlands, it never recovered.

Similar dynastic histories have been emerging from research at other Classic Maya sites. Inscriptions in the shrine above the tomb of Lord Pacal (r. 615–683), the greatest ruler of the city of Palenque, located in the west of the Maya region in hills overlooking the Gulf coast plain, record the city's entire dynastic history back to mythic ancestors. Two of the rulers in this genealogy were women, one of them Pacal's mother, Lady Zac Kuk (r. 612–640), and another predecessor, Lady Kanal Ikal (r. 583–604). Palenque is also remarkable for its architectural innovations, which permitted its architects to build structures with thinner walls and larger rooms than at other Classic sites.

Between 800 and 900 C.E. Classic civilization collapsed in the southern lowlands. The ruling dynasties all came to an end, the construction of monumental architecture and sculpture with Long Count dates ceased, and the great cities were virtually abandoned. The cause of the collapse has long been a subject of intense speculation, and is still not known for sure. The factors that may have contributed to it, however, are becoming clearer. Among them are intensifying warfare, population growth, increased population concentration, and attempts to increase agricultural production that ultimately backfired. As the urban areas around the ceremonial centers grew, so did the demand for food. Ambitious building projects continued in the centers right up to the collapse, and some scholars believe that as a growing proportion of the population was employed in these projects, fewer were left to produce food. Overfarming may then have led to soil exhaustion. Some archaeologists also believe a major drought may have occurred. Clearly the Maya exceeded the capacities of their resources, but exactly why and how remain unknown.

After the abandonment of the Classic sites in the southern lowlands, the focus of Maya civilization shifted to the northern Yucatán. There the site of Chichén Itzá, located next to a sacred well, flourished from the ninth to the thirteenth centuries. Stylistic resemblances between Chichén Itzá and Tula, the capital of the Post-Classic Toltec Empire in central Mexico (see the next section) suggest ties between the two cities, but archaeologists are uncertain of their nature. Chichén Itzá had the largest ball court in the Maya area. After Chichén Itzá's fall, Mayapan became the main Maya center. By the time of the Spanish conquest it too had lost sway, and the Maya had divided into small, competing centers.

The Post-Classic Period

No new strong, centralized power arose immediately to replace Teotihuacán in the wake of its collapse in the eighth century. Warfare increased, and several smaller, militaristic states emerged, many centered around fortified hilltop cities. At the same time interregional trade and market systems became increasingly important, and secular and religious authority, closely linked during the Classic period, began to diverge.

The Toltecs

About 900 C.E. a people known as the Toltecs rose to prominence. Their capital, Tula, is located near the northern periphery of Mesoamerica. Like Teotihuacán, it lay close to an important source of obsidian. The Toltecs themselves were apparently descendants of one of many "barbarian" northern peoples (like the later Aztecs) who began migrating into Mesoamerica during the Late Classic.

Aztec mythology glorified the Toltecs, seeing them as the fount of civilization and attributing to them a vast and powerful empire to which the Aztecs were the legitimate heirs. Other Mesoamerican peoples at the time of the conquest also attributed legendary status to the Toltecs. The archaeological evidence for a Toltec empire, however, is ambiguous. Although a substantial city with a population of between 35,000 and 60,000 people, Tula was never as large or as organized as Teotihuacán. Toltec influence reached many regions of Mesoamerica—as already noted, there were many stylistic affinities between Tula and the Maya city of Chichén Itzá—but archaeologists are uncertain whether that influence translated into political control.

Toltec iconography, which stresses human sacrifice, death, blood, and military symbolism, supports their warlike reputation. Their deities are clearly antecedent to those worshiped by the Aztecs, including the feathered serpent Quetzalcoatl and the warlike trickster Tezcatlipoca.

Whatever the reality of Toltec power, it was short-lived. By about 1100 Tula was in decline and its influence gone.

The Aztecs

The people commonly known as the Aztecs referred to themselves as the Mexica, a name that lives on as *Mexico.* At the time of the arrival of the Spanish in 1519 the Aztecs controlled a powerful empire that dominated much of Mesoamerica. Their capital city, Tenochtitlán, was the most populous yet seen in Mesoamerica. Built on islands and landfill in the southern part of Lake Texcoco in the Valley of Mexico, it was home to some 200,000 to 300,000 people. Its great temples and palaces gleamed in the sun. Bearing tribute to its rulers and goods to its great markets, canoes crowded the city's canals and people on foot thronged its streets and the great causeways linking it to the mainland. The city's traders brought precious goods from distant regions; vast wealth flowed in constantly from subject territories. Yet the people responsible for these accomplishments were relative newcomers, the foundation of their power being less than two hundred years old.

Because of the dramatic clash with Spanish adventurers that brought their empire to an end, we have more direct information about the Aztecs than any other preconquest Mesoamerican people. Many of the conquistadors recorded their experiences, and postconquest administrators and missionaries collected valuable information about their new subjects while at the same time seeking to extirpate their religion and culture. Although filtered through the bitterness of defeat for the Aztecs and the biases of the conquerors, these records nevertheless provide detailed information about Aztec society and Aztec history.

According to their own legends, the Aztecs were originally a nomadic people inhabiting the shores of a mythical Lake Aztlán somewhere to the northwest of the Valley of Mexico. At the urging of their patron god Huitzilopochtli, they began to migrate, arriving in the Valley of Mexico early in the thirteenth century. Scorned by the people of the cities and states already there, but prized and feared as mercenaries, they ended up in the marshy land on the shores of Lake Texcoco. They finally settled on the island that be-

DOCUMENT A SPANIARD DESCRIBES THE GLORY OF THE AZTEC CAPITAL

On November 8, 1519, a group of approximately four hundred Spaniards under the command of Hernán Cortés entered the Aztec capital of Tenochtitlán. One of them was Bernal Díaz del Castillo (b. 1492) who later wrote The Conquest of New Spain, *a chronicle of his experience. This gives some sense of the magnificence of the Aztec capital.*

What elements of Aztec life especially astonished Díaz? What can one conclude about the social and political life of the Aztec elite from the manner in which Montezuma was attended? What forms of wealth were most apparent?

Early next day we left Iztapalapa [where Cortés forces had been camped] with a large escort of these great Caciques [Aztec nobles], and followed the causeway, which is eight yards wide and goes so straight to the city of Mexico [Tenochtitlán] that I do not think it curves at all. Wide though it was, it was so crowded with people that there was hardly room for them all. Some were going to Mexico and others coming away, besides those who had come out to see us, and we could hardly get through the crowds that were there. For the towers and the cues [temples] were full, and they came in canoes from all parts of the lake. No wonder, since they had never seen horses or men like us before.

With such wonderful sights to gaze on we did not know what to say, or if this was real that we saw before our eyes. On the land side there were great cities, and on the lake many more. The lake was crowded with canoes. At intervals along the causeway there were many bridges, and before us was the great city of Mexico. . . .

We marched along our causeway to a point where another small causeway branches off to another city . . . and there, beside some towerlike buildings, which were their shrines, we were met by many more Caciques and dignitaries in very rich cloaks. The different chieftains wore different brilliant liveries, and the causeways were full of them. . . .

. . . When we came near to Mexico, at the place where there were some other small towers, the great Montezuma descended from his litter, and these other great Caciques supported him beneath a marvelously rich canopy of green feathers, decorated with gold work, silver, pearls . . . which hung from a sort of border. It was a marvelous sight. The great Montezuma was magnificently clad, in their fashion and wore sandals . . . the soles of which are of gold and the upper parts ornamented with precious stones. And the four lords who supported him were richly clad also in garments that seem to have been kept ready for them on the road so they could accompany their master . . . and many more lords . . . walked before the great Montezuma, sweeping the ground on which he was to tread, and laying down cloaks so that his feet should not touch the earth. Not one of these chieftains dared to look him in the face. All kept their eyes lowered most reverently except those four lords, his nephews, who were supporting him.

. . . Who could now count the multitude of men, women, and boys in the streets, on the roof-tops and in canoes on the waterways, who had come out to see us? . . .

They led us to our quarters, which were in some large houses capable of accommodating us all and had formerly belonged to the great Montezuma's father. . . . Here Montezuma now kept the great shrines of his gods, and a secret chamber containing gold bars and jewels. This was the treasure he had inherited from his father, which he never touched.

From *The Conquest of New Spain*, by Bernal Díaz, trans. by J. M. Cohen (New York: Penguin Books, 1963), copyright © J. M. Cohen, 1963, pp. 216–218.

came Tenochtitlán in 1325 after seeing an eagle perched there on a prickly pear cactus, an omen Huitzilopochtli had said would identify the end of their wandering.

The Aztecs accepted a position as tributaries and mercenaries for Azcazpotzalco, then the most powerful state in the valley, but soon became trusted allies with their own tribute-paying territories. They further consolidated their position with marriage alliances to the ruling families of other cities. These alliances gave their own rulers claim to descent from the Toltecs. In 1428, under their fourth ruler, Itzcoatl (r. 1427–1440), the Aztecs formed a triple alliance with Texcoco and Tlacopan, turned against Azcazpotzalco, and became the dominant power in the Valley of Mexico. It was at this time, less than 100 years before the arrival of Cortés, that the Aztecs, as head of the Triple Alliance, began the aggressive expansion that brought them their vast tribute-paying empire (see Map 14–2).

Itzcoatl also laid the foundation of Aztec imperial ideology. He ordered the burning of all the ancient books in the valley, expunging any history that conflicted with Aztec pretensions, and restructured Aztec religion and ritual to support and justify Aztec preeminence. The Aztecs now presented themselves as the divinely ordained successors to the ancient Toltecs, and with each new conquest and the growing splendor of Tenochtitlán, they seemed to ratify that claim.

Aztec conquests ultimately included almost all of central Mexico. To the west, however, they were unable to conquer the rival Tarascan Empire with its capital of Tzintzuntzan. And within the Aztec realm several pockets, most prominently Tlaxcala, remained unsubdued but nonetheless locked into a pattern of ritual warfare with the Aztecs.

THE AZTEC EXTRACTIVE EMPIRE The Aztec Empire was extractive. After a conquest, the Aztecs usually left the

MAP EXPLORATION

Interactive map: To explore this map further, go to http://www.prenhall.com/craig_map14.2

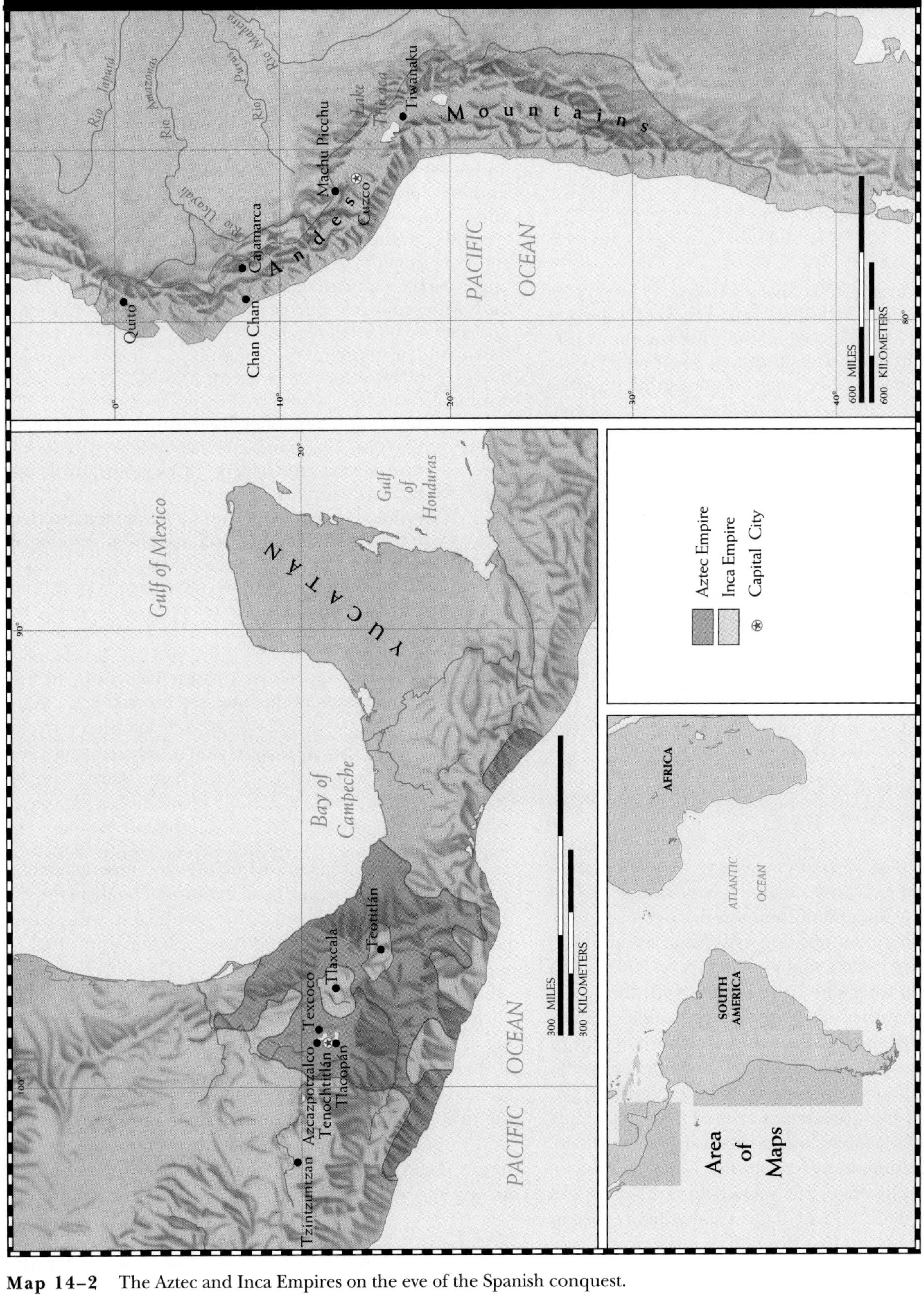

Map 14–2 The Aztec and Inca Empires on the eve of the Spanish conquest.

local elite intact and in power, imposing their rule indirectly. But they demanded heavy tribute in goods and labor. Tribute included goods of all kinds, including agricultural products, fine craft goods, gold and jade, textiles, and precious feathers. Tribute lists in Tenochtitlán, which the Spanish preserved because they, too, wished to exploit the empire they had conquered, indicate the immense quantity of goods that flowed into Tenochtitlán's coffers as a result. In a given year, for example, tribute included as much as 7,000 tons of maize and 2 million cotton cloaks. One nearby province alone was responsible for "12,800 cloaks . . ., 1600 loin cloths, 1600 women's tunics, 8 warriors' costumes . . ., 32,000 bundles of paper, 8000 bowls, and 4 bins of maize and beans."[2] It was this wealth that underwrote the grandeur of Tenochtitlán, making it, as one commentator has described it, "a beautiful parasite, feeding on the lives and labour of other peoples and casting its shadow over all their arrangements."[3]

AZTEC RELIGION AND HUMAN SACRIFICE Aztec imperial exploitation did not end with food, cotton, and valued craft goods. Human sacrifice on a prodigious scale was central to Aztec ideology. The Aztecs believed that Huitzilopochtli, as sun god, required human blood to sustain him as he battled the moon and stars each night to rise again each day, and that it was their responsibility to provide the victims. The prime candidates for sacrifice were war captives, and the Aztecs often engaged in "flowery wars" with traditional enemies like Tlaxcala just to obtain captives. On major festivals, thousands of victims might perish. Led up the steps of the temple of Huitzilopochtli, a victim was thrown backward over a stone, his arms and legs pinned, while a priest cut out his heart. He would then be rolled down the steps of the temple, his head placed on a skull rack, and his limbs butchered and distributed to be eaten. Small children were sacrificed to the rain god Tlaloc, who, it was believed, was pleased by their tears.

Victims were also selected as god impersonators, stand-ins for particular gods who were sacrificed after a series of rituals. The rituals involved in the festivals honoring the powerful god Tezcatlipoca were particularly elaborate. A beautiful male youth was chosen to represent the god for an entire year, during which he was treated with reverence. He wandered through the city dressed as the god and playing the flute. A month before the end of his reign he was given four young women as wives. Twenty days before his death he was dressed as a warrior and for a few days he was virtually ruler of the city. Then he and his guardians left the city for an island in the lake. As he ascended the steps of the temple, there to be sacrificed, the new Tezcatlipoca began playing his flutes in Tenochtitlán.

As we have seen, human sacrifice had long been characteristic of Mesoamerican societies, but no other Mesoamerican people practiced it on the seale of the Aztecs. Whatever other reasons for it there might have been, one effect must certainly have been to intimidate subject peoples. It may also have had the effect of reducing the population of fighting-age men from conquered provinces, and with it the possibility of rebellion. Together with the heavy burden of tribute, human sacrifice may also have fed resentment and fear, explaining why so many subject peoples were willing to throw in their lot with Cortés when he challenged the Aztecs.

TENOCHITITLÁN Three great causeways linked Tenochtitlán to the mainland. These met at the ceremonial core of the city, dominated by a double temple dedicated to Huitzilopochtli and the rain god Tlaloc. It was here that most of the Aztec's sacrificial victims met their fate. The palaces of the ruler and high nobles lay just outside the central precinct. The ruler's palace was the empire's administrative center, with government officials, artisans and laborers, gardens, and a zoo of exotic animals. The rest of the city was divided into four quarters, and these further divided into numerous wards (*calpulli*). Some *calpulli* were specialized, reserved for merchants (*pochteca*) or artisans. The city was laid out on a grid formed of streets and canals. Agricultural plots of great fertility known as *chinampas* bordered the canal and the lake shores. Aqueducts carried fresh water from springs on the lake shore into the city. A massive dike kept the briny water of the northern part of Lake Texcoco from contaminating the waters around Tenochtitlán. The neighboring city of Tlatelolco was noted for its great marketplace.

SOCIETY Aztec society was hierarchical, authoritarian, and militaristic. It was divided into two broad classes, noble and commoner, with merchants and certain artisans forming an intermediate category. The nobility enjoyed great wealth and luxury. Laws and regulations relating to dress reinforced social divisions. Elaborate and brilliantly colored regalia distinguished nobles from commoners and rank within the nobility. Commoners were required to wear rough, simple garments.

The Aztecs were morally austere. They valued obedience, respectfulness, discipline, and moderation. Laws were strict and punishment severe. Standards for the nobility were higher than for commoners, and punishments for sexual and social offenses were more strictly enforced the higher one stood in the hierarchy. Drunkenness was frowned upon and harshly punished among the elite. Parents would even execute their own children for breaking moral laws and customs.

The highest rank in the nobility was that of *tlatoani* (plural *tlatoque*), or ruler of a major political unit. Of these, the highest were the rulers of the three cities of the Triple Alliance; of them, the highest was the *tlatoani* of Tenochtitlán. Below them were the *tetcutin*, lords of subordinate units. And below them were the *pipiltin*, who filled the bureaucracy and the priesthood.

[2] Frances F. Berdan. *The Aztecs of Central Mexico: An Imperial Society* (New York: Holt, Rinehart, and Winston, 1982), p. 36.
[3] Inga Clendinnen, *Aztecs: An Interpretation* (Cambridge: Cambridge University Press, 1991). p. 8.

DOCUMENT NEZAHUALCOYOTL OF TEXCOCO SINGS OF THE GIVER OF LIFE

Nezahualcoyotl, ruler of Texcoco, lived from 1402 to 1472 and was admired as a philosopher-king. In this poem he sings of the presence of the Giver of Life who invents himself and of the ability of human beings to invoke this divinity, but at the same time he emphasizes the impossibility of achieving any close relationship with the divinity.

In what ways does this song remind you of the thought and religious traditions of the early civilizations of China, India, Egypt, and Greece? What are the characteristics of "He Who invents Himself"? What kind of relationship can human beings achieve with this being? Why does the singer compare seeking the Giver of Life with seeking someone among flowers?

In no place can be the house of He Who invents Himself.
But in all places He is invoked,
in all places He is venerated,
His glory, His fame are sought on the earth.
It is He Who invents everything
He is Who invents Himself: God.
In all places He is invoked,
in all places He is venerated,
His glory, His fame are sought on the earth.
No one here is able,
no one is able to be intimate
with the Giver of Life;
only He is invoked, at His side,
near to Him,
one can live on the earth.
He who finds Him,
knows only one thing; He is invoked,
at His side, near to Him,
one can live on the earth.
In truth no one is intimate with You,
O Giver of Life!
Only as among the flowers,
we might seek someone,
thus we seek You,
we who live on the earth,
while we are at Your side.
Our hearts will be troubled,
only for a short time,
we will be near You and at Your side.
The Giver of Life enrages us,
He intoxicates us here.
No one can be perhaps at His side,
be famous, rule on the earth.
Only You change things
as our hearts know it:
No one can be perhaps at His side,
be famous, rule on the earth.

From *Fifteen Poets of the Aztec World* by Miguel León-Portilla. Copyright © 1992 University of Oklahoma Press, pp. 86–88. Reprinted by permission.

The bulk of the population were commoners. It was they who farmed the *chinampas,* harvested fish from the lake, and provided labor for public projects. All commoners belonged to a *calpulli,* each of which had its own temple. Children received training in ritual and ideology in the song houses attached to these temples. Young men received military training in the *telpochcalli,* or young men's house. *Calpulli* officials were responsible for assuring that the *calpulli* fulfilled its tribute obligations. Commoners unable to pay debts or their required tribute might become slaves. They might also become slaves for some criminal offenses. A class of serfs worked the estates of noblemen.

Professional traders and merchants—*pochteca*—were important figures in Aztec society. Their activities, backed by the threat of force from Aztec armies, were a key factor in spreading Aztec influence. Their far-reaching expeditions brought back precious luxury goods for the lords of Tenochtitlán. They organized their own guilds and established their own laws and customs for doing business. Their wealth put them in an ambiguous position in Aztec society. As a result, they tended to be self-effacing and avoided ostentatious display. Artisans of luxury goods—including lapidaries, feather workers, and goldsmiths—also had their own *calpulli* and enjoyed a special status.

Markets were central to Aztec economic life. The great market at Tlatelolco impressed the Spaniards for its great size, orderliness, and the variety of goods traded there. More than 60,000 people went there daily. Market administrators, women as well as men, regulated transactions. Cacao beans and cotton cloaks served as mediums of exchange.

Above all else, Aztec society was organized for war. Although there was no standing army as such, the entire society stood on a war footing. All young men received military training, nobles in special schools reserved for them, commoners in their *calpulli* schools. Battles were fought to capture new territory, punish rebellious or recalcitrant tributaries, protect trading expeditions, and secure access to important natural resources. Some battles—the flowery wars—were fought just to secure sacrificial victims. Combat was a matter of individual contests, not the confrontation of massed infantry. A warrior's goal was to subdue and capture prisoners for sacrifice. Prowess in battle, as measured by the number of prisoners a warrior captured, was key to social advancement and rewards for

A disc with relief carving showing the dismembered body of the Aztec moon goddess Coyolxauhqui, Huitzilopochtli's sister. She and the stars tried to prevent Huitzilopochtli's birth, but he emerged fully armed from his mother and killed her. This disc lay at the foot of the temple of Huitzilopochtli in Tenochtitlán (stone 3.5 m diameter). (This is discussed in more detail in the Art and the World essay on p. 376.) Barbara and Justin Kerr Studio

both commoners and nobles. Failure in battle brought social disgrace.

Women in Aztec society could inherit and own property. They traded in the marketplace and served as market officials. With their craftwork they could provide their families with extra income. Girls and boys alike were educated in the song houses, and women had access to priestly roles, although they were barred from high religious positions. In general, however, the Aztec emphasis on warfare left women in a subordinate position, tending hearth and home and excluded from positions of high authority. As a man's primary role was to be a warrior, a woman's was to bear children, and childbirth was compared to battle. Death in childbirth, like death in battle, guaranteed rewards in the afterlife.

Andean South America

The Andean region of South America—primarily modern Peru and Bolivia—had, like Mesoamerica, a long history of indigenous civilization when Spanish conquerors arrived in the sixteenth century. This is a region of dramatic contrasts. From near the equator south, a narrow strip of desert, one of the driest in the world, lines the Pacific coast. Beyond this strip the Andes Mountains rise abruptly. Small river valleys descend the western face of the mountains, cutting the desert plain to create a series of oases from north to south. The cold waters of the Humboldt current sweep north along the coast from the Antarctic, carrying rich nutrients that support abundant sea life. Within the Andes are regions of high peaks and steep terrain, regions of grassland (*puna*), and deep, warm, fertile intermontane valleys. The eastern slopes of the mountains, covered with dense vegetation, descend into the great tropical rain forest of the Amazon basin.

From ancient times, the people of the coast lived by exploiting the marine resources of the Pacific and by cultivating maize, beans, squash, and cotton. They also engaged in long-distance trade by sea along the Pacific coast.

The people of the highlands domesticated several plants native to the Andean region, including the potato, other tubers, and a grain called quinoa. They cultivated (and still cultivate) these crops on the high slopes of the Andes. In the intermontane valleys they cultivated maize. And in the *puna* grasslands they kept herds of llamas and alpacas—the Andean camelids—using them for their fur, their meat, and as beasts of burden. Highland communities since ancient times have maintained access to the different resources available in different altitude zones, with holdings in each zone that can be far distant from each other. They share this adaptation, which anthropologists sometimes call *verticality*, with people in other mountainous regions, such as the Alps and the Himalayas.[4]

Andean civilization is conventionally divided into seven periods: the Early, Middle, and Late Horizons are periods in which a homogeneous art style spread over a wide area. The Intermediate periods are characterized by regional stylistic diversity.

The Preceramic and the Initial Period

The earliest monumental architecture in Peru dates to the early third millennium B.C.E., roughly contemporary with the Great Pyramids of Egypt. Located on the coast mostly near the shore, these earliest centers consist of ceremonial mounds and plazas and predate the introduction of pottery to Peru.

Coastal people at this time subsisted primarily on the bounties of the sea, supplementing their diets with squash, beans, and chili peppers cultivated in the floodplains of the coastal rivers. They also cultivated gourds—for use as containers and utensils—and cotton. The cotton fishing nets and other textiles of this period represent the beginning of the sophisticated Andean textile tradition.

The earliest public buildings in the highlands date to before 2500 B.C.E. These are typically stone-walled structures enclosing a sunken fire pit used to burn ritual offerings. The distribution of these structures, first identified at the site of Kotosh, suggests that highland people shared a set of religious beliefs that archaeologists have called the *Kotosh religious tradition.* Highland people were more dependent on agriculture than coastal people during the late preceramic, cultivating maize as well as potatoes and other highland tubers. Llamas and alpacas were fully domesticated by about 2500 B.C.E.

There is little evidence of social stratification for the late preceramic. The public structures of both the coast and the highlands appear to have been centers of community ritual for relatively egalitarian societies.

The introduction of pottery to Peru around 2000 B.C.E. marks the beginning of the Initial period and corresponds to a major shift in settlement and subsistence patterns on the coast. People became increasingly dependent on agriculture as well as on maritime resources. They moved their settlements inland, built irrigation systems, began cultivating maize, and built large and impressive ceremonial centers. The form of these centers varied by region. On the central coast, for example, they consisted primarily of large U-shaped structures that faced inland, toward the mountains and the source of the water that nourished the coastal crops. On the north coast they consisted of large circular sunken courts and large platform structures. Centers were adorned with stone and adobe sculpture, and their façades were brightly painted. Population grew and society became gradually but increasingly stratified. Incised carvings of bodies with severed heads at Cerro Sechín and Sechín Alto in

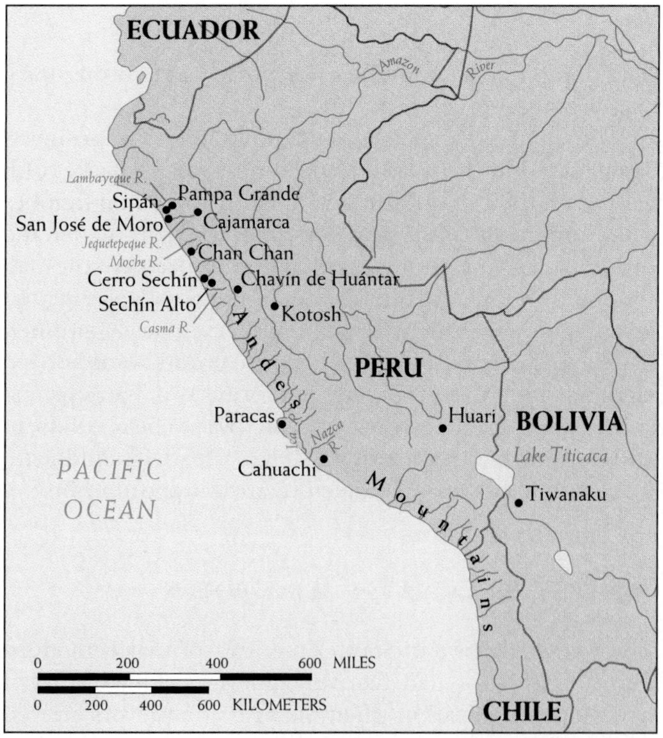

Map 14-3 Pre-Inca sites discussed in this chapter.

[4] Michael Mosley, *The Incas and Their Ancestors* (New York and London: Thames and Hudson, 1992), p. 42.

Chronology

The Periods of Andean Civilization

ca. 3000–ca. 2000 B.C.E.	Preceramic
ca. 2000–ca. 800 B.C.E.	Initial
ca. 800–ca. 200 B.C.E.	Early Horizon
ca. 200 B.C.E.–ca. 600 C.E.	Early Intermediate
ca. 600 C.E.–ca. 800/1000 C.E.	Middle Horizon
ca. 800/1000–ca. 1475	Late Intermediate
ca. 1475–1532	Late Horizon (Inca Empire)

the Casma suggest growing conflict. Centers apparently remained independent of one another, however, with little evidence to suggest larger political groupings.

Chavín de Huantar and the Early Horizon

The large coastal centers of the Initial period declined early in the first millennium B.C.E. At about the same time, beginning around 800 B.C.E., a site in the highlands, Chavín de Huantar, was growing in influence (see Map 14–3). Located on a trade route between the coast and the lowland tropical rain forest, Chavín was the center of a powerful religious cult with a population of perhaps 3,000 at its height. The architecture of its central temple complex, which includes U-shaped structures and a sunken circular courtyard, reflects coastal influence. Its artistic iconography draws on many tropical forest animals, including monkeys, serpents, and jaguars. The structure known as the Old Temple is honeycombed with passageways and drains. Archaeologists think that water could be deliberately channeled through these drains to produce a roaring sound. At the end of the central passageway is an imposing stela in the shape of a knife with the blade in the floor and the handle in the ceiling. Known as the Lanzon, this stela is carved in the image of a fanged deity that combines human and feline features. A small hole in the ceiling above the Lanzon suggests that it may have been an oracle whose "voice" was that of a priest in the gallery above.

Between about 400 and 200 B.C.E. Chavín influence spread widely throughout Peru, from the Nazca valley in the south to beyond Cajamarca in the north. This spread is seen in both the distribution of goods made at Chavín and in the incorporation of Chavín iconography into local traditions. Archaeologists believe Chavín influence reflects the prestige of its cult, not political or military expansion. The florescence of Chavín was also marked by important technological innovations in ceramics, weaving, and metallurgy.

Excavations at Chavín and other Early Horizon sites point to increasing social stratification. Examination of skeletal remains at Chavín, for example, suggests that people who lived closer to the ceremonial center ate better than people living on the margins of the site.

The Early Intermediate Period

Signs of increasing warfare accompany the collapse of the Chavín culture and the ideological unity it had brought to the Andes. The subsequent Early Intermediate period saw increasing regional diversity combined with increasing political centralization and the emergence of what were probably the first territorial states in the Andes. We will discuss briefly here only the two best-known cultures of this period, that of Nazca on the south coast of Peru, and of Moche on the north coast.

Nazca

The Nazca culture, which flourished from about 100 B.C.E. to about 700 C.E., was centered in the Ica and Nazca valleys. The people of the Nazca valley built underground aqueducts to tap ground water in the middle of the valley and divert it into irrigation canals. Cahuachi, the largest Nazca site, was once thought to be a large, permanently occupied urban center. Recent research, however, indicates that it was empty most of the year, filling periodically with pilgrims during religious festivals. It may have been the capital of a Nazca confederation, with each of its many temple platforms representing a member unit.

The earlier Paracas culture on the south coast produced some of the world's finest and most intricate textiles. The Nazca too are renowned for their textiles as well as their fine polychrome pottery, elaborately decorated with images of Andean plants and animals. They may be most famous, however, for their colossal earthworks, or geoglyphs, the so-called Nazca lines. These were created by brushing away the dark gravel of the desert to reveal a lighter-colored surface. Some geoglyphs depict figures like hummingbirds, spiders, and killer whales that appear on Nazca pottery. These are usually located on hillsides visible to passers-by. Others, usually consisting of radiating lines and geometric forms, are drawn on the Nazca pampa flats and are only visible from the air.

Moche

The Moche culture flourished from about 200 to 700 C.E. on the north coast of Peru. At its height it dominated all the coastal river valleys from Piura in the north to Huarmey in the south, a distance of some 370 miles. The culture takes its name from the Moche valley, the location of its largest center next to Cerro Blanco. Two huge structures, the Pyramid of the Sun and the Pyramid of the Moon, overlook this site. The cross-shaped Pyramid of the Sun, the largest adobe structure in the Americas, was some 1,200 feet long by 500 feet wide and rose in steps to a height of 60 feet. It was made with more than 143 million adobe bricks, each of which had a mark that probably identified the group that made it. Archaeologists think the marks enabled Moche lords to be sure that subject groups fulfilled their tribute obligations.

It was once thought that Cerro Blanco was the capital of a unified Moche empire. It appears now, however, that the Moche may not have been so centralized. Instead the Moche area may have been divided into northern and

Art and the World

MESOAMERICAN ART

In 1978, electricity workers digging near Mexico City's Metropolitan Cathedral discovered this eight-ton stone disk, which represents the dismembered body of the moon goddess Coyolxauhqui. Archeologists had known for decades that the site of the Aztec *teocallii*, or sacred place, lay beneath the cathedral's sequential incarnations and a significant area beyond—colonialist theologians, identifying non-Christian deities as demons, often directed that churches be built atop "pagan" temples. However, it was the rigorously composed and masterfully executed stone relief that finally inspired the excavations that would bring to light the Aztecs' Templo Mayor, or Great Temple. The Aztecs traditionally believed this spot to be the center of the world, the place where around 1325 C.E. their wandering ancestors had seen an eagle with a snake in its beak perched on a prickly pear cactus, the sign promised them by the sun god Huitzilopochtli.

The relief, which dates to about 1469 C.E., when the Templo Mayor underwent a major expansion, consecrated with several days of around-the-clock sacrifices, refers to the traditional Aztec account of the sun god's conception and birth. One day when Coatlicue, "she of the serpent skirt," is sweeping, a shower of fine feathers falls upon her. She picks them up, and places them in her bosom. When she finishes her task, Coatlicue goes to take out the feathers, but they are gone, and she is with child.

Coatlicue, the Mother Goddess, has already given birth to four hundred sons and their sister, Coyolxauhqui, "she of the bells in her cheek." Now, sorrowfully, Coatlicue overhears Coyolxauhqui urge her brothers to join her in killing the mother who has so dishonored them with her pregnancy. From within his mother's womb, Huitzilopochtli reassures her—then leaps out fully armed just as his siblings prepare to carry out their matricidal plan. Wielding the fire serpent *xiuhcóatl*, Huitzilopochtli beheads Coyolxauhqui, dismembers her, then turns to destroy his brothers. And so Huitzilopochtli, who is also Teotzauhtéotl, "the maker of portents," became the supreme deity of the Aztecs.

This duality characterizes the Mesoamerican gods and goddesses no less than the deities of other cultures. Coyolxauhhqui's attributes, for example, manifest ambiguity as well. Some of them—the balls of feathers in her hair; the serpents at waist, arms, and feet; and her flaccid breasts—identify her with her mother, Coatlicue, while her solar earrings would seem to refer to her brother and nemesis, Huitzilopochtli.

Duality also characterizes the bird-men in this handsome example of the fiber arts of Peru; the motif recurs thousands of miles away, in the art of North American Indians. Birds were revered religious emblems, their feathers decorating special ritual costumes. Made around 50 to 100 C.E., this woven and embroidered piece is an example of the skill of the people of the Paracas culture; their successors in the region of the Nazca River were equally famous for their textiles.

The fibers used for this mantle—which was probably worn for religious ceremonies—may be from alpacas or vicuña, the two camelids that give the finest wool. Other fibers used by the pre-Columbian weavers were the coarser llama wool, cotton on the coast, and sometimes bat wool. Dyes were from vegetable, animal, and mineral sources.

Like today's fabrics and clothing, those of the Incas and other peoples of the Peruvian coast and highlands revealed much about their position and role in society. For example, when a boy turned fourteen, he adopted the breechclout; men also wore tunics without sleeves, while women wore dresses that wrapped around their bodies. Both sexes wore long mantles.

Women were the fabric artists. They spun the fibers into yarn and wove cloth and tapestries on any of three kinds of looms: belt looms—used in Mesoamerica as well—or horizontal or vertical looms. Factories made cloth of different qualities, while the production of textiles dedicated to ritual or royalty was assigned to elite artisans. As in Mesoamerica, cloth was in effect currency, and might be required as tribute from subject groups. The *conquistadores* were dazzled by the gold they saw adorning people and great buildings; they ignored the warehouses that held bolts of priceless fabrics, the emblem of a precious skill that still endures today.

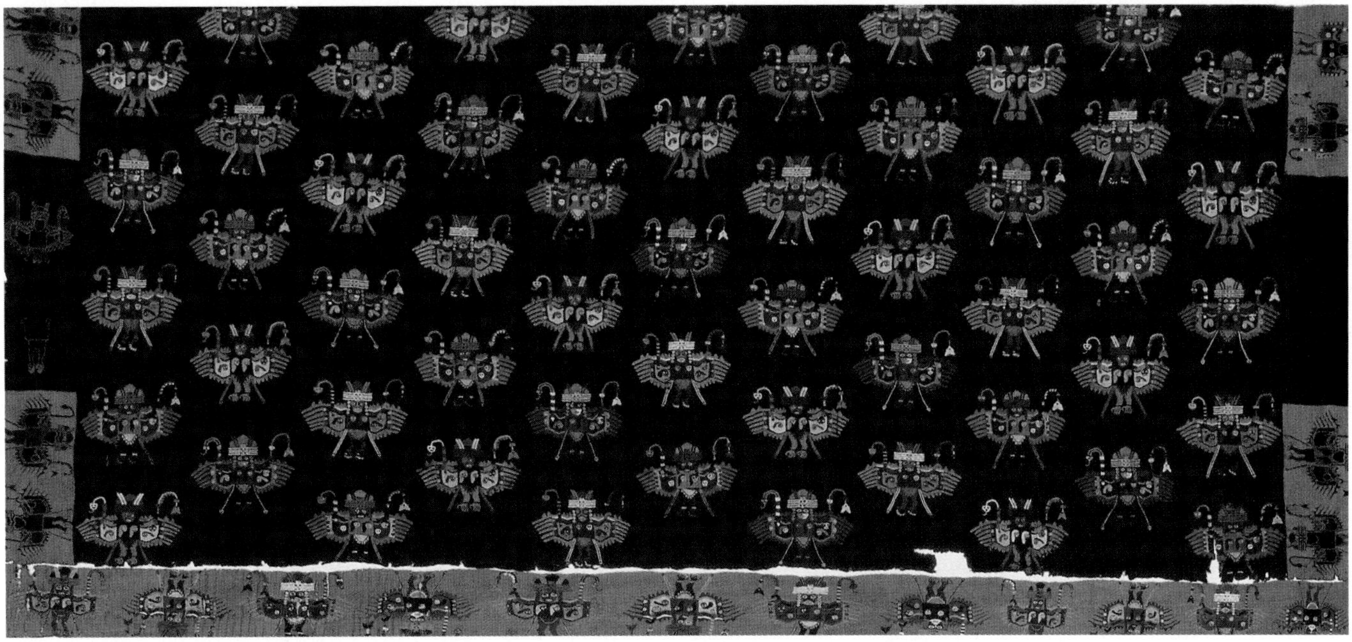

Embroidered Mantle with Bird Impersonators. Fine textiles were a source of prestige and wealth in ancient Peruvian societies. This mantle was made by the people of the Paracas culture on the south coast of Peru ca. 50–100 C.E. Plain weave with stem stitch embroidery, camelid fiber. Gift of Denman W. Ross, Courtesy of Museum of Fine Arts, Boston. ©1996. All Rights Reserved southern realms, and each valley ruled by Moche lords from its own center. Pampa Grande, a Moche site in the Lambayeque valley, was almost as large as Cerro Blanco.

The Moche were skilled potters, producing molded and painted vessels that reveal much about Moche life, religion, and warfare. Realistic portrait vessels may depict actual people. Other vessels provide evidence about the appearance of Moche architecture and the kind of regalia worn by the elite. The discovery in the late 1980s of the undisturbed tombs of Moche rulers at the site of Sipan in the Lambayeque valley and San José de Moro in the Jequetepeque valley suggests that a central theme in Moche iconography—the sacrifice ceremony—was an actual Moche ritual. Depictions of the sacrifice ceremony show elaborately dressed figures drinking the blood of sacrificed prisoners. Archaeologists have labeled one of the central figures the Warrior Priest and another the Priestess. The Moche lord in one of the tombs at Sipan was buried in the regalia of the Warrior Priest, and the occupant of one of the tombs at San José de Moro was buried in the regalia of the Priestess. (See page 358 for an example of Mochean art.)

The Moche were also the most sophisticated smiths in the Andes. They developed innovative alloys, cast weapons and agricultural tools, and used the lost-wax process to create small, intricate works.

The Middle Horizon Through the Late Intermediate Period

Tiwanaku and Huari

In the fifth century C.E., when the Germanic invasions were leading to the disintegration of the Roman Empire and as Teotihuacán was reaching its height in Mesoamerica, the first expansionist empires were emerging in the Andean highlands. One of these was centered at Tiwanaku in the Bolivian altiplano near the south shore of Lake Titicaca, and the other at Huari, in the south-central highlands of Peru. Although they differ in many ways, both are associated with productive new agricultural technologies, and both show evidence of a form of statecraft that reflects Andean verticality—the practice of sending out settlements to exploit the region's varied ecological zones—and that foreshadows the administrative practices of the later Inca Empire. The artistic symbolism of both also shares many features, suggesting a shared religious ideology. Archaeologists still do not have a firm grip on the chronology of Tiwanaku and Huari or the relationship between them.

Tiwanaku lies at more than 12,600 feet above sea level, making it the highest capital in the ancient world. Construction apparently began at the site about 200 C.E. It began its expansionist phase about 500–600 C.E., and collapsed some 500 years later in the eleventh century. The city occupied one to two square miles, and may have had a population of some 20,000-40,000 people at its height. Laid out on a grid, it is dominated by several large and impressive public structures and ceremonial gateways. The effort expended in transporting the stone for these monuments was enormous, and indicates the power of the Tiwanaku's rulers over the labor of their subjects.

A system of raised-field agriculture on the shores of Lake Titicaca provided Tiwanaku with its economic base. This system involved farming on artificial platforms capped with rich topsoil and separated by basins of water. Experimental reconstructions have shown it to be extremely productive.

Tiwanaku dominated the Titicaca basin and neighboring regions. It probably exerted its influence through its religious prestige and by establishing colonies and religious-administrative structures in distant territories.

The Huari Empire flourished from about 600 to 800 C.E., dominating the highlands from near Cuzco in the south to Cajamarca in the north. For a brief period it also extended a fortified colony into Tiwanaku territory. The capital, Huari, covers about one and a half square miles. It consists of a sprawl of large, high-walled stone enclosures, and had a population of 20,000–30,000 people.

Huari is located in an intermontane valley and its rise is associated with the development of techniques for terracing and irrigating the slopes of the valley to increase their productivity. The spread of this beneficial technology may have facilitated the expansion of the Huari Empire, explaining its acceptance in most places without signs of overt military domination. Huari administrative centers were undefended and built in accessible places. Many archaeologists think they may have functioned like later Inca administrative centers, housing a small Huari elite that organized local labor for state projects. Again like the Inca, Huari administrators used *quipu* record-keeping devices made of string. Inca *quipu*, however, used knots, whereas Huari *quipu* used different-colored string.

The Chimu Empire

Although there is evidence of Huari influence on the Peruvian north coast, it is unlikely to have taken the form of direct political control. After the demise of Moche authority, two new states emerged on the north coast. One, named for the site of Sican, was centered in the Lambayeque valley. The central figure in Sican iconography, the Sican Lord, may have been a representation of a mythical founder figure named Nyamlap, mentioned in postconquest Spanish chronicles. Like their Moche predecessors in the Lambayeque valley, the Sican people were skilled smiths who produced sumptuous gold objects.

The other new north coast state, known as Chimu, was centered in the Moche valley. In two waves of expansion the Chimu built an empire that incorporated the Lambayeque

DOCUMENT THE INCAS ORGANIZE THEIR EMPIRE

The Incas were remarkable for their ability to organize a vast and diverse empire. One of their chief devices of government was the movement of large groups of people to new, unfamiliar provinces. The Incas were also very sensitive to the power of religion and religious rituals. Once they had moved a population, they required that the chief object of worship belonging to that people be moved to the Inca capital of Cuzco where it was attended by representatives of its original worshipers. This latter group was changed from time to time, allowing portions of the transferred population to become familiar with the language and customs of the court city of Cuzco. These processes of government are described in the following passage by Bernabé Cobo (1582–1657), a Jesuit, whose account is regarded as among the most complete and accurate discussions of Inca culture.

To what extent did the Incas appear to be following a classic mode of rule by dividing and conquering? How did the Incas use one group to balance the threat to their rule from another group? How did they use religion and language to strengthen their authority?

The first thing that these kings did after conquering a province was to remove six or seven thousand families . . . and to transfer these families to the quiet, peaceful provinces, assigning them to different towns. In their stead they introduced the same number of people, taken from the places to which the former families had been sent or from such other places as seemed convenient. . . . In these transfers of population they saw to it that the migrants, both the newly conquered persons and the others, were moved to lands whose climate and conditions were the same as, or similar to, those which they had left behind them. . . .

The Incas introduced these changes of domicile in order to maintain their rule with greater ease, quiet, and security.. . . [T]hey ordered the majority of the *mitimaes* [the groups transferred] whom they sent to the recently conquered towns to make their homes in the provincial capitals, where they served as garrisons.. . . As soldiers they received certain privileges to make them appear of nobler rank, and they were ordered always to obey the slightest commands of their captains and governors. Under this plan, if the natives revolted, the *mitimaes*, being devoted to the governors, soon reduced them to obedience to the Inca; and if the *mitimaes* rioted they were repressed and punished by the natives; thus, through this scheme of domiciling the majority of the people of some province in other parts, the king was made secure against revolts in his dominions.. . . The Incas required everyone to absorb their language, laws, and religion with all the beliefs about these matters that were established at Cuzco.. . . In order to introduce and establish these things more effectively,. . . they would remove the principal idol from a conquered province and set it up in Cuzco with the same attendance and worship that it had formerly had; all this was seen to by persons who had come from that province.. . . For this reason Indians from every province of the kingdom were at all times in residence in the capital and court, occupied in guarding and ministering to their own idols. Thus they learned the usages and customs of the court; and when they were replaced by others. . . they taught their people what they had seen and learned in the court.

From *Historia del Nuevo Mundo* by Bernabé Cobe (Seville, 1890–1893), 3: 222–225; Benjamin Keen, trans., as reprinted in Benjamin Keen, ed., *Readings in Latin American Civilization 1492 to the Present* (Boston: Houghton Mifflin Company, 1955), pp. 29–30.

Valley and stretched for 800 miles along the coast, from the border of Ecuador in the north to the Chillon valley in the south. The administrative capital of this empire, Chan Chan, in the Moche valley, was a vast city. Its walls enclosed eight square miles and its central core covered over two square miles. The focus of the city are some ten immense adobe-walled enclosures known as *ciudadelas.* With their large open plazas, their administrative and storage facilities, and their large burial mounds, these probably housed the empire's ruling elite. Surrounding them were smaller compounds that probably housed the lesser nobility. And surrounding these were the homes and workshops of the artisans and workers who served the elite. Two areas were apparently transport centers, where llama caravans brought raw materials to the capital from the empire's territories. The total population of the city was between 30,000 and 40,000.

In about 1470, only sixty years before the arrival of the Spaniards, the Chimu Empire was swept away by a powerful new state from the southern highlands of Peru, the Inca Empire.

THE INCA EMPIRE

In 1532, when Francisco Pizarro and his companions happened on it, the Inca Empire was one of the largest states in the world, rivaling China and the Ottoman Empire in size. Its domains encompassed the area between the Pacific coast and the Amazon basin for some 2,600 miles, from Ecuador to northern Chile (see Map 14–2). Its ethnically and linguistically diverse population numbered in the millions.

The Inca themselves called their domain *Tawantinsuyu*, the Land of the Four Quarters. Their capital, Cuzco, lay at the intersection of these divisions. Home to the ruler (Inca)

The Inca city of Machu Picchu perches on a saddle between two peaks on the eastern slopes of the Andes.
Robert Frerk/Odyssey Productions

and the ruling elite, it was a city of great splendor and magnificence. Its principal temples, dedicated to the sun and moon, gleamed with gold and silver.

The origins of the Inca are obscure. According to their own traditions, Inca expansion began only in the fifteenth century in the wake of a revolt of the Chanca people that nearly destroyed Cuzco. Inca Yupanqui, son of the city's aging ruler, led a heroic resistance and crushed the revolt. Assuming the name Pachacuti, he laid the foundations of Inca statecraft; he and his successors expanded their domains to bring the blessings of civilization to the rest of the Andean world. There is clearly an element of imperial propaganda in this legend. The Inca did expand dramatically in the fifteenth century, but archaeological evidence suggests that they had been expanding their influence for decades and perhaps centuries before the Chanca revolt.

The Inca enlarged their empire through a combination of alliance and intimidation as well as conquest. They organized their realm into a hierarchical administrative structure and imposed a version of their language, Quechua, as the administrative language of the empire. As a result, Quechua is still widely spoken in the Peruvian Andes.

Unlike the Aztecs, who extracted tribute from their subject peoples, the Inca relied on various forms of labor taxation. They divided agricultural lands into several categories, allowing local populations to retain some for their own support and reserving others for the state and the gods. In a system known as the *mita,* local people worked for the state on a regular basis, receiving in return gifts and lavish state-sponsored ritual entertainments. Men also served in the army and on public works projects, building cities and roads, for example, and terracing hillsides. In a policy that reflects the Andean practice of colonizing ecologically varied regions, the Inca also designated entire communities as *Mitimaqs,* moving them about, sometimes great distances, to best exploit the resources of their empire. They sometimes settled loyal people in hostile regions and moved hostile people to loyal regions.

The Inca employed several groups of people in what amounted to full-time state service. One of these, the *mamakuna,* consisted of women who lived privileged but celibate and carefully regulated lives in cities and towns throughout the empire. *Mamakuna* might also be given in marriage by Inca rulers to cement alliances. These so-called Virgins of the Sun played an important economic as well as religious role, weaving and brewing the maize beer known as *chicha* for the Inca elite. Textiles were highly prized in Andean society, and cloth was a form of wealth among the

Incas. *Chicha* had great ritual importance and was consumed at state religious festivals. Another group of full-time state workers, the *yanakuna*, were men whose duties included tending the royal llama herds.

Cloth and clothing were not only a principal source of wealth and prestige in Inca society, they were also a means of communication. Complex textile patterns served as insignia of social status, indicating a person's rank and ethnic affiliation. Textile production was among the forms of labor service required by the state, and Inca warehouses were filled with textiles as well as with food and other craft goods.

The Incas made their presence felt in their empire through regional administrative centers and warehouses linked by a remarkable system of roads. The centers served to organize, house, and feed people engaged in *mita* labor service and to impress upon them the power and beneficence of the state with feasting and ritual. The wealth of the empire, collected in storehouses, sustained the *mita* laborers, fed and clothed the army, and enriched the Inca elite. Although the Inca lacked writing, they kept detailed administrative records on string accounting devices called *quipu*.

To move their armies, administer their domains, and distribute the wealth of their empire efficiently, the Inca built more than 14,000 miles of road. These ranged from narrow paths to wide thoroughfares. Rope suspension bridges crossed gorges and rivers, and stairways eased the ascent of steep slopes. A system of relay runners sped messages to Cuzco from the far reaches of the empire.

Over their long history the people of the Andes developed an adaptation to their challenging environment that allowed them to prosper and grow, bringing more land under cultivation than today. Building on ancient Andean traditions, the Inca appear to have engineered a productive economy that brought its people a measure of well-being that would not survive the destruction of the empire by Spanish invaders.

In World Perspective

ANCIENT CIVILIZATIONS OF THE AMERICAS

Civilization in the Americas before 1492 developed independently of civilization in the Old World. As the kings of Egypt were erecting their pyramid tombs, the people of the desert coast of Peru were erecting temple platforms. While King Solomon ruled in Jerusalem, the Olmec were creating their monumental stone heads. As Rome reached its apogee and then declined, so did the great city of Teotihuacán in the Valley of Mexico. As Islam spread from its heartland, the rulers of Tikal brought their city to its greatest splendor before its abrupt collapse. Maya mathematics and astronomy rivaled that of any other peoples of the ancient world. And as the aggressive nation-states of Europe were emerging from their feudal past, the Aztecs and Incas were consolidating their great empires.

The encounter between Old World and New, however, would prove devastating for American civilization. The technology that allowed Europeans to embark on the voyages of discovery and fight destructive wars among themselves caught the great native empires unprepared. Uncertain how to respond to these aggressive foreigners, they succumbed.

REVIEW QUESTIONS

1. Describe the rise of civilization in Mesoamerica and Andean South America. What does it have in common with the rise of civilization in Africa and Eurasia? In what ways was it different?
2. The appearance of monumental architecture in the ancient world was often associated with hierarchical agricultural societies. Was this the case for the Peruvian coast?
3. What were some of the accomplishments of the Classic civilizations of Mesoamerica? How do they compare with contemporary civilizations elsewhere in the world?
4. How was the Aztec Empire organized? The Inca Empire? How do they compare to the early empires of the ancient world in the Near East, Europe, and Asia?
5. Both the Aztec and Inca Empires fell in the early sixteenth century when confronted with Spanish forces of a few hundred men. What do you think might have been some of the reasons for their defeat?

SUGGESTED READINGS

B. S. BAUER, *The Development of the Inca State* (1992). An important new work that emphasizes archaeological evidence over the Spanish chronicles in accounting for the emergence of the Inca Empire.

F. F. BERDAN, *The Aztecs of Central Mexico: An Imperial Society* (1982). An excellent introduction to the Aztecs.

R. E. BLANTON, S. A. KOWALEWSKI, G. FEINMAN, AND J. APPEL, *Ancient Mesoamerica: A Comparison of Change in Three Regions* (1981). Concentrates on ancient Mexico.

K. O. BRUHNS, *Ancient South America* (1994). A clear discussion of the archaeology and civilization of the region with emphasis on the Andes.

R. L. BURGER, *Chavín and the Origins of Andean Civilization* (1992). A detailed study of early Andean prehistory by one of the leading authorities on Chavín.

R. M. CARMACK, J. GASCO, AND G. H. GOSSEN, *The Legacy of Mesoamerica: History and Culture of a Native American Civilization* (1996). A survey of Mesoamerica from its origins to the present.

I. CLENDINNEN, *Aztecs: An Interpretation* (1995). A fascinating attempt to reconstruct the Aztec world.

M. D. COE, *Breaking the Maya Code* (1992). The story of the remarkable achievement of deciphering the ancient Maya language.

M. D. COE, *The Maya* (1993). The best introduction.

M. D. COE, *Mexico from the Olmecs to the Aztecs* (1994). A wide-ranging introductory discussion.

G. CONRAD AND A. A. DEMAREST, *Religion and Empire: The Dynamics of Aztec and Inca Expansionism* (1984). An interesting comparative study.

S. D. GILLESPIE, *The Aztec Kings* (1989).

R. HASSIG, *Aztec Warfare.*

J. HYSLOP, *Inka Settlement Planning* (1990). A detailed study.

M. LEÓN-PORTILLA, *Fifteen Poets of the Aztec World* (1992). An anthology of translations of Aztec poetry.

M. E. MILLER, *The Art of Mesoamerica from Olmec to Aztec* (1986). A well-illustrated introduction.

C. MORRIS AND A. VON HAGEN, *The Inka Empire and Its Andean Origins* (1993). A clear overview of Andean prehistory by a leading authority. Beautifully illustrated.

M. E. MOSELY, *The Incas and Their Ancestors: The Archaeology of Peru* (1992). Readable and thorough.

J. A. SABLOFF, *The Cities of Ancient Mexico* (1989). Capsule summaries of ancient Mesoamerican cultures.

J. A. SABLOFF, *Archaeology and the Maya* (1990). A look at changing views of the ancient Maya.

L. SCHELE and M. E. MILLER, *The Blood of Kings* (1986). A rich and beautifully illustrated study of ancient Maya art and society.

R. S. SHARER, *The Ancient Maya*, 5th ed. (1994). A classic. Readable, authoritative, and thorough.

M. P. WEAVER, *The Aztecs, Maya, and Their Predecessors* (1993). A classic textbook.

DOCUMENTS CD-ROM

1. The Myth of the Incas: A case of double creation?
2. The Mesoamerican Mind: Tezcatlipoca, Quetzatcoatl, and music
3. The Mesoamerican Mind: The Aztecs and holy warfare
4. Twenty Sacred Hymns, Mexico
5. Florentine Codex, Mexico

WORLD AND THE WEB

NOVA: Ice Mummies of the Inca

http://www.pbs.org/wgbh/nova/peru/

In September 1996, high-altitude archaeologist Johan Reinhard led an expedition to the summit of Sara Sara in Peru in search of frozen sacrificial mummies. Reinhard's expedition was filmed by the BBC as part of the three-part series, "Ice Mummies" and was documented on this website as a NOVA/PBS Online Adventure.

Maya-archaeology.org

http://www.maya-archaeology.org/

Covers Mayan, Olmec, Teotihuacán art, architecture, deities, hieroglyphic writing, and the latest digital photography, 35mm film, and flatbed scanner technology for recording the artifacts and pyramid-temple and palace architectural remains of these fascinating ancient civilizations.

Mundo Maya Online

http://www.mayadiscovery.com/ing/default.htm

The Mundo Maya covers a territory of 500,000 square kilometers, now occupied by five Mexican states: Chiapas, Tabasco, Campeche, Yucatán, and Quintana Roo; and the Central American countries of Guatemala, Belize, Honduras, and El Salvador. This site covers this area's Archaeology, Daily Life, History, Handicrafts, and Legends.

Teotihuacán: The City of the Gods

http://archaeology.la.asu.edu/teo/

Offers access to information about the ancient city of Teotihuacán. It consists of introductory pages, online movies, a chronology, recent excavation reports, and academic journals. In addition, there are many links to other Mesoamerican sites.

Nazca

http://emuseum.mnsu.edu/prehistory/latinamerica/south/cultures/nazca.html

Briefly covers the three stages—Early, Middle, and Late—and also the Classic Nazca (ca. 250–750 A.D.). It also discusses the Nazca lines, which are the most attractive and mysterious feature of this culture.

15

Europe to the Early 1500s

Revival, Decline, and Renaissance

The University of Bologna in central Italy was distinguished as the center for the revival of Roman law. This carving on the tomb of a Bolognese professor of law shows students attending one of his lectures. Scala/Art Resource, N.Y.

Chapter topics

- Revival of Empire, Church, and Towns
- Society
- Growth of National Monarchies
- Political and Social Breakdown
- Ecclesiastical Breakdown and Revival: The Late Medieval Church
- The Renaissance in Italy (1375–1527)
- Revival of Monarchy: Nation Building in the Fifteenth Century

In World Perspective
The High Middle Ages

THE HIGH MIDDLE AGES (FROM THE ELEVENTH through the thirteenth centuries) were a period of both political expansion and consolidation and intellectual flowering and synthesis. The Latin, or Western, church established itself as a spiritual authority independent of secular monarchies, which themselves became more powerful and self-aggrandizing. The parliaments and popular assemblies that accompanied the rise of these monarchies laid the foundations of modern representative institutions.

The High Middle Ages saw a revolution in agriculture that increased food supplies and populations. Trade and commerce revived, towns expanded, protomodern forms of banking and credit developed, and a "new rich" merchant class became ascendant in Europe's cities. Universities arose and contact with the Arab world led to the beginning of the recovery of the writings of the ancient Greek philosophers, which would in turn stimulate the great expansion of Western education and culture during the late Middle Ages and the Renaissance.

The late Middle Ages and the Renaissance (the fourteenth, fifteenth, and early sixteenth centuries) were a time of unprecedented calamity and of bold new beginnings in Europe. France and England grappled with each other in a bitter conflict known as the Hundred Years' War (1337–1453). Bubonic plague, known to contemporaries as the Black Death, killed as much as one third of the population in many regions between 1348 and 1350. A schism emerged within the church (1378–1417). In 1453 the Turks captured Constantinople and threatened the West. Western civilization seemed to be collapsing.

But the late Middle Ages also witnessed a rebirth that would continue into the seventeenth century. Scholars criticized medieval assumptions about the nature of God, humankind, and society. Italian and northern humanists made a full recovery of classical knowledge and languages and began cultural changes that would spread throughout Europe. The "divine art" of printing was invented. The vernacular, the local language, began to take its place alongside Latin. In the independent nation-states of Europe, patriotism and incipient nationalism became major forces.

Revival of Empire, Church, and Towns

Otto I and the Revival of the Empire

The fortunes of both the old empire and the papacy began to revive when the Saxon Henry I ("the Fowler"; d. 936) became the first non-Frankish king of Germany in 918. Henry rebuilt royal power and left his son and successor Otto I (r. 936–973) in a strong territorial position. Otto maneuvered his own kin into power in Bavaria, Swabia, and Franconia and invaded Italy and proclaimed himself its king in 951. In 955 he defeated the Hungarians at Lechfeld, which secured German borders against new barbarian attack and earned Otto the title "the Great."

As part of a careful rebuilding program, Otto enlisted the church. Bishops and abbots, men who possessed a sense of universal empire yet did not marry and found competitive dynasties, were made royal princes and agents of the king. In 961 Otto,

Otto I presents the Magdeburg Cathedral to Christ, as the pope (holding the keys to the kingdom of heaven) watches, a testimony to Otto's guardianship of the church. Metropolitan Museum of Art, bequest of George Blumenthal, 1941 (41.100.157). Photograph © 1986 The Metropolitan Museum of Art.

who had long aspired to the imperial crown, responded to a call for help from Pope John XII (955–964), in return for which John crowned him emperor on February 2, 962. The church was now more than ever under royal control. Under Otto I popes ruled at the emperor's pleasure.

The Reviving Catholic Church

Otto thus shifted the royal focus from Germany to Italy. His successors became so preoccupied with Italy that their German base began to disintegrate. As the revived empire began to crumble in the eleventh century, the church, long unhappy with imperial domination, prepared to declare its independence to a new force for reform within the church itself.

Cluny Reform Movement In a great monastery at Cluny, founded in 910 in east-central France, a reform movement was born. The reformers of Cluny were aided in their efforts by popular respect for the church that found expression in both religious fervor among laypersons and generous baronial patronage of religious houses. People admired clerics and monks because the church was medieval society's most democratic institution as far as lay participation was concerned. In the Middle Ages any man could theoretically become pope, since the pope was supposed to be elected by the people and the clergy of Rome. All people were candidates for the church's grace and salvation. The church promised a better life to come to the great mass of ordinary people, who found their present existence brutish and without hope.

The Cluny reformers rejected the subservience of the clergy to royal authority. They taught that the pope in Rome was sole ruler over all the clergy. They further denounced the transgression of ascetic piety by "secular" parish clergy, who maintained concubines in a relationship akin to marriage. The distinctive Western separation of church and state and the celibacy of the Catholic clergy had their definitive origins in the Cluny reform movement. From Cluny, reformers were dispatched throughout France and Italy, and in the late eleventh century the papacy embraced their reforms.

Investiture Struggle: Gregory VII and Henry IV In 1075 Pope Gregory VII (r. 1073–1085), a fierce advocate of church reform, condemned under penalty of excommunication the lay investiture of clergy at any level. He had primarily in mind the emperor's well-established custom of installing bishops by presenting them with the ring and staff that symbolized episcopal office. Henry IV considered Gregory's action a direct challenge to his authority. The territorial princes, on the other hand, eager to see the emperor weakened, fully supported Gregory's edict.

The lines of battle were quickly drawn. Henry assembled his loyal German bishops at Worms in January 1076 and had them proclaim their independence from Gregory. Gregory promptly excommunicated Henry and absolved all Henry's subjects from loyalty to him. The German princes were delighted, and Henry faced a general revolt. He had to come to terms with Gregory. In a famous scene, Henry prostrated himself outside Gregory's castle retreat at Canossa in northern Italy on January 25, 1077. There he reportedly stood barefoot in the snow off and on for three days before the pope absolved him. Papal power had reached a pinnacle.

The investiture controversy was finally settled in 1122 with the Concordat of Worms. Emperor Henry V (r. 1106–1125) formally renounced his power to invest bishops with ring and staff. In exchange, Pope Calixtus II (r. 1119–1124) recognized the emperor's right to be present and to invest bishops with fiefs before or after their investment with ring and staff by the church. The emperor also effectively retained the right to nominate or veto a candidate.

The Gregorian party secured the independence of the clergy, but at the price of encouraging the divisiveness of the political forces within the empire. The pope had made himself strong by making imperial authority weak. In the end, the local princes profited most from the investiture controversy.

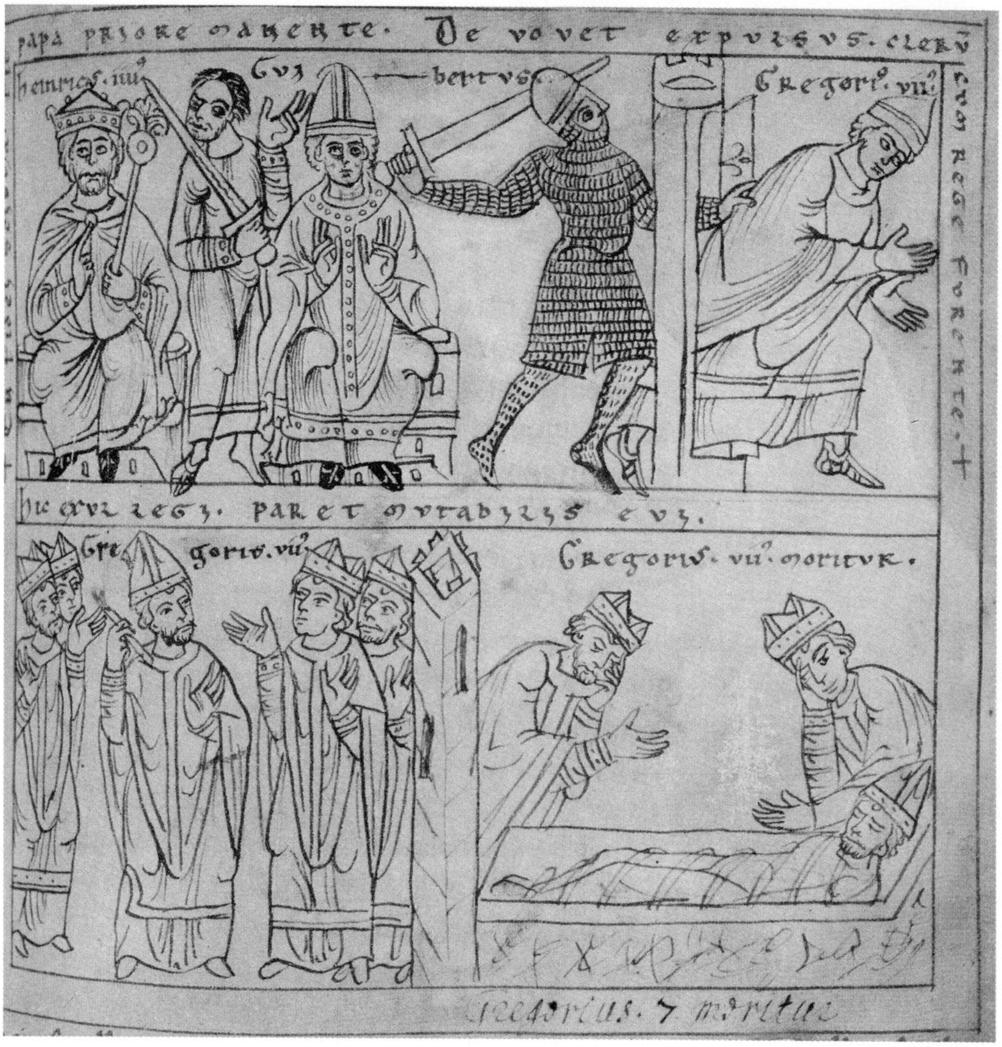

A 12th-century German manuscript portrays the struggle between Emperor Henry IV and Pope Gregory VII. In the top panel, Henry installs the puppet pope Clement III and drives Gregory from Rome. Below, Gregory dies in exile. The artist was a monk; his sympathies were with Gregory, not Henry. Thuringer Universities and Landesbibliothek, Jena.

THE FIRST CRUSADE

If an index of popular piety and support for the pope in the High Middle Ages is needed, the Crusades amply provide it. What the Cluny reform was to the clergy, the First Crusade to the Holy Land was to the laity: an outlet for the heightened religious zeal of the late eleventh and the twelfth centuries, Europe's most religious period before the Protestant Reformation.

Late in the eleventh century, the Byzantine Empire was under severe pressure from the Seljuk Turks, and Emperor Alexius I Comnenus (r. 1081–1118) appealed for Western aid. At the Council of Clermont in 1095, Pope Urban II (r. 1088–1099) responded by launching the First Crusade.

Religion was not the only motive inspiring the Crusaders; hot blood and greed were equally influential. But unlike the later Crusades, undertaken for patently mercenary reasons, the early Crusades were inspired by genuine religious piety and were carefully orchestrated by the revived papacy. Popes promised participants in the First Crusade a plenary indulgence should they die in battle—that is, a complete remission of any outstanding temporal punishment for their unrepented mortal sins and hence release from suffering for them in purgatory. In addition to this direct spiritual reward, the Crusaders were also impelled by their enthusiasm for a Holy War against the hated infidel and by the romance of a pilgrimage to the Holy Land. Crusading zeal also sparked anti-Jewish riots and massacres in Europe, an expression of intolerance to Jews that became an enduring feature of militant Christianity.

These fanatical Crusaders defeated one Seljuk army after another in a steady advance toward Jerusalem, which fell to them on July 15, 1099. They divided the conquered territory into "states," which they held as alleged fiefs from the pope.

However, the Latin presence in the East soon began to crumble. A Second Crusade, preached by Saint Bernard of Clairvaux (1091–1153), Christendom's most powerful monastic leader, was a dismal failure. In October 1187 Jerusalem itself was reconquered by Saladin (r. 1138–1193), king of Egypt and Syria.

DOCUMENT POPE URBAN II (1088–1099) PREACHES THE FIRST CRUSADE

When Pope Urban II summoned the First Crusade in a sermon at the Council of Clermont on November 26, 1095, he painted a savage picture of the Muslims who controlled Jerusalem. Urban also promised the Crusaders, who responded by the tens of thousands, remission of their unrepented sins and assurance of heaven. Robert the Monk is one of four witnesses who has left us a summary of the sermon.

Is the pope engaging in a propaganda and smear campaign? What are the images he creates of the enemy and how accurate and fair are they? Did the Christian church have a greater claim to Jerusalem than the people then living there? Does a religious connection with the past entitle one group to confiscate the land of another?

From the confines of Jerusalem and the city of Constantinople a horrible tale has gone forth and very frequently has been brought to our ears, namely, that a race from the kingdom of the Persians [that is, the Seljuk Turks], an accursed race, a race utterly alienated from God, a generation forsooth which has not directed its heart and has not entrusted its spirit to God, has invaded the lands of those Christians and has depopulated them by the sword, pillage and fire; it has led away a part of the captives into its own country, and a part it has destroyed by cruel tortures; it has either entirely destroyed the churches of God or appropriated them for the rites of its own religion. They destroy the altars, after having defiled them with their uncleanness. They circumcise the Christians, and the blood of the circumcision they either spread upon the altars or pour into the vases of the baptismal font. When they wish to torture people by a base death, they perforate their navels, and dragging forth the extremity of the intestines, bind it to a stake; then with flogging they lead the victim around until the viscera having gushed forth the victim falls prostrate upon the ground. Others they bind to a post and pierce with arrows. Others they compel to extend their necks and then, attacking them with naked swords, attempt to cut through the neck with a single blow. What shall I say of the abominable rape of the women? The kingdom of the Greeks is now dismembered by them and deprived of territory so vast in extent that it can not be traversed in a march of two months. On whom therefore is the labor of avenging these wrongs and of recovering this territory incumbent, if not upon you? . . .

Jerusalem is the navel of the world; the land is fruitful above others, like another paradise of delights. This the Redeemer of the human race has made illustrious by His advent, has beautified by residence, has consecrated by suffering, has redeemed by death, has glorified by burial. This royal city, therefore, situated at the centre of the world, is now held captive by His enemies, and is in subjection to those who do not know God, to the worship of the heathens. She seeks therefore and desires to be liberated, and does not cease to implore you to come to her aid. From you especially she asks succor, because, as we have already said, God has conferred upon you above all nations great glory in arms. Accordingly undertake this journey for the remission of your sins, with the assurance of the imperishable glory of the kingdom of heaven.

From the *Original Sources of European History*, Vol. 1 (Philadelphia: Dept. of History, University of Pennsylvania), pp. 5–7.

A Third Crusade in the twelfth century (1189–1192) attempted yet another rescue, enlisting as its leaders the most powerful Western rulers: Emperor Frederick Barbarossa (r. 1152–1190); Richard the Lion-Hearted, king of England (r. 1189–1199); and Philip Augustus, king of France (r. 1179–1223). But it too was a failure. The Holy Land remained as firmly Muslim as ever.

However, the Crusades did stimulate Western trade and cultural interaction with the East. Italian merchants followed the Crusaders' cross to lucrative new markets. The need to resupply the new Christian settlements in the Near East not only reopened old trade routes that had long been closed by Arab domination of the Mediterranean, but also opened new ones.

CHRONOLOGY

THE CRUSADES

1095	Pope Urban II launches the First Crusade
1099	The Crusaders take Jerusalem
1147–1149	The Second Crusade
1187	Jerusalem retaken by the Muslims
1189–1192	Third Crusade
1202–1204	Fourth Crusade

TOWNS AND TOWNSPEOPLE

In the eleventh and twelfth centuries, most towns were small and held only about 5 percent of western Europe's population. But they contained the most creative segments of medieval society.

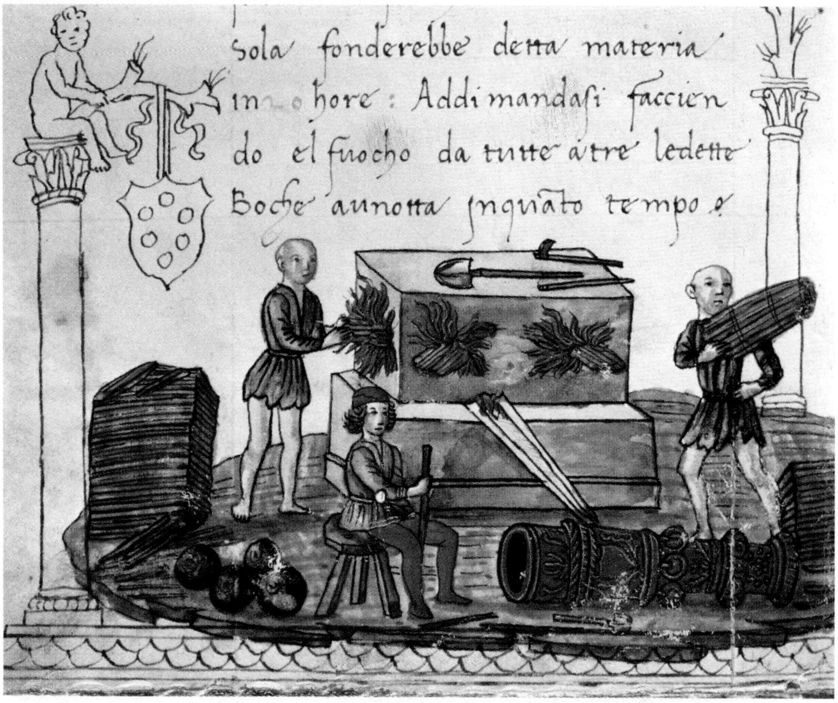

Skilled workers were an integral component of the commerce of medieval towns. This scene shows the manufacture of cannons in a foundry in Florence. Scala/Art Resource, N.Y.

THE CHARTERING OF TOWNS Towns were originally dominated by feudal lords, both lay and clerical, who granted charters to those who would agree to live and work within them. The charters guaranteed the towns' safety and gave their inhabitants an independence unknown to peasants who worked the land. The purpose was originally to concentrate skilled laborers who could manufacture the finished goods desired by lords and bishops.

As towns grew and beckoned, many serfs took their skills to the new urban centers. There they found the freedom and profits that could lift an industrious craftsperson into higher social ranks. As this migration of serfs to the towns accelerated, the lords in the countryside offered serfs more favorable terms of tenure to keep them on the land. The growth of towns thus improved the lot of serfs generally.

THE RISE OF MERCHANTS Rural society not only gave the towns their craftspeople and day laborers, but the first merchants themselves may also have been enterprising serfs. Certainly, some of the long-distance traders were people who had nothing to lose and everything to gain from the enormous risks of foreign trade. They traveled together in armed caravans and convoys, buying goods and products as cheaply as possible at the source, and selling them for all they could get in western ports (see Map 15–1).

At first the merchants were disliked because they were outside the traditional social groups of nobility, clergy, and peasantry. Over time, however, the powerful grew to respect the merchants, and the weak always tried to imitate them, because the merchants left a trail of wealth behind them.

As the traders established themselves in towns, they grew in wealth and numbers, formed their own protective associations, and soon found themselves able to challenge traditional seigneurial authority. Merchants especially wanted to end the arbitrary tolls and tariffs regional magnates imposed over the surrounding countryside. Such regulations hampered the flow of commerce on which both merchant and craftsman in the growing urban export industries depended.

Townspeople needed simple and uniform laws and a government sympathetic to their new forms of business activity, not the fortress mentality of the lords of the countryside. The result was often a struggle with the old nobility within and outside the towns. This conflict led towns in the High and late Middle Ages to form their own independent communes and to ally themselves with kings against the nobility in the countryside, a development that would eventually rearrange the centers of power in medieval Europe and dissolve classic feudal government.

Because the merchants were the engine of the urban economy, small shopkeepers and artisans identified far more with them than with aloof lords and bishops, who had been medieval society's traditional masters. The lesser nobility (small knights) outside the towns also recognized the new mercantile economy as the wave of the future. During the eleventh and twelfth centuries, the burgher upper classes increased their economic strength and successfully challenged the old noble urban lords for control of the towns.

NEW MODELS OF GOVERNMENT With urban autonomy came new models of self-government. Around 1100

MAP EXPLORATION

Interactive map: To explore this map further, go to http://www.prenhall.com/craig_map15.1

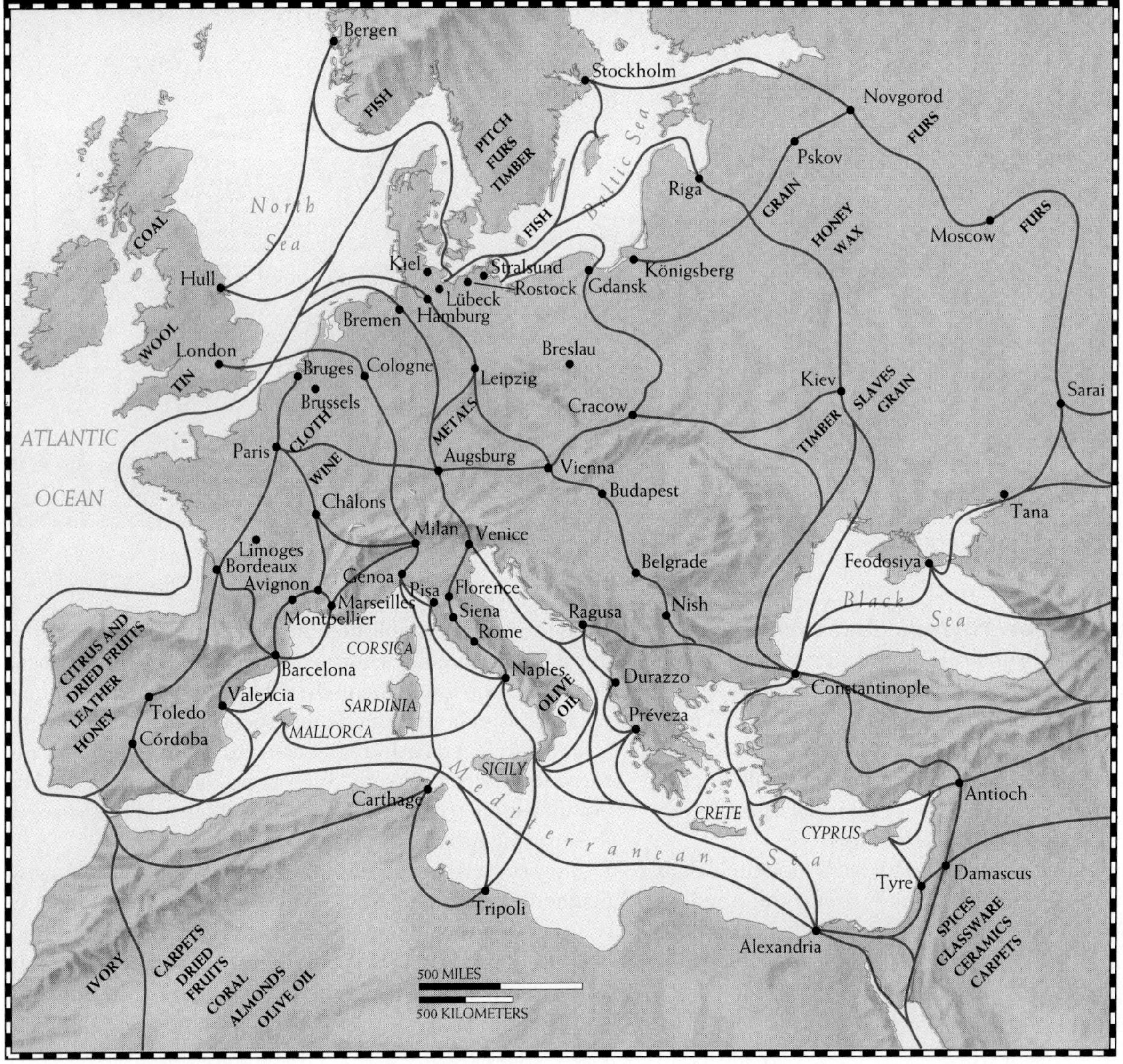

Map 15–1 Medieval trade routes and regional products. Trade in the West varied in intensity and geographical extent in different periods during the Middle Ages. The map shows some of the channels that came to be used in interregional commerce. Labels tell part of what was carried in that commerce.

the old urban nobility and the new burgher upper class merged into an urban patriciate. It was a marriage between those wealthy by birth (inherited property) and those who made their fortunes in long-distance trade. From this new ruling class was born the aristocratic town council, which henceforth governed towns.

Enriching and complicating the situation, small artisans and craftspeople also slowly developed their own protective associations or guilds and began to gain a voice in government. The towns' opportunities for the "little person" had created the slogan "Town air brings freedom." Within town walls people thought of themselves as citizens with basic rights, not subjects liable to their masters' whim.

TOWNS AND KINGS By providing kings with the resources they needed to curb factious noblemen, towns became a major force in the transition from feudal societies to national governments. Towns were a ready source of educated bureaucrats and lawyers who knew Roman law, the tool for running the state. Money was also to be found in the towns in great quantity, enabling kings to hire their own armies and free themselves from dependence on the nobility. In turn towns won royal political recognition and had their constitutions guaranteed. In France, towns became integrated early into royal government. In Germany, they fell under ever-tighter control by the princes. In Italy, uniquely, towns became genuine city-states during the Renaissance.

JEWS IN CHRISTIAN SOCIETY Towns also attracted Jews who plied trades in small businesses. Many became wealthy as moneylenders to kings, popes, and businesspeople. Jewish intellectual and religious culture both dazzled and threatened Christians. These various factors encouraged suspicion and distrust among Christians, and led to an unprecedented surge in anti-Jewish sentiment in the late twelfth and early thirteenth centuries.

SCHOOLS AND UNIVERSITIES In the twelfth century, Byzantine and Spanish Islamic scholars made it possible for the philosophical works of Aristotle, the writings of Euclid and Ptolemy, the texts of Greek physicians and Arab mathematicians, and the corpus of Roman law to circulate among western scholars. Islamic scholars wrote thought-provoking commentaries on Greek texts that were translated into Latin and made available to western scholars and students. The resulting intellectual ferment gave rise to western universities.

The first important western university was established in 1158 in Bologna, a town famous for the revival of Roman law, and became the model for the universities of Spain, Italy, and southern France. Paris became the model for northern European universities and the study of theology.

THE CURRICULUM In the High Middle Ages the learning process was basic. People assumed that truth was already known and only needed to be properly organized, elucidated, and defended. Students wrote commentaries on authoritative texts, especially those of Aristotle and the church fathers. Teachers did not encourage students to strive independently for undiscovered truth. Students rather learned to organize and harmonize the accepted truths of tradition, which were drilled into them.

This method of study, was known as Scholasticism. Students summarized the traditional authorities in their field, elaborated traditional arguments pro and con, and then drew conclusions. Logic and dialectic were the tools to discipline knowledge and thought. Dialectic is the art of discovering a truth by finding the contradictions in arguments against it. Astonishingly, medical students did no practical medical work; they studied and debated the authoritative texts in their field just as the law and theology students did in theirs.

SOCIETY

THE ORDER OF LIFE

In the art and literature of the Middle Ages, three basic social groups were represented: those who fought as

Dominicans (left) and Franciscans (right). Unlike the other religious orders, the Dominicans and Franciscans did not live in cloisters, but wandered about preaching and combating heresy. They depended for support on their own labor and the kindness of the laity. Cliche Bibliothèque Nationale de France, Paris mounted knights (the landed nobility), those who prayed (the clergy), and those who labored in fields and shops (the peasantry and village artisans). After the revival of towns in the eleventh century, a fourth social group emerged: the long-distance traders and merchants.

NOBLES By the late Middle Ages, a distinguishable higher and lower nobility had evolved, living in both town and country. The higher were the great landowners and territorial magnates, long the dominant powers in their regions; the lower were petty landlords, the descendants of minor knights, newly rich merchants, or wealthy farmers.

Arms were the nobleman's profession; waging war was his sole occupation. In the eighth century the adoption of stirrups made mounted warriors the key ingredient of a successful army. The nobility accordingly celebrated the physical strength, courage, and constant activity of warfare. Warring gave them both new riches and an opportunity to gain honor and glory. Peace meant economic stagnation and boredom.

No medieval social group was absolutely uniform. Noblemen formed a broad spectrum—from minor vassals without subordinate vassals to mighty barons, the principal vassals of a king or prince, who had many vassals of their own. Dignity and status within the nobility were directly related to the exercise of authority over others; a chief with many vassals far excelled the small country nobleman who was lord over none but himself.

By the late Middle Ages, several factors forced the landed nobility into a steep economic and political decline from which it never recovered. Climatic changes and agricultural failures created large famines, while the great plague (to be discussed later) brought about unprecedented population losses. Changing military tactics occasioned by the use of infantry and heavy artillery during the Hundred Years' War made the noble cavalry nearly obsolete. And the alliance of wealthy towns with the king weakened the nobility within their own domains. After the fourteenth century, land and wealth counted for far more than lineage as qualification for entrance into the highest social class.

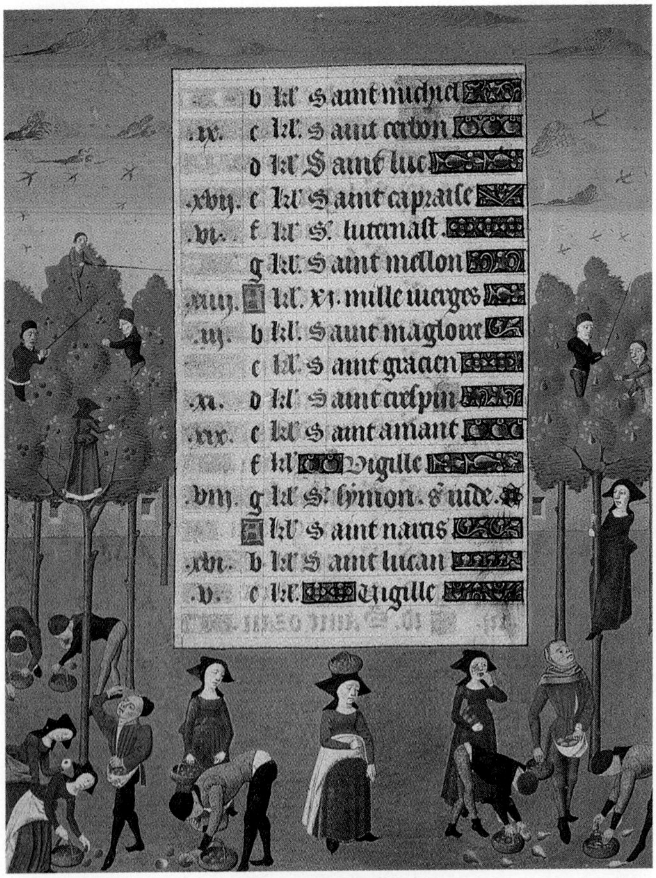

Men and women harvesting pears. From a Book of Hours (15th century). Lauros-Glraudon/Art Resource, N.Y.

CLERGY Unlike the nobility and the peasantry, the clergy was an open estate: one was a cleric by religious training and ordination, not because of birth or military prowess.

There were two basic types of clerical vocation: regular and secular. The regular clergy comprised the orders of monks who lived according to a special ascetic rule (*regula*) in cloisters separated from the world. In the thirteenth century, two new orders—the Franciscans and the Dominicans—gained the sanction of the church. Their members went out into the world to preach the church's mission and to combat heresy.

The secular clergy, those who lived and worked directly among the laity in the world (*saeculum*), formed a vast hierarchy. At the top were the wealthy cardinals, archbishops, and bishops who were drawn almost exclusively from the nobility. Below them were the urban priests, the cathedral canons, and the court clerks. Finally, there was the great mass of poor parish priests, who were neither financially nor intellectually much above the common people they served.

During most of the Middle Ages, the clergy were the first estate, and theology was the queen of the sciences. How did the clergy attain such prominence? A lot of it was self-proclaimed. However, there was also popular respect and reverence for the clergy's role as mediator between God and humanity. The priest brought the Son of God down to earth when he celebrated the sacrament of the Eucharist; his absolution released penitents from punishment for sin. It was declared improper for mere laypeople to sit in judgment on such a priest.

DOCUMENT THE SERVICES OF A SERF

By the fourteenth century, serfs were paid for their labor. This contract, from a manor in Sussex, England, describes the services required of one serf, John of Cayworth, stipulating the number of days he must devote to each and the pay he is to receive in return. Deductions for meals, which varied in price with the particular service performed, are factored into the serf's take-home pay.

Do the chores and the number of days the serf must work appear excessive? Was it worthwhile for the serf, given what he received in exchange? Would modern renters of land and lodging consider these payments reasonable today?

John of Cayworth holds a house and 30 acres of land, and owes yearly 2 s[shillings] at Easter and Michaelmas [in rent to his lord]; and he owes a cock and two hens at Christmas [also in rent] of the value of 4 d[enarii].

And he ought to harrow for 2 days at the Lenten sowing with one man and his own horse and his own harrow, the value of the work being 4d.; and he is to receive from the lord on each day 3 meals, of the value of 5d., and then the lord will be at a loss of 1d. . . .

And he ought to carry the manure of the lord for 2 days with one cart, with his own 2 oxen, the value of the work being 8d.; and he is to receive from the lord each day 3 meals at the value as above. . . .

And he shall find one man for 2 days, for mowing the meadow of the lord, who can mow, by estimation, 1 acre and a half, the value of the mowing of an acre being 6d.; the sum is there 9d. And he is to receive each day 3 meals of the value given above. . . .

And he ought to carry the hay of the lord for 1 day with a cart and 3 animals of his own, the price of the work being 6d. And he shall have from the lord 3 meals of the value of 2 1/2d. . . .

And he ought to carry in autumn beans or oats for 2 days with a cart and 3 animals of his own, the value of the work being 12d. And he shall receive from the lord each day 3 meals of the value given above. . . .

And he ought to carry wood from the woods of the lord as far as the manor, for two days in summer, with a cart and 3 animals of his own, the value of the work being 9d. And he shall receive from the lord each day 3 meals of the price given above. . . .

The totals of the rents with the value of the hens, is 2s. 4d.

From James Harvey Robinson, ed., *Readings in European History*, Vol. 1 (Boston: Athenaeum, 1906), pp. 400–402.

A 15th-century rendering of an 11th- or 12th-century marketplace. Medieval women were active in all trades, but especially in the food and clothing industries. Scala/Art Resource, N.Y.

PEASANTS The largest and lowest social group in medieval society was one on whose labor the welfare of all others depended: the agrarian peasantry. Many peasants lived and worked on the manors of the nobility, the vital cells of rural social life. The lord of the manor required a certain amount of produce (grain, eggs, and the like) and services from the peasant families and held both judicial and police powers. He owned and operated the machines that processed crops into food and drink. The lord also had the right to subject his tenants to exactions known as *banalities.* He could, for example, force them to breed their cows with his bull, and to pay for the privilege; to grind their bread grains in his mill; to bake their bread in his oven; to make their wine in his wine press; to buy their beer from his brewery; and even to surrender to him the choice parts of all animals slaughtered on his lands. The lord also collected as an inheritance tax a serf's best animal. Without the lord's permission, a serf could neither travel nor marry outside the manor in which he served.

However, the serfs' status was not chattel slavery. It was to a lord's advantage to keep his serfs healthy and happy; his welfare, like theirs, depended on a successful harvest. Serfs had their own dwellings and modest strips of land, and they lived off the produce of their own labor and organization. They could also market for their own profit any surpluses that remained after the harvest. And serfs could pass their property (their dwellings and field strips) on to their children, along with their worldly goods.

Two basic changes occurred in the evolution of the manor from the early to the later Middle Ages. The first was the increasing importance of the single-family holding. As family farms replaced manorial units, land and property remained in the possession of a single family from generation to generation. Second was the conversion of the serf's dues into money payments, a change made possible by the revival of trade and the rise of the towns. This development, completed by the thirteenth century, permitted serfs to hold their land as rent-paying tenants and to overcome their servile status.

By the mid–fourteenth century, a declining nobility in England and France, faced with the ravages of the great plague and the Hundred Years' War, tried to turn back the historical clock by increasing taxes on the peasantry and restricting their migration to the cities. The response was armed revolt. The revolts of the agrarian peasantry, like those of the urban proletariat, were brutally crushed. They stand out at the end of the Middle Ages as violent testimony to the breakup of medieval society. As growing national sentiment would break its political unity and heretical movements end its nominal religious unity, the peasantry's revolts revealed the absence of medieval social unity.

MEDIEVAL WOMEN

Although the male Christian clergy praised the ideal of a celibate life of chastity, poverty, and obedience and often depicted women as the physical, mental, and moral inferiors of men, most medieval women were workers in fields, trades, and businesses. Evidence suggests that they were respected and loved by their husbands, perhaps because they worked shoulder to shoulder and hour by hour with them. Between the ages of ten and fifteen, girls were apprenticed in a trade, much like boys, and they learned a marketable skill. Women appeared in virtually every "blue-collar" trade, but were especially prominent in the food and clothing industries. They belonged to guilds and they could become craftmasters. In the late Middle Ages, townswomen often went to school and gained vernacular literacy

William the Conqueror on horseback urging his troops into combat with the English at the Battle of Hastings (October 14, 1066). From the Bayeux Tapestry, about 1073–1083. Giraudon/Art Resource, N.Y.

although they were excluded from universities and the professions of scholarship, law, and medicine.

GROWTH OF NATIONAL MONARCHIES

ENGLAND AND FRANCE: HASTINGS (1066) TO BOUVINES (1214)

WILLIAM THE CONQUEROR The most important change in English political life was occasioned in 1066 by the death of the childless Anglo-Saxon ruler Edward the Confessor (r. 1042–1066), so named because of his reputation of piety. Edward's mother was a Norman princess, which gave Duke William of Normandy (d. 1087) a hereditary claim to the English throne. The Anglo-Saxon assembly, however, chose instead Harold Godwinsson (ca. 1022–1066). That defiant action brought the swift conquest of England by the powerful Normans. William's forces defeated Harold's army at Hastings on October 14, 1066, and William was crowned king of England in Westminster Abbey within weeks of the invasion.

Thereafter William established a strong monarchy but kept the Anglo-Saxon tax system, the practice of court writs (legal warnings) as a flexible form of central control over localities, and the Anglo-Saxon quasi-democratic tradition of frequent *parleying*—that is, the holding of conferences between the king and lesser powers who had vested interests in royal decisions. The result was a balancing of monarchical and parliamentary elements that remains true of English government today.

POPULAR REBELLION AND MAGNA CARTA William's grandson, Henry II (r. 1154–1189), brought to the throne greatly expanded French holdings through inheritance from his father (Maine, Touraine, and Anjou) and his marriage to Eleanor of Aquitaine (1122–1204), a union that created the so-called Angevin or English-French empire. As Henry II acquired new lands abroad, he became more autocratic at home. The result was strong political resistance from both the nobility and the clergy.

Under Henry's successors, the brothers Richard the Lion-Hearted (r. 1189–1199) and John (r. 1199–1216), burdensome taxation in support of foreign Crusades and a failing war with France turned resistance into outright rebellion. With the full support of the clergy and the townspeople, English barons forced the king's grudging recognition of the Magna Carta ("Great Charter") in 1215.

This famous cornerstone of modern English law put limits on royal power and secured the rights of the privileged to be represented at the highest levels of government in important matters like taxation. The Great Charter enabled the English to avoid both a dissolution of the monarchy by the nobility and the abridgment of the rights of the nobility by the monarchy.

PHILIP II AUGUSTUS Powerful feudal princes dominated France from the beginning of the Capetian dynasty (987) until the reign of Philip II Augustus (1180–1223). During this period the Capetian kings wisely concentrated their limited resources on securing the territory surrounding Paris known as the Île-de-France. By the time of Philip II, Paris had become the center of French government and culture, and the Capetian dynasty a secure hereditary monarchy. Thereafter, the kings of France were able to impose their will on the French nobles.

The Norman Conquest of England enabled the Capetian kings to establish a truly national monarchy. The Duke of Normandy, who after 1066 was master of England, was also a vassal of the French king in Paris. Capetian kings understandably watched with alarm as the power of their Norman vassal grew.

Philip Augustus faced both an internal and an international struggle, and he succeeded at both. His armies occupied all the English territories on the French coast, except for Aquitaine. At Bouvines on July 27, 1214, the French won handily over the English and their German allies. The victory unified France around the monarchy and thereby laid the foundation for French ascendancy in the late Middle Ages.

FRANCE IN THE THIRTEENTH CENTURY: REIGN OF LOUIS IX

Louis IX (r. 1226–1270), the grandson of Philip Augustus, embodied the medieval view of the perfect ruler. He inherited a unified and secure kingdom.

Louis's greatest achievements lay at home. The efficient French bureaucracy became under him an instrument of order and fair play in local government. He sent forth royal commissioners to monitor the royal officials responsible for local governmental administration and ensure justice. These royal ambassadors were received as genuine tribunes of the people. Louis further abolished private wars and serfdom within his own royal domain, gave his subjects the right of appeal from local to higher courts, and made the tax system more equitable. The French people came to associate their king with justice; and national feeling, the glue of nationhood, grew strong during his reign.

During Louis's reign, French society and culture became an example to all of Europe, a pattern that would continue into the modern period. Northern France became the showcase of monastic reform, chivalry, and Gothic art and architecture. Louis's reign also coincided with the golden age of Scholasticism, which saw the convergence of Europe's greatest thinkers on Paris, among them Saint Thomas Aquinas.

Document: The English Nobility Imposes Restraints on King John

The gradual building of a sound English constitutional monarchy in the Middle Ages required the king's willingness to share power. He had to be strong but could not act as a despot or rule by fiat. The danger of despotism became acute in England under the rule of King John. In 1215 the English nobility forced him to recognize the Magna Carta, which reaffirmed traditional rights and personal liberties that are still enshrined in English law.

Are the rights protected by the Magna Carta basic ones or special privileges? Do they suggest there was a sense of "fairness" in the past? Does the granting of such rights in any way weaken the king?

A free man shall not be fined for a small offense, except in proportion to the gravity of the offense; and for a great offense he shall be fined in proportion to the magnitude of the offense, saving his freehold [property]; and a merchant in the same way, saving his merchandise; and the villein [a free serf, bound only to his lord] shall be fined in the same way, saving his wainage [wagon], if he shall be at [the king's] mercy. And none of the above fines shall be imposed except by the oaths of honest men of the neighborhood. . . .

No constable or other bailiff of [the king] shall take anyone's grain or other chattels without immediately paying for them in money, unless he is able to obtain a postponement at the good will of the seller.

No constable shall require any knight to give money in place of his ward of a castle [i.e., standing guard], if he is willing to furnish that ward in his own person, or through another honest man, if he himself is not able to do it for a reasonable cause; and if we shall lead or send him into the army, he shall be free from ward in proportion to the amount of time which he has been in the army through us.

No sheriff or bailiff of [the king], or any one else, shall take horses or wagons of any free man, for carrying purposes, except on the permission of that free man.

Neither we nor our bailiffs will take the wood of another man for castles, or for anything else which we are doing, except by the permission of him to whom the wood belongs. . . .

No free man shall be taken, or imprisoned, or dispossessed, or outlawed, or banished, or in any way injured, nor will we go upon him, nor send upon him, except by the legal judgment of his peers, or by the law of the land.

To no one will we sell, to no one will we deny or delay, right or justice.

James Harvey Robinson, ed., *Readings in European History*, Vol. 1 (Boston: Athenaeum, 1904), pp. 236–237.

The portal of Reims Cathedral, where the kings of France were crowned. The cathedral was built in the Gothic style—emblematic of the High and late Middle Ages—that originated in France in the mid-twelfth century. The earlier Romanesque (Roman-like) style from which it evolved is characterized by fortresslike buildings with thick stone walls, rounded arches and vaults, and few windows. The Gothic style, in contrast, is characterized by soaring sturctures, their interiors flooded with colored light from vast expanses of stained glass. Distinctive features of the style include ribbed, crisscrossing vaulting; pointed rather than roudned arches; and prominent exteriror flying buttresses. The vaulting and the flying buttresses made possible the great height of Gothic buildings. By shifting structural weight from the walls, the buttresses also made possible the large, stained-glass-filled windows. The windows were used much as mosaics had been earlier, to show stories from the Bible, saints' lives, and local events. Scala/Art Resource, N.Y.

THE HOHENSTAUFEN EMPIRE (1152–1272)

While stable governments developed in both England and France during the Middle Ages, the Holy Roman Empire fragmented in disunity and blood feuding (see Map 15–2).

FREDERICK I BARBAROSSA Frederick I Barbarossa (1152–1190), the first of the Hohenstaufens, reestablished imperial authority but also initiated a new phase in the contest between popes and emperors. Never have rulers and popes despised and persecuted one another more than they did during the Hohenstaufen dynasty. Frederick attempted to hold the empire together by stressing feudal bonds, but his reign ended with stalemate in Germany and defeat in Italy. In 1186 his son—the future Henry VI (r. 1190–1197)—married Constance, heiress to the kingdom of Sicily. That alliance became a fatal distraction for the Hohenstaufens. This union of the empire with Sicily left Rome encircled, thereby ensuring the undying hostility of a papacy already thoroughly distrustful of the emperor.

When Henry VI died in September 1197, chaos followed. Germany was thrown into anarchy and civil war. Meanwhile, Henry VI's four-year-old son, Frederick, who had a direct hereditary claim to the imperial crown, had for his own safety been made—fatefully, it would prove—a ward of Pope Innocent III (r. 1198–1215), who proclaimed and practiced as none before him the doctrine of the plenitude of papal power. Innocent had both the will and the means to challenge the Hohenstaufens.

FREDERICK II Hohenstaufen support had meanwhile remained alive in Germany, where in December 1212 young Frederick, with papal support, became Emperor Frederick II. But Frederick soon disappointed papal hopes. He was Sicilian and only nine of his thirty-eight years as emperor were spent in Germany. To secure the imperial title for himself and his sons, he gave the German princes what they wanted. The German princes became undisputed lords over their territories, petty kings.

Frederick had an equally disastrous relationship with the papacy, which excommunicated him four times and led the German princes against him, launching the church into European politics on a massive scale. This transformation of the papacy into a formidable political and military power soon made the church highly vulnerable to criticism from religious reformers and royal apologists.

When Frederick died in 1250, the German monarchy died with him. The princes established an electoral college in 1257 to pick the emperor, and the "king of the Romans" became their puppet. Between 1250 and 1272 the Hohenstaufen dynasty slowly faded into oblivion.

POLITICAL AND SOCIAL BREAKDOWN

HUNDRED YEARS' WAR

THE CAUSES OF THE WAR The Hundred Years' War, which began in May 1337 and lasted until October 1453, started when the English king Edward III (r. 1327–1377), the grandson of Philip the Fair of France (r. 1285–1314), claimed the French throne. But the war was more than a dynastic quarrel. England and France were territorial and economic rivals with a long history of prejudice and animosity between them. These factors made the Hundred Years' War a struggle for national identity.

Although France had three times the population of England, was far wealthier, and fought on its own soil, most of the major battles were stunning English victories. The primary reason for these French failures was internal disunity caused by endemic social conflicts. Unlike England, France was still struggling to make the transition from a fragmented feudal society to a centralized modern state.

France's defeats also resulted from incompetent leadership and English military superiority. The English infantry was more disciplined than the French, and English archers could fire six arrows a minute with enough force to pierce an inch of wood or the armor of a knight at 200 yards. Eventually, thanks in part to the inspiring leadership of Joan of Arc (1412–1431), and a sense of national identity and self-confidence, the French were able to expel the English from France. By 1453, all that remained to the English was their coastal enclave of Calais.

Charles forgot his liberator as quickly as he had embraced her. When the Burgundians captured Joan in May 1430, he could have secured her release but did not. The Burgundians and the English wanted her publicly discredited, believing this would demoralize French resistance. She was turned over to the Inquisition in English-held Rouen, where, after ten weeks of interrogation, she was executed on May 30, 1431.

The Hundred Years' War had lasting political and social consequences. It devastated France, but it also awakened French nationalism and hastened the country's transition from a feudal monarchy to a centralized state. In both France and England the burden of the war fell most heavily on the peasantry, who were forced to support it with taxes and services.

THE BLACK DEATH

PRECONDITIONS AND CAUSES In the late Middle Ages, improvements in agriculture increased both the food supply and the population. It is estimated that Europe's population doubled between the years 1000 and 1300, and then began to outstrip food production. There were now

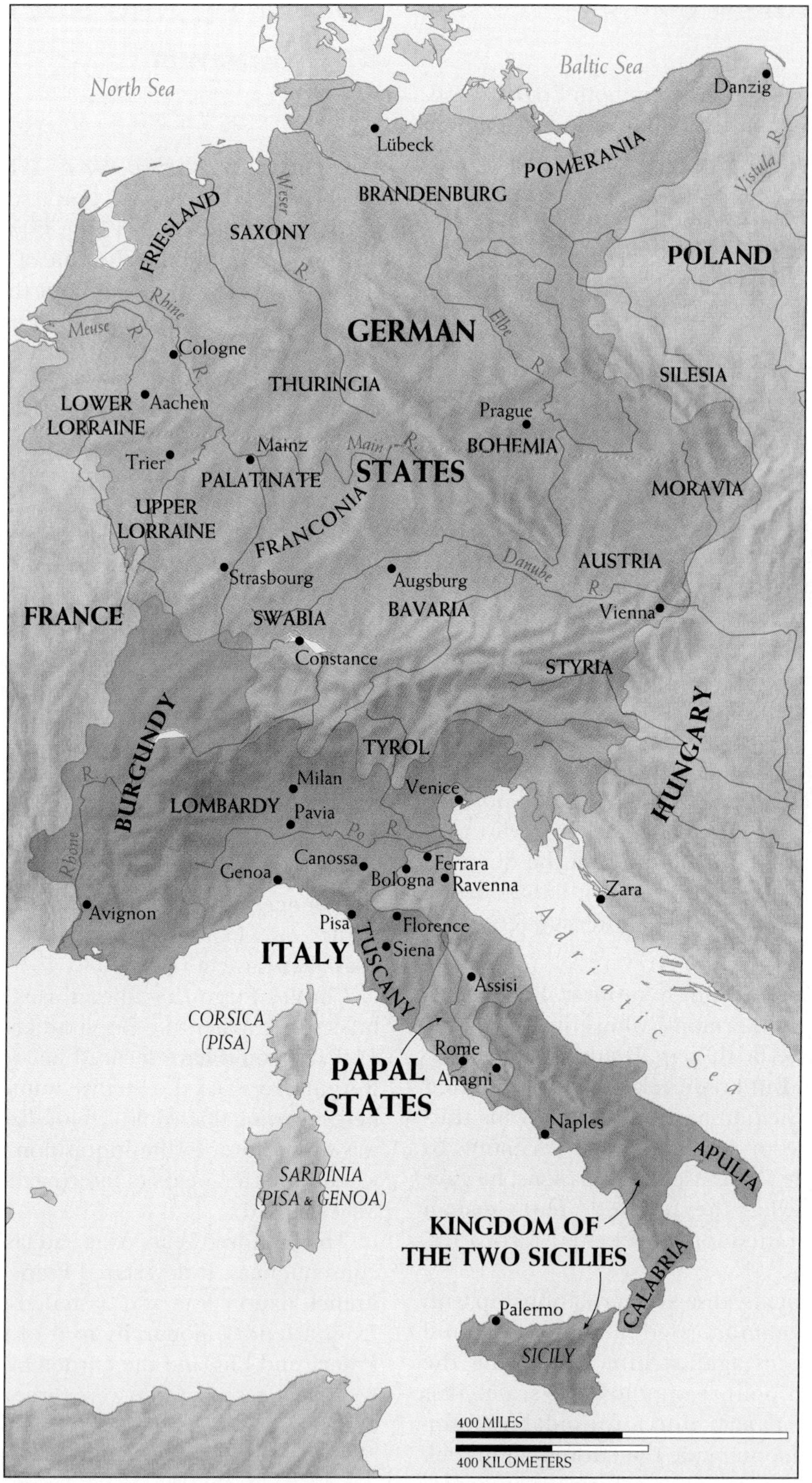

Map 15–2 **Germany and Italy in the Middle Ages.** Medieval Germany and Italy were divided lands. The Holy Roman Empire (Germany) embraced hundreds of independent territories that the emperor ruled only in name. The papacy controlled the Rome area and tried to enforce its will in the Romagna. Under the Hohenstaufens (mid-twelfth to mid-thirteenth centuries), internal German divisions and papal conflict reached new heights; German rulers sought to extend their power to southern Italy and Sicily.

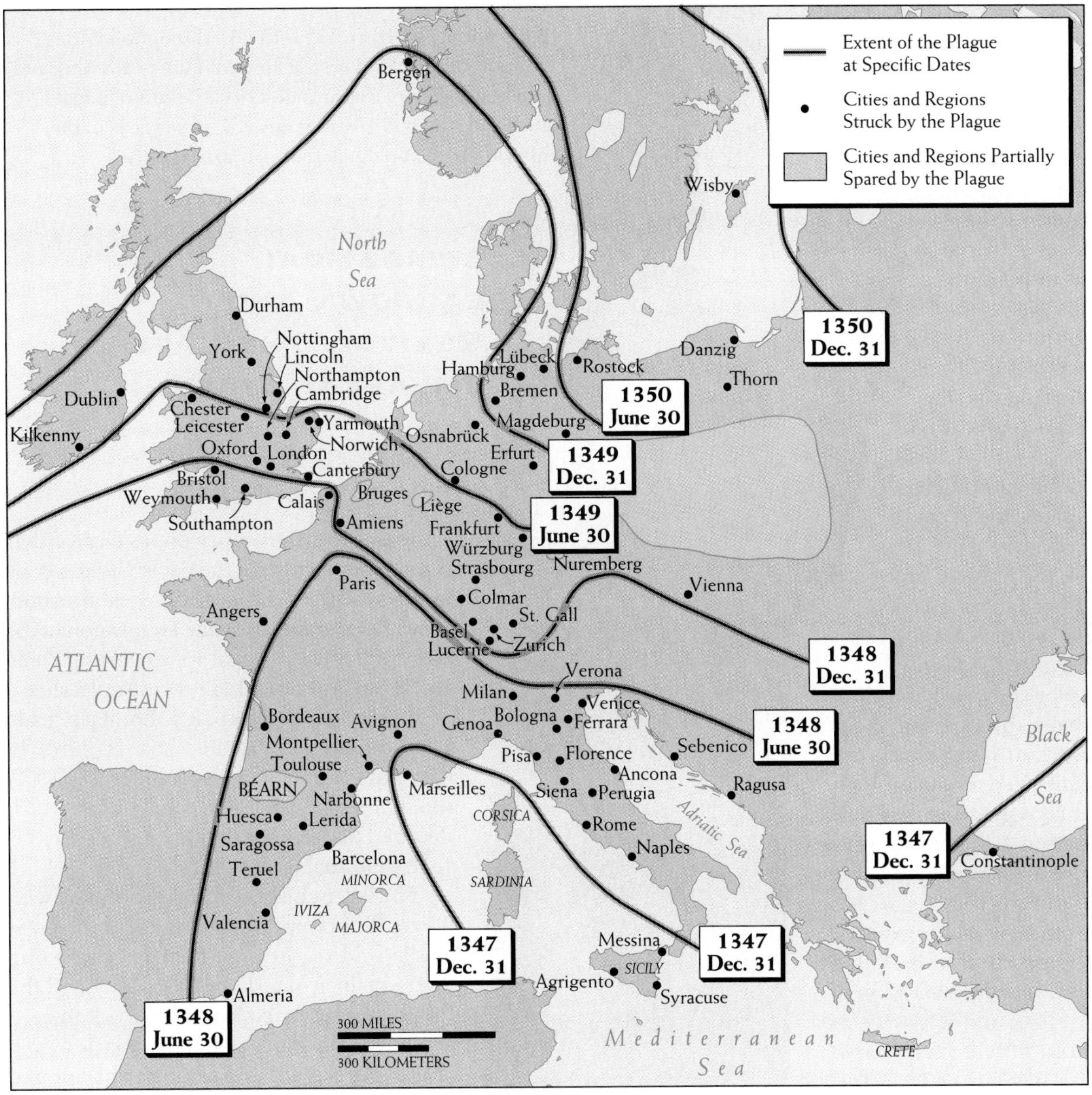

Map 15–3 Spread of the Black Death. Apparently introduced by sea-borne rats from areas around the Black Sea where plague-infested rodents have long been known, the Black Death had great human, social, and economic consequences. According to one of the lower estimates, it killed 25 million in Europe. The map charts the spread of the plague in the mid–14th century. Generally following trade routes, it reached Scandinavia by 1350, and some believe it then went on to Iceland and even Greenland. Areas off the main trade routes were largely spared.

more people than food to feed them or jobs to employ them, and the average European faced the probability of famine at least once during his or her expected thirty-five-year life-span. Decades of overpopulation, economic depression, famine, and bad health made Europe's population vulnerable to a virulent bubonic plague that struck with full force in 1348.

This Black Death, so called because it discolored the body, followed the trade routes from Asia into Europe. Appearing in Sicily in late 1347, it entered Europe through Venice, Genoa, and Pisa in 1348, and from there it swept rapidly through Spain and southern France and into northern Europe. Areas that lay outside the major trade routes, like Bohemia, appear to have remained virtually unaffected. Bubonic plague reappeared in succeeding decades. By the early fifteenth century, it may have killed two fifths of western Europe's population (see Map 15-3).

Social and Economic Consequences

Whole villages vanished in the wake of the plague. Among the social and economic consequences of this depopulation were a shrunken labor supply and a decline in the value of the estates of the nobility.

As the number of farm laborers decreased, their wages increased, and those of skilled artisans soared. Many serfs now replaced their labor services with money payments or abandoned the farm altogether for jobs in the cities. Agricultural prices fell because of lowered demand, and the price of luxury and manufactured goods—the work of skilled artisans—rose. The noble landholders suffered the greatest decline in power from this new state of affairs. They were forced to pay more for finished products and for farm labor, but received less for their agricultural produce. Everywhere their rents declined after the plague.

Although the plague hit urban populations especially hard, the cities and their skilled industries eventually prospered from its effects. Cities had always protected their interests by regulating competition and immigration from rural areas. After the plague the reach of such laws was extended beyond the cities.

The omnipresence of death whetted the appetite for goods that only skilled urban industries could produce. Expensive cloths, jewelry, furs, and silks were in great demand. Faced with life at its worst, people insisted on having the best. Initially this new demand could not be met, as the first wave of plague transformed the already restricted supply of skilled artisans into a shortage almost overnight. As a result, the prices of manufactured and luxury items soared to new heights, but this in turn encouraged workers to migrate to the city to become artisans. As wealth poured into the cities and per capita income rose, urban dwellers paid less for agricultural products from the countryside.

There was also gain as well as loss for the church. Although it suffered losses as a great landholder and was politically weakened, it had received new revenues from the vastly increased demand for religious services for the dead and the dying and from the multiplication of gifts and bequests. Nonetheless, after 1350, and largely as a consequence of the plague, the two traditional "containers" of monarchy—the landed nobility and the church—were politically on the defensive.

Pope Boniface VIII (r. 1294–1303), who opposed the taxation of the clergy by the kings of France and England and issued one of the strongest declarations of papal authority, the bull *Unam Sanctam.* This statue is in the Museo Civico, Bologna, Italy. Scala/Art Resource, N.Y.

Ecclesiastical Breakdown and Revival: The Late Medieval Church

Boniface VIII and Philip the Fair

By the fourteenth century popes faced rulers far more powerful than the papacy. When Pope Boniface VIII (r. 1294–1303) issued a bull, *Clericis Laicos,* which forbade lay taxation of the clergy without prior papal approval, King Philip the Fair of France (r. 1285–1314) unleashed a ruthless antipapal campaign. Boniface made a last-ditch stand against state control of national churches on November 18, 1302, when he issued the bull *Unam Sanctam,* which declared that temporal authority was "subject" to the spiritual power of the church.

The French, however, responded with force. Philip sent troops who beat the pope badly, and might even have executed him had not an aroused populace liberated the pope and returned him safely to Rome.

There was no papal retaliation. No pope ever again so seriously threatened kings and emperors. Future relations between Church and State would henceforth tilt toward state control of religion within particular monarchies.

The Great Schism (1378–1417) and the Conciliar Movement to 1449

After Boniface VIII's death, his successor, Clement V (r. 1305–1314), moved the papal court to Avignon on the southeastern border with France, where it remained until Pope Gregory XI (r. 1370–1378) reestablished the papacy in Rome in January 1377. His successor, Pope Urban VI (r. 1378–1389), proclaimed his intention to reform the Curia. This announcement alarmed the cardinals, most of whom were French. Not wanting to surrender the benefits of a papacy under French influence, the French king, Charles V (r.

1364–1380), supported a schism in the church and on September 20, 1378, thirteen cardinals, all but one of whom was French, elected a cousin of the French king as Pope Clement VII (r. 1378–1397). Clement returned to Avignon. Thereafter allegiance to the two papal courts divided along political lines: England and its allies (the Holy Roman Empire, Hungary, Bohemia, and Poland) acknowledged Urban VI, whereas France and its orbit (Naples, Scotland, Castile, and Aragon) supported Clement VII. Only the Roman line of popes, however, is recognized as official by the church.

In 1409 a council at Pisa deposed both the Roman and the Avignon popes and elected its own new pope. But neither Rome nor Avignon accepted its action, so after 1409 there were three contending popes. This intolerable situation ended when the emperor Sigismund (r. 1410–1437) prevailed on the Pisan pope to summon a legal council of the church in Constance in 1414, a council also recognized by the reigning Roman pope Gregory XII (r. 1406–1415). After the three contending popes had either resigned or been deposed, the council elected a new pope, Martin V (r. 1417–1431), in November 1417, reuniting the church.

Under Pope Eugenius IV (r. 1431–1447), the papacy regained much of its prestige and authority, and in 1460 the papal bull *Execrabilis* condemned all appeals to councils as "completely null and void." But the conciliar movement had planted deep within the conscience of all western peoples the conviction that the leader of an institution must be responsive to its members and not act against their best interests.

MAP EXPLORATION

Interactive map: To explore this map further, go to http://www.prenhall.com/craig_map15.4

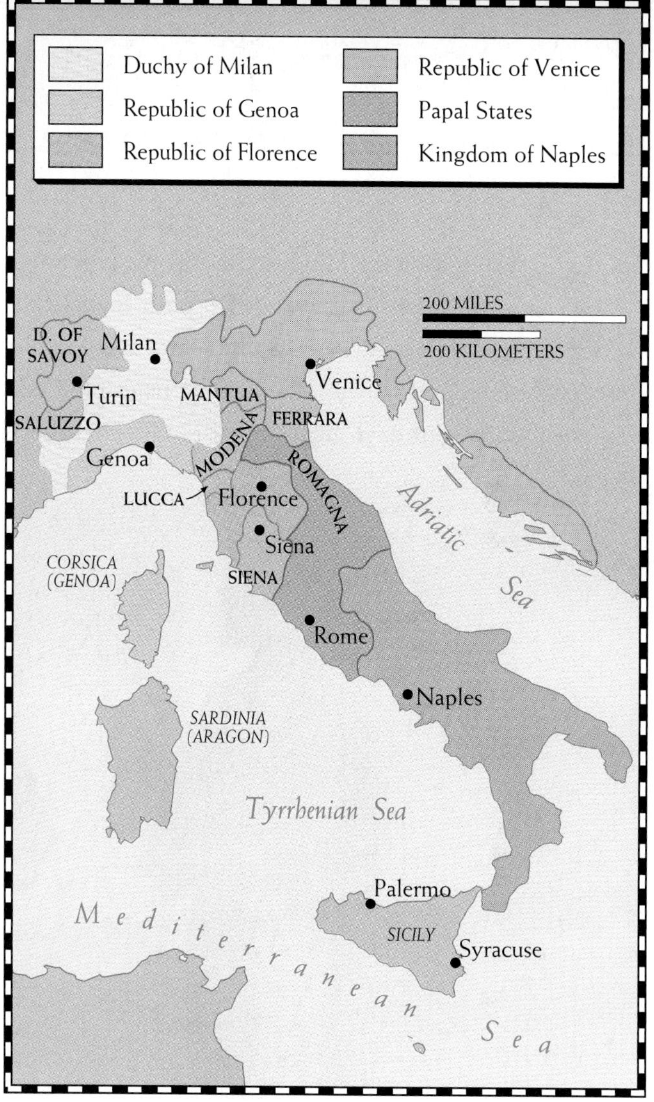

Map 15–4 Renaissance Italy. The city-states of Renaissance Italy were self-contained principalities whose internal strife was monitored by their despots and whose external aggression was long successfully controlled by treaty.

The Renaissance in Italy (1375–1527)

Most scholars agree that the Renaissance was a transition from the medieval to the modern world. Medieval Europe, especially before the twelfth century, had been a fragmented feudal society with an agricultural economy, its thought and culture dominated by the church. Renaissance Europe, especially after the fourteenth century, was characterized by growing national consciousness and political centralization, an urban economy based on organized commerce and capitalism, and ever greater lay and secular control of thought and culture.

The distinctive features and achievements of the Renaissance are most strikingly revealed in Italy from roughly 1375 to 1527, the year of the infamous sack of Rome by imperial soldiers. What was achieved in Italy during these centuries also deeply influenced northern Europe.

The Italian City-State: Social Conflict and Despotism

Renaissance society took distinctive shape within the cities of late medieval Italy. Italy was the natural gateway between East and West. Venice, Genoa, and Pisa traded uninterruptedly with the Near East throughout the Middle Ages, and maintained vibrant urban societies. During the thirteenth and fourteenth centuries, the trade-rich Italian cities became powerful city-states, dominating the political and economic life of the surrounding countryside. By the fifteenth century, the great Italian cities had become the bankers for much of Europe. There were five such major, competitive states in Italy: the duchy of Milan, the republics of Florence and Venice, the Papal States, and the kingdom of Naples (see Map 15–4).

Art and the World

Images of Death in the Late Middle Ages

Throughout the Middle Ages, people perceived, and artists portrayed death both realistically and religiously: on the one hand, as a terrible, inescapable fate, and on the other, as the beginning of a new, eternal life, either in heaven or in hell. That life is death (transitory) and death is life (the afterlife) were two urgent and ironic teachings of the Christian church. Many laity, finding the present world undesirable and death no sure release into a better one, understandably resisted. Graphic and sermonic instruction in the "Art of Dying" be-

The Prince of the World in the Church of St. Sebald, Nürnberg, 1320–1330.
Germnisches Nationalmuseum, Nürnberg.

came the church's response. Shown here, a sandstone sculpture, *The Prince of the World,* carries a vivid warning. When viewers looked behind this young, attractive prince, they discovered that beauty is only skin deep: His body, like everyone else's, is filled with worms and flesh-eating frogs. A serpent spirals up his left leg and enters his back—an allusion to the biblical teaching that the wages of sin are death. To drive home human mortality, the church instructed laity to think often about the inevitability of death by visiting dying relatives and friends, watching them die and being buried, and thereafter visiting their graves often. This, in turn, would move them to resist the devil's temptations, obey the church, avoid sin, and become eligible for heaven in the afterlife.

During the late Middle Ages, in both literature and art, the "Dance of Death" became a new reminder of human mortality and the need for Christian living and church instruction. (It was first painted in 1424, on the wall of the Church of the Holy Innocents in Paris.) Death appeared as a living skeleton in lively conversation with mortal representatives—from pope to friar in the religious world, from emperor to laborer in the secular—none of whom, no matter how mighty, can elude death's grasp. Even the Son of God, as an incarnate man, died a dreadful death. Although emerging in the late Middle Ages, the "Dance of Death" conveyed an old message, apparently urgently needed at the time because of the indiscipline and self-indulgence occasioned by the new horrors of the Black Death and the Hundred Years' War.

The church's last word on death, however, was resplendently positive: mortal men and women of true faith, like the crucified Son of God, might look forward to eternal life as shown in *The Resurrection,* from the *Isenheim Altarpiece,* 1509/10–1515.

Sources: Alberto Tenenti, "Death in History," in *Life and Death in Fifteenth Century Florence,* ed. M. Tetel et al. (Durham, NC: Duke University Press, 1989); Donald Weinstein, "The Art of Dying Well and Popular Piety in the Preaching and Thought of Girolamo Savonarola," in *ibid.,* 88–104; and James M. Clark, *The Dance of Death in the Middle Ages and the Renaissance* (Glasgow: Jackson, Son, and Col, 1950), pp. 1–4, 22–24, 106–110. Joseph L. Koerner, *The Moment of Self-Portraiture in German Renaissance Art* (Chicago: University of Chicago Press, 1993), pp. 199–200. H. W. Janson et al., *History of Art* (Upper Saddle River, NJ: Prentice Hall, 1997), p. 528.

Gruenwald, Mathias (1460–1528), *The Resurrection.* A panel from the *Isenheim Altar.* Limewood (ca. 1515), 250 × 650 cm. Musée d'Unterlinden, Colmar, France. © Erich Lessing/Art Resource, N. Y.

Social strife and competition for political power were so intense within the cities that for survival's sake, most had evolved into despotisms by the fifteenth century. Venice, ruled by a successful merchant oligarchy, was the notable exception. Elsewhere, the new social classes and divisions within society produced by rapid urban growth fueled chronic, near-anarchic conflict.

In Florence, these social divisions produced conflict at every level of society. True stability was not established until the ascent to power in 1434 of Cosimo de' Medici (1389–1464). The wealthiest Florentine and a most astute statesman, Cosimo controlled the city internally from behind the scenes, skillfully manipulating the constitution and influencing elections. His grandson Lorenzo the Magnificent (1449–1492, r. 1478–1492) ruled Florence in almost totalitarian fashion.

Despotism was less subtle elsewhere in Italy. To prevent internal social conflict and foreign intrigue from paralyzing their cities, the dominant groups in many cities cooperated to install a hired strongman, known as a *podesta*, to maintain law and order. Because these despots could not depend on the divided populace, they operated through mercenary armies.

Political turbulence and warfare gave birth to diplomacy, through which the various city-states stayed abreast of foreign military developments and, if shrewd enough, gained power and advantage without actually going to war. Most city-states established resident embassies during the fifteenth century. Their ambassadors became their watchful eyes and ears at rival courts.

Renaissance culture was promoted as vigorously by despots as by republicans and by popes as enthusiastically as by the secularized ones.

CHRONOLOGY

CHURCH AND EMPIRE

910	Monastary of Cluny founded
918	Henry I becomes King of Germany
951	Otto I invades Italy
955	Otto I defeats the Hungarians at Lechfeld
962	Otto I crowned emperor by Pope John XII
1077	Gregory VII pardons Henry IV at Canossa
1122	Concordat of Worms settles the investiture controversy
1152–1190	Reign of Frederick Barbarossa
1198–1215	Reign of Innocent III
1214	Collapse of the claims of Otto IV
1220	Frederick II crowned emperor
1232	Frederick II devolves authority to the German princes
1257	The German monarchy becomes elective

HUMANISM

Humanism was the scholarly study of the Latin and Greek classics and the ancient Church Fathers both for their own sake and to promote a rebirth of ancient norms and values. Humanists advocated the *studia humanitatis*, a liberal arts program that embraced grammar, rhetoric, poetry, history, politics, and moral philosophy.

The first humanists were orators and poets. They wrote original literature in both the classical and the vernacular languages, inspired by the newly discovered works of the ancients, and they taught rhetoric within the universities. Their talents were sought as secretaries, speech writers, and diplomats in princely and papal courts.

Classical and Christian antiquity had been studied before the Italian Renaissance—during the Carolingian renaissance of the ninth century, for example. However, the Italian Renaissance of the late Middle Ages was more secular and lay dominated, had broader interests, recovered more manuscripts, and possessed far superior technical skills than earlier rebirths of antiquity.

Unlike their Scholastic rivals, humanists were not content only to summarize and compare the views of recognized authorities on a question, but instead went directly to the original source and drew their own conclusions. Avidly searching out manuscript collections, Italian humanists made the full sources of Greek and Latin antiquity available to scholars during the fourteenth and fifteenth centuries. Mastery of Latin and Greek was their surgeon's tool. There is a kernel of truth—but only a kernel—in the arrogant boast of the humanists that the period between themselves and classical civilization was a "dark middle age."

PETRARCH, DANTE, AND BOCCACCIO Francesco Petrarch (1304–1374) was the father of humanism. He left the legal profession to pursue his love of letters and poetry. Petrarch celebrated ancient Rome in his writings and tirelessly collected ancient manuscripts; among his finds were letters by Cicero. His critical textual studies, elitism, and contempt for the allegedly useless learning of the Scholastics were shared by many later humanists.

Petrarch was far more secular in orientation than Dante Alighieri (1265–1321), whose *Vita Nuova* and *Divine Comedy* form, with Petrarch's sonnets, the cornerstones of Italian vernacular literature. Petrarch's student and friend Giovanni Boccaccio (1313–1375), author of the *Decameron*, 100 bawdy tales told by three men and seven women in a country retreat from the plague that ravaged Florence in 1348, also pioneered humanist studies. An avid collector of manuscripts, Boccaccio assembled an encyclopedia of Greek and Roman mythology.

EDUCATIONAL REFORMS AND GOALS The classical ideal of a useful education that produces well-rounded people inspired far-reaching reforms in traditional education. The most influential Italian Renaissance tract on education, Pietro Paolo Vergerio's (1349–1420) *On the Morals That*

Cosimo de' Medici (1389–1464), Florentine banker and statesman, in his lifetime the city's wealthiest man and most successful politician. This portrait is by Jacopo da Pontormo (1494–1556). Erich Lessing/Art Resource, N.Y.

Befit a Free Man, was written directly from classical models. Vittorino da Feltre (d. 1446) directed his students to a highly disciplined reading of ancient authors, together with vigorous physical exercise and games with intellectual pursuits.

Educated and cultured noblewomen also had a prominent place at Renaissance courts, among them Christine de Pisan (1363?–1434). She was an expert in classical, French, and Italian languages and literature and became a well-known woman of letters in the courts of Europe. Her most famous work, *The City of Ladies,* describes the accomplishments of the great women of history.

RENAISSANCE ART

In Renaissance Italy, as later in Reformation Europe, the values and interests of the laity were less subordinated to those of the clergy. In education, culture, and religion, medieval Christian values were adjusting to a more this-worldly spirit. Men and women began again to appreciate and even to glorify the secular world, secular learning, and purely human pursuits as ends in themselves.

This perspective on life is especially prominent in the painting and sculpture of the High Renaissance (late fifteenth and early sixteenth centuries), when Renaissance art reached its full maturity. In imitation of Greek and Roman art, painters and sculptors attempted to create harmonious, symmetrical, and properly proportioned figures, portraying the human form with a glorified realism. Whereas Byzantine and Gothic art had been religious and idealized in the extreme, Renaissance art, especially in the fifteenth century, realistically reproduced nature and human beings as a part of nature.

Renaissance artists took advantage of new technical skills and materials developed during the fifteenth century: the use of oil paints, using shading to enhance realism (chiaroscuro), and adjusting the size of figures to give the viewer a feeling of continuity with the painting (linear perspective). Compared with their flat Byzantine and Gothic counterparts, Renaissance paintings seem filled with energy and life and stand out from the canvas in three dimensions. The great masters of the High Renaissance included Leonardo da Vinci (1452–1519), Raphael (1483–1520), and Michelangelo Buonarroti (1475–1564).

LEONARDO DA VINCI Leonardo personified the Renaissance ideal of the universal person, one who is not only a jack-of-all-trades but also a master of many. A mil-

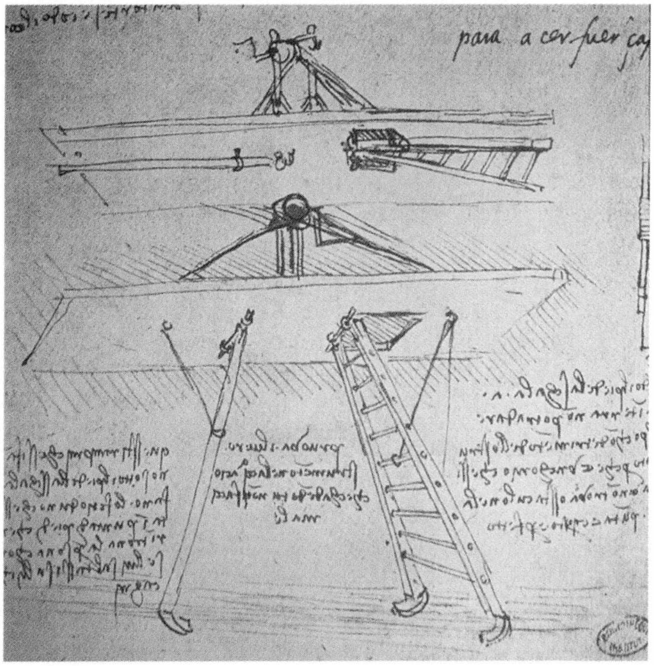

Aviation drawings by Leonardo da Vinci (1452–1519), who imagined a possible flying machine with a retractable ladder for boarding. David Forbert/SuperStock, Inc.

itary engineer and advocate of scientific experimentation, he dissected corpses to learn anatomy and was a self-taught botanist. He foresaw such modern machines as airplanes and submarines. The variety of his interests tended to shorten his attention span, so that he constantly moved from one activity to another. As a painter, his great skill lay in conveying inner moods through complex facial features, such as that seen in the most famous of his paintings, the *Mona Lisa.*

RAPHAEL Raphael, who died young (thirty-seven), is famous for his tender madonnas. Art historians also praise his fresco *The School of Athens,* which depicts Plato and Aristotle surrounded by philosophy and science, as one of the most perfect examples of Renaissance artistic theory and technique.

Raphael's portrait (ca. 1515) of Baldassare Castiglione (1478–1529), now in the Louvre. Castiglione, author of the *Book of the Courtier,* was Raphael's close friend. The self-restraint and inner calm that he considered the chief qualities of the gentleman are also qualities of Raphael's art, reflected in the portrait's perfect balance and harmony. This painting greatly influenced Rembrandt, who later tried unsuccessfully to buy it. Cliche des Musées Nationaux, Paris

MICHELANGELO This melancholy genius also excelled in a variety of arts and crafts. His eighteen-foot godlike sculpture *David* is a perfect example of the Renaissance artist's devotion to harmony, symmetry, and proportion, as well as his extreme glorification of the human form. Four different popes commissioned works by Michelangelo, the best known of which are the frescoes for the Sistine Chapel, painted for Pope Julius II (r.1503–1513).

His later works mark, artistically and philosophically, the passing of High Renaissance painting and the advent of a new, experimental style known as *mannerism,* which reached its peak in the late sixteenth and early seventeenth centuries. It derived its name from the fact that it permitted the artist to express his own individual perceptions and feelings, to paint, compose, or write in a "mannered" or "affected" way. Tintoretto (d. 1594) and especially El Greco (d. 1614) became its supreme representatives.

Michelangelo's *Pietà* (made between 1498 and 1500), St. Peter's, Rome. This work of the artist's youth, sculpted between his twenty-third and twenty-fifth years, portrays a Mary who is younger than her son. Unsurpassed in delicacy, realism, and emotional impact, it exemplifies the creativity of the Italian Renaissance. Scala/Art Resource, N.Y.

DOCUMENT: PICO DELLA MIRANDOLA STATES THE RENAISSANCE IMAGE OF MAN

One of the most eloquent Renaissance descriptions of the abilities of humankind comes from the Italian humanist Pico della Mirandola (1463–1494). In his famed Oration on the Dignity of Man (ca. 1486), Pico described humans as free to become whatever they choose.

In what does the dignity of humankind consist? Does Pico reject the biblical description of Adam and Eve's fall? Does he exaggerate a person's ability to choose freely to be whatever he or she wishes? What inspired such seeming hubris during the Renaissance?

The best of artisans [God] ordained that that creature (man) to whom He [God] had been able to give nothing proper to himself should have joint possession of whatever had been peculiar to each of the different kinds of being. He therefore took man as a creature of indeterminate nature and, assigning him a place in the middle of the world, addressed him thus: "Neither a fixed abode nor a form that is thine alone or any function peculiar to thyself have we given thee, Adam, to the end that according to thy longing and according to thy judgment thou mayest have and possess what abode, what form, and what functions thou thyself shalt desire. The nature of all other beings is limited and constrained within the bounds of laws prescribed by Us. Thou, constrained by no limits, in accordance with thine own free will, in whose hand We have placed thee, shall ordain for thyself the limits of thy nature. We have set thee at the world's center that thou mayest from thence more easily observe whatever is in the world. We have made thee neither of heaven nor of earth, neither mortal nor immortal, so that with freedom of choice and with honor, as though the maker and molder of thyself, thou mayest fashion thyself in whatever shape thou shalt prefer. Thou shalt have the power to degenerate into the lower forms of life, which are brutish. Thou shalt have the power, out of thy soul's judgment, to be reborn into the higher forms, which are divine." O supreme generosity of God the Father, O highest and most marvelous felicity of man! To him it is granted to have whatever he chooses, to be whatever he wills.

From Giovanni Pico della Mirandola, *Oration on the Dignity of Man*, in *The Renaissance Philosophy of Man*, ed. by E. Cassirer et al. Phoenix Books, 1961, pp. 224–225. Reprinted by permission of The University of Chicago Press.

ITALY'S POLITICAL DECLINE: THE FRENCH INVASIONS (1494–1527)

Autonomous city-states of Italy had always preserved their peace and safety from foreign invasion by cooperation with each other. However, in 1494 Naples, supported by Florence and the Borgia pope Alexander VI (1492–1503), prepared to attack Milan. At this point, the Milanese despot Ludovico il Moro (r. 1476–1499) invited the French to revive their dynastic claim to Naples. But France also had dynastic claims to Milan, and the French appetite for new territory became insatiable once French armies had crossed the Alps and reestablished themselves in Italy.

The French king Charles VIII (r. 1483–1498) responded rapidly to Ludovico's call. Within five months he had crossed the Alps (August 1495) and raced as conqueror through Florence and the Papal States into Naples.

Charles's lightning march through Italy alarmed Ferdinand of Aragon (r. 1479–1516), who was also king of Sicily and helped to create a counteralliance: the League of Venice, which was able to force Charles to retreat.

The French returned to Italy under Charles's successor, Louis XII (r. 1498–1515), this time assisted by the Borgia pope Alexander VI (1492–1503). Alexander, probably the most corrupt pope in history, sought to secure a political base in Romagna, officially part of the Papal States, for his son Cesare.

Seeing that a French alliance could allow him to reestablish control over the region, Alexander agreed to abandon the League of Venice, which made the league too weak to resist a French reconquest of Milan. Louis successfully invaded Milan in August 1499. In 1500 he and Ferdinand of Aragon divided Naples between themselves, while the pope and Cesare Borgia conquered the Romagna without opposition.

In 1503 Cardinal Giuliano della Rovere became Pope Julius II (1503–1513). He suppressed the Borgias and placed their newly conquered lands in Romagna under papal jurisdiction. After fully securing the Papal States with French aid, Julius changed sides and sought to rid Italy of his former ally, the French invaders. Julius, Ferdinand of Aragon, and Venice formed a Holy League in October 1511, and soon Emperor Maximilian I (r. 1493–1519) and the Swiss joined them. By 1512 the French were in full retreat.

The French invaded Italy again under Louis's successor, Francis I (r. 1515–1547). French armies massacred Swiss soldiers of the Holy League at Marignano in September 1515. That victory won from the Medici pope Leo X (r. 1513–1521) an agreement known as the Concordat of Bologna (August 1516), which gave the French king control over the French clergy and the right to collect taxes from them, in exchange for French recognition of the pope's superiority over church councils. This helped keep France Catholic after the outbreak of the Protestant Reformation. But the new French entry into Italy also led to the first of four major wars with Spain in the first half of the sixteenth century: the Habsburg-Valois wars, none of which France won.

Santi di Tito's portrait of Machiavelli, perhaps the most famous Italian political theorist, who advised Renaissance princes to practice artful deception and inspire fear in their subjects if they wished to succeed. Scala/Art Resource, N.Y.

Niccolò Machiavelli

The foreign invasions made a shambles of Italy. One who watched as French, Spanish, and German armies wreaked havoc on his country was Niccolò Machiavelli (1469–1527). The more he saw, the more convinced he became that Italian political unity and independence were ends that justified any means. Machiavelli admired the heroic acts of ancient Roman rulers, what Renaissance people called their *Virtu.* Romanticizing the old Roman citizenry, he lamented the absence of heroism among his compatriots. Such a perspective caused his interpretation of both ancient and contemporary history to be exaggerated.

The juxtaposition of what Machiavelli believed the ancient Romans had been with the failure of contemporary Romans to realize such high ideals made him the famous cynic we know in the popular epithet *Machiavellian.* Only an unscrupulous strongman, he concluded, using duplicity and terror, could impose order on so divided and selfish a people. Machiavelli seems to have been in earnest when he advised rulers to discover the advantages of fraud and brutality. He apparently hoped to see a strong ruler emerge from the Medici family. The Medicis, however, were not destined to be Italy's deliverers. The second Medici pope, Clement VII (r. 1523–1534), watched helplessly as Rome was sacked by the army of Emperor Charles V (r. 1519–1556) in 1527, the year of Machiavelli's death.[1]

Chronology

Major Political Events of the Italian Renaissance (1375–1527)

1378-1382	Ciompi revolt in Florence
1434	Medici rule in Florence established by Cosimo de' Medici
1454-1455	Treaty of Lodi allies Milan, Naples, and Florence (in effect until 1494)
1494	Charles VIII of France invades Italy
1495	League of Venice unites Venice, Milan, the Papal States, the Holy Roman Empire, and Spain against France
1499	Louis XII invades Milan (the second French invasion of Italy)
1500	The Borgias conquer Romagna
1512-1513	The Holy League (Pope Julius II, Ferdinand of Aragon, Emperor Maximilian I, and Venice) defeat the French
1513	Machiavelli writes *The Prince*
1515	Francis I leads the third French invasion of Italy
1516	Concordat of Bologna between France and the papacy
1527	Sack of Rome by imperial soldiers

[1] To place the western Renaissance in world perspective, see the conclusion of Chapter 16, where the Renaissance and the Reformation are discussed together.

DOCUMENT MACHIAVELLI DISCUSSES THE MOST IMPORTANT TRAIT FOR A RULER

Does Machiavelli share Pico della Mirandola's image of humankind? (See p. 406.)

Why is the ability to inspire fear more important for a ruler than the ability to inspire love? Are there any limitations on a ruler?

Here the question arises; whether it is better to be loved than feared or feared than loved. The answer is that it would be desirable to be both but, since that is difficult, it is much safer to be feared than to be loved, if one must choose. For on men in general this observation may be made: they are ungrateful, fickle, and deceitful, eager to avoid dangers, and avid for gain, and while you are useful to them they are all with you, offering you their blood, their property, their lives, and their sons so long as danger is remote . . . but when it approaches they turn on you. Any prince, trusting only in their words and having no other preparations made, will fall to his ruin, for friendships that are bought at a price and not by greatness and nobility of soul are paid for indeed, but they are not owned and cannot be called upon in time of need. Men have less hesitation in offending a man who is loved than one who is feared, for love is held by a bond of obligation which, as men are wicked, is broken whenever personal advantage suggests it, but fear is accompanied by the dread of punishment which never relaxes.

From Niccolò Machiavelli, *The Prince* (1513), trans. and ed. by Thomas G. Bergin (New York: Appleton-Century-Crofts, 1947), p. 48.

REVIVAL OF MONARCHY: NATION BUILDING IN THE FIFTEENTH CENTURY

With the emergence of sovereign rulers after 1450, unified national monarchies progressively replaced fragmented and divisive feudal governance. The dynastic and chivalric ideals of feudalism did not however disappear. Minor territorial princes survived, and representative assemblies even grew in influence in some regions. But by the late fifteenth and early sixteenth centuries, the old problem of the one and the many was being decided clearly in favor of monarchy.

In the feudal monarchy of the High Middle Ages the basic powers of government were divided between the king and his semiautonomous vassals. The nobility and the towns acted with varying degrees of unity and success through such evolving representative bodies as the English Parliament, the French Estates General, and the Spanish Cortes to thwart the centralization of royal power. However, as a result of the Hundred Years' War and the schism in the church, the landed nobility and the clergy were in decline in the late Middle Ages. The increasingly important towns now began to ally with the king. Loyal, businesswise townspeople, not the nobility and the clergy, staffed the royal offices, becoming the king's lawyers, bookkeepers, military tacticians, and diplomats. This new alliance between king and town would slowly break the bonds of feudal society and make possible the rise of the modern sovereign state.

In a sovereign state, the powers of taxation, war making, and law enforcement are no longer the local right of semiautonomous vassals, but are concentrated in the monarch and exercised by his chosen agents. Taxes, wars, and laws become national rather than merely regional matters. Only as monarchs were able to act independently of the nobility and the representative assemblies could they overcome the decentralization that had been the basic obstacle to nation building.

Monarchies also began to create standing national armies in the fifteenth century. As the noble cavalry receded and the infantry and the artillery became the backbone of armies, mercenary soldiers were recruited from Switzerland and Germany to form the mainstay of the "king's army."

The growing cost of warfare increased the need to develop new national sources of royal income. The expansion of royal revenues was especially hampered by the stubborn belief among the highest classes that they were immune from government taxation. The nobility guarded their properties and traditional rights and despised taxation as an insult and a humiliation. Royal revenues accordingly grew at the expense of those least able to resist and least able to pay. Monarchs had several options. As feudal lords they could collect rents from their royal domain. They might also levy national taxes on basic food and clothing, such as the *gabelle* or salt tax in France and the *alcabala* or 10 percent sales tax on commercial transactions in Spain. Kings could also levy direct taxes on the peasantry and on commercial transactions in towns under royal protection. This they did through agreeable representative assemblies of the privileged classes in which the peasantry did not sit. The French *taille* was such a tax. Sale of public offices and the issuance of high-interest government bonds appeared in the fifteenth century as innovative fund-raising devices. But kings did not levy taxes on the powerful nobility. They turned to rich nobles, as they did to the great bankers of Italy and Germany, for loans, bargaining with the privileged classes, who often remained as much the kings' creditors and competitors as their subjects.

Medieval Russia

In the late tenth century Prince Vladimir of Kiev (r. 972–1015), then Russia's dominant city, received delegations of Muslims, Roman Catholics, Jews, and Greek Orthodox Christians, each group hoping to win the Russians to its religion. Prince Vladimir chose Greek Orthodoxy, which became the religion of Russia, adding a new cultural bond to the long-standing commercial ties the Russians had with the Byzantine Empire.

Vladimir's successor, Yaroslav the Wise (r. 1016–1054), developed Kiev into a magnificent political and cultural center, but after his death, rivalry among princes challenged Kiev's dominance, and it became just one of several national centers.

The Cathedral of St. Basil in Moscow. Built between 1544 and 1560 during the reign of Ivan the Terrible, it reflects the enduring Byzantine influence on Russian architecture.
Sovfoto/Eastfoto

Mongol Rule (1243–1480) Mongol (or Tatar) armies (see Chapters 8 and 13) invaded Russia in 1223, and Kiev fell in 1240. Russian cities became tribute-paying principalities of the segment of the Mongol Empire called the *Golden Horde,* which had its capital at Sarai, on the lower Volga.

Mongol rule further divided Russia from the West but left Russian political institutions and religion largely intact. Thanks to their far-flung trade, the Mongolians brought most Russians greater peace and prosperity than they had enjoyed before.

Russian Liberation The princes of Moscow cooperated with the Mongols and grew wealthy. They then gradually expanded the principality through land purchases, colonization, and conquest.

In 1380 Grand Duke Dimitri of Moscow (1350–1389) defeated Tatar forces at Kulikov Meadow in a victory that marked the beginning of the decline of Mongolian hegemony. Another century would pass before Ivan III, called Ivan the Great (d. 1505), would bring all of northern Russia under Moscow's control and end Mongol rule in 1480. By the last quarter of the fifteenth century, Moscow had replaced Kiev as the political and religious center of Russia. In Russian eyes it was destined to become the "third Rome" after the fall of Constantinople to the Turks in 1453.

France

There were two cornerstones of French nation building in the fifteenth century. The first was the collapse of the English holdings in France following the Hundred Years' War. The second was the defeat of Charles the Bold (r. 1467–1477) and the duchy of Burgundy. Perhaps Europe's strongest political power in the mid–fifteenth century, Burgundy aspired to lead a dominant middle kingdom between France and the Holy Roman Empire. It might have succeeded had not the Continental powers joined together in opposition. When Charles the Bold was killed at Nancy in 1477, the dream of Burgundian empire died with him.

The dissolution of Burgundy ended its constant intrigue against the French king and left Louis XI (r. 1461–1483) free to secure the monarchy. The newly acquired Burgundian lands and his own Angevin inheritance permitted the king to double the size of his kingdom. Louis harnessed the nobility and expanded trade and industry.

A strong nation is a two-edged sword. It was because Louis's successors inherited such a secure and efficient government that France was able to pursue Italian conquests in the 1490s and to fight a long series of losing wars with the Habsburgs in the first half of the sixteenth century. By the mid–sixteenth century France was again a defeated nation and almost as divided internally as it had been during the Hundred Years' War.

SPAIN

Spain, too, became a strong country in the late fifteenth century. Both Castile and Aragon had been poorly ruled, divided kingdoms in the mid–fifteenth century. The marriage of Isabella of Castile (r. 1474–1504) and Ferdinand of Aragon (r. 1479–1516) changed that situation. The two future sovereigns married in 1469, despite strong protests from neighboring Portugal and France, both of which foresaw the formidable European power such a union would create. Castile was by far the richer and more populous of the two, having an estimated 5 million inhabitants to Aragon's population of under 1 million. Castile was also distinguished by its lucrative sheep-farming industry, which was run by a government-backed organization called the *Mesta*, another example of developing centralized economic planning. Although the two kingdoms were dynastically united by the marriage of Ferdinand and Isabella in 1469, each retained its own government agencies—separate laws, armies, coinage, and taxation—and cultural traditions.

Ferdinand and Isabella could do together what neither was able to accomplish alone: subdue their realms, secure their borders, and venture abroad militarily. Townspeople allied themselves with the crown and progressively replaced the nobility within the royal administration. The crown also extended its authority over the wealthy chivalric orders, a further circumscription of the power of the nobility.

Spain had long been remarkable as a place where three religions—Islam, Judaism, and Christianity—coexisted with a certain degree of toleration. This toleration ended dramatically under Ferdinand and Isabella, who made Spain the prime example of state-controlled religion. Ferdinand and Isabella exercised almost total control over the Spanish church as they placed religion in the service of national unity. They appointed the higher clergy and the officers of the Inquisition. The Inquisition, run by Tomás de Torquemada (d. 1498), Isabella's confessor, was a key national agency established in 1479 to monitor the activity of converted Jews (*conversos*) and Muslims (*Moriscos*) in Spain. In 1492 the Jews were exiled and their properties were confiscated. In 1502 nonconverting Moors in Granada were driven into exile. Spanish spiritual life remained largely uniform and regimented, a major reason for Spain's remaining a loyal Catholic country throughout the sixteenth century and providing a base of operation for the European Counter-Reformation.

Ferdinand and Isabella had wide horizons. They contracted anti-French marriage alliances that came to determine much of European history in the sixteenth century. In 1496 their eldest daughter, Joanna, later known as "the Mad" (1479–1555), married Archduke Philip (1478–1506), the son of Emperor Maximilian I (r. 1493–1519). Their son, Charles I, the first ruler over a united Spain, came by his inheritance and election as Emperor Charles V in 1519 to rule over a European kingdom almost equal in size to that of Charlemagne. A second daughter, Catherine of Aragon (1485–1536), married King Henry VIII of England. The failure of this latter marriage became the key factor in the emergence of the Anglican Church and the English Reformation.

The new Spanish power was also evident in Ferdinand and Isabella's promotion of overseas exploration. Their patronage of the Genoese adventurer Christopher Columbus (1451–1506), who discovered the islands of the Caribbean while sailing west in search of a shorter route to the spice markets of the Far East, led to the creation of the Spanish Empire in Mexico and Peru, whose gold and silver mines helped to make Spain Europe's dominant power in the sixteenth century.

ENGLAND

The last half of the fifteenth century was a period of especially difficult political trial for the English. Following the Hundred Years' War, a defeated England was subjected to internal warfare between two rival branches of the royal family, the House of York and the House of Lancaster. This conflict, known to us today as the Wars of the Roses (as York's symbol, according to legend, was a white rose, and Lancaster's a red rose), kept England in turmoil from 1455 to 1485.

The Lancastrian monarchy of Henry VI (r. 1422–1461) was consistently challenged by the Duke of York and his supporters in the prosperous southern towns. In 1461 Edward IV (r. 1461–1483), son of the Duke of York, seized power and, assisted by loyal and able ministers, effectively bent Parliament to his will. His brother and successor was Richard III (r. 1483–1485), whose reign saw the growth of support for the exiled Lancastrian Henry Tudor. Henry returned to England to defeat Richard on Bosworth Field in August 1485.

Henry Tudor ruled as Henry VII (r. 1485–1509), the first of the new Tudor dynasty that would endure until 1603. To bring the rival royal families together and to make the hereditary claim of his offspring to the throne uncontestable, Henry married Edward IV's daughter, Elizabeth of York. He succeeded in disciplining the English nobility through a special and much-feared instrument of the royal will known as the Court of Star Chamber. Henry shrewdly construed legal precedents to the advantage of the crown, using English law to further his own ends. He confiscated so much noble land and fortunes that he governed without dependence on Parliament for royal funds, always a cornerstone of strong monarchy. Henry thus began to shape a monarchy that became one of early modern Europe's most exemplary governments during the reign of his granddaughter, Elizabeth I (r. 1558–1603).

In World Perspective

THE HIGH MIDDLE AGES

With its borders finally secured, western Europe concentrated during the High Middle Ages on its political institutions and cultural development, something denied it during the early Middle Ages. In England and France, modern Western nations can be seen in formation. Within the empire, imperial rule both revived (under Otto I) and totally collapsed (during the Hohenstaufen dynasty). Everywhere, society successfully organized itself from noble to serf. With the flourishing of trade and the expansion of towns, a new wealthy class patronized education. Western Europe's first universities appeared, and a movement called Scholasticism brought a new, and often forbidding, order to knowledge. The major disruption of the period, however, was an unprecedented conflict between former allies. The Roman Catholic Church had become a monarchy in its own right, able to compete with secular states and even to dethrone (by excommunication and interdict) kings and princes. The foundation was thereby laid both for perpetual conflict between popes and rulers, which lasted well into early modern times, and for the creation of the peculiar Western separation of church and state.

For western Europe, the High Middle Ages were a period of clearer self-definition during which individual lands gained much of the geographic shape we recognize today. Other world civilizations had by this time become well established and had even begun to depart their "classical" or "golden" periods. For the West, the best still lay ahead.

Under the Sung dynasty (960–1279), before Mongol rule, China continued its technological advance. In addition to the printing press, the Chinese invented the abacus and gunpowder. They also enjoyed a money economy unknown in the West. But culturally, these centuries between 1000 and 1300 were closed and narrow by comparison with those of the T'ang dynasty. Politically, the Sung was far more autocratic. In China (as in western European lands like England and France, although not in Italy and the empire), regional aristocracies ceased to be serious obstacles to a strong centralized government.

Chinese women generally held a lower status and had fewer vocational options than Western women, as the practice of foot binding dramatically attests. As in the West, a higher degree of freedom and self-government developed in the countryside, especially by the fourteenth century, as peasants gained the right to buy and sell land and to fulfill traditional labor obligations by money payments. Intellectually, China, like the West, had a scholastic movement within its dominant philosophy; Confucianism made religious and philosophical thought more elaborate, systematic, and orthodox. Whereas Western Scholasticism made Christianity aloof, elitist, and ridiculed by its lay critics, Confucianism remained a philosophy highly adaptable and popular among laypeople.

In the late twelfth century Japan shifted from civilian to military rule; the Kamakura *bakufu* governed by mounted warriors who were paid with rights to income from land in exchange for their military services. This rise of a military aristocracy marked the beginning of Japan's "medieval," as distinct from its "classical," period. Three Mongol invasions in the thirteenth century also fostered a strong military to resist them. With a civilian court also in existence, Japan actually had a dual government (that is, two emperors and two courts) until the fourteenth century. However, this situation differed greatly from the deep and permanent national divisions developing at this time among the emerging states and autonomous principalities of western Europe.

Japanese women, more like those in western Europe than in China, traditionally played a prominent role in royal government and court culture. Nun Shogun, for example, succeeded her husband for a brief period of Kamakura rule in the late twelfth century. But the prominence of women in government would also change in Japan by the fourteenth century.

Within the many developing autonomous Islamic lands at this time, the teaching of Muhammad created an international culture. The regular practice of religious fundamentals enabled Muslims to transcend their new and often very deep regional divisions. Similarly, Christianity allowed Englishmen, Frenchmen, Germans, and Italians to think of themselves as one people and to unite in Crusades to the Holy Land. As these Crusades began in the late eleventh century, Islam too was on the march, penetrating Anatolia and Afghanistan, and impinging upon India, where it met a new challenge in Hinduism.

REVIEW QUESTIONS

1. How do you account for the success of the Cluny reform movement? Can major features of the modern Catholic Church be found in the Cluny reforms?
2. Was the investiture controversy a political or a religious conflict? Summarize the respective arguments of Gregory VII and Henry IV. Is the conflict a precedent for the modern doctrine of the separation of church and state?
3. Why did Germany remain divided while France and England began to coalesce into reasonably strong states during the High Middle Ages?
4. How did the responsibilities of the nobility differ from those of the clergy and the peasantry during the High Middle Ages? How did each social class contribute to the stability of society?
5. What gave rise to towns, and how did they change traditional medieval society?
6. How did the Hundred Years War, the Black Death, and the great schism in the church affect the course of history? Which had the most lasting effects on the institutions it touched?
7. Was the church an aggressor or a victim in the late Middle Ages and the Renaissance? How successful was it in its confrontations with Europe's emerging dynastic states?
8. What was "reborn" in the Renaissance? Were the humanists the forerunners of modern secular education and culture, or eloquent defenders of a still-medieval Christian view of the world against the church's secular and pagan critics?
9. Historians find features of modern states developing in west European lands during the late Middle Ages and Renaissance. What modern features can you identify in the governments of the Italian city-states and the northern monarchies?

SUGGESTED READINGS

L. B. ALBERTI, *The Family in Renaissance Florence*, trans. by R. N. Watkins (1962). A contemporary humanist, who never married, explains how a family should behave.

E. AMT, ED., *Women's Lives in Medieval Europe: A Source-book* (1992). Outstanding collection of sources.

J. W. BALDWIN, *The Scholastic Culture of the Middle Ages: 1000–1300* (1971). Best brief synthesis available.

M. W. BALDWIN, ED., *History of the Crusades, I: The First Hundred Years* (1955). Basic historical narrative.

H. BARON, *The Crisis of the Early Italian Renaissance*, Vols. 1 and 2 (1996). A major work, setting forth the civic dimension of Italian humanism.

G. BARRACLOUGH, *The Origins of Modern Germany* (1963). Penetrating political narrative.

R. BARTLETT, *The Making of Medieval Europe* (1992). Sees the interaction of different cultures as the decisive factor in the creation of west European civilization.

M. BLOCH, *French Rural Society*, trans. by J. Sondheimer (1966). A classic by a great modern historian.

G. BRUCKER, *Renaissance Florence* (1983). Considered the best introduction to the subject.

J. BURCKHARDT, *The Civilization of the Renaissance in Italy* (1867). The old classic that still has as many defenders as detractors.

A. CAPELLANUS, *The Art of Courtly Love*, trans. by J. J. Parry (1941). Translation of this classic along with other documents from the court of Marie de Champagne.

C. CIPOLLA, *Before the Industrial Revolution: European Society and Economy, 1000–1700* (1976). Readable, sweeping account.

R. H. C. DAVIS, *A History of Medieval Europe: From Constantine to St. Louis, Part 2* (1972).

G. DUBY, *The Three Orders: Feudal Society Imagined*, trans. by Arthur Goldhammer (1981). Large, comprehensive, and authoritative.

W. K. FERGUSON, *The Renaissance* (1940). A brief, stimulating summary of the Renaissance in both Italy and northern Europe.

F. GILBERT, *Machiavelli and Guicciardini* (1984). The two great Renaissance historians compared.

E.M. HALAM, *Capetian France 987–1328* (1980). Especially good on politics and heretics.

J. R. HALE, *Europe in the Renaissance* (1994). New, learned survey focusing on social and cultural history.

C. H. HASKINS, *The Renaissance of the Twelfth Century* (1927). Still the standard account.

C. H. HASKINS, *The Rise of Universities* (1972). A short, minor classic.

D. HERLIHY, *Medieval Households* (1985). Sweeping survey of Middle Ages that defends the medieval family against modern caricatures.

D. HERLIHY AND C. KLAPISCH-ZUBER, *Tuscans and Their Families* (1985). Important work based on unique demographic data that gives the reader an appreciation of quantitative history.

J. C. HOLT, *Magna Carta*, 2nd ed. (1992). The famous document and its interpretation by succeeding generations.

J. HUIZINGA, *The Waning of the Middle Ages: A Study of the Forms of Life, Thought, and Art in France and the Netherlands in the Dawn of the Renaissance* (1924). A classic study of "mentality" at the end of the Middle Ages.

D. JENSEN, *Renaissance Europe: Age of Recovery and Reconciliation* (1981). Up-to-date textbook.

R. KIECKHEFER, *Unquiet Souls* (1984). Penetrating and sympathetic study of fourteenth-century religious life.

P. O. KRISTELLER, *Renaissance Thought: The Classic, Scholastic, and Humanist Strains* (1961). A master shows the many sides of Renaissance thought.

G. LEFF, *Paris and Oxford Universities in the Thirteenth and Fourteenth Centuries: An Institutional and Intellectual History* (1968). Very good on debates on Scholasticism.

K. LEYSER, *Medieval Germany and Its Neighbors, 900–1250* (1982). Basic and authoritative.

R. S. LOPEZ AND I. W. RAYMOND, EDS., *Medieval Trade in the Mediterranean World* (1955). An illuminating collection of sources, concentrated on southern Europe.

W. H. MCNEILL, *Plagues and Peoples* (1976). The Black Death in a broader context.

E. MÂLE, *The Gothic Image: Religious Art in France in the Thirteenth Century* (1913). A classic.

L. MARTINES, *Power and Imagination: City States in Renaissance Italy* (1980). Stimulating account of cultural and political history.

H. E. MAYER, *The Crusades*, trans. by John Gilligham (1972). Extremely detailed, and the best one-volume account.

R. I. MOORE, *The Formation of a Persecuting Society: Power and Deviance in Western Europe, 950–1250* (1987). A sympathetic look at heresy and dissent.

J. B. MORRALL, *Political Thought in Medieval Times* (1962). A readable and illuminating account.

T. NOONAN, *Contraception: A History of Its Treatment by the Catholic Theologians and Canonists* (1967). A fascinating account of medieval theological attitudes toward sexuality and sex-related problems.

S. OZMENT, *Ancestors: The Loving Family of Old Europe* (2001). Fluid, insightful, and provocative.

E. PANOFSKY, *Gothic Architecture and Scholasticism* (1951). A controversial classic.

E. PERROY, *The Hundred Years' War*, trans. by W. B. Wells (1965). The most comprehensive one-volume account.

H. PIRENNE, *Medieval Cities: Their Origins and the Revival of Trade*, trans. by Frank D. Halsey (1970). A minor classic.

J. RILEY-SMITH, *The Crusades: A Short History* (1987). Up-to-date, lucid, and readable.

S. SHAHAR, *The Fourth Estate: A History of Women in the Middle Ages* (1983). Readable survey.

Q. SKINNER, *The Foundations of Modern Political Thought I: The Renaissance* (1978). A broad survey, very comprehensive.

B. TIERNEY, *The Crisis of Church and State 1050–1300* (1964). A very useful collection of primary sources on key church-state conflicts. Part 4 provides the major documents in the clash between Boniface VIII and Philip the Fair.

J. WEISHEIPL, *Friar Thomas* (1980). Biography of Thomas Aquinas that attempts to do justice to the human side of the story as well as to the theological.

S. WILLIAMS, ED., *The Gregorian Epoch: Reformation, Revolution, Reaction* (1964). Variety of scholarly opinion on the significance of Pope Gregory's reign presented in debate form.

P. ZIEGLER, *The Black Death* (1969). A highly readable journalistic account.

DOCUMENTS CD ROM

1. Gregory VII's Letter to the Bishop of Metz, 1081
2. Duke William of Aquitane: Foundation Charter for the Abbey of Cluny, 909
3. St. Thomas Aquinas: The Summa against the Gentiles
4. St. Thomas Aquinas: On Kingship or the Governance of Rulers
5. The Magna Carta
6. Robert of Clari, The Conquest of Constantinople
7. The Chronicle of Jean de Venette
8. The Bull *Unam Sanctam* of Boniface VIII
9. Propositions of Wycliffe condemned at London 1382, and at the Council of Constance 1415
10. Dante: *The Divine Comedy, Inferno*, Canto I
11. Niccolo Machiavelli, *The Prince* and *The Discourses on Titus Livy*
12. Francis Petrarch, *Rime*

WORLD AND THE WEB

Plague and Public Health in Renaissance Europe

http://www.iath.virginia.edu/osheim/intro.html

This project involves the creation of a hypertext archive of narratives, medical consilia, governmental records, religious and spiritual writings and images documenting the arrival, impact and response to the problem of epidemic disease in Western Europe. The site includes original source documents from Florence, Pistoia, and Lucca.

Renaissance Forum (An Electronic Journal of Early-Modern Literary and Historical Studies)

http://www.hull.ac.uk/renforum/about.htm

An interdisciplinary refereed journal that specializes in early-modern English literary and historical scholarship and in the critical methodologies of these fields. Its aim is twofold: to offer a platform for work of the highest scholarly standard in an electronic medium, and to provide a forum for scholarly and theoretical debate of a kind that is not possible in most conventional journals.

The Great Schism of the Ecumenical Church

http://www.goarch.org/access/orthodoxfaith/schism.html

This site presents a concise account of the real motives and events that led to the Great Schism of the Ecumenical Church into Eastern Orthodoxy and Western Catholicism. It includes a list of the innovations added by the Western Church.

The Internet Encyclopedia of Philosophy - Niccolò Machiavelli (1469-1527)

http://www.utm.edu/research/iep/m/machiave.htm

The first great political philosopher of the Renaissance was Niccolò Machiavelli (1469-1527). His famous treatise *The Prince* stands apart from all other political writings of the period insofar as it focuses on the practical problems a monarch faces in staying in power, rather than on more speculative issues explaining the foundation of political authority. This site contains a brief biography and several of his works including *The Prince.*

Please go to http://www.prenhall.com/craig for the Technology and Civilization essay, "The Invention of Printing in China and Europe."

PART IV

The World in Transition

Between 1500 and 1800, the major centers of world civilization achieved political organization and stability that in some cases endured to the end of the twentieth century. This period also witnessed a shift in the balance of world political and economic power toward Europe. That shift was anything but inevitable. It was the result of paths taken by the peoples and governments of other areas of the world.

Sixteenth-century Japan was torn by feudal wars among its various small states and regions. This civil conflict eroded the manorial social structure. The adoption of the spear and then the musket in place of the sword allowed the development of foot-soldier armies that displaced the mounted samurai. By approximately 1600, however, a new political regime was establishing itself on the basis of a "feudal" society involving complex vassal-lord relationships in many, although not all, ways similar to those in medieval Europe. Tokugawa leyasu established his government in Edo (now Tokyo). Through a series of land transfers and confiscations, he surrounded himself with unquestionably loyal retainers and placed those of less certain loyalty at far geographical locations removed from his capital. He and his successors required their vassals to send their families to live as virtual hostages near the court in Edo. Finally, Tokugawa Japan adopted a policy of isolation from the rest of the world. Although stable and relatively prosperous, Japan remained separated from the larger world from the 1630s until the middle of the nineteenth century.

Spared comparable civil strife, China entered on an epoch of remarkable strength, expansion, and cultural achievement. The Ming and Ch'ing dynasties ruled for more than five centuries, and only a short period of strife accompanied the transfer of power from one to the other in 1644. The emperors of both dynasties governed in an absolute manner. The bureaucracy—referred to as mandarins by the Jesuits, who came to China in the sixteenth

Map of Brazil, ca. 1547, as viewd from North America. The Granger Collection, N.Y.

century—was chosen meritocratically through a complex series of examinations, and it governed efficiently. The populations of China expanded steadily. China experienced a third commercial revolution. Chinese shipping expanded. Although a truly national economy did not emerge, China possessed several regional economies, each as large as that of a major European national state. A banking system spread through the country to foster commerce. What did not occur in China, for all its commercial enterprise, was the development of industrialism. Nonetheless, at the end of this era China appeared to be a very strong, stable nation. As in Japan, Confucian teachings had become ever more influential.

In 1550, over a century of continued political and military strength lay before the Islamic world. The Ottoman Empire was at the time perhaps the most powerful military state in the world. The Safavids securely governed Iran as would the Mughals in India a few years later. However, by the middle of the seventeenth century the power of all three empires was on the wane even as their cultural vitality was still immense. The growing military and naval strength of Europe defeated the Ottoman Turks at the sea battle of Lepanto in 1571 and in numerous land engagements during the seventeenth century. The final Turkish siege of Vienna failed in 1683. In Iran the intense religiosity of the Shi'ite Safavids led to the neglect of political and military structures and, consequently, to difficulty in halting aggression from the Turks. At the same time, a distinctive mode of Shi'ite pietism arose among the populace in Iran. the Mughal Empire in India experienced a slow but steady decline after the late seventeenth century. By the battle of Plassey in 1757 the British East India Company had established a position of strength from which, within less than a century, Britain would come to govern the entire Indian subcontinent.

Early in the sixteenth century, western Europe began to be divided between Protestantism and Roman Catholicism. The sectarian splintering that has resulted in hundreds of modern Protestant denominations also began at this time. Even within Catholicism, deep divisions developed between Catholics who favored traditional practices and those who championed the reforms of the Counter-Reformation and the Jesuits. A century and a half of religious war and theological conflict followed. Rulers made the most of these divisions to consolidate their territories politically. Confessionalization (that is, strict enforcement of a particular "orthodox" religious belief and practice) went hand in hand with the creation of modern Western states.

Four factors account largely for this momentous shift in the cultural balance of the Western world. First, the new monarchies that had arisen in the late Middle Ages, particularly in France, England, and Spain, now successfully unified their realms. Between 1500 and the middle of the eighteenth century those monarchs learned to tame their aristocracies, to collect taxes efficiently, and to build effective armies and navies. Second, in league with the commercial sectors of their national economies, the monarchs and their bureaucrats encouraged voyages of commercial expansion and discovery. Through those voyages Europeans penetrated markets across the globe. They also conquered and colonized the American continents and thereby Europeanized two vast, rich landmasses much larger than Europe itself.

Third, during the seventeenth century European thinkers carried out new intellectual explorations that culminated in the scientific revolution. The new knowledge and methods of rational investigation of physical nature permitted them to develop their technological skills more fully. As a consequence, the fourth factor came into play as Europeans, and most particularly the British, achieved an early foundation of industrial manufacturing that would permit further domination of world markets with inexpensive consumer goods.

1500–1600

Europe

1517–1555	Protestant Reformation
1533–1584	Ivan the Terrible of Russia reigns
1540	Jesuit Order founded by Ignatius Loyola
1543–1727	Scientific Revolution
1556–1598	Philip II of Spain reigns
1558–1603	Elizabeth I of England reigns
1562–1598	French Wars of Religion
1581	The Netherlands declares its independence from the Spanish Habsburgs
1588	Defeat of the Spanish Armada
1589–1610	Henry IV, Navarre, founds Bourbon dynasty of France

Near East/India

1500–1722	Safavid Shi'ite rule in Iran
1512–1520	Ottoman ruler Selim I
1520–1566	Ottoman ruler Suleiman the Magnificent
1525–1527	Babur founds Mughai dynasty in India
1540	Hungary under Ottoman rule
1556–1605	Akbar the Great of India reigns
1571	Battle of Lepanto; Ottomans defeated
ca. 1571–1640	Safavid philosopher-writer Mullah Sadra
1588–1629	Shah Abbas I of Iran reigns

Queen Elizabeth I

1600–1700

Europe

1618–1648	Thirty Years' War
1640–1688	Frederick William, the Great Elector, reigns in Brandenburg-Prussia
1642–1646	Puritan Revolution in England
1643–1715	Louis XIV of France reigns
1682–1725	Peter the Great of Russia reigns
1688	Glorious Revolution in England
1690	"Second Treatise of Civil Government," by John Locke

Near East/India

1628–1657	Shah Jahan reigns; builds Taj Mahal as mausoleum for his beloved wife
1646	Founding of Maratha Empire
1648	Delhi becomes the capital of Mughal Empire
1658–1707	Shah Aurangzeb, the "World Conqueror," reigns in India; end of religious toleration toward Hindus; beginning Mughal decline
1669–1683	Last military expansion by Ottomans: 1669, seize Crete; 1670s, the Ukraine; 1683, Vienna

1700-1800

Europe

1701	Act of Settlement provides for Protestant succession to English throne
1702–1713	War of Spanish Succession
1740–1748	War of Austrian Succession
1756–1763	Seven Years' War
ca. 1750	Industrial Revolution begins in England
1772	First partition of Poland
1789	First French Revolution
1793 and 1795	Last two partitions of Poland

Near East/India

1700	Sikhs and Marathas bring down Mughal Imperial Power
1708	British East India Company and New East India Company merge
1722	Last Safavid ruler forced to abdicate
1724	Rise in the Deccan of the Islamic state of Hyderabad
1725	Nadir Shah of Afganhistan becomes ruler of Persia
1739	Persian invasion of northern India, by Nadir Shah
1748–1761	Ahmad Shah Durrani of Afghanistan invades India
1757	British victory at Plassey, in Bengal

EAST ASIA

1500–1800 Commercial revolution in Ming-Ch'ing China; trade with Europe; flourishing of the novel

1543 Portuguese arrive in Japan

1568–1600 Era of unification follows end of Warring States Era in Japan

1587 Spanish arrive in Japan

1588 Hideyoshi's sword hunt in Japan

1592–1598 Ming troops battle Hideyoshi's army in Korea

1600 Tokugawa Ieyasu wins battle of Sekigahara, completes unification of Japan

1600–1868 Tokugawa shogunate in Edo

1630s Seclusion adopted as national policy in Japan

1644–1694 Bashō, Japanese poet

1644–1911 Ch'ing (Manchu) dynasty in China

1661-1722 K'ang Hsi reign in China

1673–1681 Revolt of southern generals in China

1699 British East India Company arrives in China

1701 Forty-seven rōnin incident in Japan

1716–1733 Reforms of Tokugawa Yoshimune in Japan

1737–1795 Reign of Ch'ien Lung in China

1742 Christianity banned in China

1784 American traders arrive in China

1787–1793 Matsudaira Sadanobu's reforms in Japan

1798 White Lotus Rebellion in China

AFRICA

1506 East coast pf Africa under Portuguese domination

1507 Mozambique founded by Portuguese

1517 Spanish crown authorizes slave trade to its South American colonies; rapid increase in importation of slaves to the New World

1554–1659 Sa'did Sultanate in Morocco

1575 Union of Bornu and Kanem by Idris Alawma (r. 1575–1610); Kanem-Bornu state the most fully Islamic in West Africa

1591 Moroccan army defeats Songhai army; Songhai Empire collapses

1600s English, Dutch, and French enter the slave trade; slaves imported to sugar plantations in the Caribbean

1619 First African slaves in North America land in Virginia

1652 First Cape Colony settlement of Dutch East India Company

1660–1856 Omani domination of East Africa; Omani state centered in Zanzibar; 1698, takes Mozambique from Portuguese

African captives, eighteenth century print

1702 Asiento Guinea Trade Company founded for slave trade between Africa and the Americas

1700s Transatlantic slave trade at its height

1741–1856 United Sultanate of Oman and Zanzibar

1754–1817 Usman Dan Fodio, founder of sultanate in northern and central Nigeria; the Fulani become the ruling class in the region

1762 End of Funj Sultanate in eastern Sudanic region

THE AMERICAS

1519 Conquest of the Aztecs by Cortes; Aztec ruler, Montezuma (r. 1502–1519) killed; Tenochtitlán destroyed

1529 Mexico City becomes capital of the viceroyalty of New Spain

1533 Pizarro begins his conquest of the Incas

1536 Spanish under Mendoza arrive in Argentina

1544 Lima becomes capital of the viceroyalty of Peru

1584 Sir Walter Raleigh sends expedition to Roanoke Island (North Carolina)

Algonquin village of Secotton

1607 The London Company establishes Jamestown Colony (Virginia)

1608 Champlain founds Quebec

1619 Slave labor introduced at Jamestown (Virginia)

1733 Georgia founded as last English colony in North America

1739–1763 Era of trade wars in Americas between Great Britain and the French and Spanish

1763 Peace of Paris establishes British government in Canada

1776–1781 American Revolution

1783–1830 Simón Bolívar, Latin American soldier, statesman

1789 U.S. Constitution

1791 Negro slave revolt in French Santo Domingo

1791 Canada Constitution Act divides the country into Upper and Lower Canada

16 The Age of Reformation and Religious Wars

A Catholic portrayal of Martin Luther tempting Jesus (1547). Reformation propaganda often portrayed the pope as the Antichrist or the devil. Here Catholic propaganda turns the tables on the Protestant reformers by portraying a figure of Martin Luther as the devil (note the monstrous feet and tail under his academic robes). Versuchung Christi, 1547, Gemälde, Bonn, Rheinisches Landesmuseum, Inv. Nr. 58.3.

Chapter topics

- On the Eve of the Reformation
- The Reformation
- The Reformation's Achievements
- The Wars of Religion
- Superstition and Enlightenment: The Battle Within

In World Perspective
The Renaissance and Reformation

IN THE SECOND DECADE OF THE SIXTEENTH CENTURY, A powerful religious movement began in Saxony in Germany and rapidly spread throughout northern Europe, deeply affecting society and politics as well as the spiritual lives of men and women. Attacking what they believed to be burdensome superstitions that robbed people of both their money and their peace of mind, Protestant reformers led a revolt against the medieval church. In a short time, hundreds of thousands of people from all social classes set aside the beliefs of centuries and adopted a more simplified religious practice.

The Protestant Reformation challenged aspects of the Renaissance, especially its tendency to follow classical sources in glorifying human nature and its loyalty to traditional religion. Protestants were more impressed by the human potential for evil than by the inclination to do good; they encouraged parents, teachers, and magistrates to be firm disciplinarians. On the other hand, Protestants also embraced many Renaissance values, especially in educational reform and in learning ancient languages, for here they found the tools to master Scripture and challenge the papacy.

Protestantism was not the only reform movement to grow out of the religious grievances and reforms of the late Middle Ages. Within the church itself a reform was emerging that would give birth to new religious orders, rebut Protestantism, and win back a great many of its converts.

As different groups identified their political and social goals with either Protestantism or Catholicism, a hundred years of bloody opposition between Protestants and Catholics darkened the second half of the sixteenth century and the first half of the seventeenth. In the second half of the sixteenth century the political conflict that had previously been confined to central Europe and a struggle for Lutheran rights and freedoms shifted to western Europe—to France, the Netherlands, England, and Scotland—and became a struggle for Calvinist recognition. In France Calvinists fought Catholic rulers for the right to form their own communities, to practice their chosen religion openly, and to exclude from their lands those they deemed heretical. During the Thirty Years' War (1618–1648), international armies of varying religious persuasions clashed in central and northern Europe. By 1649 English Puritans had overthrown the Stuart monarchy and the Anglican Church.

For Europe the late fifteenth and the sixteenth centuries were also a period of unprecedented territorial expansion. Permanent colonies were established within the Americas, and the exploitation of the New World's human and mineral resources began. Imported American gold and silver spurred scientific invention and a new weapons industry. The new bullion also helped create an international traffic in African slaves as rival tribes sold their captives to the Portuguese. These slaves were brought in ever-increasing numbers to work the mines and the plantations of the New World as replacements for faltering American natives.

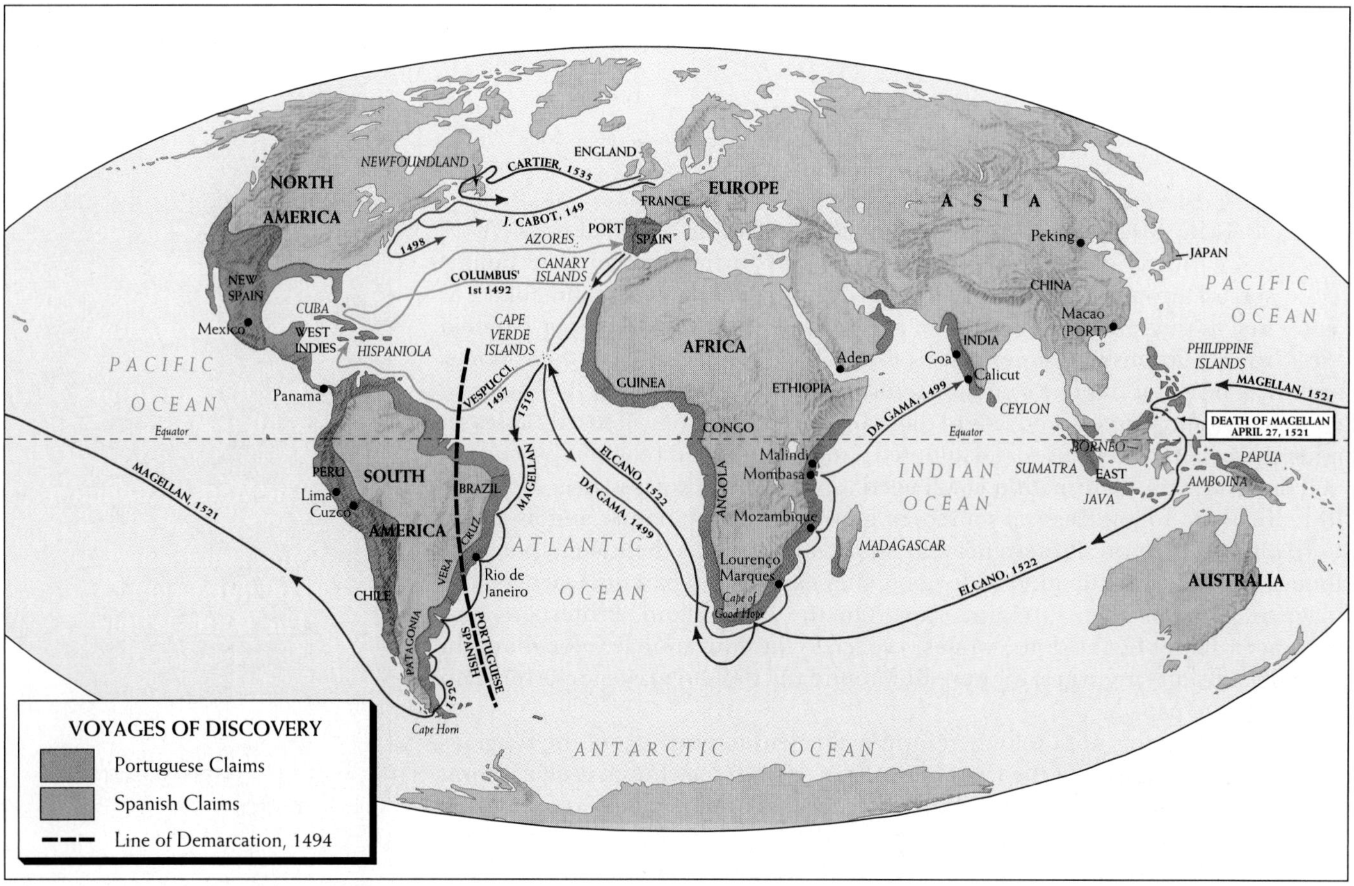

Map 16–1 European voyages of discovery and the colonial claims of Spain and Portugal in the fifteenth and sixteenth centuries. The map dramatizes Europe's global expansion in the fifteenth and sixteenth centuries.

On the Eve of the Reformation

The Discovery of a New World

The discovery of the Americas dramatically expanded the geographical and intellectual horizons of Europeans. Knowledge of the New World's inhabitants and exploitation of its vast wealth set new cultural and economic forces in motion throughout western Europe. Beginning with the successful voyages of Christopher Columbus (1451–1506) in the late fifteenth century, commercial supremacy started to shift from the Mediterranean and the Baltic to the Atlantic seaboard, and western Europe's global expansion began in earnest (see Map 16–1).

Gold and Spices Mercenary motives, reinforced by traditional missionary ideals, had earlier inspired Prince Henry the Navigator (1394–1460) to sponsor Portuguese exploration of the African coast. His main object was the gold trade, which Muslims had monopolized for centuries. By the late fifteenth century, gold from Guinea was entering Europe on Portuguese ships calling at the port cities of Lisbon and Antwerp, rather than via the traditional Arab overland routes. Antwerp became the financial center of Europe, a commercial crossroads where enterprise and daring could find capital funds.

The rush for gold quickly expanded into a rush for the spice markets of India as well. In the fifteenth century most Europeans ate a dull combination of bread and gruel, cabbage, turnips, peas, lentils, and onions, together with what meat became available during seasonal periods of slaughter. Spices, especially pepper and cloves, were in great demand both as preservatives and to enhance the taste of food.

Bartholomew Dias (d. 1500) opened the Portuguese Empire in the East when he rounded the Cape of Good Hope at the tip of Africa in 1487. A decade later, in 1498, Vasco da Gama (d. 1524) stood on the shores of India. When he returned to Portugal, his cargo was worth sixty times the cost of the voyage. Later, the Portuguese established themselves firmly on the Malabar coast with colonies in Goa and Calcutta and successfully challenged the Arabs and the Venetians for control of the European spice trade.

While the Portuguese concentrated on the Indian Ocean, the Spanish set sail across the Atlantic, hoping to establish a shorter route to the rich spice markets of the East Indies. Rather than beat the Portuguese at their own game, however, Columbus discovered the Americas instead.

THE VOYAGES OF COLUMBUS On October 12, 1492, after a thirty-three-day voyage from the Canary Islands, Columbus landed in San Salvador (Watlings Island) in the eastern Bahamas. Having undertaken his journey in the belief that Japan would be the first landmass he would reach as he sailed west, he thought San Salvador was an outer island of Japan. That belief was based on Marco Polo's account of his years in China during the thirteenth century and the global map of Martin Behaim, which showed only ocean between the west coast of Europe and the east coast of Asia.

Naked and extremely friendly natives met Columbus and his crew on the beaches of the New World. They were Taino Indians, who spoke a variant of a language known as Arawak. Mistaking the island for the East Indies, Columbus called the native people Indians, a name that stuck even after it became known that he had discovered a new continent. The natives' generosity amazed Columbus. They freely gave his men all the corn and yams they desired, along with many sexual favors as well. "They never say no," Columbus marveled. At the same time he observed how easily they could be enslaved.

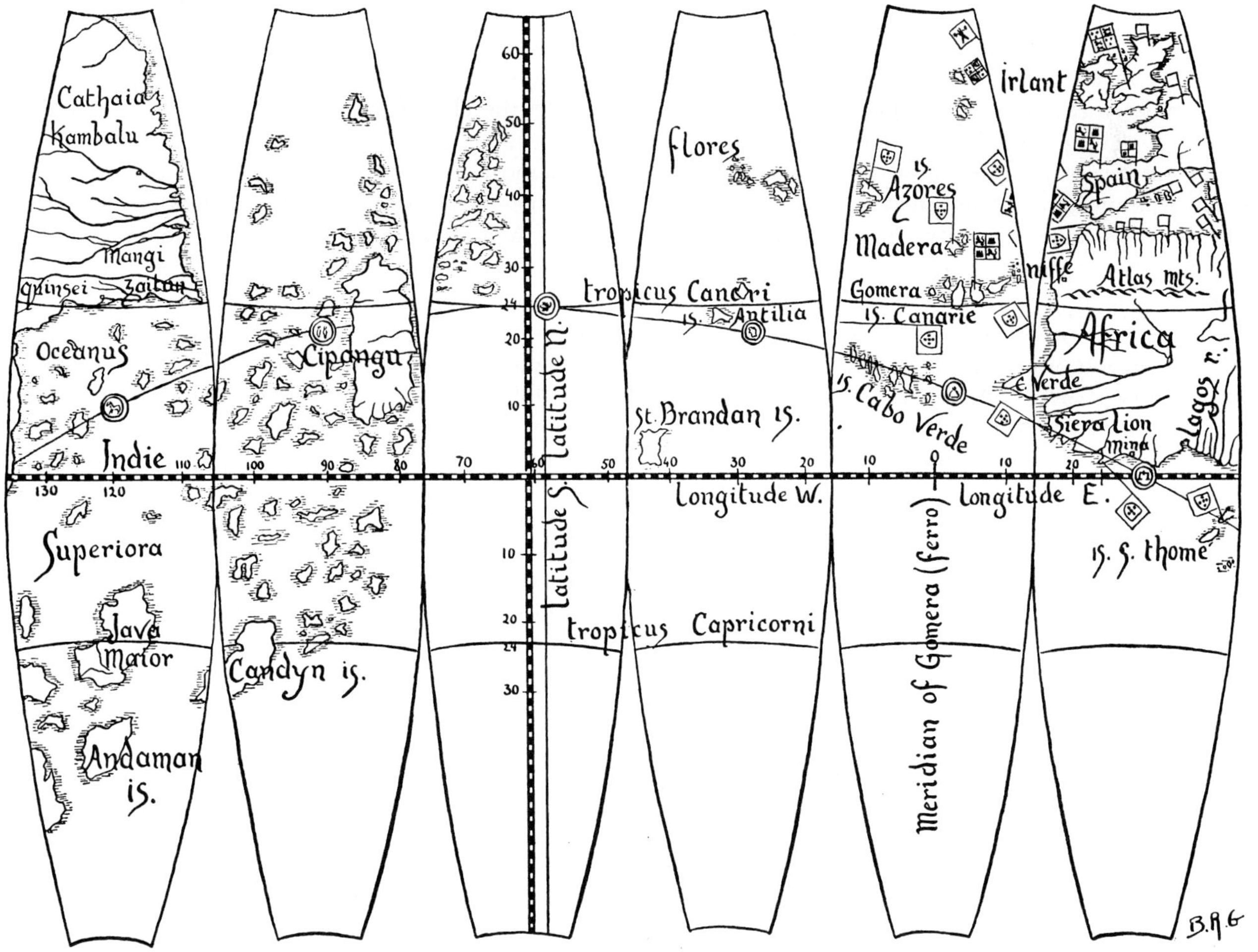

Martin Behaim's "globe apple." What Columbus knew of the world in 1492 was contained in this map by Nuremberg geographer Martin Behaim (1440–1507), creator of the first spherical globe of the earth. The ocean section of Behaim's globe is reproduced here. Departing the Canary Islands (in the second section from the right), Columbus expected his first major landfall to be Japan, or what he calls Cipangu (in the second section from the left). When he landed at San Salvador, he thought he was on an outer island of Japan; after reaching Cuba, he believed it to be Japan. Only slowly did it dawn on him that these new lands had never before been seen by Europeans. Samuel Eliot Morison, Admiral of the Ocean Sea. Copyright 1942 © renewed 1970 by Samuel Eliot Morison. By permission of Little, Brown and Company, Boston, MA.

On the heels of Columbus, Amerigo Vespucci (1451–1512), after whom America is named, and Ferdinand Magellan (1480–1521) carefully explored the coastline of South America. Their travels documented that the new lands discovered by Columbus were not the outermost territory of the Far East, but a new continent that opened on the still greater Pacific Ocean. Magellan, in search of a westward route to the East Indies, sailed to the Philippines, where he died.

IMPACT ON EUROPE AND AMERICA Columbus's voyage of 1492 marked, unknowingly to those who undertook and financed it, the beginning of more than three centuries of Spanish conquest, exploitation, and administration of a vast American empire. What had begun as voyages of discovery soon became expeditions of conquest that resembled the warfare of Christian Aragon and Castile against the Islamic Moors. Those wars had just ended in 1492, and they imbued the early Spanish explorers with a zeal for conquering and converting non-Christian peoples.

The voyages to the New World had important consequences for the cultures of both Europe and America. For Spain the venture created the largest and longest-surviving European trading bloc, while spurring other European countries to undertake their own colonial ventures. The great wealth from its American possessions financed Spain's commanding role in the age's religious and political conflicts. It also ignited a gradual, Europe-wide inflation during the sixteenth century.

For the native peoples of America, the voyages triggered a long period of conquest that virtually destroyed their civilizations, as warfare, new diseases, and exploitation of labor and resources devastated their populations. In both South and North America, Spanish rule set an imprint of Roman Catholicism, economic dependency, and hierarchical social structure that is still highly visible today.

RELIGION AND SOCIETY

The Reformation broke out first in the free imperial cities of Germany and Switzerland. There were about sixty-five such cities, and each was in a sense a little kingdom unto itself. Most had Protestant movements, but with mixed success and duration. Some quickly turned Protestant and remained so. Some were Protestant only for a short time. Others developed mixed confessions, frowning on sectarianism and aggressive proselytizing, and letting Catholics and Protestants coexist.

What seemed a life-and-death struggle with higher princely or royal authority was not the only conflict cities were experiencing. They also suffered deep internal social and political divisions. Certain groups favored the Reformation more than others. In many places, guilds like that of the printers, whose members were prospering both socially and economically, and who had a history of conflict with local authority, were in the forefront of the Reformation. Evidence suggests that people who felt pushed around and bullied by either local or distant authority—a guild by an autocratic local government; a city or region by a prince or king—perceived in the Protestant movement an ally, at least initially.

Social and political experience thus coalesced with the larger religious issues in both town and countryside. When Martin Luther and his comrades wrote, preached, and sang about a priesthood of all believers, scorned the authority of ecclesiastical landlords, and ridiculed papal laws as arbitrary human inventions, they touched political as well as religious nerves in German and Swiss cities. This was also true in the villages, for the peasants on the land also heard in the Protestant sermon and pamphlet a promise of political liberation and even a degree of social betterment.

POPULAR MOVEMENTS AND CRITICISM OF THE CHURCH The Protestant Reformation could also not have occurred without the monumental crises of the late medieval church and the Renaissance papacy. For many people, the church had ceased to provide a viable foundation for religious piety. Laity and clerics alike began to seek a more heartfelt, idealistic, and often—in the eyes of the pope—increasingly heretical religious piety. The late Middle Ages were marked by independent lay and clerical efforts to reform local religious practice and by widespread experimentation with new religious forms that shared a common goal of religious simplicity in imitation of Christ.

A variety of factors contributed to the growth of lay criticism of the church. The laity in the cities were becoming increasingly knowledgeable about the world and those who controlled their lives. They traveled widely—as soldiers, pilgrims, explorers, and traders. New postal systems and the printing press increased the information at their disposal. The new age of books and libraries raised literacy and heightened curiosity. Laypersons were increasingly able to take the initiative in shaping the cultural life of their communities.

SECULAR CONTROL OVER RELIGIOUS LIFE On the eve of the Reformation, Rome's international network of church offices began to fall apart in many areas, hurried along by a growing sense of regional identity—incipient nationalism—and local secular administrative competence. The late medieval church had permitted important ecclesiastical posts ("benefices") to be sold to the highest bidders and had not enforced residency requirements in parishes. Rare was the late medieval German town that did not have complaints about the maladministration, concubinage, or fiscalism of its clergy, especially the higher clergy (bishops, abbots, and prelates).

City governments also sought to restrict the growth of ecclesiastical properties and clerical privileges and to improve local religious life by bringing the clergy under the local tax code and by endowing new clerical positions for well-trained and conscientious preachers.

THE NORTHERN RENAISSANCE

The scholarly works of northern humanists created a climate favorable to religious and educational reforms. Northern humanism was initially stimulated by the importation of Italian learning through such varied intermediaries as students who had studied in Italy, merchants, and the Brothers of the Common Life. The northern humanists tended to come from more diverse social backgrounds and to be more devoted to religious reforms than were their Italian counterparts. They were also more willing to write for lay audiences.

The growth of schools and lay education combined with the invention of cheap paper to create a mass audience for printed books. In response, Johann Gutenberg (d. 1468) invented printing with movable type in the German city of Mainz around 1450. Thereafter, books were rapidly and handsomely produced on topics both profound and practical. By 1500, printing presses operated in at least sixty German cities and in more than 200 throughout Europe. A new medium now existed for politicians, humanists, and reformers alike.

The most famous of the northern humanists was Desiderius Erasmus (1466–1536), the "prince of the humanists." Idealistic and pacifistic, Erasmus gained fame as both an educational and a religious reformer. He aspired to unite the classical ideals of humanity and civic virtue with the Christian ideals of love and piety. He believed that disciplined study of the classics and the Bible, if begun early enough, was the best way to reform both individuals and society. He summarized his own beliefs with the phrase *philosophia Christi*, a simple, ethical piety in imitation of Christ. He set this ideal against what he believed to be the dogmatic, ceremonial, and factious religious practice of the late Middle Ages. To promote his own religious beliefs, Erasmus edited the works of the Church Fathers and made a Greek edition of the New Testament (1516), which became the basis for a new, more accurate Latin translation (1519). Martin Luther later used both these works as the basis for his famous German translation.

The best known of early English humanists was Sir Thomas More (1478–1535), a close friend of Erasmus. It was while visiting More that Erasmus wrote his most famous work, *The Praise of Folly* (1511), an amusing and profound exposé of human self-deception that was quickly translated from the original Latin into many vernacular languages. More's *Utopia* (1516), a criticism of contemporary society, depicts an imaginary society based on reason and tolerance that requires everyone to work and has rid itself of all social and political injustice. Although More would remain staunchly Catholic, humanism in England, as in Germany, paved the way for the English Reformation. A circle of English humanists, under the direction of Henry VIII's minister Thomas Cromwell, translated and disseminated late medieval criticisms of the papacy and many of Erasmus's satirical writings as well.

Whereas in Germany, England, and France humanism helped the Protestants, in Spain it entered the service of the Catholic Church. Here the key figure was Francisco Jiménez de Cisneros (1437–1517), a confessor to Queen Isabella, and after 1508 Grand Inquisitor—a position from which he was able to enforce the strictest religious ortho-

The printing press made possible the diffusion of Renaissance learning. But no book stimulated thought more at this time than did the Bible. With Gutenberg's publication of a printed Bible in 1454, scholars gained access to a dependable, standardized text, so that Scripture could be discussed and debated as never before. Huntington Library doxy. Jiménez was a conduit for humanist scholarship and learning. He founded the University of Alcalá near Madrid in 1509, printed a Greek edition of the New Testament, and translated many religious tracts that aided clerical reform and control of lay religious life. His greatest achievement, taking fifteen years to complete, was the Complutensian Polyglot Bible, a six-volume work that placed the Hebrew, Greek, and Latin versions of the Bible in parallel columns. Such scholarly projects and internal church reforms joined with the repressive measures of Ferdinand and Isabella to keep Spain strictly Catholic.

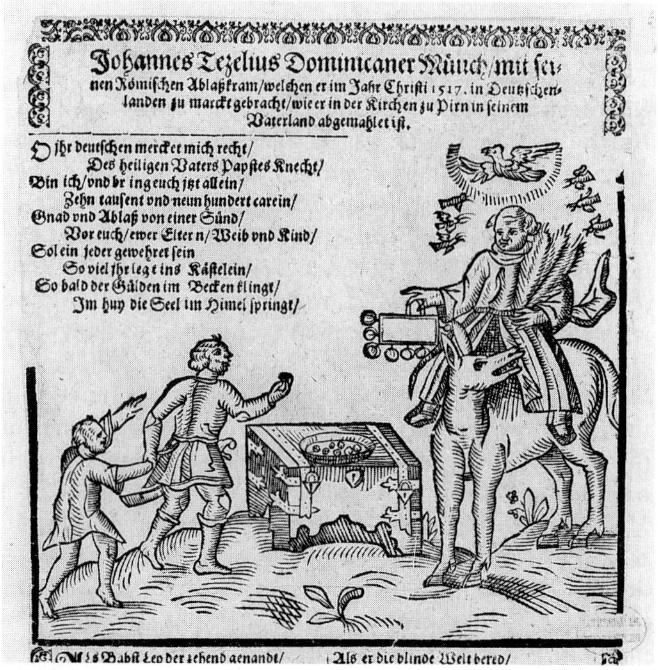

A contemporary caricature depicts John Tetzel, the famous indulgence preacher. The last lines of the jingle read: "As soon as gold in the basin rings, right then the soul to heaven springs." It was Tetzel's preaching that spurred Luther to publish his ninety-five theses. Courtesy Lutherhalle, Wittenberg

THE REFORMATION

MARTIN LUTHER AND THE GERMAN REFORMATION TO 1525

Late medieval Germany lacked the political unity to enforce "national" religious reforms during the late Middle Ages. What happened on a unified national level in England and France occurred only locally and piecemeal in Germany. As popular resentment of clerical immunities and ecclesiastical abuses, especially regarding the selling of indulgences, spread among German cities and towns, an unorganized "national" opposition to Rome formed. German humanists had long given voice to such criticism, and by 1517 it provided a solid foundation for Martin Luther's reform.

Luther (1483–1546), the son of a successful Thuringian miner, attended the University of Erfurt, taking a master of arts degree in 1505. He registered with the Law Faculty, but he never began that course of study. To the shock and disappointment of his parents, he joined the Order of the Hermits of Saint Augustine in Erfurt on July 17, 1505. In 1511 he was transferred to the Augustinian monastery in Wittenberg, where he earned his doctorate in theology (1512), thereafter to become a leader within the monastery, the new university, and the spiritual life of the city.

THE ATTACK ON INDULGENCES Reformation theology grew out of a problem common to many clergy and laity at this time: the failure of traditional medieval religion to provide full personal or intellectual satisfaction. Luther was especially plagued by the disproportion between his own sense of sinfulness and the perfect righteousness that medieval theology taught that God required for salvation. Traditional church teaching and the sacraments were no consolation. Luther wrote that he came to despise the phrase "righteousness of God," for it seemed to demand of him a perfection he knew neither he nor any other human being could ever achieve. His insight into the meaning of "justification by faith alone" was a gradual process that extended over several years, between 1513 and 1518. The righteousness God demands, he concluded, does not come from many religious works but is present in full measure in those who believe and trust in the redemptive life and death of Jesus Christ.

This new theology made indulgences unacceptable. An indulgence was a remission of the temporal penalty imposed by the priest on penitents as a "work of satisfaction" for their sins. According to medieval theology, after the priest had absolved penitents of guilt for their sins, God still imposed on them a temporal penalty, a manageable "work of satisfaction" that the penitent could perform here and now (for example, through prayers, fasting, almsgiving, retreats, and pilgrimages). Penitents who defaulted on such prescribed works of satisfaction could expect to suffer for their sins in purgatory.

At this point, indulgences became an aid to laity made genuinely anxious by their belief in a future suffering in purgatory for unrepented sins. Originally, indulgences had been given only for the true self-sacrifice of going on a crusade to the Holy Land. By Luther's time, they were regularly dispensed for small cash payments (modest sums that were regarded as almsgiving) and were presented to the laity as remitting not only their own future punishments, but also those of their dead relatives presumed to be suffering in purgatory.

In 1517 a Jubilee indulgence, proclaimed under Pope Julius II (r. 1503–1513) to raise funds for the rebuilding of Saint Peter's in Rome, was revived and preached on the borders of Saxony in the territories of Archbishop Albrecht of Mainz, who had large debts. The selling of the indulgence was a joint venture by Albrecht, the Augsburg banking house of Fugger, and Pope Leo X (r. 1513–1521), half the proceeds going to the pope and half to Albrecht and his creditors. The famous indulgence preacher John Tetzel (d. 1519) exhorted the crowds:

> Don't you hear the voices of your dead parents and other relatives crying out, "Have mercy on us, for we suffer great punishment and pain. From this you could release us with a few alms . . . We have created you, fed you, cared for you, and left you our temporal goods. Why do you treat us so cruelly and leave us to suffer in the flames, when it takes only a little to save us?"[1]

[1] *Die Reformation in Augenzeugen Berichten,* ed. by Helmar Junghans (Dusseldorf: Karl Rauch Verlag, 1967), p. 44

When on October 31, 1517, Luther posted his ninety-five theses against indulgences on the door of Castle Church in Wittenberg, he condemned the impression created by Tetzel that indulgences remitted sins and released the dead from punishment in purgatory.

Election of Charles V and the Diet of Worms

As sanctions were being prepared against Luther, Emperor Maximilian I died (January 12, 1519), diverting attention from heresy in Saxony to the contest for a new emperor. The pope backed the French king, Francis I. However, Charles I of Spain, then nineteen, succeeded his grandfather and became Emperor Charles V (r. 1519–1556) (see Map 16–2). Charles was assisted by a long tradition of Habsburg imperial rule and massive Fugger loans, which secured the votes of the seven electors.

During the same month in which Charles was elected emperor, Luther debated (June 27, 1519) the Ingolstadt professor John Eck (1486–1543) in Leipzig. During this contest Luther challenged the infallibility of the pope and the inerrancy of church councils, appealing for the first

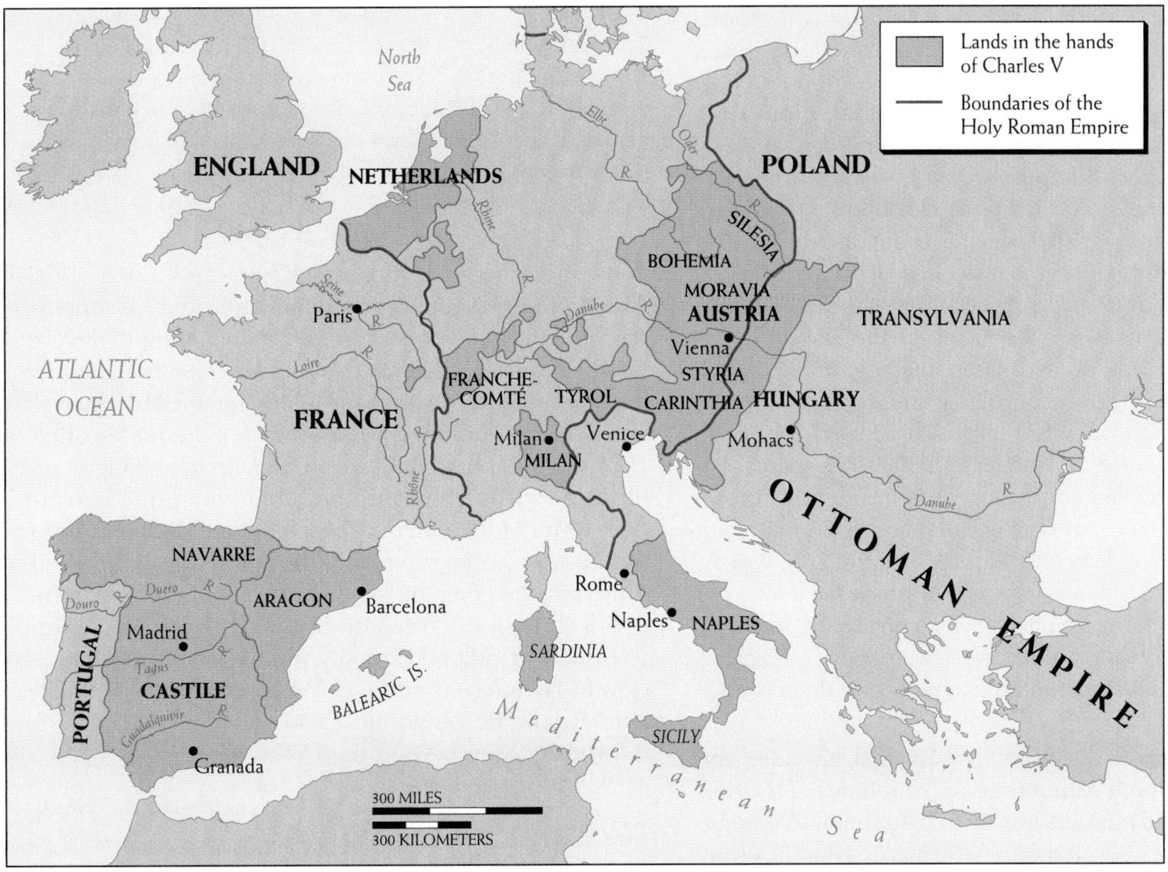

Map 16–2 The empire of Charles V. Dynastic marriages and good luck concentrated into Charles's hands rule over the lands shown here, plus Spain's overseas possessions. Crowns and titles rained down on him; election in 1519 as emperor gave him new burdens and responsibilities.

The punishment of a peasant leader in a village near Heilbronn. After the defeat of rebellious peasants in and around the city of Heilbronn, Jacob Rorbach, a well-to-do peasant leader from a nearby village, was tied to a stake and slowly roasted to death. © Badische Landesbibliothek

time to the sovereign authority of Scripture alone. He burned all his bridges to the old church when he defended Jan Hus, a condemned heretic. In 1520 Luther signaled his new direction with three famous pamphlets: the *Address to the Christian Nobility of the German Nation*, which urged the German princes to force reforms on the Roman Church, especially to curtail its political and economic power in Germany; the *Babylonian Captivity of the Church*, which attacked the traditional seven sacraments, arguing that only two were proper, and which exalted the authority of Scripture, church councils, and secular princes over that of the pope; and the eloquent *Freedom of a Christian*, which summarized the new teaching of salvation by faith alone. On June 15, 1520, the papal bull *Exsurge Domine* condemned Luther for heresy and gave him sixty days to retract. The final bull of excommunication, *Decet Pontificem Romanum*, came on January 3, 1521.

In April 1521 Luther presented his views before a diet of the empire in Worms, over which Charles V presided. Ordered to recant, Luther refused. On May 26, 1521, he was placed under the imperial ban, thereafter an "outlaw" within the empire. Saxon Elector Frederick the Wise, who for largely political reasons became his protector, hid him in Wartburg Castle. There he spent almost a year in seclusion, from April 1521 to March 1522. During his stay he translated the New Testament into German, using Erasmus's new Greek text, and he attempted by correspondence to oversee the first stages of the Reformation in Wittenberg.

The Reformation was greatly assisted in these early years by the emperor's war with France and the advance of the Ottoman Turks into eastern Europe. Against both adversaries Charles V, who also remained a Spanish king with dynastic responsibilities outside the empire, needed German troops; to that end, he promoted friendly relations with the German princes. Between 1521 and 1559, Spain (the Habsburg dynasty) and France (the Valois dynasty) fought four major wars. In 1526 the Turks overran Hungary at the Battle of Mohacs, while in western Europe the French-led League of Cognac formed against Charles for the second Habsburg-Valois war. Thus preoccupied, the emperor agreed through his representatives at the German Diet of Speyer in 1526 that each German territory was free to enforce the Edict of Worms (1521) against Luther "so as to be able to answer in good conscience to God and the emperor." That concession, in effect, gave the German princes territorial sovereignty in religious matters and the Reformation time to put down deep roots.

THE PEASANTS' REVOLT In its first decade, the Protestant movement suffered more from internal division than from imperial interference. By 1525 Luther had become as much an object of protest within Germany as was the pope.

Like the German humanists, the German peasantry had at first believed Luther to be an ally. Defiant of efforts by territorial princes to override their traditional laws and customs, peasant leaders saw in Luther's teaching of religious freedom and criticism of monastic landowners a point of view close to their own, and they openly solicited his support of their political and economic rights, including their revolutionary request for release from serfdom. Luther and his followers sympathized with the peasants, but the Lutherans were no social revolutionaries. When the peasants revolted in 1524–1525, Luther condemned them in the strongest possible terms as "unchristian" and urged the princes to crush their revolt without mercy. Tens of thousands of peasants (estimates run between seventy thousand and one hundred thousand) had died by the time the revolt was put down.

For Luther, the freedom of the Christian was an inner release from guilt and anxiety, not a right to restructure society by violent revolution. Had Luther supported the Peasants' Revolt, he would have also ended any chance of his reform surviving beyond the 1520s.

ZWINGLI AND THE SWISS REFORMATION

Although Luther's was the first, Switzerland and France had their own independent reform movements almost simultaneously with Germany's. Switzerland was a loose

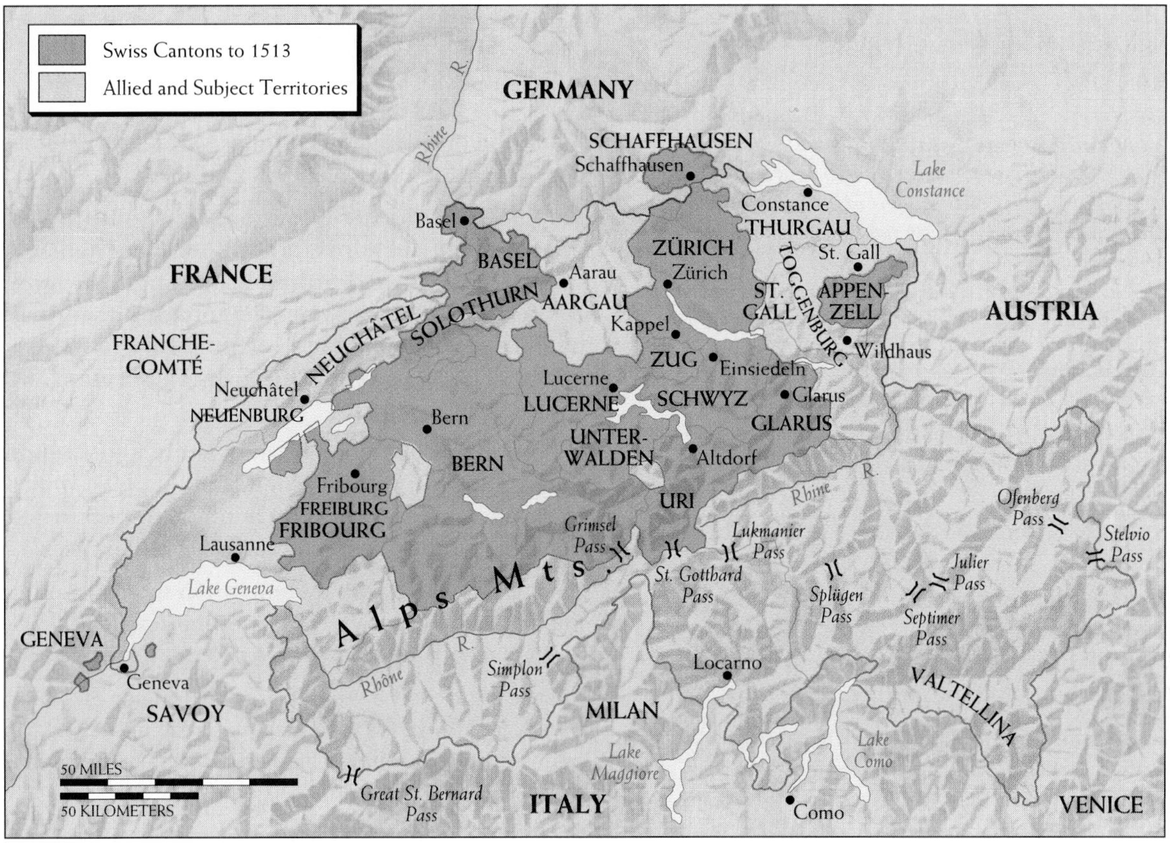

Map 16–3 The Swiss confederation. While nominally still a part of the Holy Roman Empire, Switzerland grew from a loose defensive union of the central "forest cantons" in the thirteenth century to a fiercely independent association of regions with different languages, histories, and, finally, religions.

confederacy of thirteen autonomous cantons or states and allied areas (see Map 16–3). Some became Protestant, some remained Catholic, and a few managed to effect a compromise. The two preconditions of the Swiss Reformation were the growth of national sentiment and a desire for church reform.

THE REFORMATION IN ZURICH Ulrich Zwingli (1484–1531), the leader of the Swiss Reformation, was widely known for opposition to the sale of indulgences and religious superstition. The people's priest in Zurich, he made the city his base for reform. Zwingli's reform guideline was simple and effective: whatever lacked literal support in Scripture was to be neither believed nor practiced. After a public disputation in January 1523, based on his Scripture test, Zurich became, to all intents and purposes, a Protestant city and the center of the Swiss Reformation. Its harsh discipline in pursuit of its religious ideals made it one of the first examples of a "puritanical" Protestant city.

THE MARBURG COLLOQUY Landgrave Philip of Hesse (1504–1567) sought to unite Swiss and German Protestants in a mutual defense pact, a potentially significant political alliance. His efforts were spoiled, however, by theological disagreements between Luther and Zwingli over the nature of Christ's presence in the Eucharist. Zwingli maintained a symbolic interpretation of Christ's words, "This is my body"; Christ, he argued, was only spiritually, not bodily, present in the bread and wine of the Eucharist. Luther, to the contrary, insisted that Christ's human nature could share the properties of his divine nature; hence, where Christ was spiritually present, he could also be bodily present, for his was a special nature.

Philip of Hesse brought the two Protestant leaders together in his castle in Marburg in early October 1529, but they were unable to work out their differences on this issue. Luther left thinking Zwingli a dangerous fanatic. The disagreement splintered the Protestant movement theologically and politically.

ANABAPTISTS AND RADICAL PROTESTANTS

The moderate pace and seemingly small ethical results of the Lutheran and Zwinglian reformations discontented

DOCUMENT GERMAN PEASANTS PROTEST RISING FEUDAL EXACTIONS

In the late fifteenth and early sixteenth centuries, German feudal lords, both secular and ecclesiastical, tried to increase the earnings from their lands by raising demands on their peasant tenants. As the lords restricted the traditional freedoms and property rights of peasants, massive revolts occurred in southern Germany in 1525. The following, representative statement of peasant grievances, summarized in twelve articles, came from the town of Memmingen.

Are the peasants more interested in material than in spiritual freedom? Which of their demands are the most revolutionary, and which are the least problematic for their lords to grant? Why do some centuries exhibit greater social and political equality than others?

1. It is our humble petition and desire that in the future each community should choose and appoint a pastor, and that we should have the right to depose him should he conduct himself improperly . . .
2. We are ready and willing to pay the fair tithe of grain . . . The small tithes [of cattle], whether [to] ecclesiastical or lay lords, we will not pay at all, for the Lord God created cattle for the free use of man . . .
3. We . . . take it for granted that you will release us from serfdom as true Christians, unless it should be shown us from the Gospel that we are serfs.
4. It has been the custom heretofore that no poor man should be allowed to catch venison or wildfowl or fish in flowing water, which seems to us quite unseemly and unbrotherly as well as selfish and not agreeable to the Word of God . . .
5. We are aggrieved in the matter of woodcutting, for the noblemen have appropriated all the woods to themselves . . .
6. In regard to the excessive services demanded of us which are increased from day to day, we ask that this matter be properly looked into so that we shall not continue to be oppressed in this way . . .
7. We will not hereafter allow ourselves to be further oppressed by our lords, but will let them demand only what is just and proper according to the word of the agreement between the lord and the peasant. The lord should no longer try to force more services or other dues from the peasant without payment . . .
8. We are greatly burdened because our holdings cannot support the rent exacted from them . . . We ask that the lords may appoint persons of honor to inspect these holdings and fix a rent in accordance with justice . . .
9. We are burdened with a great evil in the constant making of new laws . . . In our opinion we should be judged according to the old written law . . .
10. We are aggrieved by the appropriation . . . of meadows and fields which at one time belonged to a community as a whole. These we will take again into our own hands . . .
12. We will entirely abolish the due called Todfall [that is, *heriot* or *death tax*, by which the lord received the best horse, cow, or garment of a family upon the death of a serf] and will no longer endure it, nor allow widows and orphans to be thus shamefully robbed against God's will, and in violation of justice and right . . .
13. It is our conclusion and final resolution, that if any one or more of the articles here set forth should not be in agreement with the Word of God, as we think they are, such article we will willingly retract.

Translations and Reprints from the Original Sources of European History, Vol. 2 (Philadelphia: Department of History, University of Pennsylvania, 1897).

many people, among them some of the original co-workers of Luther and Zwingli. Many desired a more rapid and thorough implementation of primitive Christianity and accused the major reformers of going only halfway. The most important of these radical groups were the Anabaptists, the sixteenth-century ancestors of the modern Mennonites and Amish. The Anabaptists were especially distinguished by their rejection of infant baptism and their insistence on only adult baptism (*Anabaptism* derives from the Greek word meaning "to rebaptize"), believing that baptism as a consenting adult conformed to Scripture and was more respectful of human freedom.

Anabaptists physically separated from society to form a more perfect community in imitation of what they believed to be the example of the first Christians. Due to the close connection between religious and civic life in this period, the political authorities viewed such separatism as a threat to basic social bonds.

At first Anabaptism drew its adherents from all social classes. But as Lutherans and Zwinglians joined with

Catholics in opposition to it, a more rural, agrarian class came to make up the great majority of Anabaptists. In 1529 rebaptism became a capital offense throughout the Holy Roman Empire. It has been estimated that between 1525 and 1618 at least one thousand and perhaps as many as five thousand men and women were executed for rebaptizing themselves as adults.

JOHN CALVIN AND THE GENEVAN REFORMATION

Calvinism was the religious ideology that inspired or accompanied massive political resistance in France, the Netherlands, and Scotland. Believing in both divine predestination and the individual's responsibility to create a godly society, Calvinists became zealous reformers. In a famous and controversial study, *The Protestant Ethic and the Spirit of Capitalism* (1904), the German sociologist Max Weber argued that this peculiar combination of religious confidence and self-disciplined activism produced an ethic congenial to emergent capitalism, bringing Calvinism and later Puritanism into close association with the development of modern capitalist societies.

POLITICAL REVOLT AND RELIGIOUS REFORM IN GENEVA Whereas in Saxony religious reform paved the way for a political revolution against the emperor, in Geneva a political revolution against the local prince-bishop laid the foundation for religious change. In late 1533 the Protestant city of Bern sent Protestant reformers to Geneva and by the summer of 1535, after much internal turmoil, the Protestants triumphed. On May 21, 1536, the city voted officially to adopt the Reformation: "to live according to the Gospel and the Word of God . . . without . . . any more masses, statues, idols, or other papal abuses."

John Calvin (1509–1564), a reform-minded humanist and lawyer, arrived in Geneva after these events, in July 1536. The local Protestant reformer persuaded him to stay and assist the Reformation. Before a year had passed, Calvin had drawn up articles for the governance of the new church, as well as a catechism to guide and discipline the people. As a result of the strong measures proposed to govern Geneva's moral life, many suspected the reformers of trying to create a "new papacy." In February 1538 they were exiled from the city.

Calvin went to Strasbourg, a model Protestant city, where he became pastor to the French exiles. During his two years in Strasbourg he wrote biblical commentaries and a second edition of his masterful *Institutes of the Christian Religion,* which many consider the definitive theological statement of the Protestant faith. He also married and participated in the ecumenical discussions urged on Protestants and Catholics by Charles V. Most important, he learned from the Strasbourg reformer Martin Bucer (1491–1551) how to implement the Protestant Reformation successfully.

A portrait of the young John Calvin. Bibliotheque Publique et Universitaire, Geneva

CALVIN'S GENEVA In 1540 Geneva elected officials favorable to Calvin and he was invited to return. Within months of his arrival, new ecclesiastical ordinances were implemented that allowed the magistrates and the clergy to cooperate in matters of internal discipline.

Calvin and his followers were motivated above all by a desire to make society godly. The "elect," Calvin taught, should live a manifestly God-pleasing life, if they were truly God's elect. The majesty of God demanded nothing less. The consistory, a judicial body composed of clergy and laity, became his instrument of power. It enforced the strictest moral discipline, meting out punishments for a broad range of moral and religious transgressions, and became unpopular among many Genevans.

After 1555 the city's magistrates were all devout Calvinists, and Geneva became home to thousands of exiled Protestants who had been driven out of France, England, and Scotland. Refugees (more than five thousand), most of them utterly loyal to Calvin, came to make up over one third of the population of Geneva. From this time until his death in 1564, Calvin's position in the city was greatly strengthened and the magistrates were very cooperative.

Political Consolidation of the Lutheran Reformation

By 1530 the Reformation was in Europe to stay. It would, however, take several decades and major attempts to eradicate it before all would recognize this fact. With the political triumph of Lutheranism in the empire by the 1550s, Protestant movements elsewhere gained a new lease on life.

Expansion of the Reformation In the 1530s German Lutherans formed regional consistories, which oversaw and administered the new Protestant churches. These consistories replaced the old Catholic episcopates. Under the leadership of Philip Melanchthon (1497–1560), Luther's most admired colleague, educational reforms were enacted that provided for compulsory primary education, schools for girls, a humanist revision of the traditional curriculum, and catechetical instruction of the laity in the new religion.

The Reformation also dug in elsewhere. Introduced into Denmark by Christian II (r. 1513–1523), Lutheranism became the state religion under Christian III (r. 1536–1559). In Sweden, Gustavus Vasa (r. 1523–1560), supported by a nobility greedy for church lands, confiscated church property and subjected the clergy to royal authority at the Diet of Vesteras (1527). In politically splintered Poland, Lutherans, Calvinists, and others found room to practice their beliefs. The absence of a central political authority made Poland a model of religious pluralism and toleration in the second half of the sixteenth century.

Reaction Against Protestants: The "Interim" Charles V made abortive efforts in 1540–1541 to enforce a compromise agreement between Protestants and Catholics. As these and other conciliar efforts failed, he turned to a military solution. In 1547 imperial armies crushed the Protestant Schmalkaldic League.

The emperor established puppet rulers in Saxony and Hesse and issued as imperial law the Augsburg Interim, a new order that Protestants everywhere must readopt Catholic beliefs and practices. But the Reformation was too entrenched by 1547 to be ended even by brute force. Confronted by fierce Protestant resistance and weary from three decades of war, the emperor was forced to relent.

The Peace of Augsburg in September 1555 made the division of Christendom permanent. This agreement recognized in law what had already been well established in practice: *cuius regio, eius religio,* meaning that the ruler of a land would determine the religion of the land. Lutherans were permitted to retain all church lands forcibly seized before 1552. Those discontented with the religion of their region were permitted to migrate to another.

Calvinism was not recognized as a legal form of Christian belief and practice by the Peace of Augsburg. Calvinists remained determined not only to secure the right to worship publicly as they pleased, but also to shape society according to their own religious convictions. They organized to lead national revolutions throughout northern Europe.

Chronology

Progress of Protestant Reformation on the Continent

1517	Luther posts ninety-five theses against indulgences
1519	Charles I of Spain elected Holy Roman emperor (as Charles V)
1519	Luther challenges infallibility of pope and inerrancy of church councils at Leipzig Debate
1521	Papal bull excommunicates Luther for heresy
1521	Diet of Worms condemns Luther
1521–1522	Luther translates the New Testament into German
1524–1525	Peasants' Revolt in Germany
1529	Marburg Colloquy between Luther and Zwingli
1530	Diet of Augsburg fails to settle religious differences
1531	Formation of Protestant Schmalkaldic League
1536	Calvin arrives in Geneva
1540	Jesuits, founded by Ignatius of Loyola, recognized as order by pope
1546	Luther dies
1547	Armies of Charles V crush Schmalkaldic League
1555	Peace of Augsburg recognizes rights of Lutherans to worship as they please
1545–1563	Council of Trent institutes reforms and responds to the Reformation

The English Reformation to 1553

Late medieval England had a well-earned reputation for defending the rights of the crown against the pope. It was, however, the unhappy marriage of King Henry VIII (r. 1509–1547) that ensured the success of the English protest against the church.

The King's Affair Henry had married Catherine of Aragon (d. 1536), a daughter of Ferdinand and Isabella of Spain, and the aunt of Emperor Charles V. By 1527 the union had produced only one surviving child, a daughter, Mary Tudor. Henry was justifiably concerned about the political consequences of leaving only a female heir. People in this period believed it unnatural for women to rule over men. At best, a woman ruler meant a contested reign; at worst, turmoil and revolution.

An allegorical depiction of the Tudor succession by the painter Lucas de Heere (1534–1584). On Henry VIII's right stands his Catholic daughter Mary (1533–1558) and her husband Philip II of Spain. They are accompanied by Mars, the god of war. Henry's son, Edward VI (r. 1547–1553), kneels at the king's left. Elizabeth I (1558–1603) is shown standing in the foreground attended by Peace and Plenty, allegorical figures of what her reign brought to England. Sudeley Castle National Museums & Galleries of Wales

Henry even came to believe that his union with Catherine, who had had numerous miscarriages and stillbirths, had been cursed by God, because before their marriage Catherine had briefly been the wife of his late brother, Arthur.

By 1527 Henry, thoroughly enamored of Anne Boleyn (ca. 1504–1536), one of Catherine's ladies in waiting, decided to put Catherine aside and marry Anne. This he could not do in Catholic England without papal annulment of the marriage to Catherine. And therein lay a problem. In 1527 the reigning pope, Clement VII (r. 1523–1534), was a prisoner of Charles V, Catherine's nephew. Even if this had not been the case, it would have been virtually impossible for the pope to grant an annulment of the marriage. Not only had it survived for eighteen years, but it had been made possible in the first place by a special papal dispensation required because Queen Catherine had previously been the wife of Henry's brother, Arthur.

After Cardinal Wolsey (1475–1530), Lord Chancellor of England since 1515, failed to secure the annulment, Thomas Cranmer (1489–1556) and Thomas Cromwell (1485–1540), both of whom harbored Lutheran sympathies, became the king's closest advisers. Finding the way to a papal annulment closed, Henry's new advisers struck a different course: Why not simply declare the king supreme in English spiritual affairs as he was in English temporal affairs? Then the king could settle his own affair.

REFORMATION PARLIAMENT In 1529 Parliament convened for what would be a seven-year session that earned it the title of "Reformation Parliament." It passed a flood of legislation that harassed and finally placed royal reins on the clergy. In January 1531 the clergy publicly recognized Henry as head of the church in England "as far as the law of Christ allows." In 1533 Parliament passed the Submission of the Clergy, effectively placing canon law under royal control and thereby the clergy under royal jurisdiction.

CHRONOLOGY

MAIN EVENTS OF THE ENGLISH REFORMATION

1529	Reformation Parliament convenes
1532	Parliament passes the Submission of the Clergy, an act placing canon law and the English clergy under royal jurisdiction
1533	Henry VIII weds Anne Boleyn
1534	Act of Succession makes Anne Boleyn's children legitimate heirs to the English throne
1534	Act of Supremacy declares Henry VIII the only supreme head of the Church of England
1535	Thomas More executed for opposition to Acts of Succession and Supremacy
1535	Publication of Coverdale Bible
1539	Henry VIII imposes the Six Articles, condemning Protestantism and reasserting traditional doctrine
1547	Edward VI succeeds to the throne
1549	First Act of Uniformity imposes Book of Common Prayer on English churches
1553-1558	Mary Tudor restores Catholic doctrine
1558-1603	Elizabeth I fashions an Anglican religious settlement

DOCUMENT — IGNATIUS OF LOYOLA'S "RULES FOR THINKING WITH THE CHURCH"

As leaders of the Counter-Reformation, the Jesuits attempted to live by and instill in others the strictest obedience to church authority. The following are some of the eighteen rules Ignatius included in his Spiritual Exercises *to give Catholics positive direction. These rules also indicate the Catholic reformers' refusal to compromise with Protestants.*

Would Protestants find any of Ignatius's "rules" acceptable? Might any of them be controversial among Catholic as well as Protestant laity?

In order to have the proper attitude of mind in the Church Militant we should observe the following rules:

1. Putting aside all private judgment, we should keep our minds prepared and ready to obey promptly and in all things the true spouse of Christ our Lord, our Holy Mother, the hierarchical Church.
2. To praise sacramental confession and the reception of the Most Holy Sacrament once a year, and much better once a month, and better still every week . . .
3. To praise the frequent hearing of Mass . . .
4. To praise highly the religious life, virginity, and continence; and also matrimony but not as highly . . .
5. To praise the vows of religion, obedience, poverty, chastity, and other works of perfection and supererogation . . .
6. To praise the relics of the saints . . . [and] the stations, pilgrimages, indulgences, jubilees, Crusade indulgences, and the lighting of candles in the churches.
7. To praise the precepts concerning fasts and abstinences . . . and acts of penance . . .
8. To praise the adornments and buildings of churches as well as sacred images . . .
9. To praise all the precepts of the church . . .
10. To approve and praise the directions and recommendations of our superiors as well as their personal behaviour . . .
11. To praise both the positive and scholastic theology . . .
12. We must be on our guard against making comparisons between the living and those who have already gone to their reward, for it is no small error to say, for example: "This man knows more than St. Augustine"; "He is another Saint Francis, or even greater" . . .
13. If we wish to be sure that we are right in all things, we should always be ready to accept this principle: I will believe that the white that I see is black if the hierarchical Church so defines it. For I believe that between . . . Christ our Lord and . . . His Church, there is but one spirit, which governs and directs us for the salvation of our souls.

From *The Spiritual Exercises of St. Ignatius*, by Anthony Mottola. Copyright © 1964 by Doubleday, a division of Random House, pp. 139–141. Used by permission of Doubleday, a division of Random House, Inc.

In January 1533 Henry wed the pregnant Anne Boleyn, with Thomas Cranmer officiating. In 1534 Parliament ended all payments by the English clergy and laity to Rome and gave Henry sole jurisdiction over high ecclesiastical appointments. The Act of Succession in the same year made Anne Boleyn's children legitimate heirs to the throne, and the Act of Supremacy declared Henry "the only supreme head in earth of the church of England."

THE PROTESTANT REFORMATION UNDER EDWARD VI Despite his political break with Rome, Henry remained decidedly conservative in his religious beliefs, and Catholic doctrine remained prominent in a country seething with Protestant sentiment. Henry forbade the English clergy to marry and threatened to execute clergy caught twice in concubinage. The Six Articles of 1539 reaffirmed transubstantiation, denied the Eucharistic cup to the laity, declared celibate vows inviolable, provided for private Masses, and ordered the continuation of auricular confession.

Edward VI (r. 1547–1553), Henry's son by his third wife, Jane Seymour, became king at age ten. Under his regents, England enacted much of the Protestant Reformation. Henry's Six Articles and laws against heresy were repealed, and clerical marriage and Communion with the cup were sanctioned. An Act of Uniformity imposed Thomas Cranmer's Book of Common Prayer on all English churches, which were stripped of their images and altars. His forty-two-article confession of faith set forth a moderate Protestant doctrine.

These changes were short-lived because in 1553 Catherine of Aragon's daughter, Mary Tudor (d. 1558), succeeded to the throne and restored Catholic doctrine and

The Ecstasy of Saint Teresa of Avila, by Gianlorenzo Bernini (1598–1680). Mystics like Saint Teresa and Saint John of the cross helped revive the traditional piety of medieval monasticism. © Scala/Art Resource, N.Y.

practice with a single-mindedness that rivaled that of her father. It was not until the reign of Anne Boleyn's daughter, Elizabeth I (r. 1558–1603), that a lasting religious settlement was worked out in England.

Catholic Reform and Counter-Reformation

The Protestant Reformation did not take the medieval church completely by surprise. There were many internal criticisms and efforts at reform before there was a Counter-Reformation in reaction to Protestant successes.

Sources of Catholic Reform Before the Reformation began, ambitious proposals had been made for church reform. But sixteenth-century popes, mindful of how the Councils of Constance and Basel had stripped the pope of his traditional powers, quickly squelched such efforts to bring about basic changes in the laws and institutions of the church. Despite such papal foot-dragging, the church was not without its reformers. Many new religious orders sprang up in the sixteenth century to lead a broad revival of piety within the church.

Ignatius of Loyola and the Society of Jesus
Of the various reform groups, none was more instrumental in the success of the Counter-Reformation than the Society of Jesus, the new order of Jesuits. Organized by Ignatius of Loyola in the 1530s, it was officially recognized by the church in 1540. Within a century the society had more than fifteen thousand members scattered throughout the world, with thriving missions in India, Japan, and the Americas.

Ignatius of Loyola (1491–1556) was a heroic figure. A dashing courtier and caballero in his youth, he began his spiritual pilgrimage in 1521 after having been seriously wounded in the legs during a battle with the French. During a lengthy and painful convalescence, he read Christian classics. So impressed was he with the heroic self-sacrifice of the church's saints and their methods of overcoming mental anguish and pain that he underwent a profound religious conversion. Henceforth, he too would serve the church as a soldier of Christ.

After recuperating, Ignatius applied the lessons he had learned during his convalescence to a program of religious and moral self-discipline that came to be embodied in the *Spiritual Exercises.* This psychologically perceptive devotional guide contained mental and emotional exercises designed to teach one absolute spiritual self-mastery. A person could shape his or her own behavior, even create a new religious self, through disciplined study and regular practice.

Whereas in Jesuit eyes Protestants had distinguished themselves by disobedience to church authority and by religious innovation, the exercises of Ignatius were intended to teach good Catholics to submit without question to higher church authority and spiritual direction. Perfect discipline and self-control were the essential conditions of such obedience. To these were added the enthusiasm of traditional spirituality and mysticism and uncompromising loyalty to the church's cause above all else. This potent combination helped counter the Reformation and win many Protestants back to the Catholic fold, especially in Austria and Germany.

The Council of Trent (1545–1563) The broad success of the Reformation and the insistence of the emperor Charles V forced Pope Paul III (r. 1534–1549) to call a general council of the church to reassert church doctrine. The pope also appointed a reform commission, whose report, presented in February 1537, bluntly criticized the fiscality and simony[2] of the papal Curia (court) as the primary source of

[2] The sin of selling of sacred or spiritual things, in this instance church offices.

DOCUMENT: A German Mother Advises Her Fifteen-Year-Old Son, Who Is Away from Home at School for the First Time (1578)

Although only fourteen miles away from his Nuremberg home, Friedrich Behaim was fifteen and on his own for the first time at the Altdorf Academy, where he would spend the next three years of his life. As there was daily traffic back and forth, mother and son could correspond regularly and Frau Behaim could give her son needed advice and articles of clothing.

What is the mother most concerned about? What do her concerns suggest about life in the sixteenth century? Does she appear to be more strict and demanding of her son than a modern mother would be? Is the son clueless, or adroitly manipulating the mother?

Dear son Friederich . . . You write that you have been unable to get by on the money [I gave you]. I will let it pass this quarter, but see that you manage on it in the future. Enclosed is another gulden. As for your clothes, I do not have Martin [a servant] here with me now (we are quarreling), but he has begun to work on your clothes. He has made stockings for your leather holiday trousers, which I am sending you with this letter. Since your everyday trousers are so bad, wear these for now until a new pair of woolen ones can be made and sent to you, which I will do as soon as I can. Send me your old trousers in the sack I sent you the pitcher in. As for the smock that you think should be lined [for the winter], I worry that the skirt may be too short and will not keep you warm. You can certainly wear it for another summer if it is not too small for you then and the weather not too warm. Just keep it clean and brushed. I will have a new coat made for you at the earliest.

You also write about [unhappiness with] your food. You must be patient for a while. You may not at the outset lodge a complaint against [your master], and especially while you are sitting at his table. [Only] he may speak out who eats his food and is also an authority in the house. So it would be better if the Inspector, who is there for a reason, reports it to him.

Will you once tell me who your table companions are! Also, let me know by All Saints what you have spent on beer and what you owe the tailor, so I may know how much money to send you.

As for your [sore] throat, there is nothing you can take for it but warm mead. Gargle often with it and keep your head warm. Put a muffler or scarf around your neck and wear your night coat when you are in your room. Avoid cold drinks and sit perhaps for a while by the fire. And do not forget to be bled on time. [People then bled themselves once or twice a year as a health measure] . . . When you need paper, let me know . . .

I am sending some cleaning flakes for your leather pants. After you have worn them three times, put some on the knees . . . I will have your old coat patched and send it to you with the next carter [so that you can wear it] until the new one is made. Send me the two sacks with the next carter. You will find the [aforementioned] gulden in the trouser foot tied with a string.

Nothing more for now. God bless. 14 October, 1578.

Mrs. Paul Behaim

From *Three Behaim Boys: Growing Up in Early Modern Germany —A Chronicle of Their Lives*, ed. and trans. by Steven Ozment, pp. 107–108. Copyright © 1990 Yale University Press. Reprinted by permission of Yale University Press.

the church's loss of esteem. The report was so critical that Paul attempted unsuccessfully to suppress its publication, and Protestants reprinted and circulated it to justify their criticism.

The long-delayed council met in 1545 in the imperial city of Trent in northern Italy. There were three sessions, spread over eighteen years, with long interruptions due to war, plague, and politics. Unlike the general councils of the fifteenth century, Trent was strictly under the pope's control, with high Italian prelates prominent in the proceedings.

The council's most important reforms concerned internal church discipline. The selling of church offices and other religious goods was forbidden. Trent strengthened the authority of local bishops so they could effectively discipline popular religious practice. Bishops who resided in Rome were forced to move to their appointed seats of authority. They had to preach regularly and conduct annual visitations. Parish priests were required to be neatly dressed, better educated, strictly celibate, and active among their parishioners. To train better priests, Trent also called for the establishment of a seminary in every diocese.

The Council did not make a single doctrinal concession to the Protestants, however. In the face of Protestant criticism, the Council of Trent reaffirmed the traditional scholastic education of the clergy; the role of good works in salvation; the authority of tradition; the seven sacraments; transubstantiation; the withholding of the Eucharistic cup from the laity; clerical celibacy; the reality of purgatory; the veneration of saints, relics, and sacred images; and the granting of letters of indulgence.

Rulers initially resisted Trent's reform decrees, fearing a revival of papal political power within their lands. But in time the new legislation took hold, and parish life revived under the guidance of a devout and better-trained clergy.

THE REFORMATION'S ACHIEVEMENTS

THE REVOLUTION IN RELIGIOUS PRACTICES AND INSTITUTIONS

Although politically conservative, the Reformation brought about far-reaching changes in traditional religious practices and institutions in many lands. By the end of the sixteenth century, what had disappeared or was radically altered was often dramatic.

RELIGION IN FIFTEENTH-CENTURY LIFE In the fifteenth century, on the streets of the great cities of central Europe that later turned Protestant (for example, Zurich, Strasbourg, Nuremberg, or Geneva), the clergy and the religious were everywhere. They made up six to eight percent of the total urban population, and they exercised considerable political as well as spiritual power. They legislated and taxed; they tried cases in special church courts; and they enforced their laws with threats of excommunication.

The church calendar regulated daily life. About one third of the year was given over to some kind of religious observance or celebration. There were frequent periods of fasting. On almost a hundred days out of the year a pious Christian could not, without special dispensation, eat eggs, butter, fat, or meat.

Monasteries and especially nunneries were prominent and influential institutions. The children of society's most powerful citizens resided there. Local aristocrats were closely identified with particular churches and chapels, whose walls recorded their lineage and proclaimed their generosity. On the streets, friars from near and far begged alms from passersby. In the churches the Mass and liturgy were read entirely in Latin. Images of saints were regularly displayed, and on certain holidays their relics were paraded about and venerated.

There was a booming business at local religious shrines. Pilgrims gathered there by the hundreds, even thousands, many sick and dying, all in search of a cure or a miracle, but also for diversion and entertainment. Several times during the year special preachers arrived in the city to sell letters of indulgence.

Many clergy walked the streets with concubines and children, although they were sworn to celibacy and forbidden marriage. The church tolerated such relationships upon payment of penitential fines.

People everywhere could be heard complaining about the clergy's exemption from taxation and, in many instances, also from the civil criminal code. People also grumbled about having to support church offices whose occupants actually lived and worked elsewhere. Townspeople also expressed concern that the church had too much influence over education and culture.

RELIGION IN SIXTEENTH-CENTURY LIFE In these same cities after the Reformation had firmly established itself, few changes in politics and society were evident. The same aristocratic families governed as before, and the rich generally got richer and the poor poorer. But overall numbers of clergy fell by two thirds and religious holidays shrunk by one third. Monasteries and nunneries were nearly absent. Many were transformed into hospices for the sick and poor or into educational institutions, their endowments also turned over to these new purposes. A few cloisters remained for very devout old monks and nuns, who could not be pensioned off or who lacked families and friends to care for them. But these remaining cloisters died out with their inhabitants.

In the churches, which had also been reduced in number by at least a third, worship was conducted almost completely in the vernacular. In some, particularly those in Zwinglian cities, the walls were stripped bare and whitewashed to make sure the congregation meditated only on God's Word. The laity observed no obligatory fasts. Indulgence preachers no longer appeared. Local shrines were closed down, and anyone found openly venerating saints, relics, and images was subject to fine and punishment.

Copies of Luther's translation of the New Testament, or more often excerpts from it, could be found in private homes, and meditation on them was encouraged by the new clergy. The clergy could marry, and most did. They paid taxes and were punished for their crimes in civil courts. Domestic moral life was regulated by committees composed of roughly equal numbers of laity and clergy, over whose decisions secular magistrates had the last word.

Not all Protestant clergy remained enthusiastic about this new lay authority in religion. And the laity themselves were also ambivalent about certain aspects of the Reformation. Over half of the original converts returned to the Catholic fold before the end of the sixteenth century. Whereas half of Europe could be counted in the Protestant camp in the mid–sixteenth century, only a fifth would be there by the mid–seventeenth century.[3]

THE REFORMATION AND THE CHANGING ROLE OF WOMEN

The Protestant reformers took a positive stand on clerical marriage and strongly opposed monasticism and the celibate life. From this position they challenged the medieval tendency alternately to degrade women as temptresses (following the model of Eve) and to exalt them as virgins (following the model of Mary). Protestants opposed the popular antiwoman and antimarriage

[3] Geoffrey Parker, *Europe in Crisis, 1598–1648* (Ithaca, N.Y.: Cornell University Press, 1979), p. 50.

A young couple in love (ca. 1480) by an anonymous artist.
Bildarchiv Preussischer Kulturbesitz

literature of the Middle Ages. They praised woman in her own right, but especially in her biblical vocation as mother and housewife. Although from a modern perspective, women remained subject to men, new marriage laws gave them greater security and protection.

Relief of sexual frustration and a remedy of fornication were prominent in Protestant arguments for marriage. But the reformers also viewed their wives as indispensable companions in their work, and this not solely because they took domestic cares off their husbands' minds. Luther, who married in 1525 at the age of forty-two, wrote of women:

> Imagine what it would be like without women. The home, cities, economic life, and government would virtually disappear. Men cannot do without women. Even if it were possible for men to beget and bear children, they still could not do without women.[4]

John Calvin wrote at the death of his wife:

> I have been bereaved of the best companion of my life, of one who, had it been so ordered, would not only have been the willing sharer of my indigence, but even of my death. During her life she was the faithful helper of my ministry.[5]

Such tributes were intended in part to overcome Catholic criticism that marriage distracted the cleric from his ministry. They were primarily the expression of a new value placed on the estate of marriage and family life. In opposition to the celibate ideal of the Middle Ages, Protestants stressed as no religious movement before them the sacredness of home and family. This attitude contributed to a more respectful and sharing relationship between husbands and wives and between parents and children.

The ideal of the companionate marriage—that is, of husband and wife as co-workers in a special God-ordained community of the family, sharing authority equally within the household—led to an important expansion of the grounds for divorce in Protestant cities as early as the 1520s. Women now had an equal right with men to divorce and remarry in good conscience—unlike in Catholicism, where only a separation from bed and table, not divorce and remarriage, was permitted a couple in a failed marriage. The reformers were actually more willing to permit divorce and remarriage on grounds of adultery and abandonment than were secular magistrates, who feared liberal divorce laws would lead to social upheaval.

Protestant doctrines were as attractive to women as they were to men. Renegade nuns wrote exposés of the nunnery in the name of Christian freedom and justification by faith, declaring that the nunnery was no special woman's place at all and that supervisory male clergy (who alone could hear the nuns' confessions and administer the Sacrament to them) made their lives as unpleasant and burdensome as any abusive husband. Women in the higher classes, who enjoyed new social and political freedoms during the Renaissance, found in Protestant theology a religious complement to their greater independence in other walks of life. Some cloistered noblewomen, however, protested the closing of nunneries. They believed the cloister provided them with a more interesting and independent way of life than they would have known in the secular world.

Because they wanted women to become pious housewives, Protestants also encouraged the education of girls to literacy in the vernacular, expecting them thereafter to model their lives on the Bible. During their studies, however, women found biblical passages that suggested they were equal to men in the presence of God. Education also gave some women a role as independent authors in the Reformation. From a modern perspective, these may seem like small advances, but they were significant, if indirect, steps in the direction of the emancipation of women.

[4] *Luther's Works*, Vol. 54: *Table Talk*, ed. and trans. by Theodore G. Tappert (Philadelphia: Fortress Press, 1967), p. 161.

[5] *Letters of John Calvin*, Vol. 2, trans. by J. Bonnet (Edinburgh: T. Constable, 1858), p. 216.

The St. Bartholemew's Day Massacre, as depicted by the contemporary Protestant painter François Dubois. In this notorious event, three thousand Protestants were slaughtered in Paris and an estimated twenty thousand others died throughout France. The massacre transformed the religious struggle in France from a contest for political power into an all-out war between Protestants and Catholics. Musée Cantonal des Beaux Arts, Palais de Rumine, Lausanne

THE WARS OF RELIGION

After the Council of Trent adjourned in 1563, Catholics began a Jesuit-led counteroffensive against Protestants. At the time of John Calvin's death in 1564, Geneva had become both a refuge for Europe's persecuted Protestants and an international school for Protestant resistance, producing leaders fully equal to the new Catholic challenge.

Genevan Calvinism and the reformed Catholicism of the Council of Trent were two equally dogmatic, aggressive, and irreconcilable church systems. Calvinists may have looked like "new papists" to critics when they dominated cities like Geneva, but when as minorities they found their civil and religious rights denied in the empire and elsewhere, they became true firebrands and revolutionaries.

Calvinism adopted a presbyterian organization that magnified regional and local religious authority. Boards of presbyters, or elders, representing the many individual Calvinist congregations, directly shaped the policy of the church at large. By contrast, the Counter-Reformation sponsored a centralized episcopal church system, hierarchically arranged from pope to parish priest and stressing absolute obedience to the person at the top. The high clergy—the pope and his bishops—not the synods of local churches, ruled supreme. Calvinism attracted proponents of political decentralization who opposed totalitarian rulers, whereas Catholicism remained congenial to proponents of absolute monarchy determined to maintain "one king, one church, one law."

The wars of religion were both internal national conflicts and truly international wars. Catholic and Protestant subjects struggled to control France, the Netherlands, and England. The Catholic governments of France and Spain conspired and finally sent armies against Protestant regimes in England and the Netherlands. The outbreak of the Thirty Years' War in 1618 made the international dimensions of the religious conflict especially clear; before it ended in 1648, the war drew every major European nation directly or indirectly into its deadly net.

French Wars of Religion (1562–1598)

When Henry II (r. 1547–1559) died accidentally during a tournament in 1559, his sickly fifteen-year-old son, Francis II (d. 1560), came to the throne under the regency of the queen mother, Catherine de Médicis (1519–1589). With the monarchy so weakened, three powerful families began to compete to control France. They were the Bourbons, whose power lay in the south and west; the Montmorency-Châtillons, who controlled the center of France; and the Guises, who were dominant in eastern France. The Guises were by far the strongest, and the name of *Guise* was interchangeable with militant, ultra-Catholicism. The Bourbon and Montmorency-Châtillon families, in contrast, developed strong Huguenot sympathies, largely for political reasons. (French Protestants were called Huguenots after Besançon Hughes, the leader of Geneva's political revolt against the Savoyards in the late 1520s.) The Bourbon Louis I, prince of Condé (d. 1569), and the Montmorency-Châtillon admiral Gaspard de Coligny (1519–1572) became the political leaders of the French Protestant resistance.

Often for quite different reasons, ambitious aristocrats and discontented townspeople joined Calvinist churches in opposition to the Guise-dominated French monarchy. In 1561 over two thousand Huguenot congregations existed throughout France. Although they made up only about a fifteenth of the population, Huguenots held important geographic areas and represented the more powerful segments of French society. Over two fifths of the French aristocracy became Huguenots. Many apparently hoped to establish within France a principle of territorial sovereignty akin to that secured within the Holy Roman Empire by the Peace of Augsburg (1555). Calvinism thus indirectly served the forces of political decentralization.

Catherine de Médicis and the Guises Following Francis II's death in 1560, Catherine de Médicis continued as regent for her second son, Charles IX (r. 1560–1574). Fearing the Guises, Catherine, whose first concern was always to preserve the monarchy, sought allies among the Protestants. Early in 1562 she granted Protestants freedom to worship publicly outside towns—although only privately within them—and to hold synods, or church assemblies. In March of the same year this royal toleration ended when the Duke of Guise surprised a Protestant congregation worshiping illegally at Vassy in Champagne and proceeded to massacre several score—an event that marked the beginning of the French wars of religion. Perpetually caught between fanatical Huguenot and Guise extremes, Queen Catherine always sought to play the one side against the other. She wanted a Catholic France but not a Guise-dominated monarchy.

On August 22, 1572, four days after the Huguenot Henry of Navarre had married Charles IX's sister—another sign of growing Protestant power in the queen mother's eye—the Huguenot leader Coligny, who increasingly had the king's ear, was wounded by an assassin's bullet. Catherine had apparently been a part of this Guise plot to eliminate Coligny. After its failure, she feared both the king's reaction to her complicity and the Huguenot response under a recovered Coligny. Catherine convinced Charles that a Huguenot coup was afoot, inspired by Coligny, and that only the swift execution of Protestant leaders could save the crown from a Protestant attack on Paris. On the eve of Saint Bartholomew's Day, August 24, 1572, Coligny and three thousand fellow Huguenots were butchered in Paris. Within three days an estimated twenty thousand Huguenots were executed in coordinated attacks throughout France.

This event changed the nature of the struggle between Protestants and Catholics both within and beyond the borders of France. It was thereafter no longer an internal contest between Guise and Bourbon factions for French political influence, nor was it simply a Huguenot campaign to win basic religious freedoms. Henceforth, in Protestant eyes, it became an international struggle to the death for sheer survival against an adversary whose cruelty justified any means of resistance.

The Rise to Power of Henry of Navarre Henry III (r. 1574–1589), who was Henry II's third son and the last Valois king, found the monarchy wedged between a radical Catholic League, formed in 1576 by Henry of Guise, and vengeful Huguenots. Like the queen mother, Henry III sought to steer a middle course, and in this effort he received support from a growing body of neutral Catholics and Huguenots who put the political survival of France above its religious unity. Such *politiques*, as they were called, were prepared to compromise religious creeds to save the nation.

In the mid-1580s the Catholic League, supported by the Spanish, became completely dominant in Paris. Henry III failed to rout the league with a surprise attack in 1588 and had to flee Paris. Forced by his weakened position into guerrilla tactics, the king had both the Duke and the Cardinal of Guise assassinated. The Catholic League reacted with a

The Milch Cow, a sixteenth-century satirical painting depicting the Netherlands as a land all the great powers of Europe wish to exploit. Elizabeth of England is feeding her (England had long-standing commerical ties with Flanders); Philip II of Spain is attempting to ride her (Spain was trying to reassert its control over the entire region); William of Orange is trying to milk her (he was the leader of the anti-Spanish rebellion); and the king of France holds her by the tail (France hoped to profit from the rebellion at Spain's expense). Rijksmuseum, Amsterdam.

fury that matched the earlier Huguenot response to the Massacre of Saint Bartholomew's Day. The king was now forced to strike an alliance with his Protestant cousin and heir, Henry of Navarre, in April 1589.

As the two Henrys prepared to attack Paris, however, a fanatical Dominican friar murdered Henry III. Thereupon the Bourbon Huguenot Henry of Navarre became Henry IV of France (r. 1589–1610).

Henry IV came to the throne as a *politique*, weary of religious strife and prepared to place political peace above absolute religious unity. He believed that a royal policy of tolerant Catholicism would be the best way to achieve such peace. On July 25, 1593, he publicly abjured the Protestant faith and embraced the traditional and majority religion of his country. "Paris is worth a Mass," he is reported to have said.

THE EDICT OF NANTES Five years later, on April 13, 1598, Henry IV's famous Edict of Nantes proclaimed a formal religious settlement. In 1591 he had already assured the Huguenots of at least qualified religious freedoms. The Edict of Nantes made good that promise. It recognized and sanctioned minority religious rights within what was to remain an officially Catholic country. This religious truce—and it was never more than that—granted the Huguenots, who by this time numbered well over a million, freedom of public worship, the right of assembly, admission to public offices and universities, and permission to maintain fortified towns. Most of the new freedoms, however, were to be exercised within their own localities. Concession of the right to fortify towns reveals the continuing distrust between French Protestants and Catholics. The edict only transformed a long hot war between irreconcilable enemies into a long cold war. To its critics, it created a state within a state.

A Catholic fanatic assassinated Henry IV in May 1610. Although Henry is best remembered for the Edict of Nantes, the political and economic policies he put in place were equally important. They laid the foundations for the transformation of France into the absolutist state it would become in the seventeenth century. Ironically, in pursuit of the political and religious unity that had escaped Henry IV, his grandson Louis XIV (r. 1643–1715), calling for "one king, one church, one law," would later revoke the Edict of Nantes in 1685 (see Chapter 20). This action would force France and Europe to learn again by bitter experience the hard lessons of the wars of religion. Rare is the politician who learns from the lessons of history rather than repeat its mistakes.

Imperial Spain and the Reign of Philip II (1556–1598)

Until the English defeated his mighty Armada in 1588, no one person stood larger in the second half of the sixteenth century than Philip II of Spain. During the first half of his reign, attention focused on the Mediterranean and Turkish expansion. On October 7, 1571, a Holy League of Spain, Venice, and the pope defeated the Turks at Lepanto in the largest naval battle of the sixteenth century. Before the engagement ended, thirty thousand Turks had died and over one third of the Turkish fleet was sunk or captured.

Map 16–4 The Netherlands during the Reformation. The northern provinces of the Netherlands—the United Provinces—were mostly Protestant in the second half of the sixteenth century. The southern provinces—the Spanish Netherlands—made peace with Spain and remained largely Catholic.

REVOLT IN THE NETHERLANDS The spectacular Spanish military success in southern Europe was not repeated in northern Europe when Philip attempted to impose his will within the Netherlands and on England and France. The resistance of the Netherlands especially proved the undoing of Spanish dreams of world empire.

The Netherlands were the richest area in Europe (see Map 16–4). The merchant towns of the Netherlands were however, Europe's most independent; many, like magnificent Antwerp, were also Calvinist strongholds. A stubborn opposition to the Spanish overlords formed under William of Nassau, the Prince of Orange (r. 1533–1584). Like other successful rulers in this period, William of Orange was a *politique* who placed the Netherlands' political autonomy and well-being above religious creeds. He personally passed through successive Catholic, Lutheran, and Calvinist stages.

The year 1564 saw the first fusion of political and religious opposition to Spanish rule, the result of Philip II's unwise insistence that the decrees of the Council of Trent be enforced throughout the Netherlands. A national covenant was drawn up called the Compromise, a solemn pledge to resist the decrees of Trent and the Inquisition.

Philip dispatched the Duke of Alba (1508–1582) to suppress the revolt. His army of ten thousand men marched northward from Milan in 1567 in a show of combined Spanish and papal might. A special tribunal, known to the Spanish as the Council of Troubles and among the Netherlanders as the Council of Blood, reigned over the land. Several thousand suspected heretics were publicly executed before Alba's reign of terror ended.

William of Orange had been an exile in Germany during these turbulent years. He now emerged as the leader of a broad movement for the Netherlands' independence from Spain.

After a decade of persecution and warfare, the ten largely Catholic southern provinces (what is roughly modern Belgium) came together in 1576 with the seven largely Protestant northern provinces (what is roughly the modern Netherlands) in unified opposition to Spain. This union, known as the Pacification of Ghent, declared internal regional sovereignty in matters of religion. It was a Netherlands version of the Peace of Augsburg.

After more fighting, in January 1579 the southern provinces formed the Union of Arras and made peace with Spain. The northern provinces responded with the formation of the Union of Utrecht and continued the struggle. Spanish preoccupation with France and England in the 1580s permitted the northern provinces to drive out all Spanish soldiers by 1593. In 1596 France and England formally recognized the independence of these provinces. However, the northern provinces did not formally conclude peace with Spain until 1609, when the Twelve Years' Truce concluded their virtual independence. But Spain did not fully recognize that independence until the Peace of Westphalia in 1648.

Elizabeth I (1558–1603) standing on a map of England in 1592. An astute, if sometimes erratic, politician in foreign and domestic policy, Elizabeth was one of the most successful rulers of the sixteenth century. National Portrait Gallery, London

ENGLAND AND SPAIN (1558–1603)

ELIZABETH I Elizabeth I (r. 1558–1603), the daughter of Henry VIII and Anne Boleyn, was perhaps the most astute politician of the sixteenth century in both domestic and foreign policy. She repealed the anti-Protestant legislation of her predecessor Mary Tudor and guided a religious settlement through Parliament that prevented England from being torn asunder by religious differences in the sixteenth century, as the Continent was.

Catholic extremists hoped to replace Elizabeth with the Catholic Mary Stuart, Queen of Scots. But Elizabeth acted swiftly against Catholic assassination plots and rarely let emotion override her political instincts.

Elizabeth dealt cautiously with the Puritans, Protestants who sought to "purify" the national church of every vestige of "popery" and to make its Protestant doctrine more precise. The Puritans had two special grievances: (1) the retention of Catholic ceremony and vestments within the Church of England, and (2) the continuation of the episcopal system of church governance.

Sixteenth-century Puritans were not separatists, however. They worked through Parliament to create an alternative national church of semiautonomous congregations governed by representative presbyteries (hence, Presbyterians), following the model of Calvin and Geneva. The more extreme Puri-

MAP EXPLORATION

Interactive map: To explore this map further, go to http://www.prenhall.com/craig_map16.5

Map 16–5 Religious division ca. 1600. By 1600 few could expect Christians to return to a uniform religious allegiance. In Spain and southern Italy Catholicism remained relatively unchallenged, but note the existence elsewhere of large religious minorities, both Catholic and Protestant.

tans wanted every congregation to be autonomous, a law unto itself, with no higher control. They came to be known as Congregationalists. Elizabeth refused to tolerate this group, whose views she considered subversive.

DETERIORATION OF RELATIONS WITH SPAIN A series of events led inexorably to war between England and Spain, despite the sincere desires of both Philip II and Elizabeth to avoid it. Following Spain's victory at Lepanto in 1571, England signed a mutual defense pact with France. Also in the 1570s, Elizabeth's famous seamen, John Hawkins (1532–1595) and Sir Francis Drake (?1545–1596), began to prey regularly on Spanish shipping in the Americas. Drake's circumnavigation of the globe between 1577 and 1580 was one in a series of dramatic demonstrations of English ascendancy on the high seas. In 1585 Elizabeth signed a treaty that committed English soldiers to the Netherlands. These events made

Map 16–6 The Holy Roman Empire ca. 1618. On the eve of the Thirty Years' War the empire was politically and religiously fragmented, as this somewhat simplified map reveals. Lutherans dominated the north and Catholics the south, while Calvinists controlled the United Provinces and the Palatinate and also had an important presence in Switzerland and Brandenburg.

a tinderbox of English-Spanish relations. The spark that finally touched it off was Elizabeth's reluctant execution of Mary, Queen of Scots (1542–1587) on February 18, 1587, for complicity in a plot to assassinate Elizabeth. Philip II ordered his Armada to make ready.

On May 30, 1588, a mighty fleet of 130 ships bearing 25,000 sailors and soldiers under the command of the Duke of Medina-Sidonia set sail for England. But the day belonged completely to the English. The barges that were to transport Spanish soldiers from the galleons onto English shores were prevented from leaving Calais and Dunkirk. The swifter English and Netherlands ships, assisted by an "English wind," dispersed the waiting Spanish fleet, over a third of which never returned to Spain. The Armada's defeat gave heart to Protestant resistance everywhere. Spain never fully recovered from it. By the time of Philip's death on September 13, 1598, his forces had been rebuffed by the French and the Dutch. His seventeenth-century successors were all inferior leaders who never knew responsibilities equal to Philip's; nor did Spain ever again know such imperial grandeur. The French soon dominated the Continent, while the Dutch and the English whittled away Spain's overseas empire.

Elizabeth died on March 23, 1603, leaving behind her a strong nation poised to expand into a global empire.

THE THIRTY YEARS' WAR (1618–1648)

The Thirty Years' War in the Holy Roman Empire was the last and most destructive of the wars of religion. Religious and political differences had long set Catholics against Protestants and Calvinists against Lutherans. What made the Thirty Years' War so devastating was the now entrenched hatred of the various sides and their seeming determination to sacrifice all for their territorial sovereignty and religious beliefs. As the conflicts multiplied, virtually every major European land became involved either directly or indirectly. When the hostilities ended in 1648, the peace terms shaped much of the map of northern Europe as we know it today.

FRAGMENTED GERMANY During the second half of the sixteenth century, Germany was an almost ungovernable land of 360 autonomous political entities. The Peace of Augsburg (1555) had given each a significant degree of sovereignty within its own borders. Each levied its own tolls and tariffs and coined its own money, practices that made land travel and trade between the various regions difficult, where not impossible. Many of these little "states" also had great power pretensions. Political decentralization and fragmentation characterized Germany as the seventeenth century opened; it was not a unified nation like Spain, England, or even strife-torn France.

RELIGIOUS DIVISION Religious conflict accentuated the international and internal political divisions (see Map 16–5). The Holy Roman Empire was about equally divided between Catholics and Protestants, the latter having perhaps a slight numerical edge by 1600 (see Map 16–6). The terms of the Peace of Augsburg (1555) had attempted to freeze the territorial holdings of the Lutherans and the Catholics. In the intervening years, however, the Lutherans had gained political control in many Catholic areas, as had the Catholics in a few previously Lutheran areas. There was also religious strife between liberal and conservative Lutherans and between Lutherans and the growing numbers of Calvinists.

As elsewhere in Europe, Calvinism was the political and religious leaven within the Holy Roman Empire. Unrecognized as a legal religion by the Peace of Augsburg, Calvinism established a strong foothold within the empire when Elector Frederick III (r. 1559–1576), a devout convert to Calvinism, made it the official religion within the Palatinate in 1559. By 1609 Palatine Calvinists headed a Protestant defensive alliance supported by Spain's sixteenth-century enemies: England, France, and the Netherlands.

If the Calvinists were active within the Holy Roman Empire, so also were their Catholic counterparts, the Jesuits. Staunchly Catholic Bavaria, supported by Spain, became militarily and ideologically for the Counter-Reformation what the Palatinate was for Protestantism. From Bavaria, the Jesuits launched successful missions throughout the empire. In 1609 Maximilian, Duke of Bavaria (1573–1651), organized a Catholic League to counter a new Protestant alliance that had been formed by the Calvinist Elector Palatine, Frederick IV (r. 1583–1610). When the league fielded a great army under the command of Jean't Senclaes, Count of Tilly, (1559–1632), the stage was set, internally and internationally, for the Thirty Years' War, the worst European catastrophe since the Black Death of the fourteenth century.

THE TREATY OF WESTPHALIA In 1648 all hostilities within the Holy Roman Empire were brought to an end by the Treaty of Westphalia. It firmly reasserted the major feature of the religious settlement of the Peace of Augsburg (1555), as rulers were again permitted to determine the religion of their lands. The treaty also gave the Calvinists their long-sought legal recognition while still denying it to sectarians. The independence of the Swiss Confederacy and the United Provinces of Holland, long recognized in fact, now became law.

By confirming the territorial sovereignty of Germany's many political entities, the Treaty of Westphalia perpetuated German division and political weakness into the modern period. However, two German states attained international significance during the seventeenth century: Austria and Brandenburg-Prussia. The petty regionalism within the empire also reflected on a small scale the drift of larger European politics. During the seventeenth century distinctive nation-states, each with its own political, cultural, and religious identity, reached maturity and firmly established the competitive nationalism of the modern world.

SUPERSTITION AND ENLIGHTENMENT: THE BATTLE WITHIN

Religious reform and warfare permanently changed religious institutions in major European lands. They also moved intellectuals to rethink human nature and society.

One side of that reconsideration was dark and cynical, perhaps because the peak years of religious warfare had also been those of the great European witch hunts. Another side, however, was brilliantly skeptical and constructive, reflecting the growing scientific movement of the years between 1500 and 1700.

WITCH HUNTS AND PANIC

Nowhere is the dark side of the period better seen than in the witch hunts and panics that erupted in almost every western land. Between 1400 and 1700, courts sentenced an estimated seventy to one hundred thousand people to death for harmful magic (*malificium*) and diabolical witchcraft. In addition to inflicting harm on their neighbors, these witches were said to attend mass meetings known as sabbats, to which they were believed to fly. They were also accused of indulging in sexual orgies with the devil, who appeared in animal form, most often as a he-goat. Still other charges against them were cannibalism (they were alleged to be especially fond of small Christian children) and a variety of ritual acts and practices designed to insult every Christian belief and value.

Where did such beliefs come from, and how could seemingly enlightened people believe them? Their roots were in society at large, in both popular and elite cultures, especially the clergy.

VILLAGE ORIGINS In village societies, so-called cunning folk played a positive role in helping people cope with calamity. People turned to them for help in the face of natural disasters or physical disabilities. The cunning folk provided consolation and gave people hope that such calamities might be averted or reversed by magical means. They thus provided an important service and kept village life moving forward.

Possession of magical powers, for good or ill, made one an important person within village society. Not surprisingly, claims to such powers most often were made by the people most in need of security and influence—namely, the old and the impoverished, especially single or widowed women. Witch beliefs in village society may also have been a way of defying urban Christian society's attempts to impose its laws and institutions on the countryside. From this perspective, village Satanism became a fanciful substitute for an impossible social revolt, a way of spurning the values of one's new masters. It is also possible, although unlikely, that witch beliefs in rural society had a foundation in local fertility cults, whose semipagan practices, designed to ensure good harvests, may have acquired the features of diabolical witchcraft under church persecution.

INFLUENCE OF THE CLERGY Popular belief in magic was the essential foundation of the great witch hunts of the sixteenth and seventeenth centuries. Yet the contribution of learned society was equally great. The Christian clergy also practiced magic, that of the holy sacraments, and the exorcism of demons was one of their traditional functions within society. Fear of demons and the devil, which the clergy actively encouraged, allowed them to assert their moral authority and enforce religious conformity.

In the late thirteenth century the church declared that only its priests possessed legitimate magical power. Since such power was not human, theologians reasoned, it had to come either from God or from the devil. If it came from God, then it was properly confined to and exercised only by the church. Those who practiced magic outside the church evidently derived their power from the devil. From such reasoning grew accusations of "pacts" between non-Christian magicians and Satan.

The church based its intolerance of magic outside its walls on sincere belief in and fear of the devil. But attacking witches was also a way for established Christian society to extend its power and influence into new areas. To accuse, try, and execute witches was also a declaration of moral and political authority over a village or territory. As the cunning folk were local spiritual authorities, revered and feared by people, their removal became a major step in establishing a Christian beachhead in village society.

WHY WOMEN? A good eighty percent of the victims of witch hunts were women, most single and between forty-five and sixty years of age. This has suggested to some that misogyny fueled the witch hunts. Based on male hatred and sexual fear of women, and occurring at a time when women threatened to break out from under male control, witch hunts, it has been argued, were simply woman hunts. Older single women may, however, have been vulnerable for more basic social reasons. They were a largely dependent social group in need of public assistance and natural targets for the "social engineering" of the witch hunts. Some accused witches were women who sought to protect and empower themselves within their communities by claiming supernatural powers.

However, gender may have played a largely circumstantial role. Because of their economic straits, more women than men laid claim to the supernatural powers that made them influential in village society. They thus found themselves on the front lines in disproportionate numbers when the church declared war against all who practiced magic without its blessing. Also, the involvement of many of these women in midwifery associated them with the deaths of beloved wives and infants and thus made them targets of local resentment and accusations. Both the church and their neighbors were prepared to think and say the worst about these women. It was a deadly combination.

Art and the World

Warring Architectural Styles: Baroque versus Plain Churches

Art and architecture portrayed the beliefs of different religious systems as effectively as did the latter's creeds and laws. The Swiss, French, and English churches that grew out of the Reformed Protestant traditions of Ulrich Zwingli and John Calvin together with the nonconformist sectarian Protestants (Anabaptists, Puritans, Quakers) opposed both Catholic and Lutheran retention of traditional church art and architecture and of music in churches as a serious distraction from the Word of God. Although a much-praised musician, Zwingli could find no biblical basis for any ornamentation in a Christian service of worship. In this, he had the support not only of sectarians who condemned the more flexible Luther, but also of the humanist Erasmus. In Zwinglian, Calvinist, and sectarian churches across Europe, the walls were stripped bare, and congregational recitation of the Psalms was the only music.

Interior of "Asamkirche," Asam Cosmas Damian (1686–1739). Saint Nepomit Church in Munich designed by the brothers Cosmas Damian and Egid Quirin Asam in 1733. The church stands next to the house the brothers built for themselves.
Asamkirche (St. JohannNepomit). Erich Lessing/Art Resource, N.Y.

In Austria, southern Germany, and elsewhere, the Catholic Counter-Reformation, led by the Jesuits, embraced the exuberant baroque style of art and architecture then popular in Italy. This style grandly portrayed the Catholic faith in three dimensions, its impact magnified by choruses and musical instruments, the whole making for an artistic and musical feast. The intent was to overwhelm the worshipers' senses and move them emotionally, leaving them awed by the power and glory of their church. The new style reassured the doubting faithful and brought many who had turned Protestant back into Catholic churches.

Baroque style was also a boon to the building trades and the careers of painters, sculptors, and musicians. Great baroque artists like Peter Paul Rubens (1571–1640) and Gianlorenzo Bernini (1598–1680) were Catholics. But Protestants also had their great church architects, such as the Englishman Christopher Wren (1632–1723), and popular artists, such as the Dutch Mennonite Rembrandt van Rijn (1606–1669), whose works were distinguished by their simplicity and restraint. This eighteenth-century church, in Munich, is in the baroque style congenial to the Catholic Counter-Reformation. The interior explodes with energy. Sculpture, paintings and woodwork dazzle the eyes. The in-

Temple de Lyon. Biblitheque Publique et Universitaire, Geneve

tent was to give worshippers a keen sense of membership in the church militant and move them to self-transcendence.

In stark contrast to the Baroque style, this seventeenth-century Calvinist church in Lyon has no interior decoration to distract the worshiper from the Word of God. Here, the intent was to create an atmosphere of quiet introspection and reflection on one's own spiritual life in the presence of God's Word. For the Calvinists at worship in Lyon, the preacher is absolutely at center stage. There are no decorations, paintings, statuary, or elaborate stained glass. In Zwinglian churches the walls were even whitewashed, and no music or singing was permitted. Such simplicity contrasts dramatically with the baroque style of contemporary Catholic churches.

WITCH PANICS Political self-aggrandizement also played a role. As governments expanded and attempted to control their realms, they, like the church, wanted to eliminate all competition for the loyalty of their subjects. Secular rulers as well as the pope could pronounce their competitors "devilish."

Some also argue that the Reformation was responsible for the witch panics. Having weakened the traditional religious protections against demons and the devil, while still portraying them as powerful, the Reformation is said to have forced people to protect themselves by executing perceived witches.

END OF THE WITCH HUNTS Many factors helped end the witch hunts. The emergence of a new, more scientific worldview made it difficult to believe in the powers of witches. When in the seventeenth century mind and matter came to be viewed as two independent realities, words and thoughts lost the ability to affect things. A witch's curse was merely words. With advances in medicine and the beginning of insurance companies, people learned to rely on themselves when faced with natural calamity and physical affliction; they no longer searched for supernatural causes and solutions. Witch hunts also tended to get out of hand. Accused witches sometimes alleged that important townspeople had also attended sabbats; even the judges could be so accused. At this point the trials ceased to serve the purposes of those who were conducting them. They not only became dysfunctional but threatened anarchy as well.

Although Protestants, like Catholics, hunted witches, the Reformation may also have contributed to an attitude of mind that put the devil in a more manageable perspective. Protestants ridiculed the sacramental magic of the old church as superstition and directed their faith to a sovereign God absolutely supreme over time and eternity. Even the devil was believed to serve God's purposes and acted only with his permission. Ultimately God was the only significant spiritual force in the universe. This belief made the devil a less fearsome creature. "One little word can slay him," Luther wrote of the devil in "A Mighty Fortress Is Our God," the great hymn of the Reformation.

Miguel de Cervantes Saavedra (1547–1616), the author of *Don Quixote*, considered by many to be Spain's greatest writer.
Art Resource, N.Y.

WRITERS AND PHILOSOPHERS

By the end of the sixteenth century, many could no longer embrace either old Catholic or new Protestant absolutes. Intellectually as well as politically, the seventeenth century would be a period of transition, one already well prepared by the humanists and scientists of the Renaissance and post-Renaissance (see Chapter 24), who reacted strongly against medieval intellectual traditions.

The writers and philosophers of the late sixteenth and the seventeenth centuries were aware that they lived in a period of transition. Some embraced the emerging new science wholeheartedly (Hobbes and Locke), some tried to straddle the two ages (Cervantes and Shakespeare), and still others ignored or opposed the new developments that seemed mortally to threaten traditional values (Pascal).

MIGUEL DE CERVANTES SAAVEDRA Spanish literature of the sixteenth and seventeenth centuries was influenced by the peculiar religious and political history of Spain in this period. Spain was dominated by the Catholic Church, whose piety was strongly promoted by the state. The intertwining of Catholic piety and Spanish political power underlay literary preoccupation with medieval chivalric virtues—in particular, honor and loyalty.

Generally acknowledged to be the greatest Spanish writer of all time, Cervantes (1547–1616) was preoccupied in his work with the strengths and weaknesses of religious idealism. He was the son of a nomadic physician. Having received only a smattering of formal education, he educated himself by insatiable reading in vernacular literature and immersion in the school of life. As a young man, he worked in Rome for a Spanish cardinal. In 1570 he became a soldier and was decorated for gallantry at Lepanto (1571). He conceived and began to write his most famous work, *Don Quixote*, in 1603, while languishing in prison after conviction for theft.

The first part of *Don Quixote* appeared in 1605, and a second part in 1615. If, as many argue, the intent of this work was to satirize the chivalric romances so popular in Spain, Cervantes failed to conceal his deep affection for the character he had created as an object of ridicule, Don Quixote. Don Quixote, a none-too-stable middle-aged man, is driven mad by reading too many chivalric romances. He comes to believe that he is an aspirant to knighthood and must prove his worthiness. To this end, he acquires a rusty suit of armor, mounts an aged horse, and chooses for his inspiration a quite unworthy peasant girl whom he fancies to be a noble lady to whom he can, with honor, dedicate his life.

Don Quixote's foil in the story—Sancho Panza, a clever, worldly-wise peasant who serves as his squire—watches with bemused skepticism, but also with genuine sympathy, as his lord does battle with a windmill (which he mistakes for a dragon) and repeatedly makes a fool of himself as he gallops across the countryside. The story ends tragically with Don Quixote's humiliating defeat by a well-meaning friend, who, disguised as a knight, bests Don Quixote in combat and forces him to renounce his quest for knighthood. The humiliated Don Quixote does not, however, come to his senses as a result. He returns sadly to his village to die a shamed and broken-hearted old man.

Throughout *Don Quixote*, Cervantes juxtaposed the down-to-earth realism of Sancho Panza with the old-fashioned religious idealism of Don Quixote. Cervantes admired the one as much as the other. He wanted his readers to remember that to be truly happy, men and women need dreams, even impossible ones, just as much as a sense of reality.

WILLIAM SHAKESPEARE There is much less factual knowledge about William Shakespeare (1564–1616), the greatest playwright in the English language, than one would expect of such an important figure. He apparently worked as a schoolteacher for a time and in this capacity acquired his broad knowledge of Renaissance learning and literature. His work shows none of the Puritan distress over worldliness. He took the new commercialism and the bawdy pleasures of the Elizabethan Age in stride and with amusement. In politics and religion, he was a man of his time and not inclined to offend his queen.

That Shakespeare was interested in politics is apparent from his history plays and the references to contemporary political events that fill all his plays. He seems to have viewed government simply, however, through the character of the individual ruler, whether Richard III or Elizabeth Tudor, not in terms of ideal systems or social goals. By modern standards he was a political conservative, accepting the social rankings and the power structure of his day and demonstrating unquestioned patriotism.

Shakespeare knew the theater as one who participated in every phase of its life. A member and principal dramatist of a famous company of actors known as the King's Men, he was a playwright, actor, and part owner of a theater. His work brought together in an original synthesis the best past and current achievements in the dramatic arts. He particularly mastered the psychology of human motivation and passion and had a unique talent for psychological penetration.

Shakespeare wrote histories, comedies, and tragedies. The tragedies are considered his unique achievement. Four of these were written within a three-year period: *Hamlet* (1603), *Othello* (1604), *King Lear* (1605), and *Macbeth* (1606). The most original of the tragedies, *Romeo and Juliet* (1597), transformed an old popular story into a moving drama of "star-cross'd lovers."

In his lifetime and ever since, Shakespeare has been immensely popular with both audiences and readers. As Ben Jonson (1572–1637), a contemporary classical dramatist who created his own school of poets, put it in a tribute affixed to the *First Folio* edition of Shakespeare's plays (1623): "He was not of an age, but for all time."

BLAISE PASCAL Blaise Pascal (1623–1662) was a French mathematician and a physical scientist widely acclaimed by his contemporaries. Torn between the continuing dogmatism and the new skepticism of the seventeenth century, he aspired to write a work that would refute both the Jesuits, whose casuistry (i.e., confessional tactics designed to minimize and even excuse sinful acts) he considered a distortion of Christian teaching, and the skeptics, who either denied religion altogether (atheists) or accepted it only as it conformed to reason (deists). Pascal never realized such a definitive work, and his views on these matters exist only in piecemeal form. He wrote against the Jesuits in his *Provincial Letters* (1656–1657), and he left behind a provocative collection of reflections on humankind and religion that was published posthumously under the title *Pensées.*

Pascal was early influenced by the Jansenists, seventeenth-century Catholic opponents of the Jesuits. Although good Catholics, the Jansenists shared with the Calvinists Saint Augustine's belief in the total sinfulness of human beings, their eternal predestination by God, and their complete dependence on faith and grace for knowledge of God and salvation.

Pascal believed that reason and science, although attesting to human dignity, remained of no avail in religion. Here only the reasons of the heart and a "leap of faith" could prevail. Pascal saw two essential truths in the Christian religion: that a loving God, worthy of human attainment, exists; and that human beings, because they are corrupted in nature, are utterly unworthy of God. Pascal believed that the atheists and deists of the age had spurned the lesson of reason. For him, rational analysis of the human condition attested to humankind's utter mortality and corruption and exposed the weakness of reason itself in resolving the problems of human nature and destiny. Reason should rather drive those who truly heed it to faith and dependence on divine grace.

Pascal made a famous wager with the skeptics. It is a better bet, he argued, to believe that God exists and to stake everything on his promised mercy than not to do so; if God does exist, everything will be gained by the believer, whereas the loss incurred by having believed in God should he prove not to exist is, by comparison, very slight.

Pascal was convinced that belief in God measurably improved earthly life psychologically and disciplined it morally, regardless of whether God proved in the end to exist. He thought that great danger lay in the surrender of traditional religious values. Pascal urged his contemporaries to seek self-understanding by "learned ignorance" and to discover humankind's greatness by recognizing its misery. Thereby he hoped to counter what he believed to be the false optimism of the new rationalism and science.

BARUCH SPINOZA The most controversial thinker of the seventeenth century was Baruch Spinoza (1632–1677), the son of a Jewish merchant of Amsterdam. Spinoza's philosophy caused his excommunication by his own synagogue in 1656. In 1670 he published his *Treatise on Religious and Political Philosophy*, a work that criticized the dogmatism of Dutch Calvinists and championed freedom of thought. During his lifetime, both Jews and Protestants attacked him as an atheist.

Spinoza's most influential writing, *Ethics*, appeared after his death in 1677. Religious leaders universally condemned it for its apparent espousal of pantheism. God and nature were so closely identified by Spinoza that little room seemed left either for divine revelation in Scripture or for the personal immortality of the soul, denials equally repugnant to Jews and to Christians.

The most controversial part of *Ethics* deals with the nature of substance and of God. According to Spinoza there is only one substance, which is self-caused, free, and infinite, and God is that substance. From this definition, it follows that everything that exists is in God and cannot even be conceived of apart from him. Such a doctrine is not literally pantheistic, because God is still seen to be more than the created world that he, as primal substance, embraces. Nonetheless, in Spinoza's view, statements about the natural world are also statements about divine nature. Mind and matter are seen to be extensions of the infinite substance of God; what transpires in the world of humankind and nature is a necessary outpouring of the Divine.

Such teaching clearly ran the danger of portraying the world as eternal and human actions as unfree and inevitable, the expression of a divine fatalism. Such points of view had been considered heresies by Jews and Christians because these views deny the creation of the world by God and destroy any voluntary basis for personal reward and punishment.

THOMAS HOBBES Thomas Hobbes (1588–1679) was the most original political philosopher of the seventeenth century. Although he never broke with the Church of England, he came to share basic Calvinist beliefs, especially the low view of human nature and the ideal of a commonwealth based on a covenant, both of which find eloquent expression in his political philosophy.

Hobbes was an urbane and much-traveled man and one of the most enthusiastic supporters of the new scientific movement. During the 1630s he visited Paris, where he came to know Descartes; after the outbreak of the Puritan Revolution (see Chapter 20) in 1640, he lived as an exile in Paris until 1651. Hobbes also spent time with Galileo (see Chapter 23) in Italy and took a special interest in the works of William Harvey. Harvey was a physiologist famed for the discovery of how blood circulated through the body; his scientific writings influenced Hobbes's own tracts on bodily motions.

Hobbes was driven to the vocation of political philosophy by the English Civil War (see Chapter 21). In 1651 his *Leviathan* appeared. Its subject was the political consequences of human passions, and its originality lay in (1) its making natural law, rather than common law (i.e., custom or precedent), the basis of all positive law, and (2) its defense of a representative theory of absolute authority against the theory of the divine right of kings. Hobbes maintained that statute law found its justification only as an expression of the law of nature and that rulers derived their authority from the consent of the people.

Hobbes viewed humankind and society in a thoroughly materialistic and mechanical way. Human beings are defined as a collection of material particles in motion. All their psychological processes begin with and are derived from bare sensation, and all their motivations are egotistical, intended to increase pleasure and minimize pain.

Despite this seemingly low estimate of human beings, Hobbes believed much could be accomplished by the reasoned use of science. All was contingent, however, on the correct use of that greatest of all human powers, one compounded of the powers of most people: the commonwealth, in which people are united by their consent in one all-powerful person.

The key to Hobbes's political philosophy is a brilliant myth of the original state of humankind. According to this myth, human beings in the natural state are generally inclined to a "perpetual and restless desire of power after power that ceases only in death."[6] As all people desire—and in the state of nature have a natural right to—everything, their equality breeds enmity, competition, and diffidence, and the desire for glory begets perpetual quarreling—"a war of every man against every man."[7]

Whereas earlier and later philosophers saw the original human state as a paradise from which humankind had fallen, Hobbes saw it as a corruption from which only society had delivered people. Contrary to the views of Aristotle and of Christian thinkers like Thomas Aquinas, Hobbes saw human beings not as sociable, political animals, but as self-centered beasts, laws unto themselves, utterly without a master unless one is imposed by force.

According to Hobbes, people escape the impossible state of nature only by entering a social contract that creates a commonwealth tightly ruled by law and order. The social contract obliges every person, for the sake of peace and self-defense, to agree to set aside personal rights to all things. We should impose restrictions on the liberty of others only to the degree that we would allow others to restrict our own.

Because words and promises are insufficient to guarantee this state, the social contract also establishes the coercive force necessary to compel compliance with the covenant. Hobbes believed that the dangers of anarchy were far greater than those of tyranny, and he conceived of the ruler's power as absolute and unlimited. There is no room in Hobbes's political philosophy for political protest in the name of individual conscience, nor for resistance to legitimate authority by private individuals—features of *Leviathan* criticized by his contemporary Catholics and Puritans alike.

[6] *Leviathan Parts I and II*, ed. by H. W. Schneider (Indianapolis: Bobbs-Merrill, 1958), p. 86.

[7] Ibid., p. 106.

JOHN LOCKE John Locke (1632–1704) has proved to be the most influential political thinker of the seventeenth century.[8] His political philosophy came to be embodied in the so-called Glorious Revolution of 1688–1689 (Chapter 20). Although he was not as original as Hobbes, his political writings were a major source of the later Enlightenment criticism of absolutism, and they gave inspiration to both the American and French Revolutions.

Locke's two most famous works are the *Essay Concerning Human Understanding* (1690) (discussed in Chapter 23) and *Two Treatises of Government* (1690). Locke wrote *Two Treatises of Government* against the argument that rulers were absolute in their power. Rulers, Locke argued, remain bound to the law of nature, which is the voice of reason, teaching that "all mankind [are] equal and independent, [and] no one ought to harm another in his life, health, liberty, or possessions,"[9] inasmuch as all human beings are the images and property of God. According to Locke, people enter social contracts, empowering legislatures and monarchs to "umpire" their disputes, precisely to preserve their natural rights, and not to give rulers an absolute power over them.

"Whenever that end [namely, the preservation of life, liberty, and property for which power is given to rulers by a commonwealth] is manifestly neglected or opposed, the trust must necessarily be forfeited and the power devolved into the hands of those that gave it, who may place it anew where they think best for their safety and security."[10] From Locke's point of view, absolute monarchy was "inconsistent" with civil society and could be "no form of civil government at all."[11]

[8] Locke's scientific writings are discussed in Chapter 24.

[9] *The Second Treatise of Government*, ed. by T. P. Peardon (Indianapolis: Bobbs-Merrill, 1952), chap. 2, sects. 4–6, pp. 4–6.

[10] Ibid., chap. 13, sect. 149, p. 84.

[11] Ibid.

In World Perspective

THE RENAISSANCE AND REFORMATION

During the Renaissance, western Europe rediscovered its classical cultural heritage, from which it had been separated for almost eight centuries. No previous world civilization had experienced such alienation from its cultural past. The West owed the recovery of its heritage to the work of Byzantine and Islamic scholars. During the Renaissance, western European lands bound up the wounds of internal warfare and established permanent centralized states and regional governments. Even the great population losses of the fourteenth century were largely recovered by 1500. In the late fifteenth and the sixteenth centuries, Europeans sailed far from their own shores, reaching Africa, southern and eastern Asia, and the New World of the Americas. From Japan to Peru, they now directly confronted for the first time the civilizations of the world.

Western history between 1500 and 1650 was also powerfully shaped by an unprecedented schism in Christianity, as Protestant groups broke ranks with Rome. The religious divisions contributed to new national and international warfare, which by the seventeenth century had devastated the Holy Roman Empire on a scale unseen since the Black Death.

The other world civilizations moved less dynamically during these centuries, maintaining greater social and political unity and exhibiting a greater tolerance of religious differences. Under Mongol rule (1279–1368), China recognized all indigenous religions as well as Islam and Eastern Christianity. No crises on the scale of those that rocked the West struck China, although plagues between 1586 and 1589 and between 1639 and 1644 killed between a quarter and a third of the inhabitants in populous regions. China moved steadily from Mongol to Ming (1368–1644) to Ching (1644–1911) rule without any major social and political upheavals. Compared to the West, its society was socially stable and its rulers in sure, if despotic, control. While the West also had highly centralized and authoritarian governments between 1350 and 1650, the interests of citizens and subjects were arguably contested more vigorously and accommodated more successfully. That was particularly true in regional and urban governments, where parliaments, estates general, and city councils represented the interests of powerful noblemen, patricians, and well-to-do burghers. But lesser political bodies too, representing the rights of the middling and lower classes, also had recognized platforms for the expression of their grievances.

Although parallels may be drawn between the court culture of the Forbidden Palace in Beijing and that of King Louis XIV in seventeenth-century France, the Chinese government and its official religious philosophy of Confucianism remained more unified and patriarchal than their counterparts in the West. In China, there was never the same degree of political dissent and readiness to fragment society in the name of religion that existed in western societies, even during the West's "Age of Absolutism." On the other hand, the Chinese readily tolerated other religions, as their warm embrace of Jesuit missionaries attests. There is no similar Western demonstration of tolerance for Asian religious philosophy.

Voyages of exploration also set forth from Ming China, especially between 1405 and 1433, reaching India, the Arabian Gulf, and East Africa. These voyages did not, however, prove to be commercially profitable as those of the West would be, nor did they spark any notable commercial development in China. It is an open question whether this was because the Chinese were less greedy, curious, or belligerent than the Portuguese and Spanish.

Like the West in the late Middle Ages, Japan experienced its own political and social breakdown after 1467, when the *bakufu* government began to collapse. Japan's old manorial society progressively fell apart, and a new military class of vassalized foot soldiers, armed with spears and muskets, replaced the mounted samurai as the new military force. In 1590 Hideyoshi (r. 1536–1598) disarmed the peasantry and froze the social classes, thereby laying the foundation for a new social and political order in Japan. Building on this achievement, Tokugawa rule (1600–1850) managed to stabilize and centralize the government by 1650. Much as Western kings had to "domesticate" their powerful noblemen to succeed, Japanese rulers learned to integrate the many regional daimyo lords into government. Like Louis XIV, Tokugawa shoguns required these lords to live for long periods at court, where their wives and children also remained. As in most Western countries, the shoguns of Japan thus avoided both fragmented and absolutist government.

Like the Chinese, the Japanese were also admirers of the Jesuits, who arrived in Japan with the Portuguese in 1543. The admiration was mutual, leading to three hundred thousand Christian converts by 1600. As in China, the Jesuits treated native religion as a handmaiden and prelude to superior Christian teaching. But the tolerance of Christianity did not last as long in Japan as in China. Christianity was banned in the late sixteenth century as part of Hideyoshi's internal unification program. With the ascent of more-tolerant Confucianism over Buddhism among the Japanese ruling classes, Christianity and Western culture would again be welcomed in the nineteenth century.

During the age of Reformation in the West, absolutist Islamic military regimes formed in the Ottoman Empire, among the Safavids in Iran, and among the Mughals in India. In all three cultures religion became tightly integrated into government, so that they never knew the divisiveness and political challenge periodically prompted in the West by Christianity. In opposition to the expansive Ottomans, Shah Abbas I (r. 1588–1629) allied with the Europeans and welcomed Dutch and English traders. Embracing Shi'ite religion and the Persian language (the rest of the Islamic world was mostly Sunni and spoke Arabic or different regional languages), Iran progressively isolated itself. Unlike the west, the Timurid Empire of the Indian Mughals, particularly under Akbar the Great (r. 1556–1605), and extending into the late seventeenth century, encouraged religious toleration even to the point of holding discussions among different faiths at the royal court. Like China and Japan, India too was prepared to live with and learn from the West.

REVIEW QUESTIONS

1. What were the main problems of the church that contributed to the Protestant Reformation? Why was the church unable to suppress dissent as it had earlier?
2. How did the theologies of Luther, Zwingli, and Calvin differ? Were their differences only religious, or did they have political consequences for the Reformation as well?
3. Why did the Reformation begin in Germany and not in France, Italy, England, or Spain?
4. What was the Catholic Reformation? Did the Council of Trent alter the character of traditional Catholicism?
5. Why did Henry VIII break with the Catholic Church? Was the "new" religion he established really Protestant?
6. Were the wars of religion really over religion?
7. Henry of Navarre (later Henry IV of France), Elizabeth I, and William of Orange have been called *politiques.* What does that term mean, and how might it apply to each?
8. Why was England more successful than other lands in resolving its internal political and religious divisions peacefully during the sixteenth and seventeenth centuries?
9. "The Thirty Years' War is the outstanding example in European history of meaningless conflict." Evaluate this statement and provide specific reasons.

SUGGESTED READINGS

R. ASHCRAFT, *Revolutionary Politics and Locke's Two Treatises of Government* (1986). The most important study of Locke to appear in recent years.

R. H. BAINTON, *Here I Stand: A Life of Martin Luther* (1957). The most readable and positive biography of the reformer.

W. BOUWSMA, *John Calvin. A Sixteenth Century Portrait* (1988). Interpretation of Calvin against background of Renaissance intellectual history.

C. BOXER, *Four Centuries of Portuguese Expansion 1415–1825* (1961). A comprehensive survey by a leading authority.

F. BRAUDEL, *The Mediterranean and the Mediterranean World in the Age of Philip the Second,* vols. 1 and 2 (1976). A widely acclaimed work by a French master.

R. BRIGGS, *Witches and Neighbors: A History of European Witchcraft* (1996). Readable introduction.

K. C. BROWN, *Hobbes Studies* (1965). A collection of important essays.

E. CAMERON, *The European Reformation* (1990). Large synthesis of recent studies, with most attention given to the German Reformation.

J. DELUMEAU, *Catholicism Between Luther and Voltaire: A New View of the Counter Reformation* (1977). Programmatic essay for a new social history of the Counter-Reformation.

A. G. DICKENS, *The Counter Reformation* (1969). A brief narrative with pictures.

A. G. DICKENS, *The English Reformation* (1974). The best one-volume account.

B. DIEFENDORF, *Beneath the Cross: Catholics and Huguenots in Sixteenth Century Paris* (1991). Stresses the primary forces of popular religion in the French wars of religion.

G. DONALDSON, *The Scottish Reformation* (1960). A dependable, comprehensive narrative.

E. DUFFY, *The Stripping of the Altars* (1992). Strongest argument yet that there was no deep reformation in England.

R. DUNN, *The Age of Religious Wars 1559–1689* (1979). An excellent brief survey of every major conflict.

M. DURAN, *Cervantes* (1974). Detailed biography.

J. H. ELLIOTT, *Europe Divided 1559–1598* (1968). A direct, lucid narrative account.

G. R. ELTON, *Reformation Europe 1517–1559* (1966). Among the best short treatments, especially strong on political issues.

H. O. EVENNETT, *The Spirit of the Counter Reformation* (1968). An essay on the continuity of Catholic reform and its independence from the Protestant Reformation.

P. GEYL, *The Revolt of the Netherlands, 1555–1609* (1958). The authoritative survey.

HANS-JÜRGEN GOERTZ, *The Anabaptists* (1996). Best treatment of minority Protestants.

M. GREENGRASS, *The French Reformation* (1987). Summary account, pulling everything together succinctly.

C. HAIGH, *The English Reformation Revised* (1988). Argues that the English Reformation was less revolutionary than historians have traditionally argued.

M. HOLT, *The French Wars of Religion, 1562–1629* (1995). Scholarly appreciation of religious side of story

R. P. HSIA, *The German People and the Reformation* (1989). Collection illustrative of the new social history of the German Reformation.

H. JEDIN, *A History of the Council of Trent,* Vols. 1 and 2 (1957–1961). Comprehensive, detailed, and authoritative.

T. F. JESSOP, *Thomas Hobbes* (1960). A brief biographical sketch.

W. K. JORDAN, *Edward VI: The Young King* (1968). The basic biography.

R. KIECKHEFER, *European Witch Trials: Their Foundations in Popular and Learned Culture 1300–1500* (1976). One of the best treatments of the subject.

R. J. KNECHT, *The French Wars of Religion, 1559–1598* (1989).

A. KORS AND E. PETERS, EDS., *European Witchcraft, 1100–1700* (1972).

P. LASLETT, *Locke's Two Treatises of Government,* 2nd ed. (1970). Definitive texts with very important introductions.

CARTER LINDBERG, *The European Reformations* (1996). New survey with traditional strengths and clarity.

A. MACFARLANE, *The Family Life of Ralph Josselin: A Seventeenth Century Clergyman* (1970). Exemplary family history.

J. MCNEILL, *The History and Character of Calvinism* (1954). The most comprehensive account, very readable.

G. MATTINGLY, *The Armada* (1959). A masterpiece, novel-like in style.

H. C. E. MIDELFORT, *The Mad Princes of Renaissance Germany* (1996).

K. MOXLEY, *Peasants, Warriors, and Wives* (1989). The English Reformation through popular art.

C. G. NAUERT, JR., *Humanism and the Culture of Renaissance Europe* (1995). Lucid up-to-date overview.

J. E. NEALE, *The Age of Catherine de Medici* (1962). A short, concise summary.

J. W. O'MALLEY, *The First Jesuits* (1993). Extremely detailed account of the creation of the Society of Jesus and its original purposes.

S. OZMENT, *The Age of Reform 1250–1550: An Intellectual and Religious History of Late Medieval and Reformation Europe* (1980). Broad, lucid survey.

S. OZMENT, *When Fathers Ruled: Family Life in Reformation Europe* (1983). Effort to portray the constructive side of Protestant thinking about family relationships.

S. OZMENT, *Three Behaim Boys: Growing Up in Early Modern Germany* (1990). Teenagers and young adults in their own words.

S. OZMENT, *The Bürgermeister's Daughter: Scandal in a Sixteenth Century German Town* (1996). A woman's struggle for justice.

S. OZMENT, *Flesh and Spirit: Private Life in Early Modern Germany* (1998). The German family from courtship and marriage to sending a new adult generation into the world.

S. OZMENT, *Ancestors: The Loving Family in Old Europe* (2001). Readable discussion of changing views of the premodern family.

G. PARKER, *The Thirty Years' War* (1984). Large, lucid survey.

J. H. PARRY, *The Age of Reconnaissance* (1964). A comprehensive account of explorations from 1450 to 1650.

E. F. RICE, JR., *The Foundations of Early Modern Europe 1460–1559* (1970). A broad, succinct narrative.

J. H. M. SALMON, ED., *The French Wars of Religion: How Important Were the Religious Factors?* (1967). Scholarly debate over the relation between politics and religion.

J. J. SCARISBRICK, *Henry VIII* (1968). The best account of Henry's reign.

A. SOMAN, ED., *The Massacre of St. Bartholomew's Day: Reappraisals and Documents* (1974). The results of an international symposium on the anniversary of the massacre.

L. SPITZ, *The Religious Renaissance of the German Humanists* (1963). Comprehensive and entertaining.

G. STRAUSS, *Luther's House of Learning: The Indoctrination of the Young in the German Reformation* (1978). Account of Protestant efforts to rear children in the new faith, stressing the authoritarian elements.

G. STRAUSS, ED. AND TRANS., *Manifestations of Discontent in Germany on the Eve of the Reformation* (1971). A rich collection of sources for both rural and urban scenes.

R. H. TAWNEY, *Religion and the Rise of Capitalism* (1947). Advances beyond Weber's arguments relating Protestantism and capitalist economic behavior.

K. THOMAS, *Religion and the Decline of Magic* (1971). Something of a classic on the subject.

E. TROELTSCH, *The Social Teaching of the Christian Churches,* Vols. 1 and 2, trans. by Olive Wyon (1960).

M. WEBER, *The Protestant Ethic and the Spirit of Capitalism,* trans. by Talcott Parsons (1958). First appeared in 1904–1905; it has continued to stimulate debate over the relationship between religion and society.

C. V. WEDGWOOD, *The Thirty Years' War* (1939). Controversial, but basic.

C. V. WEDGWOOD, *William the Silent* (1944). An excellent political biography.

F. WENDEL, *Calvin: The Origins and Development of His Religious Thought,* trans. by Philip Mairet (1963). The best treatment of Calvin's theology.

M. WIESNER, *Working Women in Renaissance Germany* (1986). Sketch of women's opportunities in six German cities.

G. H. WILLIAMS, *The Radical Reformation* (1962). A broad survey of the varieties of dissent within Protestantism.

H. WUNDER, *He Is the Sun, She Is the Moon: Women in Early Modern Germany* (1998). The best book in any language on the subject to date.

DOCUMENTS CD-ROM

1. Christopher Columbus: The Letters of Columbus to Ferdinand and Isabel
2. Erasmus, Julius II Excluded
3. Martin Luther: Ninety-Five Theses or Disputation on the Power and Efficacy of Indulgences
4. Luther versus Erasmus: A reformer's attack on free will
5. John Calvin and the Elect: The cool logic of salvation

WORLD AND THE WEB

Selected Works of Martin Luther

http://www.iclnet.org/pub/resources/text/wittenberg/wittenberg-luther.html

Project Wittenberg is home to works by and about Martin Luther and other Lutherans. It offers short quotations, commentaries, hymns, statements of faith, theological treatises, biographies, and links to other places where words and images from the history of Lutheranism live.

Thirty Years War Publications and Other Information

http://www.lukehistory.com/resources/30yrswar.html

This site contains seventeenth century, Thirty Years' War and English Civil War pamphlets, news sheets and other documents in full text format. Additionally, there are articles of interest to the reenactor, texts of blackletter ballads, bibliographies and links to other useful sites on the Internet.

Internet Archive of Texts and Documents

http://history.hanover.edu/texts.htm

The Internet Archive of Texts and Documents is a creation of faculty and students in the History Department of Hanover College. The principal goal of the archive is to make primary texts and secondary sources on the Internet available to students and faculty for use in history and humanity classes. This section includes the Italian Renaissance, the Protestant Reformation, the Catholic Reformation, and Witch Hunts.

The John Calvin Center

http://www.johncalvin.com/about.html

The Internet Calvin Center was created with the intention of being the most complete collection of John Calvin's writings ever published. Visitors interested in the theology of John Calvin are invited to use the files provided and participate in the discussion groups.

Le Poulet Gauche: The Wars of Religion, Part I

http://www.lepg.org/wars.htm

This website is a guide to the history, culture, and daily life of sixteenth-century France. Le Poulet Gauche exists in the context of the SCA (Society for Creative Anachronism), a group dedicated to historical recreation of the Middle Ages and the Renaissance.

Please go to http://www.prenhall.com/craig for the Technology and Civilization essay, "Navigating the Oceans: Antiquity to the Renaissance."

Religions of the World

CHRISTIANITY

The teaching of Jesus gave birth to Christianity. His simple message of faith in God and self-sacrificial love of one's neighbor attracted many people whose religious needs were not adequately met by the philosophies and religions of the ancient world. After Jesus' crucifixion, his devout followers proclaimed his resurrection and expected him to return in glory, defeat sin and evil, and take them away with him to heaven—a radical vision of judgment and immortality that also heightened Christianity's initial appeal. In the writings of St. Paul and the teachings of the early church, Jesus became the Christ, the son of God, the long-awaited Messiah of Jewish prophecy. According to John's gospel, Jesus was also the *logos*, the eternal principle of all being, after which the thinkers of antiquity had quested. Christianity thus offered people something more than philosophy, law, and ritual.

Christianity proclaimed the very incarnation of God in a man, the visible presence of eternity in time. According to early Christian teaching, the power of God's incarnation in Jesus lived on in the preaching and sacraments of the church under the guidance of the Holy Spirit. Christian thinkers here borrowed from the popular Asian cults of the Roman world, which had also offered their followers a sacramental participation in deity and spiritual redemption from sin. But Christianity went beyond them all when it declared the source of all being to be no longer transcendent and proclaimed the Messiah to have arrived. The Christian message was that, in Jesus, eternity had made itself accessible to every person here and now and forevermore.

The first Christians were drawn from among the rich and poor alike. People flocked to the new religion for both materialistic and deeply religious reasons. For some believers Christianity promised a better material life. But its appeal also lay in its unique ability to impart to people a sense of spiritual self-worth regardless of their place or prospects in society. The gospel of Jesus appealed to the hopelessly poor and powerless as readily as to the socially rising and well-to-do.

In the late second century the Romans began persecuting Christians both as "heretics" (because of their rejection of the traditional Roman gods) and as social revolutionaries.

The Annunciation. This scene, painted in 1430 by Fra Angelico, illustrates a passage from the Gospel of Luke (1:26 ff.): "The angel Gabriel was sent from God" to Mary "and said unto her, the Holy Ghost shall come upon thee, and the power of the Highest shall overshadow thee: therefore also that holy thing which shall be born of thee shall be called the Son of God." The impending redemption of humanity through Mary, the new Eve, and Christ, the new Adam, is juxtaposed with the fall of Adam and Eve and their expulsion from paradise (shown on the left). The beam of light represents the Holy Spirit. The small panels at the bottom illustrate scenes from the life of Mary. Joseph Martin/Bildarchiv Preussischer Kulturbesitz

At the same time dissenting Christians, particularly sects claiming a direct spiritual knowledge of God apart from Scripture, brought new internal divisions to the young church by advocating Christian heresies of their own. Such challenges had to be met, and by the fourth century effective weapons against both state terrorism and Christian heresy were in place: an ordained official clergy; a hierarchical church organization; orthodox creeds; and a biblical canon,

Women are entering the ministry and priesthood of many Christian denominations. The first woman bishop of the Episcopal Church of North America is here shown consecrating the Eucharist. The Church of England has also voted to admit women to the priesthood. Ira Wyman/Sygma

the New Testament. Christianity not only gained legal status within the Roman Empire, but, by the fourth century, was the favored religion of the emperor as well.

The fortune of Christianity after the fall of the Western Roman Empire in the fifth century C.E. is one of history's great success stories. Aided by the enterprise of its popes and the example of its monks, the church cultivated an appealing lay piety centered on the Lord's Prayer, the Apostles' Creed, veneration of the Virgin, and the sacrament of the Eucharist. Clergy became both royal teachers and bureaucrats within the kingdom of the Franks. Despite a growing schism between the Eastern (Byzantine) and Western churches, and a final split in 1054, by 1000 the church held real economic and political power. In the eleventh century reform-minded prelates ended secular interference in its spiritual affairs; the traditional lay practice of investing clergy in their offices was condemned under penalty of excommunication. For several centuries thereafter the church would remain a formidable international force, successfully challenging kings and emperors and inspiring crusades against the non-Christian world.

By the fifteenth century the new states of Europe had stripped the church of much of this political power. It would henceforth be progressively confined to its present role of spiritual and moral authority. Christianity's greatest struggles ever since have been not with kings and emperors over political power, but with materialistic philosophies and worldly ideologies, over spiritual and moral hegemony within an increasingly pluralistic and secular world. Since the sixteenth century a succession of Humanists, Skeptics, Deists, Rationalists, Marxists, Freudians, Darwinians, and atheists have attempted to explain away some of traditional Christianity's most basic teachings. In addition, the church has endured major internal upheaval. After the Protestant Reformation (1517–1555) made the Bible widely available to the laity, the possibilities for internal criticism of Christianity multiplied geometrically. Beginning with the split between Lutherans and Zwinglians in the 1520s, Protestant Christians have fragmented themselves into hundreds of sects, each claiming the true interpretation of Scripture. The Roman Catholic church, by contrast, has maintained its unity through these perilous times. However, present-day discontent with papal authority threatens the modern Catholic church almost as seriously as the Protestant Reformation once did.

But Christianity is nothing if not resilient. It continues to possess the simple, almost magically appealing gospel of Jesus. It finds itself within a world whose religious needs and passions still remain deep and basic, and like other religions, it has experienced a remarkable revival in recent decades. The Roman Catholic church, although troubled by conflicts over papal authority, has become far more pluralistic than in earlier periods. The pope has become a world figure, traveling to all continents to represent the church and advance its position on public issues. A major ecumenical movement emerging in the 1960s has promoted unprecedented cooperation among all Christian denominations. In the United States, many Protestant denominations have been politically active. Black ministers took the lead in the civil-rights struggle of the 1960s and continue to lend their voice and moral authority to issues of concern to the African American community. White fundamentalist clergy have frequently promoted conservative political agendas, turning to television to spread their messages. Catholics and Protestants alike have struggled with the role of women in the church.

17 Africa

CA. 1000–1800

A bronze plaque showing three warriors from Benin, West Africa. Note that the two small figures in the background apparently depict Portuguese or other European soldiers. Hillel Burger/Peabody Museum, Harvard University © President and Fellows of Harvard College. All rights reserved.

Chapter topics

- North Africa and Egypt
- The Spread of Islam South of the Sahara
- Sahelian Empires of the Western and Central Sudan
- The Eastern Sudan
- The Forestlands—Coastal West and Central Africa
- East Africa

In World Perspective
Africa, 1000–1800

THE HISTORY OF AFRICA IN THE FIRST HALF OF the second millennium C.E. varied considerably for different parts of the continent. Many African regions were little influenced by outsiders; others were strongly influenced by Europe and the Islamic world.

The Atlantic slave trade was the major phenomenon that affected almost all of Africa between the fifteenth and nineteenth centuries and is treated in Chapter 18. However, in this chapter we cannot overlook its importance in disrupting and reconfiguring African economies, social organization, and political life

We begin with Africa above the equator, where the influence of Islam increased and where substantial empires and kingdoms developed. Then we discuss west, east, central, and southern Africa and the effects of first Arab-Islamic and then European influence in these regions.

North Africa and Egypt

As we saw in Chapter 13., Egypt and other North African societies played a central role in Islamic and Mediterranean history after 1000 C.E. From Tunisia to Egypt, Sunni religious and political leaders and their Shi'ite, especially Isma'ili, counterparts struggled for the minds of the masses. By the thirteenth century, however, the Shi'ites had become a small minority of the Muslim population of Mediterranean Africa. In Egypt a Sunni revival confirmed the Sunni character of Egyptian religiosity and legal interpretation: In general, a feisty regionalism characterized states, city-states, and tribal groups north of the Sahara and along the lower Nile. No single power controlled them for long. Regionalism persisted even after 1500, when most of North Africa came under the influence—and often direct control—of the Ottoman Empire centered in Istanbul and felt the pressure of Ottoman–European naval rivalry in the Mediterranean.

By 1800 the nominally Ottoman domains from Egypt to Algeria were effectively independent. In Egypt the Ottomans had established direct rule after their defeat of the Mamluks in 1517, but by the seventeenth and eighteenth centuries, power had passed to Egyptian governors descended from the former ruling Mamluks. These Mamluk governors survived until the rise of Muhammad Ali in the wake of the French invasion of 1800 (see Chapter 28.). The Mediterranean coastlands between Egypt and Morocco were officially Ottoman provinces, or regencies. By the eighteenth century, however, Algiers was a separate, locally run principality with an economy based on piracy. Tripoli (in modern Libya) was ruled by a family of hereditary, effectively independent rulers, and Tunisia was virtually independent of its nominal Ottoman overlords.

Morocco, ruled by a succession of *Sharifs* (leaders claiming descent from the family of the Prophet Muhammad), was the only North African sultanate to remain fully independent after 1700. The most important *Sharifian* dynasty was that of the Sa'dis (1554–1659). One major reason for Morocco's independence was that its Arab and Berber populations united after 1500 to oppose the Portuguese and the Spaniards.

Feluccas on the Nile. These lateen-rigged sailing vessels are the traditional riverboats of Egypt and are still in use today.
Photograph by Eliot Elisofon, Courtesy of the Freer Gallery of Art, Smithsonian Institution, Washington, D.C.

THE SPREAD OF ISLAM SOUTH OF THE SAHARA

Islamic influence in sub-Saharan Africa began as early as the eighth century and by 1800 affected most of the Sudanic belt and the coast of East Africa as far south as modern Zimbabwe. The process was mostly peaceful, gradual, and partial. Islam rarely penetrated beyond the ruling or commercial classes and tended to coexist or blend with indigenous ideas and practices. Nevertheless, agents of Islam brought commercial and political changes as well as the Qur'an, new religious practices, and literate culture, which proved as important for subsequent history as any other development. Many innovations, from architecture and technology to intellectual life and administrative practice, depended on writing and literacy, two major bases for developing large-scale societies and cultures.

Comparison of the spread of Islam in West and central Africa with that in East Africa is instructive. In East Africa, Muslim traders moving down the coastline with the ancient monsoon trade routes had begun to "Islamize" ports and coastal regions even before 800 C.E. From the thirteenth century on, Islamic trading communities and city-states developed along the coast from Mogadishu to Kilwa.

By contrast, in the western and central parts of the continent, Islam penetrated south of the Sahara into the Sudan by overland routes, primarily from North Africa and the Nile valley. Yet as in East Africa, its agents were traders, chiefly Berbers who plied the desert routes (see Chapter 6) to trading towns such as Awdaghast on the edge of the Sahel, as early as the eighth century. From there Islam spread south to centers such as Kumbi and beyond, southeast across the Niger, and west into Senegambia. Another source for the gradual spread of Islam into the central and western Sudan was Egypt and the Nilotic Sudan. Its agents were primarily emigrants from the east seeking new land; migrating Arab tribal groups in particular came west to settle in the central sub-Saharan Sahel.

Some Muslim conversion in the western and central Sudan came early, again virtually always through the agency of Muslim traders. The year 985 marks the first time a West Africa royal court—that of the kingdom of Gao, east of the Niger bend—officially became Muslim (see Chapter 6. and below). The Gao rulers did not, however, try to convert their subjects. By contrast, as we shall see later in the chapter, the rulers of the later kingdom of Ghana long maintained their indigenous traditions even though they traded with Muslims and had Muslim advisers.

From the 1030s zealous militants known as Almoravids (see Chapter 14) began an overt conversion campaign that extended to the western Sahel and Sahara. This movement eventually swept into Ghana's territory, taking first Awdaghast and finally Kumbi in 1076. Thereafter, the forcibly converted Soninke ruling group of Ghana spread Islam among their own populace and farther south in the savannah. Here they converted Mande-speaking traders, who brought Islam south into the forests. Farther west, the Fulbe rulers of Takrur along the Senegal became Muslim in the 1030s and propagated their new faith among their subjects. The Fulbe, or Fulani, remained important carriers of Islam over the next eight centuries as they migrated gradually into new regions as far east as Lake Chad, where some rulers were Muslim as early as 1100.

Major groups in West Africa strongly resisted Islamization, especially the Mossi kingdoms founded in the Volta region at Wagadugu around 1050 and Yatenga about 1170.

The Djinguereber mosque in Timbuktu. This mud and wood building is typical of western Sudanese mosques. The distinctive tower of the mosque was a symbol of the presence of Islam, which came to places like Timbuktu in central and West Africa by way of overland trade routes. Photograph by Eliot Elisofon 1970, National Museum of African Art, Eliot Elisofon Archives, Smithsonian Institution, Washington, D.C. Neg. no. IV-9A.32

SAHELIAN EMPIRES OF THE WESTERN AND CENTRAL SUDAN

As we noted in Chapter 6, substantial states had risen in the first millennium C.E. in the Sahel regions just south of the Sahara proper.[1] From about 1000 to 1600, four of these developed into relatively long-lived empires: Ghana, Mali, and Songhai in the western Sudan, and Kanem-Bornu in the central Sudan.

GHANA

Ghana established the model for later empires of the Sahel region of the western Sudan. It was located well north of modern Ghana (and unrelated to it except by name) in the region between the inland Niger Delta and the upper Senegal to the north. A Ghanaian kingdom originated as early as 400–600 C.E., but Ghana emerged as a regional power only near the end of the first millennium and flourished for about two centuries. Its capital, Kumbi (or Kumbi Saleh), on the desert's edge, was well sited for the Saharan and Sahelian trade networks. Ghana's major population group was the Soninke. (*Ghana* is the Soninke term for "ruler.")

The Ghanaian rulers were matrilineally descended (through the previous king's sister). They ruled through a council of ministers. The reports we have, especially from the eleventh-century Muslim writer al-Bakri (see the box on p. 465), indicate that the king was supreme judge and held court regularly to hear grievances. The royal ceremonies reported to have been held in Kumbi Saleh were embellished with the full trappings of regal wealth and power appropriate to a king held to be divinely blessed if not semidivine himself.

Ghana's power rested on a solid economic base. Tribute from the empire's many chieftaincies and taxes on royal lands and crops supplemented duties levied on all incoming and outgoing trade. This trade, both north–south between the Sahara and the savannah and especially east–west through the Sahel between Senegambia and more easterly trading towns like Gao on the Niger Bend, involved a variety of goods—notably imported salt, cloth, and metal goods such as copper—probably in exchange for gold and perhaps kola nuts from the south. The regime apparently also controlled the gold (and, presumably, the slave) trade that originated in the savannah to the south and west, in the tributary regions of the Bambuk and Galam regions of the middle Senegal and its southern tributary, the Faleme, and in the Boure region of the upper Niger and its tributaries.

Although the king and court of Ghana did not convert to Islam, they made elaborate arrangements to accommodate Muslim traders and government servants in their own settlement a few miles from the royal preserve in Kumbi Saleh. Muslim traders were prominent in the court, literate Muslims administered the government, and Muslim legists advised the ruler. In Ghana's hierarchical society, slaves were at the bottom; farmers and draftsmen above them; merchants above them; and the king, his court, and the nobility on top.

A huge, well-trained army secured royal control and enabled the kings to extend their sway in the late tenth century to the Atlantic shore and to the south (see Map 17-1). Ghanaian troops captured Awdaghast, the important southern terminus of the trans-Saharan trade route to Morocco, from the Berbers in 992. The empire was, however, vulnerable to attack from the desert fringe, as Almoravid Berber forces proved in 1054 when they took Awdaghast in a single raid.

Ghana's empire was probably destroyed in the late twelfth century by the anti-Muslim Soso people from the mountains southeast of Kumbi Saleh, a Malinke clan who had long been part of the Ghanaian Empire. Their brief ascendancy between 1180 and 1230 apparently spelled the end of the once great transregional power centered at Kumbi.[2]

[1] S.K. and R.J. McIntosh, *Prehistoric Investigations at Jenne, Mali* (1980), pp. 41–59, 434–461; R. Oliver, *The African Experience* (New York: HarperCollins, 1991), pp. 90–101.

[2] D. Conrad and H. Fisher, "The Conquest That Never Was: Ghana and the Almoravids, 1076," *History in Africa 9* (1982): 1–59; 10 (1983): 53–78.

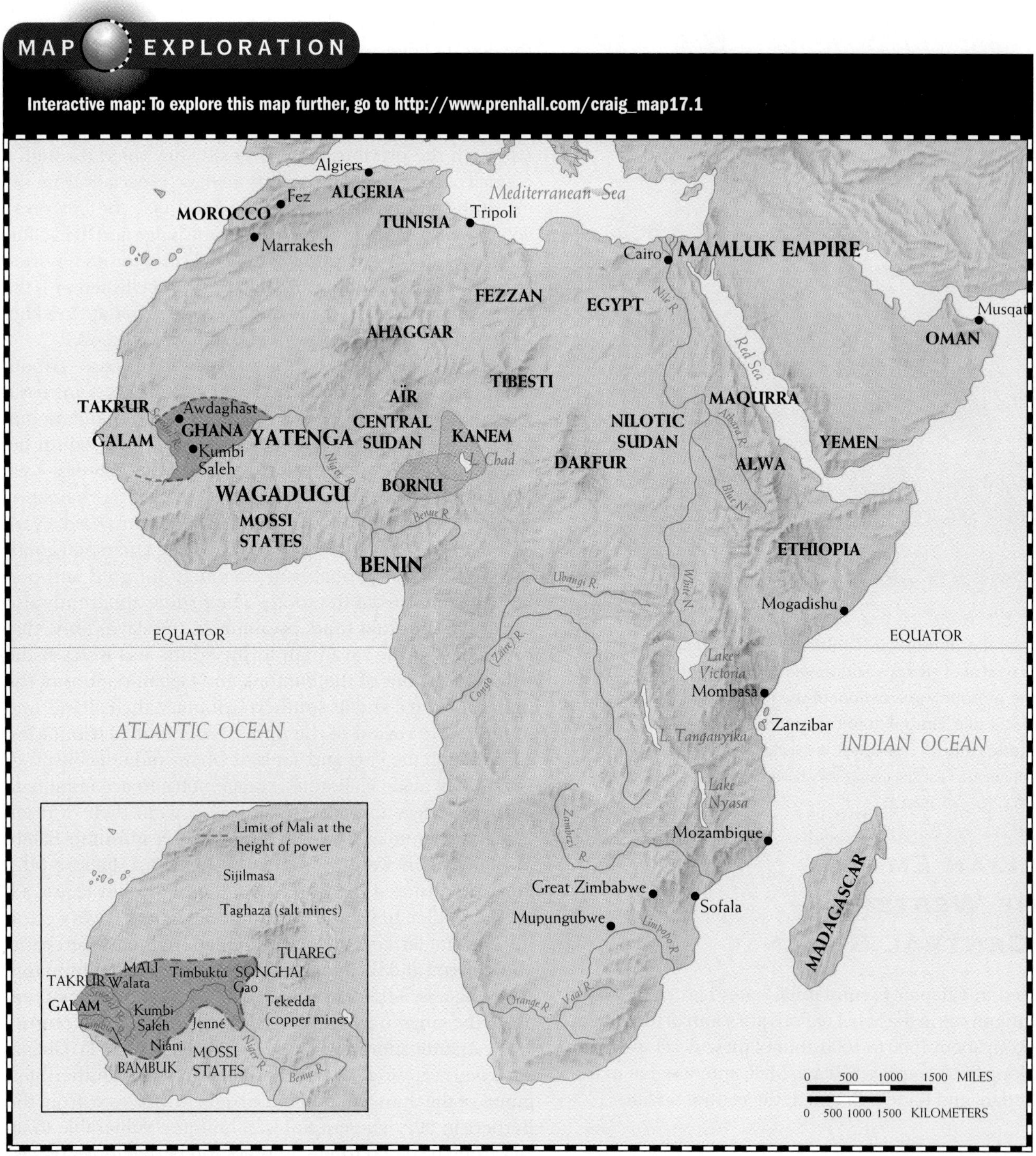

Map 17–1 Africa ca. 900–1500. Shown are major cities and states referred to in the text. The main map shows the region of West Africa occupied by the empire of Ghana from ca. 990 to ca. 1180. The inset shows the region occupied by Mali between 1230 and 1450.

MALI

With Ghana's collapse and the Almoravids' failure to build a new empire below the Sahara (largely because of their focus on North Africa), the western Sudan broke up into smaller kingdoms. The former Ghanaian provinces of Mande and Takrur were already independent before 1076, and in the early twelfth century Takrur's control of the Senegal valley and the gold-producing region of Galam made it briefly the strongest state in the western Sudan.

DOCUMENT GHANA AND ITS PEOPLE IN THE MID-ELEVENTH CENTURY

The following excerpt is from the geographical work of the Spanish Muslim geographer al-Bakri (d. 1094). In it he describes customs of the ruler and people of the capital of Ghana as he carefully gleaned them from other Arabic sources and travelers (he never visited West Africa himself, it seems).

How did the ruler of Ghana deal with the differing religious groups in his capital?

Ghana is a title given to their kings; the name of the region is Awkar, and their king today, namely in the year 460 [1067–8], is Tanka Manin. ... This Tanka Manin is powerful, rules an enormous kingdom, and possesses great authority.

The city of Ghana consists of two towns situated on a plain. One of these towns, which is inhabited by Muslims, is large and possesses twelve mosques, in one of which they assemble for the Friday prayer. There are salaried imams and muezzins, as well as jurists and scholars. In the environs are wells with sweet water, from which they drink and with which they grow vegetables. The king's town is six miles distant from this one and bears the name of Al-Ghaba. Between these two towns there are continuous habitations. The houses of the inhabitants are of stone and acacia (*sunt*) wood. The king has a palace and a number of domed dwellings all surrounded with an enclosure like a city wall (*sur*). In the king's town, and not far from his court of justice, is a mosque where the Muslims who arrive at his court ... pray. Around the king's town are domed buildings and groves and thickets where the sorcerers of these people, men in charge of the religious cult, live. In them too are their idols and the tombs of their kings. ...

All of them shave their beards, and women shave their heads. The king adorns himself like a woman [wearing necklaces] round his neck and [bracelets] on his forearms, and he puts on a high cap (*tartur*) decorated with gold and wrapped in a turban of fine cotton. He sits in audience or to hear grievances against officials (*mazalim*) in a domed pavilion around which stand ten horses covered with gold-embroidered materials. Behind the king stand ten pages holding shields and swords decorated with gold, and on his right are the sons of the [vassal] kings of his country wearing splendid garments and their hair plaited with gold. The governor of the city sits on the ground before the king and around him are ministers seated likewise. ... When the people who profess the same religion as the king approach him they fall on their knees and sprinkle dust on their heads, for this is their way of greeting him. As for the Muslims, they greet him only by clapping their hands.

Their religion is paganism and the worship of idols (*dakakir*). When their king dies they construct over the place where his tomb will be an enormous dome of saj wood. Then they bring him on a bed covered with a few carpets and cushions and place him beside the dome. At his side they place his ornaments, his weapons, and the vessels from which he used to eat and drink, filled with various kinds of food and beverages.

From J. F. P. Hopkins, trans.; N. Levtzion and J. F. P. Hopkins, eds., *Corpus of Early Arabic Sources for West African History*. Reprinted with permission of Cambridge University Press, pp. 79–80.

Like Ghana, however, it was soon eclipsed, first by the brief Soso ascendancy and then by the rise of Mali.

In the mid–thirteenth century the Keita ruling clan of a Ghanaian successor kingdom, Mali, forged a new and lasting empire. This empire seems to have been built on the same economic base as that of Ghana and Takrur earlier: monopolization of the lucrative north–south gold trade. The Keita kings dominated enough of the Sahel to control the flow of West African gold from the Senegal regions and the forest lands south of the Niger to the trans-Saharan trade routes, and the influx of copper and salt in exchange. Because they were farther south, in the fertile land along the Niger, than their Ghanaian predecessors had been, they were better placed to control all trade on the upper Niger and to add to it the Gambia and Senegal trade to the west. They also used captives for plantation labor in the Niger inland delta to produce surplus food for trade.

Agriculture and cattle farming were the primary occupations of Mali's population and, together with the gold trade, the mainstays of the economy. Rice was grown in the river valleys and millet in the drier parts of the Sahel. Together with beans, yams, and other agricultural products, this made for a plentiful food supply. Fishing flourished along the Niger and elsewhere. Cattle, sheep, and goats were plentiful. The chief craft specialties were metalworking (iron and gold) and weaving of cotton grown within the empire.

The Malinke, a southern Mande-speaking people of the upper Niger region, formed the core population of the new state. They apparently lived in walled urban settlements typical of the western savannah region. Each walled town was surrounded by its own agricultural land, held perhaps 1,000 to 15,000 people, and presumably had enough arable land within its walls to deal with siege. Each was linked to neighboring cities by trade and possibly intermarriage.

The Keita dynasty had converted early to Islam (ca. 1100) and even claimed descent from Muhammad's famous muezzin (the person who calls the faithful to worship), Bilal, a former black slave from Abyssinia whose son was said to have settled in the Mande-speaking region. During Mali's heyday in the thirteenth and fourteenth centuries, its kings often made the pilgrimage to Mecca. From their travel in the central Islamic lands, they brought back with them not

The great mosque at Jenne, one of the important commercial centers controlled by the empire of Mali in the 13th and 14th centuries. Ann Stalcup

only military aids, such as large Barbary war horses, but also new ideas about political and military organization. Through Muslim traders' networks, Islam also connected Mali to other areas of Africa, especially those to the east.

Mali's imperial power was built largely by the Keita King Sundiata (or Sunjaata, r. 1230–1255). Sundiata and his successors exploited their agricultural resources, significant population growth and Malinke commercial skills to build an empire even more powerful than that of Ghana. Sundiata extended his control west to the Atlantic coast and east beyond Timbuktu. By controlling the commercial entrepôts of Gao, Walata, and Jenne, he dominated the Saharan as well as the Niger trade. He built his capital, Niani, into a major city. Niani was located on a tributary of the Niger in the savannah at the edge of the forest in a gold- and iron-rich region. It had access to the forest trade products of gold, kola nuts, and palm oil; it was easily defended by virtue of its surrounding hills; and it was readily reached by river.

The empire that Sundiata and his successors built ultimately encompassed three major regions and language groups of Sudanic West Africa: (1) the Senegal region (including Takrur), occupied by speakers of the West Atlantic Niger-Kongo language group (including Fulbe, Tukulor, Wolof, Serer); (2) the central Mande states between Senegal and Niger, occupied by the Niger-Kongo-speaking Soninke and Mandinke peoples; and (3) the peoples of the Niger in the Gao region who spoke Songhai, the only Nilo-Saharan language west of the Lake Chad basin. Mali was less a centralized bureaucratic state than the center of a vast sphere of influence that included provinces and tribute-paying kingdoms. Many individual chieftaincies were independent but recognized the sovereignty of the supreme, sacred *mansa*, or "emperor," of the Malian realms.

The greatest Keita king proved to be Mansa Musa (r. 1312–1337), whose pilgrimage through Mamluk Cairo to Mecca in 1324 became famous. He paid out or gave away so much gold in Cairo alone that he started massive inflation lasting over a decade. He returned with many Muslim scholars, artists, and architects. At home, he consolidated Mali's power, securing peace for most of his reign throughout his vast dominions. Musa's devoutness as a Muslim fostered the spread of Islam in the empire and beyond. Under his rule, Timbuktu became famous for its *madrasas* and libraries, and for its poets, scientists, and architects, making it the leading intellectual center of sub-Saharan Islam and a major trading city of the Sahel—roles it retained long after Mali's imperial sway ended.

Mali's dominance waned after Musa, evidently as the result of rivalries for the throne. Eventually the empire withered, and after 1450 a new Songhai power in Gao to the east ended Mali's imperial authority.

SONGHAI

Evidence suggests that as early as the eleventh or twelfth century there was a Songhai kingdom around Gao, on the eastern arc of the great bend of the Niger. In 1325 Mansa Musa brought this kingdom and the Gao region under the control of Mali and the Malinke. Mali's domination ended with the rise of a dynasty in Gao known as the Sunni or Sonni

MAP EXPLORATION

Interactive map: To explore this map further, go to http://www.prenhall.com/craig_map17.2

Map 17–2 Africa ca. 1500–1800. Important towns, regions, peoples, and states. The inset shows the empire of Songhai at its greatest extent in the early 16th century.

around 1375. The kingdom became an imperial power, under the greatest Sunni ruler, Sonni Ali (r. 1464–1492). Thereafter the Songhai Empire for more than a century was arguably the most powerful state in Africa (see Map 17–2). With a strong military built around a riverboat flotilla and cavalry, Sonni Ali took Jenne and Timbuktu. He pushed the Tuareg Berbers back into the northern Sahel and Sahara and stifled threats from the southern forestland.

His successor Askia Muhammad al-Turi (r. 1493–1528) continued Sonni Ali's expansionist policies. Between

A mosque tomb in Gao reputed to have been built for the Askia rulers of Songhai. John O. Hunwick

them, Sonni Ali and Askia Muhammad built an empire that stretched west nearly to the Atlantic, northwest into the Sahara, and east into the central Sudan. Taking advantage of their control of access to the gold and other desirable commodities of West Africa, they emulated their Ghanaian predecessors in cultivating and expanding the ancient caravan trade across the Sahara to the North African coasts of Libya and Tunisia. This provided their major source of wealth.

Unlike Sonni Ali, who held to the traditional African religious faith of his people, Muhammad al-Turi was an enthusiastic Muslim. He built up the Songhai state after the model of the Islamic empire of Mali. In his reign, many Muslim scholars came to Gao, Timbuktu, and Jenne. He appointed Muslim judges (*qadis*) in towns throughout the empire and made Timbuktu a major intellectual and legal training center for the whole Sudan. He also replaced native Songhais with Arab Muslim immigrants as government officials to strengthen his centralized power. Like Mansa Musa before him, Muhammad made a triumphal pilgrimage to Mecca, where he was hailed as "Caliph of the western Sahara." From his vast royal treasury he supported the poor and the Sufi leaders, or *marabouts*, and built mosques throughout the realm. Nevertheless, he failed to Islamize the empire or to ensure a strong central state for his successors.

The last powerful Askia leader was Askia Dawud (r. 1549–1583), under whom Songhai economic prosperity and intellectual life achieved its apogee. The trans-Saharan trade reached new heights, and royal patronage of the arts rose to new levels. Still, difficulties mounted. The Askia battled the Mossi to the south and Berber forces from the north. Civil war broke out over succession to the throne in 1586, and the empire was divided. In 1591 an assay sent by the Sa'dis of Morocco used superior gunpowder weapons, and the aid of disaffected Songhai princes to defeat the last Askia of Gao at Tondibi, and the Gao Empire collapsed.

CHRONOLOGY

SAHELIAN EMPIRES OF THE WESTERN SUDAN

ca. 990–ca. 1180?	Empire of Ghana
1076	Ghana loses Awdaghast to Almoravids
1180–1230	Soso clan briefly controls the old Ghanaian territories
ca. 1230–1450	Empire of Mali, founded by Sundiata
1230–1255	Reign of Sundiata
1312–1337	Reign of Mansa Musa
1374	Independent Songhai state emerges in Gao after throwing off Malian rule
ca. 1450–1600	Songhai Empire at Gao
1464–1591	Askia dynasty
1464–1492	Reign of Sonni Ali
1493–1528	Reign of Askia Muhammad al-Turi
1549–1583	Reign of Askia Dawud
1590s	Collapse of the Songhai Empire

KANEM AND KANEM-BORNU

A fourth sizable Sahelian empire—in the central Sudan—arose after 1100. Called Kanem, it began as a southern Saharan confederation of the black nomadic tribes known as Zaghawah that were spread over much of the south-central and southeastern Sahara. By the twelfth century a Zaghawah group known as the Kanuri had

DOCUMENT MUSLIM REFORM IN SONGHAI

Around 1500 Askia Muhammad al-Turi, the first Muslim among the rulers of Songhai, wrote to the North African Muslim theologian Muhammad al-Maghili (d. 1504) about proper Muslim practices. These excerpts are from the seventh question of al-Turi and the answers al-Maghili gave. One sees the zeal of the new convert to conform to traditional religious norms and the puritanical "official line" of the conservative Maliki ulama *on "pagan" mores. Also evident is the king's desire for bettering social order and his concern for justice. It is also manifest that many of the more strongly Shari`a-minded* ulama *did not want to compromise at all, let alone allow syncretism to emerge among formerly pagan, newly converted groups.*

What are the problems and corresponding solutions listed in the letter? Which problem did al-Maghili find most serious? Why? Which do you think would have been most serious? Why?

From Al-Turi's Seventh Question

Among the people [of the Songhay Empire said Askia Muhammad], there are some who claim knowledge of the supernatural through sand divining and the like, or through the disposition of the stars ... [while] some assert that they can write (talismans) to bring good fortune ... or to ward off bad fortune. ... Some defraud in weights and measures. ...

One of their evil practices [continued Askia Muhammad] is the free mixing of men and women in the markets and streets and the failure of women to veil themselves ... [while] among the people of Djenné [Jenne] it is an established custom for a girl not to cover any part of her body as long as she remains a virgin ... and all the most beautiful girls walk about naked among people. ...

So give us legal ruling concerning these people and their ilk, and may God Most High reward you!

From Al-Maghili's Answer

The answer—and God it is who directs to the right course—is that everything you have mentioned concerning people's behavior in some parts of this country is gross error. It is the bounden duty of the commander of the Muslims and all other believers who have the power [replied al-Maghili] to change every one of these evil practices.

As for any who claims knowledge of the supernatural in the ways you have mentioned ... he is a liar and an unbeliever. ... Such people must be forced to renounce it by the sword. Then whoever renounces such deeds should be left in peace, but whoever persists should be killed with the sword as an unbeliever; his body should not be washed or shrouded, and he should not be buried in a Muslim graveyard. ...

As for defrauding in weights and measures [continued al-Maghili] it is forbidden (*haram*) according to the Qur'an, the Sunna and the consensus of opinion of the learned men of the Muslim community. It is the bounden duty of the commander of the Muslims to appoint a trustworthy man in charge of the markets, and to safeguard people's means of subsistence. He should standardize all the scales in each province. ... Similarly, all measures both large and small must be rectified so that they conform to a uniform standard. ...

Now, what you mentioned about the free mixing of men and women and leaving the pudenda uncovered is one of the greatest abominations. The commander of the Muslims must exert himself to prevent all these things. ... He should appoint trustworthy men to watch over this by day and night, in secret and in the open. This is not to be considered as spying on the Muslims; it is only a way of caring for them and curbing evildoers, especially when corruption becomes widespread in the land as it has done in Timbuktu and Djenné [Jenne] and so on.

From *The African Past*, trans. by J. O. Hunwick, reprinted in Basil Davidson (Grosset and Dunlap, The Universal Library), pp. 86–88. Reprinted by permission of Curtis Brown Ltd. Copyright © 1964 by Basil Davidson.

apparently settled in Kanem, and from there they began a campaign of military expansion during the thirteenth century. Their key leader in this, Mai Dunama Dibbalemi (r. ca. 1221–1259), was a contemporary of Sundiata in Mali. Like Sundiata, Dibbalemi was a Muslim, and Islam appears to have entrenched itself among the Kanuri ruling class during his reign. Dibbalemi used it to sanction his rule, which otherwise had the familiar African trappings of sacred kingship. It also provided a rationale for expansion through *jihad*, or holy "struggle" against polytheists.

Dibbalemi and his successors expanded Kanuri power north into the desert to include the Fezzan in modern Libya and northeast along the Sahel-Sahara fringe toward Nilotic Africa. In both directions they controlled important trade routes—north to Libya and east to the Nile and Egypt. The next two centuries saw the mixing of Kanuri and local Kanembu peoples, primarily those known as the So. There was a corresponding transformation of the Kanuri leader from a nomadic *shaykh* to a Sudanic king and a shift of Kanem from a nomadic to a largely sedentary kingdom with quasi-feudal institutions. Like Mali to the west, Kanem's dominion was of two kinds: direct rule over and taxation of core territories and groups, and indirect control over and collection of tribute from a wider region of vassal chieftaincies. Islamic acculturation progressed most rapidly in the core territories under direct rule.

Civil strife, largely over the royal succession, weakened the Kanuri state in the later fourteenth and fifteenth centuries. After 1400 the locus of power shifted from Kanem proper westward, to the land of Bornu, southwest of Lake Chad. Here, at the end of the fifteenth century, a new Kanuri empire arose almost simultaneously with the collapse of the Askia dynasty of the Songhai Empire at Gao. Near the end of the sixteenth century firearms and Turkish military instructors enabled the Kanuri leader Idris Alawma (r. ca. 1575–1610) to unify Kanem and Bornu. He set up an avowedly Islamic state and extended his rule even into Hausaland, between Bornu and the Niger River. The center of trading activity as well as political power and security now shifted from the Niger Bend east to the territory under Kanuri control.

Deriving its prosperity from the trans-Saharan trade, Idris Alawma's regional empire survived for nearly a century. It was finally broken up by a long famine, repeated Tuareg attacks, lack of strong leadership, and loss of control over trade to smaller, better-organized Hausa states. The ruling dynasty held out until 1846, but by 1700 its power had been sharply reduced by the growing Hausa states to the west in what is now northern Nigeria. Their real power came only in the nineteenth century with their unification under the Fulani sultanate of Sokoto (see Chapter 28.).

The Eastern Sudan

The Christian states of Maqurra and Alwa in the Nilotic Sudan, or Nubia, lasted for more than 600 years from their early-seventh-century beginnings and maintained political, religious and commercial contact with Egypt, the Red Sea world, and much of the Sudan.

After 1000 C.E. Maqurra and Alwa continued treaty relations with their more powerful northern Egyptian neighbors. However, the Mamluks intervened repeatedly in Nubian affairs, and Arab nomads constantly threatened the Nubian states. From late Fatimid times onward, both Maqurra and Alwa were increasingly subject to immigrating Muslim Arab, tribesmen and to traders and growing Muslim minorities. The result was a long-term intermingling of Arabic and Nubian cultures and the creation of a new Nilotic Sudanese people and culture.

A significant factor in the gradual disappearance of Christianity in Nubia was its elite character there and its association with the foreign Egyptian world of Coptic Christianity. Maqurra became officially Muslim at the beginning of the fourteenth century, although Christianity survived until late in the same century. The Islamization of Alwa came somewhat later, most effectively under the long-lived Funj sultanate that replaced the Alwa state.

The Funj state flourished between the Blue and White Niles and to the north along the main Nile from just after 1500 until 1762. The Funj were originally cattle nomads who apparently adopted Islam soon after setting up their kingdom. During the late sixteenth and the seventeenth centuries, the Funj developed an Islamic society whose Arabized character was unique in sub-Saharan Africa. A much-reduced Funj state held out until an Ottoman Egyptian invasion in 1821.

Chronology

Central Sudanic Empires

ca. 1100–1500	Kanuri empire of Kanem
ca. 1220s–1400	Height of empire of Kanem
1221–1259	Reign of Mai Dunama Dibbalemi
1575–1846	Kanuri empire of Kanem-Bornu
1575–1610	Reign of Idris Alawma, major architect of the state

The Forestlands—Coastal West and Central Africa

West African Forest Kingdoms: The Example of Benin

Many states, some with distinct political, religious, and cultural traditions, had developed in the southern and coastal regions of West Africa several centuries before the first Portuguese reports in 1485. Even those states like Asante or the Yoruba kingdoms of Oyo and Ife, which reached their height only after 1500, had much earlier origins. Benin, the best known of these forest kingdoms, reflects, especially in its art, the sophistication of West African culture before 1500.

Benin State and Society The Edo speakers of Benin have occupied the southern Nigerian region between Yorubaland and the Ibo peoples east of the lower Niger for millennia. Traditional Edo society is organized according to a patrilineal system emphasizing primogeniture. The village is the fundamental political unit, and authority is built around the organization of males into age-grade units.[3]

According to archaeological evidence, the local traditions of the Edo culture of Benin were closely linked to those of Ife, one of the most prominent Yoruba states northwest of Benin. Some kind of distinct kingdom of Benin likely existed as early as the twelfth century, and traditional accounts of both Ife and Edo agree that an Ife prince was sent to rule in Benin around 1300. There are indications

[3] A. F. C. Ryder, *Benin and the Europeans, 1485–1897* (New York: Longman, 1969), p. 1. Ryder's work is a basic reference for the following brief summary about Benin.

that the power of the king, or *oba*, at this time was sharply limited by the Edo leaders who invited the foreign ruler. These leaders were known as the *uzama*, an order of hereditary indigenous chiefs. According to tradition, the fourth *oba* managed to wrest more control from these chiefs and instituted something of the ceremonial authority of absolute monarchy. However, only in the fifteenth century, with King Ewuare, did Benin become a royal autocracy and a large state of major regional importance.

Ewuare rebuilt the capital—known today as Benin City—and named it and his kingdom Edo. He apparently established a government in which he had sweeping authority, although he exercised it in light of the deliberations of a royal council. Ewuare formed this council not only from the palace *uzama* but also from the townspeople. He gave each chief specific administrative responsibilities and rank in the government hierarchy. Ewuare and his successors developed a tradition of military kingship and engaged in major wars of expansion, both into Yorubaland to the west and Ibo country east across the Niger River. They also claimed for the office of *oba* an increasing ritual authority that presaged more radical developments in the king's role.

In the seventeenth century the *oba* was transformed from a military leader into a religious figure with supernatural powers. Human sacrifice, specifically of slaves, seems to have accompanied the cult of deceased kings and became even more frequent later, in the nineteenth century. The succession by primogeniture was discontinued, and the *uzama* chose *obas* from any branch of the royal family.

Benin Art The lasting significance of Benin, however, lies in its court art, especially its famous brass sculptures. The splendid terra-cotta, ivory, and brass statuary sculpture of Ife-Benin are among the glories of human creativity. These magnificent sculptures seem to be wholly indigenous African products, and some scholars trace their artistic and technical lineage to the sculptures of the Nok culture of ancient West Africa (see Chapter 6).

The best sculptures before the sixteenth century and the coming of the Portuguese are cast bronze plaques depicting legendary and historical scenes. These were mounted in the royal palace in Benin City (cf. p. 472). There are also brass heads, apparently of royalty, that resemble the many life-size terra-cotta and brass heads found at Ife. The heads at Ife are held to represent the Oni, or religious chief of ancient Ife, or particular ancestors, who are thereby reverently remembered by their descendants.

Similar sculptures have been found both to the north and in the Niger Delta. Recent excavations east of the Niger at Igbo-Ukwu have unearthed stunning terra cottas and bronzes that belong to the same general artistic culture, which is dated as early as the ninth century. These artifacts testify to the high cultural level attained in traditional African societies that had little or no contact with the extra-African world.

European Arrivals on the Coastlands

Along the coasts of West and central Africa, many important changes occurred between 1500 and 1800. Those wrought by the burgeoning Atlantic slave trade are the most famous (see Chapter 18). Of comparable importance are changes connected with trade in West African gold and other commodities and the effects associated with the importation and spread in West and central Africa of food crops, such as maize, peanuts, squash, sweet potatoes, cocoa, and cassava (manioc) from the Americas. The gradual involvement of Africa in the emerging global economic system paved the way for eventual colonial domination of the continent, especially its coastal regions, by the Europeans. The European names for segments of the coastline—the Grain (or Pepper) Coast, the Ivory Coast, the Gold Coast, and the Slave Coast—identify the main exports that could be extracted by ship.

Senegambia In West Africa, Senegambia—which takes its name from the Senegal and Gambia Rivers—was one of the earliest regions affected by European trade. Its interior had long been involved in both trans-Saharan trade and east–west trade in the Sahel and the savannah, especially in the heydays of the empires of Ghana, Mali, and Songhai. Senegambia's maritime trade with European powers, like the older overland trade, was primarily in gold and products such as salt, cotton goods, hides, and copper. For roughly a century Senegambian states also provided slaves for European purchase; indeed, perhaps a third of all African slaves exported during the sixteenth century came from Senegambia. Thereafter, however, the focus of the slave trade shifted south and east along the coast (see Chapter 18). Over time, Portuguese-African mulattos and the British came to control the Gambia River trade, while the French won the Senegal River markets.

The Gold Coast The Gold Coast, like Senegambia, was one of the West African coastal districts most affected by the arrival of international maritime trade. The name derives from the region's importance after 1500 as the outlet for the more southern of West Africa's gold fields in the forestland of Akan. Here, beginning with the Portuguese at Elmina in 1481, but primarily after 1600,

Chronology

Benin

ca. 1100–1897	Benin state
ca. 1300	First Ife king of Benin state
1440–1475	Reign of Ewuare

Art and the World

BENIN AND IFE "BRONZES"

Some of the world's finest works of art were made by the artists of Benin and Ife, though much is still unknown about them. Rarely found elsewhere in Africa, bronze panels like the plaque shown here, possibly inspired by European illustrated books, adorned the royal palace, and are considered examples of "court art." The figures are typical of the Benin style in their proportions of head to body—about one to four—perhaps emphasizing the head's importance as a symbol of life and behavior. Although the facial traits of the central figure are not individualized, the artist meticulously detailed his weapon, jewelry, and clothing, which would very likely have enabled viewers to identify his rank and family. The features of all three figures are highly stylized; this quality and the chased background design that covers the entire field are typical of Benin bronzes, as are the precise craft and high, expertly modeled relief.

It can be difficult to assign these works to precise periods, but they probably date from the thirteenth century C.E. to 1897, when the British navy arrived in Benin. The plaque shown here gives a specific clue to its time period: because their helmets identify the two smaller lateral figures as Portuguese or other European soldiers, the plaque cannot be much earlier than 1485—the date of the first Portuguese accounts of Benin. Over time, court art would gradually lose its vitality, so the panel's vigor and deftly balanced composition suggest an earlier rather than a later date.

Benin plaque. Hillel Burger/Peabody Museum, Harvard University © President and Fellows of Harvard College. All rights reserved.

Collectively called "bronzes," the metal artworks of Benin and Ife are actually made of a range of materials—most of the Benin cast pieces are of leaded brass, a more malleable alloy of copper and zinc, while some Ife objects are made of pure copper. Copper has been mined in Africa at least since the sixth century B.C.E. (and has been, at times, more prized than gold), and West and South Africa also boast deposits of zinc, lead, and tin, any of which may be mixed in various proportions with copper to produce bronze. The presence of tin on the Jos Plateau in northern Nigeria has suggested a connection between Nok art and that of Ife and Benin.

Oral tradition and some contemporary scholars maintain that Ife metalwork was the source of Benin's art; other archaeologists believe that both derive from a third common source. Yet the artworks of the two related cultures (both Edo and Ife are linguistically related to the Kwa family of languages) also display significant differences, for example, in their casting and in the proportions of trace elements used in the various alloys. The art of Ife, presently dated to between the twelfth and sixteenth centuries C.E.—although it may have originated six centuries earlier—tends to be more naturalistic than that of Benin, and displays a serene classicism equaled only by that of ancient Greece. In fact, the first European to discover an Ife bronze head, in 1910, surmised that it and the terra-cotta pieces beside it must have been made by the ancient Greeks—of Atlantis. Other art historians of the period and later also hypothesized that it was impossible that Africans had made such fine works.

Ife artworks are made of bronze, brass (like the example illustrated), and pure copper—the latter a technically difficult material to cast. The Yoruba artisans of Ife were skilled at sculpting in clay, so that when the lost-wax method of metalwork arrived from the north, the techniques—and iconography—were readily transferred. Like the Benin bronzes, this piece is not an actual portrait, although it most likely represents an Oni, or ruler: the holes across the top of the head probably held a crown. Nails through the holes in the neck fixed the head to a wooden shaft, though for what purpose is not certain. The figure may have been used in a "second burial," a ritual used for the death of kings in France and England as well. This practice allowed the monarch to be buried in a timely way, while an effigy was the focus of a later memorial. The meaning of the lines on this and some other faces is also unknown; they may represent scarification or a veil. The regal head shown here is an exquisite example, not only of the high style of Ife art, but of one of its mysteries: only objects of this degree of artistry have been found.

Head of a King, from Ife. c. 13th century C.E. Brass, height 11 7/16" (29 cm). © Frank Willett. From Werner Gillon, *A Short History of African Art* (London: Penguin Books, 1991).

European states and companies built coastal forts to protect their trade and to serve as depots for inland goods. The trade in gold, kola nuts, and other commodities seems to have encouraged the growth of larger states in the region, perhaps because they could better handle and control the overland commerce.

The intensive contact of the Gold Coast with Europeans also led to the importation and spread of American crops, notably maize and cassava. The success of these crops in West and central Africa likely contributed to substantial population growth in the sixteenth and seventeenth centuries.

The Gold Coast escaped the ravages of the slave trade for some decades; it was even an importer of slaves until long after 1500. Slaves, however, became big business here in the late seventeenth century, especially in the Accra region. The economy was so disrupted by the slave trade that gold mining declined sharply. Eventually more gold came into the Gold Coast from the sale of slaves than went out from its mines (see Chapter 18).

CENTRAL AFRICA

The vast center of the subcontinent is bounded by swamps in the north, coastal rain forests to the west, highlands to the east, and deserts in the south. Before 1500 these natural barriers impeded international contact and trade with the interior. They also shaped the two-pronged route by which Bantu peoples and languages moved, over many centuries, from western and west-central Africa south into the Zaire basin and east around the equatorial forest into the lakes of highland East Africa. In the tropical central area, regional interaction in movements of peoples and in trade and culture had always been the norm. Here as elsewhere in Africa, however, large as well as small political, economic, and social units could be found. Peoples such as the Lunda and the Luba, for example, on the southern savannah below the rain forest, carved out sizable kingdoms by the fifteenth century and expanded their control over neighboring areas into the eighteenth century.

The Portuguese came to the western coastal regions looking for gold and silver but found none. Ultimately, their main export was slaves. These slaves were taken, first for gang labor to the Portuguese sugar plantations on Sao Thomé island in the Gulf of Guinea and then, in vast numbers to perform similar plantation labor in Brazil. In the 1640s the Dutch briefly succeeded the Portuguese as the major suppliers of African slaves to English and French plantations in the Caribbean.

THE KONGO KINGDOM Kongo was the major state with which the Portuguese dealt after coming to central Africa in 1483. Dating from probably the fourteenth century, the Kongo kingdom was located on a fertile, well-watered plateau south of the lower Zaïre River valley, between the coast and the Kwango River in the east. Here, astride the border between forest and grassland, the Kongo kings had built a central government based on a pyramid structure of tax or tribute collection. The king's, authority was tied to acceptance of him as a kind of spiritual spokesman of the gods or ancestors. By 1600 Kongo was half the size of England and boasted a high state of specialization in weaving and pottery, salt production, fishing, and metalworking.

The Portuguese brought Mediterranean goods, preeminently luxury textiles from North Africa, to trade for African goods. Such luxuries augmented the prestige and wealth of the ruler and his elites. However, slaves became the primary export that could be used to obtain foreign luxuries. Meanwhile, imports such as fine clothing, tobacco, and alcohol did nothing to replace the labor pool lost to slavery.

At first the Portuguese put time and effort into education and Christian proselytizing, but the need for more slaves eventually outweighed these concerns. Regional rulers sought to procure slaves from neighboring kingdoms, as did Portuguese traders who went inland themselves. As the demand grew, local rulers increasingly attacked neighbors to garner slaves for Portuguese traders (see Chapter 18.).

The Kongo ruler Affonso I (r. ca. 1506–1543), a Christian convert, at first welcomed Jesuit missionaries and supported conversion. But in time he broke with the Jesuits and encouraged traditional practices, even though he himself remained a Christian. Affonso had constant difficulty curbing the more exploitative slaving practices and independent-minded provincial governors, who often dealt directly with the Portuguese, undermining royal authority. Affonso's successor finally restricted Portuguese activity to Mpinda harbor and the Kongo capital of Mbanza Kongo (São Salvador). A few years later, Portuguese attempts to name the Kongo royal successor caused a bloody uprising against them that led in turn to a Portuguese boycott on trade with the kingdom.

Thereafter, disastrous internal wars shattered the Kongo state. Slavery apparently contributed significantly to provincial unrest. Independent Portuguese traders and adventurers soon did their business outside of government channels and tried to manipulate the Kongo kings.

CHRONOLOGY

CENTRAL AFRICA

1300s	Kongo kingdom founded
1483	Portuguese come to central African coast
ca. 1506–1543	Reign of Affonso I as king of Kongo
1571	Angola becomes Portuguese proprietary colony

Kongo, however, enjoyed renewed vigor in the seventeenth century. The Kongo kings, all descended from Affonso, ruled as divine-right monarchs at the apex of a complex sociopolitical pyramid that rose from district headmen through provincial governors to the court nobility and king. Royal power came to depend on a guard of musket-armed hired soldiers. The financial base of the kingdom rested on tribute from officials and taxes and tolls on commerce. Christianity, the state religion, was accommodated to the traditional ancestor cult, magic, and sorcery. Sculpture, iron and copper technology, and dance and music flourished.

ANGOLA To the south, in Portuguese Angola, the experience was even worse than in Kongo. The Ndongo kingdom flourished among the Mbundu people during the sixteenth century, though the Portuguese tried and failed to make Angola a proprietary colony (the first white colonial enterprise in black Africa). By the end of the 1500s Angola was exporting thousands of slaves yearly through the port of Luanda. In less than a century the hinterland had been depopulated. New internal trade in salt and the spread of American food crops such as maize and cassava (which became part of the staple diet of the populace) produced some positive changes in the interior, but in the coastal region the Portuguese brought catastrophe.

EAST AFRICA

SWAHILI CULTURE AND COMMERCE

The participation of East African port towns in the lucrative South-Seas trade was ancient. Arabs, Indonesians, and even some Indians had trafficked there for centuries. Many had been absorbed into what had become, during the first millennium C.E., from Somalia south, a predominantly Bantu-speaking population. From the eighth century onward Islam traveled with Arab and Persian sailors and merchants to these southerly trading centers of what the Arabs called the land of the *Zanj*, or "Blacks" (hence "Zanzibar"). Conversion to Islam, however, occurred only

DOCUMENT — AFFONSO I OF KONGO WRITES TO THE KING OF PORTUGAL

In 1526 Affonso, the Christian African king of Kongo, wrote to the Portuguese monarch ostensibly to complain about the effects of slaving on the Kongo people and economy. But the real issue was that the Portuguese were circumventing his own royal monopoly on the inland slave trade. One of the insidious effects of the massive demand of the Atlantic trade for slaves was the ever increasing engagement in it of African monarchs, chieftains, and merchants.

How had the introduction of Portuguese merchants and European goods upset the social and political situation in Kongo? How had these goods tempted Affonso's subjects into the slave trade? How did Affonso wish to change the relationship of his people to Portugal? Was the king more worried about human rights or his economic losses?

Sir, Your Highness [of Portugal] should know how our Kingdom is being lost in so many ways that it is convenient to provide for the necessary remedy, since this is caused by the excessive freedom given by your factors and officials to the men and merchants who are allowed to come to this Kingdom to set up shops with goods and many things which have been prohibited by us, and which they spread throughout our Kingdoms and Domains in such an abundance that many of our vassals, whom we had in obedience, do not comply because they have the things in greater abundance than we ourselves; and it was with these things that we had them content and subjected under our vassalage and jurisdiction, so it is doing a great harm not only to the service of God, but the security and peace of our Kingdoms and State as well.

And we cannot reckon how great the damage is, since the mentioned merchants are taking every day our natives, sons of the land and the sons of our noblemen and vassals and our relatives, because the thieves and men of bad conscience grab them wishing to have the things and wares of this Kingdom which they are ambitious of; they grab them and get them to be sold; and so great, Sir, is the corruption and licentiousness that our country is being completely depopulated, and Your Highness should not agree with this nor accept it as in your service. And to avoid it we need from those [your] Kingdoms no more than some priests and a few people to teach in schools, and no other goods except wine and flour for the holy sacrament. That is why we beg of Your Highness to help and assist us in this matter, commanding your factors that they should not send here either merchants or wares, because it is *our will that in these Kingdoms there should not be any trade of slaves nor outlet for them.*[4]

Concerning what is referred above, again we beg of Your Highness to agree with it, since otherwise we cannot . . . remedy such an obvious damage. Pray Our Lord in His mercy to have Your Highness under His guard and let you do for ever the things of His service. I kiss your hands many times. . . .

[4] Emphasis in the original.

From *The African Past,* trans. by J. O. Hunwick, reprinted in Basil Davidson (Grosset and Dunlap, The Universal Library), pp. 191–193. Reprinted by permission of Curtis Brown Ltd. Copyright © 1964 by Basil Davidson.

along the coast. In the thirteenth century Muslim traders from Arabia and Iran began to dominate the coastal cities from Mogadishu to Kilwa. By 1331 the traveler Ibn Battuta writes of Mogadishu as a thoroughly Islamic port and of the ruler and inhabitants of Kilwa as Muslims. He also notes that towns there had mosques for the faithful.[5]

By this time a common language called *Swahili*, or *Kiswahili*, from the Arabic *sawahil*, "coastlands," had developed from the interaction of Bantu and Arabic speakers along the coast. Its structure is Bantu, its vocabulary has a strong admixture of Arabic, and it is written in Arabic script.

Current theory suggests that, like the language, Swahili culture is basically African with a large contribution by Arab, Persian, and other extra-African elements. This admixture created a new consciousness and identity. Today, the many coastal peoples who share Swahili language join African to Persian, Indian, Arab, and other ancestry.

[5] *Travels in Asia and Africa, 1325–1354*, trans. and selected by H. A. R. Gibb (New York: Robert M. McBride, 1929), pp. 110–113.

The Friday Mosque at Shela on the southeastern coast of Lamu Island, Kenya. This fine example of Late Swahili architecture dates to the early 19th century. It is the only surviving pre-20th-century mosque in the region with a minaret. Swahili settlements on Lamu Island date to about the 15th century and enjoyed a period of substantial wealth that reached its zenith in the 19th century. Peter Greenberg

Swahili language and culture probably developed first in the northern towns of Manda, Lamu, and Mombasa, then farther south along the coast to Kilwa. They remained localized largely along the coast until recently. Likewise, the spread of Islam was largely limited to the coastal civilization, with the possible exception of the Zambezi valley, where Muslim traders penetrated upriver. This contrasts with the Horn of Africa, where Islamic kingdoms developed both in the Somali hinterland and on the coast.

Swahili civilization reached its apogee in the fourteenth and fifteenth centuries. The harbor trading towns were the administrative centers of the local Swahili states, and most of them were sited on coastal islands or easily defended peninsulas. To these ports came merchants from abroad and from the African hinterlands. These towns were impressive. Stone mosques, fortress-palaces, harbor fortifications, fancy residences, and commercial buildings have their own distinctive cast, which combines African and Arabo-Persian elements.

The Swahili states' ruling dynasties were probably African in origin, with an admixture of Arab or Persian blood. Swahili coastal centers boasted an advanced, cosmopolitan culture; by comparison, most of the populace in the small villages lived in mud and sometimes stone houses and earned their living by farming or fishing. Society seems to have consisted of three principal groups: the local nobility, the commoners, and resident foreigners engaged in commerce. Slaves constituted a fourth class, although their local extent (as opposed to their sale) is disputed.

The flourishing trade of the coastal centers was fed mainly by export of inland ivory. Other exports included gold, slaves, turtle shells, ambergris, leopard skins, pearls, fish, sandalwood, ebony, and cotton cloth. The chief imports were cloth, porcelain, glassware, glass beads, and glazed pottery. Certain exports tended to dominate particular ports: cloth, sandalwood, ebony, and ivory at Mogadishu, ivory at Manda, and gold at Kilwa (brought up the coast from Sofala, still farther south). Cowrie shells were a common currency in the inland trade, but coins minted at Mogadishu and Kilwa from the fourteenth century on were increasingly used in the major trading centers.

THE PORTUGUESE AND THE OMANIS OF ZANZIBAR

The original Swahili civilization declined in the sixteenth century primarily because the trade that had originally made everything possible waned with the arrival of the Portuguese and their destruction of both the old oceanic trade (in particular, the Islamic commercial monopoly) and the main

DOCUMENT VISITING MOGADISHU AND KILWA (1331)

Ibn Battuta (d. 1369 or 1377), a native of Tangier, became one of history's most famous travelers through his voluminous and entertaining writings about his years of journeying from West and East Africa to India and China. In the following two excerpts from his description of his trip down the East African coast in 1331, he describes first the daily proceedings at the grievance and petitions court presided over by the Sultan of Mogadishu, then the generosity of the Sultan of Kilwa. The East Africans referred to their Sultan as "Shaikh" (a term used also for any religiously learned man). A qadi *is a judge; a* faqih, *a jurisconsult or legal scholar; a* wazir, *a government minister; an* amir, *a military commander; and a* sharif, *a descendant of the Prophet Muhammad (which carries special social status).*

What Muslim values and practices do the two reports seem to describe? Does Ibn Battuta as a Muslim, but also as an Arab outsider to the African Muslim societies he is visiting, seem to approve or disapprove of what he reports?

Mogadishu

When it is Saturday, the people come to the door of the shaikh (the local term for the Sultan), and they sit in covered halls outside the house. The *qadi*, the *faqihs*, the *sharifs*, the men of piety, the shaikhs and the men who have performed the pilgrimage enter the second council room. They sit on wooden platforms prepared for the purpose. The *qadi* is on a platform by himself and each group on a platform reserved for them which nobody shares with them. Then the shaikh sits in his council and sends for the *qadi* who sits on his left. Then enter the *faqihs* and their leaders sit in front of him while the rest of them salute and go away. Then the *sharifs* enter, their leaders sit before him, the rest of them salute and go away. If they are guests, they sit on his right. Then enter the shaikhs and those who have performed the pilgrimage, and their great ones sit and the rest salute and go away. Then enter the *wazirs* and *amirs*; the heads of the soldiers, rank upon rank, they salute and go. Food is brought and the *qadi*, the *sharifs* and whoever is sitting in that session eat with the shaikh and the shaikh eats with them. If he wishes to honour one of the leaders of his *amirs*, he sends for him that he should eat with them. The rest of the people eat in the dining hall and their eating is according to precedence in the manner of their entrance before the shaikh. Then the shaikh goes into his house and the *qadi*, the *wazirs*, the private secretary, and four of the leading *amirs* sit for hearing litigation between the members of the public and hearing the cases of people with complaints. In a matter connected with the rules of the *shari`a* [religious law] the *qadi* passes judgement; in a matter other than that, the members of the council pass judgement, that is, the ministers and the *amirs*. In a matter where there is need of consultation with the sultan, they write about it to him and he sends out the reply to them immediately on the back of the note in accordance with his view. And such is always their custom.

The Sultan of Kilwa

When I arrived, the Sultan was Abu al-Muzaffar Hasan surnamed Abu al-Mawahib [the Father of Gifts] on account of his numerous charitable gifts. He frequently makes raids into the Zanj country, attacks them and carries off booty, of which he reserves a fifth, using it in the manner prescribed by the Koran. That reserved for the kinsfolk of the Prophet is kept separate in the Treasury, and, when *sharifs* come to visit him, he gives it them. They come to him from Iraq, the Hijaz, and other countries. I found several *sharifs* from the Hijaz at his court, among them Muhammad ibn Jammaz, Mansur ibn Labida ibn Abi Nami and Muhamma ibn Shumaila ibn Abi Nami. At Mogadishu I saw Tabl ibn Kubaish ibn Jammaz, who also wished to visit him. This Sultan is very humble: he sits and eats with beggars, and venerates holy men and descendants of the Prophet.

From Said Hamdun and Noèl King, ed. and trans., *Ibn Battuta in Black Africa*, (Princeton, NJ: Markus Wiener, rev. ed., 1994), pp. 20–21. Reprinted by permission of Markus Wiener Publishers, Inc.

Islamic city-states along the eastern coast. Decreases in rainfall or invasions of Zimba peoples from inland regions may also have contributed to the decline.

Nevertheless, the Portuguese undoubtedly intended to gain control of the South-Seas trade (see Chapter 18). In Africa, as everywhere, they saw the "Moors" as their implacable enemies and viewed the struggle to wrest the commerce and the parts of Africa and Asia from Islamic control as a Christian crusade.

The initial Portuguese victories along the African coast led to the submission of many small Islamic ports and states. Still, there was no concerted effort to spread Christianity beyond the fortified settlements established in places like Sofala, Zanzibar, Mozambique, and Mombasa. Thus the long-term cultural and religious consequences of the Portuguese presence were slight.

The Portuguese did, however, cause widespread economic decline on the east coast. When the inland Africans refused to cooperate with them, the formerly heavy gold trade up the Zambezi from Sofala dried up. The militant Portuguese presence also sharply reduced Muslim coastal shipping from India and Arabia. Ottoman efforts in the late sixteenth century failed to defeat the Portuguese, but after 1660 the strong eastern Arabian state of Oman raided the African coast with impunity. In 1698 the Omanis took Mombasa and ejected the Portuguese everywhere north of Mozambique.

Under the Omanis, Zanzibar became a new and major power center in East Africa. Their control of the coastal ivory and slave trade seems to have fueled a substantial recovery of prosperity by the later eighteenth century. Zanzibar itself benefited from the introduction of clove cultivation in the 1830s; cloves became its staple export thereafter. (The clove plantations became also the chief market for a new, devastating internal slave trade, which flourished in East Africa into the late nineteenth century even as the external trade in slaves was crushed.) Omani African sultans dominated the east coast until 1856. Thereafter, Zanzibar and its coastal holdings became independent under a branch of the same family that ruled in Oman. Zanzibar passed eventually to the British when they, the Germans, and the Italians divided East Africa in the late 1880s. Still, the Islamic imprint on the whole coast survives today.

SOUTHERN AFRICA

SOUTHEASTERN AFRICA: "GREAT ZIMBABWE"

At about the same time that the east-coast trading centers were beginning to flourish, a different kind of civilization was enjoying its heyday farther south, in the rocky, savannah-woodland watershed between the Limpopo and Zambezi Rivers, in modern southern Zimbabwe. This civilization was a purely African one sited far enough inland never to have felt the impact of Islam. It was founded in the tenth or eleventh century by Bantu-speaking Shona people, who still inhabit the same general area today. It seems to have become a large and prosperous state between the late thirteenth and the late fifteenth centuries. We know it only through the archaeological remains of an estimated 150 settlements in the Zambezi-Limpopo region.

"Great Zimbabwe," so called because it is the most impressive of 300 such stone ruins in modern Zimbabwe and neighboring countries. These sites give clear evidence of the advanced Iron Age mining and cattle-raising culture that flourished in this region between about 1000 and 1500 C.E. The people, thought to have been of Bantu origins, apparently had a highly developed trade in gold and copper with outsiders, including Arabs on the east coast. As yet, all too little is known about this impressive society. Robert Aberman and Barbara Heller/Art Resource, N.Y.

The most impressive of these ruins, and the apparent capital of this ancient Shona state, is known today as "Great Zimbabwe"—a huge, sixty-odd-acre site encompassing two major building complexes. One—the so-called acropolis—is a series of stone enclosures on a high hill. It overlooks another, much larger enclosure that contains many ruins and a circular tower, all surrounded by a massive wall some thirty-two feet high and up to seventeen feet thick. The acropolis complex may have contained a shrine, whereas the larger enclosure was apparently the royal palace and fort. The stonework reflects a wealthy and sophisticated society. Artifacts from the site include gold and copper ornaments, soapstone carvings, and imported beads, as well as glass and porcelain of Chinese, Syrian, and Persian origins.

The state itself seems to have had partial control of the increasing gold trade between inland areas and the east-coast port of Sofala. Its territory lay east and south of substantial gold-mining enterprises. We can speculate that this large settlement was the capital city of a prosperous empire and the residence of a ruling elite. Its wider domain was made up mostly of smaller settlements whose inhabitants lived by subsistence agriculture and cattle raising and whose culture was different from that of the capital.

We are not sure why Great Zimbabwe civilization flourished. The evidence suggests first general population growth and increasing economic prosperity in the Zambezi-Limpopo region before 1500 C.E. Even earlier Iron Age sites farther south suggest that other large-state entities may have preceded the heyday of Great Zimbabwe proper. The specific impetus for Great Zimbabwe may have been a significant immigration around 1000 C.E. of Late Iron Age Shona speakers who brought with them mining techniques and farming innovations, along with their ancestor cults. Improved farming and animal husbandry could have led to substantial population growth. The gold trade between the inland gold mining areas and Sofala may also have expanded. Great Zimbabwe may have been the chief beneficiary of this trade. This hypothesis links the flourishing of Zimbabwe to that of the East African coast from about the thirteenth century.

However, without new sources, we may never know why this impressive civilization developed and dominated its region for nearly 200 years. The reasons for its demise are also obscure. It appears that the northern and southern sectors of the state split up, and people moved away from Great Zimbabwe, probably because the farming and grazing land there was exhausted. The southern successor kingdom was known as Changamire, which became powerful from the late 1600s until about 1830. The northern successor state, stretched along the middle and lower course of the Zambezi, was known to the first Portuguese sources as the kingdom ruled by the Mwene Mutapa, or "Master Pillager," the title of its sixteenth-century ruler, Mutota, and his successors.

Artifacts from Great Zimbabwe include this carving (steatite, 40.5 cm high). It is thought that it represents a mythical eagle that carries messages from man to the gods. It dates to ca. 1200–1400 C.E. Werner Forman Archive/Art Resource, N.Y.

CHRONOLOGY

EAST AND SOUTHEAST AFRICA

900–1500	"Great Zimbabwe" civilization
ca. 1200–1400	Development of Bantu Kiswahili language
ca. 1300–1600	Height of Swahili culture
1698	Omani forces take Mombasa, oust Portuguese from East Africa north of the port of Mozambique
1741–1856	United sultanate of Oman and Zanzibar

THE PORTUGUESE IN SOUTHEASTERN AFRICA

The Portuguese destroyed Swahili control of both the inland gold trade and the multifaceted overseas trade. Their chief object was to obtain gold from the Zambezi region of the interior. However, because the gold production of the entire region was small and because they encountered repeated difficulties trying to control it, the Portuguese derived little lasting profit from the enterprise. When they had problems sustaining the Zambezi gold trade by trying simply to supplant the Swahili merchants on the coast, they established fortified posts up the Zambezi and meddled in the regional politics of the Shona who controlled the region. This tactic led to ongoing strife between the invaders and the Shona kingdoms. In the 1690s the Changamire Shona dynasty conquered the northern Shona territory and pushed the Portuguese out of gold country.

All along the Zambezi, however, a lasting and destabilizing consequence of Portuguese intrusion was the creation of quasi-tribal chiefdoms. These were led by mixed-blood Portuguese landholders, or *prazeros*, descended from the first Portuguese estate holders along the Zambezi, who had built up huge estates. Their descendants eventually formed a few clanlike groups of mixed-blood members (from unions with Africans, Indian immigrants, or other estate families). By the end of the eighteenth century, they controlled vast land holdings, commanded armies (often made up largely of slaves), and were a disruptive force in the region because they were too strong for either the Portuguese or the regional African rulers to control. They remind us of how diverse the peoples of modern Africa are.

This Benin bronze plaque came from the palace of the Obas of Benin and dates to the Edo period of Benin culture, 1575–1625. It depicts two Portuguese males, perhaps a father and son, holding hands. It is likely that they represent the traders or government officials who came to the African coasts in increasing numbers from the end of the 15th century on. On the West African coast and in Central Africa they trafficked in a variety of things ranging from ivory to human slaves, the latter gradually displacing everything else. Art Resource, N.Y.

SOUTH AFRICA: THE CAPE COLONY

In South Africa the Dutch planted the first European colonials almost inadvertently, yet the consequences of their action were to be ultimately as grave and far-reaching as any European incursion onto African soil. The first Cape settlement was built in 1652 by the Dutch East India Company as a resupply point and way station for Dutch vessels on their way back and forth between the Netherlands and the East Indies. The support station grew gradually into what became by century's end a large settler community (the population of the colony in 1662, including slaves, was 392; by 1714 it had reached 3,878).[6] These settlers were the forebears of the Afrikaners of modern South Africa.

Many of the less powerful Khoikhoi people of the region were gradually incorporated into the new colonial economy. The local Khoikhoi (see Chapter 6) were almost ex-

CHRONOLOGY

SOUTHERN AFRICA

1652	First Cape Colony settlement of Dutch East India Company
1795	British replace Dutch as masters of Cape Colony

[6] R. Elphick and H. Giliomee, *The Shaping of South African Society, 1652–1820* (Cape Town: Longman, 1979), p. 4.

clusively pastoralists; they had neither traditions of strong political organization nor an economic base beyond their herds. At first they bartered livestock freely to Dutch ships and then to the Company settlement for iron, copper, and tobacco. However, when settlers began to displace the Khoikhoi in the southwestern Cape, conflicts ensued. The results were the consolidation of European landholdings and a breakdown of Khoikhoi society. Dutch military success led to even greater Dutch control of the Khoikhoi by the 1670s. Treated as free persons, they became the chief source of colonial wage labor—labor in ever greater demand as the colony grew.

The colony also imported slaves from all along the southern-seas trade routes, including India, East Africa, and Madagascar. Slavery set the tone for relations between the emergent, and ostensibly "white," Afrikaner population and the "coloreds" of other races. Free or not, the latter were eventually all too easily identified with slave peoples.

After the first settlers spread out around the Company station, nomadic white livestock farmers, or *Trekboers*, moved more widely afield, leaving the richer, but limited, farming lands of the coast for the drier interior tableland. There they contested still wider groups of Khoikhoi cattle herders for the best grazing lands. To this end, they developed military techniques—notably the "commando," a collective civilian punitive raid—to secure their way of life by force where necessary. Again the Khoikhoi were the losers. By 1700 they were stripped almost completely of their own pasturages, and their way of life was destroyed. More and more Khoikhoi took up employment in the colonial economy, among the Trekboers as well as the settled colonists. Others moved north to join with other refugees from Cape society (slaves, mixed bloods, and some freedmen) to form raiding bands operating along the frontiers of Trekboer territory close to the Orange River. The disintegration of Khoikhoi society continued in the eighteenth century, accelerated sharply by smallpox—a European import against which this previously isolated group had no immunity.

The Cape society in this period was thus a diverse one. The Dutch Company officials (including Dutch Reformed ministers), the emerging Afrikaners (both settled colonists and Trekboers), the Khoikhoi, and the slaves played differing roles in the emerging new society radiating from Capetown. Intermarriage and cohabitation of masters and slaves added to the social complexity, despite laws designed to check such mixing. Accommodation of nonwhite minority groups within Cape society went on apace; the slow emergence of *Afrikaans*, a new vernacular language of the colonials, shows that the Dutch immigrants themselves were also subject to acculturation processes. By the time of English domination after 1795, the sociopolitical foundations—and the bases of *apartheid*—of modern South Africa were firmly laid.

In World Perspective

AFRICA, 1000–1800

Developments in African history from 1000 to 1800 varied markedly by region. Along the Mediterranean the key new factor was the Ottomans' imperial expansion into Egypt and North Africa and their long hegemony in the Mediterranean. The influence of Islam reached across the Sahara from North Africa and the Middle East to the Sudan, where Muslim conversion played a growing social and political role, especially among the ruling elites. The Islamic tradition provided a shared arena of expression for at least some classes and groups in societies over a vast area from Egypt to Senegambia. At the same time, most Africans from the Sahara south clung to their older traditions. In central and southern Africa, except along the east coast, and in the West African forests, there was little or no evidence of Islam beyond individual Muslims involved in trade. On the east coast, however, Islam influenced the development of the distinctive Swahili culture and language, and Islamic traders linked the region to India, China, and the Indies.

Along the Atlantic and Indian Ocean coasts of Africa, the key development of the fifteenth century was the appearance of ships from Christian Europe and the traders and missionaries they carried. First the Portuguese and later the Dutch, Spaniards, and other Europeans came by sea in search of commerce and eventually spheres of influence. The European voyages of discovery of the fifteenth and sixteenth centuries were especially important for Africa, presaging the continent's involvement in a new, expanding global trading system dominated by Europeans (see Chapter 18). This system generally exploited rather than bolstered African development, as the infamous Atlantic slave trade and the South African experience illustrate.

REVIEW QUESTIONS

1. Why did Islam succeed in sub-Saharan and East Africa? What role did warfare play in its success? What role did trade have in it?
2. What was the importance of the empires of Ghana, Mali, and Songhai to world history? Why was the control of the trans-Saharan trade so important to these kingdoms? What was the importance of Islamic culture to them? Why did each of these empires break up?
3. What was the impact of the Portuguese on East Africa? On Central Africa? How did European coastal activities affect the African interior?
4. Why did Ottoman influence decline in northern Africa in the eighteenth century?
5. How did the Portuguese and Dutch differ from or resemble the Arabs, Persians, and other Muslims who came as outsiders to sub-Saharan Africa?
6. Discuss the diversity of Cape society in South Africa before 1800. Who were the Trekboers and what was their conflict with the Khoikhoi? How was the basis for apartheid formed in this period?

SUGGESTED READINGS

J. ABUN-NASR, *A History of the Maghrib in the Islamic Period* (1987). The most recent North African survey. Pages 59–247 are relevant to this chapter.

D. BIRMINHAM, *Central Africa to 1870* (1981). Chapters from the *Cambridge History of Africa* that give a brief, lucid overview of developments in this region.

P. BOHANNAN AND P. CURTIN, *Africa and Africans*, rev. ed. (1971). Accessible, topical approach to African history, culture, society, politics, and economics.

P. D. CURTIN, S. FEIERMANN, L. THOMPSON, AND J. VANSINA, *African History* (1978). An older, but masterly survey. The relevant portions are chapters 6–9.

R. ELPHICK, *Kraal and Castle: Khoikhoi and the Founding of White South Africa* (1977). An incisive, informative interpretation of the history of the Khoikhoi and their fateful interaction with European colonization.

R. ELPHICK AND H. GILIOMEE, *The Shaping of South African Society, 1652–1820* (1979). A superb, synthetic history of this crucial period.

J. D. FAGE, *A History of Africa* (1978). Still a readable survey history.

M. HISKETT, *The Development of Islam in West Africa* (1984). The standard survey study of the subject. Of the relevant sections (Chapters 1–10, 12, 15), that on Hausaland, which is treated only in passing in this text, is noteworthy.

R. W. JULY, *Precolonial Africa: An Economic and Social History* (1975). Chapter 10 gives an interesting overall picture of slaving in African history.

R. W. JULY, *A History of the African People*, 3rd ed. (1980). Chapters 3–6 treat Africa before about 1800 area by area; Chapter 7 deals with "The Coming of Europe."

I. M. LEWIS, ED., *Islam in Tropical Africa* (1966), pp. 4–96. Lewis's introduction is one of the best brief summaries of the role of Islam in West Africa and the Sudan.

D. T. NIANI, ED. *Africa from the Twelfth to the Sixteenth Century, UNESCO General History of Africa*, Vol. IV (1984). Many survey articles cover the various regions and major states of Africa in the centuries noted in the title.

R. OLIVER, *The African Experience* (1991). A masterly, balanced, and engaging survey, with outstanding syntheses and summaries of recent research.

J. A. RAWLEY, *The Transatlantic Slave Trade: A History* (1981). Impressively documented, detailed, and well-presented survey history of the Atlantic trade; little focus on African dimensions.

A. F. C. RYDER, *Benin and the Europeans: 1485–1897* (1969). A basic study.

JOHN K. THORNTON, *The Kingdom of Kongo: Civil War and Transition, 1641–1718* (1983). A detailed and perceptive analysis for those who wish to delve into Kongo state and society in the seventeenth century.

M. WILSON AND L. THOMPSON, EDS., *The Oxford History of South Africa*, Vol. I., *South Africa to 1870* (1969). Relatively detailed, if occasionally dated, treatment.

DOCUMENTS CD-ROM

1. Ibn Battuta in Mali
2. Martin Fernandez de Figueroa, Confonting the Moors in Somalia
3. Kilwa, Mombasa, and the Portugese: Realities of empire
4. Sundiata

WORLD AND THE WEB

South African Arts, Culture and Heritage

http://www.mg.co.za/saarts/museums1.htm

The Department of Arts, Culture, Science and Technology site contains analyses and descriptions of a wide range of South Africa's history and culture. Written by respected experts in each field, the site looks at the following array of South Africa's culture: shebeens, classical music, food, archaeology, theater, crafts, jazz, cultural villages, literature, dance, art collections, galleries, architecture, museums, the history of the struggle against apartheid, and popular culture.

The Story of Africa

http://www.bbc.co.uk/worldservice/africa/features/storyofafrica/index.shtml

At this BBC site, Africa's top historians examine the events and individuals that have shaped the continent from the origins of humankind to the end of South African apartheid. It has excellent histories of the West African kingdoms of ancient Ghana, Mali and Songhai.

The Literature and Culture of Zimbabwe

http://www.scholars.nus.edu.sg/landow/post/zimbabwe/art/greatzim/gz1.html

This site covers the Great Zimbabwe, the largest ruins in Africa. This complex of ruins, which covers almost 1,800 acres, is one of the country's greatest historical and cultural attractions.

Africa Revisited: Swahili Culture

http://www.unesco.org/whc/exhibits/afr_rev/africa-k.htm

"Africa Revisited" aims to reveal the richness, the diversity, and the fragility of this great heritage and thereby encourage us all to preserve and enhance it.

18 Conquest and Exploitation

The Development of the Transatlantic Economy

As this painting of the Old Custom House Quay in London suggests, trade from European empires and the tariffs imposed on it were expected to generate revenue for the home country. But behind many of the goods carried in the great sailing ships in the harbor and landed on these docks lay the labor of African slaves working on the plantations of North and South America. Michael Holford/Samuel Scott "Old Custom House Quay" Collection/By Courtesy of the Trustees of the Victoria and Albert Museum

Chapter topics

- Periods of European Overseas Expansion
- Mercantilist Theory of Economic Exploitation
- Establishment of the Spanish Empire in America
- Economies of Exploitation in the Spanish Empire
- Colonial Brazil and Slavery
- French and British Colonies in North America
- Slavery in the Americas
- Africa and the Transatlantic Slave Trade

IN WORLD PERSPECTIVE
The Transatlantic Economy

THE LATE-FIFTEENTH-CENTURY EUROPEAN encounter with the American continents changed the world. The more than two and a half centuries of European domination and government that followed the encounter made the Americas a region where European languages, legal and political institutions, trade, and religion prevail. These developments in the Americas gave Europe more influence over other world cultures and civilizations than it would otherwise have achieved.

Within decades of the European voyages of discovery, Native Americans, Europeans, and Africans began to interact in a manner unprecedented in human history. The Native Americans of North and South America encountered bands of European conquerors and European Roman Catholic missionaries. Technological and military superiority as well as political divisions among the Native Americans allowed the Europeans to realize their material and religious ambitions. By the middle of the sixteenth century Europeans had begun to import black Africans into the American continents as chattel slaves, converting them to Christianity in the process. Consequently, by the close of the sixteenth century Europe, the Americas, and Africa had become linked in a vast transatlantic economy that extracted material and agricultural wealth from the American continents largely on the basis of the nonfree labor of impressed Native Americans and imported African slaves.

The next century would see English and French colonists settling in North America and the Caribbean, introducing different political values and, through the English, Protestantism. These North American colonists would also become part of the transatlantic economy, and many would become economically involved directly or indirectly with African slavery. They too would interact with the Native Americans of North America, sometimes destroying their cultures, sometimes converting them to Christianity, and always drawing them into the transantlantic economy as they exploited the American wilderness.

Beginning in the sixteenth century the importation of African slaves and the use of slave labor were fundamental to the plantation economy that eventually extended from Maryland to Brazil. The slave trade intimately connected the economy of certain sections of Africa to the transatlantic economy. The slave trade had a devastating effect on the African people and cultures involved in it, but it also enriched the Americas with African culture and religion.

PERIODS OF EUROPEAN OVERSEAS EXPANSION

It may be useful to see the establishment of this vast new transatlantic economy in the larger context of European overseas expansion. That expansion loosed the forces that created the transatlantic economy.

Since the late fifteenth century European contacts with the rest of the world have gone through four distinct stages. The first was that of the European discovery, exploration, initial conquest, and settlement of the Americas and commercial expansion elsewhere in the world. By the close of the seventeenth century Spain governed South America, except for Portuguese-ruled Brazil. French and British

The Dutch established a major trading base at Batavia in the East Indies. The city they called Batavia is now Djakarta, Indonesia. Bildarchiv Preussischer Kulturbesitz

colonies had been established in North America. France, Britain, the Netherlands, and Spain controlled various islands in the Caribbean. The French, British, and Dutch held outposts in Asia.

The second era was one of colonial trade rivalry among Spain, France, and Great Britain. The Anglo-French side of the contest has often been compared to a second Hundred Years' War. During this second period both the British colonies of the North American seaboard and the Spanish colonies of Mexico and Central and South America emancipated themselves from European control. This era may be said to have closed during the 1820s (see Chapter 24).

The third stage of European contact with the non-European world occurred in the nineteenth century when European governments carved new formal empires in Africa and Asia. Those nineteenth-century empires also included new areas of European settlement such as Australia, New Zealand, and South Africa. The bases of these empires were trade, national honor, racial theories, religious expansion, and military superiority (see Chapter 26).

The last period of European empire occurred during the mid–twentieth century with the decolonization of peoples who had previously been under European colonial rule (see Chapters 34 and 35).

During the four and a half centuries before decolonization, Europeans exerted political dominance over much of the rest of the world that was out of all proportion to Europe's size or population. Europeans frequently treated other peoples as social, intellectual, and economic inferiors. They ravaged existing cultures because of greed, religious zeal, or political ambition. These actions significantly affect the contemporary relationship between Europe and its former colonies. What allowed the Europeans to exert such influence and domination for so long over so much of the world was not any innate cultural superiority but a technological supremacy related to naval power and gunpowder. Ships and guns allowed the Europeans to exercise their will almost wherever they chose.

Mercantilist Theory of Economic Exploitation

The early modern European empires of the sixteenth through the eighteenth centuries—empires based on commerce—existed primarily to enrich trade. Extensive trade rivalries sprang up around the world. The protection of these empires required naval power. Spain dominated the largest of these empires and constructed elaborate naval, commercial, and political structures to exploit and govern it. Finally, these empires depended largely on slave labor. Indeed, the Atlantic slave trade was a major way in which European merchants enriched themselves. That trade in turn forcibly brought the peoples of Africa into the life and culture of the New World.

To the extent that any formal economic theory lay behind the conduct of these empires, it was mercantilism, that practical creed of hard-headed business people. The terms *mercantilism* and *mercantile system* (coined by later opponents) designate a system in which governments heavily regulate trade and commerce in hope of increasing individual national wealth. Economic writers of the time believed that a nation had to gain a favorable trade balance of gold and silver bullion. A nation was truly wealthy only if it amassed more bullion than its rivals.

From beginning to end, the economic well-being of the home country was the primary concern of mercantilist writers. Colonies existed to provide markets and natural resources

DOCUMENT BUCCANEERS PROWL THE HIGH SEAS

Piracy was a major problem for transatlantic trade. There was often a fine line between freewheeling, buccaneering pirates operating for their own gain and privateers who in effect worked for various European governments who wanted to penetrate the commercial monopoly of the Spanish Empire. Alexander Exquemelin was a ship's surgeon who for a time plied his trade on board a pirate ship and then later settled in Holland. He wrote an account of those days in which he emphasizes the careful code of conduct among the pirates themselves and the harshness of their behavior to both wealthy ships they captured and poor farmers and fishermen whom they robbed and virtually enslaved.

How did the restrictive commercial policy of the Spanish Empire encourage piracy and privateering? Was there a code of honor among the pirates? What kinds of people may have suffered most from piracy? To what extent did pirates have any respect for individual freedom? How romantic was the real world of pirates?

When a buccaneer is going to sea he sends word to all who wish to sail with him. When all are ready, they go on board, each bringing what he needs in the way of weapons, powder and shot.

On the ship, they first discuss where to go and get food supplies. . . . The meat is either [salted] pork or turtle . . . Sometimes they go and plunder the Spaniards' *corrales*, which are pens where they keep perhaps a thousand head of tame hogs. The rovers . . . find the house of the farmer . . . [whom] unless he gives them as many hogs as they demand, they hang . . . without mercy. . . .

When a ship has been captured, the men decide whether the captain should keep it or not: if the prize is better than their own vessel, they take it and set fire to the other. When a ship is robbed, nobody must plunder and keep the loot to himself. Everything taken . . . must be shared . . . , without any man enjoying a penny more than his faire share. To prevent deceit, before the booty is distributed everyone has to swear an oath on the Bible that he has not kept for himself so much as the value of six-pence . . . And should any man be found to have made a false oath, he would be banished from the rovers, and never be allowed in their company. . . .

When they have captured a ship, the buccaneers set the prisoners on shore as soon as possible, apart from two or three whom they keep to do the cooking and other work they themselves do not care for, releasing these men after two or three years.

The rovers frequently put in for fresh supplies at some island or other, often . . . lying off the south coast of Cuba. . . . Everyone goes ashore and sets up his tent, and they take turns to go on marauding expedition in their canoes. They take prisoner . . . poor men who catch and set turtles for a living, to provide for their wives and children. Once captured, these men have to catch turtle for the rovers as long as they remain on the island. Should the rovers intend to cruise along a coast where turtle is abound, they take the fishermen along with them. The poor fellows may be compelled to stay away from their wives and families four or five years, with no news whether they are alive or dead.

From John Exquemelin, *The Buccaneers of America*, Alexis Brown, trans. Penguin Books © 1969. pp. 70–72.

for the industries of the home country. In turn, the home country furnished military security and political administration for the colonies. For decades both sides assumed that the colonies were the inferior partner in the relationship. The mercantilist statesmen and traders regarded the world as an arena of scarce resources and economic limitation. They assumed that one national economy could grow only at the expense of others. The home country and its colonies were to trade exclusively with each other. To that end, they tried to forge trade-tight systems of national commerce through navigation laws, tariffs, bounties to encourage production, and prohibitions against trading with the subjects of other monarchs. National monopoly was the ruling principle.

Mercantilist ideas were always neater on paper than in practice. By the early eighteenth century mercantilist assumptions were far removed from the economic realities of the colonies. The colonial and home markets simply did not mesh. Spain could not produce enough goods for South America. Economic production in the British North American colonies challenged English manufacturing and led to British attempts to limit certain colonial industries, such as iron and hat making.

Colonists of different countries wished to trade with each other. English colonists could buy sugar more cheaply from the French West Indies than from English suppliers. The traders and merchants of one nation always hoped to break the monopoly of another. For all these reasons, the eighteenth century became the "golden age of smugglers."[1] The governments could not control the activities of all their subjects. Clashes among colonists could and did lead to war between governments. Consequently, the problems associated with the European mercantile empires led to conflicts around the world.

This brief overview of the periods of the European empire and of mercantile theory should provide a clearer context for understanding the character of the conquest of America and the establishment of the transatlantic economy.

[1] Walter Dorn, *Competition for Empire, 1740–1763* (New York: Harper, 1940), p. 266.

ESTABLISHMENT OF THE SPANISH EMPIRE IN AMERICA

CONQUEST OF THE AZTECS AND THE INCAS

Within twenty years of the arrival of Columbus (1451–1506), Spanish explorers in search of gold had claimed the major islands of the Caribbean and brutally suppressed the native peoples. These actions presaged what was to occur on the continent. The Caribbean islands became the staging areas for the further exploration and conquest of other parts of the Americas.

In 1519 Hernán Cortés (1485–1547) landed in Mexico with about 500 men and a few horses. He opened communication with nearby communities and then with Moctezuma II (1466–1520), the Aztec emperor. Moctezuma may initially have believed Cortés to be the god Quetzalcoatl, who, according to legend, had been driven away centuries earlier but had promised to return. Whatever the reason, Moctezuma hesitated to confront Cortés, attempting at first to appease him with gifts of gold that only whetted Spanish appetites. Cortés succeeded in forging alliances with some subject peoples and, most importantly, with Tlaxcala, an independent state and traditional enemy of the Aztecs. His forces then marched on the Aztec capital of Tenochtitlán (modern Mexico City), where Moctezuma welcomed him. Cortés soon seized Moctezuma, making him a prisoner in his own capital. Moctezuma died in unexplained circumstances, and the Aztecs' wary acceptance of the Spaniards turned to open hostility. The Spaniards were driven from Tenochtitlán and nearly wiped out, but they ultimately returned and laid siege to the city. The Aztecs, under their last ruler, Cuauhtemoc (ca. 1495–1525), resisted fiercely but were finally defeated in late 1521. Cortés razed Tenochtitlán, building his own capital over its ruins, and proclaimed the Aztec Empire to be New Spain.

In 1532, largely inspired by Cortés's example in Mexico, Francisco Pizarro (ca. 1478–1541) landed on the western coast of South America to take on the Inca Empire, about which he knew almost nothing. His force included about 200 men armed with guns, swords, and horses, the military power of which the Incas did not understand. Pizarro lured the Inca ruler Atahualpa (ca. 1500–1533) into a conference, then seized him. The imprisoned Atahualpa tried to ransom himself with a hoard of gold, but instead of releasing him Pizarro treacherously had him garroted in 1533. The Spaniards fought their way to Cuzco, the Inca capital, and captured it, effectively ending the Inca Empire. The Spanish faced insurrections, however, and fought among themselves for decades. Effective royal control was not established until the late 1560s.

The conquests of Mexico and Peru are among the most dramatic and brutal events in modern world history. Small military forces armed with advanced weapons subdued, in a remarkably brief time, two advanced, powerful peoples. The spread of European diseases, especially smallpox, among the Native Americans also aided the conquest. The native

A 16th-century Aztec drawing depicts a battle in the Spanish conquest of Mexico. Corbis-Bettmann

populations had long lived in isolation, and many of them succumbed to the new diseases. But beyond the drama and bloodshed, these conquests, as well as those of other Native American peoples, marked a fundamental turning point. Whole civilizations with long histories and a record of enormous social, architectural, and technological achievement were effectively destroyed. Native American cultures endured, accommodating to European dominance, but there was never any doubt about which culture had the upper hand.

Bartolomé de Las Casas (1474–1566) was the most outspoken and effective defender of the Native Americans against Spanish exploitation. Bildarchiv Preussischer Kulturbesitz

THE ROMAN CATHOLIC CHURCH IN SPANISH AMERICA

The Spanish conquest of the West Indies, Mexico, and the South American continent opened that vast region to the Roman Catholic faith. Roman Catholic priests followed in the steps of the explorers and conquerors. As it had in the Castilian reconquest of the Iberian Peninsula from the Moors, religion played a central role in the conquest of the New World. In this respect the crusade against Islamic civilization in Spain and the crusade against the indigenous religions of the Americas were closely related. In both cases the Castilian monarchy received approval from church authorities for a policy of military conquest on the grounds of converting non-Christians to the Christian faith and eradicating their indigenous religious practices. The mission of conversion justified military conquest and the extension of political control and dominance. As a consequence of this policy, the Roman Catholic Church in the New World was always a conservative force working to protect the political power and prestige of the conquerors and the interests of the Spanish authorities.

The relationship between political authority and the propagation of religious doctrine was even closer in the

The Cruelties used by the Spaniards on the Indians, from a 1599 English edition of *The Destruction of the Indies* by Bartolomé de las Casas. These scenes were copied from a series of engravings produced by Theodore de Bry that accompanied an earlier edition. British Library

DOCUMENT A CONTEMPORARY DESCRIBES FORCED INDIAN LABOR AT POTOSÍ

The Potosí range in Bolivia was the site of the great silver-mining industry in the Spanish Empire. The vast wealth of the region became legendary almost as soon as mining commenced there in the 1540s. Native Americans, most of whom were forced laborers working under the mita *system of conscription, did virtually all of the work underground. This description, written by a Spanish friar in the early seventeenth century, portrays both the large size of the enterprise and the harsh conditions that the Native Americans endured. At any one time only one third of the 13,300 conscripted Native Americans were employed. The labor force was changed every four months.*

How efficient does the description suggest the mines were? What would have been the likely effects of working so long underground surrounded by burning candles?

According to His Majesty's warrant, the mine owners on this massive range have a right to the *mita* [conscripted labor] of 13,300 Indians in the working and exploitation of the mines, both those which have been discovered, those now discovered, and those which shall be discovered. It is the duty of the Corregidor [municipal governor] of Potosí to have them rounded up and to see that they come in from all the provinces between Cuzco over the whole of El Collao and as far as the frontiers of Tarija and Tomina. . . .

The *mita* Indians go up every Monday morning to the locality of Guayna Potosí which is at the foot of the range; the Corregidor arrives with all the provincial captains or chiefs who have charge of the Indians assigned them, and he there checks off and reports to each mine and smelter owner the number of Indians assigned him for his mine or smelter; that keeps him busy till 1 P.M., by which time the Indians are already turned over to these mine and smelter owners.

After each has eaten his ration, they climb up the hill, each to his mine, and go in, staying there from that hour until Saturday evening without coming out of the mine; their wives bring them food, but they stay constantly underground, excavating and carrying out the ore from which they get the silver. They all have tallow candles, lighted day and night; that is the light they work with, for as they are underground, they have need of it all the time. . . .

These Indians have different functions in the handling of the silver ore; some break it up with bar or pick, and dig down in, following the vein in the mine; others bring it up; others up above keep separating the good and the poor in piles; others are occupied in taking it down from the range to the mills on herds of llamas; every day they bring up more than 8,000 of these native beasts of burden for this task. These teamsters who carry the metal do not belong to the *mita*, but are mingados—hired.

From Antonio Vázquez de Espinosa, *Compendium and Description of the Indies* (ca. 1620), trans. by Charles Upson Clark (Washington, DC: Smithsonian Institution Press, 1968), p. 62, quoted in Helen Delpar, ed., *The Borzoi Reader in Latin American History* (New York: Alfred A. Knopf, 1972), pp. 92–93.

New World than on the Iberian Peninsula. The papacy recognized that it could not from its own resources support so extensive a missionary effort, the full requirements for which became clear only after the conquests of Mexico and Peru. The papacy therefore turned over much of the control of the church in the New World directly to the Spanish monarchy. There was thus always a close relationship between the political and economic goals of the monarchy and the role of the church. The zeal of both increased early in the sixteenth century as the papacy and the Habsburg monarchy fought the new enemy of Protestantism, which they were determined should have no foothold in America. As a consequence, the Roman Catholicism that spread throughout the Spanish domains of America took the form of the increasingly zealous faith associated with the Counter-Reformation.

During the sixteenth century the Roman Catholic Church, represented more often than not by the mendicant orders such as the Franciscans and Dominicans, and later by the newly formed Jesuits, sought to convert the Native Americans. In the early decades these conversions often occurred shortly before the Spanish exterminated Native Americans or after they had conquered them. The conversion effort also involved attempts to eradicate surviving Indian religious practices. The Roman Catholic authorities tended to tolerate some residual Indian ceremonies in the sixteenth century, but worked to prohibit them during the seventeenth century. Thus religious conversion represented, among other things, an attempt to destroy still another part of the Native American culture. Furthermore, conversion did not bring acceptance; even until late in the eighteenth century, there were few Native American Christian priests.

Real tension, however, existed between the early Spanish conquerors and the mendicant friars who sought to minister to the Native Americans. Without conquest the church could not convert the Native Americans, but the priests often deplored the harsh conditions imposed on the native peoples. By far the most effective and outspoken clerical critic of the Spanish conquerors was Bartolomé de Las Casas (1474–1566), a Dominican. He contended that conquest was not necessary for conversion. One result of his campaign was new royal regulations after 1550.

The silver mines of Potosí, worked by conscripted Indian laborers under extremely harsh conditions, provided Spain with a vast treasure in silver. Hulton/Corbis-Bettmann

Another result of Las Casas's criticism was the emergence of the "Black Legend," according to which all Spanish treatment of the Native Americans was unprincipled and inhumane. Those who created this view of Spanish behavior drew heavily on Las Casas's writings. Although substantially true, the "Black Legend" nonetheless exaggerated the case against Spain. Certainly the rulers of the native empires—as the Aztec demands for sacrificial victims attest—had often themselves been exceedingly cruel to their subject peoples.

By the end of the sixteenth century the church in Spanish America had become largely an institution upholding the colonial status quo. Although individual priests did defend the communal rights of Indian tribes, the colonial church prospered as the Spanish elite prospered through its exploitation of the resources and peoples of the New World. The church became a great landowner through crown grants and through bequests from Catholics who died in the New World. The monasteries took on an economic as well as a spiritual life of their own. Whatever its concern for the spiritual welfare of the Native Americans, the church remained one of the indications that Spanish America was a conquered world. Those who spoke for the church did not challenge Spanish domination or any but the most extreme modes of Spanish economic exploitation. The church at best only modestly moderated the forces exploiting human labor and material wealth. By the end of the colonial era in the late eighteenth century, the Roman Catholic Church had become one of the single most conservative forces in Latin America and would continue to be so for at least the next century and a half.

Economies of Exploitation in the Spanish Empire

The colonial economy of Spanish America was an economy of exploitation in two senses. First, the organization of labor within the Spanish Empire in one situation after another involved structures of highly dependent servitude or slavery. Second, the resources of the continent were exploited in mercantilist fashion for the economic advantage of Spain.

Varieties of Economic Activity

The early *conquistadores* ("conquerors") had been interested primarily in gold, but by the middle of the sixteenth century silver mining provided the chief source of metallic wealth. The great silver mining centers were Potosí in present-day Bolivia and smaller sites in northern Mexico. The Spanish crown was particularly interested in mining because it received one fifth (the *quinto*) of all mining revenues. The crown thus maintained a monopoly over the production and sale of mercury, which was required for separating silver from the other impurities in the ore. Silver mining was a flourishing source of wealth for the Spanish until the early seventeenth century, when the industry underwent a recession because of lack of new investment and the increasing costs involved in deeper mines. Nonetheless, silver predominated during the colonial era and experienced a major boom, especially in Mexico, during the eighteenth century. Its production for the benefit of Spaniards and the Spanish crown epitomized the wholly extractive economy on which Latin American colonial life was based.

The activities associated with this extractive economy—mining the ore, smelting it, harvesting wood to feed the smelters' fires—required labor. From the initial contact with America, there were too few Spanish colonists to provide the needed labor. Furthermore, the social status and expectations of those colonists who did come to the Americas made them unlikely to provide wage labor. Consequently, the Spaniards looked first to the native Indian population and then to black African slaves. Indian labor dominated on the continent and African labor in the Caribbean.

ENCOMIENDA The Spanish devised a series of institutions to exploit Native American labor. The first was the *encomienda*, a formal grant by the crown of the right to the labor of a specific number of Native Americans for a particular time. An *encomienda* usually involved a few hundred Native Americans, but might grant the right to the labor of several thousand. The *encomienda* was first used on Hispaniola, but spread to the continent as the conquest took place. *Encomienda* as an institution persisted in some parts of Latin America well into the eighteenth century, but had generally declined by the middle of the sixteenth. Some Native Americans substituted payments in kind or cash for labor.

The Spanish crown disliked the *encomienda* system. The monarchy was distressed by reports from concerned clergy that the Native Americans were being mistreated under the system and feared that *encomienda* holders were attempting to transform themselves into a powerful independent nobility in the New World.

REPARTIMIENTO The passing of the *encomienda* led to another arrangement of labor servitude, the *repartimiento*, which was largely copied from the draft labor practices of the Incas. *Repartimiento*, in an adaptation of the Incan *mita*, required adult male Native Americans to devote a set number of days of labor annually to Spanish economic enterprises. In the mines of Potosí, the *repartimiento* was known as the *mita*. The time limitation on *repartimiento* led some Spanish managers to use their workers in an extremely harsh manner, under the assumption that more fresh workers would soon be appearing on the scene. Native Americans sometimes did not survive their days of labor rotation.

THE HACIENDA Outside the mines, the major institution using dependent labor in the Spanish colonies was the *hacienda*. This institution, which dominated rural and agricultural life in Spanish colonies on the continent, developed when the crown, partly to counter the extension of the *encomienda*, made available grants of land. These grants led to the establishment of large landed estates owned by *peninsulares*, whites born in Spain, or Creoles, whites born in America. The crown thus continued to use the resources of the New World for patronage without directly impinging on the Native Americans because the grazing that occurred on the *haciendas* required far less labor than did the mines. The establishment of *haciendas* represented the transfer of the principle of the large unit of privately owned land, which was characteristic of Europe and especially of Spain, to the New World. Such estates would become one of the most important features of Latin American life. Laborers on the *hacienda* usually stood in some relation of formal servitude to the owner. Furthermore, they were usually required to buy goods for everyday living on credit from the owner. They were rarely able to repay the resulting debts and thus could not move to work for new landowners. This system was known as *debt peonage*. There were two major products of the *hacienda* economy: foodstuffs for mining areas and urban centers, and leather goods used in vast quantities on mining machinery. Both farming and ranching were thus subordinate to the mine economy.

THE DECLINE OF THE NATIVE AMERICAN POPULATION

The conquest and the economy of exploitation and forced labor (and the introduction of European diseases) produced extraordinary demographic consequences for the Indian population. Beginning in the sixteenth century Native Americans had begun to die off in huge numbers. The pre-Columbian population of America is a matter of great controversy, but conservative estimates put the Indian population at the time of Columbus's discovery at well over 50 million. In New Spain (Mexico) alone, the population probably declined from approximately 25 million to fewer than 2 million within the first century after the conquest. Similar depopulation of native peoples appears to have occurred elsewhere in Spanish America during approximately the same period. Thereafter the Indian population began to expand slowly. Whatever the exact figures, the precipitous drop eliminated the *conquistadores'* easy supply of exploitable labor.

COMMERCIAL REGULATION AND THE FLOTA SYSTEM

Because Queen Isabella of Castile (r. 1474–1504) had commissioned Columbus, the technical legal link between the New World and Spain was the crown of Castile. Its powers both at home and in America were subject to few limitations. Government of America was assigned to the Council of the Indies, which, in conjunction with the monarch, nominated the viceroys of New Spain and Peru. These viceroys were the chief executives in the New World and carried out the laws promulgated by the Council of the Indies. Each of the viceroyalties included subordinate

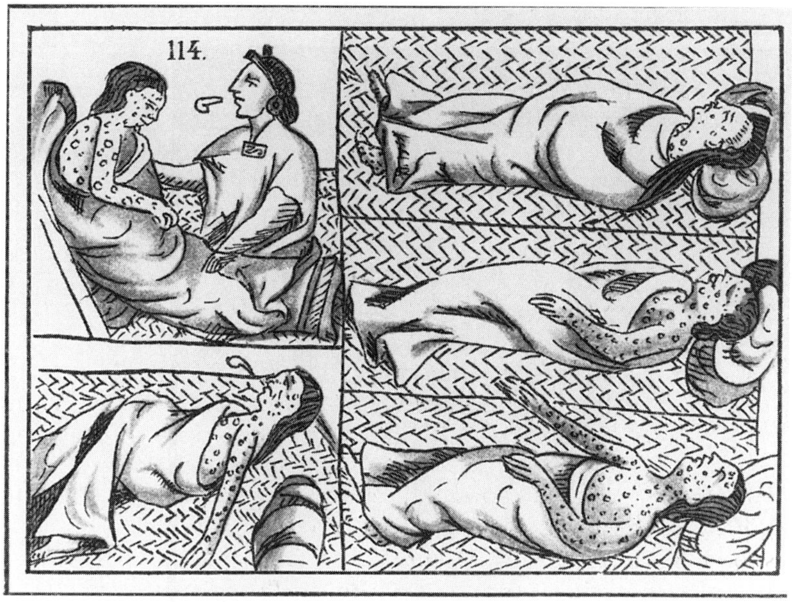

Smallpox, introduced by Europeans to the Americas, had a devastating effect on Native American populations. It swept through the Aztec capital of Tenochtitlán soon after the Spaniards arrived, contributing to the fall of the city. This illustration of the effect of the plague in the Aztec capital is from a post-conquest history known as the Florentine Codex compiled for Spanish church authorities by Aztec survivors. Courtesy President and Fellows of Harvard College, Peabody Museum, Harvard University, Photograph by Hillel Burger

judicial councils known as *audiencias*. There were also a variety of local officers, the most important of which were the *corregidores*, who presided over municipal councils. These offices provided the monarchy with a vast array of opportunities for patronage, usually bestowed on persons born in Spain. Virtually all political power flowed from the top of this political structure downward; in effect, there was little or no local initiative or self-government (see Map 18–1).

The colonial political structures existed largely to support the commercial goals of Spain. Spanish control of its American empire involved a system of monopolistic trade regulation that was more rigid in appearance than in practice. The trade monopoly was often breached. The Casa de Contratación (House of Trade) in Seville regulated all trade with the New World. Cádiz was the only Spanish port to be used for the American trade. In America there were similarly specific ports for trade both to Spain and with non-Spanish merchants. The latter trade was highly restricted. The Casa de Contratación was the single most influential institution of the Spanish Empire, and its members worked closely with the Consulado (Merchant Guild) of Seville and other groups involved with the American commerce in Cádiz. The entire organization was geared to benefit the Spanish monarchy and these privileged merchant groups.

A complicated system of trade and bullion fleets administered from Seville provided the key for maintaining the trade monopoly. Each year a fleet of commercial vessels (the *flota*) controlled by Seville merchants, escorted by warships, carried merchandise from Spain to a few specified ports in America. These included Portobello, Veracruz, and Cartagena. There were no authorized ports on the Pacific coast. Areas far to the south, such as Buenos Aires, received goods only after the shipments had been unloaded at one of the authorized ports. After selling their wares, the ships were loaded with silver and gold bullion, usually wintered in heavily fortified Caribbean ports, and then sailed back to Spain. The flota system always worked imperfectly, but trade outside it was illegal. Regulations prohibited the Spanish

The fortress of El Morro in the harbor of San Juan, Puerto Rico. This massive citadel protected the Spanish treasure fleets that carried gold and silver each year to Spain from the mines of Mexico and Peru. Comstock

MAP EXPLORATION

Interactive map: To explore this map further, go to http://www.prenhall.com/craig_map18.1

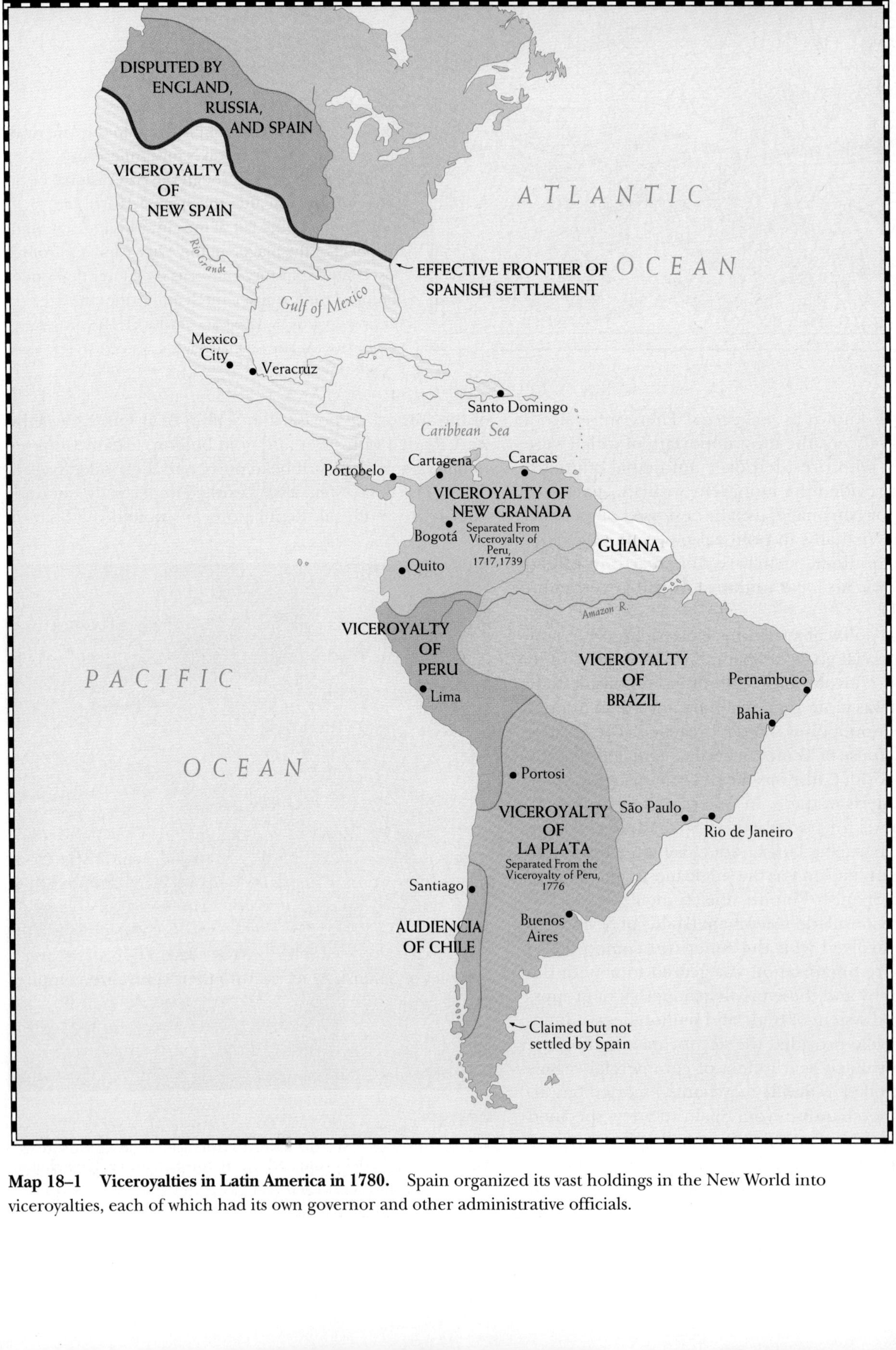

Map 18–1 Viceroyalties in Latin America in 1780. Spain organized its vast holdings in the New World into viceroyalties, each of which had its own governor and other administrative officials.

DOCUMENT VISITORS DESCRIBE THE PORTOBELLO FAIR

The Spanish tried to restrict all trade within their Latin American empire to a few designated ports. Each year a fair was held in certain of these ports. The most famous of these was Portobello on the Isthmus of Panama. In the 1730s two visitors saw the event and described it. This fair was the chief means of facilitating trade between the western coast of South America and Spain.

What products were sold at this fair? How does this passage illustrate the inefficiency of monopoly trade in the Spanish Empire and the many chances for smuggling?

The town of Portobello, so thinly inhabited, by reason of its noxious air, the scarcity of provisions, and the soil, becomes, at the time of the [Spanish] galleons one of the most populous places in all South America. . . .

The ships are no sooner moored in the harbour, than the first work is, to erect, in the square, a tent made of the ship's sails, for receiving its cargo; at which the proprietors of the goods are present, in order to find their bales, by the marks which distinguish them. These bales are drawn on sledges, to their respective places by the crew of every ship, and the money given them is proportionally divided.

Whilst the seamen and European traders are thus employed, the land is covered with droves of mules from Panama, each drove consisting of above an hundred, loaded with chests of gold and silver, on account of the merchants of Peru. Some unload them at the exchange, others in the middle of the square; yet, amidst the hurry and confusion of such crowds, no theft, loss, or disturbance, is ever known. He who has seen this place during the tiempo muerto, or dead time, solitary, poor, and a perpetual silence reigning everywhere; the harbour quite empty, and every place wearing a melancholy aspect; must be filled with astonishment at the sudden change, to see the bustling multitudes, every house crowded, the square and streets encumbered with bales and chests of gold and silver of all kinds; the harbour full of ships and vessels, some bringing by the way of Rio de Chape the goods of Peru, such as cacao, quinquina, or Jesuit's bark, Vicuña wool, and bezoar stones; others coming from Carthagena, loaded with provisions; and thus a spot, at all times detested for its deleterious qualities, becomes the staple of the riches of the old and new world, and the scene of one of the most considerable branches of commerce in the whole earth.

The ships being unloaded, and the merchants of Peru, together with the president of Panama, arrived, the fair comes under deliberation. And for this purpose the deputies of the several parties repair on board the commodore of the galleons, where, in the presence of the commodore, and the president of Panama, . . . the prices of the several kinds of merchandizes are settled. . . . The purchases and sales, as likewise the exchanges of money, are transacted by brokers, both from Spain and Peru. After this, every one begins to dispose of his goods; the Spanish brokers embarking their chests of money, and those of Peru sending away the goods they have purchased, in vessels called chatas and bongos, up the river Chagres. And thus the fair of Portobello ends.

From George Juan and Antonio de Ulloa, *A Voyage to South America*, Vol. 1 (London, 1772), pp. 103–110, as quoted in Benjamin Keen, ed., *Readings in Latin-American Civilization 1492 to the Present* (New York: Houghton Mifflin, 1955), pp. 107–108.

colonists within the American empire from trading directly with each other and from building their own shipping and commercial industry. Foreign merchants were also forbidden to breach the Spanish monopoly.

COLONIAL BRAZIL AND SLAVERY

Spain and Portugal originally had rival claims to the Americas. In 1494, by the Treaty of Tordesillas, the pope divided the seaborne empires of Spain and Portugal by drawing a line west of the Cape Verde Islands. In 1500 a Portuguese explorer landed on the coast of what is present-day Brazil, which extended east of the papal line of division, and thus Portugal gained a major hold on the South American continent.

Portugal had fewer human and material resources to devote to its New World empire than did Spain. The crown granted captaincies to private persons that permitted them to attempt to exploit the region. The native people in the lands that Portugal governed lived for the most part in small, nomadic groups. In this they differed from the native peoples of Spanish America, with their centralized empires, cities, and organized political structures. As a result, labor practices in the two regions were also different. The Portuguese imported Africans as slaves rather than using the Native Indian population, as did the Spanish in most areas.

By the mid–sixteenth century, sugar production had gained preeminence in the Brazilian economy, although some minerals were discovered and some cattle raised. Because sugar cane was grown on large estates (*fazendas*) with African slave labor, the dominance of sugar meant also the dominance of slavery.

The sugar plantations of Brazil and the West Indies were a major source of the demand for slave labor. Slaves are here shown grinding sugar cane and refining sugar, which was then exported to the consumer markets in Europe. Hulton/Corbis-Bettmann

Toward the close of the seventeenth century, sugar prices declined and the economy suffered. In the early eighteenth century, however, significant deposits of gold were discovered in southern Brazil. Immigrants from Portugal joined the ensuing gold rush, and economic activity moved suddenly toward the south. This shift, however, did not reduce Brazil's reliance on slave labor. In fact, the expansion of gold mining also led to the increased importation of African slaves. Nowhere, except perhaps in the West Indies, was slavery so important as it was in Brazil, where it persisted until 1888.

The taxation and administration associated with gold mining brought new, unexpected wealth to the eighteenth-century Portuguese monarchy, allowing it to rule without recourse to the Cortés or traditional parliament for taxation. Through transatlantic trade the new wealth generated from Brazilian gold also filtered into all the major trading nations, which could sell their goods to Portugal as well as profit from the slave trade.

As in the Spanish Empire, the Portuguese crown attempted to establish a strong network of regulation around Brazilian trade. Brazil, however, required less direct control by the Portuguese than the Spanish Empire required from Spain, and as a result, Brazil's colonial settlers may have felt less resentment toward the Portuguese government than the settlers of the Spanish Empire felt toward the Spanish administrators. In Brazil, where the basic unit of production was the plantation, there were fewer large cities than in Spanish America. The crown's determination in Spanish America to have precious metals sent to Spain required a vast colonial administration. The sugar plantations of Brazil, in contrast, did not require such direct administration. Consequently, the Portuguese were willing to allow more local autonomy than was Spain. More local officials were allowed to serve in the government in Brazil than in Spanish America, where the administration was dominated by officials born in Spain. In Spanish America the use of Indian labor, which was important to the colonial economy, required government supervision. Brazil, less dependent on Indian labor, felt no such constraints. Indeed, the Portuguese government condoned policies whereby Indian tribes were driven into the back country or exterminated. Throughout the eighteenth century the Portuguese government also favored the continued importation of slaves.

French and British Colonies in North America

French explorers had pressed down the St. Lawrence river valley in Canada during the seventeenth century. French fur traders and Roman Catholic Jesuit missionaries had followed in their wake, with the French government supporting the missionary effort. By the end of the seventeenth century a significant but sparsely populated French presence existed in Canada. Trade rather than extensive settlements characterized the French effort. The largest settlement was Quebec, founded in 1608. Some French settlers married Native American women; the absence of a drive to permanently claim land reduced conflict between the French and the Native Americans. It was primarily through the fur trade that French Canada functioned as part of the early transatlantic economy.

For most readers of this volume, the story of the founding of the English-speaking colonies along the Atlantic seaboard is relatively familiar, but it needs to be set in the larger world context. Beginning with the first successful settlement in Jamestown, Virginia, in 1607 and ending with the establishment of Georgia in 1733, the eastern seaboard of the United States became populated by a series of English colonies. Other nations, including the Dutch and Swedes, had founded settlements, but all of them were eventually taken over during the seventeenth century by the English.

A wide variety of reasons led to the founding of the English colonies. Settlement for enrichment from farming and trade accounted for some settlements, such as Virginia and New Amsterdam (after 1664, New York). Others, such as the Carolinas, were developed by royal favorites who were given vast land tracts. James Oglethorpe founded Georgia as a refuge for English debtors. But the pursuit of religious liberty constituted the major driving force of the Pilgrim and Puritan founders of Massachusetts, the Baptist Roger Williams in Rhode Island, the Quaker William Penn in Pennsylvania, and the Roman Catholic Lord Baltimore in Maryland.

With the exception of Maryland, these colonies were Protestant. The Church of England dominated the southern colonies. In New England, varieties of Protestantism associated with or derived from Calvinism were in the ascendancy. In their religious affiliations, the English-speaking colonies manifested two important traits derived from the English experience. First, much of their religious life was organized around self-governing congregations. Second, their religious outlook derived from those forms of Protestantism that were suspicious of central political authority and especially of potentially despotic monarchs. In this regard, their cultural and political outlook differed sharply from the cultural and political outlook associated with the Roman Catholicism of the Spanish Empire. In a sense the values of the extreme Reformation and Counter-Reformation confronted each other on the two American continents.

The English colonists had complex interactions with the Native American populations. Unlike the Spanish to the south or the French to the north, they had only modest interest in missionary enterprise. As in South America, new diseases imported from Europe took a high death toll among the native population. Unlike Mexico and Peru, however, North America had no large Native American cities. The Native American populations were far more dispersed, and intertribal animosity was intense. The English often encountered well-organized resistance, as from the Powhatan conspiracy in Virginia and the Pequots in New England. The most powerful of the Native American groups was the Iroquois Nation, organized in the early eighteenth century in New York. The Iroquois battled successfully against other tribes and long negotiated successfully with both the Dutch and the English. The English also often used one tribe against another, and the Native Americans also tried to use the English or the French in their own conflicts. The outcome of these struggles between the English settlers and the Native Americans was rarely full victory for either side, but rather mutual exhaustion, with the Native Americans temporarily retreating beyond the reach of English settlements and the English temporarily restraining their initial claims. From the late seventeenth century through the American Revolution, however, the Native Americans of North America were drawn into the Anglo-French Wars that were fought in North America as well as Europe. Indeed, Native American alliances became important for the Anglo-French conflict on the Continent, which was intimately related to their rivalry over transatlantic trade (see Chapter 20).

The largest economic activity throughout the English-speaking colonies was agriculture. From New England through the Middle Atlantic states there were mostly small farms tilled by free white labor; from Virginia southward it was the plantation economy, dependent on slavery. During the early eighteenth century the chief products raised on these plantations were tobacco, indigo, rice, and sugar. Although slavery was a dominant institution in the South, all of the colonies included slaves. The principal port cities along the seaboard—Boston, Newport, New York, Philadelphia, Baltimore, and Charleston—resembled small provincial English cities. They were primarily trading centers through which goods moved back and forth between the colonies and England and the West Indies. The commercial economies of these cities were all related to the transatlantic slave trade.

Until the 1760s the political values of the Americans resembled those of their English counterparts. The colonials were thoroughly familiar with events in England. They sent many of their children there to be educated. They were monarchists but, like their English counterparts, suspicious of monarchical power. Their politics involved vast amounts of patronage and individual favors. Their society was clearly hierarchical, with an elite that functioned like a colonial aristocracy and many ordinary people who were dependent on that aristocracy. Throughout the colonies during the eighteenth century, the Anglican Church grew in influence and membership. The prosperity of the colonies might eventually have led them to separate from England, but in 1750 few people thought that would occur.

Both England and France had important sugar islands in the Caribbean. England held Jamaica and Barbados, and France held Saint Domingue (Haiti), Guadeloupe, and Martinique. The plantations on these islands were worked by African slaves, and the trade and commerce of the northern British colonies were closely related to meeting the needs of these islands.

SLAVERY IN THE AMERICAS

Black slavery was the final mode of forced or subservient labor in the New World. Unlike the labor exploitation of Native Americans discussed earlier in this chapter, black slavery extended throughout not only the Spanish Empire but also Portuguese Brazil and the English-speaking colonies of North America.

ESTABLISHMENT OF SLAVERY

As the numbers of Native Americans in South America declined due to disease and exploitation, the Spanish and the Portuguese turned to the labor of imported African slaves.

By the late sixteenth century, in the islands of the West Indies and the major cities of South America, black slaves equaled or surpassed the white European population.

On much of the South American continent dominated by Spain, the number of slaves declined during the late seventeenth century, and the institution became less fundamental there than elsewhere. Slavery continued to prosper, however, in Brazil and in the Caribbean. Later, starting with the importation of slaves to Jamestown in 1619, slavery spread into the British North American colonies and became a fundamental institution there.

One of the forces that led to the spread of slavery in Brazil and the West Indies was the cultivation of sugar. Sugar cane required a large investment in land and equipment, and only slave labor could provide enough workers for the extremely profitable sugar plantations. As the production of sugar expanded, so did the demand for slaves, and more slaves were imported.

By the close of the seventeenth century the Caribbean islands were the world center for sugar production. As the European appetite for sugar continued to grow, the slave population continued to expand. By 1725 black slaves may have constituted almost 90 percent of the population of Jamaica. The situation was similar throughout the West Indies. There and elsewhere, in Brazil and the southern British colonies, prosperity and slavery went hand in hand. The wealthiest and most prized of the colonies were those that raised consumer staples, such as sugar, rice, tobacco, or cotton, by slave labor.

THE PLANTATION ECONOMY AND TRANSATLANTIC TRADE

The plantations that stretched from Maryland through the West Indies and into Brazil formed a vast corridor of slave societies in which social and economic subordination was based on both involuntary servitude and race. This kind of society, in its total dependence on slave labor and racial differences, was something novel in world history; it had not existed before the European discovery and exploitation of the Americas. The social and economic influence of plantation slavery touched not only the plantation societies themselves

Native Americans in the Saint Lawrence region of North America were drawn into the transatlantic economy through interaction with French fur traders in the early 17th century. This illustration shows Samuel de Champlain, the founder of New France, assisting his Huron allies in an attack on the Iroquois in part of an ongoing struggle for control of valuable fur grounds. The palm trees in the background suggest that the artist was unfamiliar with the region. New York Public Library, Rare Book Division

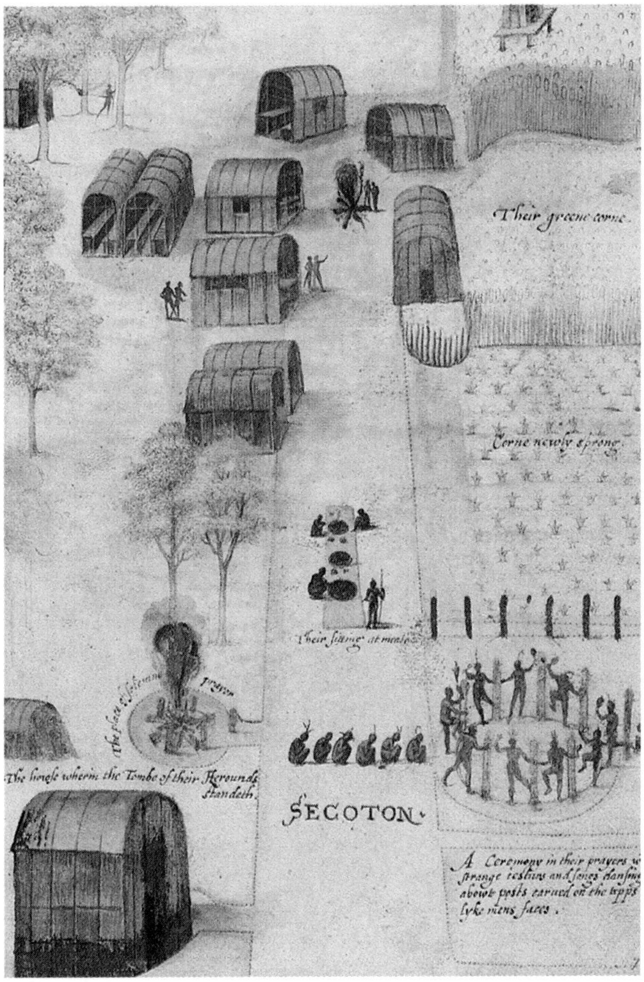

The first successful English colonies in North America in the 17th century were preceded by two failed efforts on Roanoke Island in what is now North Carolina in the late 16th century. John White accompanied both attempts, the second as governor. White was a perceptive and sensitive observer whose watercolor paintings provide invaluable information about Native American life in the coastal Carolina region at the time of contact. This painting shows the Algonquian village of Secoton. The houses were bark covered. In the lower left is a mortuary temple. The dancers in the lower right are performing a fertility ceremony. The man sitting in the platform in the upper right is keeping birds away from the corn crop. The Bridgeman Art Library International

but also West Africa, western Europe, and New England. It persisted from the sixteenth century through the second half of the nineteenth century, ending with the British effort to outlaw the slave trade during the first half of the nineteenth century, the Latin American Wars of Independence, the Emancipation Proclamation of 1862 in the United States, and the Brazilian emancipation of 1888. Every society in which it existed still contends with its long-term effects.

The slave trade was part of the larger system of transatlantic trade that linked Europe, Africa, and the European colonies in South America, the Caribbean, and North America. In this system the Americas supplied labor-intensive raw materials like tobacco, sugar, coffee, precious metals, cotton, and indigo. Europe supplied manufactured goods like textiles, liquor, guns, metal wares, and beads, not to mention various forms of cash, including even gold. And Africa supplied gold, ivory, wood, palm oil, gum, and other products, as well as the slaves who provided the labor to create the American products. By the eighteenth century slaves were the predominant African export.

SLAVERY ON THE PLANTATIONS

The plantations in the Americas to which the African slaves eventually arrived were always in a fairly isolated rural setting. Their products, however, were agricultural goods produced for an external overseas market that was part of a larger integrated transatlantic economy. The plantation might raise food for its owners and their slaves, but the main production—whether sugar, tobacco, or, later, cotton and

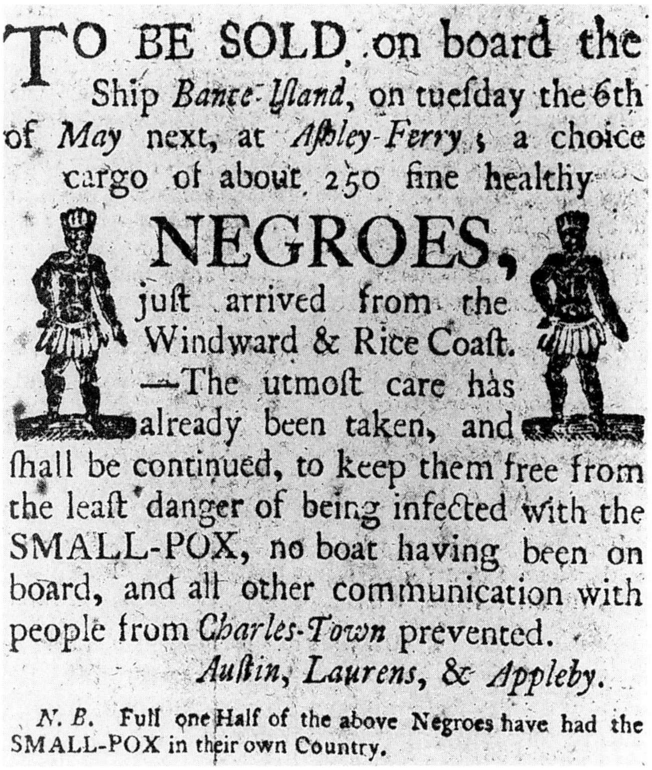
TO BE SOLD, on board the Ship *Bance-Yland*, on tueſday the 6th of *May* next, at *Aſhley-Ferry*; a choice cargo of about 250 fine healthy

NEGROES,

juſt arrived from the Windward & Rice Coaſt. —The utmoſt care has already been taken, and ſhall be continued, to keep them free from the leaſt danger of being infected with the SMALL-POX, no boat having been on board, and all other communication with people from *Charles-Town* prevented.

Auſtin, Laurens, & Appleby.

N. B. Full one Half of the above Negroes have had the SMALL-POX in their own Country.

Africans who survived the voyage across the Atlantic were immediately sold into slavery in the Americas. This slave-auction notice relates to a group of slaves whose ship had stopped at Charleston, South Carolina, and then landed elsewhere in the region to auction its human cargo. Notice the concern to assure potential buyers that the slaves were healthy. Corbis-Bettmann

In the American South, the islands of the Caribbean, and in Brazil, the slaves labored on sugar plantations under the authority of overseers. The Granger Collection

coffee—was intended for export. In turn, plantation owners imported from other parts of the world virtually all the finished or manufactured goods they used or consumed.

The life conditions of plantation slaves differed from colony to colony. Most owners possessed relatively few slaves, and vast slaveholdings were the exception. Black slaves living in Portuguese areas had the fewest legal protections. In the Spanish colonies the church attempted to provide some small protection for black slaves, but devoted much more effort toward protecting the Native Americans. Slave codes were developed in the British and the French colonies during the seventeenth century, but they provided only the most limited protection. Virtually all slave owners feared a slave revolt; slave-related legislation and other regulations were intended to prevent such an event. Slave laws favored the master rather than the slave. Masters were permitted to punish slaves by whipping and other harsh corporal punishment. Furthermore, slaves were often forbidden to gather in large groups lest they plan a revolt. In most slave-owning societies, the marriages of slaves were not recognized by law. The children of slaves continued to be slaves and were owned by the owner of the parents. Slave families could be separated by the owner or after the owner's death.

The daily life of most slaves during these centuries was one of hard agricultural labor, poor diet and clothing, and inadequate housing. The death rate among slaves was high. Their welfare and their lives were sacrificed to the ongoing expansion of the plantations that made their owners wealthy and that produced goods demanded by consumers in Europe. Scholars have argued that slaves in one area or another had a better existence than others, but it is generally accepted that slaves in all plantation societies suffered under difficult conditions. The specifics of those conditions may have varied, but they were not significantly better in one place than another.

The African slaves who were transported to the Americas were, like the Native Americans, converted to Christianity: in the Spanish domains to Roman Catholicism, and in the English colonies to various forms of Protestantism. In both cases, they became largely separated from African religious outlooks. Although some African practices survived in muted forms, and slaves did manage to mix Christianity with African religion, the conversion of Africans to Christianity nonetheless represented another example of the crushing of a set of non-European cultural values in the context of the New World economies and social structures.

The European settlers in the Americas and the slave traders were also prejudiced against black Africans. Many Europeans thought Africans were savage or less than civilized. Others looked down on them simply because they were slaves. These attitudes had been shared by both Christians and Muslims in the Mediterranean world, where slavery had long existed. Furthermore, many European languages and European cultures attached negative connotations to the idea and image of blackness. In virtually all plantation societies, race was an important element in keeping black slaves subservient. Although racial thinking in regard to slavery became more important in the nineteenth century, the fact that slaves were differentiated from the rest of the population by race as well as by their status as chattel property was fundamental to the system.

AFRICA AND THE TRANSATLANTIC SLAVE TRADE

It was the establishment of plantations demanding the use of slave labor that drew Africa and its peoples into the heart of the transatlantic economy. As Native American peoples were decimated by conquest and European diseases or proved unsatisfactory as plantation laborers, colonial entrepreneurs began to look elsewhere for peoples to work their plantations. First the Portuguese, and then the Spanish, Dutch, French, and English (others would follow, including Americans) turned to west, central, and, to a lesser degree, southeastern Africa for an ample supply of slaves. Thus the Atlantic slave trade was not overtly the result of racist principles, but of the economic needs of the colonial powers and their willingness to exploit weaker peoples to satisfy them. However, this willingness was based on the tacit racist assumption that non-European, nonwhite tribal peoples were subhuman and could be enslaved for European purposes.

The Portuguese, who were the principal carriers throughout most of the history of the trade, had a virtual monopoly until the Dutch broke it in the 1640s and briefly became the chief carriers. The French and the English came into the trade only in the late seventeenth century; yet during the eighteenth century, which saw the greatest shipments, they carried almost half the total traffic. Americans, too, were latecomers but avid slavers who managed to make considerable profits before and even after Britain and the United States outlawed slaving in 1807.

If gold and the search for a sea route to Asia brought the first European ships to Africa, slaves were the main commodity for which they returned for a long time. Slaving was an important part of the massive new overseas trade that financed much European and American economic development that so dramatically changed the West during the nineteenth century. The success of this trade, bought at the price of immense human suffering, helped propel Europe and some of its colonial offshoots in the Americas into world dominance.

The Background of Slavery

Slavery seems to have been one of the tragic facts of human societies as far back as we can trace its history. Although linked to warfare and the age-old practice of taking captives, it cannot be fully explained by military or economic necessity.

Virtually every premodern state around the globe depended on slavery to some extent. The Mediterranean and African worlds were no exception, in both the pre-Islamic and the Islamic periods. Slave institutions in sub-Saharan Africa were ancient and included traffic with the Mediterranean world. The Islamic states of southwestern Asia and North Africa continued and even increased this traffic, importing slaves from both the Sudan and Horn of Africa as well as the East African coast, although they took fewer slaves from Africa than from Eastern Europe and Central Asia. Central Asia, for example, was the source of most of the (largely Turkish) slave-soldier dynasties that came to rule many Islamic states from India to North Africa. (Hence it is not surprising that the word *slave* is derived ultimately from *Slav.*) Both Mediterranean-Christian and Islamic peoples were using slaves—mostly Greeks, Bulgarians, Turkish prisoners of war, and Black Sea Tartars, but also Africans—well before the voyages of discovery opened sub-Saharan sources of slaves for the new European colonies overseas.

Not all forms of slavery were as dehumanizing as the chattel slavery that came to predominate (with the sanction of Christian authorities) during the colonization of the Americas. Islamic law, for example, although permitting slavery, also ameliorated it. All slavery, however, involved the forceful exploitation and degradation of some human beings for the profit of others, the denial of basic freedoms, and sometimes the sundering, often violently, of even the closest family ties.

Africa suffered immense social devastation when it was the chief supplier of slaves to the world. The societies that were built to a great extent on the exploitation of African slavery also suffered enduring consequences, not the least of which, many believe, is racism.

Slavery and Slaving in Africa

The trade that long before the fifteenth century supplied African slaves to the Islamic lands of the Mediterranean and to southwestern and southern Asia has conventionally been termed the "Oriental" slave trade. The savannahs of the Sudan and the Horn of Africa were the two prime sources of slaves for this trade. The trade managed by Europeans, conventionally called the "Occidental" slave trade, can be traced at least to the thirteenth century, when Europeans established sugar cane plantations on Cyprus soon after Muslim forces had driven them out of the Holy Land. In Cypress, as later in Brazil and the Caribbean islands, slaves proved an especially profitable workforce for the labor-intensive process of sugar production. This industry subsequently spread westward to Crete and Sicily and, in the fifteenth century, to the Portuguese Atlantic islands of Madeira and São Thomé.

The Portuguese in particular developed the plantation system of slave labor as they began their expansion into the Atlantic and beyond. Although the savannah and Horn

Table 18–1
Estimated Slave Imports into the Americas and Old World by Region, 1451–1870

British North America	523,000
Spanish America	1,687,000
British Caribbean	2,443,000
French Caribbean	1,655,000
Dutch Caribbean	500,000
Danish Caribbean	50,000
Brazil (Portuguese)	4,190,000
Old World	297,000
Total	**11,345,000**

Figures as calculated by James A. Rawley, *The Transatlantic Slave Trade: A History* (New York: W. W. Norton, 1981), p. 428, based on his and other more recent revisions of the careful but older estimates of Philip D. Curtin, *The Atlantic Slave Trade: A Census* (Madison: University of Wisconsin Press, 1969), especially pp. 266, 268.

Art and the World

A Dramatic Moment in the Transatlantic World

Copley's "Watson and the Shark"

Both the career of the North American–born painter John Singleton Copley (1738–1815) and his monumental painting *Watson and the Shark* (1778) illustrate the economic and cultural interconnections of the eighteenth-century transatlantic world. Copley was born in Massachusetts and became an accomplished portrait painter of the Boston elite. When hostilities erupted between Britain and the colonies, Copley moved to London in 1774, where his reputation had preceded him. He never returned to America.

In Britain, he undertook commissions for *history painting,* then considered the most prestigious subject for artists. Traditionally, history painting drew its subject matter from mythology, biblical narratives, or ancient history, but Copley was interested in portraying contemporary events. His figures were modern people, dressed in modern clothing but striking poses taken from classical and Renaissance art.

History painting claimed to convey a moral message usually of heroism, patriotism, or self-sacrifice. In 1778 Copley completed *Watson and the Shark,* recounting the experience of Brook Watson's rescue, as a boy of fourteen in 1749, from the jaws of a shark in the harbor of Havana, Cuba. Watson, who later became lord mayor of London, lost most of his leg in the attack, but regarded his rescue and subsequent success as a merchant as an inspiring example to others who had encountered adversity.

In portraying the terrifying moment just before Watson's rescue, Copley presents the event as a profound drama, which he invites the viewer to attend. By seeking to evoke a powerful emotional response from the viewer, Copley was working in the category of art known at the time as the *sublime.* Yet Copley also used his power as a portraitist to depict each man in the painting as a real person, not as some allegorical figure.

Watson and the Shark is also one of the first paintings to prominently depict an African American. The black man in the middle of the painting holds the rope that will soon be used to rescue Watson. His presence also places the action in the world of the plantation economy and transatlantic trade. It is not clear whether he is a slave or a former slave now working as a sailor in the commercial shipping trade.

In several respects, this painting illustrates the interconnectedness of the eighteenth-century transatlantic world. Copley is an American artist working in London. The action occurs in a Spanish colony during a commercial venture. The person being rescued is an English subject who will become a rich merchant. The boat holds a cross section of races and cultures from Africa, Europe, and the Americas that characterized the world of the plantation economies.

Watson and the Shark is also important in art history for another reason. Through the contrasts of light and dark, Copley set out to achieve a dramatic painting of human beings in combat with powerful natural forces—the sea, the wind, and the shark. This would become a major theme of the late-eighteenth- and early-nineteenth-century artistic and literary movement known as Romanticism. *Watson and the Shark* stands as a major forerunner of this new direction of painting and taste.

Sources: Jules Prown, *John Singleton Copley* (Cambridge, Mass.: Harvard University Press, 1966): John Wilmerding, *American Art* (New York: Penguin Books, 1976); Theodore Stebbins, Jr., et al., *A New World: Masterpieces of American Painting 1760–1910* (Boston: Museum of Fine Arts, 1983), pp. 210–211; Hugh Honour, *The Image of the Black in Western Art,* Vol 4, Part I, *From the American Revolution to World War I: Slave and Liberators* (Cambridge, Mass.: Harvard University Press, 1989).

John Singleton Copley, American, 1738–1815. *Watson and the Shark*, 1778. Oil on canvas, 72¼ × 90⅜ in. Gift of Mrs. George von Lengerke Meyer. Courtesy, Museum of Fine Arts, Boston. Reproduced with permission. © 1999 Museum of Fine Arts, Boston. All Rights Reserved.

Slave dealing in the streets of Zanzibar. Slaving was a part of East African trade for centuries. Corbis-Bettmann

regions were the earliest sources for this trade, voyages beginning in the fifteenth century by first the Portuguese and then other Europeans opened the western coasts of Africa as far south as Angola, making them the prime slaving areas. A third but less important source region for both Occidental and Oriental trades was the eastern coast of Africa below the Horn.

Before the full development of the transatlantic slave trade by about 1650, slavery and slave trading had been no more significant in Africa than anywhere else in the world.[2] Indigenous African slavery resembled that of other premodern societies. It was apparently most common, if still limited, in the areas of the savannah and Horn, presumably because these areas were involved in external slave trading. In the western and central Sudan, slavery came largely to be regulated by Islamic norms, but in the Horn, specifically in Ethiopia, slavery was practiced in both Christian and Muslim communities. Estimates suggest that about 10,000 slaves per year, most of them female, were taken from sub-Saharan Africa through the Oriental trade.

By about 1650 the newer Occidental slave trade of the Europeans had become as large as the Oriental trade and for the ensuing two centuries far surpassed it. It affected adversely all of Africa, disrupting especially western and central African society. As a result of the demand for young male slaves on the plantations of the Americas, West Africa experienced a sharp drain on its productive male population. Between 1640 and 1690, although the price of a slave at the coast remained constant, the number of slaves sold to European carriers doubled, indicating the increasing participation of Africans in the expanding trade. With the growing demand for slaves came an increase in internal warfare in western and central Africa. Moreover, as the external trade destroyed the regional male-female population balance, an internal market for female slaves in particular arose.

These developments accelerated during the eighteenth century—at the height of the Occidental trade. It was also during this period that African states and slave traders were most heavily involved as regulators and suppliers of the trade. Slave prices at times accelerated accordingly. Owing to population depletion and regional migrations, however, the actual number of sold slaves declined in some areas. The population declined sharply in the coastal and inland areas hardest hit by the ravages of the trade in the later eighteenth century and continued to decline in places even until 1850.

[2] The summary follows closely that of P. Manning, *Slavery and African Life: Occidental, Oriental, and African Slave Trades* (Cambridge: Cambridge University Press, 1990), pp. 127–140.

This 18th-century print shows bound African captives being forced to a slaving port. It was largely African middlemen who captured slaves in the interior and marched them to the coast. North Wind Picture Archives

DOCUMENT A SLAVE TRADER DESCRIBES THE ATLANTIC PASSAGE

During 1693 and 1694 Captain Thomas Phillips carried slaves from Africa to Barbados on the ship Hannibal. *The financial backer of the voyage was the Royal African Company of London, which held an English crown monopoly on slave trading. Phillips sailed to the west coast of Africa, where he purchased the Africans who were sold into slavery by an African king. Then he set sail westward.*

Who are the various people described in this document who in one way or another were involved in or profited from the slave trade? What dangers did the Africans face on the voyage? What contemporary attitudes could have led this ship captain to treat and think of his human cargo simply as goods to be transported? What are the grounds of his self-pity for the difficulties he met?

Having bought my complement of 700 slaves, 480 men and 220 women, and finish'd all my business at Whidaw [on the Gold Coast of Africa], I took my leave of the old king and his cappasheirs [attendants], and parted, with many affectionate expressions on both sides, being forced to promise him that I would return again the next year, with several things he desired me to bring from England. . . . I set sail the 27th of July in the morning, accompany'd with the East-India Merchant, who had bought 650 slaves, for the Island of St. Thomas . . . from which we took our departure on August 25th and set sail for Barbadoes.

We spent in our passage from St. Thomas to Barbadoes two months eleven days, from the 25th of August to the 4th of November following: in which time there happened such sickness and mortality among my poor men and Negroes. Of the first we buried 14, and of the last 320, which was a great detriment to our voyage, the Royal African Company losing ten pounds by every slave that died, and the owners of the ship ten pounds ten shillings, being the freight agreed on to be paid by the charter-party for every Negro delivered alive ashore to the African Company's agents at Barbadoes. . . . The loss in all amounted to near 6500 pounds sterling.

The distemper which my men as well as the blacks mostly died of was the white flux, which was so violent and inveterate that no medicine would in the least check it, so that when any of our men were seized with it, we esteemed him a dead man, as he generally proved. . . .

The Negroes are so incident to the small pox that few ships that carry them escape without it, and sometimes it makes vast havock and destruction among them. But tho' we had 100 at a time sick of it, and that it went thro' the ship, yet we lost not above a dozen by it. All the assistance we gave the diseased was only as much water as they desir'd to drink, and some palm-oil to annoint their sores, and they would generally recover without any other helps but what kind nature gave them. . . .

But what the small pox spar'd, the flux swept off, to our great regret, after all our pains and care to give them their messes in due order and season, keeping their lodgings as clean and sweet as possible, and enduring so much misery and stench so long among a parcel of creatures nastier than swine, and after all our expectations to be defeated by their mortality. . . .

No gold-finders can endure so much noisome slavery as they do who carry Negroes; for those have some respite and satisfaction, but we endure twice the misery; and yet by their mortality our voyages are ruin'd, and we pine and fret ourselves to death, and take so much pains to so little purpose.

From Thomas Phillips, "*Journal*," *A Collection of Voyages and Travels*; Vol. VI, ed. by Awnsham and John Churchill (London, 1746), as quoted in Thomas Howard, ed., *Black Voyage: Eyewitness Accounts of the Atlantic Slave Trade* (Boston: Little, Brown and Company, 1971), pp. 85–87.

As European nations, followed by nations in the Americas, slowly began to outlaw slaving and slavery in the nineteenth century, occidental demand slowed and prices for slaves sank. The result was that the oriental and internal trades increased. Slave exports from East Africa and the Sudan and Horn increased significantly after about 1780, and indigenous African slavery, predominantly of women, also expanded. Indeed, by about 1850 the internal African trade surpassed the combined oriental and (now outlawed and decreasing) occidental trade. This traffic was dominated by the same figures—merchants, warlords, and rulers—who had previously profited from external trade.

Indigenous African slavery began a real decline only at the end of the nineteenth century, in part because of the dominance of European colonial regimes and in part because of internal changes. The formal end of African indigenous slavery occurred over a long period, beginning in 1874 in the Gold Coast and ending only in 1928 in Sierra Leone.

THE AFRICAN SIDE OF THE TRANSATLANTIC TRADE

Africans were actively involved in the transatlantic slave trade. Except for the Portuguese in central Africa, European slave traders generally obtained their human cargoes from private or government-sponsored African middlemen at coastal forts or simply at anchorages along the coast. A system of forts built by Europeans mostly between 1640 and 1750, for example, dominated the Gold Coast. This situation was the result of both the desire and ability of Africans to control inland trade and the vulnerability of Europeans to tropical disease (a new European arrival stood a less than 50 percent chance of surviving a year on the tropical African coast). Thus it was largely African middlemen who undertook the actual capture or procurement of slaves and the difficult, dangerous task of marching them to the coast. These middlemen were generally either wealthy merchants who could mount slaving

Captured by Mandingo enemies and sold to a Maryland tobacco planter, Job ben Solomon accomplished the nearly impossible feat of returning to Africa as a freeman. By demonstrating his talents as a Muslim scholar, including his ability to write the entire Qur'an from memory, he astonished his owners and eventually convinced them to let him go home. "The Fortunate Slave," An Illustration of African Slavery in the early 18th century by Douglas Grant (1968). From "Some Memoirs of the Life of Job," by Thomas Bluett 1734. Photo by Robert D. Rubic/Precision Chromes, Inc., The New York Public Library, Research Libraries.

expeditions inland or the agents of African chieftaincies or kingdoms that sought to profit from the trade.

The media of exchange were varied. At first they usually involved mixed barter for goods that ranged from gold dust or firearms to beads and alcohol. As time went on they came increasingly to involve some form of monetary payment. This exchange drained productive resources (human beings) in return for nonproductive wealth.

The chief western and central African slaving regions provided different numbers of slaves at different times, and the total number of exported slaves varied sharply between periods. When one area was unable to produce sufficient numbers to meet demand (whether as a result of depopulation of choice areas, local warfare, or changing state policies), the European traders shifted their buying to other points. Thus, between 1526 and 1550 the major sources of the slaves for the Atlantic trade were the Kongo-Angola region (34 percent), the Guinea coast of Cape Verde (25.6 percent), and Senegambia (23.5 percent).[3] By contrast, between 1761 and 1810 the French drew some 52 percent of their slaves from Angola and 24 percent from the Bight of Benin, but only 4.8 percent from Senegambia, whereas the British relied most heavily on the Bight of Biafra and central Africa.[4] Traders naturally went where population density and the presence of active African merchant or state suppliers promised the best numbers and prices, although prices do not seem to have varied radically in a given period.

THE EXTENT OF THE SLAVE TRADE

The slave trade varied sharply in extent from period to period. Only about 3 percent of the total Occidental trade occurred before 1600, and only about 14 percent between 1600 and 1700. The period of greatest activity, 1701–1810, accounted for over 60 percent of the total, and even the final half century of slaving until 1870 accounted for over 20 percent of the total. Despite moves by European nations to abolish slaving in the early 1800s, the Portuguese still transported more than a million slaves to Brazil between 1811 and 1870. In fact, more slaves landed in the Americas in these final years of the trade than during the entire seventeenth century.[5] We would do well to remember how long it actually took the "modern" occidental world to abolish the trade in African slaves.

The overall number of African slaves exported during the occidental trade—effectively, between 1451 and 1870—is still debated and must be seen in the larger context of all types of slaving in Africa in the same period. A major unknown—for both the occidental and the oriental trades—is the number of slaves who died under the brutal conditions to which they were subjected when captured and transported overland and by sea. The most reliable estimates pertain only to those slaves who actually landed abroad, and these estimates are more reliable for the occidental trade than for the older, smaller, and more dispersed oriental trade. As Table 18–1 shows, just those who actually reached an American or Old World destination in the occidental trade totaled more than 11 million souls.

Recent scholarship estimates that at a minimum Africa lost some 13 million people to the Atlantic trade alone during its four centuries of existence. Another 5 million or more were lost to the oriental trade. Finally, the occidental trade spurred an apparently huge increase in internal slavery, and according to the estimate of one expert, an additional 15 million people were enslaved within African societies themselves.[6]

CONSEQUENCES OF THE SLAVE TRADE FOR AFRICA

The statistics in the previous section hint at the massive impact slave trading had on African life and history. Still, the

[3] Philip Curtin, *The Atlantic Slave Trade: A Census* (Madison: University of Wisconsin Press, 1969), p. 101.

[4] Curtin, pp. 101, 129; James A. Rawley, *The Transatlantic Slave Trade: A History* (New York: W. W. Norton, 1981), p. 129.

[5] Rawley, p. 429; Curtin, p. 268.

[6] Manning, pp. 37, 170–171.

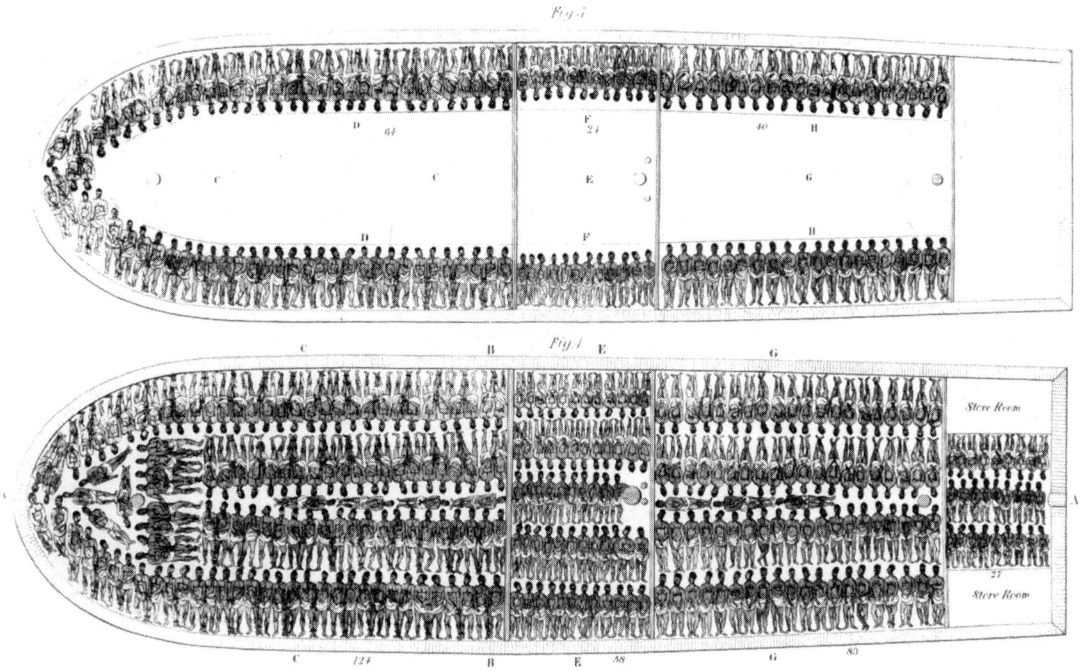

Loading plan for the main decks of the 320-ton slave ship *Brookes*. The *Brookes* was only 25 feet wide and 100 feet long, but as many as 609 slaves were crammed on board for the nightmarish passage to the Americas. The average space allowed each person was only about 78 inches by 16 inches. Photographs and Prints Division, Schomburg Center for Research in Black Culture, The New York Public Library, Astor, Lenox, and Tilder Foundations

question of the actual effects remains difficult and disputed. Modern scholarship has tended to emphasize the importance for African history of the coming of the maritime European powers in general and the Atlantic slave trade in particular. Regarding the slave trade, it is safe to say that the impact was considerable, however much that general conclusion must be qualified in the light of particular cases. Consider some examples.

We do not know for certain if the Atlantic trade brought net population loss or gain to specific areas of West Africa. The wide and rapid spread of maize and cassava cultivation in forest regions after these plants had been imported from the Americas may have fueled African population increases that offset regional human loss through slaving. We know, however, that slaving took away many of the strongest young men in many areas and, in the oriental-trade zones, most of the young women.

Similarly, we do not know if more slaves were captured as byproducts of local wars or from pure slave raiding, but we do know they were captured and removed from their societies.

Nor do we know if slaving always inhibited development of trade or perhaps sometimes stimulated it because commerce in a range of African products—from ivory to wood and hides—often accompanied that in slaves. Still, we do know that in general, the exchange of productive human beings for money or goods that were generally not used to build a productive economy was a great loss for African society as a whole.

CHRONOLOGY

CONQUEST OF THE AMERICAS AND THE TRANSATLANTIC SLAVE TRADE

1494	The Treaty of Tordesillas divides the seaborne empires of Spain and Portugal
1500	The Portuguese arrive in Brazil
1519–1521	Hernan Cortés conquers the Aztec Empire
1531–1533	Francisco Pizarro conquers the Inca Empire
1607	Jamestown, Virginia, first permanent English settlement in North America founded
1608	The French found Quebec
1619	First African slaves brought to British North America
1650	Transatlantic slave trade becomes bigger than the older oriental slave trade
1700s	Over 6 million slaves imported from Africa to the Americas
1807	Slavery abolished in British domains
1808	The importation of slaves abolished in the United States
1874–1928	Indigenous African slavery abolished
1888	Slavery abolished in Brazil

This late-eighteenth-century engraving, showing European slave traders on the coast of Africa, graphically illustrates the first step in the wrenching and dehumanizing process of enslavement.
© The British Museum

Finally, because we do not yet have accurate estimates of the total population of Africa at different times over the four centuries of the Atlantic slave trade, we cannot determine with certainty its demographic impact. We can, however, make some educated guesses. If, for example, tropical Africa had possibly 50 million inhabitants in 1600, it would then have had 30 percent of the combined population of the Americas, the Middle East, Europe, and Africa. If in 1900, after the depredations of the slave trade, it had 70 million inhabitants, its population would have dropped to only slightly more than 10 percent of the combined population of the same world regions. Accordingly, current best estimates indicate that overall African population growth suffered significantly as a result of the devastating numbers of people lost to enslavement or to the increased warfare and decreased birthrate tied to the slave trade. Figures like these also give some idea of slavery's probable impact on Africa's ability to keep up with the modern industrializing world.[7]

It is important to remember that even in West and central Africa, which bore the brunt of the Atlantic trade, its impact and the response to it were so varied in different places and times that even accurate overall statistics could be misleading for particular cases. In a few cases, kingdoms such as Dahomey (the present Republic of Benin) seem to have sought and derived immense economic profit for a time by making slaving a state monopoly. Other kingdoms, such as Benin, sought to stay almost completely out of slaving and derived no gain from it. In many instances, including the rise of Asante power or the fall of the Yoruba Oyo Empire, it now appears that increased slaving was in part a result as well as a cause of regional instability and change. Increased warfare meant increased prisoners to be enslaved and a surplus to be sold off; however, whether slaving gave good cause for war is still a major question in each regional context.

Similarly, if one can establish, as seems evident, a major increase in indigenous slavery as a result of the external trade to occident and orient during the centuries in question, we have to assume major social consequences for African society as a whole, but the specific consequences would differ according to the specifics of regional situations. For example, in West Africa relatively more men were taken as slaves than women, whereas in the Sahelian Sudanic regions relatively more women than men were taken. In the west the loss of so many men increased the pressures for polygamy and possibly the regional use of women slaves as well, whereas in the Sahelian Sudanic regions the loss of women may have stimulated polyandry and reduced the birthrate significantly.

Even though slavery existed previously in Africa, the scale of the Atlantic trade was unprecedented and hence had an unprecedented impact on indigenous social, political, and economic realities. In general, the slave trade measurably changed patterns of life and balances of power in the main affected areas, whether by stimulating trade or warfare (or at least raiding for new supplies), by disrupting previous market and political structures, by substantially increasing slavery inside Africa, or by disturbing the male-female ratio (and hence the workforce balance and birthrate patterns) and consequently the basic social institution of monogamous marriage.

If the overseas slave trade did not substantially and irrevocably change every region it touched, at the least it siphoned indigenous energy into ultimately counterproductive or destructive directions. This, in turn, meant the inhibition of true economic development, especially in central and coastal West Africa. The Atlantic slave trade must by any standard be described as one of the most tragic aspects of European involvement in Africa.

[7] On all of the preceding points regarding probable impact of the trade, see Manning, pp. 126–148, 168–176.

In World Perspective

THE TRANSATLANTIC ECONOMY

The contact between the native peoples of the American continents and the European explorers of the fifteenth and sixteenth centuries transformed world history. In the Americas, the native peoples—whose ancestors had migrated from Asia millennia before—had established a wide variety of civilizations. Some of their most remarkable architectural monuments and cities were constructed during the very centuries when European civilizations were reeling from the collapse of Roman power. Until the European explorations, the civilizations of the Americas and the civilizations of Eurasia and Africa had had no significant contact with each other.

Within half a century of the landing of Columbus, millions of America's native peoples in Florida, the Caribbean islands, Mesoamerica, and South America had encountered Europeans intent on conquest, exploitation, and religious conversion. Because of their advanced weapons, navies, and the new diseases they brought with them, as well as internal divisions among the Native Americans, the Europeans were able to achieve a rapid conquest. Thereafter, Spain and Portugal dominated Latin America, and England, France, and Holland set out to settle North America.

In both North and South America economies of exploitation were established. The Europeans were generally determined to do little labor themselves. In Latin America various institutions were developed to extract native labor. From the mid-Atlantic English colonies through the Caribbean and into Brazil a long corridor of slave-labor plantation systems was established. The slaves were forcibly imported from Africa and sold in America to plantation owners. The economies and peoples of Europe, Africa, and the Americas were thus drawn into a vast worldwide web of production based on slave labor.

The impact of slavery in the Americas was not limited to the life of the black slaves. Whites in the New World numbered about 12 million in 1820, compared to some 6 million blacks. However, up to that time only about 2 million whites had migrated there, compared to some 11 million or more Africans forcibly imported as slaves. Such numbers reveal the effects of brutal slave work conditions and the high mortality and sharply reduced birthrates of slave populations relative to those of the free white populations.

None of these statistics, however, enables us to assess adequately the role that slavery has played in the Americas or, in particular, the United States. The United States actually received only a bit more than a quarter as many slaves as did Brazil alone or the British and French Caribbean regions together, yet the consequences of the forced migration of just over half a million Africans have been and remain massive. Consider just the American Civil War and the endurance of societal racism and inequality or, more positively, the African contribution to American industrial development, language, music, literature, and artistic culture. The Atlantic slave trade's impact has been and continues to be felt at both ends of the original "trade."

REVIEW QUESTIONS

1. How were small groups of Spaniards able to conquer the Aztec and Inca Empires?
2. What was the basis of the mercantilist theory of economics? What was the relationship between the colonial economies and those of the homelands?
3. Describe the economies of Spanish America and Brazil. What were the similarities and differences between them and the British and French colonies in the Caribbean and North America? What role did the various colonies play in the transatlantic economy?
4. Why did forced labor and slavery develop in tropical colonies? How was slavery in the Americas different from slavery in earlier societies?
5. What was the effect of the transatlantic slave trade on West African societies? On East Africa? What role did Africans themselves play in the slave trade?

SUGGESTED READINGS

P. BAKEWELL, *A History of Latin America* (1997). A recent accessible survey.

I. BERLIN, *Many Thousands Gone: The First Two Centuries of Slavery in North America* (1998). The most extensive recent treatment emphasizing he differences in the slave economy during different decades.

L. BETHWELL, *The Cambridge History of Latin America*, Vols. 1 and 2 (1984). Excellent essays by leading scholars.

R. BLACKBURN, *The Making of New World Slavery from the Baroque to the Modern* 1492–1800 (1997). An extradordinary work.

B. COBO, *History of the Inca Empire* (1979). A major discussion.

G. A. COLLIER, R. I. ROSALDO, AND J. D. WIRTH, *The Inca and Aztec States 1400–1800* (1982). An important collection of advanced essays.

P. D. CURTIN, *The Atlantic Slave Trade: A Census* (1969). Still a basic work.

P. D. CURTIN, *Economic Change in Precolonial Africa: Senegambia on the Eve of the Slave Trade.* (1975) The chapter on slave trading is an illuminating treatment of the topic with respect to one area of Africa.

D. B. DAVIS, *The Problem of Slavery in Western Culture* (1966). A brilliant and far-ranging discussion.

H. L. Gates, Jr. and W. L. Andrews, eds., *Pioneers of the Black Atalantic: Five Slave Narratives from the Enlightenment 1772–1815* (1998). An anthology of autobiographical accounts.

H. A. GEMERY AND J. S. HOGENDORN, EDS., *The Uncommon Market: Essays in the Economic History of the Atlantic Slave Trade* (1979). Useful on trans-Saharan and particular African regions of the Atlantic slave trade.

C. GIBSON, *The Aztecs Under Spanish Rule: A History of the Native Americans of the Valley of Mexico* (1964). An exceedingly interesting book.

C. GIBSON, *Spain in America* (1966). A splendidly clear and balanced discussion.

S. GRUZINSKI, *The Conquest of Mexico: The Incorporation of Indian Societies into the Western World, 16th–18th Centuries* (1993). Interprets the experience of native Americans, from their own point of view, during the time of the Spanish conquest.

L. HANKE, *Bartolomé de Las Casas: An Interpretation of His Life and Writings* (1951). A classic work.

J. HEMMING, *The Conquest of the Incas,* (1970). A lucid account of the conquest of the Inca Empire and its aftermath.

J. HEMMING, *Red Gold: The Conquest of the Brazilian Native Americans,* 1500–1760 (1978). A careful account with excellent bibliography.

H. KLEIN, *The Middle Passage: Comparative Studies in the African Slave Trade* (1978). A far-ranging overview of the movement of slaves from Africa to the Americas.

M. LEON-PORTILLA, ED., *The Broken Spears: The Aztec Account of the Conquest of Mexico* (1961). A collection of documents recounting the experience of the Aztecs from their own point of view.

J. LOCKHARDT AND S. B. SCHWARTZ, *Early Latin America: A History of Colonial Spanish America and Brazil* (1983). The standard work.

J. R. MCNEIL, *Atlantic Empires of France and Spain: Louisbourg and Havana, 1700–1763* (1985). An examination of imperial policies in terms of two key overseas outposts.

P. MANNING, *Slavery and African Life: Occidental, Oriental, and African Slave Trades* (1990). An admirably concise yet probing and careful economic-historical synthesis of the evidence, with multiple tables and statistics to supplement the magisterial analysis. An indispensable attempt at presenting the "big picture" of African slavery.

S. W. MINTZ, *Sweetness and Power: The Place of Sugar in Modern History* (1985). Traces the role of sugar in the world economy and sugar's impact on world culture.

A. PAGDEN, *Lords of All the World: Ideologies of Empire in Spain, Britain, and France* c. 1500–c. 1800 (1955). An effort to explain the imperial thinking of the major European powers.

J. H. PARRY, *Trade and Dominion: The European Overseas Empires in the Eighteenth Century* (1971). A comprehensive account with attention to the European impact on the rest of the world.

J. A. RAWLEY, *The Transatlantic Slave Trade: A History* (1981). Impressively documented, detailed, and well-presented survey history of the Atlantic trade; little focus on African dimensions.

S. B. SCHWARTZ, *Sugar Plantations in the Formation of Brazilian Society: Bahia, 1550–1835* (1985). A broad-ranging study of the emergence of the plantation economy.

I. K. STEELE, *The English Atlantic, 1675–1740s: An Exploration of Communication and Community* (1986). An exploration of culture and commerce in the transatlantic world.

R. L. STEIN, *The French Sugar Business in the Eighteenth Century* (1988). A study that covers all aspects of the French sugar trade.

S. J. STEIN, *Peru's Indian Peoples and the Challenge of Spanish Conquest: Huamanga to 1640* (1933). A work that examines the impact of the conquest of the Inca empire over the scope of a century.

H. THOMAS, *Conquest: Montezuma, Cortés, and the Fall of Old Mexico* (1993). A splendid modern narrative of the event with careful attention to the character of the participants.

J. THORNTON, *Africa and Africans in the Making of the Atlantic World, 1400–1680* (1992). A discussion of the role of Africans in the emergence of the transatlantic economy.

N. WACHTEL, *The Vision of the Vanquished: The Spanish Conquest of Peru Through Indian Eyes, 1530–1570* (1977). A presentation of Incan experience of conquest.

DOCUMENTS CD-ROM

1. Bernal D'az del Castillo, The Conquest of Mexico
2. Bartholomew De Las Casas: Amerindians and the "Garden of Eden"
3. Christopher Columbus, Journal of First Voyage to America
4. Bartholomew De Las Casas: Destruction of the Indies and The Only Method of Converting the Indians
5. Commerce, Slavery and Religion in North Africa

WORLD AND THE WEB

The European Voyages of Exploration: Fifteenth and Sixteenth Centuries

http://www.ucalgary.ca/applied_history/tutor/eurvoya/index.html

During the fifteenth and sixteenth centuries two nations, Portugal and Spain, pioneered the European discovery of sea routes that were the first channels of interaction between all of the world's continents, thus beginning the process of globalization. This site introduces these two pioneering nations, their motivations, their actions, and the inevitable consequences of their colonization.

Third Person, First Person: Slave Voices From The Special Collections Library

http://scriptorium.lib.duke.edu/slavery/title.html

This site provides primary documents held at Duke University. For many of these documents both scanned images and transcriptions are available for view. The documents provided in this site will greatly expand your knowledge of slavery during the Colonial Era.

Africans in America

http://www.pbs.org/wgbh/aia/part2/title.html

This site orients you to the history and historical resources of the early American slave era. The Resource Bank provides annotated images and documents, stories, biographics, and commentaries.

Viruses, Plagues, and History

http://www.nytimes.com/books/first/o/oldstone-viruses.html

"Viruses, Plagues, and History" by Michael B. A. Oldstone tracks how battles have been won or lost when a particular virus infected one army but not its adversaries. A smallpox epidemic began on the very evening that the Aztecs drove the conquistadors out of what is now Mexico City.

Cultural Readings: Colonization & Print in the Americas

http://www.library.upenn.edu/special/gallery/kislak/index/intro.html

Any account of the colonization of the Americas must acknowledge the prodigious number of texts which colonization generated. "Cultural Readings" presents a sample of those texts. The website is grouped into six broad categories.

19 East Asia in the Late Traditional Era

Ming Vase (detail). In East Asia ceramics are a major art form. Connoisseurs see the Sung dynasty as the peak of ceramic art, but relatively few pots of that age have survived and they are mostly in museum collections. Collectors usually focus on Ming and Ch'ing products. Some pots were a chaste blue and white; others, often imitated by the nascent ceramic industry in Europe, were decorated with flowers and colorful scenes. Museum of Oriental Ceramics, Osaka

Chapter topics

LATE IMPERIAL CHINA

- Ming (1368–1644) and Ch'ing (1644–1911) Dynasties

JAPAN

- Warring States Era (1467–1600)
- Tokugawa Era (1600–1868)

KOREA AND VIETNAM

- Korea
- Vietnam

IN WORLD PERSPECTIVE
Late Traditional East Asia

ONE DIFFICULTY IN COMPARING EAST ASIAN countries is that although they shared many cultural elements, their institutions and history were so different. Their cultural affinity is immediately apparent if we look at Chinese, Japanese, Korean, and Vietnamese paintings side by side. Less visible, but no less basic, was a range of social values shared at least by their elites. To the extent that it was based on Confucianism, the similarity may have been greatest in the mid–nineteenth century, when Japan, Korea, and Vietnam had become more Confucian than ever before.

But when we compare their histories and institutions, the similarities diminish. China and Japan were furthest apart. Each had gone its own way. Korea and Vietnam, even while forging an identity in reaction to China, were more directly influenced by China in their history and closer to China in their culture and institutions.

For China, the Ming (1368–1644) and Ch'ing dynasties (1644–1911) were just two more centralized bureaucratic regimes of a kind that had been in place for centuries. In the T'ang (618–907) the Chinese had forged a pattern of government so efficient and closely geared to the deeper familial and educational constitution of the society that, thereafter, they rebuilt it after each dynastic breakdown. This pattern continued during the Ming and the Ch'ing, giving their histories a recognizable cyclical cast, even though they are also replete with historical trends that cut across dynastic lines.

Japanese political history, in contrast, is not cyclical. Each period of Japanese history reflects a new and different configuration. The centralized governments of the Nara and early Heian gave way to a manorial social order in which a powerful, local warrior class emerged. From this "feudal" class arose first the Kamakura *bakufu*, and then the Ashikaga. These in turn were followed by an era of Warring States and then a lengthy period of centralized "feudalism." Superficially at least, Japan's history was more like that of Europe than of China. Neither Europe nor Japan ever found a pattern of rule that worked so well, was so satisfactory to the rulers, and was so deeply embedded in the institutions of the society that it was re-created over and over again. In fact, from a Japanese or European point of view, that is not how history works.

This chapter underlines the dynamism of both China and Japan during these late centuries. "Late traditional society" does not mean "late static society." In both countries the society became more integrated and the apparatus of government more sophisticated than ever before. These advances shaped Chinese and Japanese responses to the West during the nineteenth century. Even Korea and Vietnam did not lack dynamism. But we must also note that during these centuries the West was transformed. In fact, Greece and Rome apart, most of what seems important in Western history—the Renaissance, the Reformation, the Scientific Revolution, the formation of nation-states, the Industrial Revolution, the Enlightenment, and the democratic revolution—happened while the Ming and the Ch'ing dynasties were reigning in China. As we view East Asia from the perspective of Europe, it appears to have been caught in a tar pit of slow motion. But it was actually the West that had accelerated.

Late Imperial China

MING (1368–1644) AND CH'ING (1644–1911) DYNASTIES

The Ming and the Ch'ing were China's last dynasties. The first was Chinese, the second a dynasty of conquest in which the ruling house and an important segment of the military were foreign (Manchus). They were nevertheless remarkably similar in their institutions and pattern of rule, so much so that historians sometimes speak of "Ming-Ch'ing despotism" as if it were a single system. The two dynasties are also coupled as a result of certain demographic and economic trends that began during the Ming and continued through the Ch'ing.

LAND AND PEOPLE

China's population doubled from about 60 million in 1368 at the start of the Ming dynasty to about 125 million in 1644 at its end. The population then tripled during the early and middle Ch'ing dynasty, reaching about 410 million people several decades into the mid–nineteenth century. This population density stimulated the growth of commerce and gave new prominence to the scholar-gentry class.

An increase in the food supply paralleled population growth. During the Ming, the spread of Sung agricultural technology and new strains of rice accounted for 40 percent of the higher yields, and newly cultivated lands accounted for the rest. During the Ch'ing, half the increased food supply was due to new lands and the other half to better seeds, fertilizers, and irrigation. New crops introduced from America during the late Ming, such as maize, sweet potatoes, and peanuts (which could be planted on dry sandy uplands and did not compete with rice), also bolstered the food supply. By the nineteenth century maize was grown in all parts of China.

In north China the population had declined from 32 million to 11 million during the Mongol conquests. The Ming government repopulated its open lands, resettling villages, building water control systems, and reopening the Grand Canal in 1415. The movement of people to the north continued until the nineteenth century. In the north, most farmers owned the land they worked and at times used hired labor. The land consisted mainly of irrigated dry fields, and the chief crops were millet, sorghum, and wheat.

South and southwest China also saw an influx of migrants from the densely populated lower Yangtze region, many settling in hilly or mountainous border areas that were agriculturally marginal. The White Lotus Rebellion of 1796–1804 occurred in such a recently settled area far from centers of governmental authority. The Miao Wars of the late eighteenth century also were precipitated by the movement of Chinese settlers into southwestern uplands previously left to the slash-and-burn agriculture of the Miao tribes. Other Chinese crossed over to Taiwan or emigrated overseas. During the Ch'ing dynasty, large Chinese mercantile communities became established in Southeast Asia.

The Yangtze basin, meanwhile, became even more densely populated. The lower Yangtze region and the delta, well supplied with waterways, had long been the rice basket of China, but from the late Ming agricultural cash crops, such as silk and cotton, predominated. Cotton was so widely grown in the delta that food had to be brought in from other areas by the early nineteenth century. In the lower Yangtze absentee landlords owned almost half of the land. A typical landlord's holdings were subdivided among tenants, who paid fixed rents in kind. South China also had extensive absentee landlordism, but far more land was owned collectively by clans, which managed the land and distributed rents among their members.

There are many unanswered questions regarding the population growth during these six centuries. Was there a decline in the death rate and, if so, why? Or was it simply that new lands and technology enabled more mouths to be fed? Did the population oblige by promptly increasing? Certainly the Ming-Ch'ing era was the longest continuous period of good government in Chinese history. The good years of Ming rule were longer than such periods in earlier dynasties, and the transition to Ch'ing rule was quicker and less destructive. How much did these long periods of good government contribute to the population growth? Epidemic disease was not absent. In the great plagues from 1586 to 1589 and from 1639 to 1644, as many as 20 to 30 percent of the people died in the most populous regions of China, and in specific counties and villages the figure was often higher. Another epidemic occurred in 1756 and a cholera epidemic from 1820 to 1822. The growth of China's population more than overcame such losses. Because of the growth in agriculture and population, most accounts view the eighteenth century as the most prosperous in Chinese history. But by the early nineteenth century the Chinese standard of living may have begun to decline. An ever increasing population was no blessing.

CHINA'S THIRD COMMERCIAL REVOLUTION

Commerce in China flourished between 300 B.C.E. and 220 C.E. (the late Chou through the Han dynasties), only to decline in the centuries of disunity that followed. In Chapter 7 we read Ssu-ma Ch'ien's description of wealthy Han merchants. Between 850 and 1250 (late T'ang through Sung) commerce again surged, only to contract during the

Mongol conquest. At the end of the Mongol dynasty, warlords confiscated merchant wealth. Early Ming emperors, isolationist and agrarian in orientation, restricted the use of foreign goods, required licenses for junks, and attempted to encase foreign trade within the constraints of the tribute system. The early Ming also operated government monopolies that stifled enterprise and depressed the southeastern coastal region by their restrictions on maritime trade and shipping. In the mid–sixteenth century commerce started to grow again, buoyed by the surge of population and agriculture and aided by a relaxation of government controls. If the growth during the Han and Sung dynasties may be called respectively China's first and second commercial revolutions, then the expansion between 1500 and 1800 was the third. This revolution was partly the extension to other parts of China of changes begun earlier in the Yangtze area, but it had new features as well. By the early nineteenth century China was the most highly commercialized nonindustrial society in the world.

One stimulus to commerce was imported silver, which played the role in the Ming-Ch'ing economy that copper cash had played in the Sung dynasty. The Chinese balance of trade was favorable. Beginning in the mid–sixteenth century silver from mines in western Japan entered China, and from the 1570s Spanish galleons sailing from Acapulco to China via Manila brought in Mexican and Peruvian silver. In exchange, Chinese silks and porcelains were vended in the shops of Mexico City. The late Ming court also opened silver mines in Kweichow and Yunnan provinces. In the eighteenth century copper mines were opened in south China. Also, private "Shensi banks" opened branches throughout China to facilitate the transfer of funds from one area to another and extend credit for trade. Eventually they opened offices in Singapore, Japan, and Russia, as well.

As in Europe, so in China, the influx of silver and the overall increase in liquidity led to inflation and commercial growth. The price of land rose steadily. During the sixteenth century the thirty or forty early Ming taxes on land that were payable in grain, labor service, and cash were consolidated into one tax payable in silver, the so-called Single Whip Reform. To obtain the silver, farmers sold their grain in the market, and some switched from grain to cash crops. Moreover, by the early nineteenth century there were six times as many farm families as in the mid–fourteenth century.

Urban growth between 1500 and 1800, responding to flourishing local markets, was mainly at the level of intermediate market towns. These towns grew more rapidly than the population as a whole and provided the link between the local markets and the larger provincial capitals and cities such as Peking, Hangchow, or Canton. The commercial integration of local, intermediate, and large cities was not entirely new, having occurred during the Sung dynasty in the lower Yangtze region. But now it spread over all of China. Interregional trade also gained. Where Sung trade between regions was mainly in luxury goods such as silk, lacquerware, porcelains, medicines, and paintings, early Ch'ing traders also dealt in staples, such as grain, timber, salt, iron, and cotton. Not that China developed a national economy. Seven or eight regional economies, each the size of a large European nation, were still the focus for most economic activity. But a new level of trade developed among them, especially where water transport made such trade economical. A final feature of eighteenth-century Chinese economic

"Fishermen on Autumn River," a Ming dynasty scroll painting by Tai Ch'in (1390–1460). Courtesy of Freer Gallery of Art, Smithsonian Institution, Washington, D.C.

DOCUMENT THE THIN HORSE MARKET

In China, ancestors without descendants to perform the rites ran the danger of becoming hungry ghosts or wandering spirits. Consequently, having a son who would continue the family line was an act of filial piety. If a wife failed to produce an heir, an official, merchant, or wealthy landowner might take a concubine and try again. Or he might do so simply because he was able to, because it gave him pleasure, and because it was socially acceptable. For a poor peasant household, after a bad harvest and faced with high taxes, the sale of a comely daughter often seemed preferable to the sale of ancestral land.

Concubines usually had no choice in the matter. But neither did many brides in premodern China. Was a woman better off as the wife of a poor peasant, experiencing hardship, hunger, and want, or as the concubine in a wealthy household with servants, good food, and the likelihood that her children would receive an education? What does the following passage tell us about attitudes toward women in premodern China?

Upwards of a hundred people in Yangzhou earn a living in the "thin horse" business. If someone shows an interest in taking a concubine, a team of a broker, a drudge, and a scout stick to him like flies. Early in the morning, the teams gather to wait outside the doors of potential customers, who usually give their business to the first team to arrive. Any teams coming late have to wait for the next opportunity. The winning team then leads their customer to the broker's house. The customer is then served tea and seated to wait for the women. The broker leads out each of them, who do what the matchmaker tells them to do. After each of her short commands, the woman bows to the customer, walks forward, turns toward the light so the customer can see her face clearly, draws back her sleeves to show him her hands, glances shyly at him to show her eyes, says her age so he can hear her voice, and finally lifts her skirt to reveal whether her feet are bound. An experienced customer could figure out the size of her feet by listening to the noise she made as she entered the room. If her skirt made noise when she walked in, she had to have a pair of big feet under her skirt. As one woman finishes, another comes out, each house having at least five or six. If the customer finds a woman to his liking, he puts a gold hairpin in her hair at the temple, a procedure called "inserting the ornament." If no one satisfies him, he gives a few hundred cash to the broker or the servants.

If the first broker gets tired, others will willingly take his place. Even if a customer has the stamina to keep looking for four or five days, he cannot finish visiting all the houses. Nevertheless, after seeing fifty to sixty white-faced, red-dressed women, they all begin to look alike and he cannot decide which are pretty or ugly. It is like the difficulty of recognizing a character after writing it hundreds or thousands of times. Therefore, the customer usually chooses someone once his mind and eyes can no longer discriminate. The owner of the woman brings out a piece of red paper on which are listed the "betrothal presents," including gold jewelry and cloth. Once he agrees to the deal, he is sent home. Before he even arrives back at his lodgings, a band and a load of food and wine are already waiting there. Before long, presents he was to send are prepared and sent back with the band. Then a sedan chair and all the trimmings—colorful lanterns, happy candles, attendants, sacrificial foods—wait outside for the customer's arrangement. The cooks and the entertainer for the wedding celebration also arrive together with foods, wine, candy, tables, chairs, and tableware. Without the customer's order, the colorful sedan chair for the girl and the small sedan chair for her companion are dispatched to get the girl. The new concubine performs the bowing ceremony with music and singing and considerable clamor. The next morning before noon the laborers ask for rewards from the man, then leave to prepare another wedding for another customer in the same manner.

[1]A horse market is for the sale of horses. A "thin horse" market is the market for concubines. The name implies a measure of criticism.

Reprinted with the permission of The Free Press, a division of Simon & Schuster, Inc. from *Chinese Civilization and Society: A Sourcebook* by Patricia Buckley Ebrey. Copyright © 1993 by Patricia Buckley Ebrey.

life was the so-called "putting out" system in textiles, under which merchant capitalists organized and financed each stage of production from fiber to dyed cloth.

WOMEN AND THE COMMERCIAL REVOLUTION The Confucian family ideal changed little during the Ming and Ch'ing dynasties. A woman was expected first to obey her parents, then her husband, and finally her son—when he became the new family head. Physically, women became more restricted. Footbinding, which had begun among the elite during the Sung dynasty, spread through the upper classes during the Ming and to some commoners during the mid to late Ch'ing. Most girls were subjected to this cruel and deformative procedure. Even in villages, women with big—that is to say, normal —feet were sometimes considered unmarriageable. One exception to the rule was the Hakka people of south China. Hakka women with unbound feet worked in the fields alongside their male kinsmen. Another exception was the Manchus. One Manchu (Ch'ing) emperor even issued an edict banning footbinding, but the Chinese ignored it.

As population grew and the size of the average landholding shrank, more women worked at home, spinning, weaving, and making other products for the burgeoning commercial markets. As their contribution to the household income grew, their voice in household decisions often became larger than Confucian doctrines would suggest. But the same commercial revolution also increased the number of rich townsmen who could afford concubines and patronize tea houses, restaurants, and brothels.

POLITICAL SYSTEM

One might expect these massive demographic and economic changes to have produced, if not a bourgeois revolution, at least some profound change in the political superstructure of China. They did not. Government during the Ming and Ch'ing was much like that of the Sung or Yuan, only improved and made stronger. Historians sometimes describe it as the "perfected" late imperial system. This system, they argue, was able to contain and use the new economic energies that destroyed the weaker late-feudal polities of Europe. The sources of strength of the perfected Ming-Ch'ing system were the spread of education, the use of Confucianism as an ideology, stronger emperors, better government finances, more competent officials, and a larger gentry class with an expanded role in local society.

ROLE OF CONFUCIANISM Confucian teachings were more widespread in late imperial China than ever before. There were more schools in villages and towns. Academies preparing candidates for the civil service examinations multiplied. Publishing flourished, bookstores abounded, and literacy outpaced population growth. The Confucian view of society was patriarchal. The family, headed by the father, was the basic unit. The emperor, the son of heaven and the ruler-father of the empire, stood at its apex. In between were the district magistrates, the "father-mother officials." The idea of the state as the family writ large was not just a matter of metaphor but carried with it duties and obligations that were binding at every level.

The sociopolitical worldview of Confucianism was also buttressed by Neo-Confucian metaphysics, which gave a unitary character to Ming and Ch'ing culture. This is not, of course, to deny the existence of different schools of Confucian thought. The vitality of late Ming thinkers was especially notable. Still, in comparison to Europe, where religious philosophies were less involved with the state and where a revolution in science was reshaping both religious and political doctrines, the greater unity and integration of the Chinese worldview cannot be denied.

EMPEROR In Ming-Ch'ing times the emperor was stronger than ever. The Secretariat of high officials that had coordinated government affairs during the Sung and the Yuan was abolished by the first Ming emperor, who himself made all important and many unimportant decisions. His successors, often aided by Grand Secretaries, continued this pattern of direct, personal rule. During the late fourteenth and fifteenth centuries the emperor was the bottleneck official, without whose active participation the business of government would bog down.

Then, during the sixteenth and early seventeenth centuries, a series of emperors appeared who were not interested in government. One spent his days on wine, women, and sports; another on Taoist rites; and still another emperor, who never learned to write, passed his days making furniture. During this era Grand Secretaries or eunuchs exercised the emperor's authority. But the Ch'ing reestablished the pattern of personal government by emperors.

Emperors wielded despotic powers at their courts. They had personal secret police and prisons where those who gave even minor offense might be tortured. Even high officials might suffer the humiliating, and sometimes fatal, punishment of having their bared buttocks beaten with bamboo rods at court—a practice inherited from the Mongols. The dedication and loyalty even of officials who were mistreated attest to the depth of their Confucian ethical formation. One censor who had served three emperors ran afoul of a powerful eunuch. The eunuch obtained an imperial order and had the official tortured to death in 1625. In his deathbed notes to his sons, the official blamed the villain for his agonies but wrote that he welcomed death because his body belonged to his "ruler-father." An earlier mid–sixteenth century incident involved Hai Jui, the most famous censor of the Ming period:

> Hai presented himself at the palace gate to submit a memorial denouncing some of the emperor's notorious idiosyncrasies. The emperor flew into a rage and ordered that Hai not be permitted to escape. "Never fear, sire," the eunuch go-between told the emperor. "He has said goodbye to his family, has brought his coffin with him, and waits at the gate!" Shih-tsung [the emperor] was so taken aback by this news that he forgave Hai for his impertinence. [2]

During the Ch'ing the life-and-death authority of emperors did not diminish, but officials were generally better treated. As foreign rulers, the Manchu emperors took care not to alienate Chinese officials.

The Forbidden Palace in Peking, rebuilt when the third Ming emperor moved the capital from Nanking to Peking, was an icon of the emperor's majesty. Unlike the Kremlin, which consists of an assortment of buildings inside a wall, the entire palace complex in Peking focused on the single figure of the ruler. Designed geometrically its massive outer and inner walls, and vast courtyards, and halls progress stage by stage to the raised area of the audience hall. During the T'ang, emperors sat together with their grand councilors

[2]C. O. Hucker, *China's Imperial Past* (Stanford, CA: Stanford University Press, 1975), p. 206.

while discussing matters of government. In the Sung, officials stood in his presence. By the Ming, the emperor sat on an elevated dais above the officials, who knelt before him. Behind the audience hall were the emperor's private chambers and his harem. In 1425 the palace had 6300 cooks serving 10,000 persons daily. These numbers later increased. By the seventeenth century there were 9,000 palace ladies and perhaps 70,000 eunuchs. The glory of the emperor extended to his family, whose members were awarded vast estates in North China.

BUREAUCRACY A second component of the Ming-Ch'ing system was the government itself. The formal organization of offices was little different from that in the T'ang or the Sung. At the top were the military, the censorate, and the administrative branch, and beneath the administration were the six ministries and the web of provincial, prefectural, and district offices. But government was better financed than during earlier dynasties. The productivity of China became steadily greater, whereas the apparatus of government grew only slowly. Government finances had ups and downs, but as late as the 1580s huge surpluses were still accumulated at both the central and the provincial levels. These surpluses probably braked the process of dynastic decline. Only during the last fifty years of the Ming did soaring military expenses bankrupt government finances.

Then, in the second half of the seventeenth century the Manchus reestablished a strong central government and restored the flow of taxes to levels close to those of the Ming. In fact, revenues were so ample that early in the eighteenth century the emperors were able to freeze taxes on agriculture at the 1711 level and fix quotas for each province.

This contributed to the general prosperity of the eighteenth century but led to problems during the nineteenth century. Because agricultural productivity continued to rise, even though local officials collected some of the surplus, fixed quotas meant a declining share of the product. Both cultivators and gentry probably benefited from the new wealth, with the latter obtaining the larger share.

If the Ming-Ch'ing system can be spoken of as perfected, the good government it brought to China was largely a product of the ethical commitment and the exceptional ability of its officials. No officials in the world today approach in power or prestige those of the Ming and the Ch'ing. When the Portuguese arrived early in the sixteenth century, they called these officials "mandarins." (This term began as a Sanskrit word for "counselor" that became Hindi, entered Malay, and was then picked up by the Portuguese and adopted by other Europeans.) As in the Sung, the rewards of an official career were so great that the competition to enter it was intense. As population grew and schools increased, entrance became evermore competitive.

After being screened at the district office, a candidate took the county examination. If he passed he became a member of the gentry. He gained the cap and sash of the scholar and exemption from state labor service. Even this examination required years of arduous study. About half a million passed each year. The second hurdle was the provincial examination held every third year. Only one in a hundred or more was successful. The final hurdle was the metropolitan examination, also held triennially. During the Ming fewer than ninety passed each year. As in earlier dynasties, regional quotas were set to prevent the Yangtze region from dominating the officialdom.

GENTRY A final component in the Ming-Ch'ing system—if not new, at least vastly more significant than in earlier dynasties—was the gentry class. It was an intermediate layer

The dilapidated remains of the examination stalls at Nanking. Doors to individual cubicles can be seen to the right and left of the three-story gate. Thousands of such cubicles made up the old examination stalls. Those who passed the exams governed China. CORBIS

DOCUMENT THE SEVEN TRANSFORMATIONS OF AN EXAMINATION CANDIDATE

The Chinese civil service examination was a grueling ordeal. Like a chess tournament, it required physical strength. Chinese critics said, "To pass the provincial examination a man needed the spiritual strength of a dragon-horse, the physique of a donkey, the insensitivity of a wood louse, and the endurance of a camel." The following selection is by a seventeenth-century writer who never succeeded in passing.

Is the style of this passage overdone or effective? What is distinctively Chinese about it?

When he first enters the examination compound and walks along, panting under his heavy load of luggage, he is just like a beggar. Next, while undergoing the personal body search and being scolded by the clerks and shouted at by the soldiers, he is just like a prisoner. When he finally enters his cell and, along with the other candidates, stretches his neck to peer out, he is just like the larva of a bee. When the examination is finished at last and he leaves, his mind in a haze and his legs tottering, he is just like a sick bird that has been released from a cage. While he is wondering when the results will be announced and waiting to learn whether he passed or failed, so nervous that he is startled even by the rustling of the trees and the grass and is unable to sit or stand still, his restlessness is like that of a monkey on a leash. When at last the results are announced and he has definitely failed, he loses his vitality like one dead, rolls over on his side, and lies there without moving, like a poisoned fly. Then, when he pulls himself together and stands up, he is provoked by every sight and sound, gradually flings away everything within his reach, and complains of the illiteracy of the examiners. When he calms down at last, he finds everything in the room broken. At this time he is like a pigeon smashing its own precious eggs. These are the seven transformations of a candidate.

From I. Miyazaki, *China's Examination Hell*, trans. by C. Schirokauer. Copyright © 1976 Weatherhill, pp. 57–58.

between the elite bureaucracy above and the village below. The lowest level of bureaucratic government was the office of the district magistrate. Although the population increased six-fold during the Ming and the Ch'ing, the number of district magistrates increased only from 1,171 to 1,470. Thus the average district, which had had a population of 50,000 in the early Ming and 100,000 in the late Ming, had two or three times that number by the early nineteenth century. The district magistrate came to his district as an outsider. The "law of avoidance," designed to prevent conflicts of interest, prevented him from serving in his home province. His office compound had a large staff of secretaries, advisers, specialists, clerks, and runners; but even then, he could not govern such a large population directly. To govern effectively, the magistrate had to obtain the cooperation of the local literati or gentry.

By *gentry* we do not mean a rural elite, like English squires. The Chinese gentry was largely urban, living in market towns or district seats. Socially and educationally, its members were of the same class as the magistrate—a world apart from clerks, runners, or village headmen. They usually owned land, which enabled them to avoid manual labor and to send their children to private academies. As absentee landlords whose lands were worked by sharecroppers, they were often exploitative; rebels at the end of the Ming attacked landlords as they did government offices. But the gentry were also local leaders. They represented community interests, which they interpreted conservatively, vis-à-vis the bureaucracy. They also performed quasi-official functions on behalf of their communities: maintaining schools and Confucian temples; repairing roads, bridges, canals, and dikes; and writing local histories.

The gentry class was the matrix from which officials arose; it was the local upholder of Confucian values. During the mid–nineteenth century, at a time of crisis, it would become the sustainer of the dynasty.

PATTERN OF MANCHU RULE The collapse of the Ming dynasty in 1644 and the establishment of Manchu rule was less of a break than might be imagined. First, the transition was short. Second, the Manchus, unlike the Mongols, were already partially Sinicized at the time of the conquest. They had been vassals of the Chinese state during the Ming, organized by tribal units into commanderies. Even before entering China, they had had the experience of ruling over Chinese who had settled in Manchuria to the north of the Great Wall.

In the late sixteenth century an able leader unified the Manchurian tribes and proclaimed a new dynasty. While still based in Mukden, the dynasty established a Confucian government with six ministries, a censorate, and other Chinese institutions. When the Ming collapsed and rebel forces took over China, the Manchus presented themselves as the conservative upholders of the Confucian order. The Chinese gentry preferred the Manchus to Chinese rebel leaders, whom they regarded as bandits. After the Manchu conquest, a few scholars and officials became famous as

Ming loyalists. Most, however, served the new dynasty. The Ch'ing as a Chinese dynasty dates from 1644, when the capital was moved from Mukden to Peking. All of south China was taken by 1659, with the aid of Ming generals who switched their allegiance to the new regime.

As a tiny fraction of China's population, the Manchus adopted institutions to maintain themselves as an ethnically separate elite group. One was their military organization. The basic unit was the banner—the unit took the name of its flag. There were eight Manchu banners, eight Mongol, and eight Chinese. There were more companies (of 300 men each) in the Manchu banners than in either of the other two; together with their steppe allies, the Mongols, the Manchu troops outnumbered Chinese troops by more than two to one. Furthermore, the Chinese banners were mainly of Manchurian Chinese, who had been a part of the regime from its inception. Manchu garrison forces were segregated and were not under the jurisdiction of Chinese officials. They were given stipends and lands to cultivate. They were forbidden to marry Chinese, their children had to study Manchu, and they were not permitted to practice footbinding. In 1668 northern and central Manchuria were cordoned off by a willow palisade as a Manchu strategic tribal territory and closed to Chinese immigrants.

In addition to the Manchu banners, there were also Chinese constabulary forces known as "armies of the green standard." At first the distinction between the banners and the Chinese military was critical. Later, as the dynasty became Sinicized and accepted, the ethnic basis of its military strength became less important.

The second institutional feature of Manchu government was what has been termed "dyarchy": the appointment of two persons, one Chinese and one Manchu, to each key post in the central government. Early in the dynasty the Chinese appointments were often bannermen or bondservants who were personally loyal to the Manchus. At the provincial level Manchu governor-generals oversaw Chinese

The great Manchu emperor Ch'ien Lung (r. 1736–1795).

© Metropolitan Museum of Art, Rogers Fund, 1942 (42.141.8)

CHRONOLOGY

LATE IMPERIAL CHINA

Ming Dynasty 1368–1644

1368–1398	Reign of first Ming emperor; Chinese armies invade Manchuria, Mongolia, and eastern Central Asia
1402–1424	Reign of third Ming emperor; Chinese armies invade Vietnam and Mongolia
1405–1433	Voyages of Cheng Ho to India and Africa
1415	Grand Canal reopened
1472–1529	Wang Yang-ming, philosopher
1592–1598	Chinese army battles Japanese army in Korea

Ch'ing (Manchu) Dynasty 1644–1911

1668	Manchuria closed to Chinese immigrants (by Willow Palisade)
1661–1722	Reign of K'ang Hsi
1681	Suppression of revolts by Chinese generals
1683	Taiwan captured
1689	China and Russia sign Treaty of Nerchinsk
1736–1795	Reign of Ch'ien Lung
1793	Macartney mission

governors. Most officials and virtually all district magistrates beneath the governors were Chinese.

A particular strength of the Manchu dynasty was the long reigns of two extremely able emperors, K'ang Hsi (1661–1722) and Ch'ien Lung (1736–1795). K'ang Hsi was born in 1654, ten years after the start of the dynasty. He ascended the throne at the age of seven, began to rule at thirteen, and held sway until his death in 1722. He was a man of great vigor. He rose at dawn to read memorials (official documents) before beginning his daily routine of audiences with officials. He sired thirty-six sons and twenty daughters by thirty consorts. He presided over palace examinations. Well versed in the Confucian classics, he won the support of scholars by his patronage of the *Ming History*, a new dictionary, and a 5,000-volume encyclopedia.

K'ang Hsi also displayed an interest in European science: he studied with Jesuit court astronomers whom the Ch'ing had inherited from the Ming. He opened four ports to foreign trade and carried out public works, improving the dikes on the Huai and Yellow Rivers and dredging the Grand Canal. During his reign he made six tours of China's southern provinces. K'ang Hsi, in short, was a model emperor. But he was also responsible for the various policies that sought to preserve a separate Manchu identity. Like Kublai Khan (r. 1271–1294) before him, he built a summer palace on the plains of Manchuria, where he hunted, hawked, and rode horseback with the freedom of a steppe lord.

Ch'ien Lung began his reign in 1736, fourteen years after the death of his grandfather K'ang Hsi, and ruled until 1795. During his reign the Ch'ing dynasty attained its highest level of prosperity and power. Like K'ang Hsi, he was vigorous, wise, conscientious, careful, and hard-working. He visited south China on inspection tours. He patronized scholars on a grand scale: His *Four Treasures* of the classics, treating history, letters, and philosophy, put 15,000 copyists to work for almost fifteen years. (But he also carried out a literary inquisition against works critical of Manchu rule.)

Only in his last years did Ch'ien Lung lose his grip and permit a court favorite to practice corruption on an almost unprecedented scale. In 1796 the White Lotus Rebellion broke out. Ch'ien Lung's successor put down the rebellion and permitted the corrupt court favorite to take his own life. The ample financial reserves that had existed throughout the eighteenth century were never reestablished. China nevertheless entered the nineteenth century with its government intact and with a peaceful and stable society. There were few visible signs of what was soon to come.

MING-CH'ING FOREIGN RELATIONS

MING Some scholars have contended that post-Sung China was not an aggressive or imperialist state. They cite its inability to resist foreign conquest; the civility, self-restraint, and gentlemanliness of its officials; and the

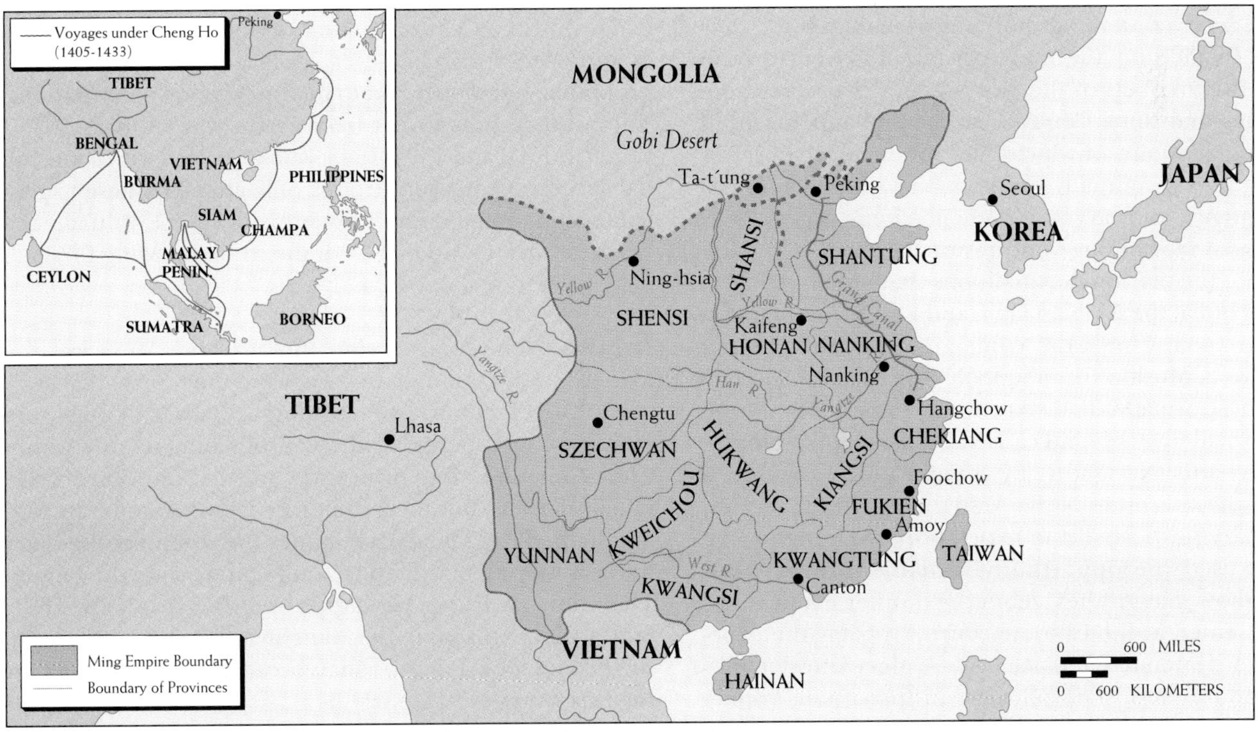

Map 19–1 Ming Empire and the voyages of Cheng Ho. The ships of Cheng Ho, venturing beyond Southeast Asia and India, reached the coast of East Africa.

Sung adage that good men should not be used to make soldiers just as good iron is not used to make nails. The early Ming convincingly disproves this contention. The first Ming emperor (r. 1368–1398) oversaw the vigorous expansion of China's borders. At his death, China controlled the northern steppe from Hami at the gateway of Central Asia to the Sungari River in Manchuria and had regained control of the southern tier of Chinese provinces as well. The Mongols were expelled from Yunnan in 1382 (see Map 19–1).

During the reign of the third Ming emperor (1402–1424) China became even more aggressive. The emperor sent troops into northern Vietnam, which became a Chinese province for two decades. He also personally led five expeditions into the Gobi Desert in pursuit of Mongol troops.

Whenever possible, the third emperor and his successors "managed" China's frontiers with the tribute system. In this system the ambassadors of vassal kings acted out their political subordination to the universal ruler of the celestial kingdom. An ambassador approached the emperor respectfully, performed the kowtow (kneeling three times and each time bowing his head to the floor three times), and presented his gifts. In return, the vassal kings were sent seals confirming their status, given permission to use the Chinese calendar and year-period names, and appointed to the Ming nobility.

The system conferred notable benefits on those willing to participate. While in Peking the ambassadors were housed and fed in a style appropriate to their status. The gifts they received were far more valuable than those they brought. In addition, they were permitted to trade private goods in the markets of the city. So attractive were these perquisites that some Central Asian merchants invented imaginary kingdoms of which they appointed themselves the emissaries. Eventually China had to set limits on the size, frequency, and cargos of these missions.

The most far-ranging ventures of the third Ming emperor were the maritime expeditions that sailed to Southeast Asia, India, the Arabian Gulf, and East Africa between 1405 and 1433. They were commanded by the eunuch Cheng Ho, a Muslim from Yunnan (see Map 19–1). The first of these armadas had sixty-two major ships and hundreds of smaller vessels and carried 28,000 sailors, soldiers, and merchants. Navigating by compass, the expeditions followed the sea routes of the Arab traders. Trade was not the primary purpose of the expeditions, although some eunuchs used the opportunity to make fortunes, and records show that giraffes, zebras, and other exotic items were presented at the Chinese court. Probably the expeditions were intended to make China's glory known to distant kingdoms and to enroll them in the tribute system. Cheng Ho's soldiers installed a new king in Java. They captured and brought back to China hostile kings from Borneo and Ceylon, and they signed up nineteen other states as Chinese tributaries.

The expeditions ended as abruptly as they had begun. They were costly and offered little return at a time when the dynasty was fighting in Mongolia and building the new capital at Peking. What was remarkable about these expeditions was not that they came half a century earlier than the Portuguese voyages of discovery, but that China had the necessary maritime technology and yet decided not to use it. China lacked the combination of restlessness, greed, religious faith, and curiosity that would motivate the Portuguese.

The chief threat to the Ming dynasty was the Mongols. In disarray after the collapse of their rule in China, the Mongols had broken up into eastern, western, and southern tribes. The Chinese, "using the barbarian to control the barbarian," made allies of the southern tribes (those settled just north of the Great Wall) against the more fearsome grassland Mongols. This policy worked most of the time, but twice the Mongols formed confederations—pale imitations of the war machine of Genghis—strong enough to defeat Chinese armies: in the 1430s they captured the emperor, and in 1550 they overran Peking. The Mongol forces involved in the latter attack were defeated by a Chinese army in the 1560s and signed a peace treaty in 1571.

A second foreign threat to the Ming dynasty was the Japanese and the Chinese pirates associated with them. Warrior-lords of decentralized Japan had begun raids on Korea and the northeastern Chinese coast during the thirteenth and early fourteenth centuries; they extended their activities down the coast to southeastern China and beyond during the fifteenth and sixteenth centuries. Hitherto, the coast had been China's most secure frontier. China built defenses and used a scorched-earth policy to make raiding less profitable, but mostly had to put up with the depredations. The most serious threat from Japan was its invasions of Korea in 1592 and 1597–1598. Korea resisted with some initial success. China sent troops only after Japanese armies had occupied the entire Korean peninsula. Eventually the Japanese armies withdrew, but the strain on Ming finances had severely weakened the dynasty.

CH'ING The final foreign threat to the Ming was the Manchus, who, as we have seen, were the mouse that swallowed the elephant. After coming to power in 1644, the Manchu court spent decades consolidating its rule within China. The last Ming prince was pursued into Burma and killed in 1662. But then the three Chinese generals who had helped the Manchus conquer the south revolted and were supported by a Sino-Japanese pirate state on Taiwan. The emperor K'ang Hsi suppressed the revolts by 1681; most Chinese troops in the Manchu armies remained loyal. In 1683 he took Taiwan, which became a part of China for the first time (see Map 19–2).

As always, the principal foreign threats to China, even to the Manchu dynasty, which had itself come from the north, came from the north and northwest. Russia had begun expanding east across Siberia and south against the

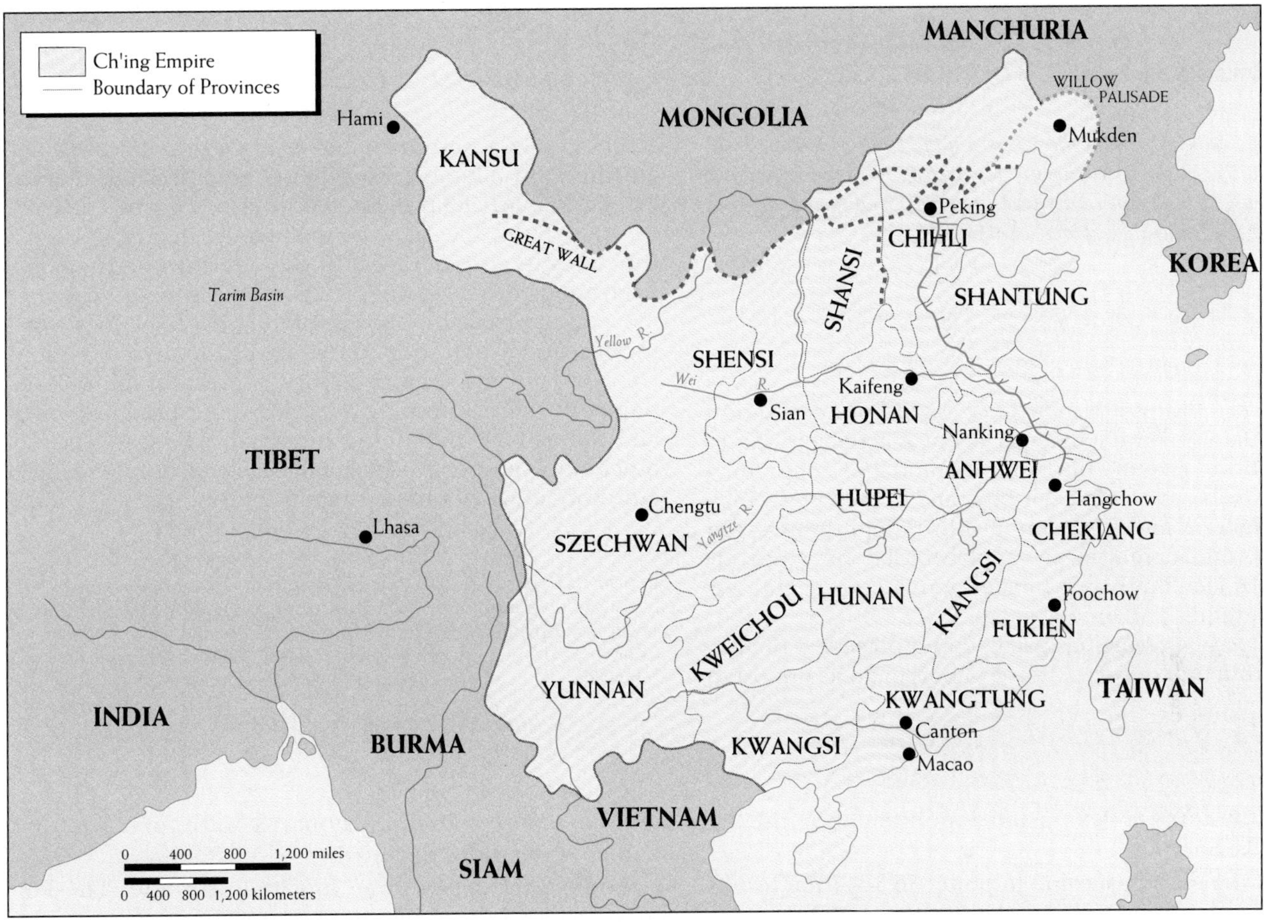

Map 19–2 The Ch'ing Empire at its peak. The Willow Palisade was the line of demarcation between the Manchurian homeland of the Ch'ing rulers and China. Chinese were excluded from Manchuria.

remnants of the Golden Horde during the reign of Ivan the Terrible (1533–1584). By the 1660s Russian traders, trappers, and adventurers had reached northern Manchuria, where they built forts and traded with the eastern Mongols. One is reminded of the French penetration of Canada during the same decades. To prevent a rapprochement between the Russians and Mongols, K'ang Hsi set up military colonies in Manchuria during the 1680s and drove the Russians from the lower Amur River. This victory during the early years of the reign of Peter the Great (1682–1725) led to the 1689 Treaty of Nerchinsk. Negotiated with the assistance of Jesuit translators, this treaty excluded Russia from northern Manchuria while permitting its caravans to visit Peking.

In the west the situation was more complex, with a three-corner relationship among Russia, the western Mongols, and Tibet. K'ang Hsi, and then Ch'ien Lung, campaigned against the Mongols, invaded Tibet, and in 1727 signed a new treaty with Russia. During the campaigns the Chinese temporarily came to control millions of square miles of new territories. These areas became protectorates under a "barbarian management office," separate from the administration for China itself. It is a telling comment on the Chinese concept of empire that ever since that time, even after China's borders contracted during the nineteenth century, the Chinese have insisted that the Manchu conquests of non-Chinese peoples define their legitimate borders. The roots of the present-day contention over borders between China and the countries of the former Soviet Union go back to these events during the eighteenth century, as does the Chinese claim to Tibet.

CONTACTS WITH THE WEST Europeans had made their way to China during the T'ang and the Yuan dynasties. But only with Europe's oceanic expansion in the sixteenth century did they arrive in large numbers. Some came as missionaries, of whom the most calculating, disciplined, enterprising, and successful were the Jesuits. On first arriving in Ming China, they put on the robes of the Buddhist monk; on learning something of the country they switched to the gowns of the Confucian scholar. They studied Chinese and the Confucian classics and engaged in conversations with scholars. They used their knowledge of astronomy, geography, engraving, and firearms to win

DOCUMENT CH'IEN LUNG'S EDICT TO KING GEORGE III OF ENGLAND

The Chinese emperor rejected the requests of the 1793 Macartney mission for change in the restrictive Canton system. His edict reflects the Chinese sense of their superiority to other peoples and their belief that China was the "central kingdom" of the world.

What philosophical principles underlie the emperor's sense of superiority?

You, O King, are so inclined toward our civilization that you have sent a special envoy across the seas to bring to our Court your memorial of congratulations on the occasion of my birthday and to present your native products as an expression of your thoughtfulness. On perusing your memorial, so simply worded and sincerely conceived, I am impressed by your genuine respectfulness and friendliness and greatly pleased. . . .

The Celestial Court has pacified and possessed the territory within the four seas. Its sole aim is to do its utmost to achieve good government and to manage political affairs, attaching no value to strange jewels and precious objects. The various articles presented by you, O King, this time are accepted by my special order to the office in charge of such functions in consideration of the offerings having come from a long distance with sincere good wishes. As a matter of fact, the virtue and prestige of the Celestial Dynasty having spread far and wide, the kings of the myriad nations come by land and sea with all sorts of precious things. Consequently there is nothing we lack, as your principal envoy and others have themselves observed. We have never set much store on strange or ingenious objects, nor do we need any more of your country's manufactures. . . .

Reprinted by permission of the publisher from *China's Response to the West* by Ssu-yu Teng and John K. Fairbank, Cambridge, MA: Harvard University Press. Copyright © 1954, 1979 by the President and Fellows of Harvard College. Reprinted by permission of Harvard University Press. Copyright renewed 1982 by Ssu-yu Teng and John K. Fairbank.

entry to the court at Peking and appointments in the bureau of astronomy.

When the Manchus came to power in 1644 the Jesuits kept their position. They appealed to the curiosity of the court with instruments such as telescopes, clocks, and clavichords. They tried to propagate Christianity. They attacked Taoism and Buddhism as superstitions but argued that Confucianism as a rational philosophy complemented Christianity, just as Aristotle's teaching complemented Christian theology in Europe. They handled the problem of the Confucian rites of ancestor worship by interpreting them as secular and nonantagonistic to Christianity. A few high court officials were converted. K'ang Hsi was sympathetic to the scholarly personalities of the Jesuits and appreciated the canon they cast but was unsympathetic to their religion: "I had asked [the Jesuit] Verbiest why God had not forgiven his son without making him die, but though he had tried to answer I had not understood him."[3]

Meanwhile, their Franciscan and Dominican rivals had reported to Rome that the Jesuits condoned the Confucian rites. The ensuing debate was long and complex, but in the end, papal bulls issued in 1715 and 1742 decided against the Jesuits and forbade Chinese Christians to participate in the family rites of ancestor worship. Thereupon the emperor banned Christianity in China, churches were seized, missionaries were forced to flee, and congregations declined.

Other Europeans came to China to trade. The Portuguese came first in the early sixteenth century but behaved badly and were expelled. They returned in midcentury and were permitted to trade on a tiny peninsula at Macao that was walled off from China. They were followed by Dutch from the East Indies (Indonesia), by the British East India Company in 1699, and by Americans in 1784.

At first the Westerners mingled with ships from Southeast Asia in a fairly open multiport pattern of trade. Then, during the early eighteenth century, the more restrictive "Canton system" evolved. Westerners could trade only at Canton. They were barred from entering the city proper but were assigned land outside its walls along the river. They could not bring their wives to China. They were subject to the harsh dispositions of Chinese law. They were under the control of official merchant guilds. Nevertheless, the trade was profitable to both sides.

The British East India Company developed a triangular commerce among China, India, and Britain that enabled the English to drink tea and wear silk. Private fortunes were built. For China this trade produced an influx of specie, and the Chinese officials in charge grew immensely wealthy. Chafing under the various restrictions, the British government in 1793 sent the Macartney mission to China to negotiate the opening of other ports, fixed tariffs, representation at Peking, and so on. The emperor Ch'ien

[3]D. Spence, *Emperor of China: Self-Portrait of K'ang-Hsi* (New York: Alfred A. Knopf, 1974), p. 84.

Lung graciously permitted Lord Macartney (1736–1806) to present his gifts—which the Chinese described as tribute, even though Macartney refused to perform the kowtow—but he turned down Macartney's requests. Western trade remained encapsulated at Canton, distant from Peking and little noted elsewhere in China.

MING-CH'ING CULTURE

One thing that can be said of Ming-Ch'ing culture, like population or agricultural productivity, is that there was more of it. Whether considering gentry, scholar officials, or a professionalized class of literati, their numbers and works were far greater than in previous dynasties. Even local literary figures or philosophers were likely to publish their collected works or have them published by admiring disciples. Bookstores came of age in the Ming, selling the Confucian classics; commentaries on them; collections of T'ang and Sung poetry; and also colored prints, novels, erotica, and model answers for the civil service examinations.

Chinese culture had begun to turn inward during the Sung in reaction to Buddhism. This tendency was accelerated by the Chinese antipathy to Mongol rule and continued into the Ming and Ch'ing, when Chinese culture became virtually impervious to outside influences. Even works on mathematics and science translated into Chinese by the Jesuits left few traces in Chinese scholarly writings. Chinese cultural self-sufficiency, of course, reflected a tradition and a social order that had stood the test of time, but it also indicated a closed system of ideas with weaknesses that would become apparent in the nineteenth century. Orthodox thought during these five centuries was Chu Hsi Neo-Confucianism. From the mid- to the late Ming, some perturbations were caused by the Zen-like teachings of the philosopher Wang Yang-ming (1472–1529), whose activism caused him to be jailed, beaten, and exiled at one point in an otherwise illustrious official career.

Several other original thinkers' refusal to accept bureaucratic posts under the Ch'ing won them plaudits during the anti-Manchu nationalism of the early twentieth century, but they had only a limited influence on their own times. The most interesting was Ku Yen-wu, who wrote on both philology and statecraft. He used philology and historical phonetics to get at the original meanings of the classics and contrasted their practical ethics with the "empty words" of Wang Yang-ming. Ku's successors extended his philological studies, developing empirical methods for textual studies, but lost sight of their implications for politics. The Manchus clamped down on unorthodox thought, and the seventeenth-century burst of creativity guttered out into a narrow, bookish, conservative scholasticism. Not until the end of the nineteenth century did thinkers draw from these studies the kind of radical inferences that philological studies of the Bible had produced in Europe.

Ming and Ch'ing Chinese esteemed most highly, and not without reason, the traditional categories of high culture: painting, calligraphy, poetry, and philosophy. Porcelains of great beauty were also produced. In the early Ming the blue-on-white glazes predominated. During the later Ming and Ch'ing more decorative wares with enamel painted over the glaze became widespread. The pottery industry of Europe was begun during the sixteenth century to imitate these wares, and Chinese and Japanese influences have dominated Western ceramics down to the present. Chinese today, however, look back and see the novel as the characteristic cultural achievement of the Ming and Ch'ing.

The novel in China grew out of plot-books used by earlier storytellers. Like the stories, Chinese novels consisted of episodes strung together, and chapters in early novels often ended with an admonition to the reader not to miss the next exciting development. Ming and Ch'ing novels were usually written by scholars who had failed the examinations, which may account for their caustic comments on officials. As most novels were written in colloquial Chinese, which was not quite respectable in the society of scholars, their authors wrote under pseudonyms.

Two collections of lively short stories are available in English: *Stories from a Ming Collection* and *The Courtesan's Jewel Box.* Many other stories were pornographic. In fact, the Ming may have invented the humorous pornographic novel. One example available in English is *The Carnal Prayer Mat.* This genre was suppressed in China during the Ch'ing and rediscovered in Japanese collections in the twentieth century.

Short descriptions of several major novels may convey something of their flavor:

1. *The Romance of the Three Kingdoms,* published in 1522, tells of the political and military struggles in China in the aftermath of the Han dynasty. Like Shakespeare, the author, whose identity is uncertain, used a historical setting to create a dramatic world in which human character determines the outcome of events. More than twenty editions had appeared by the end of the Ming, and the novel was also extremely popular in Japan and Korea.
2. *All Men Are Brothers* (also translated as *The Water Margin*) tells of 108 bandit heroes who flee government repression during the late northern Sung, establish a hideout on a mountain amid marshes, and like Robin Hood, avenge the wrongs perpetrated by corrupt officials. Separate episodes tell why each had to leave society and of their many daring and funny adventures. Of all Chinese novels, this was the most popular. It was officially banned as subversive during the Ch'ing but was widely read nonetheless.
3. *The Golden Lotus* is a pornographic novel about the sexual adventures of an urban merchant. It gives

DOCUMENT A Star in Heaven

Among the officials whose stories are told in The Scholars *is Fan Chin, thin and sallow with a grizzled beard and threadbare linen gown, who finally passes the county examination at the age of fifty-four. On his return home, he is given a feast and advice by his domineering father-in-law, Butcher Hu. But when Fan Chin asks Hu for money to travel to the provincial examination, he gets the following reaction.*

Why did a satire such as *The Scholars* not undermine the premises on which Ch'ing society rested?

Butcher Hu spat in his face and let loose a stream of abuse. "Don't forget who you are!" he bellowed. "Just passing one examination and you become like a toad thinking to dine on the flesh of a swan. I hear you passed the examination not because of your essay, but because the examiner took pity on your old age. Now, like a fool, you aspire to be an official. Don't you know that those who have passed the higher examination are all stars in heaven! Haven't you seen the Changs in the city? Those officials all have tons of money and generously proportioned faces and ears. Now look at you with your protruding mouth and monkey chin. Piss on the ground and take a good look at yourself in the puddle! A miserable creature like you can't even hope to swallow a swan's fart! Forget it!

[Fan Chin takes the examination anyway. When he returns home, he discovers that his family has been hungry for two days. Fan goes to the market to sell a chicken. In the meantime, heralds on horseback arrive to proclaim he has passed the provincial examination. Returning home, Fan sees the posted announcement and falls into a dead faint. When revived, he begins ranting incoherently. A herald suggests that Butcher Hu, whom Fan fears, bring him to his senses with a slap. Butcher Hu demurs.]

"He may be my son-in-law," he said, "but now he has become a member of the gentry, a star in heaven. How can I hit a star in heaven? I've heard from Buddhist priests that whoever strikes a star in heaven will be carried away by the King of Hell, struck one hundred times with an iron rod, consigned to the eighteenth hell, and never return to human form again. I wouldn't dare do it."

[Eventually Butcher Hu slaps him, and Fan recovers in time to receive a visit from a member of the local gentry, who is wearing "an official's gauze cap, sunflower-coloured gown, gilt belt and black shoes." "Sir," he says to Fan, "although we live in the same district, I regret that we have never become acquainted." After paying his respects, the visitor presents Fan with fifty taels of silver and a more appropriate house. Soon others give him land, goods, money, rice, and servants. The chapter ends with the maids cleaning up under the supervision of Fan Chin's wife after several days of feasting. Fan Chin's mother enters the courtyard.]

"You must be very careful," the old lady warned her daughter-in-law and the maids. "These things all belong to someone else, so don't break them."

The maids replied:" How can you say they belong to others, madam? They all belong to you."

"Oh no! How could our house have such things?" she said with a smile. "How can you talk of their belonging to others?" the maids replied in unison. "And not only these things, but all of us and the house, too, belong to you."

When the old lady heard this, she picked up the bowls and dishes of fine porcelain and the cups and chopsticks inlaid with silver and examined them one by one. She burbled: "These things are all mine." Laughing wildly, she fell over backward, choked on phlegm, and lost consciousness.

If you want to know what became of the old lady, please read the next chapter.

Translation by Shang Wei.

vivid descriptions of individual women and satirical descriptions of venal officials and greedy monks. In the end the hero dies of his excesses and his family—all six wives and their children—disintegrates. The early English translation of this novel had long passages in Latin to protect those whose minds were not disciplined by the study of that language. Despite its literary merits, the book, like all of its genre, was proscribed during the era of Mao Tse-Tung. In the recent decade it has become available again.

4. *The Dream of the Red Chamber* (also translated as *The Story of the Stone*) is generally considered China's greatest novel. It tells the story of a youth growing up in a wealthy but declining family during the early Ch'ing. Critics praise its subtlety and psychological insight. Anthropologists mine the novel for information on the Chinese extended family and for its depiction of social relations. Like other Ming and Ch'ing novels, it was recognized as a respectable work of art only during the twentieth century, after Western novels entered China.

Ming dynasty ink painting by Wu Wei (1479–1508). The seated human figure is a part of the tranquility of nature. Nature, densely concentrated at the left and lower portions of the painting, stretches off into space in the middle and upper right portion. © 1996. All rights reserved. Courtesy of Museum of Fine Arts, Boston

5. *The Scholars* is a social satire of the early Ch'ing that pokes fun at scholars and officials.

Japan

The two segments of late traditional Japan could not be more different. The Warring States era (1467–1600), really the last phase of Japan's medieval history, saw the unleashing of internal wars and anarchy that scourged the old society from the bottom up. Within a century all vestiges of the old manorial or estate system had been scrapped and virtually all of the Ashikaga lords had been overthrown. The Tokugawa era (1600–1868) that followed saw Japan reunited and stable, with a more competent government than ever. The culture was also brilliantly transformed, preparing it for the challenge it would face during the mid–nineteenth century.

WARRING STATES ERA (1467–1600)

War is the universal solvent of old institutions. Nowhere in history was this clearer than in Japan between 1467 and 1600. In 1467 a dispute arose over who would be the next Ashikaga shōgun. The dispute led to war between two territorial lords who supported the respective contenders. Other lords used the opportunity to gain territory at the expense of weaker neighbors, and wars raged throughout Japan for eleven years. Most of Kyoto was destroyed in the fighting, and the authority of the Ashikaga *bakufu* came to an end. This first war ended in 1477, but the fighting resumed and continued for more than a century.

WAR OF ALL AGAINST ALL

Even before 1467 the Ashikaga equilibrium had been precarious. Regional daimyo lords had relied on their relationship to the *bakufu* to hold their stronger vassals in check, while relying on these vassals to preserve their independence against strong neighbors. The collapse of *bakufu* authority after 1467 pulled the linchpin from the system. It left the regional lords standing alone, removing the last barrier to internecine wars.

The regional lords, however, were too weak to stand alone. A region was a hodgepodge of competing jurisdictions. Lands might be "public," or in estates, and some were starting to look like private fiefs. Revenues might be paid to nobles in Kyoto, to regional lords, or to local samurai strongmen. Most regions contained military bands that were not the vassals of the daimyo. Several daimyo had lands in the territories of other lords. Occasionally vassals were militarily more powerful than their daimyo lords. Some local vassals commanded bands of village warriors. Once the regional daimyo were forced to stand alone, they became prey to the stronger among their vassals as well as to neighboring states.

By the end of the sixteenth century all Ashikaga daimyo had fallen, with one exception in remote southern Kyushu. In their place emerged hundreds of little "Warring States daimyo," each with his own warrior band. In one prefecture along the Inland Sea, the remains of 200 hillside castles of such

Construction of the "White Heron" castle in Himeji was begun during the Warring States era and was completed shortly after 1600. During the Tokugawa peace, it remained as a monument to the glory of the daimyo. Today it can be seen from the "bullet train." Japan Airlines/Photo by Morris Simoncelli

daimyo have been identified. The constant wars among these men were not unlike those of the early feudal era in Europe.

A Japanese term for "survival of the fittest"—"the strong eat and the weak become the meat"—is often applied to this century of warfare. Of the daimyo bands, the most efficient in revamping their domain for military ends survived. The less ruthless, who clung to old ways, were defeated and absorbed. It was an age, as one Warring States general put it, "when only muscle counts." Another said, "The warrior doesn't care if he's called a dog or beast, the main thing is winning." [4]

Early in this period, when there were hundreds of small states, castles were built on a bluff above a river or on a mountainside with natural defenses against surprise attacks. Inuyama Castle, today a thirty-minute bus ride from Nagoya, is the most impressive surviving example.

As fighting continued, hundreds of local states gave way to tens of regional states. The castles of such regional states were often located on plains, and as castle towns grew up around them, merchants flocked to supply the needs of their growing soldiery. Eventually, alliances of these regional states fought it out, until in the late sixteenth century all of Japan was brought under the hegemony of a single lord. Oda Nobunaga (1534–1582) completed the initial unification of central Honshu and would have finished the job had a treacherous vassal not assassinated him in 1582. Toyotomi Hideyoshi (1536–1598), who had begun life as a lowly foot soldier, completed the unification in 1590. After his death his vassal generals once again went to war, and it was only with the victory of Tokugawa Ieyasu (1542–1616) at the Battle of Sekigahara in 1600 that true unification was finally achieved. Ieyasu's unification of 1600 superficially resembled that of the Minamoto in 1185 but was in fact based on a sweeping transformation of Japan's society.

Foot Soldier Revolution

During the Warring States period, the foot soldier replaced the aristocratic mounted warrior as the backbone of the military in Japan. Soldiers were still called *samurai.* They were still the vassals of daimyo or, sometimes, the vassals of vassals of daimyo. But their numbers, social status, and

[4]G. Elison and B. L. Smith, eds., *Warlords, Artists, and Commoners* (Honolulu: Hawaii University Press, 1981), p. 57.

techniques of warfare changed dramatically. As a result, Japanese society changed from what it had been only a century earlier.

The changes began on the land. Ashikaga daimyo had diverted more and more land revenues for their own use, but Warring States daimyo took them all. Public lands and estates, including those of the imperial house, were seized and converted into fiefs. Soldiers were paid stipends from the revenues of the daimyo's lands, and important vassals, usually the officers or commanders of the daimyo's army, were awarded fiefs of their own. The governance of fiefs was essentially private, in the hands of the fief holder.

Inheritance patterns changed to fit the new circumstances. Multigeniture—the division of a warrior's rights to revenues from land among his children—was not appropriate to a society with a hereditary military class. It had impoverished the Kamakura vassals. To protect the integrity of the warrior's household economy, multigeniture had begun to give way to single inheritance during the Ashikaga period. After 1467 single inheritance became universal. As the fief was often passed to the most able son, not necessarily the eldest, the pattern is usually called *unigeniture* rather than *primogeniture.*

With larger revenues, Warring States daimyo built bigger armies. They recruited mainly from the peasantry. Some of the new soldiers moved to the castle town of the daimyo. Others lived on the land or remained in their villages, farming in peace and fighting in war. The growth of the military class had begun earlier. Accounts of twelfth-century battles tell of fighting by tens of hundreds of warriors, sometimes more. Scroll paintings of the Heiji wars corroborate these figures. By the fourteenth century battles involved thousands or tens of thousands of troops. By the late sixteenth century hundreds of thousands were deployed in major campaigns. Screen paintings show massed troops in fixed emplacements with officers riding about on horseback. Of course, special cavalry strike forces were still used.

In the mid–fourteenth century a new weapon was developed: a thrusting spear with a thick shaft and a heavy chisel-like blade. Held in both hands, it could penetrate medieval armor as a sword could not. It could also be swung about like a quarterstaff. It was used by soldiers positioned at intervals of three feet, in a pincushion tactic to impale charging cavalry. The weapon spelled the end of the aristocratic warrior in Japan, just as the pikes used by Swiss soldiers ended knighthood in northern Europe during the fifteenth century. After 1467 this spear became the principal weapon of Warring States Japan. Not surprisingly, its spread coincided with the recruitment of peasant soldiers, for it required only short training. By the early sixteenth century it was every warrior's dream to be the "number one spearsman" of his lord. Even generals trained in its use. One famous general wrote that "one hundred spearsmen are more effective than ten thousand swords."

A second change in military technology was the introduction of the musket by the Portuguese in the mid–sixteenth century. Warring States generals quickly adopted it. Its superiority was proved in the Battle of Nagashino in 1575, in which Oda Nobunaga and Tokugawa Ieyasu used spear and musket platoons against the cavalry of a famous military tactician. Massing 3,000 muskets behind a bamboo barrier-fence and firing in volleys, Nobunaga decimated the forces of his enemy. As individual combat gave way to mass armies, warfare became pitiless, cruel, and bloody.

How, then, should one characterize the society that emerged from the Warring States? Does the word *feudal* apply, with its suggestion of lords and vassals and manorial life on the fiefs of aristocratic warriors? In some respects, it does: by the late sixteenth century all warriors in Japan were part of a pyramid of vassals and lords headed by a single overlord; warriors of rank held fiefs and vassals of their own.

In other respects Japan resembled postfeudal Europe. First, most of the military class were soldiers, not aristocrats. Even though they were called samurai and were vassals, they were something new. They were not given fiefs but were paid with stipends of so many bales of rice. Second, unlike, say, feudal England, where the military class was about one quarter of 1 percent of the population, in mid-sixteenth-century Japan it may have reached 7 or 8 percent. It was more of a size with the mercenary armies of Europe during the fifteenth or sixteenth centuries. Third, the recruitment of village warriors added significantly to the power of Warring States daimyo but gave rise to problems as well. Taxes became harder to collect. Local samurai were often involved in uprisings. When organized by Pure Land Buddhist congregations, these uprisings sometimes involved whole provinces. Again, the parallels with postfeudal Europe seem closer. Fourth, even in a feudal society, not everything is feudal. The commercial growth of the Kamakura and Ashikaga periods continued through the dark decades of the Warring States era.

FOREIGN RELATIONS AND TRADE

Japanese pirate-traders plied the seas of East Asia during the fifteenth and sixteenth centuries. To halt their depredations, the Ming emperor invited the third Ashikaga shōgun to trade with China. An agreement was reached in 1404 and the shōgun was appointed the "King of Japan." During the next century and a half, periodic "tribute missions" were sent to China. The opening of official trade channels did not, however, end piracy. It stopped only after Japan was reunified at the close of the sixteenth century.

The content of the trade reflected the progress of Japanese crafts. Early Japanese exports to China were raw materials such as raw copper, sulfur, or silver, but by the sixteenth century manufactured goods were rising in importance and included swords, spears, wine bottles, folding fans, picture scrolls, screen paintings, ink slabs, and the like. In exchange, Japan received copper cash, porcelains, paintings, books, and medicines.

After establishing his hegemony over Japan, Hideyoshi permitted only ships with his vermilion seal to trade with China, a policy the Tokugawa continued. Between 1604 and 1635 over 350 ships went to China in this "vermilion-seal trade." Then, in 1635, the imposition of seclusion ended Japan's foreign trade: no Japanese could leave Japan; the construction of large ships was prohibited; trade with the continent was limited to a small community of Chinese merchants in Nagasaki, and to quiet trading with China and Korea through the Ryukyu and Tsushima Islands.

Overlapping Japan's maritime expansion in the seas of East Asia was the arrival of European ships. Portuguese pirate-traders made their way to Goa in India, to Malacca, to Macao in China, and arrived in Japan in 1543. Spanish galleons came in 1587 via Mexico and the Philippines. These eastern and western waves of Iberian expansion were followed by the Dutch and the English after the turn of the century.

The Portuguese, from a tiny country with a population of 1.5 million, were motivated by a desire for booty and profits and by religious zeal. Their ships were superior. Taking advantage of the Chinese ban on maritime commerce, they became important as shippers. They carried Southeast Asian goods and Japanese silver to China and Chinese silk to Japan, and then used their profits to buy Southeast Asian spices for the European market. The Portuguese, initially at least, found it easier to trade with the daimyo of a disunited Japan than to deal with the authorities of a united China. A few Kyushu daimyo, thinking to attract Portuguese traders, even converted to Christianity.

Traders brought with them Jesuit missionaries. The Society of Jesus had been founded in 1540 to act as soldiers in the pope's campaign against the Reformation. Only nine years later Saint Francis Xavier (1506–1552) arrived in Japan. He soon wrote back that the Japanese were "the best [people] who have yet been discovered." Another Jesuit wrote that the Japanese "are all white, courteous, and highly civilized, so much so that they surpass all other known races of the world." The Japanese, for their part, also appeared to admire the Jesuits for their asceticism, devoutness, and learning.

As they had attempted to convert scholar-officials in China, so the Jesuits in Japan directed their efforts toward the samurai. Moving to Kyoto, they won the favor of Nobunaga, who was engaged in campaigns against warrior monks on Mount Hiei and against Pure Land strongholds in Osaka. Portuguese and Christian objects became fashionable. Painters produced "Southern Barbarian screens" that depicted the "black ships" of the Portuguese. Christian symbols were used on lacquer boxes and saddles. Nobunaga himself occasionally wore Portuguese clothes and a cross and said he might become a Christian if only the Jesuits would drop their insistence on monogamy. Christian converts increased from a few in the early years to 130,000 in 1579, and to about 300,000 in 1600. That is to say, in the late sixteenth century a higher percentage of Japanese were Christian than today.

It is difficult to explain why Christianity met with greater success in Japan than in other Asian lands. When introduced, it was seen as a new Buddhist sect. There seemed little difference to the Japanese between the cosmic Buddha of Shingon and the Christian God, between the paradise of Amida and the Christian heaven, or between prayers to Kannon—the female *bodhisattva* of mercy—and to the Virgin Mary. The Japanese also noted the theological similarity between the pietism of the Pure Land sect and that of Christianity. To Japanese ears, the passage in Romans 10:13, "whosoever shall call upon the name of the Lord shall be saved," was reminiscent of the Pure Land practice of invoking the name of Amida. The Jesuits, too, noted these parallels and felt that the devil had established these sects in Japan to test their faith. Xavier, who, despite his admirable personal characteristics, was narrow-minded, referred to the historical Buddha and Amida as "two demons." Although this intolerance gave rise to certain tensions and animosities, Christianity spread, and to no small measure as a result of the personal example of the Jesuits.

The fortunes of Christianity began to decline in 1597, when Hideyoshi banned Christianity and had six Spanish Franciscans and twenty Japanese converts crucified in Nagasaki. Hideyoshi was aware of Spanish colonialism in the Philippines, and it was said that a Spanish pilot had boasted that merchants and priests represented the first step toward the conquest of Japan. Sporadic persecutions continued until 1614, when Tokugawa Ieyasu began a serious movement to extirpate the foreign religion. Faced with torture, some Christians recanted. More than 3,000 others were martyred.

CHRONOLOGY

WARRING STATES JAPAN AND THE ERA OF UNIFICATION (1467–1600)

1467–1568	Battles throughout Japan
1543	Portuguese arrive in Japan
1568	Oda Nobunaga takes Kyoto and partially unifies Japan
1575	Battle of Nagashino
1582	Nobunaga assassinated
1588	Hideyoshi starts sword hunt
1590	Hideyoshi completes unification
1592, 1597–1598	Hideyoshi sends armies to Korea
1597	Hideyoshi bans Christianity
1598	Hideyoshi dies, his generals battle for succession
1600	Battle of Sekigahara; Tokugawa reunifies Japan

The last resistance was an uprising near Nagasaki in 1637 and 1638 in which 37,000 Christians died. After that, Christianity survived in Japan only as a hidden religion with secret rites and devotions to "Maria-Kannon," the mother of Jesus represented or disguised as the Buddhist goddess of mercy holding a child in her arms. A few of these "hidden Christians" reemerged in the later nineteenth century. Otherwise, apart from muskets and techniques of castle building, all that remained of the Portuguese influence were certain loan words that became a permanent part of the Japanese language: *pan* for bread, *birodo* for velvet, *kasutera* for sponge cake, *karuta* for playing cards, and *tempura* for that familiar Japanese dish.

"The Arrival of the Portuguese in Japan." Portuguese merchants arrived in Japan in 1543 from India and the East Indies. Their crews were multiethnic, and they brought Jesuit priests as well.
Giraudon/Art Resource, N.Y.

TOKUGAWA ERA (1600–1868)

POLITICAL ENGINEERING AND ECONOMIC GROWTH DURING THE SEVENTEENTH CENTURY

From 1467 to 1590 Japan's energies were absorbed in ever bigger wars. But after the unifications of 1590 and 1600 Japan's leaders sought to create a peaceful, stable, orderly society. Like a great tanker that requires many times its own length to come about, Japan made this transition slowly. Many of the values and habits of mind of the Warring States era continued into the seventeenth century. By the middle or late seventeenth century, however, its society and political system had been radically reengineered. Vigorous economic and demographic growth had also occurred. This combination of political and economic change made the seventeenth century a period of great dynamism.

HIDEYOSHI'S RULE One pressing problem faced by Japan's unifiers was how to cope with an armed peasantry. In war, village warriors fought for their lord: the benefit they offered the lord was greater than their cost. In peace, only the cost remained: their resistance to taxation and the threat of local uprisings. Accordingly, in the summer of 1588 Hideyoshi ordered a "sword hunt" to disarm the peasants. Records of the collected weaponry exist for only one county of 3400 households in Kaga, a domain on the Sea of Japan: 1,073 swords, 1,540 short swords, 700 daggers, 160 spears, 500 suits of armor, and other miscellaneous items. Once the hunt was completed, the 5 percent of the population who remained samurai used their monopoly on weapons to control the other 95 percent.

Hideyoshi next moved to freeze the social classes. Samurai were prohibited from quitting the service of their lord. Peasants were barred from abandoning their fields to become townspeople. This policy was continued by the Tokugawa after 1600, and by and large succeeded. Samurai, farmers, and townspeople tended to marry within their respective classes, and each class developed a unique cultural character. The authorities even attempted to dictate life styles, prescribing who could ride in palanquins, who could wear silk, and who was permitted to build fancy gates in front of their houses.

But to grasp the class structure of Tokugawa society, we must note the vast range of social gradations within each class. A farmer who was a landlord and a district official was a more important figure than most lower samurai and lived in a different social world from a landless "water-drinking" peasant too poor to buy tea. A townsman could be the head of a great wholesale house, or a humble street peddler or clog mender. A samurai could be an elder, a key decision maker of his domain, with an income of thousands of bushels of rice and several hundred vassals of his own, or an impecunious foot soldier who stood guard at the castle gate.

Having disarmed the peasantry, Hideyoshi ordered cadastral surveys on his own lands and on those of his vassals. The surveys defined each parcel of land by location, size, soil quality, product, and cultivator's name. For the first time, an attempt was made to standardize the rods used to measure land and the boxes used to measure quantities of rice. These standards marked the beginning of the detailed record keeping that characterized the Tokugawa era. Hideyoshi's survey laid the foundations for a systematic land tax. Based on these surveys, domains and fiefs were henceforth ranked in terms of their assessed yield.

ESTABLISHMENT OF TOKUGAWA RULE Bedazzled by his own power and military successes, and against all the evidence of Warring States political behavior, Hideyoshi assumed that his vassals would honor their sworn oaths of loyalty to his heir. He was especially trustful of his great ally Tokugawa Ieyasu, whose domains were larger than his own. His trust was misplaced. After his death in 1598, Hideyoshi's former vassals, paying little attention to his heir, broke apart into two opposing camps and fought a great battle in 1600 from which the alliance headed by Tokugawa Ieyasu emerged victorious. Ieyasu was wise, effective in maintaining alliances, and a master strategist, but above all patient. In comparing the three unifiers, the Japanese tell the story that when a cuckoo failed to sing, Nobunaga said, "I'll kill it if it doesn't sing"; Hideyoshi said, "I'll make it sing"; but Ieyasu sat down and said, "I'll wait until it sings."

Like the Minamoto of twelfth-century Kamakura, Ieyasu spurned the Kyoto court and established his headquarters in Edo (today's Tokyo), in the center of his military holdings in eastern Japan (see Map 19–3). He took the title of shōgun in 1603 and called his government the *bakufu.* In Edo he built a great castle, surrounded by massive fortifications of stone and concentric moats. The inner portion of these moats and stone walls remains today as the Imperial Palace. Ieyasu then used his military power to reorganize Japan.

Ieyasu's first move was to confiscate the lands of his defeated enemies and to reward his vassals and allies. During the first quarter of the seventeenth century the *bakufu* confiscated the domains of 150 daimyo, some of former enemies and some for infractions of the Tokugawa legal code, and transferred 229 daimyo from one domain to another. The transfers completed the work of Hideyoshi's sword hunt by severing long-standing ties between daimyo and their disarmed former village retainers. When a daimyo was transferred to a new fief, he took his samurai retainers with him. During the second quarter of the seventeenth century transfers and confiscations ended and the system settled down.

The reshuffling of domains had not been random. The configuration that emerged was, first, of a huge central Tokugawa domain. It contained the following: most of the domains of "house daimyo"—those who had been Tokugawa vassals before 1600; the fiefs of the 5,000 Tokugawa bannermen (upper samurai); and the lands that furnished the stipends of the other 17,000 Tokugawa direct retainers (middle and lower samurai). Then, strategically placed around the Tokugawa heartland were the domains of the "related daimyo." These domains had been founded by the second and third sons of early shōgun and furnished a successor to the main Tokugawa line when a shōgun had no heir. Beyond the related daimyo was a second tier of "outside daimyo" who had fought as allies of Tokugawa Ieyasu in 1600 but became his vassals only after the battle was over.

Finally, at the antipodes of the system were those outside daimyo who had been permitted to survive despite having fought against the Tokugawa in 1600. Their domains were drastically reduced. They remained the "enemies" within the system, although they had submitted and become Tokugawa vassals after 1600. Thus, the entire layout of domains constituted a defensive system, with the staunchest Tokugawa supporters nearest to the center.

The Tokugawa also established other systemic controls. Legal codes regulated the imperial court, temples and shrines, and daimyo. Military houses were enjoined to use men of ability and to practice frugality. They were prohibited from engaging in drinking parties, wanton revelry, sexual indulgence, habitual gambling, or the ostentatious display of wealth. Only with *bakufu* consent could daimyo marry or repair their castles.

A second control was a hostage system, firmly established by 1642, that required the wives and children of daimyo to reside permanently in Edo and the daimyo themselves to spend every second year in Edo. Like the policy of Louis XIV (r. 1643–1715) at Versailles, this requirement transformed feudal lords into courtiers. The palatial Edo compounds of the daimyo contained hundreds or thousands of retainers and servants and occupied much of the city.

A third key control, established during the 1630s, was the national policy of seclusion. Seclusion was no barrier to cultural imports from China and Korea. But except for small Chinese and Dutch trading contingents at Nagasaki, no foreigners were permitted to enter Japan, and on pain of death, no Japanese were allowed to go abroad. Nor could oceangoing ships be built. This policy was strictly enforced until 1854. Like the case of a watch, seclusion enclosed the workings of the entire system. Cut off from substantial outside political contacts, for Japanese, Japan became the world.

An interesting parallel can be drawn between Europe and Tokugawa Japan. Between the fifteenth and eighteenth centuries France moved from a late feudal pattern toward ever greater centralization, whereas Germany moved toward a decentralized order of many independent states. In Japan these two tendencies were delicately balanced. On the one hand, representing the forces of centralization, was the *bakufu,* which governed its own domain and also administered the controls over the whole system. Its offices were staffed by its vassals—its highest councils by house daimyo and high-ranking bannermen, and lesser posts by lower-ranking vassals of ability. The pool of rank was always larger than that of the available posts.

On the other hand, representing decentralization were the domains of the 260 or so daimyo. Except for the house daimyo, they were excluded from service in the *bakufu.*

MAP EXPLORATION

Interactive map: To explore this map further, go to http://www.prenhall.com/craig_map19.3

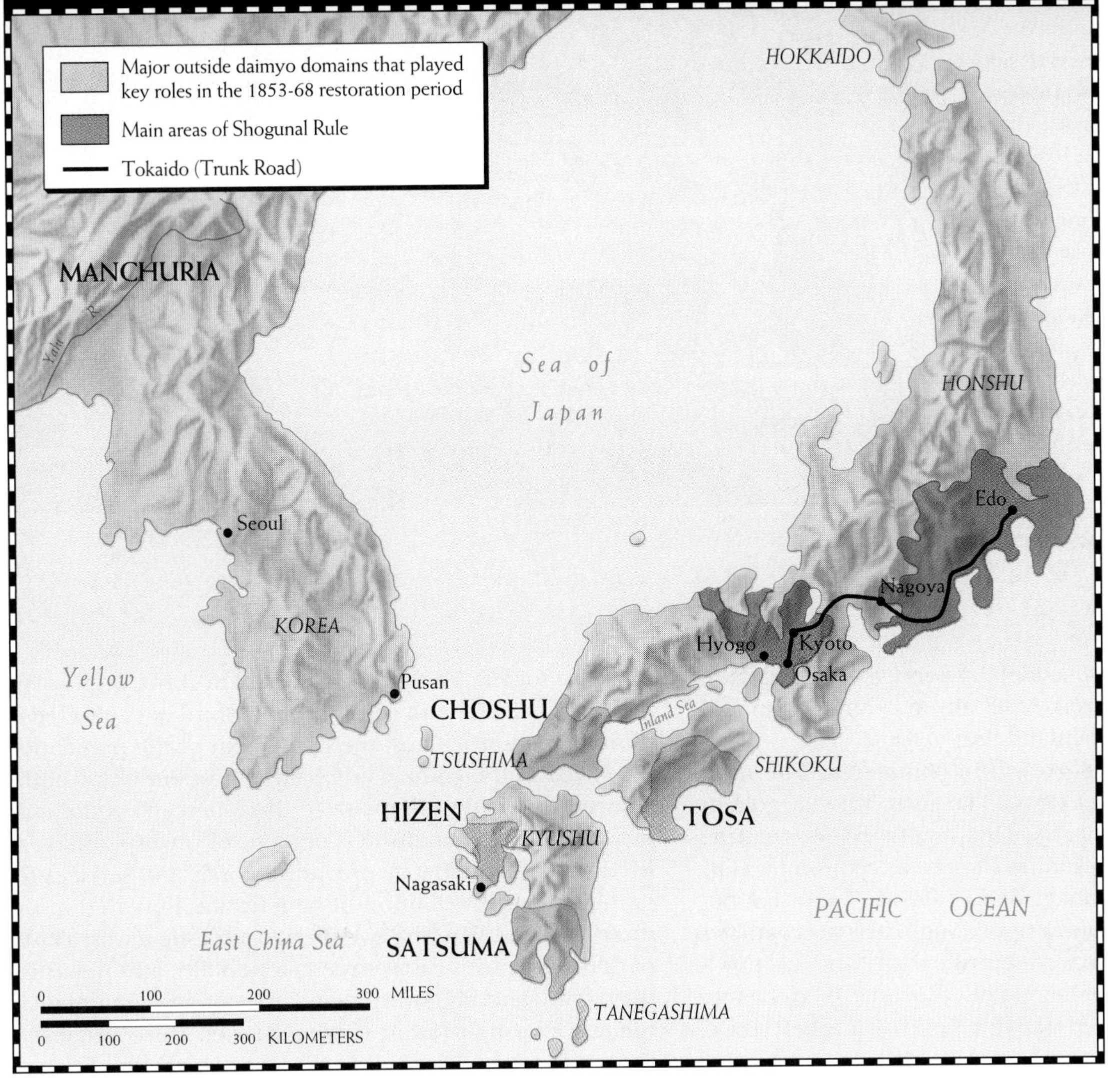

Map 19–3 Tokugawa Japan and the Korean peninsula. The area between Edo and Osaka in central Honshu was both the political base of the Tokugawa *bakufu* and its rice basket. The domains that would overthrow the Tokugawa *bakufu* in the late 19th century were mostly in outlying areas of southwestern Japan.

Their domain governments, like miniature *bakufu*, were staffed by their samurai vassals. Each domain had its own autonomous military, finances, judiciary, schools, paper money, and so on. This balance between centralization and decentralization has led Japanese scholars to label the Tokugawa polity the "*bakufu*-domain system."

THE SEVENTEENTH-CENTURY ECONOMY The political dynamism of the period from Hideyoshi through the first century of Tokugawa rule was matched by economic growth. By the late sixteenth century there existed a backlog of agricultural techniques, the spread of which had been impeded by regionalism and wars: methods of water control and irrigation that made double-cropping easier, better tools, new seed strains, the use of bony fish or of night soil from cities as fertilizers, and so on. During the seventeenth century these techniques were widely applied. Resources no longer needed for war were allocated to land reclamation. The result was a doubling of agricultural production, as well as a doubling of population from 12 million in 1600 to 24 million in 1700. The production of

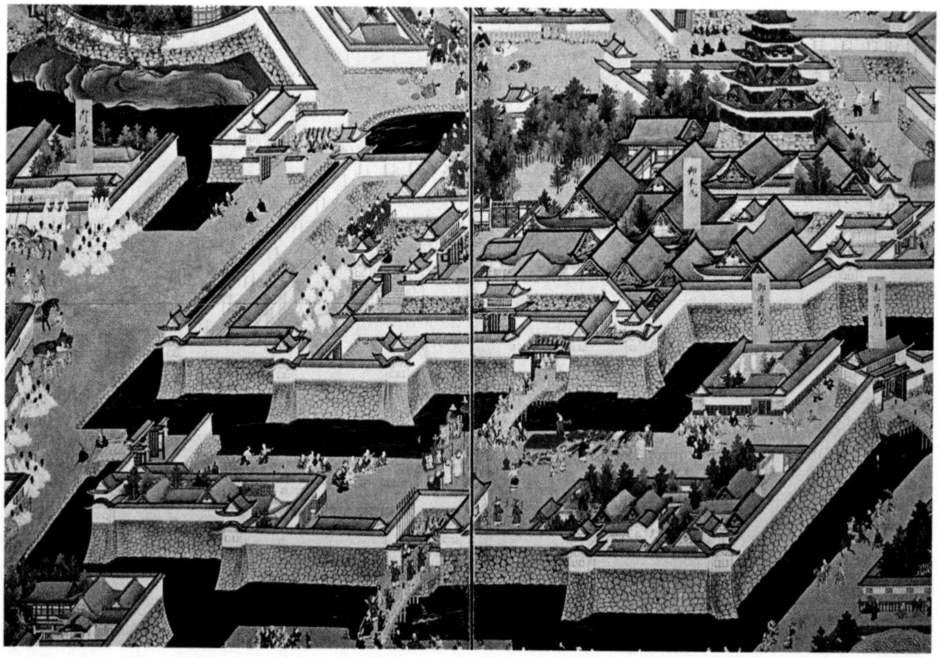

Edo Castle Edo first became a castle town in the mid-fifteenth century. Tokugawa Ieyasu made the castle his residence and headquarters in 1590, and, after his great victory in 1600, rebuilt and extended it. This early Edo period screen painting shows (upper right) the keep or inner citadel, which was not rebuilt after a fire in 1657. Korean envoys (bottom center) enter the castle grounds. They have brought tiger skins and other gifts. Onlookers gawk at their unfamiliar garb. Warriors (top, far right) practice archery. The inner castle compounds shown in the painting were only the central part of an elaborate system of moats, stone-block ramparts, and gates. In 1868, after the Meiji Restoration, the Edo Castle was renamed the Tokyo (Eastern Capital) Castle, and became the residence of the emperor.

agricultural byproducts—cotton, silk, indigo, lumber, dyes, *sake*, and so on—also grew, especially in central Japan and along the shores of the Inland Sea.

Peace also sustained growth in commerce. The merchants in Warring States Japan, like geese who lay golden eggs, had always been at risk. They had to pay for security; they operated within cramped regional economies. On coming to power, Nobunaga and Hideyoshi knew that political unification alone was not enough. They recognized that prosperity would make their rule easier and, acknowledging the enterprise of merchants, they abolished the medieval guilds and freed Japan's central markets from monopolistic restrictions. The result was a burgeoning of trade and the formation of a national market network atop the domain economies. As this network expanded during the seventeenth century, economic functions became more differentiated and efficient. The economic chain that began with a local buyer might extend to a merchant house in a regional port, to coastal shippers, to warehousers in Osaka or Edo, and then to great wholesale houses.

Seclusion ended much foreign trade. One might expect the sharp decline in trade to have dampened Japan's domestic economy. Instead, commerce continued to grow for the remainder of the seventeenth century.

To explain this growth, we must look at the tax system and the pattern of consumption in the castle towns and Edo. Tokugawa tax policy was based on land, not commerce. Taxes took about one third of the peasant's production. It was a heavier tax rate than that in neighboring China and bespeaks the effective grasp that the military class had on Japanese society. Most taxes were paid in grain. Even as late as the mid–nineteenth century, only a third was collected in money payments. Thus, the 87 percent of the population who lived in the countryside paid almost one third of the country's agricultural wealth to the 5 percent in the military class. The remaining 8 percent of townspeople also lived off the tax flow by providing goods and services for samurai. This distribution of benefits was mirrored in the three-area city planning common to all castle towns: a large parklike area with castle, trees, stone walls, and moats for the daimyo and his government; an extensive samurai quarter; and a meaner townspeople's quarter. Moreover, just as the castle towns were the consumption centers of the regional tax economies, so was Edo the national consumption center and a super-castle town. It had the same three-area layout, although on a far grander scale. When the daimyo of Kaga, from a great domain on the Japan Sea, was in attendance at Edo, he was served by 8,000 samurai. When he returned to his domain, 4,000 stayed on in Edo to manage the Kaga estates: 267 acres of houses and gardens, barracks, schools, warehouses, and so on. One of these estates, with its magnificent red gate still intact, is today the main campus of Tokyo University. Other daimyo had establishments proportional to their domains. By 1700 Edo had a population of about million.

To support their Edo establishments, the daimyo sold tax rice in Osaka. The "kitchen of Japan," Osaka became the redistribution center from which competing fleets of coastal shippers brought to Edo food, clothing, lumber, oil, and other supplies. By 1700 Osaka's population was about

A daimyo seated in a palanquin carried by commoner porters. The screen at the side is rolled up so that he can observe the sights of Edo. Surrounding the palanquin are several dozen of his samurai retainers. In the right foreground are Edo townsmen. Courtesy A. Craig

400,000. Kyoto, rebuilt after its destruction in the early Warring States period, was almost as big. It continued as a center of handicraft production. It also was the location of the "captive" imperial court, which, after suffering penury during the Warring States era, was given support lands equivalent in revenues to those of a small daimyo.

The system of alternate-year attendance at Edo contributed to the development of overland transportation. The most traveled grand trunk road was the Tōkaidō Road between Edo and Kyoto. The artist Hiroshige (1797–1858) made a series of woodblock prints that depicted the scenery at its fifty-three post stations. The post stations had official inns for traveling daimyo and requisitioned supplies and horses as a tax obligation from adjacent villages. These stations often grew into thriving local towns.

The growth of a national economy led to a richness and diversity in urban life. Townsmen governed their districts. Samurai city managers watched over the city as a whole. Public schools, police, and companies of firefighters provided public services—a proverb of the time was "Fires are the flowers of Edo." But there were also servants, cooks, messengers, restaurant owners, priests, doctors, teachers, sword sharpeners, book lenders, instructors in the martial arts, prostitutes, and bathhouse attendants. In the world of popular arts there were woodblock printers and artists, book publishers, puppeteers, acrobatic troupes, storytellers, and Kabuki and Nō actors. Merchant establishments included money changers, pawnbrokers, peddlers, small shops, single-price retail establishments like the House of Mitsui, and great wholesale merchants. Merchant households furnished the raw materials for the personae of Edo fiction: the skinflint merchant who pinches every penny, the profligate son who runs through an inheritance to an inevitable bankruptcy, an erring wife, or the clerk involved in a hopeless affair with a prostitute.

Eighteenth and Early Nineteenth Centuries

By the late seventeenth century the political engineering of the Tokugawa state was complete. After that, few major new laws were enacted, and few important changes were made in governing institutions. In the economy, too, from the early eighteenth century, dynamic growth gave way to

The commercial district of Osaka, the "kitchen" of Tokugawa Japan. Warehouses bear the crests of their merchant houses. Ships (upper right) loaded with rice, cotton goods, *sake*, and other goods are about to depart for Edo (Tokyo). Their captains vied with one another to arrive first and get the best price.
Courtesy A. Craig

slower growth within a high-level equilibrium. In the words of some historians, the society had become "frozen," "unchanging," or "strangely preserved." Yet changes of a different kind were under way.

THE FORTY-SEVEN RŌNIN The eighteenth century began with high drama. In the spring of 1701 a daimyo on duty at Edo Castle drew his sword and slightly wounded a *bakufu* official who had insulted him. Even to unsheath a sword within the castle was punishable by death. On the same day the daimyo was ordered to commit *harakiri* (literally, to cut his stomach), and his domain was confiscated. Fearing an attempt at revenge, the *bakufu* police kept an eye on the daimyo's retainers—now *rōnin*, or "masterless samurai." The retainers dissembled, working at lowly jobs, staying at home with their families, or leading lives of drunkenness and debauchery.

Twenty-one months later, on a snowy night in January, forty-seven of the retainers gathered in Edo, attacked the residence of the *bakufu* official, took his head, and then surrendered to the authorities. Their act struck the imagination of the citizenry of Edo and was widely acclaimed. But the *bakufu* council, after deliberating for two months, ordered all forty-seven to commit *harakiri*. The incident embodied the perennial theme of duty versus human feelings. Writers of Kabuki drama and puppet theater quickly took up the incident, and to this day it has been reworked into novels, movies, and television scripts. Just as in Western theater there have been different Hamlets, so have there been many characterizations of Ōishi Kuranosuke, the leader of the band of forty-seven.

Viewed historically, three points may be noted about the incident. First, in a similar situation the more practical samurai of the Warring States period would have forgotten their former lord and rushed to find a new one. Loyalty was highly valued because disloyalty was a live option. But this was no longer true in the Tokugawa era. With the authority of the daimyo backed by that of the shōgun, there was no room for disloyalty. So loyalty became deeply internalized and was viewed almost as a religious obligation. It was also easier for Tokugawa samurai to be loyal unto death because, for the most part, there was so little likelihood in an era of peace that such a loyalty would be called for. In any case, in 1701 it was this Tokugawa species of absolute loyalty that moved the forty-seven rōnin.

Second, the incident tells something of the state in Tokugawa Japan. The 1615 "Laws for the Military Houses" contains the passage: "Law is the basis of the social order. Reason may be violated in the name of law, but law may not be violated in the name of reason. Those who break laws deserve heavy punishments."[5] One Tokugawa law forbade private vendettas. So, despite the moral purity of their

[5]R. Tsunoda, W. T. de Bary, and D. Keene, eds., *Sources of the Japanese Tradition* (New York: Columbia University Press, 1958), p. 336.

act—which all recognized, even those who condemned them to death—the forty-seven "virtuous warriors" had to die. The state was above ethics. Their death sentence was a bureaucratic necessity.

Third, loyalty and idealism were not a monopoly of the males. In the drama, at least, samurai wives and daughters displayed the same heroic spirit of self-sacrifice.

CYCLES OF REFORM Most political history of late Tokugawa Japan is written in terms of alternating cycles of laxity and reform. Even during the mid–seventeenth century the expenses of the *bakufu* and daimyo states were often greater than their income. In part, the reason was structural: Taxes were based on agriculture in an economy that was becoming commercial. In part, it was simple mathematics: After the samurai were paid their stipends, not enough was left for the expenses of domain governments and the costs of the Edo establishments. In part, it was the toll of extraordinary costs, such as a *bakufu* levy, the wedding of a daimyo's daughter, or the rebuilding of a castle after a fire. And finally, in part, it was a growing taste for luxury among daimyo and retainers of rank.

Over the years a familiar pattern emerged. To make ends meet, domains would borrow from merchants. Then, as finances became even more straitened, a reformist clique of officials would appear, take power, retrench the domain's finances, eliminate extravagance, and return the domain to a more frugal and austere way of life. Debts would be repaid or repudiated. A side effect of reform was the depression of the local merchant economy. But no one likes to practice frugality forever. So, after some of the goals of the reform had been achieved, a new clique would take over the government and a new round of spending would begin. The *bakufu* carried out three great reforms on Tokugawa lands:

1716–1733	Tokugawa Yoshimune	17 years
1787–1793	Matsudaira Sadanobu	6 years
1841–1843	Mizuno Tadakuni	2 years

The first two were long and successful; the third was not. Its failure set the stage for the ineffective response of the *bakufu* to the West in the mid–nineteenth century. Daimyo domains also carried out reforms. Some were successful, enabling them to respond more effectively to the political crisis of the mid–nineteenth century.

BUREAUCRATIZATION The balance between centralization and decentralization lasted until the end of the Tokugawa era. Not a single domain ever tried to overthrow the *bakufu* hegemony. Nor did the *bakufu* ever try to extend its control over the domains. But bureaucracy grew steadily both within the *bakufu* and within each domain. One development was the extension of public authority into

The bridal procession of Yohime, the 21st daughter of the 11th Tokugawa shōgun, approaches the Edo mansion of the Kaga daimyo. The red gate (upper right), built in 1827 for this occasion, is today an entrance to the main campus of Tokyo University. The 11th shōgun had twenty-eight sons and twenty-seven daughters by his more than forty concubines. Of his children, thirteen sons and twelve daughters survived to maturity. This woodblock print by Kunisada is a "national treasure." Courtesy A. Craig areas that had been private. In 1600 most samurai fiefs were run by their samurai fief holders. They collected the taxes, often at a heavier rate than the domain set, and appointed fief stewards to oversee the fiefs. By 1850, however, district officials administered all but the largest of samurai fiefs. They collected the standard domain taxes and forwarded to the samurai their income. In periods of retrenchment, samurai were often paid only half the amount due.

Along with the growth of bureaucracy was the proliferation of administrative codes and government by paperwork. Surviving domain archives house room after room of records of every imaginable kind, mostly from the late eighteenth and early nineteenth centuries: records of births, adoptions, name changes, samurai ranks, fief registers, stipend registers, land and tax registers, court proceedings, domain history, and so on. Administrative codes for the *bakufu* exchequer, for example, grew from a single page during the seventeenth century to forty pages in the late Tokugawa. They define among other things an elaborate structure of offices and suboffices, their jurisdictional boundaries, and detailed instructions about how many copies of each document should be made and to which offices they should be forwarded.

Of course, bureaucratization had limits. Only samurai could aspire to official posts. They came to the office wearing their two swords. Decision-making posts were limited to upper-ranking samurai. In periods of financial crises—endemic in the late Tokugawa—a demand arose for men of ability, and middle- or lower-middle-ranking samurai joined domain decision-making by becoming staff assistants to bureaucrats of rank.

THE LATER TOKUGAWA ECONOMY By 1700 the economy approached the limit of expansion within the available technology. The population, an important index, reached 26 million early in the eighteenth century and was at the same figure in the mid–nineteenth century, a period during which the population of China more than doubled. Within this constant figure were various smaller movements. Population declined during epidemics in the 1750s and the 1760s, and during famines in the 1780s. The northeast never fully recovered. Southwestern Japan along the Inland Sea gained in population. Central Japan stayed even; it was more urban, and like most premodern cities, Tokugawa cities had higher death rates.

After 1700 taxes became stabilized and land surveys were few. Evidence suggests little increase in grain production and only slow growth in agricultural byproducts. Some families, to raise their standard of living, made conscious efforts to limit their size. Contraception and abortion were commonplace, and infanticide (euphemistically called *mabiki*, the term for thinning out rice shoots in a paddy) was practiced in hard times. But periodic disease, shortages of food, and late marriages among the poor were more important factors. A study of one rural village showed the daughters of poor farmers marrying at twenty-two and having an average of 4.6 children, whereas for the daughters of rich farmers the figures were nineteen and 6.2. A study of another domain showed that the size of the average farm household declined from 7 to 4.25 members.

During the Tokugawa some farmers remained independent small cultivators, but others became landlords or tenants. By the mid–nineteenth century tenants worked about a quarter of all cultivated lands. Most landlords were small, lived in their villages, and often were village leaders. They were not at all like the Chinese gentry. The misery of the lower stratum of rural society contributed to an increase in peasant uprisings during the late eighteenth and early nineteenth centuries. Authorities had no difficulty in quelling them, although some involved thousands of protestors and were locally destructive. No uprising in Japan even remotely approached those of late Manchu China.

Commerce grew slowly during the late Tokugawa. In the early eighteenth century it was reencased within guilds. Merchants paid set fees, usually not especially high, in return for monopoly privileges in central marketplaces. Guilds were also reestablished in the domains, and some domains established domain-run monopolies on products such as wax, paper, indigo, or sugar. The problem facing domain leaders was how to tax profits without injuring the competitive standing of domain exports. Most late Tokugawa commercial growth was in countryside industries—*sake*, soy sauce, dyes, silks, or cotton—and was especially prominent in central and western Japan. Some were organized and financed by city merchants under the putting-out system. Others competed with city merchants, shipping directly to end markets to circumvent monopoly controls. The expansion of labor in such rural industries contributed to the population shrinkage in late Tokugawa cities.

The largest question about the Tokugawa economy concerns its relation to Japan's amazing industrialization, which began later in the nineteenth century. Some scholars have suggested that Japan had a "running start." Others have stressed Japanese backwardness in comparison with European late developers. The question is still unresolved.

TOKUGAWA CULTURE

If the *Tale of Genji* represents the classical culture of the aristocratic Heian court, and if Nō drama or an ink painting by Sesshū represents the austere samurai culture of medieval Japan, then a satire by Saikaku (1642–1693), a drama by Chikamatsu (1653–1724), or a woodblock print of a beauty by Utamaro (1753–1806) may be taken to represent the new urban culture of the Tokugawa era. In such works, one discerns a new secular consciousness, an exquisite taste put to plebeian ends, occasional vulgarities, and a sense of humor only occasionally encountered in the earlier Japanese tradition.

DOCUMENT THE VIRTUOUS WIFE

The three-generation stem family, composed of the older parents, their eldest son and his "bride," and their children, was the ideal during the Edo period. The principal family bond was between the parents and their elder son. The son's "bride," at least until she produced children of her own, was less than a full family member, as the adage "the womb is borrowed" suggests. Kaibara Ekken (1630–1714), an early Confucian moralist, propounded an ethic appropriate to such a family in his Greater Learning for Women. *It reflects the "wisdom" of his age.*

Can people accept and practice any ethic that serves their society? Or are some ethics more "natural" than others? How did a girl raised in Tokugawa society feel? Could she embrace Ekken's teachings? Or does the following passage suggest, at least obliquely, that some human feelings are universal and difficult to deny?

Girl's Instruction

Seeing that it is a girl's destiny, on reaching womanhood, to go to a new home, and live in submission to her father-in-law, it is even more incumbent upon her than it is on a boy to receive with all reverence her parents' instructions. Should her parents, through their tenderness, allow her to grow up self-willed, she will infallibly show herself capricious in her husband's house, and thus alienate his affection; while, if her father-in-law be a man of correct principles, the girl will find the yoke of these principles intolerable. She will hate and decry her father-in-law, and the end of these domestic dissensions will be her dismissal from her husband's house and the covering of herself with ignominy. Her parents, forgetting the faulty education they gave her, may, indeed, lay all the blame on the father-in-law. But they will be in error; for the whole disaster should rightly be attributed to the faulty education the girl received from her parents.

The Infirmities of Woman

The five worst infirmities that afflict the female are indocility, discontent, slander, jealousy, and silliness. Without any doubt, these five infirmities are found in seven or eight out of every ten women, and it is from these that arises the inferiority of women to men. A woman should cure them by self-inspection and self-reproach.

The Wife's Miscellaneous Duties

A woman has no particular lord. She must look to her husband as her lord, and must serve him with all worship and reverence, not despising or thinking lightly of him. The great lifelong duty of a woman is obedience. In her dealings with her husband, both the expression of her countenance and style of her address should be courteous, humble, and conciliatory, never peevish and intractable, never rude and arrogant—that should be a woman's first and chiefest care. When the husband issues his instructions, the wife must never disobey them. In doubtful cases she should inquire of her husband, and obediently follow his commands. If ever her husband should inquire of her, she should answer to the point—to answer in a careless fashion would be a mark of rudeness. Should her husband be roused at any time to anger, she must obey him with fear and trembling, and not set herself up against him in anger and forwardness. A woman should look on her husband as if he were Heaven itself, and never weary of thinking how she may yield to her husband and thus escape celestial castigation.

Kaibara Ekken, *Greater Learning for Women* in K. Hoshino, *The Way of Contentment* (London: John Murray, 1913, reprinted 1979), pp. 33–34, 44–45.

But there was more to Tokugawa culture than the arts and literature of the townspeople. Two hundred and fifty years of peace and prosperity provided a base for an ever more complex culture and a broader popular participation in cultural life. In the villages Buddhism became more deeply rooted; new folk religions proliferated; by the early nineteenth century most well-to-do farmers could read and write. The aristocratic culture of the ranking samurai houses also remained vigorous. Nō plays continued to be staged. The medieval tradition of black ink paintings was continued by the Kanō school and other artists.

The Ashikaga tradition of restraint, simplicity, and naturalness in architecture was extended. The imperial villa in Katsura outside of Kyoto has its roots in medieval architecture and to this day inspires Japanese architects. The gilded and colored screen paintings that had surged in popularity during Hideyoshi's rule developed further, culminating in the powerful works of Ogata Kōrin (1658–1716).

Zen Buddhism, having declined during the Warring States period, was revitalized by the monk Hakuin (1686–1769). One of the great cultural figures of the Tokugawa era, Hakuin was also a writer, a painter, a calligrapher, and a sculptor. His autobiographical writings have been translated as *The Embossed Tea Kettle.*

Some scholars have argued that Tokugawa urban culture had a double structure. On the one hand were the samurai, serious and high-minded, who produced a vast body of Chinese-style paintings, poetry, and philosophical treatises. On the other hand was the culture of the townspeople: lowbrow, irreverent, secular, satirical, and often scatological. The samurai esteemed Sung-style paintings of mountains or waterfalls, often adorned with quotations from the Confucian classics or T'ang poetry. The townspeople collected prints of local beauties, actors, courtesans, and scenes from

Utamaro Woodblock Print

Medieval Buddhism called this world with its transient pleasures the "floating world" or *ukiyo*. But in the Tokugawa period, the *ukiyo* was the brothel quarter and it was here that the *ukiyo-e* or woodblock print developed, first in black and white, and later in color.

The prints were produced by what economic historians call a "putting- out system." Publishers, organized in guilds, paid for each stage of production: the artists, the carvers of the wooden blocks, and the printers. Prints were made in runs of 200. If popular, new editions were issued until the blocks wore out. The publishers sold the prints to distributors, who in turn sold them to door-to-door peddlers and to print shops in Edo.

During the Westernization that followed the 1868 Meiji Restoration, *ukiyo-e* fell into disfavor in Japan. But Western collectors discovered their beauty. For a time they were purchased for next to nothing in Tokyo and sold for good prices in Paris. Imitations of Hiroshige prints by Vincent van Gogh can be seen in the Van Gogh Museum in Amsterdam.

Kitagawa Utamaro (1753–1806) was a late Edo master artist famed for his paintings of lovely women. Some titles of his print series were *A Comparison of the Charms of Five Beautiful Women, Day and Night in the Pleasure Houses, Eight Views of Famous Tea Houses*, and *Five Elegant Aspects of Life*. So popular were his works that some publishers hired unknown artists to produce fakes in his name. This led him to sign some works "the genuine Utamaro." He boasted of his high fees, comparing himself to a great courtesan and his would-be imitators to streetwalkers.

Mother Bathing Her Son. Woodblock print (37.8 × 25.7 cm) by Kitagawa Utamaro (1753–1806). Note the cooper's craft seen in the tub, the wooden clog, the simple yet elegant kimono design, and a second kimono hanging to dry at the upper right corner. Photo: M. McLean The Nelson-Atkins Museum of Art, Kansas City, MO (Purchase: Nelson Trust). © The Nelson Gallery Foundation. All Reproduction Rights Reserved.

everyday life. Samurai moralists saw money as the root of evil. Merchants saw it as their goal in life; in Osaka, they even held an "abacus festival," at which their adding machines were consecrated to the gods of wealth and commerce.

In poetry, too, a double structure appeared. Bashō (1644–1694) was born a samurai but gave up his status to live as a wandering poet. He is famous for his travel journal, *The Narrow Road of Oku,* and especially for his haiku, little word-picture poems:

> Such stillness—
> The cries of the cicadas
> Sink into the rocks.
>
> A crow perches
> On a leafless branch
> An autumn evening.

Or, on visiting a battlefield of the past, he wrote:

> The summer grass
> All that is left
> Of a warrior's dream. [6]

Contrast Bashō's sense of the transience of life with the worldliness humor of the townsman:

> From a mountain temple
> The snores of a monk and
> the voice of the cuckoo.
>
> Showing a love-letter
> to her mother
> From a man she doesn't love.
>
> Even the most virtuous woman
> will undo her sash
> For a flea.[7]

This is not to say, of course, that townspeople did not write proper haiku as well.

LITERATURE AND DRAMA Is cultural creativity more likely during periods of economic growth and political change or during periods of stability? The greatest works of literature and philosophy of Tokugawa Japan were produced between 1650 and 1725, just as the initial political transformation was being completed but the economy still growing and the society not yet set in its ways.

One of the major literary figures and certainly the most entertaining was Ihara Saikaku (1642–1693), who is generally credited with having re-created the Japanese novel. Saikaku was heir to an Osaka merchant house. He was raised to be its master, but after his wife died he let the head clerk manage the business and devoted himself to poetry, theater, and the pleasure quarters. At the age of forty he wrote and illustrated *The Life of an Amorous Man,* the story of a modern and bawdy Prince Genji who cuts a swath through bathhouse girls, shrine maidens, courtesans, and boy actors. The overnight success of the work led to a sequel, *The Life of an Amorous Woman,* the tale of a woman undone by passion and of her downward spiral through the minutely graded circles of the Osaka demimonde. Saikaku also wrote more than twenty other works, including *The Japanese Family Storehouse,* which humorously chronicles the contradictions between the pursuit of wealth and the pursuit of pleasure.

A second major figure of Osaka culture at the turn of the century was the dramatist Chikamatsu Monzaemon

[6]D. Keene, ed., *Anthology of Japanese Literature* (New York: Grove Press, 1955), p. 371. Used by permission of Grove/Atlantic, Inc.

[7]R. H. Blyth, *Japanese Humor* (Tokyo: Japanese Travel Bureau, 1957), p. 141.

One of Edo's three Kabuki theaters during the 1790s. The male actors provide the drama—even female roles are played by men. The audience eats, drinks, and smokes while watching the action. Note the mix of social classes: Day laborers at center-left sit on boards while well-to-do merchants occupy more expensive seats in the right and left foreground. At bottom-center an artisan cadges a light for his pipe. Several boxes to his left, another pours a drink. A reprint of a three-panel woodblock print by Utagawa Toyokuni (1769–1825) from the late 1790s. Musee Guimet, Paris, France/Giraudon/Art Resource, N.Y.

(1653–1724). Born a samurai in Echizen province, Chikamatsu entered the service of a court aristocrat in Kyoto and then, in 1705, moved to Osaka to write for both the Kabuki and the puppet theater. Kabuki had begun early in the seventeenth century as suggestive skits and erotic dances performed by troupes of actresses. In 1629 the *bakufu* forbade women to perform on the stage. By the 1660s Kabuki had evolved into a more serious drama with male actors playing both male and female roles. Actors entered the stage on a raised runway or "flower path" through the audience. Famous actors took great liberties in interpreting plays, to roars of approval from the audience. There was a ready market for woodblock prints of actors in their most famous roles—like posters of rock musicians today, but done with incomparably greater artistry.

The three main types of Kabuki plays were dance pieces, which were influenced by the tradition of the Nō; domestic dramas; and historical pieces. Chikamatsu wrote all three. In contrast to Saikaku's protagonists, the men and women in Chikamatsu's dramas struggle to fulfill the duties and obligations of their stations in life. Only when their passions become uncontrollable, which is generally the case, do the plays end in tragedy. The emotional intensity of the ending is heightened by the restraint shown by the actors before they reach their breaking point. In some plays the hero and heroine leave duty behind and set out on a flight to death. Another favorite ending is the double suicide, in which the unfortunate lovers choose union in the next world. Indeed, this ending was banned by *bakufu* authorities when the excessive popularity of the drama led to its imitation in real life.

It is interesting to compare Kabuki and the Nō drama. Nō is like early Greek drama in that the chorus provides the narrative line. In Nō, the stylization of action is extreme. In Kabuki, as in Elizabethan drama, the actors declaim their lines in the dramatic realism demanded by the commoner theatergoers of seventeenth-century Japan. But to convey the illusion of realism required some deviation from it. As Chikamatsu himself noted about Kabuki: "Many things are said by the female characters which real women could not utter. . . . It is because they say what could not come from a real woman's lips that their true emotions are disclosed." For him, "Art is something that lies in the slender margin between the real and the unreal." [8] Yet, for all that Chikamatsu was concerned with the refinements of his craft and the balance between emotional expressiveness and unspoken restraints, he never talked of the mysterious "no mind" as the key to an actor's power. His dramas are a world removed from the religiosity of the medieval Nō.

In the early eighteenth century Kabuki was displaced in popularity by the puppet theater (Bunraku). Many of Chikamatsu's plays were written for this genre. The word '*puppet*' does not do justice to the half-life-sized human figures, which rival Nō masks in their artistry. Manipulated by a team of three, a puppet does not only kneel and bow or engage in swordplay, but can also mimic brushing a tear from the eye with its kimono sleeve or threading a needle. In the late eighteenth century the puppet theater, in turn, declined, and as the center of culture shifted from Osaka to Edo, Kabuki again blossomed as Japan's premier form of drama.

CONFUCIAN THOUGHT The most important change in Tokugawa intellectual life was that the ruling elite abandoned the religious teachings of Buddhism in favor of the more secular worldview of Confucius, opening many avenues for further changes. The reworking occurred slowly. During the seventeenth century samurai were enjoined never to forget the arts of war and to be ever ready to die for their lord. One samurai in his deathbed poem lamented dying on *tatami*—with his boots off, as it were. In this period, most samurai were illiterate and saw book learning as unmanly. Nakae Tōju (1608–1648), a samurai and a Confucian scholar, recounted that as a youth he swaggered around with his friends during the day and studied secretly at night so as not to be thought a sissy. Schools, too, were slow to develop. One Japanese scholar has noted that in 1687 only four domains had proper domain schools; in 1715, only ten.

The great figures of Tokugawa Confucianism lived during the same years as Saikaku and Chikamatsu, in the late seventeenth and early eighteenth centuries. They are great because they succeeded in the difficult task of adapting Chinese Confucianism to fit Japanese society. One problem, for example, was that in Chinese Confucianism there was no place for a shōgun, whereas in the Japanese tradition of sunline emperors there was no room for the Mandate of Heaven. Most Tokugawa thinkers handled this discrepancy by saying that Heaven gave the emperor its mandate and that the emperor then entrusted political authority to the shōgun. One philosopher suggested that the divine emperor acted for Heaven and gave the mandate to the shōgun. Neither solution was very comfortable, for, in fact, the emperor was as much a puppet as those in the Osaka theater.

Another problem was the difference between China's centralized bureaucratic government and Japan's "feudal" system of lord-vassal relationships. Samurai loyalty was clearly not that of a scholar-official to the Chinese emperor. Some Japanese thinkers solved this problem rather ingeniously by saying that it was China that had deviated from the feudal society of the Chou sages, whereas in Japan, Tokugawa Ieyasu had re-created just such a society.

A third problem concerned the "central flowery kingdom" and the barbarians around it. No philosopher could quite bring himself to say that Japan was the real middle kingdom and China the barbarian, but some argued that

[8] R. Tsunoda, p. 448.

centrality was relative, and still others suggested that China under barbarian Manchu rule had lost its claim to universality. These are just a few of a large range of problems related to Japanese political organization, Shinto, and to Japanese family practices. By the early eighteenth century these problems had been addressed, and a revised Confucianism acceptable for use in Japan had come into being.

Another point to note is the continuing vitality of Japanese thought—Confucian and otherwise—into the mid–nineteenth century. This vitality is partly explained by the disputes among different schools of Confucianism and partly, perhaps, by Japan's lack of an examination system. The best energies of its samurai youth were not channeled into writing the conventional and sterile "eight-legged essay" that was required in the Chinese examination system. Official preferment—within the constraints of Japan's hereditary system—was often obtained by writing a proposal for domain reforms, although this could sometimes lead to punishments as well.

The vitality was also a result of the rapid expansion of schools from the early eighteenth century. By the early nineteenth century every domain had its own official school and a school on its Edo estate. Commoner schools (*terakoya*), in which reading, writing, and the rudiments of Confucianism were taught, grew apace. In the first half of the nineteenth century private academies also appeared throughout the country. By the late Tokugawa era about 40 to 50 percent of the male population and 15 to 20 percent of the female population was literate—a far higher rate than in most of the world, and on a par with some European late developers.

OTHER DEVELOPMENTS IN THOUGHT For Tokugawa scholars, the emotional problem of how to deal with China was vexing. Their response was usually ambivalent. They praised China as the teacher country and respected its creative tradition. They studied its history, philosophy, and literature, and began a tradition of scholarship on China that has remained powerful to this day. But they also sought to retain a separate Japanese identity. Most scholars dealt with this problem by adapting Confucianism to fit Japan. But two schools—never in the mainstream of Tokugawa thought, but growing in importance during the eighteenth and early nineteenth centuries—arrived at more radical positions. The schools of National Studies and Dutch Studies were diametrically opposed in most respects but alike in criticizing the Chinese influence on Japanese life and culture.

National Studies began as philological studies of ancient Japanese texts. One source of its inspiration was Shinto. Another was the Neo-Confucian School of Ancient Learning. Just as the School of Ancient Learning had sought to discover the original, true meanings of the Chinese classics before they were contaminated by Sung metaphysics, so the scholars in the National Studies tradition tried to find in the Japanese classics the original true character of Japan before it had been contaminated by Chinese ideas. On studying the *Record of Ancient Matters, The Collection of Myriad Leaves,* or *The Tale of Genji,* they found that the early Japanese spirit was free, spontaneous, clean, lofty, and honest, in contrast to the Chinese spirit, which they characterized as rigid, cramped, and artificial. Some writings of this school appear to borrow the anti-Confucian logic of Taoism.

A second characteristic of National Studies was its reaffirmation of Japan's emperor institution. Motoori Norinaga (1730–1801) wrote of Shinto creationism as the "Right Way":

> Heaven and Earth, all the gods and all phenomena, were brought into existence by the creative spirits of two deities. . . . This . . . is a miraculously divine act the reason for which is beyond the comprehension of the human intellect.
>
> But in foreign countries where the Right Way has not been transmitted, this act of divine creativity is not known. Men there have tried to explain the principle of Heaven and earth and all phenomena by such theories as the yin and yang, the hexagrams of the Book of Changes, and the Five Elements. But all of these are fallacious theories stemming from the assumptions of the human intellect and they in no wise represent the true principle.
>
> The "special dispensation of our Imperial Land" means that ours is the native land of the Heaven-Shining Goddess who casts her light over all countries in the four seas. Thus our country is the source and fountainhead of all other countries, and in all matters it excels all the others.[9]

National Studies became influential during the late Tokugawa era. It had a small but not unimportant influence on the Meiji Restoration. Its doctrines continued thereafter as one strain of modern Japanese ultranationalism. Its most enduring achievement was in Japanese linguistics. Even today, scholars admire Motoori's philology. Moreover, in an age when the prestige of things Chinese was overwhelming, Motoori helped redress the balance by appreciating and giving a name to the aesthetic sensibility found in the Japanese classics. The phrase he used was *mono no aware,* which means, literally, "the poignancy of things."

But National Studies had several weaknesses that prevented it from becoming the mainstream of Japanese thought. First, even the most refined sensibility is no substitute for philosophy. In its celebration of the primitive, National Studies ran headlong into the greater rationality of Confucian thought. Second, National Studies was chiefly literary, and apart from its enthusiasm for the divine emperor, it had little to offer politically in an age when political philosophy was central in both the domain and the *bakufu* schools.

A second development was Dutch Studies. After Christianity had been proscribed and the policy of seclusion

[9]Tsunoda, pp. 521, 523.

DOCUMENT A TOKUGAWA SKEPTIC

Confucian teachings, while hardly scientific, placed a premium on rational argument. Some scholars used this rationalism to attack Buddhism. Others directed their attack against superstitions and explanations of natural phenomena that they found wanting. The following passages by Miura Baien (1723–1789), the son of a Kyushu doctor, exemplify such a rationalism.

Does modern science answer the kind of question that Baien is raising? Are some superstitions in modern societies still vulnerable to his critique?

Why do a pair of dark things on the forehead see; why do a pair of holes in the head hear? Why don't eyes hear, why don't ears see? When most people come to these points they just leave them alone, but I simply can't leave them alone. . . . They refer the question to past authority, and when they find a book that deals with it, they accept whatever answer it gives. I can't convince myself entirely in that way. When they discuss the natural world, they do so in a wild, hit-or-miss manner; when they talk of life and death, they do so in an absurd or obscure manner. Though their evidence may be flimsy and their arguments preposterous, this does not disturb people at all.

[It is] a human peculiarity . . . to view everything as human. Take, for example, children's picture books, *The Betrothal of Rats* or *Monsters and Goblins.* Rats are never kept as rats in their true shape; instead all of them are turned into human forms. The bridegroom appears in the book in ceremonial robes with a pair of swords, while the bride is shown with a flowing gown on and snowy cap of cotton, and is carried in a palanquin with an escort of footmen and young guards. In the book of *Monsters and Goblins,* no cases are found of an umbrella turning into a tea-mortar, or of a broom changing into a bucket. But all monsters and goblins are given eyes and noses and hands and feet, so as to look like members of the human family. . . .

It is such an imagination as this that populates heaven with a supreme God, and earth with gods of wind and thunder. Monstrous in form, they all move by foot, and do their work by hand. Wind is put in bags, thunder is beaten out on drums. If they are real bags, how are they made? And there must be skin to make a drum. If such imaginings are carried further, the sun will be unable to go on revolving unless it gets feet, and nature will be helpless in her work unless she has hands.

R. Tsunoda, W. T. de Bary, and D. Keene, eds., *Sources of the Japanese Tradition* (New York: Columbia University Press, 1960), pp. 490, 493–494.

adopted, all Western books were banned in Japan. Some knowledge of Dutch was maintained among the official interpreters who dealt with the Dutch at Nagasaki. The ban on Western books (except for those propagating Christianity) was ended in 1720 by the shōgun Tokugawa Yoshimune (r. 1716–1745), following the advice of a scholar whom he had appointed to reform the Japanese calendar.

During the remainder of the eighteenth century, a school of "Dutch medicine" became established in Japan. Japanese pioneers early recognized that Western anatomy texts were superior to Chinese. The first Japanese dissection of a corpse occurred in 1754. In 1774 a Dutch translation of a German anatomy text was translated into Japanese. By the mid–nineteenth century there were schools of Dutch Studies in the main cities of Japan, and instruction was available in some domains as well. Fukuzawa Yukichi (1835–1901), who studied Dutch and Dutch science during the mid-1850s at a school begun in 1838 in Osaka, wrote in his *Autobiography* of the hostility of his fellow students toward Chinese learning:

> Though we often had discussions on many subjects, we seldom touched upon political subjects as most of us were students of medicine. Of course, we were all for free intercourse with Western countries, but there were few among us who took a serious interest in that problem. The only subject that bore our constant attack was Chinese medicine. And by hating Chinese medicine so thoroughly, we came to dislike everything that had any connection with Chinese culture. Our general opinion was that we should rid our country of the influences of the Chinese altogether. Whenever we met a young student of Chinese literature, we simply felt sorry for him. Particularly were the students of Chinese medicine the butt of our ridicule. [10]

While medicine was the primary occupation of those who studied Dutch, some knowledge of Western astronomy, geography, botany, physics, chemistry, and arts also entered Japan. Works on science occasionally influenced other thinkers as well. Yamagata Bantō (1748–1821) was a rich and scholarly Osaka merchant who devised a rationalistic philosophy based on a synthesis of Neo-Confucianism and Western science. After studying a work on astronomy, he wrote in 1820 that conditions on other planets "varied only according to their size and their proximity to the sun." Bantō also speculated that "grass and trees will appear, insects will develop; if there are insects, fish, shellfish, animals

[10]E. Kiyooka, trans., *The Autobiography of Fukuzawa Yukichi* (New York: Columbia University Press, 1966), p. 91.

and birds will not be absent, and finally there will be people too." Bantō qualified his argument with the naturalistic supposition that Mercury and Venus would probably lack human life, "since these two planets are near to the sun and too hot." He contrasted his rational arguments regarding evolution with the "slap-dash" arguments of Buddhists and Shintoists.[11]

From the late eighteenth century the Japanese began to be aware of the West, and especially of Russia, as a threat to Japan. In 1791 a concerned scholar wrote *A Discussion of the Military Problems of a Maritime Nation*, advocating a strong navy and coastal defenses. During the early nineteenth century such concerns mounted. A sudden expansion in Dutch Studies occurred after Commodore Matthew Perry's visits to Japan in 1853 and 1854. During the 1860s Dutch Studies became Western Studies, as English, French, German, and Russian were added to the languages studied at the *bakufu* Institute for the Investigation of Barbarian Books. In sum, Dutch Studies was not a major influence on Tokugawa thought. It cannot begin to compare with Neo-Confucianism. But it laid a foundation on which the Japanese built quickly when the need arose.

Korea and Vietnam

A feature of world history, noted earlier, is the spread of heartland civilizations into their surrounding areas. In East Asia the heartland civilization was that of China, the surrounding areas that were able to take in Chinese learning were Japan, Korea, and Vietnam. Like the Japanese, Koreans and Vietnamese learned to write using Chinese ideographs. They partially modeled their governments on those of China. They accepted Chinese Buddhism and Confucianism, and with them Chinese conceptions of the universe, state, and human relationships. The Confucian definitions of the relations between ruler and minister, father and son, and husband and wife were emphasized in Korea and Vietnam as they were in China. But at the same time, Koreans and Vietnamese who spoke non-Chinese tongues, saw themselves as separate peoples, and gradually came to take pride in their independence. In Europe, Germany might be a parallel case: it became civilized by borrowing the heartland Greco-Christian culture of the Mediterranean area, but it kept its original tongue and elements from its earlier culture.

[11]M. Jansen, ed., *Changing Japanese Attitudes Toward Modernization* (Princeton: Princeton University Press, 1965), p.144.

CHRONOLOGY

TOKUGAWA ERA (1600–1868)

1600	Tokugawa Ieyasu reunifies Japan
1615	"Laws of Military Houses" issued
1639	Seclusion policy adopted
1642	Edo hostage system in place
1644–1694	Bashō, poet
1653–1724	Chikamatsu Monzaemon, dramatist
1701	The forty-seven rōnin avenge their lord
1853, 1854	Commodore Matthew Perry visits Japan

KOREA

A range of mountains along its northern rim divides the Korean peninsula from Manchuria, making it a distinct geographical unit. Mountains continue south through the eastern third of Korea, while in the west and south are coastal plains and broad river valleys. The combination of mountains, rice paddies, and sea makes Korea a beautiful land. The traditional name for Korea may be translated as the "land of the morning calm." Two further geographical factors affected Korean history. One was that the northwestern corner of Korea was only 300 miles from the northeastern corner of historical China: close enough for Korea to be vulnerable to invasions by its powerful neighbor but far enough away so that most of the time China found it easier to treat Korea as a tributary than to control it directly. The other factor was that the southern rim of Korea was just one hundred miles distant from the Japanese southern island of Kyushu across the Tsushima Straits.

EARLY HISTORY

During its old and new stone ages, Korea was peopled by Tungusic tribes moving south from northeast Asia. They spoke an Altaic tongue—distantly related to Japanese and to Manchurian, Mongolian, and Turkic. They lived by hunting, gathering, and fishing, and, like other early peoples of northeast Asia, made comb-patterned pottery and practiced an animistic religion. During the first millennium B.C.E. agriculture, bronze and iron were introduced, transforming their primitive society. But Koreans were still ruled by tribal chiefdoms in 108 B.C.E. when the Han emperor Wu Ti sent an army into north Korea to menace the flank of the Hunnish (Hsiung Nu) empire that spread across the steppe to the north of China. Wu Ti built a Chinese city—near the present-day capital of North Korea—which survived into the fourth century C.E., and established commanderies and prefectures to administer the land.

Between the fourth and seventh centuries three archaic states emerged from earlier tribal confederations. Silla, one of the three, together with armies from T'ang China, conquered the other two in the seventh century. The T'ang armies wanted to stay and rule Korea, but after battles with Silla troops they withdrew, and Silla was recognized by China in 675 as an autonomous tribute state. The period of Silla rule may be likened to Nara Japan: Korea borrowed Chinese writing, established some government offices on the Chinese model, sent annual embassies to the T'ang court, and took in Chinese Buddhism and Chinese arts and philosophies. Yet within the Silla government, birth mattered more than scholarship and rule by aristocrats continued, while in village Korea, the worship of nature deities was only lightly touched by the Buddhism that spread among the ruling elites.

Celadon glazes spread from China to Korea during the Koryo period (918–1392). Pots such as this late-12th or early-13th-century ewer are prized by collectors around the world for their graceful contours and detail.
The Avery Brundage Collection/Asian Art Museum of San Francisco

Silla underwent a normal end-of-dynasty decline, and in 918 a warlord general founded a new dynasty, the Koryo. The English word "Korea" is derived from this dynastic name. This was a creative period. Korean scholars advanced in their mastery of Chinese principles of government. New genres of poetry and literature appeared. Korean potters made celadon vases rivaling those of China. The craft of history advanced: the earliest surviving history of Korea was compiled in 1145. Printing using moveable metallic type was invented during the thirteenth century. But most important of all was the growth of Buddhism. Temples, monasteries, and nunneries were built throughout the land, and Buddhist arts flourished. During the thirteenth century, Buddhist scholars produced in classical Chinese a printed edition of the Tripitaka, a huge compendium of sutras and other sacred writings.

Despite cultural advances, the Koryo state was weak. For one thing, the Koryo economy was undeveloped: trade was by barter, money did not circulate, and Chinese missions commented on the extravagance of officials in the capital and the squalor of commoners and slaves in Korea's villages. For another, the dynasty was aristocratic from the start, and as centuries passed, private estates and armies arose, and civil officials were replaced by military men. For still another, frequent incursions from across Korea's northern border weakened the state. The cost of wars with the Mongols was particularly high. The Koryo court survived as long as it did by becoming in succession the tributary of the Sung, Liao, Chin, and Mongol dynasties.

THE CHOSON ERA: LATE TRADITIONAL KOREA

In 1392, a Koryo general, Yi Songgye, switched his allegiance from the Mongols to the rising Ming state, deposed the Koryo king, and founded a new dynasty. It lasted for 518 years until 1910; its amazing longevity was directly related to the stability of Ming-Ch'ing China.

After seizing power, Yi carried out an extensive land reform and strengthened his government by absorbing into his officialdom members of the great Koryo families. During the Yi or Choson period, these elite families, known as *yangban,* monopolized education, official posts, and land. Beneath them were the commoners known as "good people," tax-paying free subjects of the king. Beneath the commoners and constituting perhaps one third of the population were government and private slaves. Korean scholars argue that they were not like slaves in other lands, since there were no slave auctions, and, following Confucian teachings, husbands were not separated from their wives. But Korean slaves were nonetheless property. They were often attached to land, they could be given as gifts, and their children were slaves to be used as their owners willed.

Early Choson culture showed many signs of vigor. Lyrical poetry and then prose reached new heights. In 1443, a group of scholars under King Sejong—who was regarded as a sage—invented a simple alphabet for the transcription of Korean without the burden of Chinese ideographs. Such was the prestige of Chinese writing that the simple alphabet was not used until modern times. The most important intellectual trend during the Choson era was the gradual movement of the *yangban* away from Buddhism and their acceptance of Neo-Confucianism. By the late fifteenth century, Korean philosophers were making original contributions to the philosophy of this school, contributions that later became influential in Japan.

But at mid-dynasty, invasions dealt a severe blow to the well-being of Choson society. Hideyoshi, having brought all of Japan under his control, decided to conquer China; for him, the path to China was through Korea. His samurai armies devastated Korea twice, once in 1592 and again in 1596. The invasions ended with his death in 1598. On both occasions the Ming court sent troops to aid its tributary, but the rescuing Chinese armies, in turn, devastated the land almost as much as had the Japanese. A third disaster occurred in 1627 and 1637 when Manchu troops invaded pro-Ming Korea, laying waste to the northwest and to Seoul. The result of these multiple incursions was a drop in taxable land to about a quarter of its late-sixteenth-century level. Behind this statistic lay a grim reality of famine, death, and misery.

Had the late-sixteenth-century Choson government been stronger, it might have recovered. But from the end of the fifteenth century cliques of officials had begun to fight among themselves, and their partisan struggles intensified during the centuries that followed. On the surface, the struggles took the form of debates over issues relating to the king or queen. In actuality, they were bitter contests between the growing numbers of educated sons of *yangban* families over a limited number of official positions. Many in the losing factions were executed—at times dismembered—or imprisoned. As the struggles became more fierce, the effectiveness of government declined, except for a brief recovery during the early eighteenth century. High officials in Seoul used their power to garner private agricultural estates, and established local academies to prepare their own kinsmen for the official examinations.

From the mid–seventeenth century on, Korea offers a mixed picture. Literacy rose and a new popular fiction of fables, romances, and novels appeared. Women writers became important for the first time. Among some *yangban* there was a philosophic reaction against what was perceived as the emptiness of Neo-Confucianism. Calling for "practical learning" to effect a renewal of Korean society, scholars criticized the Confucian classics and outlined plans for administrative reforms and the encouragement of commerce. Unfortunately, their recommendations were not adopted, and the society continued its decline. More Koreans died in the famine of 1671 than during Hideyoshi's invasions. Overtaxation, drought, floods, pestilence, and famine became commonplace. Robberies occurred in daytime Seoul, and bandits plagued the countryside. Disgruntled officials led peasants in month-long revolts in 1811 and 1862. Because of the concentration of officials, wealth, and military power at Seoul and because of Manchu support for the ruling house, neither revolt succeeded in toppling the dynasty, but the revolts left Korea with neither the will nor the means to meet the challenges it would soon face.

VIETNAM

SOUTHEAST ASIA

The historical civilizations of Southeast Asia were shaped by three movements. One was the movement of peoples and languages from north to south. Ranges of mountains rising in Tibet and South China extend southward, dividing Southeast Asia into river valleys. The Mon and Burmese peoples had moved from the southeast slopes of the Tibetan plateau into the Upper Irrawaddy by 500 B.C.E., and continued south along the Irrawaddy and Salween Rivers, founding the kingdom of Pagan in 847 C.E. Thai tribes moved south from China down the valley of the Chao Phraya River somewhat later, founding the kingdoms of Sukhothai (1238–1419) and Ayutthaya (1350–1767). Even today Thai-speaking tribes are still to be found in several south China provinces. The Vietnamese, too, arose in the north and moved into present-day central and south Vietnam only in recent historical times.

A second movement was the Indianization of Southeast Asia. Between the first and fifteenth centuries Indian traders and missionaries crossed the Bay of Bengal and established outposts throughout Southeast Asia. As Hinduism and Buddhism spread through the region, Indian-type states with god-kings were established, and Indian scripts, legal codes, literature, drama, art, and music were adopted by the indigenous peoples. Today, Burma, Thailand, and Cambodia retain an Indian-type of Buddhism; on the walls of Bangkok temples are painted scenes from the great Hindu epic, the *Mahabharata.*

A third movement of shorter duration but considerable dynamism was of Arab and Indian traders who sailed across the Indian Ocean to dominate trade with the Spice Islands (the Moluccas of present-day Indonesia) between the thirteenth and fifteenth centuries. Settling on the coasts and islands of southeast Asia, they married into local ruling families and spread the teachings of Islam. Local rulers who converted became sultans. Today Malaysia and Indonesia are predominantly Muslim. The majestic Buddhist temple at Borobudur in central Java is a monument of an earlier age, submerged today in a sea of Islamic practice. Only the Hindu island of Bali to the east of Java retains the Indian religion that once covered the entire Indonesian archipelago.

CHRONOLOGY

KOREA

108 B.C.E.–4th century C.E.	Chinese rule in northern Korea
4th century C.E.–675	Three archaic states
675–918	Silla
918–1392	Koryo
1392–1910	Choson
1592, 1596	Japanese invasions of Korea
1627, 1637	Manchu invasions of Korea
1671	Famine

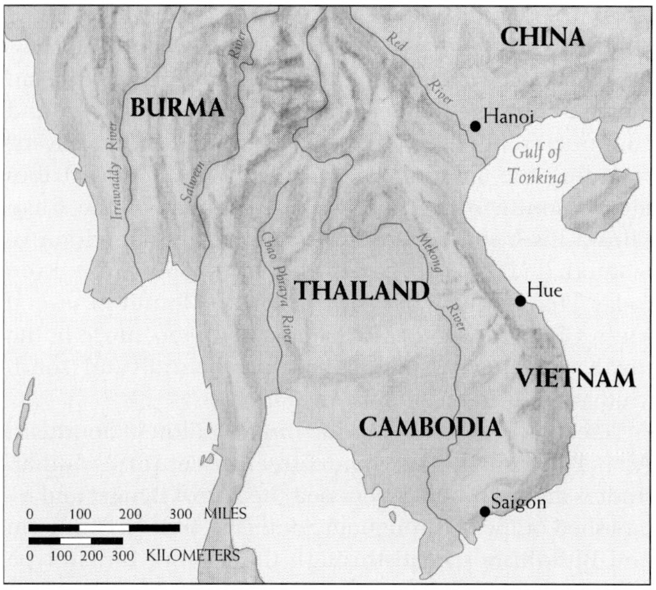

Map 19–4 Vietnam and neighboring Southeast Asia.

Early Vietnam

Vietnam has been likened to two baskets on a carrying pole. One basket is the Red River basin, centering on Hanoi in the north, the other the delta of the Mekong centering on Saigon in the south. The carrying pole is the narrow mountainous strip of central Vietnam with little river valleys opening to the South China Sea. Until the late fifteenth century, Vietnamese inhabited only the northern half of what is today Vietnam, that is to say, the basin of the Red River, which flows from west to east and empties into the Gulf of Tongking. Unlike other Southeast Asian peoples, whose culture was either Indic or Islamic, Vietnamese higher culture came from China.

Central Vietnam and part of the southeastern coast was inhabited by the Chams, a people ethnically closer to Indonesians than to Vietnamese. The Chams were a sea-faring people, who engaged in trade and piracy. They early became Hindu-Buddhist and later Muslim. They were united in the kingdom of Champa and waged intermittent wars against the Vietnamese to their north. Southern Vietnam, that is to say the Mekong River delta, was ruled by Hindu-Buddhist Cambodian empires and inhabited mainly by Cambodians.

The political history of the Vietnamese in the Red River basin began in 208 B.C.E. when a renegade Han dynasty general formed the state of Nan Yueh. Its capital was near the present-day Chinese city of Canton. It ruled over peoples in both southeastern China and the Red River basin. In Vietnamese, the Chinese ideograph *Yueh* is read "Viet." The name "Vietnam," literally, "Viet to the south," is derived from the name of this early state. Nan Yueh lasted for about a century until 111 B.C.E., when the armies of Han Wu Ti conquered it and brought it under Chinese control. After that, the Red River basin was ruled by China for more than one thousand years.

For the first seven centuries, Vietnam was a Chinese military commandery—like those established in Korea and other border regions to govern non-Chinese "barbarian" populations. The administrative center was initially a fort with a Chinese governor and Chinese troops. The governor ruled indirectly through local Vietnamese chiefs or magnates. In 39 C.E. the Trung sisters led a revolt against Chinese rule—the husband of one had been executed by the Chinese. The sisters later became national heroes. As a fifteenth-century Vietnamese poet put it:

> All the male heroes bowed their heads in submission;
> Only the two sisters proudly stood up to avenge the country.[12]

But in that age there was little sense of "country," and the only consequence of the revolt was a further strengthening of Chinese controls.

Vietnamese society advanced during the centuries of Chinese rule. Early Vietnamese had a matrilineal tribal society, practiced slash-and-burn agriculture, and moved their settlements when their lands became exhausted. New agricultural techniques, introduced from China, made possible permanent settlements and denser populations. Tribal organization gave way to village society, and matrilineal to patrilineal descent—though women continued to enjoy a higher status than in China. Buddhism entered, replacing or mingling with earlier animistic beliefs. Chinese officials sometimes married Vietnamese women, and a Sino-Vietnamese social elite arose in the capital. The influence of Chinese higher culture was largely confined to this elite.

During the T'ang dynasty (618–907), Vietnam was still treated as a border region, but Chinese administration became stronger. Elements of Chinese law and, possibly, the Chinese land and tax system were introduced at this time. Also, the Red River basin was divided into provinces, which the Chinese referred to collectively as *Annam,* the "pacified south." When the French came to Vietnam in the nineteenth century, they picked up the term and called the north Vietnamese *Annamese.*

Since it was during the T'ang that Japan and Korea also took in Chinese learning, one can ask whether Vietnam was a parallel case. In some regards it was. In all three societies Buddhism entered, flourished in the capitals, and gradually percolated into local areas, where it absorbed elements from earlier indigenous religions. In all three, other aspects of China's higher culture affected mainly the elites of the society, while an older way of life continued in villages with only small changes. But where Japanese and Korean rulers reached out for Chinese learning and technology and used it for their

[12]K.W. Taylor, *The Birth of Vietnam* (1983). p. 334.

DOCUMENT "ON HUSBAND-SHARING"

The position of women in Vietnam may have been higher than in China, but Vietnamese officials still had concubines when they could afford them. The eighteenth-century poet Ho Xuang Huong gives her view on the subject.

Should this poem be read as a criticism of the prevailing Confucian ethos?

One rolls in warm blankets,
The other freezes:
Down with this husband-sharing!
You're lucky ever to have him,
He comes perhaps twice a month,
Or less.
Ah—to fight for—this!
Turned to a half-servant, an unpaid maid!
Had I known
I would have stayed single.

From *A Thousand Years of Vietnamese Poetry* by Nguyen Ngoc Bich. Copyright © 1975 by The Asia Society. Reprinted by permission.

own ends, the Vietnamese had it thrust upon them. In the ninth century the Japanese devised a phonetic syllabary for the transcription of their language, and by the year 1000 were writing works such as *The Tale of Genji*—reflecting a new culture in which native and Chinese elements were fused. In Vietnam, where both the rulers and the written language were Chinese, no such transformation occurred.

THE SECOND MILLENNIUM: POLITICS AND SOCIETY

Ten major revolts occurred during the thousand years of Chinese rule—a not unusual number for a Chinese border region with a non-Chinese population. The last revolt, which took place in 939, when China was weak, led to the establishment of an independent Vietnamese government. Vietnam never again became a part of China.

The history of Vietnam's second millennium is conventionally broken into dynastic blocks named after the ruling family:

Ly	1009–1225
Tran	1225–1400
Le	1428–1787
Nguyen	1802–1880s

Vietnamese dynasties, however, were not the strong, centralized, bureaucratic states found in Chinese history. From the beginnings of dynasties, there were tensions between the center and periphery. At the center were the social elites who ruled the population of the Red River delta. At the periphery were magnates—powerful local figures who controlled upland peoples. Of these peripheral areas, the province of Thanh Hoa, one hundred miles south of the Hanoi capital, was of particular importance with magnates who were usually autonomous and often opposed the dynasty. Both center and periphery maintained military forces and sometimes engaged in wars. Often, several independent states coexisted during the timespan of a single "dynasty."

Chinese invasions also affected Vietnamese history. Most Chinese dynasties, as they expanded, attempted to reconquer the "south" that had once been ruled by China. Such invasions were repelled—though Ming armies occupied Vietnam for twenty years from 1407. But rather than defying China altogether, Vietnamese rulers found it easier to accommodate: every Vietnamese dynasty became a "tributary" of China and sent missions that professed the Vietnamese ruler's submission to the Chinese emperor. In official communications with the Chinese "emperor," the Vietnamese rulers styled themselves as "kings," indicating their subordinate status.

Such submission, however, was purely formal. Within Vietnam, Vietnamese rulers styled themselves as "emperors" and claimed their mandate to rule came directly from Heaven, separate but equal to the mandate received by the Chinese emperor. They also denied the universality of the Chinese imperium by referring to China not as the Middle Kingdom but as the Northern Court—their own government being the Southern Court. In 1076, a Vietnamese general fighting Chinese troops wrote the following poem:

> The Southern emperor rules the Southern land
> Our destiny is writ in Heaven's Book
> How dare you bandits trespass on our soil
> You shall meet your undoing at our hands[13]

One should note that the poem was in Chinese, Vietnam's only written language, and couched in the terminology of Chinese political thought.

Two momentous developments occurred in Vietnam during the fifteenth century. The first was the increased use of Chinese institutions and culture as an advanced technology

[13]S.T. Huynh, *The Heritage of Vietnamese Poetry* (1979), p. 3. Reprinted by permission. Yale University Press.

to strengthen government. The reforms of Le Thanh Tong (1442–1497), an immensely talented early Le dynasty ruler, were especially notable. He divided his realm into thirteen provinces and then into prefectures, counties, and departments. He weakened the nobility by holding civil service examinations for the selection of officials, and set up nine ranks of civil and military officials. He established schools, introduced Neo-Confucian learning, and promoted public works. He registered the population and reinstituted a Chinese-type land tax. Over decades such reforms would break down, until another reformer came along, but nonetheless, Chinese culture had a more lasting influence than Chinese arms.

The second development, after years of conflict, was the destruction of the Champa state by the same Le Thanh Tong in 1471. To help rule the culturally alien chams, he promulgated in 1483 a Confucian-tinged legal code that remained in effect through most of the dynasty. He also established colonies of Vietnamese soldier-peasants along the coast of the former kingdom. Thus began the centuries-long movement of Vietnamese into the central and southern portions of what is today Vietnam. Vietnamese historians label this movement "the march to the south," but it might be more apt to call it a "drift." Le Thanh Tong's successors were unable to hold together the territories he had conquered. Autonomous Vietnamese states arose in the area, which impeded the passage of settlers to the south during the sixteenth and early seventeenth centuries.

Demography and politics became entwined. During the late Le dynasty, the north was actually ruled by the Trinh family, and central Vietnam was ruled, from 1558, by the Nguyen family, whose capital was in the city of Hue. The two states fought during the early 1600s, but in 1673 agreed on a truce: they would separately rule the two parts of the country while paying lip service to the Le dynasty. In the mid-seventeenth century the Mekong delta was sparsely populated, mostly by Cambodians and Chams. The post-Ming diaspora of Chinese throughout Southeast Asia began during the seventeenth century. By the century's end substantial numbers of Chinese immigrants had settled and formed communities in the Mekong delta. Some became Saigon merchants, selling rice to Chinese merchants in Singapore. Today about a million partially assimilated Chinese live in southern Vietnam and play a major role in its economy. Vietnamese also began to move south. The Nguyen court in Hue extended its rule to Saigon in 1698, when it sent an official to settle a dispute between Chinese and Cambodians. By 1757 the Nguyen had extended their control over the entire Mekong delta westward to the Gulf of Siam. Political control facilitated the further movement of Vietnamese to the south, though they remained a minority in southern Vietnam throughout the eighteenth century.

During the late eighteenth century wars broke out again between the Nguyen and the north. By 1802 the Nyugen had defeated the opposing armies, unified the country, and established a new dynasty. It kept its capital at Hue. In coming to power the new emperor had been aided by French advisors and adventurers, several of whom were rewarded with high official posts. The Nguyen dynasty, nonetheless, became more Chinese than any previous dynasty. It adopted the law codes of Manchu China and established institutions such as the Six Boards, Hanlin Academy, Censorate, and a hierarchy of civil and military officials recruited by examinations. The reasons for these initiatives were to placate Confucian scholars in the north, to strengthen the court, and to weaken the military figures who had helped the dynasty's rise. From the time of the second emperor it also became anti-French and strongly anti-Christian in its policies.

During the first half of the nineteenth century, Vietnam was probably governed better than at any previous time and better than any other Southeast Asian state. By any traditional standard, it was governed competently. But it had weaknesses. There were tensions between the north, which was overpopulated, well schooled, and furnished most of the official class, and the south, which was ethnically diverse, educationally backward, and poorly represented in government. Trade and artisanal industries were less developed than in China and Japan, only small amounts of specie circulated, and periodic markets were more common than market towns. The government rested on a society composed largely of self-sufficient villages. In sum, Vietnam entered the second half of the nineteenth century even less prepared than China or Japan for the challenges it would soon face.

In World Perspective

LATE TRADITIONAL EAST ASIA

The history of late traditional East Asia underlines the exceptional nature of the European development from commerce to industry. The arguments and counterarguments as to why this development did not occur in China and Japan are illuminating. One often-cited argument is that East Asia lacked the Protestant ethic that inspired Western capitalism. The counterargument is that all East Asian nations have strong family-centered ethics with an emphasis on frugality, hard work, and saving. Is that not a Protestant ethic of sorts? Moreover, if the problem is as deeply rooted as a religious ethic, why have parts of East Asia been able to achieve such explosive economic growth since the 1960s?

Another argument stresses the absence of a scientific revolution in premodern East Asia. The counterargument is that science made only a minimal contribution to England's early industrialization. Some scholars argue that in China merchant capital, instead of being put into industry, was invested in land, the ownership of which was honorable and secure from rapacious officials. But this argument applies to the Ch'ing less well than the Ming and does not apply to Japan, where merchants could not buy land at all.

Still another argument stresses the differences in incentives and rewards. In England the self-educated technicians who invented the water loom and the steam engine reaped enormous rewards and honors. In China wealth and prestige were reserved largely for officials and gentry, who were literary or political in orientation and despised those who worked with their hands. No patent laws protected inventors. But other scholars ask whether the Ming and Ch'ing were so different from past dynasties during which the Chinese had been brilliantly inventive. Whatever the explanation, all agree that substantial commercial growth in both China and Japan did not lead to an indigenous breakthrough to machine industry.

Another comparison concerns bureaucracy. Bureaucracy does for administration what the assembly line does for manufacturing: it breaks complex tasks into simple ones to achieve huge gains in efficiency. In the West bureaucracies appeared only in recent centuries. They strengthened first monarchies and then nation-states against landed aristocrats. They are viewed as a sign of modernity, the triumph of ability over hereditary privilege. In some respects Chinese bureaucracy was similar: It was reasonably efficient, and it strengthened the central state. Would-be officials in nineteenth-century Britain studied the Greek and Roman classics, just as those in China studied the Confucian classics. But in other regards, Western historians of Chinese bureaucracy feel as if they have passed through Alice's looking glass: What was recent in the West had flourished for over a thousand years in China. Chinese officials themselves were a segment of a landed gentry class in a country from which hereditary aristocracies had long since disappeared. Moreover, although Chinese officials were doubtless men of talent, they would become a major obstacle to modernity.

A final point to make is the difference between Chinese and Japanese attitudes toward outside civilizations. When the Jesuits tried to introduce science, the Chinese response was occasional curiosity and general indifference. A few Jesuits were appointed as interpreters and court astronomers, or were used as technicians to cast canon. The Chinese lack of interest in foreign cultures may be explained by the coherence of China's core institutions of government—the emperor, bureaucracy, examination system, gentry, and Confucian schools—which had been in place for centuries. Having proved their worth, they were so deeply rooted and internalized as to approximate a closed system, impervious to outside influences. In contrast, the Tokugawa Japanese, despite a national policy of seclusion, reached out for Dutch science as they earlier had reached out for Chinese Neo-Confucianism. This difference would shape the respective responses of China and Japan to the West during the mid–nineteenth century.

For Korea and Vietnam, the problem is to explain why they were so much less developed in commerce—to say nothing of industry—than China and Japan. Were both the Korean *yangban* and the Vietnamese officials more aristocratic than Chinese gentry? Was the *yangban*'s distaste for commerce greater than that of Chinese officials? Vietnam clearly lacked the long periods of peace—a necessary condition for commercial growth—enjoyed by China and Japan. Did the travails and social unrest during the last centuries of Choson rule in Korea also stifle the growth of commerce? These are questions for which scholars have not yet provided answers.

REVIEW QUESTIONS

1. Why did the economy grow in late traditional China?
2. Did Manchu rule resemble Mongol rule, or was it different? In what regards were K'ang Hsi and Ch'ien Lung indistinguishable from Chinese emperors?
3. Ming-Ch'ing foreign relations set the stage for China's nineteenth-century encounter with the West. How would you describe the setting?
4. How did military technology in Japan change during the fifteenth and sixteenth centuries? Was unification the consequence or would it have happened anyway?
5. Contrast the dynamism of social engineering in seventeenth-century Japan with the high-level equilibrium of the eighteenth and early nineteenth centuries. How did these influence changes in Japanese thought?
6. In what sense was Chinese culture a "technology" used by Japan, Korea, and Vietnam for state building? Why were the results in each country so different?

SUGGESTED READINGS

China

D. BODDE AND C. MORRIS, *Law in Imperial China* (1967). Focuses on the Ch'ing dynasty (1644–1911).

C. S. CHANG AND S. L. H. CHANG, *Crisis and Transformation in Seventeenth Century China: Society, Culture, and Modernity* (1992).

P. CROSSLEY, *Translucent Mirror: History and Identity in Qing Imperial Ideology* (1999).

W. T. DE BARY, *Learning for One's Self: Essays on the Individual in Neo-Confucian Thought* (1991). A useful corrective to the view that Confucianism is simply a social ideology.

M. ELVIN, *The Pattern of the Chinese Past: A Social and Economic Interpretation* (1973). A controversial but stimulating interpretation of Chinese economic history in terms of technology. It brings in earlier periods as well as the Ming, Ch'ing, and modern China.

J. K. FAIRBANK, ED., *The Chinese World Order: Traditional China's Foreign Relations* (1968). An examination of the Chinese tribute system and its varying applications.

H. L. KAHN, *Monarchy in the Emperor's Eyes: Image and Reality in the Ch'ien-lung Reign* (1971). A study of the Chinese court during the mid-Ch'ing period.

P. KUHN, *Soulstealers: The Chinese Sorcery Scare of 1768* (1990).

LI YU, *The Carnal Prayer Mat*, trans. by P. Hanan (1990).

F. MOTE AND D. TWITCHETT, EDS., *The Cambridge History of China: The Ming Dynasty 1368–1644*, Vols. VI (1988) and VII (1998).

S. NAQUIN, *Peking Temples and City Life, 1400–1900* (2000).

S. NAQUIN AND E. S. RAWSKI, *Chinese Society in the Eighteenth Century* (1987).

J. B. PARSONS, *The Peasant Rebellions of the Late Ming Dynasty* (1970).

P. C. PERDUE, *Exhausting the Earth, State and Peasant in Hunan, 1500–1850* (1987).

D. H. PERKINS, *Agricultural Development in China, 1368–1968* (1969).

M. RICCI, *China in the Sixteenth Century: The Journals of Matthew Ricci, 1583–1610* (1953).

W. ROWE, *Hankow* (1984). A study of a city in late imperial China.

G. W. SKINNER, *The City in Late Imperial China* (1977).

J. D. SPENCE, *Ts'ao Yin and the K'ang-hsi Emperor: Bondservant and Master* (1966). An excellent study of the early Ch'ing court.

J. D. SPENCE, *Emperor of China: A Self-Portrait of K'ang-hsi* (1974). The title of this readable book does not adequately convey the extent of the author's contribution to the study of the early Ch'ing emperor.

J. D. SPENCE, *Treason by the Book* (2001). On the legal workings of the Ch'ing authoritarian, bureaucratic state. It reads like a detective story.

L. A. STRUVE, TRANS. AND ED., *Voices from the Ming-Ch'ing Cataclysm* (1993). A reader with translations of Chinese sources.

F. WAKEMAN, *The Great Enterprise* (1985). On the founding of the Manchu dynasty.

Japan

M. E. BERRY, *Hideyoshi* (1982). A study of the sixteenth-century unifier of Japan.

M. E. BERRY, *The Culture of Civil War in Kyoto* (1994). On the Warring States era.

H. BOLITHO, *Treasures Among Men: The Fudai Daimyo in Tokugawa Japan* (1974). A study in depth.

C. R. BOXER, *The Christian Century in Japan, 1549–1650* (1951).

M. CHIKAMATSU, *Major Plays of Chikamatsu*, trans. by D. Keene (1961).

R. P. DORE, *Education in Tokugawa Japan* (1965).

C. J. DUNN, *Everyday Life in Traditional Japan* (1969). A descriptive study of Tokugawa society.

G. S. ELISON, *Deus Destroyed: The Image of Christianity in Early Modern Japan* (1973). A brilliant study of the persecutions of Christianity during the early Tokugawa period.

J. W. HALL AND M. JANSEN, EDS., *Studies in the Institutional History of Early Modern Japan* (1968). A collection of articles on Tokugawa institutions.

J. W. HALL AND J. L. MCLAIN, EDS., *The Cambridge History of Japan: Early Modern Japan* (1991).

J. W. HALL, K. NAGAHARA, AND K. YAMAMURA, EDS., *Japan Before Tokugawa* (1981).

S. HANLEY, *Everyday Things in Premodern Japan: The Hidden Legacy of Material Culture* (1997).

H. S. HIBBETT, *The Floating World in Japanese Fiction* (1959). An eminently readable study of early Tokugawa literature.

M. JANSEN, ED., *The Nineteenth Century*, Vol. 5 in *The Cambridge History of Japan* (1989).

K. KATSU, *Musui's Story* (1988). The life and adventures of a boisterous, no-good samurai of the early nineteenth century. Eminently readable.

D. KEENE, TRANS., *Chushingura, the Treasury of Loyal Retainers* (1971). The puppet play about the forty-seven rōnin who took revenge on the enemy of their former lord.

M. MARUYAMA, *Studies in the Intellectual History of Tokugawa Japan*, trans. by M. Hane (1974). A seminal work in this field by one of modern Japan's greatest scholars.

K. W. NAKAI, *Shogunal Politics* (1988). A brilliant study of Arai Hakuseki's conceptualization of Tokugawa government.

P. NOSCO, ED., *Confucianism and Tokugawa Culture* (1984). A lively collection of essays.

H. OOMS, *Tokugawa Village Practice: Class, Status, Power, Law* (1996).

I. SAIKAKU, *The Japanese Family Storehouse*, trans. by G. W. Sargent (1959). A lively novel about merchant life in seventeenth-century Japan.

G. B. SANSOM, *The Western World and Japan* (1950).

C. D. SHELDON, *The Rise of the Merchant Class in Tokugawa Japan* (1958).

T. C. SMITH, *The Agrarian Origins of Modern Japan* (1959). On the evolution of farming and rural social organization in Tokugawa Japan.

R. P. TOBY, *State and Diplomacy in Early Modern Japan: Asia in the Development of the Tokugawa Bakufu* (1984).

C. TOTMAN, *Tokugawa Ieyasu: Shōgun* (1983).

C. TOTMAN, *Green Archipelago, Forestry in Preindustrial Japan* (1989).

H. P. VARLEY, *The Ōnin War: History of Its Origins and Background with a Selective Translation of the Chronicle of Ōnin* (1967).

K. YAMAMURA AND S. B. HANLEY, *Economic and Demographic Change in Preindustrial Japan, 1600–1868* (1977).

Korea

T. HATADA, *A History of Korea* (1969).

W. E. HENTHORN, *A History of Korea* (1971).

KI-BAIK LEE, *A New History of Korea* (1984).

P. LEE, *Sourcebook of Korean Civilization*, Vol. I (1993).

Vietnam

J. BUTTINGER, *A Dragon Defiant, a Short History of Vietnam* (1972).

NGUYEN DU, *The Tale of Kieu* (1983).

N. TARLING, ED., *The Cambridge History of Southeast Asia* (1992).

K. TAYLOR, *The Birth of Vietnam* (1983).

A. B. WOODSIDE, *Vietnam and the Chinese Model* (1988).

DOCUMENTS CD-ROM

1. Dynastic change in China tears a family apart
2. Cheng Ho [Zheng He]: Ming maritime expeditions
3. Wu Chengen: from Monkey
4. Murasaki Shikibu: The Tale of Genji
5. Nō Theatre, Atsumori

WORLD AND THE WEB

www.orientalarchitecture.com

This site is a comprehensive survey of Asia's architectural heritage. There are over 4,500 photos of 301 sites in eleven countries, with extensive background information and innovative "virtual tours." The geographical limits of this website correspond to areas which once were, or still are, within the Buddhist, Hindu, or Confucian spheres of influence. However, buildings and gardens of all cultures, faiths, and beliefs within this geographical area are included.

The Center for Korean Studies Online

http://www.svpa.hawaii.edu/korea/index.html

The Center for Korean Studies Online was established in 1972 at the University of Hawai'i for students and faculty with Korea-related teaching and research interests. The site also hosts several important resources for Koreanists and others interested in Korea. Includes a bibliography, which lists thousands of recent English-language publications on Korea; full-text archives of the Korean Studies Newsletter; and links to the journal *Korean Studies* and other Korea-related sites.

The Historiographical Institute The University of Tokyo

http://www.hi.u-tokyo.ac.jp/IRIKI/eindex.html

Shiryo Hensan-jo (the Historiographical Institute, HI), the University of Tokyo, has as its primary objective the analysis, compilation, and publication of historical source materials concerning Japan. The Institute has become a major center of Japanese historical research, and makes historical sources available through its library, publications, and databases. This link will take you to dozens of original source documents throughout Japanese history.

20 European State Building and Worldwide Conflict

Louis XIV of France (r. 1643–1715) was the dominant European monarch in the second half of the 17th century. The powerful centralized monarchy he created established the prototype for the mode of government later termed absolutism. Giraudon/Art Resource, N.Y.

Chapter topics

- The Netherlands: Golden Age to Decline
- Two Models of European Political Development
- Constitutional Crisis and Settlement in Stuart England
- Rise of Absolute Monarchy in France: The World of Louis XIV
- Russia Enters the European Political Arena
- Central and Eastern Europe
- The First Worldwide Wars

In World Perspective
Eighteenth-Century European States and Warfare

BETWEEN THE EARLY SEVENTEENTH AND MID–TWENTIETH centuries no region so dominated other parts of the world politically, militarily, and economically as Europe. Such had not been the situation before that date and would not be the situation after World War II. However, for approximately three and a half centuries northwestern Europe became the chief driving force in one world historical development after another. This era of European dominance, which appears quite temporary in the large scope of world history, also coincided with a shift in power within Europe itself from the Mediterranean, where Spain and Portugal had taken the lead in the conquest and early exploitation of America, to the states of the northwest and later north-central Europe. During the seventeenth and early eighteenth centuries certain states in northern Europe so organized themselves politically to dominate Europe and later to influence and even govern other large areas of the world through military might and economic strength. Even within the region of northern Europe there occurred a sorting out of influence among political states with some successfully establishing long-term positions of dominance and others passing from the scene after relatively brief periods of either military or economic strength.

By the mid–eighteenth century five major states had come to dominate European politics and would continue to do so until at least World War I. They were Great Britain, France, Austria, Prussia, and Russia. Through their military strength, economic development, and in some cases colonial empires, they would affect virtually every other world civilization. Within Europe, these states established their dominance at the expense of Spain, Portugal, the United Provinces of the Netherlands, Poland, Sweden, and the Ottoman Empire. Equally essential to their rise was the weakness of the Holy Roman Empire after the Peace of Westphalia (1648).

By the middle of the eighteenth century the five successful states entered upon three quarters of a century of warfare among themselves. These wars were fought both in Europe and in the European colonial empires, making them the first extensive world wars arising from conflict in Europe. These conflicts represented the most extensive European impact on the non-European world since the early sixteenth century when the Spanish had conquered the civilizations of Mexico and Peru.

The Netherlands: Golden Age to Decline

The seven provinces that became the United Provinces of the Netherlands emerged as a nation after revolting against Spain in 1572. During the seventeenth century, the Dutch engaged in a series of naval wars with England. Then, in 1672, the armies of Louis XIV invaded the Netherlands. William III, the *stadtholder* of Holland, the most important of the provinces, rallied the Dutch and eventually led the entire European coalition against France. As a part of that strategy, he answered the invitation of Protestant English aristocrats in 1688 to assume, along with his wife Mary, the English throne.

During both the seventeenth and eighteenth centuries, the political and economic life of the Netherlands differed from that of the rest of Europe. The other major nations pursued paths toward strong central government, generally under monarchies, as with France, or in the case of England, under a strong parliamentary system. By contrast, the Netherlands was formally a republic. Each of the provinces retained considerable authority, and the central government, embodied in the States General that met in the Hague, exercised its authority through a kind of ongoing negotiation with the provinces. Prosperous and populous Holland dominated the States General. The Dutch deeply distrusted monarchy and the ambitions of the House of Orange. Nonetheless, when confronted with major military challenges, the Dutch would permit the House of Orange and, most notably, William III to assume dominant leadership. These political arrangements proved highly resilient and allowed the republic to establish itself permanently in the European state system during the seventeenth century. When William died in 1702 and the wars with France ended in 1714, the Dutch reverted to their republican structures.

Although the provinces making up the Netherlands were traditionally identified with the Protestant cause in Europe, toleration marked Dutch religious life. The Calvinist Reformed Church was the official church of the nation, but it was not an established church. There were always a significant number of Roman Catholics and Protestants who did not belong to the Reformed Church. The country also became a haven for Jews. Consequently, while other European states attempted to impose a single religion on their people or tore themselves apart in religious conflict, in the Netherlands peoples of differing religious faiths lived together peacefully.

Urban Prosperity

Beyond the climate of religious toleration, what most amazed seventeenth-century contemporaries about the Dutch Republic was its economic prosperity. It's remarkable economic achievement was built on the foundations of high urban consolidation, transformed agriculture, extensive trade and finance, and an overseas commercial empire.

In the Netherlands, more people lived in cities than in any other area of Europe. This urban concentration had been made possible by key transformations in Dutch farming that served as the model for the rest of Europe. During the seventeenth century, the Dutch drained and reclaimed land from the sea which they used for highly profitable farming because their shipping provided them with a steady supply of cheap grain. This meant that Dutch farmers could produce more profitable dairy products and beef and cultivate cash products such as tulip bulbs.

Dutch fishermen dominated the market for herring and supplied much of the continent's dried fish. The Dutch also supplied textiles to many parts of Europe. Dutch ships appeared in harbors all over the continent, with their captains purchasing goods that they then transported and resold at a profit to other nations. The overseas trades also supported a vast shipbuilding and ship supply industry. All of this trade, commerce, and manufacturing was supported by the most advanced financial system of the day.

The final foundation of Dutch prosperity was a seaborne empire. Dutch traders established a major presence in East Asia, particularly in spice-producing areas of Java, the Moluccas, and Sri Lanka. The vehicle for this penetration was the Dutch East Indies Company (chartered in 1602). The company eventually displaced Portuguese dominance in the spice trade of East Asia and for many years prevented English traders from establishing a major presence there. Initially, the Dutch had only wanted commercial dominance of the spice trade, but in time, they moved toward producing the spices themselves, which required them to control many of the islands that now constitute Indonesia. The Netherlands remained the colonial master of this region until after World War II.

Economic Decline

The decline in political influence of the United Provinces of the Netherlands occurred in the eighteenth century. After the death of William III of Britain in 1702, the various local provinces prevented the emergence of another strong *stadtholder*. Unified political leadership therefore vanished. Naval supremacy slowly but steadily passed to the British. The fishing industry declined, and the Dutch lost their technological superiority in shipbuilding. Countries between which Dutch ships had once carried goods now traded directly with each other.

Similar stagnation overtook the Dutch domestic industries. The disunity of the provinces hastened this economic decline and prevented action that might have halted it.

What saved the United Provinces from becoming completely insignificant in European affairs was their continued financial dominance. Well past the middle of the eighteenth century, their banks continued to finance European trade and the Amsterdam bourse remained an important financial institution.

Two Models of European Political Development

In the second half of the sixteenth century changes in military organization, weapons, and tactics sharply increased the cost of warfare. Because traditional sources of income could not finance these growing costs, in addition to the costs of government, monarchs sought new revenues. Only monarchies that succeeded in building a secure financial base that was not deeply dependent on the support of noble estates, diets, or assemblies achieved absolute rule. The French monarchy succeeded in this effort, whereas the English monarchy failed. That success and failure led to the two models of government—absolutism in France and parliamentary monarchy in England—that shaped subsequent political development in Europe.

In their pursuit of adequate income, English monarchs of the seventeenth century threatened the local political interests and economic well-being of the nobility and landed and commercial elite. These groups invoked traditional English liberties to effectively resist the monarchs.

The experience of Louis XIV (r. 1643–1715), the French king, was different. After 1660 he made the French nobility dependent on his goodwill and patronage. In turn, he supported their local influence and their place in a firm social hierarchy. But even Louis's dominance had limits. He accepted the authority of the noble-dominated *Parlement* of Paris to register royal decrees before they officially became law, and he permitted regional parlements to exercise considerable authority over local administration and taxation. Funds from taxes levied by the monarchy found their way into many local pockets.

Religious factors also affected the political destinies of England and France. In England a strong Protestant religious movement known as Puritanism actively opposed the Stuart monarchy and eventually overturned it. Louis XIV, in contrast, crushed the Protestant communities of France. He was generally supported in these efforts by Roman Catholics, who benefited from the enforced religious uniformity.

There were also major institutional differences between the two countries. The English Parliament had long bargained with the monarch over political issues. In the early seventeenth century, to be sure, Parliament did not meet regularly and was not the strong institution it would become by the close of the century. Nor was there anything certain or inevitable about the transformation it underwent during the century. The institutional basis for it, however, was in place. Parliament existed and expected to be consulted. Its members—nobility and gentry—had experience organizing and speaking, writing legislation, and criticizing royal policies. Furthermore, the English had a legal and political tradition of liberty to which members of Parliament and their supporters could and did appeal against the monarchy.

France lacked a similarly strong tradition of broad liberties, representation, and bargaining between the monarchy and other national institutions. The Estates General had met from time to time to grant certain revenues to the monarch, but it played no role after 1614. Thereafter the monarchy found other sources of income, and the Estates General was not called again until the eve of the French Revolution in 1789. Consequently, opposition to the monarchy lacked both an institutional base and a forum in which the necessary political skills might have been developed.

Finally, personalities were important. During the first half of the century France profited from the guidance of two of its most able statesmen, Cardinals Richelieu and Mazarin. Mazarin trained Louis XIV to be a hard-working, if not always wise, monarch. Louis employed strong and capable ministers. The first four Stuart monarchs of England (r. 1603–1689), on the other hand, were distrusted. They did not always keep their word. They acted on whim. Their judgment was often faulty. They rarely offered to compromise. They offended significant groups of their subjects unnecessarily. In a nation that saw itself as strongly Protestant, they were suspected, sometimes accurately, of Catholic sympathies. Many of their opponents in Parliament, of course, had flaws of their own, but attention and criticism were focused on the king.

In both England and France, the nobility and large landowners stood at the top of the social hierarchy and sought to protect their privileges and local interests. Important segments of the British nobility and landed classes came to believe that the Stuarts sought to undermine their local political control and social standing. Parliamentary government was the result of the efforts of these English landed classes to protect their interests and limit the power of the monarchy to interfere with life on the local level. The French nobility under Louis XIV, in contrast, eventually concluded that the best way to secure their own interests was to support the throne. Louis provided them with many forms of patronage, and he protected their tax exemptions, wealth, and local social standing.

CONSTITUTIONAL CRISIS AND SETTLEMENT IN STUART ENGLAND

JAMES I

In 1603 James VI of Scotland (r. 1603–1625), the son of Mary Stuart, Queen of Scots, without opposition or incident succeeded the childless Elizabeth I as James I of England. He also inherited a large royal debt and a fiercely divided church.

Parliament met only when the monarch summoned it, which James hoped to do rarely. In place of parliamentarily approved revenues, James developed other sources of income, largely by levying new custom duties known as impositions. Members of Parliament regarded this as an affront to their authority over the royal purse, but they did not seek a serious confrontation. Rather, throughout James's reign they wrangled and negotiated.

Puritans within the Church of England had hoped that James would favor their efforts to further reform the English church. But to their dismay, he firmly supported the Anglican episcopacy.

James's foreign policy also roused opposition. In 1604 he concluded a much-needed peace with Spain, England's longtime adversary. His subjects considered this a sign of pro-Catholic sentiment. James's unsuccessful attempt to relax penal laws against Catholics further increased their suspicions, as did his wise hesitancy in 1618 to rush English troops to the aid of German Protestants at the outbreak of the Thirty Years' War. His efforts to arrange a marriage between his son Charles and a Spanish princess and then Charles's marriage in 1625 to Henrietta Marie, daughter of Henry IV of France, further increased religious suspicions. In 1624, short-

Art and the World

RACHEL RUYSCH, "FLOWER STILL LIFE":

FLOWERS, COMMERCE, AND MORALITY

Paintings often are intended to convey more than first meets the eye. Such is more or less obvious in allegorical scenes in which themes appear in the guise of ancient gods or other mythological figures. But a painting of objects of everyday life arranged on tables, known as a *still life*, can also hold deep symbolic and cultural meaning. From the Middle Ages onward, particular flowers had religious meaning, but during the seventeenth century flowers took on more worldly associations.

Rachel Ruysch (1664–1750) was a Dutch woman artist living in Amsterdam who specialized in depicting elaborate arrangements of flowers. These paintings stand as very beautiful images, but they are also much more.

Rachel Ruysch, Dutch, 1664–1750, "Flower Still Life" (1956.57).
The Toledo Museum of Art, Toledo, Ohio; Purchased with funds from the Libbey Endowment, Gift of Edward Drummond Libbey

The floral still life portrayed flowers usually raised from bulbs, a major Dutch commercial enterprise. Several decades before Ruysch completed this particular painting, *Flower Still Life* (after 1700), a financial mania had gripped Holland, with speculation in rare tulip bulbs reaching enormous extravagance before the bubble burst. Consequently, a painting such as this one from the early eighteenth century—and there were hundreds of such still-life floral works executed in seventeenth- and eighteenth-century Holland—would have recalled that event.

The flowers in this and other Dutch floral paintings represent work and commerce, not the natural bounty of the Dutch countryside. Commercial growers and traders brought such flowers to the Netherlands from its overseas empire and trading partners, and the flowers came to symbolize Dutch interaction with the most far-flung regions of the globe.

The variety of flowers in the bowl suggests wealth and abundance; these are valuable species, not humble objects of ordinary life. And never, except on canvas, would these flowers have bloomed at one time. Only the painter can gather them together in a single place at a single moment, in effect overcoming the cycle of nature.

Paintings such as this one have been called "a dialogue between this newly affluent society and its material possessions" and "an expression of how the phenomenon of plenty is to be viewed and understood."[1] These rich still life paintings allowed the Calvinist Dutch to accommodate a morality that emphasized frugality and abstinence with life in the single wealthiest society in Europe. The melancholy surrounding the images conveys a lesson in the vanity and transience of earthly beauty and richness. All of these beautiful, valuable, rare natural objects, whether flowers or food, will soon decay. The flowers in this bowl, so stunning at the peak of their blossoming, will in a matter of days wilt and eventually rot. The insects buzzing about the flowers will also disappear. Even the empty snail shells on the table suggest that earthly life is only temporary. Similarly, the shadows in so many of the floral arrangements suggest the shadows that surround human life and the transience of both light and life. Yet, by owning a painting of an exquisite, diverse collection of flowers, one could possess an object of great beauty that would itself not decay.

The amazing attention to detail in Ruysch's work reflects the growth in botanical observation and knowledge during the previous century. Van Leeuwenhoek, the inventor of the microscope, hired artists to draw the organisms he could see through the instrument. That invention, as well as other Dutch optical achievements, such as the magnifying glass, led many artists to paint with enormous attention to detail.

Many of the most important illustrators of botanical manuals and other works of natural history were women. Among the leading figures was Anna Maria Sibylla Merian (1647–1717), a German woman who moved to the Netherlands and traveled to the Dutch colony of Surinam to study both plants and insects. Her work would have been enormously helpful to Ruysch, who would only rarely have worked from an actual bowl of real flowers.

Sources: Norman Bryson, *Looking at the Overlooked: Four Essays on Still Life Painting* (Cambridge, MA: Harvard University Press, 1990); Mariët Westermann, *A Worldly Art: The Dutch Republic, 1585–1718* (Upper Saddle River, NJ and New York: Prentice Hall Publishers, Inc., and Harry N. Abrams, Inc., 1990); Marilyn Stokstad, *Art History,* rev. ed. (Upper Saddle River, NJ and New York: Prentice Hall Publishers, Inc., and Harry N. Abrams, Inc., 1999) pp. 798–801.

[1] Norman Bryson, *Looking at the Overlooked: Four Essays on Still Life Painting* (Cambridge, MA: Harvard University Press, 1990), p. 104.

ly before James's death, England again went to war against Spain largely in response to parliamentary pressures.

CHARLES I

Parliament had favored the war with Spain but would not adequately finance it because its members distrusted the monarchy. Unable to gain adequate funds from Parliament, Charles I (r. 1625–1649), like his father, resorted to extra-parliamentary measures. These included levying new tariffs and duties, attempting to collect discontinued taxes, and subjecting English property owners to a so-called forced loan (a tax theoretically to be repaid) and then imprisoning those who refused to pay. All these actions, as well as quartering troops in private homes, challenged local control of nobles and landowners.

When Parliament met in 1628 its members would grant new funds only if Charles recognized the Petition of Right. This required that henceforth there should be no forced loans or taxation without the consent of Parliament, that no freeman should be imprisoned without due cause, and that troops should not be billeted in private homes. It thus expressed resentment and resistance to the intrusion of the monarchy on the local level. Charles agreed to the petition, but whether he would keep his word was doubtful.

Charles I ruled for several years without calling Parliament, but once he began a war with Scotland, he needed revenues that only Parliament could supply. Photographique de la Réunion des Musées Nationaux/Cliche des Musées Nationaux

YEARS OF PERSONAL RULE In January 1629 Parliament declared that religious innovations leading to "popery" and the levying of taxes without parliamentary consent were acts of treason. Charles promptly dissolved Parliament and did not recall it again until 1640.

To conserve his limited resources, Charles made peace with France in 1629 and Spain in 1630. This policy again roused fears that he was too friendly to Roman Catholic powers. To allow Charles to rule without renegotiating financial arrangements with Parliament, his chief minister, Thomas Wentworth (1593–1641; after 1640, earl of Strafford), instituted a policy known as *thorough.* This policy imposed strict efficiency and administrative centralization in government. Its goal was absolute royal control of England. Its success depended on the king's ability to operate independently of Parliament, which no law required him to summon. Charles's ministers exploited every legal fund-raising device, enforced previously neglected laws, and extended existing taxes into new areas.

Charles might have ruled indefinitely without Parliament had not his religious policies provoked war with Scotland. James I had allowed a wide variety of religious observances in England, Scotland, and Ireland; by contrast, Charles hoped to impose religious conformity at least within England and Scotland. In 1637 Charles and Archbishop William Laud (1573–1645), against the opposition of both the English Puritans and the Presbyterian Scots, tried to impose on Scotland the English episcopal system and a prayer book almost identical to the Anglican Book of Common Prayer.

The Scots rebelled, and Charles, with insufficient resources for war, was forced to call Parliament. Parliament refused even to consider funds for war until the king agreed to redress a long list of political and religious grievances. The king, in response, immediately dissolved Parliament—hence its name, the Short Parliament (April–May 1640). When the Scots defeated an English army at the Battle of Newburn in the summer of 1640, Charles reconvened Parliament, this time on its terms, for a long and fateful duration.

THE LONG PARLIAMENT AND CIVIL WAR

The landowners and the merchant classes represented in Parliament had long resented the king's financial measures and paternalistic rule. The Puritans in Parliament resented his religious policies and deeply distrusted the influence of his Roman Catholic wife. The Long Parliament (1640–1660) thus acted with widespread support and general unanimity when it convened in November 1640.

The House of Commons impeached both Strafford and Laud. Both were executed—Strafford in 1641, Laud in

DOCUMENT PARLIAMENT PRESENTS CHARLES I WITH THE PETITION OF RIGHT

After becoming monarch in 1625 Charles I (r. 1625–1649) had imposed unparliamentary taxes, coerced freemen, and quartered troops in transit in private homes. These actions deeply offended Parliament, which in 1628 refused to grant him any funds until he rescinded those practices by recognizing the Petition of Right (June, 1628). The Petition constituted a general catalog of the offenses associated with the exercise of arbitrary royal authority.

What limits does the Petition attempt to place on royal taxation? How did the Petition criticize arbitrary arrest? Why was the quartering of soldiers in private homes so offensive?

[The Lords Spirit and Temporal, and commons in Parliament assembled] do humbly pray your Most Excellent Majesty, that no man hereafter be compelled to make or yield any gift, loan, benevolence, tax, or such like charge, without common consent by Act of parliament; and that none be called to make answer, to take such oath, or to give attendance, or be confined, or otherwise molested or disquieted concerning the same, or for refusal thereof; and that no freeman, in any such manner as in before-mentioned, be imprisoned or detained; and that your Majesty will be pleased to remove the said soldiers and mariners [who have been quartered in private homes], and that your people may not be so burdened in time to come; and that the foresaid commissions for proceeding by martial law, may be revoked and annulled; and that hereafter no commissions of like nature may issue forth to any person or persons whatsoever, to be executed as aforesaid, lest by colour of them any of your Majesty's subjects be destroyed or put to death, contrary to the laws and franchise of the land. All which they most humbly pray of your Most Excellent Majesty, as their rights and liberties according to the laws and statues of this realm.

The King's Reply: The King willeth that right be done according to the laws and customs of the realm; and that the statues be put in due execution, that his subjects may have no cause to complain of any wrong or oppressions, contrary to their just rights and liberties, to the preservation whereof he holds himself as well obliged as of his prerogative.

From *The Constitutional Documents of the Puritan Revolution*, ed. by Samuel R. Gardiner (Oxford: Clarendon Press, 1889), pp. 4–5.

1645. Parliament abolished the courts that had enforced royal policy and had prohibited the levying of new taxes without its consent. Finally, Parliament resolved that no more than three years should elapse between its meetings and that it could not be dissolved without its own consent.

Parliament, however, was divided over religion. Both moderate Puritans (the Presbyterians) and more extreme Puritans (the Independents) wanted to abolish the episcopalcy and the Book of Common Prayer. The majority of Presbyterians sought to reshape England religiously along Calvinist lines, with local congregations subject to higher representative governing bodies (presbyteries). Independents wanted every congregation to be its own final authority. Finally, many conservatives in both houses of Parliament were determined to preserve the English church in its current form. These divisions intensified in October 1641, when Parliament was asked to raise funds for an army to suppress a rebellion in Scotland. Charles's opponents argued that he could not be trusted with an army and that Parliament should become the commander-in-chief of English armed forces.

CIVIL WAR On December 1, 1641, Parliament presented the king with the "Grand Remonstrance," a summary of popular and parliamentary grievances against the crown, containing more than 200 articles. In January 1642 Charles invaded Parliament, intending to arrest certain of his opponents, but they managed to escape. The king then left London and began to raise an army. Shocked, a majority of the House of Commons passed the Militia Ordinance, which gave Parliament authority to raise an army of its own. The die was now cast. For the next four years (1642–1646), civil war engulfed England.

Charles's supporters, known as Cavaliers, were located in the northwestern half of England. The parliamentary opposition, known as Roundheads because of their close-cropped hair, had its stronghold in the southeastern half of the country. There were nobility, gentry, and townspeople on both sides. The chief factor distinguishing them was religion; the Puritans tended to favor Parliament.

OLIVER CROMWELL AND THE PURITAN REPUBLIC

Two factors led finally to Parliament's victory. The first was an alliance with Scotland in 1643 that committed Parliament to a Presbyterian system of church government. The second was the reorganization of the parliamentary army under Oliver Cromwell (1599–1658), a country squire of iron discipline and strong independent religious sentiment. Cromwell and his "godly men" were willing to tolerate an established majority church, but only if it permitted Protestant dissenters to worship outside it.

Defeated by June 1645, Charles tried to take advantage of divisions within Parliament, but Cromwell and his army foiled him. Members who might have been sympathetic to the monarch were expelled from Parliament on January 30, 1649, after a trial by a special court. Charles was executed as a public criminal. Parliament then abolished the monarchy, the House of Lords, and the Anglican Church.

From 1649 to 1660 England became officially a Puritan republic, although it was dominated by Cromwell. His army conquered Ireland and Scotland, creating the single political entity of Great Britain. Cromwell, however, was no politician. When in 1653 the House of Commons wanted to disband his expensive army of 50,000, Cromwell disbanded Parliament. He ruled thereafter as Lord Protector.

Cromwell's military dictatorship, however, proved no more effective than Charles's rule and became just as harsh and hated. His great army and foreign adventures inflated the budget to three times what it was under Charles. Cromwell was as intolerant of Anglicans as Charles had been of Puritans. People deeply resented his Puritan prohibitions of drunkenness, theatergoing, and dancing. Political liberty vanished in the name of religious conformity. When Cromwell died in 1658, the English were ready to restore both the Anglican Church and the monarchy.

Charles II and the Restoration of the Monarchy

After negotiations with the army Charles II (r. 1660–1685) returned to England amid great rejoicing. A man of considerable charm and political skill, Charles set a refreshing new tone after eleven years of somber Puritanism. England returned to the status quo of 1642, with a hereditary monarch, a Parliament that met only when the king summoned it, and the Anglican Church, with its bishops and prayer book, supreme in religion.

The king, however, had secret Catholic sympathies and favored religious toleration. He wanted to allow loyal Catholics and Puritans to worship freely. But in Parliament even the ultraroyalist Anglicans did not believe patriotism and religion could be separated. Between 1661 and 1665, through a series of laws known as the Clarendon Code, Parliament excluded Roman Catholics, Presbyterians, and Independents from the religious and political life of the nation.

In 1670 by the Treaty of Dover, England and France formally allied against the Dutch, their chief commercial competitor. In a secret portion of this treaty Charles pledged to announce his conversion to Catholicism as soon as conditions in England permitted. In return for this announcement (which was never made), Louis XIV promised to pay Charles a substantial subsidy. In an attempt to unite the English people behind the war with Holland, and as a sign of good faith to Louis XIV, Charles issued a Declaration of Indulgence in 1672 suspending all laws against Roman Catholics and non-Anglican Protestants. But Parliament refused to fund the war until Charles rescinded the measure. After he did, Parliament passed the Test Act requiring all officials of the crown, civil and military, to swear an oath against the doctrine of transubstantiation—which no loyal Roman Catholic could honestly do. Parliament had aimed the Test Act largely at the king's brother, James, Duke of York, heir to the throne and a recent, devout convert to Catholicism.

Oliver Cromwell's New Model Army defeated the royalists in the English Civil War. After the execution of Charles I in 1649, Cromwell dominated the short-lived English republic, conquered Ireland and Scotland and ruled as Lord Protector from 1653 until his death in 1658. Historical Pictures

James II and Renewed Fears of a Catholic England

When James II (r. 1685–1688) became king in 1685, he immediately demanded the repeal of the Test Act. When Parliament balked, he dissolved it and proceeded openly to appoint known Catholics to high positions in both his court and the army. In 1687 he issued another Declaration of Indulgence suspending all religious tests and permitting free worship. Local candidates for Parliament who opposed the declaration were replaced by James's supporters. In June

William and Mary became the monarchs of England in 1689. Their accession brought England's economic and military resources into the balance against the France of Louis XIV.
Robert Harding Picture Library, London.

1688 James imprisoned seven Anglican bishops who had refused to publicize his suspension of laws against Catholics. Each of these actions represented a direct royal attack on the local authority of nobles, landowners, the church, and other corporate bodies whose members believed they possessed particular legal privileges. Under the guise of a policy of enlightened toleration, James was actually seeking to subject all English institutions to the power of the monarchy.

The English had hoped that James would be succeeded by Mary (r. 1689–1694), his Protestant eldest daughter. She was the wife of William III of Orange (1650–1702), stadtholder of the Netherlands, great-grandson of William the Silent (1533–1584), and the leader of European opposition to Louis XIV. But on June 20 James II's Catholic second wife gave birth to a son. There was now a Catholic male heir to the throne. The Parliamentary opposition invited William to invade England to preserve its "traditional liberties," that is, the Anglican Church and parliamentary government.

THE "GLORIOUS REVOLUTION"

William of Orange arrived with his army in November 1688 and was received without opposition by the English people. James fled to France, and Parliament in 1689 proclaimed William III and Mary II the new monarchs, thus completing the bloodless "Glorious Revolution." William and Mary, in turn, recognized a Bill of Rights that limited the powers of the monarchy and guaranteed the civil liberties of the English privileged classes. Henceforth, England's monarchs would be subject to law and would rule by the consent of Parliament, which was to be called into session every three years. The Bill of Rights also prohibited Roman Catholics from occupying the English throne. The Toleration Act of 1689 permitted worship by all Protestants and outlawed only Roman Catholics and those who denied the Christian doctrine of the Trinity.

The measure closing this century of strife was the Act of Settlement in 1701. This bill provided for the English crown to go to the Protestant House of Hanover in Germany if Anne (r. 1702–1714), the second daughter of James II and the heir to the childless William III, died without issue. Thus, at Anne's death in 1714, the Elector of Hanover became King George I of England (r. 1714–1727), the third foreigner to occupy the English throne in just over a century.

THE AGE OF WALPOLE

George I almost immediately confronted a challenge to his title. The Stuart pretender James Edward Stuart (1688–1766), the son of James II, landed in Scotland in December 1715 but met defeat less than two months later.

Despite the victory over the pretender, the political situation after 1715 remained in flux until Robert Walpole (1676–1745) took over the helm of government. George I gave Walpole his full confidence. For this reason Walpole

CHRONOLOGY

ENGLAND

1603	James VI of Scotland becomes James I of England
1625	Charles I becomes king of England
1628	Petition of Right
1629	Charles I dissolves Parliament and embarks on eleven years of personal rule
1640	April–May, Short Parliament; November, Long Parliament convenes
1641	Great Remonstrance
1642	Outbreak of the Civil War
1649	Charles I executed
1649–1660	Various attempts at a Puritan Commonwealth
1660	Charles II restored to the English throne
1670	Secret Treaty of Dover between France and England
1672	Parliament passes the Test Act
1685	James II becomes king of England
1688	Glorious Revolution
1689	William III and Mary II come to the throne of England
1701	Act of Settlement provides for Hanoverian Succession
1702–1714	Queen Anne, the last of the Stuarts
1714	George I of Hanover becomes king of England
1724–1742	Ascendancy of Sir Robert Walpole

DOCUMENT: LADY MARY WORTLEY MONTAGU ADVISES HER HUSBAND ON ELECTION TO PARLIAMENT

In this letter of 1714, Lady Mary Wortley Montagu discussed how her husband might be elected to the House of Commons. Note her emphasis on knowing the right people and on having large amounts of money to spend on voters. Eventually her husband was elected in a borough that was controlled through government patronage.

What are the various ways in which candidates and their supporters used money to campaign? What role did friendships play in the campaigning? How important do the political ideas or positions of the candidates seem to be? Women could not vote in eighteenth-century parliamentary elections, but what kind of influence do they seem to exert?

You seem not to have received my letters, or not to have understood them: you had been chose undoubtedly at York, if you had declared in time; but there is not any gentleman or tradesman disengaged at this time; they are treating every night. Lord Carlisle and the Thompsons have given their interest to Mr. Jenkins. I agree with you of the necessity of your standing this Parliament, which, perhaps, may be more considerable than any that are to follow it; but, as you proceed, 'tis my opinion, you will spend your money and not be chose. I believe there is hardly a borough unengaged. I expect every letter should tell me you are sure of some place; and, as far as I can perceive you are sure of none. As it has been managed, perhaps it will be the best way to deposit a certain sum in some friend's hands, and buy some little Cornish borough: it would, undoubtedly, look better to be chose for a considerable town; but I take it to be now too late. If you have any thoughts of Newark, it will be absolutely necessary for you to enquire after Lord Lexington's interest; and your best way to apply yourself to Lord Holdernesse, who is both a Whig and an honest man. He is now in town, and you may enquire of him if Brigadier Sutton stands there; and if not, try to engage him for you. Lord Lexington is so ill at the Bath, that it is a doubt if he will live 'till the elections; and if he dies, one of his heiresses, and the whole interest of his estate, will probably fall on Lord Holdernesse.

'Tis a surprize to me, that you cannot make sure of some borough, when a number of your friends bring in so many Parliament-men without trouble or expense. 'Tis too late to mention it now, but you might have applied to Lady Winchester, as Sir Joseph Jekyl did last year, and by her interest the Duke of Bolton brought him in for nothing; I am sure she would be more zealous to serve me, than Lady Jekyl.

From Lord Wharncliffe, ed., *Letters and Works of Lady Mary Wortley Montagu*, 3rd ed., Vol. 1 (London, 1861), p. 211.

has often been regarded as the first prime minister of Great Britain—although he never bore the title—and the originator of the cabinet system of government. Unlike a modern prime minister, he was not chosen by a majority of the House of Commons. His power largely depended on the goodwill of the king. Although Walpole generally demanded that all cabinet ministers agree on policy, he could not prevent frequent public differences among them.

The real source of his power was the combination of the support of the king, Walpole's ability to handle the House of Commons, and his iron-fisted control of government patronage. To oppose Walpole meant the almost certain loss of government patronage. Through the skillful use of patronage, Walpole bought support for himself and his policies from people who wanted jobs, appointments, favors, and government contracts. Such corruption cemented political loyalty.

The eighteenth-century British House of Commons was neither a democratic nor a representative body. Each county elected two members, but if the more powerful landed families agreed on the candidates, as often happened, there was no contest. Other members—many more than those elected from counties—were elected from units called *boroughs*. A few boroughs were large enough for elections to be relatively democratic. Most, however, had few electors. Proper management, which involved favors to the electors, could control the composition of the House of Commons.

The structure of Parliament and the manner in which the House of Commons was chosen resulted in the domination of the government of England by the owners of property and especially by wealthy nobles. They did not pretend to represent people and districts or to be responsive to what would later be called public opinion. They regarded themselves as representing various economic and social interests, such as the West Indian interest, the merchant interest, or the landed interest. These owners of property were suspicious of an administrative bureaucracy controlled by the crown or its ministers. For this reason, they or their agents served as local government administrators, judges, militia commanders, and tax collectors. In this sense, the British nobility and other substantial landowners actually did govern the nation. Moreover, because they regarded Parliament as the political sovereign, there was no absence of central political authority and direction. The supremacy of Parliament consequently provided Britain with the unity that elsewhere in Europe was achieved through the institutions of absolutism.

British political life was freer than that on the Continent. Walpole's power had real limits. Parliament could not wholly ignore popular pressure. Even with the extensive use of patronage, many members of Parliament maintained independent views. Newspapers and public debate flourished. Free speech could be exercised, as could freedom of association. There was no large standing army. Walpole's enemies could and did openly oppose his policies, which would not have been possible on the Continent.

Walpole's ascendancy, which lasted from 1721 to 1742, brought the nation a stability that it had not enjoyed for over a century. He maintained peace abroad and promoted the status quo at home. Britain's foreign trade spread from New England to India. Agriculture became more productive. All forms of economic enterprise seemed to prosper. The navy became stronger. As a result of this political stability and economic growth, Great Britain became not only a European power of the first order but eventually a world power. Its government and economy during the next generation were models for all progressive Europeans.

As will be seen later in this chapter, the peaceful and prosperous Walpole era would come to an end in 1739 with a colonial war fought with Spain and then France. Thereafter, for over three quarters of a century, Britain and France would fight around the world for colonial domination. The France with which Britain engaged in that conflict had developed a system of government very different from the British.

Rise of Absolute Monarchy in France: The World of Louis XIV

Historians once portrayed Louis XIV's reign (r. 1643–1715) as a time when the French monarchy exerted far-reaching, direct control of the nation at all levels. A somewhat different picture is now emerging.

The groundwork for Louis's absolutism had been laid first by Cardinal Richelieu (1585–1642), the powerful chief minister for Louis XIII (r. 1610–1643), and then by Cardinal Mazarin (1602–1661). Both Richelieu and Mazarin had tried to impose direct royal administration on France. These efforts finally aroused a series of widespread rebellions among French nobles between 1649 and 1652 known as the Fronde (after the slingshot used by street boys).

These unsuccessful rebellions convinced Louis XIV and his advisors that heavy-handed policies could endanger the monarchy. Louis would concentrate unprecedented authority in the monarchy, but he would be more subtle than his predecessors. His genius was to make the monarchy the most important and powerful political institution in France while also assuring the nobles and other wealthy groups of their social standing and political and social influence on the local level. Rather than destroying existing local social and political institutions, Louis largely worked through them. Nevertheless, the king was clearly the senior partner in the relationship.

Years of Personal Rule

On the death of Mazarin in 1661 Louis XIV assumed personal control of the government at the age of twenty-three. He appointed no chief minister. Rebellious nobles would now be challenging the king directly; they could not claim to be resisting only a bad minister.

Louis ruled through powerful councils that controlled foreign affairs, the army, domestic administration, and economic regulations. Each day he spent hours with the chief ministers of these councils, whom he chose from families long in royal service or from among people just beginning to rise in the social structure. Unlike the more ancient noble families, they had no real or potential power bases in the provinces and depended solely on the king for their standing in both government and society.

Louis made sure, however, that the nobility and other major social groups would benefit from the growth of his own authority. Although he controlled foreign affairs and limited the influence of noble institutions on the monarchy, he never tried to abolish those institutions or limit their local authority. The crown, for example, usually conferred informally with regional parlements before making rulings that would affect them. Likewise, the crown would rarely enact economic regulations without consulting local opinion. Local parlements enjoyed considerable latitude in regional matters. Louis did clash with the Parlement of Paris, which had the right to register royal laws. In 1673 he curtailed its power. Many regional parlements and other regional authorities, however, had long resented the power of that body.

Versailles

Louis and his advisors became masters of propaganda and political image creation. Louis never missed an opportunity to impress the grandeur of his crown on the French people. When the dauphin (the heir to the French throne) was born in 1662, for example, Louis appeared for the celebration dressed as a Roman emperor.

The central element of the image of the monarchy, however, was the palace of Versailles. More than any other monarch of the day, Louis XIV used the physical setting of his court to exert political control. The palace at Versailles, built between 1676 and 1708 on the outskirts of Paris, became Louis's permanent residence after 1682. It was a temple to royalty, architecturally designed and artistically decorated to proclaim the glory of the Sun King, as Louis was known. A spectacular estate with magnificent fountains and gardens, it housed thousands of the more important nobles, royal officials, and servants. Although it consumed over half Louis's annual revenues, Versailles paid significant political dividends.

Because Louis ruled personally, he was the chief source of favors and patronage in France. To emphasize his prominence, he organized life at court around every aspect of his own daily routine. Elaborate court etiquette governed every

Throughout the age of the splendor at the court of Louis XIV millions of French peasants endured lives of poverty and hardship. Erich Lessing/Art Resource, N.Y.

detail of life at Versailles. Moments near the king were important to most court nobles because they were effectively excluded from the real business of government. The king's rising and dressing were times of rare intimacy, when nobles could whisper their special requests in his ear. Fortunate nobles held his night candle as they accompanied him to his bed.

Some nobles, of course, avoided Versailles. They managed their estates and cultivated their local influence. Many others were simply too poor to cut a figure at court. All the nobility understood, however, that Louis, unlike Richelieu and Mazarin, would not threaten their local social standing. Louis supported France's traditional social structure and the social privileges of the nobility.

King by Divine Right

An important source for Louis's concept of royal authority was his devout tutor, the political theorist Bishop Jacques-Bénigne Bossuet (1627–1704). Bossuet defended what he called the "divine right of kings" and cited examples of Old Testament rulers divinely appointed by and answerable only to God. Medieval popes had insisted that only God could judge a pope; so Bossuet argued that only God could judge the king. Although kings might be duty bound to reflect God's will in their rule, yet as God's regents on earth they could not be bound to the dictates of mere nobles and parliaments. Such assumptions lay behind Louis XIV's alleged declaration: "*L'état, c'est moi*" ("I am the state").

Despite these claims, Louis's rule did not exert the oppressive control over the daily lives of his subjects that police states would do in the nineteenth and twentieth centuries. His absolutism functioned primarily in the classic areas of European state action—the making of war and peace, the regulation of religion, and the oversight of economic activity. Even at the height of his power local institutions, some controlled by townspeople and others by nobles, retained their administrative authority. The king and his ministers supported the social and financial privileges of these local elites. But in contrast to the Stuart kings of England, Louis firmly prevented them from interfering with his authority on the national level. This system would endure until the French monarchy was demoralized by financial crisis at the end of the eighteenth century.

Louis's Early Wars

By the late 1660s, however, France was superior to any other European nation in administrative bureaucracy, armed forces, and national unity. Louis could afford to raise and maintain a large and powerful army and was in a position to dominate Europe. He spent most of the rest of his reign attempting to do so, looking for opportunities to extend the borders of his domain and displace the power of the Habsburgs.

The early wars of Louis XIV included conflicts with Spain and the United Netherlands. The first was the War of the Devolution in which Louis supported the alleged right of his first wife, Marie Thérèse, to inherit the Spanish Netherlands.[1] He contended that through complex legal arrangements they should have "devolved" upon her, hence the name of the war. In 1667 Louis's armies invaded Flanders and the

[1] The political divisions during the seventeenth and eighteenth centuries in what are today the Netherlands and Belgium were complex. The independence of the United Netherlands, a loosely federated union, was recognized at the Peace of Westphalia in 1764. Most of its population were Protestants. It was often referred to as "Holland," although Holland was simply the most important of its several provinces. Present-day Belgium, which included Flanders and Brabant, was governed by the Habsburgs, first Spanish, then Austrian—after 1714. Its population was overwhelmingly Roman Catholic. Both states enjoyed considerable commercial wealth and prosperity.

MAP EXPLORATION

Interactive map: To explore this map further, go to http://www.prenhall.com/craig_map20.1

Map 20–1 The Early Wars of Louis XIV. This map shows the territorial changes resulting from Louis XIV's first three major wars (1667–1697).

Franche-Comté. He was repulsed by the Triple Alliance of England, Sweden, and the United Provinces. By the Treaty of Aix-la-Chapelle (1668) he gained control of certain towns bordering the Spanish Netherlands (Map 20–1).

In 1670, with the Treaty of Dover, England and France became allies against the Dutch. Louis invaded the Netherlands again in 1672. The Dutch rallied around the leadership of the Prince of Orange, the future

William III of England. Orange forged an alliance with the Holy Roman Emperor, Spain, Lorraine, and Brandenburg against Louis, now regarded as a menace to the whole of western Europe, Catholic and Protestant alike. The war ended inconclusively with the Peace of Nijmwegen, signed with different parties in successive years (1678, 1679). France gained more territory, including the Franche-Comté.

REVOCATION OF THE EDICT OF NANTES

After the Edict of Nantes in 1598, relations between the great Catholic majority (nine tenths of the French population) and the Protestant minority had remained hostile. There were about 1.75 million Huguenots in France in the 1660s, but their numbers were declining. The French Catholic church had long supported their persecution as both pious and patriotic.

After the Peace of Nijmwegen, Louis launched a methodical campaign against the Huguenots in a determined effort to unify France religiously. He hounded them out of public life, banning them from government office and excluding them from such professions as printing and medicine. He used financial incentives to encourage them to convert to Catholicism. And in 1681 he bullied them by quartering his troops in their towns. Finally, Louis revoked the Edict of Nantes in October 1685. Protestant churches and schools were closed, Protestant ministers exiled, nonconverting laity forced to be galley slaves, and Protestant children ceremonially baptized by Catholic priests.

The revocation was a major blunder. Henceforth, Protestants considered Louis a fanatic who must be resisted at all costs. The revocation prompted the voluntary emigration of more than a quarter million people, who formed new communities and joined the resistance to France in England, Germany, Holland, and the New World.

CHRONOLOGY

FRANCE

1649–1652	The Fronde, a revolt of nobility and townspeople against the crown
1661	Louis assumes personal rule
1667–1668	War of Devolution fought over Louis's claims to the Spanish Netherlands
1672	France invades the United Provinces
1678–1679	Peace of Nijmwegen
1682	Louis establishes his court at Versailles
1685	Edict of Nantes revoked
1689–1697	Nine Years' War between France and the League of Augsburg
1697	Peace of Ryswick
1702–1714	War of the Spanish Succession
1713	Treaty of Utrecht between England and France
1714	Treaty of Rastadt between the emperor and France
1726–1743	Ascendency of Cardinal Fleury

LOUIS'S LATER WARS

THE LEAGUE OF AUGSBURG AND THE NINE YEARS' WAR After the Treaty of Nijmwegen, Louis maintained his army at full strength and restlessly probed beyond his borders. In 1681 his forces occupied the free city of Strasbourg, prompting new defensive coalitions to form against him. One of these, the League of Augsburg, grew to include England, Spain, Sweden, the United Provinces, and the major German states. It also had the support of the Habsburg emperor Leopold I (r. 1658–1705). Between 1689 and 1697 the League and France battled each other in the Nine Years' War, while England and France struggled to control North America.

The Peace of Ryswick, signed in September 1697, secured Holland's borders and thwarted Louis's expansion into Germany.

WAR OF THE SPANISH SUCCESSION On November 1, 1700, Charles II of Spain (r. 1665–1700) died without direct heirs. Before his death negotiations had begun among the nations involved to partition his inheritance in a way that would preserve the existing balance of power. Charles II, however, left his entire inheritance to Louis's grandson Philip of Anjou, who became Philip V of Spain (r. 1700–1746).

Spain and the trade with its American empire appeared to have fallen to France. In September 1701 England, Holland, and the Holy Roman Empire formed the Grand Alliance to preserve the balance of power by once and for all securing Flanders as a neutral barrier between Holland and France and by gaining for the emperor his fair share of the Spanish inheritance. Louis soon increased the political stakes by recognizing the Stuart claim to the English throne.

In 1701 the War of the Spanish Succession (1701–1714) began, and it soon enveloped western Europe. France for the first time went to war with inadequate finances, a poorly equipped army, and mediocre generals. The English, in contrast, had advanced weaponry (flintlock rifles, paper cartridges, and ring bayonets) and superior tactics (thin, maneuverable troop columns rather than the traditional deep ones). John Churchill, the Duke of Marlborough (1650–1722) bested Louis's soldiers in every major engagement, although French arms triumphed in Spain. After 1709 the war became a bloody stalemate.

France finally made peace with England at Utrecht in July 1713 and with Holland and the emperor at Rastadt in March

Map 20–2 Europe In 1714. The War of the Spanish Succession ended a year before the death of Louis XIV. The Bourbons had secured the Spanish throne, but Spain had forfeited its possessions in Flanders and Italy.

1714. Philip V remained king of Spain but England got Gibraltar, making it a Mediterranean power (see Map 20–2). Louis also recognized the right of the House of Hanover to accede to the English throne.

After Louis's death the authority of the monarchy weakened. France was economically exhausted. Louis XV (r. 1715–1744) was only five years old at his accession, and the regency allowed the *Parlement* of Paris greater authority. By 1726 the general political direction of the nation had come under the authority of Cardinal Fleury (1653–1743). He worked to maintain the authority of the monarchy while continuing to preserve the local interests of the French nobility. Like Walpole in Britain, he pursued economic prosperity at home and peace abroad. Again like Walpole, after 1740, Fleury could not prevent France from entering a worldwide colonial conflict, which will be discussed later in this chapter.

Russia Enters the European Political Arena

The emergence of Russia as an active European power constituted a wholly new factor in European politics. Previously Russia had been considered a part of Europe only by courtesy. Geographically and politically, it was peripheral. Hemmed in by Sweden on the Baltic and by the Ottoman Empire on the Black Sea, Russia had no warm-water ports. Its chief outlet to the west was Archangel on the White Sea, which was icebound much of the year. There was little trade. Russia did have vast, largely undeveloped natural and human resources.

Years of Turmoil

Ivan IV (r. 1533–1584), later known as Ivan the Terrible, came to the throne as a child. When he began his personal rule at the age of sixteen, he appointed able advisors, undertook sensible revisions of the law and local government, and reorganized the army. About 1560 he underwent a profound personality change and began to distrust virtually everyone around him. He then established a small group of advisors and a military force loyal to himself and loosed them against anyone he regarded as an enemy. He imprisoned, tortured, and executed *boyars* (the Russian term for noble) without cause or trial. He even killed his own son.

Ivan's reign was followed by a period of anarchy and civil war known as the Time of Troubles. In 1613, hoping to end the uncertainty, an assembly of nobles elected as tsar a seventeen-year-old boy named Michael Romanov (r. 1613–1645). Thus began the dynasty that ruled Russia until 1917.

Michael Romanov and his two successors, Aleksei I (r. 1645–1676) and Theodore III (r. 1676–1682), brought stability and bureaucratic centralization to Russia. The country, however, remained weak and impoverished. The boyars largely controlled the bureaucracy. Furthermore, the government and the tsars faced the danger of mutiny from the *streltsy*, or guards of the Moscow garrison.

Peter the Great

In 1682 a ten-year-old boy ascended the fragile Russian throne as co-ruler with his half brother. His name was Peter (r. 1682–1725), and Russia would never be the same. He and his feeble half brother, Ivan V (d. 1696), had come to power on the shoulders of the *streltsy*, who expected rewards in return. Much violence and bloodshed had surrounded the disputed succession. Matters became even more confused when the boy's sister, Sophia (1657–1704), was named regent. Peter's followers overthrew her in 1689; thereafter, Peter ruled personally. The dangers and turmoil of his youth convinced him that the power of the tsar must be made secure from the jealousy of the boyars and the greed of the *streltsy* and that Russian military power had to be increased.

Peter I, who came to be known as Peter the Great, was fascinated by western Europe, particularly its military resources. He was an imitator of the first order. The products and workers from the West who had filtered into Russia impressed and intrigued him. In 1697 he made a famous visit, supposedly in disguise, to western Europe. There he talked with the great and the powerful, who considered this almost-seven-foot-tall ruler both crude and rude. He inspected shipyards, docks, and the manufacture of military hardware and returned to Moscow determined to copy what he had seen abroad, for he knew that only warfare would make Russia a great power. The tsar's drive to modernize his nation, though unsystematic, had four general areas of concern: taming the boyars and the *streltsy*, achieving secular control of the church, reorganizing the internal administration, and developing the economy.

Peter pursued each of these goals with violence and ruthlessness. His successes strengthened his monarchy and allowed him to expand his military strength. By bringing the boyars, *streltsy*, and church under control, Peter curbed the power of the groups that might have opposed his expansion of the army and navy. Developing Russia's economy enabled him to finance his military ventures.

He made a sustained attack on the boyars. In 1698, immediately on his return from abroad, he personally shaved the long beards of the court boyars and sheared off the customary long, hand-covering sleeves of their shirts and coats, which had made them the butt of jokes throughout Europe. More important, he demanded they serve his state.

In 1722 Peter published a Table of Ranks, which henceforth equated a person's social position and privileges with his rank in the bureaucracy or the army rather than with his position in the nobility. However, the Russian nobility never became perfectly loyal to the state. It repeatedly sought to reassert its independence and control over the Russian imperial court.

The *streltsy* fared less well than the boyars. In 1698 they had rebelled while Peter was on his European tour. When he returned he retaliated brutally against both leaders and followers. There were private tortures and public executions, in which Peter's own ministers took part. Almost 1200 of the rebels were put to death, and their corpses long remained on public display to discourage future disloyalty.

Peter dealt with the potential political independence of the Russian Orthodox Church with similar ruthlessness. He wanted to avoid two kinds of difficulties with the Russian church. First, he sought to prevent the clergy from opposing change and westernization. Second, he sought to prevent the church hierarchy from making religious reforms that might provoke popular discontent, as had happened in the previous century. Consequently, in 1721 Peter replaced the position of patriarch of the Russian church with a synod headed by a layman to rule the church in accordance with the needs of the state.

In his reorganization of domestic administration, Peter looked to Swedish models, creating "colleges," or bureaus, composed of several officials rather than departments headed by a single minister. The colleges were to look after the collection of taxes, foreign affairs, war, and economic matters. This new organization was an attempt to breathe life

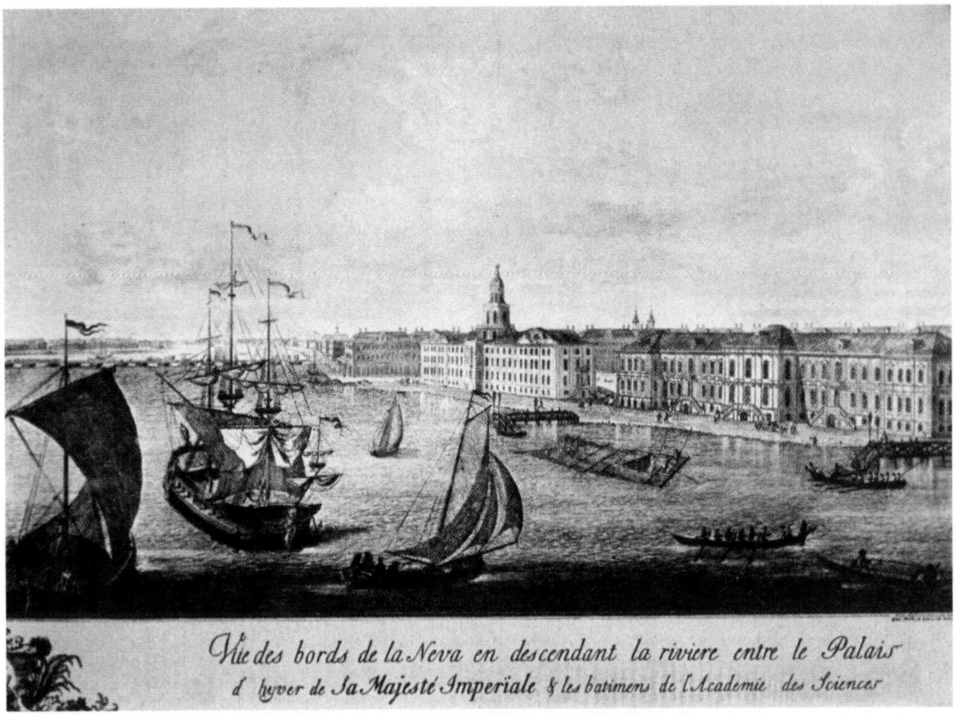

Peter the Great built St. Petersburg on the Gulf of Finland to provide Russia with better contact with western Europe. He moved Russia's capital there from Moscow in 1703. This is an 18th century view of the city. The Granger Collection

into the country's stagnant and inefficient administration. In 1711 Peter created a senate of nine members to direct the central government when the tsar was away with the army. The purpose of these reforms was to establish a bureaucracy that could collect and spend tax revenues to support an efficient army.

Peter's economic policies were closely related to his military needs. He encouraged the establishment of an iron industry in the Ural Mountains, and by midcentury Russia had become the largest iron producer in Europe. He sent prominent young Russians abroad to acquire technical and organizational skills. He attempted to lure western European craftsmen to Russia. However, except for the striking growth of the iron industry, which later languished, these efforts had only marginal success.

These internal reforms and political departures supported a policy of warfare. Peter was determined to secure warm-water ports that would allow Russia to trade with the West and to intervene in European affairs. This led to wars with the Ottoman Empire and Sweden. Peter's armies captured Azov on the Black Sea in 1696, but he had to return it in 1711.

Peter had more success against Sweden, thanks to the inconsistency and irrationality of that country's king, Charles XII (r. 1697–1718). In 1700, in the opening of the Great Northern War, Russia moved against the Swedish territory on the Baltic but was defeated at the Battle of Narva. Charles's failure to follow up his victory allowed Peter to regroup his forces and hoard his resources. In 1709, when Charles XII returned to fight Russia again, Peter was ready and at the Battle of Poltava sealed the fate of Sweden. In 1721 the Peace of Nystad, which ended the Great Northern War, confirmed the Russian conquest of Estonia, Livonia, and part of Finland. Henceforth, Russia possessed warm-water ports and a permanent influence on European affairs.

At one point the domestic and foreign policies of Peter the Great literally intersected. This was at the spot on the Gulf of Finland where Peter founded his new capital city of Saint Petersburg (renamed Leningrad during much of the twentieth century). There he built government structures and compelled his boyars to construct town houses. In this fashion he imitated those western European monarchs who themselves had copied Louis XIV by constructing smaller versions of Versailles. The founding of Saint Petersburg, however, also symbolized a new orientation for Russia toward western Europe and indicated Peter's determination to keep the Baltic coast. He began the construction of the city and had moved the capital there in 1703, even before his victory over Sweden was assured.

Despite his success on the Baltic, Peter's reign ended with a great question mark. He had long quarreled with his only son, Alexis, the heir to the throne. Peter was jealous of the young man and fearful that he might undertake sedition. Alexis was imprisoned in 1718 and died mysteriously. Thereafter, Peter claimed the right to name a successor, but he could never bring himself to designate one either orally or in writing. Consequently, when Peter died in 1725 Rus-

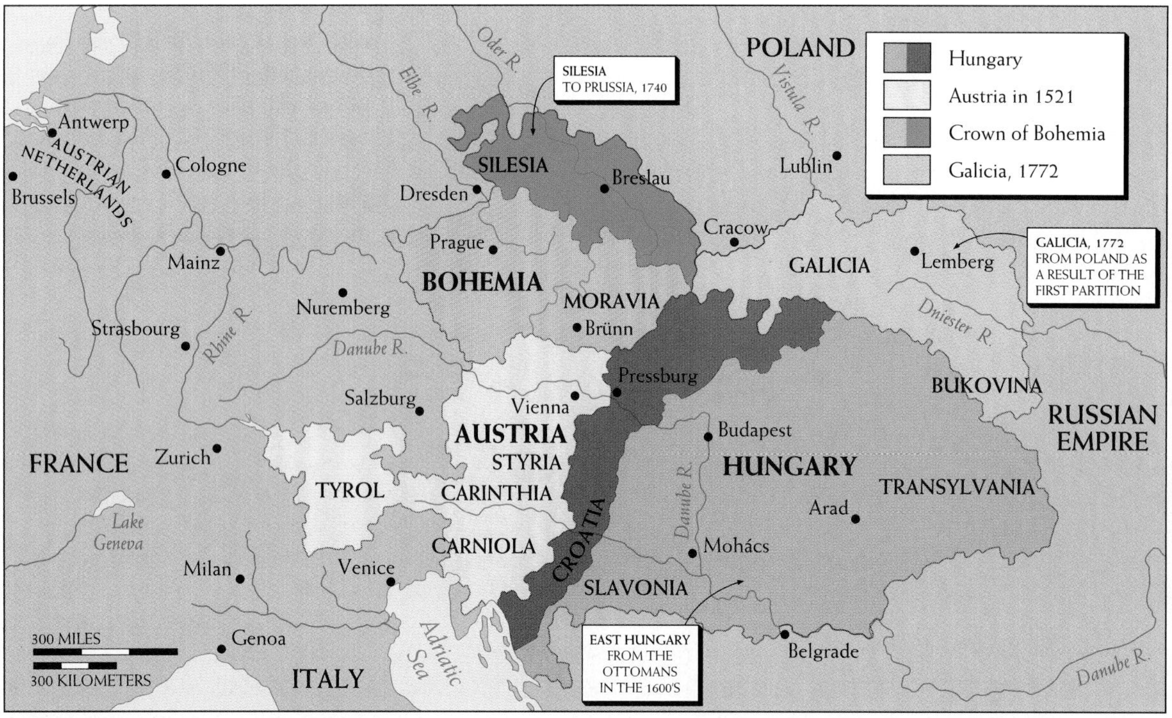

Map 20–3 The Austrian Habsburg Empire, 1521–1772. The empire had three main units—Austria, Bohemia, and Hungary. Expansion was mainly eastward: eastern Hungary from the Ottomans (17th century) and Galicia from Poland (1772). Meantime, Silesia was lost, but the Habsburgs remained Holy Roman Emperors.

sia had no firmer policy on succession than it had had when he acceded to the throne. For more than thirty years after his death, soldiers and nobles would once again determine who ruled Russia. Peter had laid the foundations of a modern Russia, but he had failed to lay the foundations of a stable state.

Central and Eastern Europe

As Russia became a major European power, the political contours of central Europe also changed. The Habsburgs realized they must expand their political base outside of Germany. Within Germany the Hohenzollerns over three generations forged Prussia into a major state. Thereafter, for over a century the Habsburg Empire and Prussia would duel for dominance in Germany. By the middle of the century that conflict would become united with the colonial conflict between Great Britain and France to create the first truly worldwide European war.

The Habsburg Empire and the Pragmatic Sanction

The close of the Thirty Years' War marked a fundamental turning point in the history of the Austrian Habsburgs. Previously, in alliance with their Spanish cousins, they had

Maria Theresa of Austria provided the leadership that saved the Habsburg Empire from possible disintegration after the Prussian invasion of Silesia in 1740. Kunsthistorisches Museum, Vienna

hoped to bring all of Germany under their control and back to the Catholic fold. In this they had failed, and the decline of Spanish power meant that the Austrian Habsburgs were on their own (see Map 20–3).

After 1648 the Habsburg family retained a firm hold on the title of Holy Roman Emperor, but the power of the emperor depended less on force of arms than on the cooperation he could elicit from the various political bodies in the empire. These included large German units (such as Saxony, Hanover, Bavaria, and Brandenburg) and scores of small German cities, bishoprics, principalities, and territories of independent knights. While establishing their new dominance among the German states, the Habsburgs also began to consolidate their power and influence within their hereditary possessions outside the Holy Roman Empire, which included the Crown of Saint Wenceslas, encompassing the kingdom of Bohemia (in modern Czechoslovakia) and the duchies of Moravia and Silesia; and the Crown of Saint Stephen, which ruled Hungary, Croatia, and Transylvania. Much of Hungary was only liberated from the Turks at the end of the seventeenth century (1699).

Through the Treaty of Rastadt in 1714 the Habsburgs further extended their domains, receiving the former Spanish (thereafter Austrian) Netherlands and Lombardy. Thereafter, the Habsburgs' power and influence would be based primarily on their territories outside Germany.

In each of their many territories the Habsburgs ruled by virtue of a different title and needed the cooperation of the local nobility, which was not always forthcoming. They repeatedly had to bargain with nobles in one part of Europe to maintain their position in another. Their domains were so geographically diverse and the people who occupied them of so many diverse languages and customs that almost no grounds existed on which to unify them politically. Even Roman Catholicism proved ineffective as a common bond, particularly in Hungary, the most recalcitrant province, where many Magyar nobles were Calvinist and seemed ever ready to rebel. Over the years Habsburg rulers established various central councils to chart common policies for their far-flung domains. Virtually all of these bodies, however, dealt with only a portion of the Habsburg holdings.

Despite these internal difficulties, Leopold I (r. 1658–1705) managed to resist the advances of the Turks into central Europe, which included a siege of Vienna in 1683, and to thwart the aggression of Louis XIV. He achieved Ottoman recognition of his sovereignty over Hungary in 1699 and extended his territorial holdings over much of the Balkan Peninsula and western Romania. These southeastward extensions allowed the Habsburgs to hope to develop Mediterranean trade through the port of Trieste and helped compensate for their loss of domination over the Holy Roman Empire. Strength in the east gave them greater political leverage in Germany. Leopold was succeeded by Joseph I (r. 1705–1711), who continued his policies.

When Charles VI (r. 1711–1740) succeeded Joseph, a new problem was added to the chronic one of territorial diversity. He had no male heir, and there was only the weakest of precedents for a female ruler of the Habsburg domains. Charles feared that on his death the Austrian Habsburg lands might fall prey to the surrounding powers, as had those of the Spanish Habsburgs in 1700. He was determined to prevent that disaster and to provide his domains with the semblance of legal unity. To those ends, he devoted most of his reign to seeking the approval of his family, the estates of his realms, and the major foreign powers for a document called the *Pragmatic Sanction.*

This instrument provided the legal basis for a single line of inheritance within the Habsburg dynasty through Charles VI's daughter Maria Theresa (1740–1780). Other members of the Habsburg family recognized her as the rightful heir. After extracting various concessions from Charles, the nobles of the various Habsburg domains and the other European rulers did likewise. Consequently, when Charles VI died in October 1740, he believed that he had secured legal unity for the Habsburg Empire and a safe succession for his daughter. He had indeed established a permanent line of succession and the basis for future legal bonds within the Habsburg holdings. Despite the Pragmatic Sanction, however, his failure to provide his daughter with a strong army or a full treasury left her inheritance open to foreign aggression. Less than two months after his death, the fragility of the foreign agreements became apparent. In December 1740 Frederick II of Prussia invaded the Habsburg province of Silesia. Maria Theresa had to fight for her inheritance.

CHRONOLOGY

RISE OF RUSSIAN POWER

1533–1584	Reign of Ivan the Terrible
1584–1613	Time of Troubles
1613	Michael Romanov becomes tsar
1682	Peter the Great becomes tsar as a boy
1689	Peter assumes personal rule
1697	European tour of Peter the Great
1698	Peter suppresses the *streltsy*
1700	The Great Northern War opens between Russia and Sweden; Russia defeated at Narva by Charles XII
1703	Saint Petersburg founded
1709	Russia defeats Sweden at Poltava
1718	Death of Alexis, son of Peter the Great
1721	Peace of Nystad ends the Great Northern War
1721	Peter establishes control over the Russian church
1722	The Table of Ranks
1725	Peter dies, leaving an uncertain succession

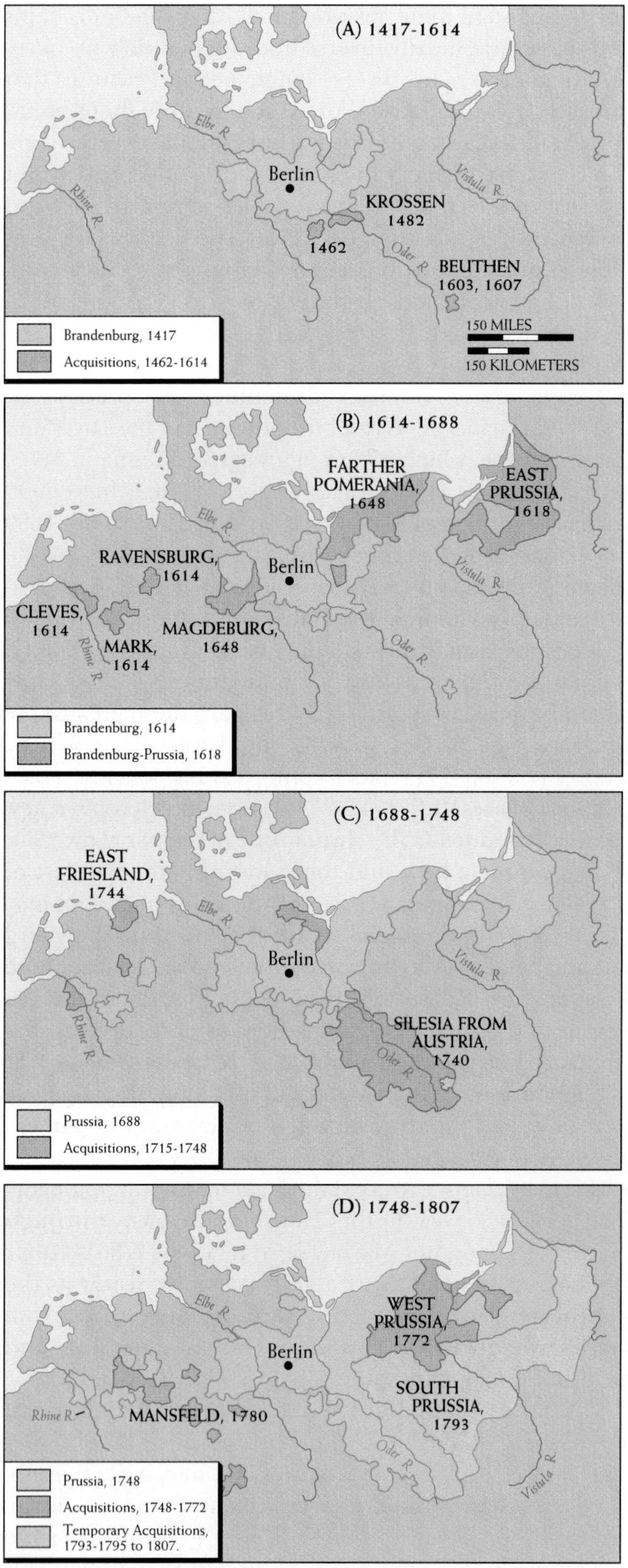

Map 20–4 Expansion of Brandenburg-Prussia. In the 17th century Brandenburg-Prussia expanded mainly by acquiring dynastic titles in geographically separated lands. In the 18th century it expanded through aggression to the east, seizing Silesia in 1740 and various parts of Poland in 1772, 1793, and 1795.

PRUSSIA AND THE HOHENZOLLERNS

The rise of Prussia occurred within the German power vacuum created by the Peace of Westphalia. It is the story of the extraordinary Hohenzollern family, which had ruled Brandenburg since 1417. Through inheritance the family had acquired Cleves and Mark and Ravensburg in 1614, East Prussia in 1618, and Pomerania in 1648 (see Map 20–4). Except for Pomerania, none of these lands was contiguous with Brandenburg. East Prussia lay inside Poland and outside the authority of the Holy Roman Emperor. All of the territories lacked good natural resources, and many of them were devastated during the Thirty Years' War. Still, by the late seventeenth century, the scattered Hohenzollern holdings represented a block of territory within the Holy Roman Empire second in size only to that of the Habsburgs.

The person who began to forge these areas into a modern state was Frederick William (r. 1640–1688), who became known as the Great Elector. He established himself and his successors as the central uniting power by breaking the medieval parliaments or estates, organizing a royal bureaucracy, and building a strong army.

Between 1655 and 1660 Sweden and Poland fought each other across the Great Elector's holdings in Pomerania and East Prussia. Frederick William had neither an adequate army nor the tax revenues to confront this foreign threat. In 1655 the Brandenburg estates refused to grant him new taxes; however, he proceeded to collect them by military force. In 1659 a different grant of taxes, originally made in 1653, elapsed; Frederick William continued to collect them as well as those he had imposed by his own authority. He used the money to build an army, which allowed him to continue to enforce his will without the approval of the nobility. Similar coercion took place against the nobles in his other territories.

There was, however, a political and social tradeoff between the Elector and his various nobles. These *Junkers*, or German noble landlords, were allowed almost complete control over the serfs on their estates. In exchange for their obedience to the Hohenzollerns, the *Junkers* received the right to demand obedience from their serfs. Frederick William also tended to choose as the local administrators of the tax structure men who would normally have been members of the noble branch of the old parliament. He thus co-opted potential opponents into his service. The taxes fell most heavily on the backs of the peasants and the urban classes. As the years passed, *Junkers* increasingly dominated the army officer corps, and this became even more pronounced during the eighteenth century. All officials and army officers took an oath of loyalty directly to the Elector. The army and the Elector thus came to embody the otherwise absent unity of the state. The army made Prussia a valuable potential ally.

Yet even with the considerable accomplishments of the Great Elector, the house of Hohenzollern did not possess a crown. The achievement of a royal title was one of the few state-building accomplishments of Frederick I (r. 1688–1713). This son of the Great Elector was the least "Prussian" of his family during these crucial years. He built palaces, founded Halle University (1694), patronized the arts, and lived luxuriously. In the War of the Spanish Succession he put his army at the disposal of the Habsburg Holy Roman Emperor Leopold I. In exchange, the emperor permitted Frederick to assume the title of "King in Prussia" in 1701.

His successor, Frederick William I (r. 1713–1740), was both the most eccentric monarch to rule the Hohenzollern domains and one of the most effective. He organized the bureaucracy along military lines. The discipline that he applied to the army was fanatical. The Prussian military grew from about 39,000 in 1713 to over 80,000 in 1740, making it the third- or fourth-largest army in Europe. Prussia's population, in contrast, ranked thirteenth in size. Separate laws applied to the army and to civilians. Laws, customs, and royal attention made the officer corps the highest social class of the state. Military service thus attracted the sons of *Junkers.* In this fashion the army, the *Junker* nobility, and the monarchy became forged into a single political entity. Military priorities and values dominated Prussian government, society, and daily life as in no other state in Europe. It has often been said that whereas other nations possessed armies, the Prussian army possessed its nation.

Although Frederick William I built the best army in Europe, he avoided conflict. His army was a symbol of Prussian power and unity, not an instrument for foreign adventures or aggression. At his death in 1740 he passed to his son Frederick II (Frederick the Great, r. 1740–1786) this superb military machine, but not the wisdom to refrain from using it. Almost immediately on coming to the throne, Frederick II upset the Pragmatic Sanction and invaded Silesia. He thus crystallized the Austrian-Prussian rivalry for the control of Germany that would dominate central European affairs for over a century.

CHRONOLOGY

AUSTRIA AND PRUSSIA

1640–1688	Reign of Frederick William, the Great Elector
1658–1705	Leopold I rules Austria and resists the Turks and Louis XIV
1683	Turkish siege of Vienna
1699	Peace between Turks and Habsburgs
1701	Frederick I becomes "King in Prussia"
1711–1740	Charles VI rules Austria and secures agreement to the Pragmatic Sanction
1713–1740	Frederick William I builds the military power of Prussia
1740	Maria Theresa succeeds to the Habsburg throne; Frederick II invades Silesia

THE FIRST WORLDWIDE WARS

The War of the Spanish Succession had been fought mainly in Europe. The wars that Europe fought between 1739 and 1763 were worldwide in scope and impact. By the end of the conflicts the French had been driven out of North America, and the British had established a domination in India that would last until 1947.

THE COLONIAL ARENA AND THE WAR OF JENKINS'S EAR

The Treaty of Utrecht established the boundaries of empire during the first half of the eighteenth century. Except for Brazil, which was governed by Portugal, Spain controlled all of mainland South America, as well as Florida, Mexico, and California in North America. Spain also ruled Cuba and half of Hispaniola. The British Empire consisted of the colonies along the North Atlantic seaboard, Nova Scotia, Newfoundland, Jamaica, and Barbados. Britain also possessed a few trading stations on the Indian subcontinent. The Dutch controlled Surinam, or Dutch Guiana, in South America; various trading stations in Ceylon and Bengal; and, most important, the trade with Java in what is today Indonesia.

The French had also established an empire in America and southern Asia. It covered the Saint Lawrence River valley; the Ohio and Mississippi river valleys; Saint Domingue (Haiti), Guadeloupe, and Martinique in the West Indies; and stations in India and West Africa. The economy of their West Indian islands resembled those of the Spanish and the British. Their holdings in Canada were sparsely populated, Quebec being the largest settlement, and the economy was based on agriculture and the fur trade. French and English settlers in North America clashed throughout the eighteenth century.

Each of the powers sought to make its imperial holdings into impenetrable trading areas. The Spanish Empire, however, especially stood on the defensive throughout the eighteenth century. The Spanish government lacked the capacity to maintain a commercial monopoly over its sprawling territory.

The Treaty of Utrecht gave the British a thirty-year *asiento,* or contract, to furnish slaves to the Spanish Empire and the right to send one ship each year to the trading fair at Portobello. Little but friction arose from these rights. Much to the chagrin of the British, the Spanish government under the Bourbons took its own alleged trading monopoly seriously and maintained coastal patrols, which searched English vessels for contraband.

In 1731, during one such search, there was a fight, and an English captain named Robert Jenkins had his ear cut off by the Spaniards. Thereafter, he preserved his ear in a jar of brandy. This incident was of little importance until 1738, when Jenkins appeared before the British Parliament, reportedly brandishing his ear as an example of Spanish atrocities to British merchants in the West Indies. British commercial interests put great pressure on Parliament to do something about Spanish interference in their trade. Robert Walpole could not resist these pressures, and in late 1739 Great Britain went to war with Spain. This might have been a relatively minor clash, but as a result of the Prussian invasion of Silesia, it became the opening encounter in a series of worldwide European wars that lasted off and on until 1815.

The War of the Austrian Succession (1740–1748)

In December 1740 the new king of Prussia, Frederick II, seized the Austrian province of Silesia. The invasion shattered the Pragmatic Sanction and upset the continental balance of power as established by the Treaty of Utrecht. In response to the Prussian aggression, the young Maria Theresa of Austria recognized Hungary as the most important of her crowns and promised the Magyars considerable local autonomy. She thus preserved the Habsburg state, but at great cost to the power of the central monarchy.

The war over the Austrian succession and the British-Spanish commercial conflict could have remained separate disputes. What united them was the role of France. A group of aggressive court aristocrats compelled the elderly Cardinal Fleury to support the Prussian aggression against Austria, the traditional enemy of France.

This proved to be one of the most fateful decisions in world history. French aid to Prussia helped to consolidate a new and powerful German state that could, and indeed later did, endanger France itself. The French move against Austria also brought Great Britain into the continental war against France and Prussia in an attempt to assure that Belgium remained in the friendly hands of Austria. In 1744 the British-French conflict expanded beyond the Continent when France decided to support Spain against Britain in the New World. The war ended in military stalemate in 1748 with the Treaty of Aix-la-Chapelle. Prussia retained Silesia, but the treaty was a truce rather than a permanent peace.

The Seven Years' War (1756–1763)

Before the rivalries again erupted into war, a dramatic shift of alliances took place. In 1756 Prussia and Great Britain signed the Convention of Westminster, a defensive alliance aimed at preventing the entry of foreign troops into the Germanies. Frederick feared invasions by both Russia and France. The convention meant that Great Britain, the ally of Austria since the wars of Louis XIV, had now joined forces with Austria's major eighteenth-century enemy. Later in 1756 Austria achieved a defensive alliance with France. Thus the traditional European alliances of the past century were reversed.

Conflict between France and Great Britain had continued unofficially on the colonial front. There were continual clashes between English and French settlers in the Ohio river valley and in upper New England. These skirmishes were the prelude to what is known in American history as the French and Indian War. Once again, however, the factor that opened a general European war that extended into a colonial theater was the action of the king of Prussia.

In August 1756, what would become the Seven Years' War opened when Frederick II invaded Saxony. Frederick considered this a preemptive strike against a conspiracy by Saxony, Austria, and France to destroy Prussian power. In the spring of 1757 France and Austria made a new alliance dedicated to the destruction of Prussia. They were eventually joined by Sweden, Russia, and the smaller German states. Two factors, in addition to Frederick's strong leadership (it was after this war that he came to be called Frederick the Great), saved Prussia—British financial aid and the death in 1762 of Empress Elizabeth of Russia (r. 1741–1762). Her successor Tsar Peter III (d. 1762), a fervent admirer of Frederick, immediately made peace with Prussia, thus allowing Frederick to hold off Austria and France. The Treaty of Hubertusburg of 1763 closed the continental conflict with no significant changes in prewar borders.

More impressive to the rest of Europe than the survival of Prussia were the victories of Great Britain in every theater of conflict. The architect of victory was William Pitt the Elder (1708–1778). Although Pitt had previously criticized British involvement with the Continent, once he was named secretary of state in charge of the war in 1757 he reversed himself and pumped huge financial subsidies to Frederick the Great. But North America was Pitt's real concern. Put simply, he wanted all of North America east of the Mississippi for Great Britain, and that was exactly what he won as he directed unprecedented resources into the overseas colonial conflict. The French government was unwilling and unable to direct similar resources against the English in America. In September 1759 the British took Quebec City. Montreal fell the next year. The French empire in Canada was coming to an end.

Pitt's colonial vision, however, was global. The French West Indies fell to the British fleets. On the Indian subcontinent the British forces under Robert Clive (1725–1774) defeated the French in 1757 at the Battle of Plassey. This victory opened the way for the eventual conquest of all India by the British East India Company. Never had any other European power experienced such a complete worldwide military victory. Never had a European military victory affected so many non-Europeans.

The Treaty of Paris of 1763 was somewhat less triumphant. Pitt was no longer in office. George III (r. 1760–1820) had succeeded to the British throne and replaced Pitt with the Earl of Bute (1713–1792) in 1762. The new minister was responsible for the peace settlement, in which Britain received all of Canada, the Ohio river valley, and the eastern half of the Mississippi river valley. France retained footholds in India at Pondicherry and Chandernagore, and regained the West Indies sugar islands of Guadeloupe and Martinique.

The midcentury wars among European powers resulted in a new balance of power on the European continent and the high seas. Great Britain gained a world empire, and Prussia was recognized as a great continental power. With the surrender of Canada, France retreated from North America and thus opened the way for a continent largely dominated by the English language and Protestantism. By contrast, Latin America would be dominated by the Spanish and Portuguese languages and Roman Catholicism. For many years, West Africa would continue to furnish slaves to the economies of both Americas. On the subcontinent of Asia the foundations were laid for almost two centuries of British dominance. By 1760, therefore, a true world economy had been established in which political and economic developments in one region could directly and relatively quickly affect others.

In World Perspective

EIGHTEENTH-CENTURY EUROPEAN STATES AND WARFARE

By the second quarter of the eighteenth century, the major European powers were not yet nation-states in which the citizens felt themselves united by a shared sense of community, culture, language, and history. They were still monarchies in which the personality of the ruler and the personal relationships of the great noble families considerably influenced public affairs.

These European states displayed certain problems that also characterized the governments of China and Japan during the same epochs. In particular, as in Japan, the problem of a balance between centralization and decentralization arose in virtually all the European states. In France, Russia, and Prussia the forces of centralization proved quite strong. In Austria the forces of decentralization were powerful. England achieved a rather delicate balance. Furthermore, as in Tokugawa, Japan, European states of the eighteenth century generally saw an increase in legal codification and in the growth of bureaucracy. Only in Prussia did the military influence on society resemble that in Japan.

The role of the personality of the monarch in Europe bore some resemblance to that of certain Manchu emperors in China, such as K'ang Hsi (1662–1722) and Ch'ien Lung (r. 1736–1795). Louis XIV and Peter the Great had no less influence on their nations than did these great Manchu emperors. All of them built up military strength and fostered innovation. However, although European rulers developed state bureaucracies, none of them put together so brilliant a group of trained civil servants as those who administered China.

The global commercial empires of France, Spain, and England gave rise to fierce commercial rivalries. The drive for empire and commercial supremacy propelled these states into contact with Africa, Latin America, India, China, and Japan. Spain and Portugal had long exploited Latin America as their own monopoly, an arrangement that England challenged in the eighteenth century. Both France and England fought for commercial supremacy in India, and by the 1760s England had, in effect, conquered the subcontinent. The slave trade between Africa and the New World flourished throughout the eighteenth century. European merchants and navies also sought to penetrate East Asia. As a result of these developments, European commerce would dominate the world for the next two centuries. Europe and its colonists extracted labor and other natural resources from virtually all other continents of the world. The European military, especially naval dominance, made all this possible.

Consequently, by the mid–eighteenth century, the European states that just two centuries earlier had only started to settle the Americas and to engage in limited long-range trade had made their power and influence felt throughout the world. Beginning in the early eighteenth century, the political power of the European states became linked to a qualitatively different economic base than any seen elsewhere in the world. That political and economic combination allowed Europe to dominate the world from the 1750s to the Second World War.

CHRONOLOGY

MID-EIGHTEENTH CENTURY CONFLICTS

1739	Outbreak of War of Jenkins's Ear between England and Spain
1740	War of the Austrian Succession commences
1748	Treaty of Aix-la-Chapelle
1756	Convention of Westminster between England and Prussia
1756	Seven Years' War opens
1757	Battle of Plassey
1759	British forces capture Quebec
1763	Treaty of Hubertusburg
1763	Treaty of Paris

REVIEW QUESTIONS

1. By the end of the seventeenth century, England and France had different systems of government with different religious policies. What were the main differences? Similarities? Why did each nation develop as it did?
2. Why did the English king and Parliament come into conflict in the 1640s? What were the most important issues behind the war between them, and who bears more responsibility for it? What was the Glorious Revolution, and why did it take place? What role did religion play in each event? How did England in 1700 differ from England in 1600?
3. Discuss the development of absolutism in France. What were the chief ways Louis XIV consolidated his monarchy? What limits were there on his authority? What was Louis's religious policy? What were the goals of his foreign policy?
4. How was the Hohenzollern family able to forge a conglomerate of diverse landholdings into the state of Prussia? Who were the major personalities involved in this process and what were their individual contributions? Why was the military so important in Prussia? Compare and contrast the varying success with which the Hohenzollerns and Habsburgs each handled their problems. Which family was more successful and why?
5. How and why did Russia emerge as a great power? Discuss the character of Peter the Great. How were his domestic reforms related to his military ambitions? What were his methods of reform? To what extent did he succeed?
6. What were the main points of conflict between Britain and France in North America, the West Indies, and India? What were the results of these conflicts by 1763? Which countries emerged stronger from the Seven Years' War and why?

SUGGESTED READINGS

M. S. ANDERSON, *Europe in the Eighteenth Century*, 1713–1783 (1988). A good one-volume introduction to the individual states.

T. M. BARKER, *Army, Aristocracy, Monarchy: Essays in War, Society and Government in Austria, 1618–1780* (1982). Examines the intricate power relationships among these major institutions.

W. BEIK, *Absolutism and Society in Seventeenth-Century France* (1985). An important study that questions the extent of royal power.

J. BLACK, *Eighteenth-Century Europe 1700–1789* (1990). An excellent survey.

R. BONNEY, *Political Change in France Under Richelieu and Mazarin 1624–1661* (1978). An important examination of the emergence of French absolutism.

J. BREWER, *The Sinews of Power: War, Money, and the English State, 1688–1783* (1989). A study that emphasizes the financial power behind British military success.

G. BURGESS, *Absolute Monarchy and the Stuart Constitution* (1996) A new study that challenges many of the traditional interpretative categories.

P. BURKE, *The Fabrication of Louis XIV* (1992). Examines the manner in which the public image of Louis XIV was forged in art.

F. L. CARSTEN, *The Origins of Prussia* (1954). Discusses the groundwork laid by the Great Elector in the seventeenth century.

J. C. D. CLARKE, *English Society, 1688–1832: Social Structure and Political Practice During the Ancien Régime* (1985). An important, controversial work that emphasizes the role of religion in English political life.

L. COLLEY, *Britons: Forging the Nation, 1707–1837* (1992) A major study of the making of British nationhood.

W. DORN, *Competition for Empire, 1740–1763* (1940). Still one of the best accounts of the mid-eighteenth-century struggle.

W. DOYLE, *The Old European Order, 1660–1800* (1992). The most thoughtful treatment of the subject.

P. DUKES, *The Making of Russian Absolutism: 1613–1801* (1982). An overview based on recent scholarship.

R. J. W. EVANS, *The Making of the Habsburg Monarchy, 1550–1700: An Interpretation* (1979). Places much emphasis on intellectual factors and the role of religion.

F. FORD, *Robe and Sword: The Regrouping of the French Aristocracy After Louis XIV* (1953). Remains an important book for political, social, and intellectual history.

P. GOUBERT, *Louis XIV and Twenty Million Frenchmen* (1966). A fine overview of seventeenth-century French social structure.

R. HATTEN, ED., *Louis XIV and Europe* (1976). Covers foreign policy.

D. HIRST, *Authority and Conflict: England 1603–1658* (1986). Scholarly survey integrating history and historiography.

J. M. HITTLE, *The Service City: State and Townsmen in Russia, 1600–1800* (1979). Examines the relationship of cities in Russia to the growing power of the central government.

L. HUGHES, *Russia in the Age of Peter the Great* (1998). A major new account.

H. C. JOHNSON, *Frederick the Great and His Officials* (1975). An excellent recent examination of the Prussian administration.

P. LANGFORD, *A Polite and Commercial People: England 1717–1783* (1989). An excellent survey of mid-eighteenth-century Britain based on the most recent scholarship covering social history as well as politics, the overseas wars, and the American Revolution.

A. LOSSKY, *Louis XIV and the French Monarchy* (1994). The most recent major analysis.

R. K. MASSIE, *Peter the Great: His Life and His World* (1980). A good popular biography.

R. MIDDLETON, *The Bells of Victory: The Pitt-Newcastle Ministry and the Conduct of the Seven Years' War, 1757–1762* (1985). A careful study of the intricacies of eighteenth-century cabinet government that questions the centrality of Pitt's role in the British victory.

J. H. PLUMB, *Sir Robert Walpole*, 2 vols. (1956, 1961). A masterful biography ranging across the sweep of European politics.

J. H. PLUMB, *The Growth of Political Stability in England, 1675–1725* (1969). An important interpretive work.

J. G. A. POCOCK, ED., *Three British Revolutions: 1641, 1688, 1776* (1980). An important collection of essays.

N. V. RIASANOVSKY, *The Image of Peter the Great in Russian History and Thought* (1985). Examines the ongoing legacy of Peter in Russian history.

J. C. RILEY, *The Seven Years' War and the Old Regime in France: The Economic and Financial Toll* (1986). An analysis of pressures that would undermine the French monarchy.

H. ROSENBERG, *Bureaucracy, Aristocracy, and Autocracy: The Prussian Experience, 1660–1815* (1960). Emphasizes the organization of Prussian administration.

D. L. RUBIN, *The Sun King: The Ascendancy of French Culture During the Reign of Louis XIV* (1992). A collection of useful essays.

C. RUSSELL, *The Fall of the English Monarchies, 1637–1642* (1991). A major revisionist account, which should be read with Stone's book.

K. SHARPE, *The Personal Rule of Charles I* (1992). A major narrative work.

L. STONE, *The Causes of the English Revolution 1529–1642* (1972) Survey stressing social history and ruminating over historians and historical method.

G. TREASURE, *Mazarin: The Crisis of Absolutism in France* (1996). An examination not only of Mazarin, but also of the larger national and international background.

D. UNDERDOWN, *Fire from Heaven: Life in an English Town in the Seventeenth Century* (1992). A lively account of how a single English town experienced the religious and political turmoil of the century.

J. WEST, *Gunpower, Government, and War in the Mid–Eighteenth Century* (1991). A study of how warfare touched much government of the day.

J. B. WOLF, *Louis XIV* (1968). Authoritative and readable.

DOCUMENTS CD-ROM

1. James I: from Anglicanism
2. Thomas Macauley: from *History of England, Volume I*
3. G. M. Trevelyan: Chapter I from *History of England Volume I*
4. Louis XIV: Memoires for the Instruction of the Dauphin
5. Peter the Great: Correspondence with His Son
6. Parliament takes control: England's Bill of Rights of 1689

WORLD AND THE WEB

The World Turned Upside Down

http://www.strecorsoc.org/world.html

A major site on the radicals during the English Revolution, with many online texts. Covers the period of the early Commonwealth of England, from the late 1640s to the 1650s. Interestingly, many of the issues that were being argued about then are still alive today.

Creating French Culture: Treasures from the Bibliothèque Nationale de France

http://www.loc.gov/exhibits/bnf/bnf0002.html

Creating French Culture traces the history of this relationship from Charlemagne (742?–814) to Charles de Gaulle (1890–1970), through the prism of more than 200 magnificent "treasures" on loan from the Bibliothèque nationale de France in Paris. Throughout French history rulers understood that the representation of power—what today we call "image"—is a form of power itself. They patronized artists, who produced works that proclaimed the legitimacy of their rule, and reinforced their authority. The Bibliothèque's collaboration has made possible a unique exhibition which includes many items never before seen outside of France.

The London Gazette

http://www.history.rochester.edu/London_Gazette/p-toc.htm

In the autumn of 1665 Charles II sought shelter in Oxford from the Great Plague; he and his courtiers wanted newspapers to read, yet feared to touch London newspapers which might be infected. Leonard Litchfeld was authorized and ordered to bring out a local paper. On Tuesday, November 14, 1665, the first number of the *Oxford Gazette* appeared. The plague was soon over and King Charles went back to Whitehall, but he was pleased with the Oxford effort and it was soon succeeded by the *London Gazette*, which has been kept alive, altering its size and character from time to time, down to this day.

Twenty-Five Lectures on Modern Balkan History

http://www.lib.msu.edu/sowards/balkan/

An ongoing project which covers the entire Balkan history from ethnic geography of the Balkans to 1500 to the Yugoslav civil war. Lectures 3 and 4 cover the "Old Regimes" in the Balkans before 1790, specifically the principles of Ottoman rule in the Balkans and Hungary and the limits of Habsburg authority.

21 European Society Under the Old Regime

During the 18th century, with their employment opportunities tightly restricted, many unmarried women and widows served as governesses to children of the aristocracy and other wealthier groups in Europe. At the other end of the spectrum, many children born out of wedlock or to very poor parents might be left at foundling hospitals where many of them died quite young.

Chardin, Jean-Baptiste-Simeon: "The Governess" (#6432), National Gallery of Canada, Ottawa

Chapter topics

- Major Features of Life in the Old Regime
- Aristocracy
- The Land and its Tillers
- Family Structures and the Family Economy
- Growth of Agriculture and Population
- The Eighteenth-Century Industrial Revolution
- Cities
- The Jewish Population: Age of the Ghetto

IN WORLD PERSPECTIVE
The European Old Regime

AT THE OPENING OF THE EIGHTEENTH CENTURY European merchants and traders dominated the transatlantic economy, and European states governed much of the American continents, though in North America only along the Atlantic seaboard. During the century the peoples living primarily in northwestern Europe undertook a series of economic advances that laid the foundation for the social and economic transformation of the world. Europeans began for the first time in their history to achieve a more or less stable food supply. For reasons still much debated the population of Europe commenced a major period of growth. New inventions in the manufacture of textiles transformed Europe's productive capacity, and the invention of the steam engine, powered by coal as a fuel, opened the way for moving manufacturing from the countryside to cities. Furthermore, the production of iron greatly expanded. These developments, known collectively as the Industrial Revolution, gave Europe a productive capacity unknown before in human history. For a time that state of economic advance provided Europeans with the tools to dominate much of the world both economically and militarily. At the same time, the industrial achievement of Europe became an example that for the next two centuries less economically advanced areas of the world would seek to imitate. All of this potential for change emerged in a society whose institutions had been in large measure designed to inhibit or even prevent major social and economic change.

During the turmoil of the French Revolution and its aftermath, it became customary to refer to the patterns of social, political, and economic relationships that had existed in France before 1789 as the *ancien régime,* or the "Old Regime." The term has come to be applied generally to the life and institutions of prerevolutionary continental Europe. Politically, it meant the rule of theoretically absolute monarchies with growing bureaucracies and aristocratically led armies. Economically, the Old Regime was characterized by food shortages, the predominance of agriculture, slow transport, a low level of iron production, comparatively unsophisticated financial institutions, and, in some cases, competitive commercial overseas empires. Socially, men and women saw themselves less as individuals than as members of distinct corporate bodies that possessed certain privileges or rights as a group.

Tradition, hierarchy, corporateness, and privilege were thus the chief social characteristics of the Old Regime. Yet change and innovation were fermenting in its midst as farming became more commercialized and the size of the population increased. The early Industrial Revolution expanded the quantity of consumer goods. The colonies in the Americas provided strong demand for European products and manufactures. Merchants in seaports and trading cities prospered. By preparing for war, European governments put new demands on their states' resources and economic organizations. The Old Regime itself thus fostered changes that eventually transformed it and later vast areas of the non-European world.

MAJOR FEATURES OF LIFE IN THE OLD REGIME

Socially, prerevolutionary Europe was based on (1) aristocratic elites with many inherited legal privileges; (2) established churches intimately related to the state and the aristocracy; (3) an urban labor force usually organized into guilds; and (4) a rural peasantry subject to high taxes and feudal dues. Of course, the men and women of this period did not know it was the Old Regime. Most of them lived as their forebears had done for generations and as they expected their children to do after them.

Maintenance of Tradition

Few persons outside the political, commercial, and intellectual elite wanted change or innovation. This was especially true of social relationships. Both nobles and peasants repeatedly called for the restoration of traditional or customary rights. The nobles asserted what they considered their ancient rights against the intrusion of the expanding monarchical bureaucracies. The peasants, through petitions and revolts, called for the revival or the maintenance of the customary manorial rights that allowed them access to particular lands, courts, or grievance procedures.

Except for the early industrial development in Britain, the economy was also predominantly traditional. The quality and quantity of the grain harvest remained crucial for most of the population and the gravest concern for governments.

Hierarchy and Privilege

The medieval sense of hierarchy became more rigid during the century. Several cities retained sumptuary laws forbidding persons in one class or occupation from dressing like their social superiors. These laws were largely ineffective. What really enforced the hierarchy was the corporate nature of social relationships.

Each state or society was considered a community composed of numerous smaller communities. Eighteenth-century Europeans did not enjoy what Americans regard as individual rights. Instead, persons enjoyed such rights and privileges as were guaranteed to whatever communities or groups of which they were a part. The "community" might include the village, the municipality, the nobility, the church, the guild, a university, or the parish. In turn, each of these bodies enjoyed certain privileges—some great, some small. The privileges might involve exemption from taxation or degrading punishment, the right to practice a trade or craft, the right of one's children to pursue a particular occupation, or, for the church, the right to collect the tithe.

Aristocracy

The eighteenth century was the great age of the aristocracy. The nobility constituted approximately 1 to 5 percent of the population of any given country. In every European state, it was the single wealthiest sector of the population; possessed the widest degree of social, political, and economic power; and dominated polite society. Land provided the aristocracy with its largest source of income, but the influence of aristocrats was felt in every area of life. Across the Continent, to be an aristocrat was a matter of birth and legal privilege, but in almost every other respect, they differed markedly from country to country.

Great Britain

The smallest, wealthiest, best-defined, and most socially responsible aristocracy resided in Great Britain. It consisted of about 400 families, whose eldest male members sat in the House of Lords. Through the corruptions of the electoral system, these families also controlled most seats in the House of Commons. Their estates ranged from a few thousand to 50,000 acres, from which they received rents. The nobles owned approximately one fourth of all the arable land in Britain. Increasingly, their money was invested in commerce, canals, urban real estate, mines, and sometimes industrial ventures. Because only the eldest son inherited the title and the land, younger sons moved into commerce, the army, the professions, and the church. Most members of the House of Commons were also landowners. They paid taxes and had few significant legal privileges, but their control of local government gave them immense political power and social influence. Socially and politically, the aristocracy dominated the English counties.

France

In France, the nobility was theoretically divided between nobles of the sword and those of the robe. The former families' nobility derived from military service; the latter had either gained their titles by serving in the bureaucracy or by purchasing them. The two groups had frequently quarreled in the past but tended to cooperate during the eighteenth century to defend their common privileges.

The nobility who held office or favor with the royal court at Versailles reaped the immense wealth that came from holding high office. The noble hold on such offices intensified during the century. By the late 1780s appointments to the church, the army, and the bureaucracy tended to go to the court aristocracy. Whereas these well-connected aristocrats were quite rich, other nobles, known as *hobereaux*, lived in the provinces and were sometimes scarcely better off than well-to-do peasants.

Despite their differences, all French aristocrats enjoyed certain hereditary privileges. They were exempt from many taxes. For example, most did not pay the *taille*, the basic land tax of the Old Regime. They were technically liable to pay the *vingtiéme*, or the "twentieth," which resembled an income tax, but rarely had to pay it in full. Unlike peasants, nobles were not subject to the royal *corvées*, or labor dona-

Eighteenth-century France had some of the best roads in the world, but they were often built with forced labor. French peasants were required to work part of each year on such projects. This system, called the *corvée*, was not abolished until the French Revolution in 1789. Claude Vernet "Construction of a Road." Louvre, Paris/Giraudon/Art Resource, N.Y.

tions. Moreover, the approximately 400,000 French nobles could collect feudal dues from their tenants and enjoyed exclusive hunting and fishing rights.

EASTERN EUROPE

In eastern Europe, the character of the nobility became more complicated and repressive. In Poland, thousands of nobles were entirely exempt from taxes. Until 1768 they could legally execute their serfs. While most Polish aristocrats were relatively poor, a few very rich nobles dominated the fragile Polish state.

In Austria and Hungary, the nobility had broad judicial powers over the peasantry and enjoyed exemptions from taxation. The wealthiest of them, Prince Esterhazy of Hungary, owned 10 million acres of land.

In Prussia, after the accession of Frederick the Great in 1740, the position of the *Junkers* became much stronger. Frederick's wars required the nobles' support. He drew his officers and increasingly his bureaucrats almost wholly from the *Junker* class. The Prussian nobles also enjoyed extensive authority over their serfs.

RUSSIA

In Russia, a new, service nobility arose in the eighteenth century. Peter the Great linked noble status to state service through the Table of Ranks (1722). Resistance to compulsory state service created among Russian nobles a self-conscious class identity. In 1736 Empress Anna (r. 1730–1740) reduced such service to twenty-five years. In 1762 Peter III removed the liability for compulsory service entirely from the greatest nobles. In 1785, in the Charter of the Nobility, Catherine the Great granted an explicit legal definition of noble rights and privileges in exchange for assurances of voluntary state service from the nobility. The noble privileges included the right of transmitting noble status to one's wife and children, the judicial protection of noble rights and property, considerable power over the serfs, and exemption from personal taxes.

Throughout the century, in a European-wide *aristocratic resurgence*, the various nobilities sought to protect their social position and privileges against the expanding power of the monarchies and the growing wealth of commercial groups. First, all nobilities attempted to restrict entry into their ranks and institutions.

Second, they also attempted to monopolize appointments to the officer corps of the armies, the bureaucracies, the government ministries, and the church. The nobles thus hoped to control the power of the monarchies.

Third, the nobles attempted to use institutions they already controlled against the monarchies. These institutions included the British Parliament, the French *parlements*, local aristocratic estates, and provincial diets.

Fourth, the aristocracies pressed the peasantry for higher rents or long-forgotten feudal dues. This was part of an effort by the nobility to shore up its position by appealing to tradition and reasserting old privileges that had lapsed. To contemporaries, this aristocratic resurgence was one of the most fundamental political facts of the day.

Emelyan Pugachev (1726–1775) led the largest peasant revolt in Russian history. In this contemporary propaganda picture he is shown in chains. An inscription in Russian and German was printed below the picture decrying the evils of revolution and insurrection. Bildarchiv Preussischer Kulturbesitz

THE LAND AND ITS TILLERS

Land was the economic basis of eighteenth-century life. Well over three fourths of all Europeans lived on the land, and most never traveled more than a few miles from their birthplaces. With the exception of the nobility and the wealthier landowners, the dwellers on the land were poor, and by any modern standard, their lives were hard. They lived in various modes of economic and social dependency, exploitation, and vulnerability.

PEASANTS AND SERFS

The major forms of rural social dependency related directly to the land. Those who worked the land were subject to immense influence and in some cases direct control by the landowners. This situation prevailed in different degrees for free peasants, such as English tenants and most French cultivators, and for the serfs of Germany, Austria, and Russia, who were legally bound to a particular plot of land and a particular lord. In all cases, the class that owned most of the land also controlled the local government and the courts.

Landlord power increased as one moved from west to east. Most French peasants owned some land, but a few were serfs. However, nearly all peasants were subject to certain feudal dues and to forced labor on the lord's estate for a certain number of days each year. Because French peasants rarely owned enough land to support their families, they were also subject to feudal dues attached to the plots of land they rented.

In Prussia and Austria, despite attempts by the monarchies late in the century to improve the lot of the serfs, the landlords continued to exercise almost complete control over them. Moreover, throughout continental Europe the burden of state taxation fell on the tillers of the soil. Many peasants, serfs, and other agricultural laborers were forced to undertake supplemental work to pay the tax collector. Through various legal privileges and the ability to demand further concessions from the monarchs, the landlords escaped the payment of numerous taxes. They also presided over the manorial courts.

The condition of the serfs was the worst in Russia. The Russian custom of reckoning one's wealth by the number of owned "souls" (that is, male serfs) rather than by the size of an estate reveals the contrast between Russia and eastern Europe. The serfs were, in effect, regarded merely as economic commodities. Their services were attached to an individual lord rather than to a particular plot of land. Russian landlords could demand as many as six days a week of labor, and like Prussian and Austrian landlords, they could punish their serfs or even exile them to Siberia. Although serfs had little recourse against their lords, custom, tradition, and law did provide a few protections. For example, the marriages of serfs, unlike those of most slaves throughout the world, were legally recognized. The landlord could not disband the family of a serf.

The Russian monarchy itself contributed to the degradation of the serfs. Peter the Great (r. 1682–1725) gave whole villages to favored nobles. Catherine the Great (r. 1762–1796) confirmed the authority of the nobles over their serfs in exchange for the nobility's political cooperation.

This situation led to considerable unrest. There were well over fifty peasant revolts between 1762 and 1769. They culminated between 1773 and 1774 in Pugachev's rebellion, during which all of southern Russia was in ferment. Emelyan Pugachev (1726–1775) promised the serfs land and freedom. The rebellion was brutally suppressed, and any thought of liberalizing the condition of the serfs was set aside for a generation.

Pugachev's was the largest peasant uprising of the eighteenth century. Smaller peasant revolts or disturbances occurred in Bohemia in 1775, in Transylvania in 1784, in Moravia in 1786, and in Austria in 1789. Western Europe was more tranquil, but England experienced numerous enclosure riots. Rural rebellions were violent, but the peasants and serfs normally directed their wrath against property rather than persons. The rebels usually sought to reassert traditional or customary rights against practices they perceived as innovations. In this respect, the peasant revolts were conservative in nature.

Family Structures and the Family Economy

In preindustrial Europe, the household was the basic unit of production and consumption. That is to say, very few productive establishments employed more than a handful of people not belonging to the owner's family. These rare establishments were located in cities. But most Europeans lived in rural areas. There, as well as in small towns and cities, the household mode of organization predominated on farms, in artisans' workshops, and in small merchants' shops. With that mode of economic organization, there developed what is known as the *family economy.*

Households

What was a household under the Old Regime? There were two basic models, one characterizing northwestern Europe and the other eastern Europe.

Northwestern Europe Here, the household almost invariably consisted of a married couple, their children through their early teenage years, and their servants. Except for the wealthy few, households were small, rarely consisting of more than five or six members. Furthermore, high mortality and late marriage generally meant that grandparents rarely lived in the same household as their grandchildren. The family structure of northwestern Europe was thus nuclear rather than extended; that is to say, these families consisted of parents and children rather than of several generations under the same roof.

Children lived with their parents only until their early teens. Then they normally left home, usually to enter the workforce of young servants who lived and worked away from home. A child of a skilled artisan might remain with his or her parents to acquire the valuable skill, but only rarely would more than one of the children do so because their labor would be more valuable elsewhere.

These young men and women who had left home would eventually marry and begin to form independent households of their own. This practice of moving away from home is known as *neolocalism.* The effort to acquire the economic resources needed to establish a household meant the age of marriage would be relatively late. For men it was over twenty-six, and for women, over twenty-three. The couple usually quickly began a family. The marriage often occurred at the end of a long courtship when the woman was already pregnant. Family and community pressures seem more often than not to have compelled the man to marry the woman, but premarital sexual relations were not rare, although illegitimate births were uncommon. The new couple would soon employ a servant, and everyone, including the growing children, would help the household support itself.

Servant in this context does not refer to someone looking after the needs of wealthy people. Rather, in preindustrial Europe, a servant was a person—either male or female—who was hired, often under a clear contract, to work for the head of the household in exchange for room, board, and wages. The servant was usually young and by no means socially inferior to his or her employer. Normally, the servant was an integral part of the household and ate with the family. Young men and women became servants when their labor was no longer needed in their parents' household or when they could earn more money for their family outside it. Being a servant for several years—often as many as eight or ten—allowed young people to acquire productive skills and save enough money to begin their own households. This period of working as a servant between leaving home and beginning a new household largely explains the late age of marriage in northwestern Europe.

Eastern Europe As one moved east, the structure of the household and the pattern of marriage changed. In Russia and elsewhere in eastern Europe, marrying involved not starting a new household but continuing in and expanding one already established. Consequently, marriage occurred early, before the age of twenty for both men and women. Children were born to parents of a much younger age than in western Europe. Often, especially among Russian serfs, wives were older than their husbands. Eastern European households tended to be larger than those in the west. The rural Russian household could have more than nine and possibly more than twenty members, with three or perhaps even four generations of the same family living together. Early marriage made this situation more likely.

The landholding pattern in eastern Europe accounted, at least in part, for these patterns of marriage and the family. The lords of the manor who owned land wanted to ensure that it would be cultivated so that they could receive their rents. To that end, for example, in Poland landlords might forbid marriage between their own serfs and those from another estate. They might also require widows and widowers to remarry so there would be adequate labor for a particular plot of land. Polish landlords also frowned on the hiring of free laborers—the equivalent of servants in the west—to help cultivate the land. The landlords preferred to use other serfs. This practice inhibited the possible formation of independent households. In Russia, landlords ordered the families of young people in their villages to arrange marriages within a short, set time. These lords discouraged single-generation family households because the death or serious illness of a person in such a household might mean that the land assigned to it would go out of cultivation.

THE FAMILY ECONOMY

Throughout Europe the household was the fundamental unit of production and consumption. People thought and worked in terms of sustaining the economic life of the family, and family members saw themselves as working together in an interdependent rather than an independent or individualistic manner. The goal of the family household was to produce or secure through wages enough food to support its members. In the countryside, that effort virtually always involved farming. In cities and towns, artisan production or working for another person was the usual pattern. Almost everyone lived within a household because ordinary people could rarely support themselves independently. Indeed, except for members of religious orders, people living outside a household were viewed with great suspicion as potentially criminal or disruptive or, at least, potentially dependent on the charity of others.

Marriage and the family within this economy meant that everyone in the household had to work. On a farm, much of the effort went directly into raising food or producing other agricultural goods that could be exchanged for food. In western Europe, however, few people had enough land to support their households from farming alone. For this reason, one or more family members might work elsewhere and send wages home. For example, the father or older children might be migrant workers, perhaps many miles from home. The burden of the farm work would then fall on the wife and the younger children. This was not uncommon. Within this family economy, all of the goods and income produced went to the benefit of the household rather than to the individual family member. Depending on their ages and skills, everyone worked. The need to survive poor harvests or economic slumps meant that no one could be idle.

The family economy also dominated the life of skilled urban artisans. The father was usually the chief craftsman. He generally had one or more servants in his employ, but he would also expect his children to work in the enterprise. His eldest child was usually trained in the trade. His wife often sold the wares, or had a small shop. The wife of a merchant also often ran the husband's business, especially when he traveled to purchase new goods. In any case, everyone in the family was involved. If business was poor, family members would look for employment elsewhere, not to support themselves but to help the family unit survive.

In western Europe, the death of a father could destroy the economy of the household. The family's economic life usually depended on his land or skills. The widow might take on the farm or the business, or her children might do so. She usually sought to remarry quickly to have the labor and skills of a male once more in the household and to prevent herself from falling into a state of dependence. The high mortality rate of the time meant that many households were reconstituted second family groups with stepchildren. But some households simply dissolved. The widow and children became dependent on charity or relatives, or the children moved earlier than they would otherwise have done into the workforce of servants. In desperate situations survivors resorted to crime or begging. The personal, emotional, and economic vulnerability of the family economy cannot be overemphasized.

In eastern Europe, the family economy existed in the context of serfdom and landlord domination. Peasants clearly thought in terms of their families and of expanding the land available for cultivation. The village structure may have mitigated the pressures of the family economy, as did the multigenerational family. Dependence on the available land was the chief fact of life, and there were many fewer artisan and merchant households and far less mobility than in western Europe.

WOMEN AND THE FAMILY ECONOMY

The family economy established many of the chief constraints on the lives and the personal experiences of women in preindustrial society. Most of the historical research that has been undertaken on this subject relates to western Europe. There, a woman's life experience was largely the function of her capacity to establish and maintain a household. For women, marriage was an institution of economic necessity as well as one that fulfilled sexual and psychological needs. A woman outside a household was highly vulnerable. Unless she were an aristocrat or a member of a religious order, she probably could not support herself by her own efforts alone. Consequently, much of a woman's life was devoted first to aiding the maintenance of her parents' household and then to getting her own household to live in as an adult. In most cases, bearing and rearing children were subordinate to these goals.

As a child, certainly by the age of seven, a girl was expected to begin to contribute to the household work. On a farm, she might look after chickens or water animals or

Painted by the English artist Francis Wheatley (1747–1801) near the close of the 18th century, this scene is part of a series illustrating a day in the life of an idealized farm family. Note the artist's assumptions about the division of labor by gender. Men work in the fields, women work in the home or look after the needs of men and children. As other illustrations in this chapter show, many 18th-century women in fact worked outside the home, but considerable social pressure was developing at this time to restrict them to domestic roles. This painting and the others in the series are thus more prescriptive than descriptive, intended in part to persuade their viewers that women belonged in their separate family sphere. Many, perhaps most, families living in the countryside could not maintain the closeness that these paintings extol. To survive, many had to send members to work on other farms or even to other regions. Francis Wheatley (RA) (1747–1801), "Evening," signed and dated 1799, oil on canvas, 17 X 21 in. (44.5 X 54.5 cm), Yale Center for British Art, Paul Mellon Collection, B1977.14.118

carry food to adult men and women working the land. In an urban artisan's household, she would do some form of light work, perhaps involving cleaning or carrying and later sewing or weaving. The girl would remain in her parents' home as long as either she made a real contribution to the family enterprise or her labor elsewhere was not more valuable to the family. An artisan's daughter might not leave home until marriage because she could learn increasingly valuable skills from her parents.

The labor of the much larger number of girls growing up on farms quickly became of little value to the family. These girls would then leave home, usually between the age of twelve and fourteen. They might go to another farm, but were more likely to migrate to a nearby town or city. They would rarely travel more than thirty miles from their parents' household and would then normally become servants in the household of an employer.

Having migrated from home, the young woman's chief goal was to accumulate a dowry. Her savings would allow her to make the necessary contribution to form a household with her husband. Marriage within the family economy was a joint economic undertaking, and the wife was expected to make an immediate contribution of capital for the establishment of the household. A young woman might well work for ten years or more to accumulate a dowry. This practice meant that marriage was usually postponed until a woman's mid- to late twenties.

Within the marriage, earning enough money or producing enough farm goods to ensure an adequate food supply was always the dominant concern. Domestic duties, childbearing, and child rearing were subordinate to economic survival. Consequently, couples would often practice birth control, usually through *coitus interruptus*, or withdrawal of the male before ejaculation. Young children were often placed with wet nurses so the mother could continue to contribute to the household economy. The wet nurse, in turn, was contributing to her own household. The child would be fully reintegrated into its family when it was weaned and would be expected to aid the family at an early age.

A married woman's work was in many ways a function of her husband's occupation. If the peasant household possessed enough land to support itself, the wife spent much of her time literally carrying things for her husband—water, food, seed, harvested grain, and the like. But few peasants had such adequate landholdings. If the husband had to do work other than farming, such as fishing or migrant labor, the wife might do the plowing, planting, and harvesting. In

Document: Priscilla Wakefield Demands More Occupations Be Opened to Women

At the end of the eighteenth century, several English women writers began to demand a wider life for women. Priscilla Wakefield was among such authors. She was concerned that women found themselves able to pursue only occupations that paid poorly. Often they were excluded from work on the grounds of their alleged physical weakness. She also believed that women should receive equal wages for equal work. Many of the issues she raised have yet to be adequately addressed on behalf of women.

From reading this passage, what do you understand to have been the arguments at the end of the eighteenth century to limit the kinds of employment that women might enter? Why did women receive lower wages for work similar to or the same as that done by men? What occupations traditionally filled by men does Wakefield believe women might also pursue?

Another heavy discouragement to the industry of women, is the inequality of the reward of their labor, compared with that of men; an injustice which pervades every species of employment performed by both sexes.

In employments which depend on bodily strength, the distinction is just; for it cannot be pretended that the generality of women can earn as much as men, when the produce of their labor is the result of corporeal exertion; but it is a subject of great regret, that this inequality should prevail even where an equal share of skill and application is exerted. Male stay-makers, mantua-makers, and hair-dressers, are better paid than female artists of the same professions; but surely it will never be urged as an apology for this disproportion, that women are not as capable of making stays, gowns, dressing hair, and similar arts, as men; if they are not superior to them, it can only be accounted for upon this principle, that the prices they receive for their labor are not sufficient to repay them for the expense of qualifying themselves for their business; and that they sink under the mortification of being regarded as artisans of inferior estimation. . . .

Besides these employments which are commonly performed by women, and those already shown to be suitable for such persons as are above the condition of hard labor, there are some professions and trades customarily in the hands of men, which might be conveniently exercised by either sex. —Watchmaking requiring more ingenuity than strength, seems peculiarly adapted to women; as do many parts of the business of stationer, particularly, ruling account books or making pens. The compounding of medicines in an apothecary's shop, requires no other talents than care and exactness; and if opening a vein occasionally be a indispensable requisite, a woman may acquire the capacity of doing it, for those of her own sex at least, without any reasonable objection. . . . Pastry and confectionery appear particularly consonant to the habits of women, though generally performed by men; perhaps the heat of the ovens, and the strength requisite to fill and empty them, may render male assistants necessary; but certain women are most eligible to mix up the ingredients, and prepare the various kinds of cakes for baking. —Light turnery and toy-making depend more upon dexterity and invention than force, and are therefore suitable work for women and children. . . .

Farming, as far as respects the theory, is commensurate with the powers of the female mind: nor is the practice of inspecting agricultural processes incompatible with the delicacy of their frames if their constitution be good.

From Priscilla Wakefield, *Reflections on the Present Condition of the Female Sex* (1798), (London, 1817), pp. 125–127, as quoted in Bridget Hill, ed., *Eighteenth-Century Women: An Anthology.* Copyright © 1984 George Allen & Unwin, pp. 227–228.

the city, the wife of an artisan or merchant often acted like a business manager. She might manage the household finances and participate in the trade or business. When her husband died, she might take over the business, perhaps hiring an artisan.

Finally, if economic disaster struck the family, more often than not it was the wife who organized what Olwen Hufton has called the "economy of expedients,"[1] within which family members might be sent off to find work elsewhere or even to beg in the streets.

In all phases of life within the family economy, women led active, often decisive roles. Industriousness rather than idleness was their lot in life. Finding a functional place in the household was essential to their well-being, but once that place had been found, their function was essential to the ongoing well-being of the household.

Children and the World of the Family Economy

Childbirth was a time of grave danger to both mother and infant, who were immediately exposed to the possible contraction of contagious diseases. Puerperal fever and other infections from unsterilized medical instruments were common. Not all midwives were skillful practitioners. Furthermore, the immense poverty and wretched housing conditions of most Europeans endangered the lives of the newborn child and the mother.

[1] "Women and the Family Economy in Eighteenth-Century France," *French Historical Studies* 9 (1975): 19.

DOCUMENT AN EDINBURGH PHYSICIAN DESCRIBES THE DANGERS OF CHILDBIRTH

Death in childbirth was a common occurrence throughout Europe until the twentieth century. This brief letter from an Edinburgh physician illustrates how devastating infectious diseases could be to women at the time of childbirth.

How does this passage illustrate a health danger that only women confronted? How might the likelihood of the death of oneself or a spouse in childbirth have affected one's attitudes toward children? How does this passage illustrate limitations on knowledge about disease in the eighteenth century?

We had puerperal fever in the infirmary last winter. It began about the end of February, when almost every woman, as soon as she was delivered, or perhaps about twenty-four hours after, was seized with it; and all of them died, though every method was tried to cure the disorder. What was singular, the women were in good health before they were brought to bed, though some of them had been long in the hospital before delivery. One woman had been dismissed from the ward before she was brought to bed; came into it some days after with her labor upon her; was easily delivered, and remained perfectly well for twenty-four hours, when she was seized with a shivering and the other symptoms of the fever. I caused her to be removed to another ward; yet notwithstanding all the care that was taken of her she died in the same manner as the others.

From a letter to Mr. White from a Dr. Young of Edinburgh, 21 November 1774, cited in C. White, *Treatise on the Management of Pregnant and Lying-In Women* (London, 1777), pp. 45–46, as quoted in Bridget Hill, ed., *Eighteenth-Century Women: An Anthology*. Copyright © 1984 George Allen & Unwin, p. 102.

However, the safe birth of a child was not always welcome. The child might be illegitimate or be another economic burden on an already hard-pressed household. Through at least the end of the seventeenth century, and to a lesser degree beyond it, various forms of infanticide were practiced, especially among the poor. Unwanted infants might be smothered or exposed to the elements. These practices were one result of both the ignorance and the prejudice surrounding contraception. Although many married couples seem to have succeeded in limiting their families, unmarried young men and women whose sexual relationships may have been the result of a fleeting acquaintance were less fortunate. Numerous young women, especially among servants, found themselves pregnant and without husbands. This situation and the consequent birth of illegitimate children seem to have become much more frequent during the eighteenth century. It probably arose from the more frequent migration of young people from their homes and the disturbance of traditional village life through enclosures (to be discussed later), the commercialization of agriculture, wars, and the late-century revolutions.

Few children in the 18th century were as privileged as these in this landed English family. Most began working to help support their families as soon as they were physically able. It was during the 18th century, however, that Europeans apparently began to view childhood as a distinct period in human development. Even though Arthur Devis has painted these children to look something like little adults, he has included various toys associated with childhood.

Arthur Devis (c. 1711–1787), "Children in an Interior," © 1742–1743, oil on canvas, 39 × 49 in. (99.0 × 125.5 cm), Yale Center for British Art, Paul Mellon Collection, B1978.43.5

Art and the World

"The Breakfast" and "The Return from Market"

Two Scenes of Domestic Life

What are known as *genre* paintings depict scenes of everyday life. Largely pioneered by the Dutch, such paintings became widespread throughout Europe during the eighteenth century. Genre painting made no claim to convey a message of universal importance. Furthermore, because the subject matter was domestic, people could enjoy these paintings without an extensive knowledge of history, classical literature, or the Bible.

French genre painters focused mostly on what would become known as the "woman's sphere" in the home. But that female domestic sphere, as illustrated in these works of Boucher and Chardin, was a complex world with numerous compartments. The home might be the feminine empire, but it was an empire of many provinces, just as there were different kinds of homes among the various social classes.

Boucher's *The Breakfast* (1739) portrays the breakfast room of a wealthy, probably nonaristocratic, family, filled with the expensive consumer goods available in Paris shops drawn from around the world. (Note, for example, the Chinese porcelain figure sitting on the shelf.) This domestic interior lacks any suggestion of political awareness or engagement in economic productivity. It is a scene of domestic, feminine consumption and child rearing such as Rousseau would advocate in *Emile* (1762). (See Chapter 23.)

Chardin's *The Return from the Market* (1738) presents another level of the domestic sphere: that of the servant. The woman in the painting appears to work in the home of a

F. Boucher. *The Breakfast*. 1739. Paris. Louvre. Scala/Art Resource, NY

person of moderate means, perhaps a merchant. In this and other of his paintings, Chardin avoids the world of domestic consumption that appears in Boucher's painting. His interiors are worlds of domestic order and tranquillity, set aside from the bustle of an eighteenth-century city street. Domestic servants in the eighteenth and nineteenth centuries were overwhelmingly women. Yet even among them, there existed a clear social hierarchy. This woman would have held a lower status than that of a governess who looked after the family's children.

Jean Baptiste Chardin, 1699–1799. *The Return from the Market* (*La Pourvoyeuse*). (1738). French. Musée du Louvre, Paris/SuperStock

Chardin was known for his remarkable ability to bring quiet dignity and warmth to the work of servants. He also suggests a certain dynamic element in the life of the family: The servant putting down the bread appears to be listening to the conversation in the other room. Later genre painters, such as the English artist Hogarth, would often suggest a strong moralizing tone, but Chardin is willing to portray his scenes without comment. He does not intrude upon the scene, which assumes a kind of timeless quality in the sense that households have needed to secure bread each day from time immemorial; this return from market is simply the most recent example. There is as much of a relaxed quality to Chardin's portrayal of this scene as there is a sense of energized arrangement in Boucher's. Chardin described his own painting as a kind of craft rather than a work of inspiration or academic rules. He seems to see his own painting as a kind of dignified everyday work, akin to the work performed by the woman returning from market.

Albert Boime, *Art in an Age of Revolution, 1750–1800* (Chicago: University of Chicago Press, 1987); Norman Bryson, *Looking at the Overlooked: Four Essays on Still Life Painting* (Cambridge, MA.: Harvard University Press, 1990); Richard Rand, *Intimate Encounters: Love and Domesticity in Eighteenth-Century France* (Princeton, NJ: Princeton University Press, 1997).

In the late seventeenth and the early eighteenth centuries, reflecting a new interest in preserving the lives of abandoned children, large foundling hospitals were established in all the major nations. (Earlier foundling hospitals had been fewer and smaller than these new institutions.) Two of the most famous, the Paris Foundling Hospital (1670) and the London Foundling Hospital (1739), cared for thousands of children. The demands on their resources vastly increased during the eighteenth century. For example, early in the century, an average of about 1,700 children were admitted to the Paris Foundling Hospital annually. But 7,676 were admitted in the peak year of 1772. Not all of those children came from Paris. Many had been taken to the city from the provinces, where local foundling homes and hospitals were also overburdened. The London Foundling Hospital lacked the income to deal with all of the children brought to it and, in the middle of the eighteenth century, found itself compelled to choose children for admission by a lottery system.

Sadness and tragedy were the lot of abandoned children. Most were illegitimate infants drawn from across the social spectrum, but many seem to have been left with the foundling hospitals because their parents could not support them. The numbers of abandoned children increased when food prices rose in Paris. Parents would sometimes leave personal tokens or saints' medals on the abandoned baby in the vain hope that they might eventually be able to reclaim the child. Few children were so reclaimed. Leaving a child at a foundling hospital did not guarantee its survival. In Paris, only about 10 percent of all abandoned children lived to the age of ten years.

Despite these perils, children did grow up and come of age across Europe. The world of the child may not have received the kind of attention it does today, but during the eighteenth century the seeds of that modern sensibility were sown. Particularly among the upper classes, new interest arose in the education of children. As economic skills became more demanding, literacy became more valuable and more common during the century. However, most education remained firmly in the hands of the churches. Most Europeans remained illiterate. It was not until the late nineteenth century that the world of childhood and the process of education became inextricably linked. Then children would be reared to become members of a national citizenry. In the Old Regime, they were reared to make their contribution to the economy of their parents' family and then to set up their own households.

Growth of Agriculture and Population

Thus far this chapter has examined those groups who sought stability and generally resisted change. Other groups, however, wished to pursue significant new directions in social and economic life. The remainder of this chapter will consider those forces and developments that would during the next century transform first Europe and then much of the rest of the world. These developments first appeared in agriculture.

The Revolution in Agriculture

The main goal of traditional European peasant society was to ensure the stability of the local food supply. That supply was never certain and became more uncertain the farther east one traveled. A failed harvest meant not only hardship but death from either outright starvation or protracted debility. Food was often harder to find in the country than in cities because city governments usually stored reserve supplies of grain.

Poor harvests also played havoc with prices. Smaller supplies or larger demand raised grain prices. Even small increases in the cost of food could squeeze peasant or artisan families. If prices increased sharply, many of those families fell back on poor relief from their local government or the church. What made the situation of food supply and prices so difficult was the peasants' sense of helplessness before the whims of nature and the marketplace. Despite differences in rural customs throughout Europe, peasants resisted changes that they felt might endanger the sure supply of food, which they generally believed traditional cultivation practices ensured.

During the century, historians now believe, bread prices slowly but steadily rose, spurred largely by population growth. This put pressure on all of the poor. The prices rose faster than urban wages and brought no appreciable advantage to the small peasant producer. On the other hand, the rise in grain prices benefited landowners and those wealthier peasants who had surplus grain to sell.

The increasing price of grain allowed landlords to improve their income and lifestyle. They began a series of innovations in farm production that are known as the *agricultural revolution.*

New Crops and New Methods This movement began during the sixteenth and seventeenth centuries in the Low Countries, where Dutch landlords and farmers devised better ways to build dykes and to drain land so that they could farm more extensive areas. They also experimented with new crops, such as clover and turnips, that would increase the supply of animal fodder and replenish the soil.

These methods were extensively adopted in England during the early eighteenth century. There, new methods of farming, new crops, and new modes of landholding eventually led to greater productivity. This advance in food production was necessary for an industrial society to develop.

It ensured adequate food for the cities and freed surplus agricultural labor for industrial production. The changing modes of agriculture sponsored by the landlords undermined the assumptions of traditional peasant production. Farming now took place not only to provide the local food supply but also to earn the landlord a handsome profit.

ENCLOSURE REPLACES OPEN-FIELD METHOD Many of the agricultural innovations, which were adopted only slowly, were incompatible with the existing organization of land in Britain. Small cultivators who lived in village communities still farmed most of the soil. Each farmer tilled an assortment of unconnected strips. The two- or three-field systems of rotation left much land fallow and unproductive each year. Animals grazed on the common land in the summer and on the stubble of the harvest in the winter. Until at least the middle of the eighteenth century the decisions about what crops would be planted were made communally. The entire system discouraged improvement and favored the poorer farmers, who needed the common land and stubble fields for their animals. The village method made it almost impossible to increase pasture land and with it the size of herds and the production of manure for fertilizer. Traditional methods aimed to produce a steady but not a growing supply of food.

In 1700 approximately half the arable land in Britain was farmed by this open-field method. By the second half of the century the rising price of wheat encouraged landlords to consolidate or enclose their lands to increase production. The enclosures were intended to use land more rationally and to raise profits. The process involved the fencing of common lands, the reclamation of previously untilled waste, and the transformation of strips into block fields. These procedures disrupted the economic and social life of the countryside. Riots often ensued. Because many British farmers either owned their strips or rented them in a manner that amounted to ownership, the larger landlords had usually to resort to parliamentary acts to legalize the enclosure of the land, which they owned but rented to the farmers. Because the large landowners controlled Parliament, such measures passed easily. Between 1761 and 1792, almost 500,000 acres were enclosed through parliamentary act, as compared with 75,000 acres between 1727 and 1760. In 1801 a general enclosure act streamlined the process.

The enclosures have remained controversial. By permitting the extension of both farming and innovation, they increased food production on larger agricultural units. However, they also disrupted the small traditional communities. They forced off the land some independent farmers, who had needed the common pasturage, and very poor cottagers, who had lived on the reclaimed waste land. However, the enclosures did not depopulate the countryside. In some counties where the enclosures took place, the population increased. New soil had come into production, and services subsidiary to farming also expanded.

LIMITED IMPROVEMENTS IN EASTERN EUROPE Improving agriculture tended to characterize farm production west of the Elbe. Dutch farming was efficient. In France, despite the efforts of the government to improve agriculture, enclosures were restricted. Yet there was much discussion about improving agricultural methods. These new procedures benefited the ruling classes because better agriculture increased their incomes and assured a larger food supply, which discouraged social unrest.

Grain production lay at the heart of 18th-century farming. In this engraving farm workers can be seen threshing wheat, winnowing the grain, and finally putting the grain in bags so it can be carried to a mill and ground into flour. In many cases the mill would be owned by the local landlord, who would charge peasants for its use.
Bildarchiv Preussischer Kulturbesitz

In Prussia, Austria, Poland, and Russia, agricultural improvement was minimal. Nothing in the relationship between serf and lord encouraged innovation. In eastern Europe, the chief method of increasing production was to farm previously untilled lands. By extending tillage the great landlords sought to squeeze more labor from their serfs rather than greater productivity from the soil. As in the West, the goal was increased profits for the landlords. But on the whole, eastern European landlords were much less ambitious and successful. The only significant nutritional gain their efforts achieved was the introduction of maize and the potato. Livestock production did not increase significantly.

Population Expansion

Agricultural improvement was both a cause and a result of an immense expansion in the population of Europe. The current population explosion seems to have had its origins in the eighteenth century. Exact figures are lacking, but the best estimates suggest that in 1700 Europe's population, excluding the European provinces of the Ottoman Empire, was between 100 million and 120 million people. By 1800 the figure had risen to almost 190 million, and by 1850 to 260 million. The population of England and Wales rose from 6 million in 1750 to over 10 million in 1800. France grew from 18 million in 1715 to approximately 26 million in 1789. Russia's population increased from 19 million in 1722 to 29 million in 1766. Such extraordinary sustained growth put new demands on all resources and considerable pressure on existing social organization.

The population expansion occurred across the Continent in both the country and the cities. Only a limited consensus exists about the causes of this growth. There was a clear decline in the death rate. There were fewer wars and somewhat fewer epidemics in the eighteenth century. Hygiene and sanitation also improved. But changes in the food supply itself may have been the chief reason for sustained population growth. One contributing factor was improved and expanding grain production. Another, even more important, was the introduction in the eighteenth century of widespread cultivation of a New World tuber, the potato. Enough potatoes could be raised on a single acre to feed one peasant's family for an entire year. With this more certain food supply, more children could be reared, and more could survive.

The Eighteenth-Century Industrial Revolution

An Event in World History

In the second half of the eighteenth century the European economy began to industrialize. This development, more than any other single factor, distinguished Europe and eventually North America from the rest of the world for the next two centuries. The consumer products of the slowly industrializing businesses gave Europeans vast amounts of new goods to sell throughout the world and thus encouraged more international trade in which Western nations supplied the finished goods in exchange for raw materials. As a consequence, the prosperity of other areas of the globe became economically dependent on European and American demand. The wealth achieved through this uneven commerce allowed Europeans to dominate world markets for almost two centuries.

Furthermore, by the early nineteenth century iron and steel production and the new technologies of manufacture allowed European states and later the United States to build more powerful military forces, especially navies, than those of Africa, Latin America, or Asia. Both the economic and the military dominance of the West arose directly from the industrial achievement.

Much of the history of the non-Western world from the middle of the eighteenth century to the present can be understood in terms of how the nonindustrialized nations initially reacted to the penetration of their world by Europeans and Americans made wealthy and powerful through industrialized economies. Africa and Latin America became generally dependent economies. Japan, by the middle of the nineteenth century, decided it must imitate the European pattern and did so successfully. China did not make that decision and became indirectly ruled by Europeans. The Chinese revolutions of the twentieth century have largely represented efforts to achieve real self-direction. Southeast Asia and the Middle East became drawn into the network of resource supply to the West; they could achieve movement toward economic independence only through imitation or, like Arab nations in the early 1970s, by refusing to supply oil to the West. The process of industrialization that commenced in small factories in eighteenth-century Europe has changed the world more than any other single development in the last two centuries.

The European Industrial Revolution of the eighteenth century constituted the achievement of sustained economic growth. Previously, production had been limited. The economy of a province or a country might grow, but soon reached a plateau. However, since the late eighteenth century the economy of Europe has expanded relatively uninterruptedly. Depressions and recessions have been temporary, and even during such economic downturns the Western economy has continued to grow.

At considerable social cost and dislocation, industrialism produced more goods and services than ever before in human history. Industrialism in Europe eventually overcame the economy of scarcity. The new means of production demanded new kinds of skills, new discipline in work, and a large labor force. The produced goods met immediate consumer demand and created new demands. In the long run, industrialism clearly raised the standard of living; the poverty in which most Europeans had always lived was overcome. Industrialization provided human beings greater control over the forces of nature than they had ever known.

The wealth produced by industrialism upset the political and social structures of the Old Regime and led to reforms. The economic elite of the emerging industrial society would eventually challenge the political dominance of the aristocracy. Industrialization also undermined traditional communities and, along with the growth of cities, displaced many people. These processes repeated themselves virtually everywhere that industrialization occurred during the next two centuries.

INDUSTRIAL LEADERSHIP OF GREAT BRITAIN

Great Britain was the home of the Industrial Revolution and, until the late nineteenth century, remained the industrial leader of Europe and the world. Several factors contributed to the early start of industrialization in Britain. Britain was the single largest free-trade area in Europe, with good roads and waterways without tolls or other internal trade barriers. There were rich deposits of coal and iron ore. The political structure was stable, and property was absolutely secure. A sound system of banking and public credit created a good investment climate. Taxation in Britain was heavy, but it received legal approval from Parliament. Taxes were efficiently and fairly collected, largely from indirect taxes with all regions and persons from all classes paying the same taxes. Besides satisfying domestic consumer demand, the British economy also benefited from the demand for goods from the North American colonies.

Finally, British society was relatively mobile. Persons who had money or could earn it could rise socially. The British aristocracy would accept people who had amassed large fortunes. No one of these factors preordained the British advance toward industrialism. The combination of them, however, plus the progressive state of British agriculture, provided the nation with a marginal advantage in the creation of a new mode of economic production. No less important, the wars and revolutions of the late eighteenth and early nineteenth centuries disrupted those parts of the Continent where an industrialized economy might also have begun to develop.

While this economic development was occurring, people did not call it a *revolution.* That term came to be applied to the British economic phenomena only after the French Revolution, when continental writers contended that what had taken place in Britain was the economic equivalent of the political events in France. From this comparison arose the concept of an *industrial* revolution. The process, however, was revolutionary less in its pace, which was on the whole rather slow, than in its implications for the future of European society.

NEW METHODS OF TEXTILE PRODUCTION Although eighteenth-century society was devoted primarily to agriculture, manufacturing permeated the countryside. The same peasants who tilled the land in spring and summer often spun thread or wove textiles in winter. Under the *domestic* or *putting-out* system, agents of urban textile merchants took wool or other unfinished fiber to the homes of peasants, who spun it into thread. The agent then transported the thread to other peasants, who wove it into the finished product. The merchant sold the wares. In literally thousands of peasant cottages from Ireland to Austria stood either a spinning wheel or a hand loom. Sometimes the spinners or weavers owned their own equipment, but more often than not, by the middle of the century, the merchant capitalist owned the machinery as well as the raw material.

What must be kept constantly in mind is that eighteenth-century industrial development took place within a rural setting. The peasant family living in a one- or two-room cottage, not the factory, was the basic unit of production. The family economy, rather than the industrial factory economy, characterized the century.

The domestic system of textile production was a basic feature of this family economy. However, by midcentury bottlenecks had developed within the domestic system. The demand for cotton textiles was growing more rapidly than production. This demand arose particularly in Great Britain, whose growing population wanted cotton textiles, as did its colonies in North America. The most famous inventions of the Industrial Revolution were devised in response to this consumer demand for cotton textiles.

Cotton textile weavers had the technical capacity to produce enough fabric to satisfy demand. However, the spinners could not produce as much thread as the weavers needed and could use. This imbalance had been created during the 1730s by James Kay's invention of the flying shuttle, which increased the productivity of the weavers. Thereafter, manufacturers and merchants offered prizes for the invention of a machine to eliminate this bottleneck. In about 1765 James Hargreaves (d. 1778) invented the spinning jenny. Initially this machine allowed 16 spindles of thread to be spun, but by the close of the century it included as many as 120 spindles.

The spinning jenny broke the bottleneck between the productive capacity of the spinners and the weavers, but it was still a piece of machinery that was used in the cottage. The invention that took cotton textile manufacture from the home to the factory was Richard Arkwright's (1732–1792) water frame, patented in 1769. It was a water-powered device designed to permit the production of a purely cotton fabric rather than a cotton fabric containing linen fiber for durability. Eventually Arkwright lost his patent rights, and other manufacturers were able to use his invention freely. As a result, numerous factories sprang up in the countryside near streams that provided the necessary water power. From the 1780s onward the cotton industry could meet an ever-expanding demand. Between 1780 and 1800 cotton output increased by 800 percent. By 1815 cotton composed 40 percent of the value of British domestic exports, and by 1830 just over 50 percent.

THE STEAM ENGINE The new technology in textile manufacture vastly increased cotton production and revolutionized a major consumer industry. But the invention that more than any other enabled industrialization to grow on itself and expand into one area of production after another was the steam engine. This machine provided for the first time in human history a steady and essentially unlimited source of inanimate power. Unlike engines powered by water or wind, the steam engine, driven by the burning of coal, was a portable source of industrial power that did not fail or falter as the seasons of the year changed. Unlike human or animal power, the steam engine depended on mineral energy that never tired. Finally, the steam engine could be applied to many industrial and, eventually, transportation uses.

The first practical engine using steam power was invented by Thomas Newcomen (1663–1729) in the early eighteenth century. It was large, inefficient in its use of energy, and practically untransportable. Nonetheless, English mine operators used it to pump water out of coal and tin mines. By the late eighteenth century almost a hundred Newcomen machines were operating in the mining districts of England.

During the 1760s James Watt (1736–1819) began to experiment with a model of a Newcomen machine at the University of Glasgow. He gradually understood that if the condenser were separated from the piston and the cylinder, much greater efficiency would result. In 1769 he patented his new invention, but his design required exceedingly precise metalwork. Watt soon found a partner in Matthew Boulton (1728–1809), a toy manufacturer in Birmingham, the city with the most skilled metalworkers in Britain. Watt and Boulton in turn consulted with John Wilkinson (1728–1808), a cannon manufacturer, to find ways to drill the precise metal cylinders required by Watt's design. In 1776 the Watt steam engine found its first commercial application pumping water from mines.

The use of the steam engine spread slowly because until 1800 Watt retained the exclusive patent rights and was reluctant to modify the engine. Boulton eventually persuaded him to adapt the engines for use in running cotton mills. By the early nineteenth century the steam engine had become the prime mover for all industry. With its application to ships and then to wagons on iron rails, it also revolutionized transportation.

During the 18th century, most goods were produced in small workshops, such as this English blacksmith shop painted by Joseph Wright of Derby (1734–1797), or in the homes of artisans. Not until very late in the century, with the early stages of industrialization, did a few factories appear. Joseph Wright of Derby, "The Blacksmith's Shop," signed and dated 1771, oil on canvas, 50 × 41 in. (128.3 × 104.0 cm). Yale Center for British Art, Paul Mellon Collection.

IRON PRODUCTION The manufacture of high-quality iron has been basic to modern industrial development. It constitutes the chief element of all heavy industry and land or sea transport and is the material out of which most productive machinery itself has been manufactured. During the early eighteenth century British ironmakers produced less than 25,000 tons annually. Three factors held back the production of the metal. First, charcoal rather than coke was used to smelt the ore. Charcoal, which is derived from wood, was becoming scarce, and it did not burn at as high a temperature as coke, which is derived from coal. Second, until the perfection of the steam engine, insufficient blasts could be achieved in the furnaces. Finally, the demand for iron was limited. The elimination of the first two problems eliminated the third.

In the course of the century, British ironmakers began to use coke, and the steam engine provided new power for the blast furnaces. Coke was abundant because of Britain's large coal deposits. The steam engine both improved iron production and increased the demand for iron.

In 1784 Henry Cort (1740–1800) introduced a new method for melting and stirring the molten ore. Cort's process produced a purer iron. He also developed a rolling mill that continually shaped the still-molten metal into bars, rails, or other forms. Previously, the metal had been pounded into these forms.

All of these innovations achieved a better, more versatile, and cheaper product. The demand for iron grew as its price went down. By the early nineteenth century annual British iron production amounted to over a million tons. The lower cost of iron in turn lowered the cost of steam engines and allowed them to be used more widely.

CITIES

PATTERNS OF PREINDUSTRIAL URBANIZATION

Remarkable changes occurred in the pattern of city growth between 1500 and 1800. In 1500 there were approximately 156 cities within Europe (excluding Hungary and Russia) with a population greater than 10,000. Only four of those cities—Paris, Milan, Venice, and Naples—had more than 100,000 inhabitants. By 1800 approximately 363 cities had 10,000 or more inhabitants, and 17 of those had populations larger than 100,000. The percentage of the European population living in urban areas had risen from just over 5 percent to just over 9 percent. The urban concentration had also shifted from southern, Mediterranean Europe to the north.

These raw figures conceal significant changes that took place in the manner in which cities grew and the population distributed itself. Major urban development in the sixteenth century was followed in the seventeenth by leveling and even decline. New growth began in the early eighteenth century and accelerated thereafter.

GROWTH OF CAPITALS AND PORTS Capitals and ports were the urban areas that displayed the most growth and vigor between 1600 and 1750. This reflects the success of monarchical state building and the consequent burgeoning of bureaucracies, armies, courts, and other groups related to the process of government who lived in the capitals. The growth of port cities in turn reflects the expansion of European overseas trade and most especially that of the Atlantic routes. With the exception of Lyons, France, significant growth did not take place in industrial cities. Furthermore, between 1600 and 1750 cities with populations of fewer than 40,000 inhabitants declined. These cities included older landlocked trading centers, medieval industrial cities, and ecclesiastical centers. They contributed less to the new political regimes, and since rural labor was cheaper than urban labor, cities with concentrations of labor declined as production sites were moved from urban workshops into the countryside.

EMERGENCE OF NEW CITIES AND GROWTH OF SMALL TOWNS After 1750 a new pattern emerged. Large cities grew more slowly. New cities arose, and older smaller cities began to grow. Several factors were at work in the process, which Jan De Vries has termed "an urban growth from below."[2] First, there was the general overall population increase. Second, the early stages of the Industrial Revolution, particularly in Britain, occurred in the countryside and tended to aid the growth of smaller towns and cities located near the factories. Factory organization itself fostered new concentrations of population. But cities also grew where there was little industrialization, probably because of the new prosperity of European agriculture. Greater agricultural production aided the growth of nearby market towns and other urban centers that served agriculture or allowed more prosperous farmers to have access to the consumer goods and recreation they wanted. This new pattern of urban growth—new cities and the expansion of smaller existing cities—would continue into the nineteenth century.

URBAN CLASSES

Social divisions were as marked in the cities of the eighteenth century as they were in the industrial centers of the nineteenth.

THE UPPER CLASSES At the top of the urban social structure stood a generally small group of nobles, large merchants, bankers, financiers, clergy, and government officials. These men (and they were always men) controlled the political and economic affairs of the town. Normally they constituted a self-appointed and self-electing oligarchy who governed the city through its corporation or city council. These rights of self-government had generally been granted by a royal charter that gave the city corporation its authority and the power to select its own members. In a few cities on the Continent artisan guilds controlled the

CHRONOLOGY

MAJOR INVENTIONS IN THE TEXTILE-MANUFACTURING REVOLUTION

1733	James Kay's flying shuttle
1765	James Hargreaves's spinning jenny (patent 1770)
1769	James Watt's steam engine patent
1769	Richard Arkwright's water frame patent
1787	Edmund Cartwright's power loom

[2] "Patterns of Urbanization in Pre-Industrial Europe, 1500–1800," in H. Schnal, ed., *Patterns of European Urbanization Since 1500* (London: Croom Helm, 1981), p. 103.

Consumption of all forms of consumer goods increased greatly in the 18th century. This engraving illustrates a shop, probably in Paris. Here women, working apparently for a woman manager, are making dresses and hats to meet the demands of the fashion trade. Bildarchiv Preussischer Kulturbesitz

corporations, but most councils were under the influence of the local nobility and the commercial elite.

THE MIDDLE CLASS The prosperous but not immensely wealthy merchants, tradesmen, bankers, and professional people were the most dynamic element of the urban population and constituted the group traditionally regarded as the middle class, or *bourgeoisie.* The middle class had less wealth than most nobles but more than urban artisans. Middle-class people lived in the cities and towns, and their sources of income had little or nothing to do with the land. The middle class normally supported reform, change, and economic growth. Middle-class businessmen and professionals often found their pursuit of profit and prestige blocked by aristocratic privilege and social exclusiveness. The bourgeoisie (and some progressive aristocrats) also wanted more rational regulations for trade and commerce.

During the eighteenth century the middle class and the aristocracy frequently collided. The former often imitated the lifestyle of the latter, and nobles increasingly embraced the commercial spirit of the middle class. The bourgeoisie was not rising to challenge the nobility; both were seeking to enhance their existing power and prestige. However, tradition and political connection gave the advantage to the nobility. Consequently, as the century passed, the middle class increasingly resented the aristocracy. That resentment became more bitter as the bourgeoisie grew wealthier and more numerous, and the aristocratic control of political and ecclesiastical power tightened. The growing influence of the nobility seemed to mean that the middle class would continue to be excluded from the political decisions of the day.

On the other hand, the middle class tended to fear the lower urban classes as much as they resented the nobility. The lower orders constituted a potentially violent element in society; a potential threat to property; and, in their poverty, a drain on national resources. The lower orders, however, were much more varied than either the city aristocracy or the middle class cared to admit.

During the Old Regime, European Jews were separated from non-Jews, typically in districts known as ghettos. Relegated to the least desirable section of a city or to rural villages, most lived in poverty. This watercolor painting depicts a street in Kazimlesz, the Jewish quarter of Cracow, Poland. Judaica Collection Max Berger, Vienna Austria/Erich Lessing/Art Resource, N.Y.

ARTISANS The segment of the urban population that suffered from both the grasping of the middle class and the local nobility was made up of shopkeepers, artisans, and wage earners. These people constituted the single largest group in any city. They included grocers, butchers, fishmongers, carpenters, cabinetmakers, smiths, printers, handloom weavers, and tailors, to give but a few examples. They had their own culture, values, and institutions. Like the peasants of the countryside, they were in many respects conservative. Their economic position was highly vulnerable. If a poor harvest raised the price of food, their own businesses suffered.

The entire life of these artisans and shopkeepers centered on their work. They usually lived near or at their place of employment. Most of them worked in shops with fewer than a half-dozen other craftsmen. Their primary institution had historically been the guild, but by the eighteenth century most guilds had lost influence.

Nevertheless, the guilds were not to be ignored. They played a conservative role. They did not seek economic growth or innovation. They attempted to preserve the jobs and the skills of their members. They still were able in many countries to determine who might and might not pursue a particular craft. They attempted to prevent too many people from learning a particular skill. The guilds also provided a framework for social and economic advancement. A young boy might become an apprentice to learn a craft or trade. After several years he would be made a journeyman. Still later, if successful, he might become a master. The artisan could also receive certain social benefits from the guilds, including aid for his family during sickness or the promise of admission into the guild for his son. The guilds constituted the chief protection for artisans against the operation of the commercial market. They were particularly strong in central Europe.

THE JEWISH POPULATION: AGE OF THE GHETTO

Although the small Jewish communities of Amsterdam and other western European cities became famous for their intellectual life and financial institutions, most European Jews lived in eastern Europe. In the eighteenth century and thereafter, no fewer than 3 million Jews dwelled in Poland, Lithuania, and Ukraine. There were perhaps 150,000 in the Habsburg lands, primarily in Bohemia, around 1760. Fewer than 100,000 lived in Germany and approximately 40,000 in France. England and Holland had Jewish populations of fewer than 10,000. There were even smaller groups of Jews in Italy.

In 1762 Catherine the Great of Russia specifically excluded Jews from a manifesto that welcomed foreigners to settle in Russia. She relaxed the exclusion a few years later. After the first partition of Poland in 1772, to be discussed in Chapter 23, Russia had a large Jewish population. The partition also resulted in larger Jewish communities in Prussia and Austria.

Jews dwelled in most nations without enjoying the rights and privileges of other subjects of the monarchs, unless such rights were specifically granted to them. They were regarded as aliens whose status might well be changed at the whim of local rulers or the monarchical government.

No matter where they dwelled, the Jews of Europe under the Old Regime lived apart from non-Jews. In cities they usually lived in distinct districts known as *ghettos*; in the countryside, in primarily Jewish villages. Thus this period in Jewish history, which may be said to have begun with the expulsion of the Jews from Spain in 1492, is known as the age of the ghetto, or separate community. Jews were also treated as a distinct people religiously and legally. In Poland for much of the century they were virtually self-governing. Elsewhere they lived under the burden of discriminatory legislation. Except in England, Jews could not mix in the mainstream of the societies in which they dwelled.

During the seventeenth century a few Jews helped finance the wars of major rulers. These financiers often grew close to the rulers and came to be known as "court Jews." They tended to marry among themselves. Perhaps the most famous was Samuel Oppenheimer (1630–1703), who helped the Habsburgs finance their struggle against the Turks, including the defense of Vienna. Their position at court and their financial abilities may have brought them privilege and fame, but court Jews, including Oppenheimer, often failed to have their loans repaid.

Unlike the court Jews, however, most European Jews lived in poverty. They occupied the most undesirable sections of cities or poor rural villages. A few were moneylenders, but most worked at the lowest occupations. Their religious beliefs, rituals, and community set them apart. A wall of laws and social institutions—as well as the physical walls of the ghetto—kept them in positions of social inferiority.

Under the Old Regime, it is important to emphasize, this discrimination was based on religious separateness. Jews who converted to Christianity were welcomed, even if not always warmly, into the major political and social institutions of European society. But until the late eighteenth century those Jews who remained loyal to their faith were subject to various religious, civil, and social disabilities. They were not free to pursue the professions or often change residence, and they stood outside the political structures of the nations in which they lived. Jews could be expelled from the cities where they dwelled, and their property could be confiscated. They were regarded as socially and religiously inferior. They could be required to listen to sermons that insulted them and their religion. Their children could be taken away from them and given Christian instruction. And they knew their non-Jewish neighbors might suddenly turn violently against them. As will be seen in subsequent chapters, however, the end of the Old Regime brought major changes in the lives of Jews and in their relationship to the larger culture.

In World Perspective

THE EUROPEAN OLD REGIME

This chapter opened by describing eighteenth-century European society as traditional, hierarchical, corporate, and privileged. These features had characterized Europe and much of the rest of the world for centuries. Virtually every society on the globe at the opening of the eighteenth century was characterized by marked social dependence and discrepancies between great wealth and poverty. All societies also confronted the grave problems of scarce food supplies.

The eighteenth century witnessed important changes in all these societies. The population explosion was a global event not limited to Europe. Its exact causes still remain uncertain, but whether in Europe or China, an improved food supply resulting from expanded acreage and new crops helped support the larger population. In China, lands once thought to be marginal were settled. Agricultural techniques improved in Europe, but emigration to the New World also opened vast expanses of land. In contrast to Europe, the farmland of China continued to be cultivated by clans or communities. But in all cases, the vast, expanding population created pressures on the existing social structures.

Another striking similarity between China and Europe is apparent in the growth of commerce during the eighteenth century. In both cultures banking was improved and a more certain money supply established. Agriculture became more commercialized, with more money payments. As in Europe, Chinese cities expanded. During the eighteenth century Chinese trade grew within Asia as well as within a larger world market. However, only Europe experienced industrialization.

Eighteenth-century Japan stood, of course, in marked contrast to both Europe and China. Tokugawa rule had achieved remarkable stability, but Japan had chosen not to enter the world-trading network, except as a depot for Dutch and Chinese goods. The population grew less rapidly than that of Europe or China, and the general economy seems to have grown slowly. Like the situation in many European cities, guilds controlled manufacture. In all these respects, Japan in the eighteenth century sought to spurn innovation and preserve stable tradition.

Throughout the eighteenth century, Africa continued to supply slave labor to both North and South America. The slave trade drew Africa deeply into the transatlantic economy.

Latin America remained at least in theory the monopolized preserve of Spain and Portugal. But that monopoly could not survive the expansion of the British economy and the determination of Britain to enter the Latin American market. At the same time, British forces established a hegemony in mid-eighteenth-century India that would last almost two centuries.

Seen in this world context, European society stood on the brink of a new era in which the social, economic, and political relationships of centuries would be destroyed. The commercial spirit and the values of the marketplace clashed with the traditional values and practices of peasants and guilds. That commercial spirit proved to be a major vehicle of social change; by the early nineteenth century it led increasingly to a conception of human beings as individuals rather than as members of communities.

The expansion of the European population further stimulated change and challenge to tradition, hierarchy, and corporateness. The traditional economic and social organization had presupposed a stable or declining population. A larger population meant that new ways had to be devised to solve old problems. The social hierarchy had to accommodate itself to more people. Corporate groups, such as the guilds, had to confront an expanded labor force. New wealth meant that birth would eventually cease to determine social relationships, except in regard to the social roles assigned to the two sexes.

Finally, the conflicting political ambitions of the monarchies, the nobilities, and the middle class generated innovation. The monarchies wanted to make their nations rich enough to wage war. The nobilities wished to reassert their privileges. The middle class, in all of its diversity, was growing wealthier from trade, commerce, and the practice of the professions. Its members wanted social prestige and influence equal to their wealth.

All of these factors meant that the society of the late eighteenth century stood at the close of one era of European history and at the opening of another. However, as these social and economic changes became connected to the world economy, the transformation of Europe led to the transformation of much of the non-European world. For the first time in the history of the world, major changes in one region left virtually no corner of the globe politically or economically untouched. By the close of the eighteenth century a movement toward world interconnectedness and interdependence that had no real precedent in terms of depth and extent had begun, and it has not yet ended.

REVIEW QUESTIONS

1. Describe the privileges of the various European nobilities. How did they differ as one moved west to east across the Continent? What was the economic basis of the life of the nobility? What authority did they have over other groups in their various societies?
2. How would you define the term *family economy*? What were some of the particular characteristics of the northwestern European household as opposed to that in eastern Europe? In what ways were the lives of women constrained by the family economy in preindustrial Europe?
3. What caused the agricultural revolution? How did technological innovations help change European agriculture? To what extent did the English aristocracy contribute to the agricultural revolution? What were some of the reasons for peasant revolts in Europe in the eighteenth century?
4. What factors explain the increase in Europe's population in the eighteenth century? What were the effects of the population explosion? How did population growth contribute to changes in consumption?
5. What caused the Industrial Revolution of the eighteenth century? What were some of the technological innovations and why were they important? Why did Great Britain take the lead in the Industrial Revolution? How did the consumer contribute to the Industrial Revolution?
6. Describe city life during the eighteenth century. Were all European cities of the same character? What changes had taken place in the distribution of population in cities and towns? Compare the lifestyle of the upper class with those of the middle and lower classes.

SUGGESTED READINGS

I. T. BEREND AND G. RANKI, *The European Periphery and Industrialization, 1780–1914* (1982). Examines the experience of eastern and Mediterranean Europe.

J. BLUM, *Lord and Peasant in Russia from the Ninth to the Nineteenth Century* (1961). A thorough and wide-ranging discussion.

J. BLUM, *The End of the Old Order in Rural Europe* (1978). The most comprehensive treatment of life in rural Europe, especially central and eastern, from the early eighteenth through the mid–nineteenth centuries.

F. BRAUDEL, *The Structures of Everyday Life: The Limits of the Possible*, trans. by M. Kochan (1982). A magisterial survey by the most important social historian of our time.

J. CANNON, *Aristocratic Century: The Peerage of Eighteenth-Century England* (1985). A useful treatment based on the most recent research.

G. CHAUSSINAND-NOGARET, *The French Nobility in the Eighteenth Century* (1985). Suggests that culture, not class, was the decisive element in late-eighteenth-century French society.

P. DEANE, *The First Industrial Revolution*, 2nd ed. (1979). A well-balanced and systematic treatment.

J. DE VRIES, *The Economy of Europe in an Age of Crisis, 1600–1750* (1976). An excellent overview that sets forth the main issues.

J. DE VRIES, *European Urbanization 1500–1800* (1984). The most important and far-ranging of recent treatments of the subject.

W. DOYLE, *Venality: The Sale of Offices in Eighteenth-Century France* (1997). Examines the manner in which the phenomenon characterized much of the society.

P. EARLE, *The Making of the English Middle Class: Business, Community, and Family Life in London, 1660–1730* (1989). The most careful study of the subject.

M. W. FLINN, *The European Demographic System, 1500–1820* (1981). A major summary.

F. FORD, *Robe and Sword: The Regrouping of the French Aristocracy After Louis XIV* (1953). An important treatment of the growing social tensions within the French nobility during the eighteenth century.

R. FORSTER AND O. RANUM, *Deviants and the Abandoned in French Society* (1978). This and the following volume contain important essays from the French journal *Annales.*

R. FORSTER AND O. RANUM, *Medicine and Society in France* (1980).

D. V. GLASS AND D.E.C. EVERSLEY, EDS., *Population in History: Essays in Historical Demography* (1965). Fundamental for an understanding of the eighteenth-century increase in population.

P. GOUBERT, *The Ancien Régime: French Society, 1600–1750*, trans. by Steve Cox (1974). A superb account of the peasant social order.

D. HAY ET AL., *Albion's Fatal Tree: Crime and Society in Eighteenth-Century England* (1976). Separate essays on a previously little-explored subject.

D. HAY AND N. ROGERS, *Eighteenth-Century English Society: Shuttles and Swords* (1997). Explores the social experience of the lower orders.

O. H. HUFTON, *The Poor of Eighteenth-Century France, 1750–1789* (1975). A brilliant study of poverty and the family economy.

C. JONES, *Charity and Bienfaisance: The Treatment of the Poor in the Montpellier Region, 1740–1815* (1982). An important local French study.

E. L. JONES, *Agriculture and Economic Growth in England, 1650–1815* (1968). A good introduction to an important subject.

A. KAHAN, *The Plow, the Hammer, and the Knout: An Economic History of Eighteenth-Century Russia* (1985). An extensive and detailed treatment.

H. KAMEN, *European Society, 1500–1700* (1985). A useful one-volume treatment.

P. LASLETT, *The World We Have Lost* (1984). Examination of English life and society before the coming of industrialism.

R. K. MCCLURE, *Coram's Children: The London Foundling Hospital in the Eighteenth Century* (1981). A moving work that deals with the plight of all concerned with the problem.

N. MCKENDERICK, ED., *The Birth of a Consumer Society: The Commercialization of Eighteenth-Century England* (1982). Deals with several aspects of the impact of commercialization.

F. E. MANUEL, *The Broken Staff: Judaism Through Christian Eyes* (1992). An important discussion of Christian interpretations of Judaism.

M. A. MEYER, *The Origins of the Modern Jew: Jewish Identity and European Culture in Germany, 1749–1824* (1967). A general introduction organized around individual case studies.

S. POLLARD, *The Genesis of Modern Management: A Study of the Industrial Revolution in Great Britain* (1965). Treats industrialization from the standpoint of factory owners.

S. POLLARD, *Peaceful Conquest: The Industrialization of Europe, 1760–1970* (1981). A useful survey.

A. RIBEIRO, *Dress in Eighteenth-Century Europe, 1715–1789* (1985). An interesting examination of the social implication of style in clothing.

G. RUDE, *The Crowd in History 1730–1848* (1964). A pioneering study.

G. RUDE, *Paris and London in the Eighteenth Century* (1973).

H. SCHMAL, ED., *Patterns of European Urbanization Since 1500* (1981). Major essays.

L. STONE, *An Open Elite?* (1985). Raises important questions about the traditional view of open access to social mobility in England.

T. TACKETT, *Priest and Parish in Eighteenth-Century France: A Social and Political Study of the Cures in a Diocese of Dauphine, 1750–1791* (1977). An important local study that displays the role of the church in the fabric of social life in the Old Regime.

L. A. TILLY AND J. W. SCOTT, *Women, Work, and Family* (1978). An excellent survey of the issues in western Europe.

D. VALENZE, *The First Industrial Woman* (1995). An elegant work exploring the manner in which industrialization transformed the work of women.

A. VICKERY, *The Gentleman's Daughter: Women's Lives in Georgian England* (1998). Argues that women experienced expanding social horizions in the eighteenth century.

R. WALL, ED., *Family Forms in Historic Europe* (1983). Essays that cover the entire Continent.

C. WILSON, *England's Apprenticeship, 1603–1763* (1984). A broad survey of English economic life on the eve of industrialism.

E. A. WRIGLEY, *Continuity, Chance and Change: The Character of the Industrial Revolution in England* (1988). A major conceptual reassessment.

E. A. WRIGLEY AND R. S. SCHOFIELD, *The Population History of England, 1541–1871: A Reconstruction* (1982). One of the most ambitious demographic studies ever undertaken.

DOCUMENTS CD-ROM

1. G. M. Trevelyan: Chapter XIII from *English Social History*
2. Jonathan Swift: *A Description of a City Shower*
3. Mary Astell: from *Some Reflections Upon Marriage*

WORLD AND THE WEB

The James Ford Bell Library (Trade Products in Early Modern History)

http://www.bell.lib.umn.edu/Products/Products.html

Books, maps, and manuscripts in the James Ford Bell Library chronicle the development of global trade in the early modern period. The desire to obtain goods that they could not produce at home lured Europeans to travel, by sea or land, to far distant lands in search of these products. In some regions Europeans entered into trade networks that had existed for centuries; in others they created new trade networks and established colonies.

Gates to Jewish Heritage,

http://www.jewishgates.org/history/index.stm

Gates to Jewish Heritage is a comprehensive site covering four General Topics: Torah, Midrash, and Historical Periods and Personalities. Its history sections cover the biblical period to the present date; however, it has excellent tracts on Jewish events in Medieval Christian Europe.

Tyburn Tree

http://www.unc.edu/~charliem/

Tyburn Tree is designed to provide information on the Web about public execution in Early Modern England, specifically London.

Luminarium

http://www.luminarium.org/lumina.htm

Combines three sites which on Medieval, Renaissance and 17th-century authors. It is an excellent starting point for students and enthusiasts of English literature and provides quotes, biographies, listings, works, and essays for each author.

22 The Last Great Islamic Empires 1500–1800

The Taj Mahal, built between 1632 and 1647 in Agra, by Shah Jahan, as a tomb for his beloved consort, is arguably the greatest monumental tomb ever built. Its setting amidst gardens and pools alludes to paradise, and its great dome seems suspended like the rising sun over the horizon. Trevor Wood/Getty Images, Inc.

Chapter topics

Islamic Empires

- The Ottoman Empire
- The Safavid Shi'ite Empire
- The Empire of the Indian Timurids, or "Mughals"

Islamic Asia

- Central Asia: Islamization and Isolation
- Power Shifts in the Southern Seas

In World Perspective
The Last Islamic Empires

BETWEEN 1450 AND 1650 ISLAMIC CULTURE AND statecraft blossomed. The creation of three powerful empires and several strong regional states was the culmination of long processes in Islamic history. During this time the ideal of a universal Muslim caliphate yielded to the reality of multiple secular, albeit distinctively "Islamic," sultanates.

The simultaneous growth of the Ottoman, Safavid, and Mughal Empires marked the global apogee of Islamic culture and power. By about 1600 the Ottoman Turks controlled Asia Minor, the Fertile Crescent, the Balkans, Crimean Europe, the Islamic Mediterranean, and Arabia; the Persian Safavids ruled all of greater Iran; and descendants of Timur—the Timurid line known as the Mughals—governed Afghanistan and most of the Indian subcontinent. Around these were arrayed Muslim khanates of Central Asia and Russia, sultanates of Southeast Asia and East Africa, the Sharifian state of Morocco, and regional empires of the Sudan in which Islam played a significant role (see Map 22–1).

In 1600 Islamic civilization seemed as strong and vital as that of western Europe, China, or Japan. Yet Islamic military preeminence and economic and political strength were declining. By the late seventeenth century Islamic commercial, political, and military power was almost everywhere in retreat before the rising tide of western European military and economic imperialism, even though Islamic cultural life flourished and Muslim religion still spread significantly between 1500 and 1800.

In this chapter we focus first on the three major Islamic empires of the period and then turn briefly to the smaller Islamic political and cultural centers of Central Asia and the coastlands of southern Asia and the Indies where European power was having an impact on what had been a virtual Muslim monopoly on maritime trade.

Islamic Empires

THE OTTOMAN EMPIRE

ORIGINS AND DEVELOPMENT OF THE OTTOMAN STATE BEFORE 1600

The Ottomans were a Turkish dynasty that rose to prominence as one of various groups of western Oghuz Turks from the steppes of Central Asia who came to Anatolia as settlers and Muslim frontier warriors.[1] The Ottomans reached Anatolia (Asia Minor) in the time of the Seljuqs of Rum (1098–1308), who were the first western Turks to have founded a lasting state there. By about 1300, the newcomers had built one of several small military states along the Byzantine-Seljuq frontier in western Anatolia. In the fourteenth century several vigorous leaders expanded their territories east into central Anatolia and west across the Dardanelles (in 1356) onto European soil, in the Byzantine lands of Macedonia and modern Bulgaria.

[1] The Ottomans, sometimes called *Osmanlis,* are named after Osman (1259–1326), also rendered *Othman* or *Uthman,* a *ghazi* said to have founded the dynasty when he set up a border state about 1288 on the Byzantine frontier in northwestern Anatolia.

MAP EXPLORATION

Interactive map: To explore this map further, go to http://www.prenhall.com/craig_map22.1

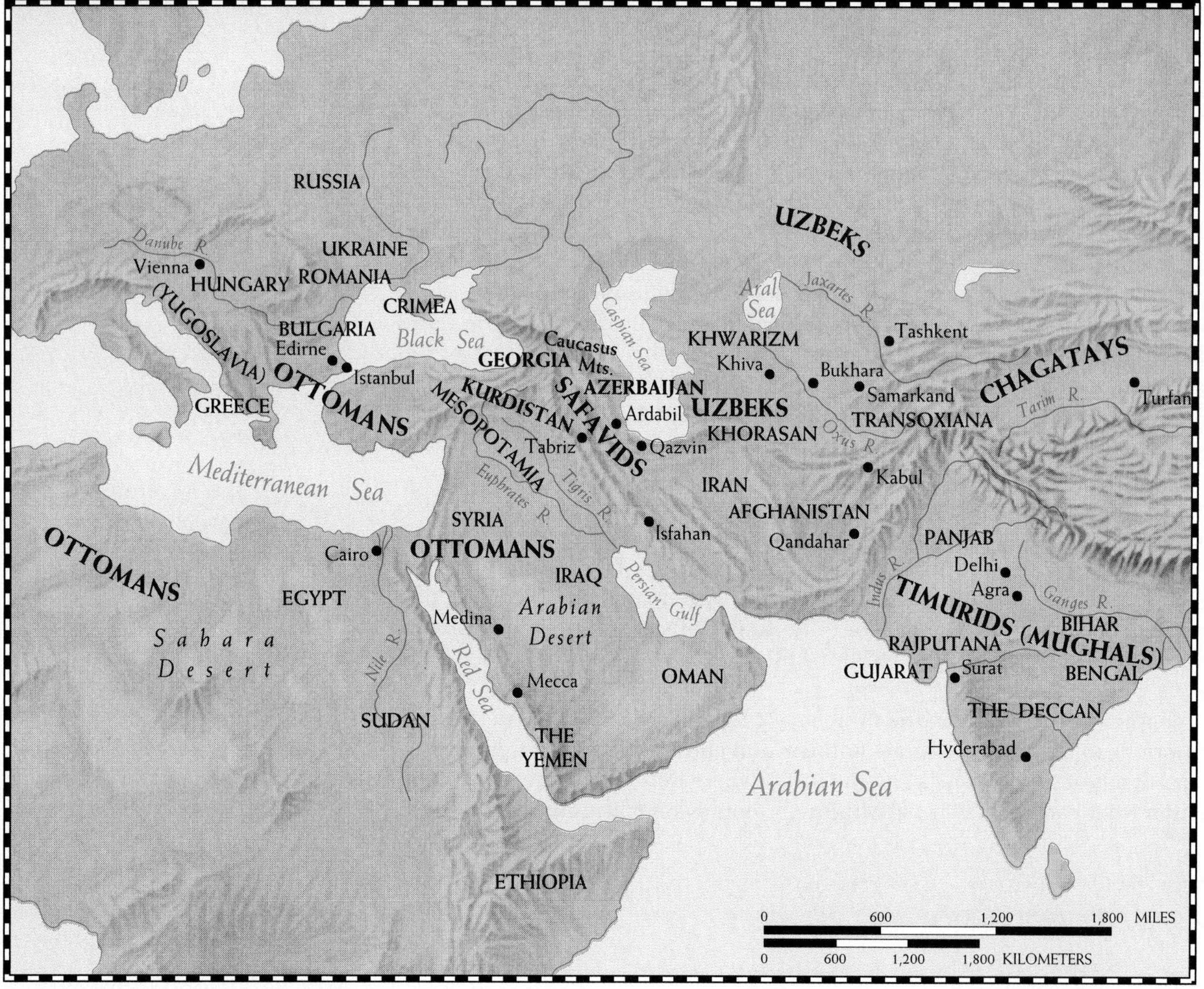

Map 22–1 Sixteenth-century Islamic empires. Major Islamic dynasties in the central Islamic lands, ca. 1600. Note that the Sharifian state of Morocoo does not show on the far left of this map.

Exchanging grants of revenue-producing conquered land (*timars*) for military service, the Ottomans built both a formidable fighting force and a loyal military aristocracy.

By 1402 the center of Ottoman rule had shifted northwest to Edirne on the Balkan Peninsula itself. Ottoman control then extended northwest as far as the Danube and east across central Anatolia. Only encircled Constantinople formed an alien pocket within these dominions, and it finally fell in 1453 to Sultan Mehmed II, "the Conqueror" (r. 1451–1481). Constantinople, now renamed "Istanbul" became the Ottoman capital. After hundreds of years proud Byzantium, the center of Eastern Christendom, was no more, although the Ottomans allowed the Christian patriarch to preside in Istanbul over the Eastern church.

By 1512 Ottoman rule was secure in virtually all of southeastern Europe and north of the Black Sea in most of the Ukraine. Under Selim I (r. 1512–1520) and Süleyman, "the Lawgiver" (known in the West as "Süleyman the Magnificent," r. 1520–1566), this sovereignty was greatly expanded. Selim subjugated the Egyptian Mamluks (1517) and annexed Syria-Palestine, most of North Africa, the Yemen, and western Arabia, including Mecca and Medina. Selim also nullified the Shi'ite threat from Iran in the east (see below). Süleyman extended Ottoman control over Kurdistan and

Georgia (in the Caucasus), as well as Mesopotamia and Iraq. He also advanced Ottoman borders in eastern Europe. Having won much of Hungary and nearly taken Vienna by siege in 1526–1529, he was able by battle and treaty to bring virtually all of Hungary under direct Ottoman rule in the 1540s.

The Ottoman ruler could now claim to be the Abbasid heir and caliph for all Muslims. This claim was symbolized by the addition (begun by Selim I, after the Mamluk conquest in 1517) of the title "Protector of the Sacred Places [Mecca and Medina]" to that of emperor (*padishah*). At this point, Ottoman military might was unmatched by any state in the world, except possibly China.

The "Classical" Ottoman Order

Mehmed II was the true founder of the Ottoman order. He replaced the tribal chieftains with loyal servants of the ruler; he initiated a tradition of formal governmental legislation with his *Qanun-name* ("Lawbook"); and he organized the *ulama* into a hierarchy under a single "Sheikh of Islam." In the next century Süleyman earned his title "Lawgiver" by his legislation touching all aspects of life and all social ranks, his reconciliation of *Shari'a* and customary law, and his efforts to regularize both law and bureaucracy.

The entire Ottoman state was organized as one vast military institution. All members, whatever their function, held military ranks as the standing "army" of the state under the hereditary leadership of the Sultan. This centralized state was supported by the productivity of its Muslim and non-Muslim subjects. The ruling class were Muslims, shared the common Ottoman culture, and had to give utter allegiance to the sultan. The state organization included the palace and three further functional divisions: the administrative or ruling institution, the military institution, and the religious or learned institution. The palace included the sultan, his harem, his ministers, and servants. The privy council, headed by the grand vizier, together with the chancery, the imperial treasury, and the remaining civil bureaucracy, formed the backbone of the ruling or administrative institution.

Several measures helped ensure the ongoing strength of the sultan at the apex of the ruling institution. Young Ottoman princes were given administrative and leadership training in the provinces, which kept them from being sheltered in the palace and gave them experience of life outside the capital. Stability of succession was traditionally guaranteed by the practice of fratricide in the ruling family, which, legalized formally in Mehmed II's *Qanun-name*, continued until the late sixteenth century. Thus the succession was theoretically left to God, the strongest aspirant to the sultanate having to assert himself and seize power, after which he was expected to execute his brothers to eliminate future competing claims to the throne.

The Ottomans co-opted the legal-religious and educational-intellectual roles of the religious scholars, or *ulama*, for the service of the state, making them an arm of the government under a single religious authority, the Grand Mufti or "Shaykh of Islam." This highly organized branch of the state was open only to Muslim men and included the entire system of courts and judges. It was based on a comprehensive network ranging from local mosque schools to the four elite madrasas built around the Süleymaniye Mosque in Istanbul during Süleyman's reign. Scholars' ranks within the graded hierarchy of the *ulama* reflected the level of schooling and teaching they had attained.

While the *ulama* were thus under state control, the state itself was formally committed to maintaining the divinely ordained *Shari'a*, and the *ulama* enjoyed great esteem. This may account for the fact that whereas the *ulama* in both Safavid Iran and Mughal India often differed with their rulers, the Ottoman *ulama* usually functioned tamely as part of the state apparatus.

Although the religious establishment upheld the supremacy of the *Shari'a* and the sultan recognized its

Süleyman the Lawgiver (r. 1520–1566), giving advice to the Crown Prince, Mehmed Khan. From a contemporaneous Ottoman miniature. Folio 79a of the *Talikizade Shenamesi*, Library of the Topkapi Palace Museum, A3592/Photograph courtesy of Talat Halman

authority, the functional law of the land was the highly organized state administrative law—the practical code, or *Qanun*, established by the ruler. The *Shari'a* as interpreted by the *ulama* theoretically governed the *Qanun*, and often the sultan formally applied traditional religious norms in his regulations. The conformity of these regulations to the *Shari'a* sometimes came from the genuine piety of a particular administrator or ruler and was sometimes only a pious fiction, something also true for Safavid Iran and Mughal India.

As for the military institution, the Ottoman rulers kept its loyalty by two means: checks on the power of the old landed aristocracy by careful registry and control of *timar* lands, and the use of slave soldiers with allegiance only to the sultan. The army was based originally on the provincial cavalry whose officers were supported with *timar* land revenues in lieu of cash wages. The state held all conquered agricultural land as its direct property, granting peasants hereditary land use but not ownership. Careful records were kept of the revenue due on all lands, and as long as the state was strong, so too was its control over productive land and the cavalry-gentry whom *timar* revenues supported. But even as early as 1400 the Ottoman rulers tried to reduce the cavalry-gentry's preeminence by employing specialized infantry troops of well-trained and well-paid slave soldiers (equipped, unlike the cavalry, with firearms) whose loyalty was to the sultan alone.

To sustain the quality of these slave troops, the Ottomans developed a unique institution: the provincial slave levy, or *devshirme*. This institution selected young Christian boys from the provincial peasantry to be raised as Muslims; most came from the Balkan peasantry. They were trained to serve in both army and bureaucracy at all levels, from provincial officer to grand vizier. The most famous slave corps was the Janissaries, the elite infantry troops of the empire. Muslim boys were not allowed into the slave corps, although some parents tried to buy them a place in what offered the most promising careers in the empire. Until 1572 marriage was forbidden to the slave soldiers, which further ensured loyalty and prevented hereditary claims on office.

After Süleyman: Challenges and Change

The reign of Süleyman marked the peak of Ottoman prestige and power. Further territorial gains were made in the seventeenth century, and the Ottoman state long remained a major force in European and Asian politics. However, beginning with the reign of Süleyman's weak son, Selim II (1566–1574), the empire was plagued by military corruption, governmental decentralization, and maritime setbacks. Economically there were agricultural failures, commercial imbalances, and inflation. Yet culturally and intellectually, the seventeenth and eighteenth centuries were periods of impressive accomplishments and lively activity. Overall, these ensuing two centuries witnessed a seesaw battle between decline and vitality.

Political and Military Developments The post-Süleyman era began on a sour note with the loss of territory in the Caucasus and Mesopotamia to the Persian Safavids (1603). By this time the Ottoman military apparatus was already weakened, partly from fighting two-front wars with the Safavids and the Habsburgs and partly because of European advances in military and naval technology. The Janissaries became increasingly disruptive. By 1600 they had largely replaced the provincial cavalry as new warfare styles made cavalry obsolete. By 1600 Muslims were allowed into the Janissary corps, marriage was possible, and the *devshirme* was declining in use (it ended just over a century later). During the seventeenth century, the Janissaries became increasingly corrupt as they tampered with politics, trying to influence decision making and even dynastic succession. Finally, the increasing employment of mercenaries resulted in peacetime in the release of masses of unemployed armed men into the countryside, which led to the sacking of provincial towns, banditry, and revolts, which disrupted society.

Murad IV (r. 1623–1640) introduced reforms and ruled with an iron hand, but his death left again a weak central authority. The Koprülüs, father and son, two capable viziers (r. 1656–1676), briefly renewed strong administrative control and military success, but thereafter the central institutions decayed.

Economic Developments Financing the Ottoman state grew ever more difficult. The increase in the Janissary corps from 12,000 to 36,000 men between the early 1500s and 1600 drained state coffers. Inflation grew as the coinage was debased. In contrast to the mercantilist and protectionist policies of European powers the Ottomans discouraged exports and encouraged imports since too many exports would have raised domestic prices. This damaged the economy in the long run. The population doubled in the sixteenth century, and unemployment grew after 1600. Increased decentralization paved the way for the rise of provincial notables (*ayan*), who became virtually independent in the eighteenth century. Tax farming also went hand-in-glove with the rise of large private estates. New taxes were imposed and old emergency levies regularized, and taxes were required in cash rather than in kind and increasingly on a communal rather than an individual basis.

Culture and Society The seventeenth and eighteenth centuries were an era of genuine vitality in poetry, prose, music, painting, cartography, historiography, astronomy, and other fields. The seventeenth century saw especially lively intellectual exchange, both religious and secular. It was also, however, when the *ulama* became an aristocratic and increasingly corrupt elite. Major religious posts became hereditary sinecures for sons and other relatives of a

DOCUMENT THE DISTINCTIVENESS OF OTTOMAN IDENTITY AND CULTURE

Presiding over a pluralistic culture, the Ottoman Turks, themselves a people from the periphery of the central Islamic lands, developed a distinctive "Ottoman" identity and culture that was most evident in their ruling elite. The following selections from members of that elite describe some of the values and qualities they saw as important to Ottoman identity. In the first, Mustafa Ali (d. 1600), a major historian, intellectual, and official of the Ottoman state, lists the special divine favors granted the Ottoman rulers. In the second, another historian, Kinalizade Ali, adopts an ancient political saying attributed to Aristotle and others to describe the prerequisites for an ordered polity under the Shari'a.

Compare the two passages. What common themes emerge?

1. The Gifts of Divine Favor Given the Ottoman Dynasty

The first gift: They reside all by themselves in a palace like unique jewels in the depth of the oyster-shell, and totally sever all relations with relatives and dependents. The slave girls and slave pages that have access to their honored private quarters (*harem*), who are evidently at least three to four thousand individuals, are all strangers and the person of the monarch is like a single gem in their midst . . . .

The second gift: Their religious convictions being immaculate and their character like a shining mirror, it has never happened that a single member of that noble family ever swerved from the road of orthodoxy or that one valiant sultan befriended himself with an unseemly doctrine.

The third gift: The Lord, the Creator and Protector, has always hidden that great race under His protection and it has never been heard that the plague would have entered their flourishing palace or that an individual belonging to that blemishless progeny would have been struck by the horror of the pestilence and would have died of it.

The fourth gift: Whenever they conquered a province and, destroying and eradicating its castles and estates, were confronted with the necessity of appointing a magistrate and assigning a substantial force on their own authority they considered it a sign of weakness, like Alexander the Great, to appoint again one of the great of that province and to assign him certain revenues; may [that province] be as far away as can be, they would opt to send one of the attendants of their Gate of Happiness [there] as *san-jaq begi*, and to Yemen and Ethiopia and to very remote places like Algeria a *begler-begi.* No such absolute power was given to the earlier sovereigns.

The fifth gift: The various special troops in their victory-oriented army and the various tools of war and battle use that are given to them were not available to the brawny fists of anyone of the countless armies [of previous times]. To their attacks going downward and going upward are the same, to their victory-imprinted military music low and high notes are of the same level and equal. In their eyes, as it were, the conquest of a castle is like destroying a spider's web, and in their God-assisted hands to beat the enemies is clearly like pulling out a hair from the beard of a decrepit old man.

The sixth gift: The coherence of the figures in the registers of their revenues and the order of the recordings in the ledgers of their expenses are so strict that they and their salaried classes are free of worries. Consequently, their income exceeds their necessary expenses, their gain is larger than [the expenses for] the important affairs of state.

2. The Need of Authority to Uphold the Shari'a

There can be no royal authority without the military
There can be no military without wealth
The subjects produce the wealth
Justice preserves the subjects' loyalty to the sovereign
Justice requires harmony in the world
The world is a garden, its walls are the state
The Holy Law [*Shari'a*] orders the state
There is no support for the Holy Law except through royal authority.

Selection 1 from Andreas Tietze, *Mustafa Ali's Counsel for Sultans of 1581*, Verlag Der Osterreichischen Akademie Der Wissenshaften, Vienna, 1979, pp. 38–39. Selection 2 from Cornell H. Fleischer, *Bureaucrat and Intellectual in the Ottoman Empire: The Historian Mustafa Ali (1541–1600)*, Princeton University Press, 1986, p. 262.

handful of families that had produced prominent *ulama*, and the pasts were often sold or leased.

In literature and the arts, the seventeenth and eighteenth centuries were highly productive. Katib Chelebi (d. 1657) was only the most illustrious of many polymaths who wrote histories, social commentary, geographies, and encyclopedic works. Other important writers were the great historian of the Ottomans, Na'ima (d. 1716), the tireless traveler and travel writer Evliya Chelebi (d. ca. 1685), and probably the greatest Ottoman poet, Nedim (d. 1730). Ottoman art had been highly eclectic in the first century after Mehmed II, but in the latter sixteenth century a more conservative turn produced distinctively Ottoman artistic and architectural forms. The greatest name here is that of the imperial master architect Sinan (d. 1678) . The first half of the eighteenth century was the golden age of Ottoman poetry and art; it also saw the first Ottoman printing press and the beginning of strong European influence in the arts, architecture, and manners. In the popular sphere, the now classical form of Turkish theater (in which two men play male and female parts) began as early as the sixteenth century, perhaps under Jewish immigrant influence.

Socially, the period saw the consolidation of Ottoman society as a multi-ethnic and multi-religious state. The empire encompassed a dizzying array of languages, religions, and ethnic identities. Considerable immigration of Jews into Ottoman societies following their expulsion from Spain (1492) had brought new craftsmen, physicians, bankers, scholars, and even entertainers. The large Christian population of the empire was generally well treated, but in the seventeenth century they began to suffer from increasing taxes and other discrimination. As a result the Christians looked as never before to Christian Europe and Russia for liberation.

Still, state policy encouraged just treatment of all subjects; for example, "rescripts of justice" (mostly against the malpractices of tax collectors) were often issued. Although royal decrees reserved special privileges for Muslims, they seldom affected mass behavior. In the eighteenth century, however, relations between Muslims and non-Muslims deteriorated, in part because of the remarkable rise in the economic and social status of non-Muslims—in particular the rich mercantile middle class. Non-Muslims virtually monopolized foreign trade, and in the eighteenth century European countries gave many of them citizenship, which allowed them the trade privileges granted to foreign governments by the sultan.

One of the major social institutions of later Ottoman society, the coffeehouse, flourished from the mid–sixteenth century on. Probably originally a Sufi institution that came with coffee to the Mediterranean from the Yemen, The Ottoman coffeehouse rapidly became a major common space for socializing. Here people gathered to drink coffee, play games, watch puppet shows, read books, discuss public affairs, and even engage in political agitation. Despite bans by the Sheikh of Islam because of the stimulant qualities of coffee, both the coffee habit and coffeehouses, like the similarly new imported habit of cigarette smoking, could not be suppressed. Different types of coffeehouses developed, each identified by its focus: music, theater, recitation, poetry, or Janissary or other professional affiliation (e.g., firefighting). The coffeehouse stimulated the development of a common Ottoman urban culture among lower and middle classes.

The Decline of Ottoman Military and Political Power

After the failure in 1683 to take Vienna, the Ottomans were driven out of Hungary and Belgrade and never again seriously threatened Europe. In 1774 Russia took the Crimea and became the formal protector of the Orthodox Christians of the Islamic empire (1774). Henceforth, the Ottomans were prey to the West, never regaining their earlier power and influence before their collapse in 1918.

Outflanked by Russia to their north and by European sea power to the south and west, the Ottomans were blocked in the east by their implacable Shi'ite foes in Iran. They could not sustain the level of external trade needed to support their expensive wars. Ultimately, their dependence on an agrarian-age economy proved insufficient to face the rising commercial and industrial powers of Europe.

The Safavid Shi'ite Empire

Origins

As noted in Chapter 13, Iranian history changed under the Safavid dynasty after 1500. The Safavids had begun in the fourteenth century as hereditary Turkish spiritual leaders of a Sunni Sufi order, in the northwestern Iranian province of Azerbaijan. In the fifteenth century the Safavid order evolved a new and militant Shi'ite ideology. By claiming descent from the seventh imam of the Twelver Shia (see Chapter 13), the Safavid spiritual masters (*shaykhs and pirs*) became the focus of Shi'ite religious allegiance. Many adherents were won to the order and to Shi'ism from among the Turkoman tribesmen of eastern Anatolia, northern Syria, and northwestern Iran. These mounted warriors were called

An Ottoman portrayal of the *Devshirme.* This miniature painting from about 1558 depicts the recruiting of young Christian children for the Sultan's elite Janissary corps. Topkapi Sarayi Musesi. H. 1517, folio 31b, Topkapi Palace Museum. Photograph courtesy of Talat Halman

Kizilbash ("Red Heads") because of their distinctive red uniform hats, which signaled their allegiance to the twelve Shi'ite imams and their Safavid master.

The growing strength of the Safavids brought about conflict with the dominant Sunni Turkoman groups in the region around Tabriz. The Safavids emerged victorious in 1501 under the leadership of the young Safavid master-designate Isma'il. Recognized as a divinely appointed representative of the "hidden" imam (see Chapter 11), Isma'il extended his sovereignty over the southern Caucasus, Azerbaijan, the Tigris-Euphrates valley, and all of western Iran by 1506. In the east by 1512 the Safavids, in league with Babur, the Timurid ruler of Kabul, had taken all of eastern Iran from the Oxus River south to the Arabian Sea from the Uzbek Turks. The Uzbeks, however, became implacable foes of the Safavids and throughout the ensuing century often forced them to fight a debilitating two-front war, against Uzbeks in the east and Ottomans in the west.

A strong central rule now united traditional Iranian lands for the first time since the heyday of the Abbasid caliphate. It was a regime based on the existing Persian bureaucratic institutions, which in turn were based on Seljuq institutions. Shah Isma'il ruthlessly enforced Shi'ite conformity, which slowly took root across the realm—perhaps bolstered by a rising Persian self-consciousness in the face of the Sunni Ottomans, Arabs, Uzbeks, and Mughals who surrounded Iran.

In the west, however, the better-armed army of Selim I soundly defeated the Safavid forces at Chaldiran, near Tabriz, in 1514, marking the beginning of an extended series of Ottoman-Safavid conflicts over the next two centuries. Chaldiran also marked the beginning of Kizilbash disaffection with Shah Isma'il and consequent efforts to take over power from the Safavids. Furthermore, this defeat gave the Ottomans control of the Fertile Crescent and forced the Safavids to move their capital and their focus eastward, first to Qazwin, and then to Isfahan.

SHAH ABBAS I

Isma'il's successor, Tahmasp I (r. 1524–1576), survived repeated attacks by both Ottomans and Uzbeks, in part through the strength of Shi'ite religious feeling and the allegiance of the Iranian bureaucracy. A few years later, however, the greatest Safavid ruler Shah Abbas I (r. 1588–1629) brought able leadership to the Safavid domains. He regained provincial land for the state and used the revenue to pay for new troops from his Caucasian territories, thereby providing a counterweight to the sometimes unruly Kizilbash, who (like the old Ottoman cavalry) were supported by land revenue assignments. Shah Abbas not only pushed the Ottomans out of Azerbaijan and Iraq but also turned back new Uzbek invasions in Khorasan. He also sought alliances with the Ottomans' European enemies. This latter tactic, used by several Safavid rulers, reflects the deep division the new militant Persian Shi'ism had brought to the Islamic world. Abbas also broke the century-long Portuguese monopoly on trade along Persian shores and opened trade with English and Dutch commercial companies. His reign brought considerable prosperity to Iran, symbolized by the magnificent capital he built at Isfahan.

SAFAVID DECLINE

After Shah Abbas, the empire rarely again enjoyed able leadership. This led finally to its decline and collapse, the chief causes of which were (1) continued two-front pressure from Ottoman and Uzbek armies, (2) economic decline, and (3) the increasing power and bigotry of the Shi'ite *ulama*. The conservative *ulama* not only introduced a Shi'ite legalism but also emphasized their own authority as interpreters of the law over that of the monarch. They also persecuted religious minorities and encouraged hatred of Sunni Muslims.

One result of Shi'ite exclusivism was tribal revolts among the Sunni Afghans. In the end, an Afghan leader captured Isfahan and forced the abdication of Husayn I (1694–1722). Safavid princes managed to retake control of western Iran, but the empire's greatness was past. A revived, but officially Sunni, monarchy under the talented Kizilbash tribal leader Nadir Shah (r. 1736–1747) and several successors restored much of Iran's lost territories. However, Nadir Shah's military ventures, which included an invasion of North India and the conquest of Delhi, sapped the empire's finances.

CHRONOLOGY

THE OTTOMAN EMPIRE

ca. 1280	Foundation of early Ottoman principality in Anatolia
1356	Ottomans cross Dardanelles into Europe
1451–1481	Rule of Sultan Mehmed II, "the Conqueror"
1453	Fall of Constantinople to Mehmed the Conqueror
1512–1520	Rule of Selim I
1517	Ottoman conquest of Egypt, assumption of claim to Abbasid caliphal succession from Mamluks
1520–1566	Rule of Süleyman, "the Lawgiver"
1526–1529	First Ottoman siege of Vienna
1578	Death of Ottoman master architect, Sinan
1656–1676	Governance of Koprülüs as viziers
1683	Second Ottoman siege of Vienna
1699	Treaty of Karlowitz, loss of Hungarian and other European territory
1774	Loss of Crimea to Russia; Tsar becomes formal protector of Ottoman Orthodox Christians
1918	End of empire

Shah Abbas I receiving a diplomatic embassy from the Turks in 1609.
Staatliche Museen zu Berlin/Bildarchiv Preussischer Kulturbesitz-Museum für Islamic Kunst

After his autocratic and despotic reign, Iran could not regain stability for another half century.

CULTURE AND LEARNING

In the long run, the most impressive aspect of Safavid times, besides the conversion of Iran to Shi'ism, was the cultural and intellectual renaissance of the sixteenth and seventeenth centuries. The traditions of painting, with their origins in the powerful miniatures of the preceding century—notably those from Herat after 1450, exemplified by the work of the painter Bihzad (1440–1514) in late Timurid times—were cultivated and modified in Safavid times. Portraiture and scenes from everyday life became popular. Among the most developed crafts were ceramic tile, porcelain, and carpets. The magnificent architecture of Isfahan constructed in Shah Abbas's time gives breathtaking evidence of the developed sense of proportion, color, and design of Safavid taste. It marks a high point in the lavish use of ceramic tiles to decorate both the facades and, especially, the great domes of major buildings.

In intellectual life, the *Ishraqi* or "illuminationist" school of theological-philosophical thought brought together the mystical bent of Persian Islamic thought and the long Islamic traditions of Aristotelianism and Platonism in the form of Shi'ite religious speculation into the nature of divine truth and its accessibility to human reason and imagination. The illuminationists' two key ideas were the concept of transcendence and the notion of a "realm of images." They conceived of transcendence in terms of a divine light identified with the Light of Truth, which was expressed most fully in Muhammad and the Shi'ite imams. The realm of images was a sphere of being in which the attuned spirit could experience true visions. These ideas reconceived human experience of the Divine in a way that transcended logic and had to be experienced individually. At stake were basic notions of the human psyche and the larger cosmos. The most prominent exponent of the *Ishraqi* school was Mulla Sadra (d. 1640).

The lasting legacies of Safavid rule were the firmly Shi'ite character of the whole Iranian region and the Persian culture that was elaborated largely under Safavid patronage in literature, theology, philosophy, painting, crafts, and ar-

CHRONOLOGY

THE SAFAVID EMPIRE

1334	Death of Safi al-Din, founder of Safavid Sufi order
ca. 1500	Rise of Safavids under Shah Isma'il
1501–1510	Safavid conquest of greater Iran; Shi'ite state founded
1588–1629	Rule of Shah Abbas I
1722	Forced abdication of last Safavid ruler
1736–1747	Rule of the Sunni Afghan leader, Nadir Shah; revival of Sunni monarchy in Iran
1739	Nadir Shah invades northern India, sacks Delhi

DOCUMENT A SAFAVID HISTORIAN PRAISES SHAH ABBAS I

The following passage presents a panegyric but interesting depiction of the great Safavid ruler by a contemporary chronicler of Abbas's reign (1587–1629).

What positive human values does the writer want to demonstrate that Shah Abbas embodies?

On Shah 'Abbas's Breadth of Vision, and His Knowledge of World Affairs and of the Classes of Society

After he has dealt with the affairs of state, Shah 'Abbas habitually relaxes. He has always been fond of conviviality and, since he is still a young man, he enjoys wine and the company of women. But this does not affect the scrupulous discharge of his duties, and he knows in minute detail what is going on in Iran and also in the world outside. He has a well-developed intelligence system, with the result that no one, even if he is sitting at home with his family, can express opinions which should not be expressed without running the risk of their being reported to the Shah. This has actually happened on numerous occasions.

As regards his knowledge of the outside world, he possesses information about the rulers (both Muslim and non-Muslim) of other countries, about the size and composition of their armies, about their religious faith and the organization of their kingdoms, about their highway systems, and about the prosperity or otherwise of their realms. He has cultivated diplomatic relations with most of the princes of the world, and the rulers of the most distant parts of Europe, Russia, and India are on friendly terms with him. Foreign ambassadors bearing gifts are never absent from his court, and the Shah's achievements in the field of foreign relations exceed those of his predecessors.

Shah 'Abbas mixes freely with all classes of society, and in most cases is able to converse with people in their own particular idiom. He is well versed in Persian poetry; he understands it well, indulges in poetic license, and sometimes utters verses himself. He is a skilled musician, an outstanding composer of rounds, rhapsodies, and part-songs; some of his compositions are famous. As a conversationalist, he is capable of elegant and witty speech.

From Eskandar Beg Monshi, *History of Shah 'Abbas the Great,* Volume I, translated by Roger M. Savory, (Westview Press, 1978), p. 533.

chitecture. The Safavid age also saw a distinctively Shi'ite piety develop. It focused on commemorating the suffering of the imams and loyalty to the Shi'ite *ulama,* who alone provided guidance in the absence of the hidden imam (see Chapter 11).

THE EMPIRE OF THE INDIAN TIMURIDS, OR "MUGHALS"

ORIGINS

Invaders from beyond the Oxus to the northwest, in the age-old pattern of Indian history, began a new era in the subcontinent in the early sixteenth century: They ended the political fragmentation that by 1500 had reduced the Delhi sultanate to only one among many Indian states. These invaders were Chaghatay Turks descended from Timur (Tamerlane) and known to history as the *Mughals* (a Persianate form of *Mongol*). In 1525–1527 the founder of the Mughal dynasty, Babur, marched on India, replaced the last sultan of Delhi, and then defeated a Rajput confederacy. Before his death in 1530 he ruled an empire stretching from the Oxus to Bihar, and the Himalaya to the Deccan. Akbar "the Great" (r. 1556–1605), however, was the real founder of the Mughal Empire and the greatest Indian ruler since Ashoka (ca. 264–223 B.C.E.). Indeed, he was as great a ruler as, if not greater than, his famous contemporaries, Elizabeth I (r. 1558–1603), Charles V (r. 1519–1556), and Süleyman.

AKBAR'S REIGN

Akbar added North India and the northern Deccan to the Mughal dominions. Even more significant, however, were his governmental reforms, cultural patronage, and religious toleration. He completely reorganized the central and provincial governments and rationalized the tax system. His marriages with Rajput princesses and his appointment of Hindus to positions of power eased Muslim-Hindu tensions. So did his cancellation of the poll tax on non-Muslims (1564) and his efforts to reduce the power of the more literalist, "hard-line" *ulama.* Under his leadership the Mughal Empire became a truly Indian empire.

Akbar was a religious eclectic who showed not only tolerance of all faiths but also unusual interest in different religious traditions. He frequently brought together representatives of all faiths—Jain and Buddhist monks, Brahmans, *ulama,* Parsis (Zoroastrians), and Jesuits—to discuss religion. These debates took place in a special hall in Akbar's magnificent palace complex at Fatehpur Sikri outside the Mughal capital, Agra.

THE LAST GREAT MUGHALS

Akbar's three immediate successors were Jahangir (r. 1605–1627), Shah Jahan (r. 1628–1658), and Awrangzeb (r. 1658–1707). They left behind significant achievements, but the problems of sustaining an Indian empire took their toll on Mughal power. The reigns of Jahangir and Shah Jahan were arguably the golden age of Mughal culture, notably in architecture and painting. But the burdens imposed by new building, by military campaigns, and by the erosion of Akbar's administrative and tax reforms led to economic decline. Jahangir set a fateful precedent in permitting English merchants to establish a trading post, or "factory," at Surat on the western coast in Gujarat. Shah Jahan brought the Deccan wholly under Mughal control but lost Qandahar to Shah Abbas II in 1648. His wars further strained the Mughal economy. No less a burden on the treasury were his elaborate building projects, the most magnificent of which was the Taj Mahal (built 1632–1653), the unparalleled tomb that he built for his beloved consort, Mumtaz.

With Shah Jahan, religious toleration retreated; under his son, Awrangzeb, a narrow religious fanaticism all but reversed Akbar's earlier policies. The resulting internal disorder and instability hastened the decline of Mughal power. Awrangzeb persecuted non-Muslims, destroying Hindu temples, reimposing the poll tax (1679), and alienating the Rajput leaders, whose forebears Akbar had so carefully cultivated. His intransigent policies coincided with and perhaps contributed to the spread of the militant reformism of the Sikh movement throughout the Panjab and the rise of Hindu Maratha nationalism in western India.

Worldly and Spiritual Drunkenness. This painting (opaque water color, ink and gold on paper, 28.9 × 21.6 cm) by the great 16th-century Safavid Iranian court painter Sultan Muhammad is from an illustrated copy of the *Diwan*, or collected works of the lyric and mystical poet Hafiz (1319–1389?). Hafiz appears himself as a drunken figure in the upper window. The entire picture plays the worldly drunkenness and debauchery of the characters in the center against the spiritual inebriation of the dancing Sufis in the garden and the angels on the roof. The angels, too, are shown drinking, a visual reference to the line of Hafiz at the top: "The angel of mercy took the cup of revelry." Courtesy of the Metropolitan Museum of Art and Arthur M. Sackler Museum, Harvard University. Promised gift of Mr. and Mrs. Stuart Cary Welch, 1988; © 1989 Metropolitan Museum of Art

SIKHS AND MARATHAS

In the late sixteenth and early seventeenth centuries the Sikhs, who trace their origins to the irenic teachings of Guru Nanak (d. 1538), developed into a distinctive religious movement. Neither Muslim nor Hindu, they had their own scripture, ritual, and moralistic and reformist ideals. Awrangzeb earned their lasting enmity by persecution that culminated in the martyrdom of their ninth leader, or guru, Teg Bahadur, in 1675. Thereafter, the tenth and last Sikh guru, Gobind Singh (d. 1708), developed the Sikhs into a formidable military force. Awrangzeb and his successors had to contend with repeated Sikh uprisings.

The Hindu Marathas, led by the charismatic Shivaji (d. 1680), rose in religious and nationalistic fervor to found their own regional empire about 1646. On Shivaji's death, the Maratha state controlled the mountainous western coast, and its army was the most disciplined force in India. Despite Awrangzeb's subsequent defeat of the Marathas and his conquest of the entire south of India, the Marathas continued to fight him. After his death they brought about a confederation of almost all the Deccan states under their leadership. While formally acknowledging Mughal sovereignty, the Marathas actually controlled far more of India after about 1740 than did the Mughals.

POLITICAL DECLINE

In addition to the Rajput, Sikh, and Maratha wars, other factors sealed the fate of the once great Mughal empire after Awrangzeb's death in 1707: the rise in the Deccan of the powerful Islamic state of Hyderabad in 1724; the Persian invasion of North India by Nadir Shah in 1739; the invasions (1748–1761) by the Afghan tribal leader Ahmad Shah

Durrani (r. 1747–1773), "founder of modern Afghanistan"; and the British victories over Bengali forces at Plassey in Bengal (1757) and over the French on the southeastern coast (1740–1763). By 1819 the dominance of the British East India Company had eclipsed Mughal as it did Maratha and almost all regional Indian power, even though the Mughal line did not officially end until 1858.

RELIGIOUS DEVELOPMENTS

The period from about 1500 to 1650 was of major importance for Indian religious life. Akbar's eclecticism mirrored the atmosphere of the sixteenth century in India. A number of religious figures preached a spiritually or mystically oriented piety that transcended the legalism of both the *ulama* and the Brahmans and rejected caste distinctions. In these ideas, we can see both Muslim Sufi and Hindu *bhakti* influences at work. We mentioned in Chapter 13 two forerunners of such reformers, Ramananda and Kabir. Guru Nanak, the spiritual father of the Sikh movement, took up Kabir's ideas and preached faith and devotion to one loving and merciful God. He opposed narrow allegiance to particular creeds or rites and excessive pride in external religious observance. Nanak's hymns of praise contain both Hindu and Muslim ideas and imagery. Dadu (d. 1603) preached a similar message. He was born a Muslim but, like Kabir and Nanak, strove to get people to go beyond either Muslim or Hindu allegiance to a more spiritual love and service of God.

There was also an upsurge of *bhakti* devotionalism that amounted to a Hindu revival. It was epitomized by the Bengali Krishna devotee Chaitanya (d. ca. 1533), who stressed total devotion to Lord Krishna. The forebears of present-day Hare Krishna devotees, his followers spread widely his ecstatic public praise of God and his message that all are equal in God's sight. The other major figure in Hindu devotionalism in this era was Tulasidas (d. 1623), whose Hindi retelling of the story of the Sanskrit *Ramayana* remains among the most popular works of Indian literature. Tulasidas used the story of Rama's adventures to present *bhakti* ideas that remain as alive in current everyday Hindu life as do his verses.

Muslim eclectic tendencies came primarily from the Sufis. By 1500 many Sufi retreat centers had been established in India. Sufis' enthusiastic forms of worship and their inclination to play down the externals of religion proved particularly congenial to Indian sensibilities. Such Sufis were, however, often opposed by the more puritanical *ulama*, many of whom held powerful positions as royal advisers and judges. To check puritan bigotry among the *ulama*, Akbar named himself the supreme spiritual authority in the empire, then ordered that toleration be the law of the land.

After Akbar's death the inevitable reaction set in. It was summed up in the work of the Indian leader of the central Asian Sufi order of the Naqshbandiya, Ahmad Sirhindi (d. 1624). He sought to purge Sufism of its extreme tendencies and of all popular practices not sanctioned by the schools of law. He crusaded against any practices that smacked of Hindu influence and also against tolerant treatment of the Hindus themselves. Among Akbar's royal successors, Awrangzeb, as noted above, was known for his strictures against non-Muslims. His intolerance has often been unfairly exaggerated, but in the end its spirit won the day. The possibilities for Hindu-Muslim rapprochement that had emerged in Akbar's time waned, presaging

Jahangir showing preference to the Chishti Sufi *shaykh* and saint Husain over three temporal rulers: the Ottoman emperor, the King of England, and a Hindu prince. The Timurid emperor presents a book to Shaykh Husain, the descendant of the great Chishti saint Mu'inuddin, while ignoring the temporal rulers in the lower left corner. The artist copied the likeness of King James I from an English portrait given to Jahangir by Sir Thomas Roe, the British ambassador from 1615 to 1619. The magnificent floral borders to the miniature (ca. 1615–1618) were added in 1727 by Muhammad Sadiq. (Opaque watercolor, gold and ink on paper, 25.3 × 18.1 cm) Bichitr, *Jahangir Preferring a Sufi Shakikh to Kings*, ca. 1660–70, Album Page; Courtesy of the Freer Gallery of Art, Smithsonian Institution, Washington, D.C.

DOCUMENT GURU ARJUN'S FAITH

These lines are from the pen of the fifth guru of the Sikh community, Arjun (d. 1606). In them he repeated the teaching of Kabir, a fifteenth-century Indian saint whose teachings are included with those of Guru Nanak and other religious poets in the Sikh holy scripture, the Adi Granth. This teaching focuses on the error of clinging to a doctrinaire communalist faith, be it that of the Hindus or of the Muslims.

Why might syncretic teachings, such as those of the Sikhs, have been appealing in seventeenth-century India?

I practice not fasting, nor observe the [month of] Ramazan:
I serve Him who will preserve me at the last hour.
The one Lord of the earth is my God,
Who judgeth both Hindus and Muslims.
I go not on a pilgrimage to Mecca, nor worship at Hindu places of Pilgrimage.
I serve the one God and no other.
I neither worship as the Hindus, nor pray as the Muslims.
I take the Formless God into my heart, and there make obeisance unto Him.
I am neither a Hindu nor a Muslim.
The soul and the body belong to God whether He be called Allah or Ram.
Kabir hath delivered this lecture.
When I meet a true guru or pīr, I recognize my own Master.

From Max Arthur Macauliffe, *The Sikh Religion*, 6 vols. (Oxford: Clarendon Press, 1909), p. 422.

the communal strife that has so marred southern Asian history in our own century.

Islamic Asia

CENTRAL ASIA: ISLAMIZATION AND ISOLATION

We can trace the solid footing of Islam in Central Asia to the post-Timur era of the fifteenth century. Even in the preceding century, as the peoples of western Central Asia had begun to shift from nomadic to settled existence, the familiar pattern of Islamic diffusion from trading and urban centers to the countryside had set in. Islamization by Sunni Sufis, traders, and tribal rulers went on apace thereafter, even as far as western China and Mongolia. It was slowed only in the late sixteenth century by the conversion of the tribes of Mongolia proper to the Buddhism of the Tibetan lamas. Thus, after 1500 the Safavid Shi'ite realm was bounded by Sunni states in India, Afghanistan, Anatolia, Mesopotamia, Transoxiana, and western Turkestan (Khwarizm, the region between the Aral and Caspian Seas). In these last two areas, the most important states were those founded by Uzbek and Chaghatay Turks, both of whom were ruled by Muslim descendants of Genghis Khan.

UZBEKS AND CHAGHATAYS

During the fifteenth century Timur's heirs had ruled Transoxiana and most of Iran (see Chapter 13). To the north, above the Jaxartes River (Syr Darya) and the Aral Sea, a new steppe khanate had been formed by the unification in 1428 of assorted clans of Turks and Mongols known as the Uzbeks. In time, an Uzbek leader who was descended from Genghis Khan, Muhammad Shaybani (d. 1510), invaded Transoxiana (1495–1500). There he founded a new Uzbek Islamic empire that replaced Timurid rule, which shifted south to Kabul and eventually India, as described earlier. Muhammad's line continued Uzbek rule in Transoxiana at Bukhara into the eighteenth century, while another Uzbek line ruled the independent khanate of Khiva in western Turkestan from 1512 to 1872.

Of the other Central Asian Islamic states after 1500, the most significant was that of the Chaghatay Turks. The Chaghatays had been the successors of Genghis Khan in the whole region from the Aral Sea and the Oxus River to Yuan China. After 1350 Timur's invasion broke up their khanate. From about 1514 a revived Chaghatay state flourished in eastern Turkestan—the Tarim basin and the territory north of it, between Tashkent in the west and the Turfan oasis in the east. Although the Chaghatay rulers lasted until 1678 in one part of the Tarim basin, their real power was lost after about 1555 to various Khoja princes, Sunni zealots who claimed to be *Sharifs* (descendants of the Prophet).

CONSEQUENCES OF THE SHI'ITE RIFT

On the face of it, the Ottoman, Mughal, Safavid, and Central Asian Islamic states had much in common: Muslim faith and culture, similar systems of taxation and law, the Persian language, and Turkish rulers. Yet the deep religious division between the Shi'ite Safavids and all their Sunni neighbors proved stronger than their common bonds. The result was a serious geographic division that isolated Central Asian Muslims in particular.

The great central square of the Registan, in Samarkand, with the 17th-century Shir Dar Madrasa on the right and the 15th-century Ulugh Beg Madrasa on the left. Samarkand and other major Central Asian cities were centers of Islamic culture and learning as well as political power. Michael Gotin

Shi'ite-Sunni political competition was sharpened by Safavid militancy, to which the Sunni states responded in kind. Attempts to form alliances with non-Muslim states, previously unheard of in the Islamic world, became a commonplace of Shi'ite political strategy. The Sunnis also resorted to such tactics: the Ottomans, for example, made common cause with Protestants against their Catholic Habsburg enemies. Although trade went on, the presence of a militant Shi'ite state astride the major overland trade routes of the larger Islamic world hurt the international flow of Islamic commerce.

The Safavid Shi'ite schism also ruptured the shared cultural traditions of the "Abode of Islam." This rupture was especially reflected in the fate of Persian literary culture. As a result of its ever stronger association with Shi'ite religious ideas after the rise of the Safavids, Persian made little further progress as a potential common language alongside—let alone above—Arabic in Sunni lands. Outside Iran it was destined to remain a language only of high culture and bureaucracy. In India, Urdu became the common Muslim idiom (see Chapter 13), and in Ottoman and Central Asian lands, one or another Turkic tongue was spoken in everyday life. The Persian classics inspired Persian learning among educated Sunnis, but Safavid Persian literature was largely ignored.

Central Asia was ultimately the Islamic region most decisively affected by the Shi'ite presence in Iran. Combined with the growing pressure of Christian Russian power from the West, the militant Shi'ism of Iran isolated Central Asia from the rest of the Muslim world. Political and

CHRONOLOGY

INDIA: THE MUGHALS AND CONTEMPORARY INDIAN POWERS

1525–1527	Rule of Babur, founder of Indian Timurid state
1538	Death of Guru Nanak, founder of Sikh religious tradition
1556–1605	Rule of Akbar "the Great"
1605–1627	Rule of Jahangir
1628–1658	Rule of Shah Jahan, builder of the Taj Mahal
1646	Founding of Maratha Empire
1658–1707	Rule of Awrangzeb
1680	Death of Maratha leader, Shivaji
1708	Death of tenth and last Sikh guru, Gobind Singh
1724	Rise of Hyderabad state
1739	Iranian invasion of North India under Nadir Shah
1757	British East India Company victory over Bengali forces at Plassey

Shah-nameh, Book of Kings

Firdawsi (c. 935–1020), born Abu ol-Qasem Mansur, composed one of the world's great epic poems, the *Shah-nameh,* or *Book of Kings,* an account of Persia's sovereigns, historical and legendary, up to the Muslim conquest of 652. First published in 1010, the *Shah-nameh* was largely responsible for a reflowering of Persian pre-Islamic culture and—as Dante's *Comedy* would do for Italian some three centuries later—contributed to the crystallization of the New Persian language.

Firdawsi was one of the many talented and learned artists and scientists attracted to the court of the Ghaznavid sultan Mahmud; the sultan, later the subject of legends himself, was renowned as both a military conqueror and a generous patron of the arts. Despite this reputation, Firdawsi, feeling that Mahmud had ill rewarded his patriotic labors (the *Shah-nameh* numbers 60,000 rhymed couplets), authored a harsh satire on the subject of the sultan and shortly after fled Ghazna.

The *Shah-nameh* was recited and illustrated for centuries, but it was under the patronage of Tahmasp I, the second Safavid shah, that the most brilliant known manuscript of the royal history of Persia was undertaken. In 1522, two years before ascending the throne, Shah Tahmasp, still in his teens, directed painters and calligraphers to begin their labors on the unique work of art shown here. The *Shah-nameh* has been called "a monument built by the most gifted Safavid artists," but so intimately was the shah involved with its production, changing artists and replacing pages as his tastes evolved, that the making of this book reflects the evolution of its patron's artistic sensibility as much as the taste of his time.[1]

In this episode, Firdawsi, in blue and brown in the lower left corner, has recently arrived in Ghazna, where Sultan Mahmud, having assembled records about Persia's history before the advent of Islam, is seeking a poet able enough to unify this wealth of information. Coincidentally, Firdawsi has been engaged in such an enterprise in his native Tus.

By permission of the Houghton Library, Harvard University, the Houghton Shahnama, ed., Martin Bernard Dickson (Cambridge, MA: Harvard University Press, 1981), vol. 1,45.

After reciting his prayers, he comes upon three of the capital's most celebrated poets, enjoying a meal al fresco and attended by servants. The masters look down upon the out-of-towner as a provincial; having observed him performing his religious duties, they also dismiss him as a puritan. Inconvenienced by their obligation to hospitality, they attempt to put Firdawsi off by explaining that their party is restricted to poets. As a test, they give him three lines of a quatrain—a *ruba'i*—with difficult rhymes and ask him to cap them, which Firdawsi accomplishes marvelously.

The painter of this and many other pages of the *Shahnameh* was Aqa-Mirak, a famed and well-born portraitist, who is believed to have depicted the shah here—Tahmasp would be the young man in blue and yellow on the right. The scene harmoniously combines various sophisticated and refined features of classical Persian painting, as well as Aqa-Mirak's specific strengths. The poets' picnic is a feast not only for the eye, but for all the senses, from the aroma of roasting meat to the scents of the flowers growing in profusion in this eternal springtime, the flavor of the vivid foods, the textures and tones of the figures' clothing, and the sound of lapping water. The composition is defined by masses—the patches of color and the figures—and centered by the seated group in the middle; also contributing to the ideal, ornamental quality is the absence of shading. The artist's play of perspective is typical of traditional Persian art: each seated figure, for example, is rendered three-dimensionally, while the overall composition stacks areas of color in two dimensions. The sinuous lines of the trees and the patterns of blossoms are purely, delightfully decorative; the scene exuberantly overflows its frame, adding to the charm of the book page.

It is not by chance that Firdawsi (whose adopted name means "of the garden" or "of Paradise")[2] comes upon his fellow poets in a lushly flowering place. The pre-Islamic notion of a kinship between human beings and plants, occupants of a single reality, easily fit with the Qur'anic definition of Paradise as a garden. These spaces soon became the preferred sites of poetry, sung in the still-recited verses of Sa'di (ca. 1213–1292), Hafez (1325 or 1326–1389 or 1390), Rumi (ca. 1207–1273), and Firdawsi himself. Stylized, the lush Persian garden appears throughout the arts, including in carpets, mosaics, and ceramics, as well as paintings, a joyous and regal celebration of the mystical marriage of earthly and spiritual.

[1] *The Houghton Shahnama,* ed., Martin Bernard Dickson (Cambridge, MA: Harvard University Press, 1981), vol. 1, 45.
[2] Elizabeth B. Moynihan, *Paradise as a Garden in Persia and Mughal India* (New York: George Braziller, fill in), 44.

economic relations with other Islamic lands became increasingly difficult after 1500, as did religious and cultural interchange. However healthy Islam remained in this region, its contact with the original Islamic heartlands (and even with India) shrank. Contact came primarily through a few pilgrims, members of Sufi orders, *ulama*, and students. Central Asian Islam mostly developed in isolation, a large but peripheral area to the Islamic mainstream communities.

POWER SHIFTS IN THE SOUTHERN SEAS

SOUTHERN-SEAS TRADE

Along the southern rim of Asia, from the Red Sea and East Africa to Indonesia and the South China Sea, the first half of the second millennium witnessed the gradual spread of Islamic religion and culture into new regions and among new peoples. In ports in Java, Sumatra, the Malay Peninsula, South India, Gujarat, East Africa, Madagascar, and Zanzibar, Islamic traders established thriving communities. Their enclaves in these cities often became the dominant presence. Initially the Muslims' economic stature attracted especially the socially and religiously mobile peoples of these cosmopolitan centers; many of them also found the ideas and practices of Islam compelling. Typically this first stage of conversion was followed by Islam's transmission to surrounding areas and finally to inland centers. In this transmission, Sufi orders and their preachers and holy men played the main role. However, conquest by Muslim coastal states quickened the process in Indonesia and East Africa.

The international trade network that the Muslims inherited in the southern seas was ancient. Before 1200 much of the trade in these waters had been dominated by Hindu or Buddhist kingdoms on the Malay Peninsula or Sumatra. Arab traders had also been active at least in the Indian Ocean. Hindu culture had been carried, along with an Indonesian language, as far as Madagascar in the first millennium C.E. Hindus were the chief religious group the Muslims displaced. In the East, Islam never ousted the Indian Buddhist cultures of Burma, Thailand, and Indochina, although Muslim traders lived in their ports. Islam did, however, gradually win most of Malaysia, Sumatra, Java, and the "Spice Islands" of the Moluccas—always the coastal areas first, then the inland regions.

CONTROL OF THE SOUTHERN SEAS

The Portuguese reached the East African coast in 1498. In the following three centuries, the history of the lands along the trade routes of the southern Asian seas, from the shores of East Africa to Indonesia and Malaysia, was bound closely not only with Islamic religious, cultural, and commercial networks but also with the rising power of Christian western Europe. The key attractions of these diverse lands were their commercial and strategic possibilities.

In the sixteenth century the Europeans began to displace by armed force the Muslims who, by 1500, had come to dominate the maritime southern rim of Asia. European success was based on two key factors. One was that their naval and commercial ventures were backed by national support systems. The other, for a time at least, was their superior warships. This combination enabled the Portuguese to carve out a major power base in the early sixteenth century along the west coast of India at the expense of the Muslims who dominated Indian maritime trade. They did so through superior naval power, and by exploiting indigenous rivalries and terrorizing all who opposed them.

However, in the southern-seas trade centers, Islamization continued, even in the face of Christian proselytizing and growing European political and commercial presence. The Muslims, unlike most of the European Christians, never kept aloof from the native populations and were largely assimilated everywhere. They rarely abandoned their faith, which proved generally attractive to new peoples they encountered. The result was usually an Islamized and racially mixed population.

As a result, while European gunboat imperialism had considerable military and economic success, often at the expense of Islamic states, European culture and Christianity made little headway against Islam. From East Africa to the Pacific, only in the northern Philippines did a substantial population become largely Christian.

CHRONOLOGY

THE SOUTHERN SEAS: ARRIVAL OF THE PORTUGUESE

1498	The Portuguese come to the East African coast and to the west coast of India
1500–1512	The Portuguese establish bases on west Indian coast, replace Muslims as Indian Ocean power
early 1500s	Muslim sultanates replace Hindu states in Java, Sumatra
1524–1910	State of Acheh in northwestern Sumatra
1600s	Major increase in Islamization and connected spread of Malay language in the archipelago
1641	Dutch conquest of Malacca
ca. 1800	Dutch replace Muslim states as main archipelago power
1873–1910	War between Holland and Acheh

THE INDIES: ACHEH

The history of the Indonesian archipelago has always revolved around the international demand for its spices, peppers, and other produce. By the fifteenth century the coastal Islamic states were centered on the trading ports of the Malay Peninsula, the north shores of Sumatra and Java, and the Moluccas, or "Spice Islands." The last great Hindu kingdom of inland Java was defeated by an Islamic coalition of states in the early 1500s. Several substantial Islamic sultanates arose in the sixteenth and seventeenth centuries, even as Europeans were carving out their own economic empires in the region. The most powerful of these Islamic states was Acheh, in northwestern Sumatra (ca. 1524–1910).

In its early years Acheh provided the only counterweight to the Portuguese presence across the straits in Malacca (Malaysia). Although the Acheh sultans were unable to drive the better armed invaders out, neither could the Portuguese subdue them. Despite Portuguese control of Indies commerce, Acheh managed to dominate the pepper trade of Sumatra and to thrive until the end of the sixteenth century. In the first half of the seventeenth century the sultanate controlled both coasts of Sumatra and parts of the Malay Peninsula. Meanwhile, the Dutch had replaced the Portuguese in the business of milking the Indies of their wealth, and by the eighteenth century they were doing it just as ruthlessly and more efficiently. In the early twentieth century the Dutch finally won full control in the region, but only after nearly forty years of intermittent war with Acheh (1873–1910).

In World Perspective

THE LAST ISLAMIC EMPIRES

The period from 1500 to 1800 in Islamic and South Asian lands and in the Afro-Asian southern seas can be characterized in various ways. We have focused on the striking cultural and political blossoming of Islamic societies and their ensuing sharp decline. We have also seen briefly the beginning of radically new kinds of European intrusion upon the societies of the Islamic heartlands and of Africa, India, and Southeast Asia. By contrast, in the sixteenth and seventeenth centuries Japan and China were not subject to much influence from either the Islamic empires or western European imperialism.

The Islamic vitality in the first half of this period was exemplified in the three mighty empires and prosperous societies of the Ottomans, Safavids, and Mughals. All three built vast bureaucracies using Islamic ideology, but even more their own imperial vigor, to legitimize their rule. They also built arguably the greatest cities in the world of their time and patronized the arts to stimulate important new traditions of Islamic literature, calligraphy, painting, and architecture. Yet they were profoundly conservative societies. Economically they remained closely tied to agricultural production and taxation based on land. They did not undergo the kind of social or religio-political revolutions that rocked the Western world after 1500. Thus, much like the contemporaneous societies of China and Japan, they did not undergo the sort of generative changes in material and intellectual life that the Western world was experiencing, although their intellectual culture was vibrant and diverse. There was no compelling challenge to traditional Islamic ideals of societal organization and human responsibility, even though many Islamic movements of the eighteenth century did call for communal and personal reform.

As one historian has put it, the striking growth of Islamic societies and cultures in this age was "not one of *origination*, but rather one of *culmination* in a culture long already mature."[2] Even in their heydays, these empires produced much scientific work, but no scientific revolution; much art, architecture, and literature of high quality, but none that departed radically in concept or inspiration from previous traditions; political consolidation and also expansion, but no conquest of significant new markets or territories; commercial prosperity, but no beginnings of a real commercial or industrial revolution. Furthermore, by the latter half of this period, all were in economic, political, and military decline.

Thus it is not surprising that European expansionism impinged fatefully in these three centuries upon Africa, India, Indonesia, and the heartland cultures of the Islamic world, rather than the reverse. Neither the great imperial Islamic states, the smaller Islamic sultanates and amirates, the diverse Hindu kingdoms, nor the varied African states (let alone the smaller societies of Africa, the Americas, and the South Pacific) fared well in their encounters with Europeans during this age. The growing European domination of the seas allowed Europeans to contain as well as to bypass the major Islamic lands in their quest for commercial empires.

[2] M. G. S. Hodgson, *The Venture of Islam* (Chicago: University of Chicago Press, 1974), Vol. 3, p. 15.

Industrial development joined economic wealth and political stability by the late 1700s to give the West global military supremacy for the first time. Before 1800 the Europeans were able to bring only minor Islamic states under colonial administrations. However, the footholds they gained in Africa, India, and Southeast Asia laid the groundwork for rapid colonial expansion after 1800. The age of the last great Muslim empires was the beginning of the first great modern European empires. The colonialism of the nineteenth century accompanied the relentless advance of Western industrial, commercial, and military power that would hold sway until the mid–twentieth century.

REVIEW QUESTIONS

1. Why did the Ottoman Empire expand so rapidly into Europe? Why did the empire fail to hold certain areas in Europe?
2. Why did the Safavid Empire succeed in Iran? What role did Islamic religion have in this development? Who were the major foes of this empire?
3. What were the most important elements that united all Islamic states? Why was there a lack of unity between these states from 1500 to 1800? How and why were the European powers able to promote division among these various states?
4. What were Akbar's main policies toward the Hindu population? Why did he succeed and his followers fail in this area? What were his main governmental reforms?
5. How and why did the Sikhs develop into a formidable military power? Why did they become separatist in their orientation to the larger Indian world?
6. What were the main tenets of the *Ishraqi* or "illumination" school of theological-philosophical thought? Define the concepts of "transcendence" and a "realm of images"?
7. Why were outside powers attracted to the southern-seas lands? Why did the European powers triumph in the struggle to control this area?
8. Compare the Sunni-Shi'ite split within the Islamic world (1500–1800) with that of the Protestant-Catholic split within the Christian world during that same period. For example, can we compare relations between England and Spain in the sixteenth century to those between the Ottomans and the Safavids?

SUGGESTED READINGS

A. L. BASHAM, ED., *A Cultural History of India* (1975). Part II, "Age of Muslim Dominance," is of greatest relevance here.

S. S. BLAIR AND J. BLOOM, *The Art and Architecture of Islam, 1250–1800* (1994). A fine survey of the period for all parts of the Islamic world.

K. CHELEBI, *The Balance of Truth* (1957). A marvelous volume of essays and reflections by probably the major intellectual of Ottoman times.

M. A. COOK, ED., *A History of the Ottoman Empire to 1730* (1976). Articles from *The Cambridge History of Islam* and *The New Cambridge Modern History*, with a brief introduction by Cook.

W. T. DE BARY ET AL., COMP., *Sources of Indian Tradition*, 2nd ed. (1958). Vol. I, *From the Beginning to 1800*, ed. and rev. by Ainslie T. Embree (1988). Excellent selections from a wide variety of Indian texts, with good introductions to chapters and individual selections.

C. H. FLEISCHER, *Bureaucrat and Intellectual in the Ottoman Empire: The Historian Mustafa Ali (1541–1600)* (1986). A major study of Ottoman intellectual history.

G. HAMBLY, *Central Asia* (1966). Excellent survey chapters (9–13) on the Chaghatay and Uzbek (Shaybanid) Turks.

R. S. HATTOX, *Coffee and Coffee-Houses: The Origins of a Social Beverage in the Medieval Near East* (1985). A fascinating piece of social history.

M. G. S. HODGSON, *The Gunpowder Empires and Modern Times*, Vol. 3 of *The Venture of Islam*, 3 vols. (1974). Less ample than Vols. 1 and 2 of Hodgson's monumental history, but a thoughtful survey of the great post-1500 empires.

P. M. HOLT, ANN K. S. LAMBTON, AND BERNARD LEWIS, *The Cambridge History of Islam*, 2 vols. (1970). A traditional, somewhat compartmentalized history useful for reference. Vol. I has important surveys on the Ottoman Empire and Safavid Iran. Vol. II includes chapters on post-1500 India, Southeast Asia, and Africa.

S. M. IKRAM, *Muslim Civilization in India* (1964). Still the best short survey history, covering the period from 711 to 1857.

H. INALCIK, *The Ottoman Empire: The Classical Age 1300–1600* (1973). An excellent, if dated, survey with solid treatment of Ottoman social, religious, and political institutions.

H. INALCIK, *An Economic and Social History of the Ottoman Empire, 1300–1914* (1994). A masterly survey by the dean of Ottoman studies today.

C. KAFADAR, *Between Two Worlds: The Construction of the Ottoman State* (1995). A readable analysis of theories of Ottoman origins and early development.

N. R. KEDDIE, ED., *Scholars, Saints, and Sufis: Muslim Religious Institutions in the Middle East Since 1500* (1972). A collection of interesting articles well worth reading.

R. C. MAJUMDAR, GEN. ED., *The History and Culture of the Indian People*, Vol. VII, *The Mughal Empire* (1974). A thorough and readable political and cultural history of the period in India.

M. MUJEEB, *The Indian Muslims* (1967). The best cultural study of Islamic civilization in India as a whole, from its origins onward.

G. NECIPOGLU, *Architecture, Ceremonial, and Power: the Topkapi Palace in the Fifteenth and Sixteenth Centuries* (1991). A superb analysis of the symbolism of Ottoman power and authority.

S. A. A. RIZVI, *The Wonder That Was India*, Vol. II (1987). A sequel to Basham's original *The Wonder That Was India*; treats Mughal life, culture, and history from 1200 to 1700.

F. ROBINSON, *Atlas of the Islamic World Since 1500* (1982). Brief, excellent historical essays, color illustrations with detailed accompanying text, and chronological tables, as well as precise maps, make this a refreshing general reference work.

R. SAVORY, *Iran Under the Safavids* (1980). A solid and readable survey.

S. J. SHAW, *Empire of the Gazis: The Rise and Decline of the Ottoman Empire, 1280–1808*, Vol. I of *History of the Ottoman Empire and Modern Turkey* (1976). A solid historical survey with excellent bibliographic essays for each chapter and a good index.

J. O. VOLL, *Islam: Continuity and Change in the Modern World* (1982). Chapter 3 provides an excellent overview of eighteenth-century revival and reform movements in diverse Islamic lands.

DOCUMENTS CD-ROM

1. The Ottomans: Empire-builders at the crossroads of three continents
2. Konstantin Mihailovic, Memoirs of a Janissary
3. Kritovoulos, History of Mehmed the Conqueror
4. Shah Abbas the Great: The resurgence of the Persian Empire
5. Albert Hourani: Changing relations with Europe

WORLD AND THE WEB

NetIran

Netiran.com

A very comprehensive collection of information on Iran. It includes excerpts from Iran YearBook, Iran/Land of Norooz, and a database complete with United Nations resolutions and statements, Tehran Times archive, Iran News archive, IRNA archive, biographies on cabinet members and other government officials, book reviews, and more.

IranMania Search Engine

http://www.iranmania.com/

Searching for Iranian material on the Internet has been greatly simplified by this excellent Iranian search engine. In addition to the usual search facilities, it includes intelligent interpretation of western spelling and also the ability to search for images.

The Ottoman Khilafa

http://www.naqshbandi.org/ottomans/

A series of decisive victories in a long chain of conquests led the Turks to the zenith of their military power and glory. An unbroken succession of ten brilliant and great Sultans led the Ottomans to acquire in the fourteenth, fifteenth and sixteenth centuries a vast empire stretching from the gates of Vienna to the straits of Bab-el-Mandib, and from the Caucasus across North Africa, almost to the Atlantic Ocean. This site details its Khalifas, Protectors, Military Ranks, the Wahhabis religious movement, and its relics.

H-Mideast-Medieval

http://www2.h-net.msu.edu/~midmed/

A discussion network for scholars and others interested in the study of the Islamic lands of the Middle East during the medieval period (defined roughly as 500-1500 C.E.). The network is sponsored by Middle East Medievalists (MEM).

Islamic Thought

http://wings.buffalo.edu/sa/muslim/isl/thought.html

This link provides a springboard for exploring texts and resources on Islamic thought, ideas, and related issues. Although there is a fine line between the histories of Islamic thought and Muslim civilization, it is useful to treat the study of Islam, the faith, somewhat differently than from the history, politics and analysis of Muslim peoples.

PART V

Enlightenment and Revolution in the West

Between approximately 1750 and 1850 certain extraordinary changes occurred in Western civilization. Although of immediate significance primarily for the nations of Europe and the Americas, these developments produced in the long run an immense impact throughout the world, No other civilizations ultimately escaped the influence of the European intellectual ferment and political turmoil of these years. Most of the intellectual, political, economic, and social characteristics associated with the *modern* world came into being during this era. Europe became the great exporter of ideas and technologies that in time transformed one area of the human experience after another.

Intellectually, the ideals of reform and of challenge to traditional cultural authority captured the imagination of numerous writers. That movement, known as the *Enlightenment*, drew confidence from the scientific worldview that had emerged during the seventeenth century. Its exponents urged the application of the spirit of critical rationalism in one area of social and political life after another. They posed serious historical and moral questions to the Christian faith. They contended that laws of society and economics could be discovered and could then be used to improve the human condition. They embraced the idea of economic growth and development. They called for political reform and more efficient modes of government. They upheld the standard of rationality in order to cast doubt on traditional modes of thought and behavior that seemed to them less than rational. As a result of their labors in Europe and eventually throughout the world, the idea of change that has played so important a role in modern life came to have a generally positive value attached to it for the first time.

For many people, however, change seemed to come too rapidly and violently when revolution erupted in France in

Ana Ipatescu leads Transylvanian revolutionaries against Russia, 1848. E.T. Archives

1789. Commencing as an aristocratic revolt against the monarchy, the revolution rapidly spread to every corner of French political and social life. The rights of man and citizen displaced those of the monarchy, the aristocracy, and the church. By 1792 the revolution had become a genuinely popular movement and had established a French republic whose armies challenged the other major European monarchies. The Reign of Terror that saw the execution of the French king unloosed domestic violence unlike anything witnessed in Europe since the age of the religious wars. By the end of the 1790s, to restore order, French political leaders turned themselves over to the leadership of Napoleon. Thereafter, for more than a decade his armies overturned the institutions of the Old Regime across the Continent. Only in 1815, after the Battle of Waterloo, was the power of France and Napoleon finally contained.

The French Revolution in one way or another served as a model for virtually all later popular revolutions. It unleashed new forces and political creeds in one area of the world after another. The French Revolution, with its broad popular base, brought *the people* to the forefront of world political history. In the early revolutionary goals of establishing a legal framework of limited monarchical power, of securing citizen rights, and of making possible relatively free economic activity, the supporters of the revolution spawned the political creed of *liberalism.* The wars of the French Revolution and of Napoleon, stretching from 1792 to 1815, awakened the political force of *nationalism,* which has proved to be the single most powerful ideology of the modern world. Loyalty to the nation defined in terms of a common language, history, and culture replaced loyalty to dynasties. As a political ideology, nationalism could be used both to liberate a people from the domination of another nation and to justify wars of aggression. Nationalism was put to both uses in Europe and throughout the rest of the world in the two centuries following the revolution in France. Nationalism became a kind of secular religion that aroused a degree of loyalty and personal self-sacrifice previously called forth only by the great religious traditions.

Finally, between 1750 and 1850 Europe became an exporter not only of reform and revolution but also of manufactured commodities. The technology and the society associated with industrialism took root throughout the western portion of the Continent. Europeans achieved a productive capacity that, in cooperation with their naval power, permitted them to dominate the markets of the world. Thereafter, to be strong, independent, and modern seemed to mean to become industrialized and to imitate the manufacturing techniques of Europe and later of the United States.

But industrialism and its society fostered immense social problems, dislocations, and injustices. The major intellectual and political response was *socialism,* several varieties of which emerged from the European social and economic turmoil of the 1830s and 1840s. History eventually proved the most important to be that espoused by Karl Marx, whose *Communist Manifesto* appeared in 1848.

Remarkable ironies are attached to the European achievements of the late eighteenth and early nineteenth centuries. Enlightenment, revolution, and industrialism contributed to an awakening of European power that permitted the Continent to dominate the world for a time at the end of the nineteenth century. Yet those same movements fostered various intellectual critiques, political ideas, and economic skills that twentieth-century non-European peoples would turn against their temporary European masters. It is for that reason that the age of enlightenment and revolution in the West was of such significance not simply in the history of Europe but in the history of the entire modern world.

1750–1800

Europe

1756–1763 Seven Years' War
1762–1796 Catherine II, "the Great" reigns in Russia
1763 Peace of Paris Seven Years' War
1772 First partition of Poland
1783 Peace of Paris
1789 French Revolution begins
1793 and 1795 Last partitions of Poland

July 14, 1789, Bastille prison, Paris

Near East/India

1757 British victory at Plassey, in Bengal
1761 English oust French from India
1772–1784 Warren Hastings' administration in India
1772–1833 Ram Mohan Roy, Hindu reformer in India
1794–1925 Qajar shahs in Iran
1805–1849 Muhammad Ali in Egypt

1800–1850

Europe

1804–1814 Napoleon's empire
1814–1815 Congress of Vienna
1830–1848 Louis Philippe reigns in France
1832 First British Reform Act
1837–1901 Queen Victoria of England
1848 Revolutions across Europe

Near East/India

1835 Introduction of English education in India

British colonial rule in India (1880)

ca. 1839–1880 Tanzimat reforms, Ottoman Empire
1839–1897 Muslim intellectual Jamal al-Din Al-Afghani
1845–1905 Muhammad Abduh

EAST ASIA

1753–1806 Kitagawa Utamaro, Tokugawa era artist

1787–1793 Matsudaira Sadanobu's reforms in Japan

1789 White Lotus Rebellion in China

1823–1901 Li Hung-chang, powerful Chinese governor-general

Utamaro woodblock print

1835–1908 Empress Dowager Tz'u-hsi

1839–1842 Opium War; 1842, Treaty of Nanking grants Hong Kong to the British and allows them to trade in China

1844 Similar treaties made between China and France and the United States

AFRICA

1754–1817 Usman Dan Fodio, founder of Sultanate in northern and central Nigeria

1762 End of Funj sultanate in eastern Sudanic region

1804 Fulani Jihad into Hausa lands

1806 British take Cape Colony from the Dutch

1817–1828 Zulu chief Shaka reigns

1830–1847 French invasion of Algeria

1830s Dutch settlers, the Boers, expand northward from Cape Colony

1848–1885 Sudanese Madhi, Muhammad Ahmad

THE AMERICAS

1759–1788 Spain reorganizes government of its American Empire

1776 American Declaration of Independence

1791 First ten amendments to U.S. Constitution (Bill of Rights) ratified

1791 Negro slave revolt in French Santo Domingo

1794 Canada Constitutional Act divides the country into Upper and Lower Canada

1804 Haitian independence

1808–1824 Wars of independence in Latin America

1822 Brazilian independence

1847 Mexican War

Simón Bolívar

23 The Age of European Enlightenment

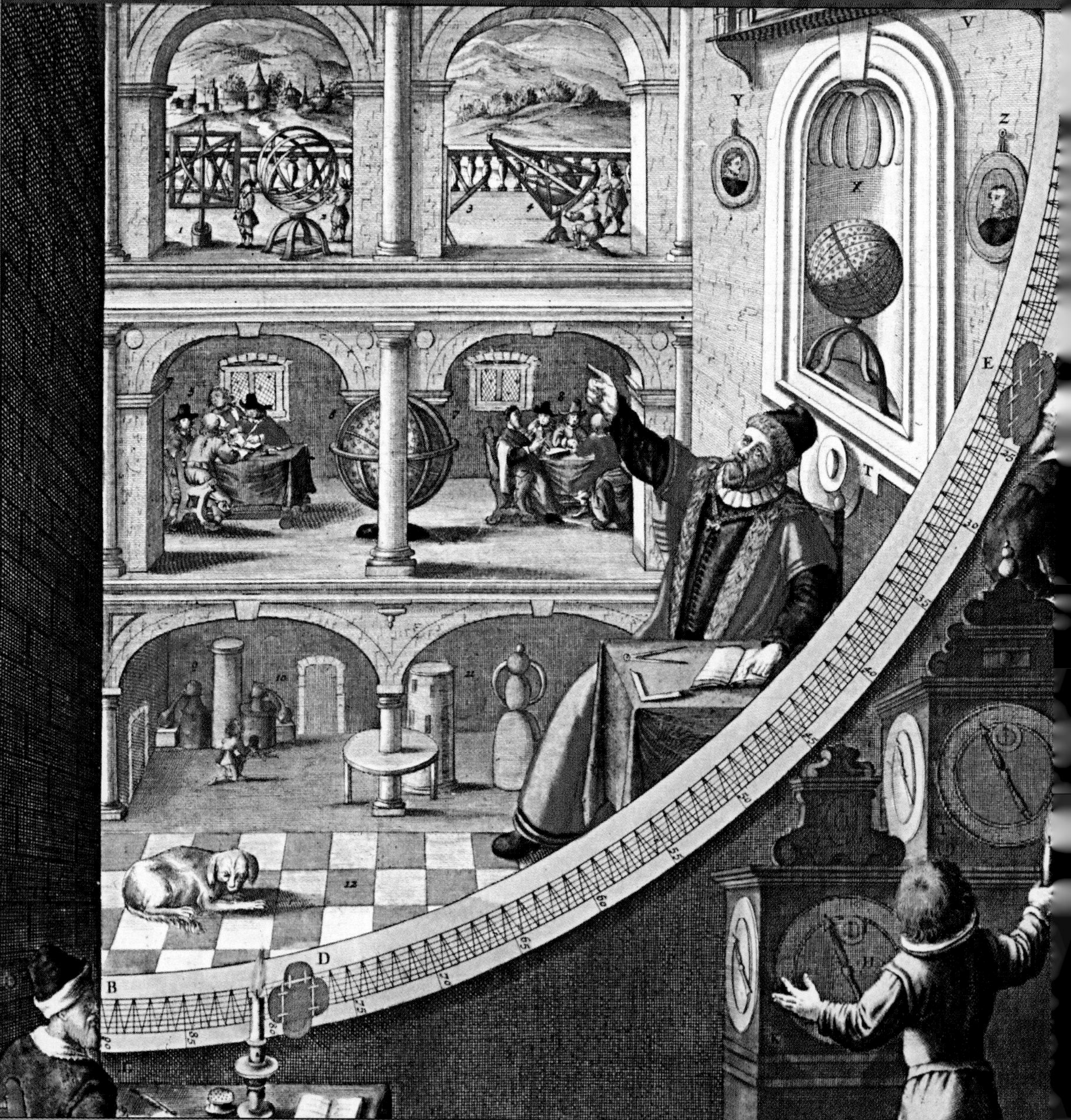

Commercing in the 16th century with new theory and observations in astronomy, a new age of European science opened. It was upon the confidence inspired by the new science that European thinkers of the 17th and 18th centuries established a framework of reformist thought that became known as the Enlightenment. This illustration from the Danish observatory of Tycho Brahe indicates the sense of wonder evoked by the new astronomy.

Chapter topics

- The Scientific Revolution
- The Enlightenment
- The Enlightenment and Religion
- The Enlightenment and Society
- Enlightened Absolutism

IN WORLD PERSPECTIVE
The Enlightenment Heritage

NO SINGLE INTELLECTUAL FORCE DURING the past three centuries has so transformed every region of the world as has Western science and the technology that has flowed from its understanding of nature. Although throughout the world today there has arisen much interest in nontraditional methods of healing, the impact of science on every area of human life remains a dominant force. Furthermore, the attainment of scientific knowledge, often for the purposes of military advantage as well as medical and economic advance, has become a goal of most modern states.

The emergence of science as this vast culturally transforming force began in Europe during the sixteenth century in a process of discovery and formation of theory known as the *Scientific Revolution*, which gained enormous momentum during the next two centuries. Then as now scientific knowledge and methods challenged other areas of intellectual and religious life, and then as now governments sought to use that knowledge to maximize their advantage against other states. Non-European states in the nineteenth and twentieth centuries often gained power and influence to the extent that science as understood in the West came to dominate their intellectual life, health care systems, and military planning.

The impact of science could make itself felt first in Europe and then elsewhere only as the conviction came to spread that change and reform were both possible and desirable. This attitude is now commonplace, but it came into its own in Europe only after 1700. The capacity and even eagerness to embrace change, especially change as justified on the grounds of science, represents one of the primary intellectual inheritances from that age. The movement of people and ideas that fostered such thinking is called the *Enlightenment.* Its leading voices combined confidence in the human mind inspired by the Scientific Revolution and faith in the power of rational criticism to challenge the intellectual authority of tradition and revealed religion. Its writers believed that human beings could comprehend the operation of physical nature and mold it to the ends of material and moral improvement. The rationality of the physical universe became a standard against which the customs and traditions of society could be measured and criticized. Such criticism penetrated every corner of contemporary society. As a result, the spirit of innovation and improvement came to characterize modern Western society. This outlook would become perhaps the most important European cultural export to the rest of the world.

THE SCIENTIFIC REVOLUTION

The sixteenth and seventeenth centuries witnessed a sweeping change in the scientific view of the universe. From being considered the center of the universe, the Earth was now seen as only another planet orbiting about the sun. The sun itself became one of millions of stars. This transformation led to a vast rethinking of moral and religious matters as well as of scientific theory. Science and the scientific method became so impressive and so influential that they set a new standard for evaluating knowledge in the Western world.

The process that established the new view of the universe is normally termed the *Scientific Revolution.* The revolution-in-science metaphor must be used carefully, however. Not everything associated with the "new" science was necessarily new. Sixteenth- and seventeenth-century natural philosophers were often reexamining and rethinking theories and data from the ancient world and the late middle ages. Moreover, the word *revolution* normally denotes rapid, collective political change involving large numbers of people. The Scientific Revolution was *not* rapid. It was a complex movement with many false starts and brilliant people suggesting wrong as well as useful ideas. Nor did it involve more than a few hundred people who labored in widely separated studies and crude laboratories located in Poland, Italy, Bohemia, France, and Great Britain. Furthermore, the achievements of the new science were not simply the function of isolated brilliant scientific minds. The leading figures of the Scientific Revolution often drew upon the aid of artisans and craftspeople to help them construct new instruments for experimentation and to carry out those experiments. Thus, the Scientific Revolution involved a reappropriation of older knowledge as well as new discoveries. Additionally, because the practice of science involves social activity as well as knowledge, the revolution also saw the establishment of new social institutions to support the emerging scientific enterprise.

Science as we know it today was only in the process of becoming during the era of the Scientific Revolution. In fact the word *scientist*, invented in the 1830s, did not yet exist in the seventeenth century nor did anything resembling the modern scientific career. Individuals devoted to natural philosophy might work in universities or in the court of a prince or possibly in their own homes and workshops. Only in the second half of the seventeenth century did formal societies and academies devoted to the pursuit of natural philosophy come into existence. Even then the entire process of the pursuit of natural knowledge was a largely informal one.

Yet by the close of the seventeenth century the new scientific concepts and the methods of their construction were so impressive that they set the standard for assessing the validity of knowledge in the Western world. From the early seventeenth century through the end of the twentieth century science achieved greater cultural authority in the Western world than any other form of intellectual activity, and the authority and application of scientific knowledge became one of the defining characteristics of modern Western civilization.

Although new knowledge emerged in many areas during the sixteenth and seventeenth centuries, including medicine, chemistry, and natural history, the scientific achievements that most captured the learned imagination and persuaded people of the cultural power of natural knowledge were those that occurred in astronomy.

Nicolaus Copernicus Rejects an Earth-Centered Universe

Nicolaus Copernicus (1473–1543) was a Polish astronomer who enjoyed a high reputation during his life. He had been educated first in Cracow and later in Italy. He led a largely isolated intellectual career and had not been known for strikingly original or unorthodox thought. In 1543, the year of his death, Copernicus published *On the Revolutions of the Heavenly Spheres.* Copernicus's book was "a revolution-making rather than a revolutionary text."[1] What Copernicus did was to provide an intellectual springboard for a complete criticism of the then-dominant view of the position of the Earth in the universe.

The Ptolemaic System At the time of Copernicus, the standard explanation of the place of the Earth in the heavens combined the mathematical astronomy of Ptolemy, contained in his work entitled the *Almagest* (150 C.E.), with the physical cosmology of Aristotle. Over the centuries, commentators on Ptolemy's work had developed several alternative Ptolemaic systems, on the basis of which they made mathematical calculations relating to astronomy. Most of these writers assumed that the Earth was the center of the universe, an outlook known as *geocentricism.* Drawing upon Aristotle, these commentators assumed that above the Earth lay a series of concentric spheres, probably fluid in character, one of which contained the moon, another the sun, and still others the planets and the stars. At the outer regions of these spheres lay the realm of God and the angels. The Earth had to be the center because of its heaviness. The stars and the other heavenly bodies had to be enclosed in the spheres so that they could move, since nothing could move unless something was actually moving it. The state of rest was presumed natural; motion required explanation. This was the astronomy found in such works as Dante's *Divine Comedy.*

Numerous problems were associated with the Ptolemaic model, and these had long been recognized. The most important was the observed motions of the planets. At certain times the planets actually appeared to be going backwards. The Ptolemaic model accounted for these motions primarily through *epicycles.* The planet moved uniformly about a small circle (an epicyle), while the center of the epicyle moved uniformly about a larger circle (called a deferent), with the Earth at or near its center. The combination of these two motions, as viewed from the Earth, was meant to replicate the changing planetary positions among the fixed stars—and did so to a high degree of accuracy. The circles employed in Ptolemaic systems were not meant to represent the actual paths of anything; that is, they were not orbits. Rather, they were the components of purely mathematical models meant to predict planetary positions. Other intellectual, but nonobservational difficulties related to the immense speed at which the spheres had to move around the Earth. To say the least, the Ptolemaic systems were cluttered. They were effective, however, as long as one assumed Aristotelian physics.

[1] Thomas S. Kuhn, *The Copernican Revolution: Planetary Astronomy in the Development of Western Thought* (New York: Vintage, 1959), p. 135.

COPERNICUS'S UNIVERSE Copernicus's *On the Revolutions of the Heavenly Spheres* challenged the Ptolemaic picture in the most conservative manner possible. Copernicus adopted many elements of the Ptolemaic model, but transferred them to a *heliocentric* (sun-centered) model which assumed that the Earth moved about the sun in a circle. Copernicus's model, which retained epicyles, was actually no more accurate than Ptolemy's. However, Copernicus could claim certain advantages over the ancient model. In particular, the epicycles were smaller. The retrograde motion of the planets now stood explained as a result of an optical illusion arising from an observer viewing the planets from a moving Earth. The order of the planets from the sun became more clearly intelligible when it was understood as a result of their increasing periods of revolution based on the planets' increasing distance from the sun.

The repositioning of the Earth had not been Copernicus's goal. Rather, Copernicus appears to have set out to achieve new intelligibility and mathematical elegance to astronomy. The means of doing so was to reject Aristotle's cosmology and to remove the Earth from the center of the universe. His system was no more accurate than the existing ones for predicting the location of the planets. He had used no new evidence. The major impact of his work was to provide another way of confronting some of the difficulties inherent in Ptolemaic astronomy. The Copernican system did not immediately replace the old astronomy, but it allowed other people who were also discontented with the Ptolemaic view to think in new directions. Indeed, for at least a century, the Copernican system was embraced by a distinct minority of natural philosophers and astronomers.

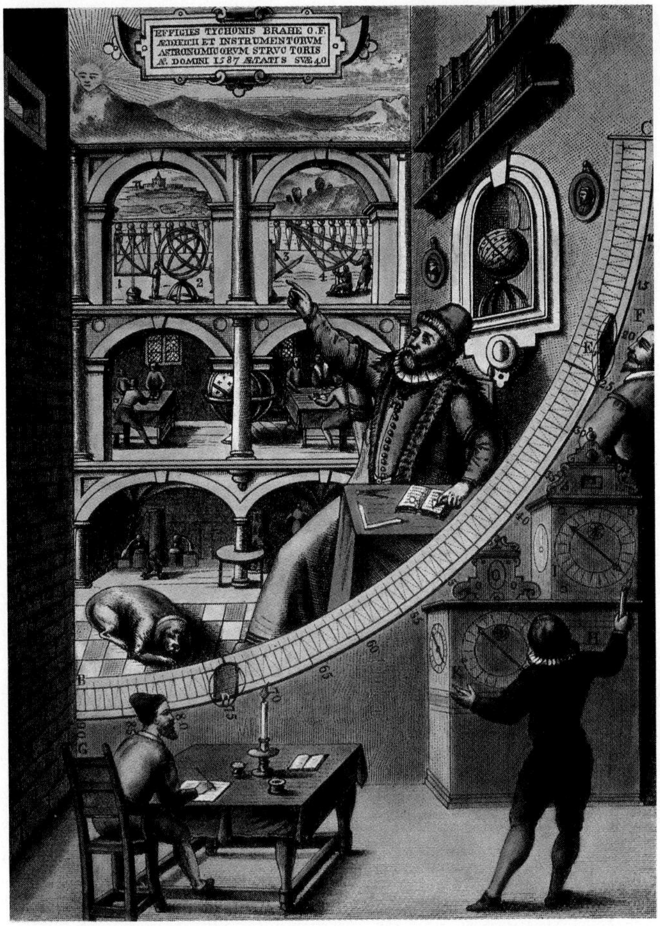

Tycho Brahe in the Uranienburg observatory on the Danish island of Hven (1587). Brahe made the most important observations of the stars since antiquity. Kepler used his data to solve the problem of planetary motion in a way that supported Copernicus's sun-centered view of the universe. Ironically, Brahe himself had opposed Copernicus's view. Bildarchiv Preussischer Kulturbesitz

TYCHO BRAHE AND JOHANNES KEPLER

The next major step toward the conception of a sun-centered system was taken by the Danish astronomer Tycho Brahe (1546–1601). He spent most of his life opposing Copernicus and advocating a different kind of Earth-centered system. He suggested that the moon and the sun revolved around the Earth and that the other planets revolved around the sun. However, in attacking Copernicus, he gave the latter's ideas more publicity. More important, his major weapon against Copernican astronomy was a series of new astronomical observations made with the naked eye. Brahe constructed the most accurate tables of observations that had been drawn up for centuries.

When Brahe died, these tables came into the possession of Johannes Kepler (1571–1630), a German astronomer. Kepler was a convinced Copernican, but for philosophical, not scientific, reasons. Kepler was deeply influenced by Renaissance Neoplatonists who, following upon Plato's (ca. 428–ca. 328 B.C.E.) association of knowledge with light, honored the sun. These Neoplatonists were also determined to discover mathematical harmonies that would support a sun-centered universe. After much work, Kepler discovered that to keep the sun at the center of things, he must abandon the Copernican concept of circular orbits. The mathematical relationships that emerged from a consideration of Brahe's observations suggested that the orbits of the planets were elliptical. Kepler published his findings in 1609 in a book entitled *On the Motion of Mars.* He had solved the problems of planetary orbits by using Copernicus's sun-centered universe and Brahe's empirical data.

Kepler had, however, also defined a new problem. None of the available theories could explain why the planetary orbits were elliptical. That solution awaited the work of Sir Isaac Newton.

Document: Galileo Discusses the Relationship of Science to the Bible

The religious authorities were often critical of the discoveries and theories of sixteenth- and seventeenth-century science. For years before his condemnation by the Roman Catholic Church in 1633, Galileo had contended that scientific theory and religious piety were compatible. In his Letter to the Grand Duchess Christiana *(of Tuscany), written in 1615, he argued that God had revealed truth in both the Bible and physical nature and that the truth of physical nature did not contradict the Bible if the latter were properly understood. Galileo encountered difficulties regarding this letter because it represented a layman telling church authorities how to read the Bible.*

Is Galileo's argument based on science or theology? Did the church believe that nature was as much a revelation of God as the Bible was? As Galileo describes them, which is the surer revelation of God, nature or the Bible? Why might the pope reject Galileo's argument?

The reason produced for condemning the opinion that the Earth moves and the sun stands still is that in many places in the Bible one may read that the sun moves and the Earth stands still. . . .

With regard to this argument, I think in the first place that it is very pious to say and prudent to affirm that the holy Bible can never speak untruth—whenever its true meaning is understood. But I believe nobody will deny that it is often very abstruse, and may say things which are quite different from what its bare words signify. . . .

This being granted, I think that in discussions of physical problems we ought to begin not from the authority of scriptural passages, but from sense-experiences and necessary demonstrations; for the holy Bible and the phenomena of nature proceed alike from the divine Word, the former as the dictate of the Holy Ghost and the latter as the observant executrix of God's commands. It is necessary for the Bible, in order to be accommodated to the understanding of every man, to speak many things which appear to differ from the absolute truth so far as the bare meaning of the words is concerned. But Nature, on the other hand, is inexorable and immutable; she never transgresses the laws imposed upon her, or cares a whit whether her abstruse reasons and methods of operation are understandable to men. For that reason it appears that nothing physical which sense-experience sets before our eyes, or which necessary demonstrations prove to us, ought to be called in question (much less condemned) upon the testimony of biblical passages which may have some different meaning beneath their words. For the Bible is not chained in every expression to conditions as strict as those which govern all physical effects; nor is God any less excellently revealed in Nature's actions than in the sacred statements of the Bible. . . .

From this I do not mean to infer that we need not have an extraordinary esteem for the passages of holy Scripture. On the contrary, having arrived at any certainties in physics, we ought to utilize these as the most appropriate aids in the true exposition of the Bible and in the investigation of those meanings which are necessarily contained therein for these must be concordant with demonstrated truths. I should judge the authority of the Bible was designed to persuade men of those articles and propositions which, surpassing all human reasoning, could not be made credible by science, or by any other means than through the very mouth of the Holy Spirit. . . .

But I do not feel obliged to believe that the same God who has endowed us with senses, reason, and intellect has intended to forgo their use and by some other means to give us knowledge which we can attain by them.

From *Discoveries and Opinions of Galileo* by Galileo Galilei. Copyright © 1957 by Stillman Drake. Used by permission of Doubleday, a division of Random House, Inc.

Galileo Galilei

From Copernicus to Brahe to Kepler, there had been little new information about the heavens that might not have been known to Ptolemy. However, in 1609 an Italian scientist named Galileo Galilei (1564–1642) first turned a telescope on the heavens. He saw stars where none had been known to exist, mountains on the moon, spots moving across the sun, and moons orbiting Jupiter. The heavens were far more complex than anyone had formerly suspected. None of these discoveries proved that the earth orbited the sun, but they did suggest the complete inadequacy of the Ptolemaic system. It simply could not accommodate these new phenomena. Some of Galileo's colleagues at the University of Padua were so unnerved that they refused to look through the telescope, because it revealed the heavens to be different from the teachings of the church and from Ptolemaic theories.

Galileo publicized his findings and arguments for the Copernican system in numerous works, the most famous of which was his *Dialogues on the Two Chief Systems of the World* (1632). This book brought down on him the condemnation of the Roman Catholic Church. He was compelled to recant his opinions. However, he is reputed to have muttered after the recantation, "*E pur si muove*" ("It [the earth] still moves").

Galileo's most important achievement was to articulate the concept of a universe totally subject to mathematical laws. More than any other writer of the century, he argued that nature in its most minute details displayed mathematical regularity. Copernicus had thought that the heavens conformed to mathematical regularity; Galileo saw this regularity throughout all physical nature. He believed that the smallest atom behaved with the same mathematical precision as the largest heavenly sphere.

Galileo stood as one of the foremost champions of the application of mathematics to scientific investigation and of the goal of reducing phenomena to mathematical formulas. However, earlier in the century the English philosopher Francis Bacon had advocated a method based solely on empiricism. As the century passed, both empirical induction and mathematical analysis proved fundamental to scientific investigation.

Francis Bacon: The Empirical Method

Bacon (1561–1626) was an Englishman of almost universal accomplishment. He was a lawyer, a high royal official, and the author of histories, moral essays, and philosophical discourses. Traditionally, he has been regarded as the father of empiricism and of experimentation in science. Much of this reputation was actually unearned. Bacon was not a natural philosopher, except in the most amateur fashion. His real accomplishment was setting an intellectual tone and helping to create a climate conducive to scientific work.

In books such as *The Advancement of Learning* (1605), the *Novum Organum* (1620), and the *New Atlantis* (1627), Bacon attacked the scholastic belief that most truth had already been discovered and only required explanation, as well as the scholastic reverence for authority in intellectual life. He believed that scholastic thinkers paid too much attention to tradition and to the knowledge of the ancients. He urged contemporaries to strike out on their own in search of a new understanding of nature. He wanted seventeenth-century Europeans to have confidence in themselves and their own abilities rather than in the people and methods of the past. Bacon was one of the first major European writers to champion the desirability of innovation and change.

Bacon believed that human knowledge should produce useful results—deeds rather than words. In particular, knowledge of nature should be brought to the aid of the human condition. These goals required the modification or abandonment of scholastic modes of learning and thinking. Bacon contended, "The [scholastic] logic now in use serves more to fix and give stability to the errors which have their foundation in commonly received notions than to help the search after truth."[2] Scholastic philosophers could not escape from their syllogisms to examine the foundations of their thought and intellectual presuppositions. Bacon urged that philosophers and investigators of nature examine the evidence of their senses before constructing logical speculations. In a famous passage, he divided all philosophers into "men of experiment and men of dogmas" and then observed:

> The men of experiment are like the ant, they only collect and use; the reasoners resemble spiders, who make cobwebs out of their own substance. But the bee takes a middle course: it gathers its material from the flowers of the garden and of the field, but transforms and digests it by a power of its own. Not unlike this is the true business of philosophy.[3]

By directing natural philosophy toward an examination of empirical evidence, Bacon hoped that it would achieve new knowledge and thus new capabilities for humankind.

Bacon boldly compared himself with Columbus, plotting a new route to intellectual discovery. The comparison is significant, because it displays the consciousness of a changing world that appears so often in writers of the late sixteenth and early seventeenth centuries. They were rejecting the past not from simple contempt or overweening pride, but rather from a firm understanding that the world was much more complicated than their medieval forebears had thought. Neither Europe nor European thought could remain self-contained. Like the new worlds on the globe, new worlds of the mind were also emerging.

Most of the people in Bacon's day, including the intellectuals, thought that the best era of human history lay in antiquity. Bacon dissented vigorously from that view. He looked to a future of material improvement achieved through the empirical examination of nature. His own theory of induction from empirical evidence was unsystematic, but his insistence on appealing to experience influenced others whose methods were more productive. He and others of his outlook received almost daily support from the reports not only of European explorers, but also of ordinary seamen who now sailed all over the world and could describe wondrous cultures, as well as plants and animals, unknown to the European ancients.

Bacon believed that science had a practical purpose and its goal was human improvement. Some scientific investigation does have this character. Much pure research does not. Bacon, however, linked science and material progress in the public mind. This was a powerful idea and has continued to influence Western civilization to the present day. It has made science and those who can appeal to the authority of science major forces for change and innovation. Thus, though not making any major scientific contribution himself, Bacon directed investigators of nature to a new method and a new purpose. As a person actively associated with politics, Bacon also believed that the pursuit of new knowledge would increase the power of governments and monarchies. Again, his thought in this area opened the way for the eventual strong linkage between governments and the scientific enterprise.

[2] Quoted in Franklin Baumer, *Main Currents of Western Thought*, 4th ed. (New Haven, CT: Yale University Press, 1978), p. 281.

[3] Quoted in Baumer, p. 288.

Isaac Newton Discovers the Laws of Gravitation

The question that continued to perplex seventeenth-century scientists who accepted the theories of Copernicus, Kepler, and Galileo was how the planets and other heavenly bodies moved in an orderly fashion. The Ptolemaic and Aristotelian answer had been the spheres and a universe arranged in the order of the heaviness of its parts. Many unsatisfactory theories had been set forth to deal with the question. It was this issue of planetary motion that the Englishman Isaac Newton (1642–1727) addressed and, in so doing, established a basis for physics that endured for more than two centuries.

In 1687 Newton published *The Mathematical Principles of Natural Philosophy*, better known by its Latin title of *Principia Mathematica.* Much of the research and thinking for this great work had taken place more than fifteen years earlier. Galileo's mathematical bias permeated Newton's thought, as did his view that inertia applied to bodies both at rest and in motion. Newton reasoned that the planets and all other physical objects in the universe moved through mutual attraction, or gravity. Every object in the universe affected every other object through gravity. The attraction of gravity explained why the planets moved in an orderly, rather than a chaotic, manner. Newton had found that "the force of gravity towards the whole planet did arise from and was compounded of the forces of gravity towards all its parts, and towards every one part was in the inverse proportion of the squares of the distances from the part."[4] Newton proved this relationship mathematically; he made no attempt to explain the nature of gravity itself.

Newton was a great mathematical genius, but he also upheld the importance of empirical data and observation. Like Francis Bacon, he believed that one must observe phenomena before attempting to explain them. The final test of any theory or hypothesis for him was whether it described what was actually observed. Newton was a great opponent of the rationalism of the French philosopher René Descartes (1596–1650), which he believed included insufficient guards against error. Consequently, as Newton's own theory of universal gravitation became increasingly accepted, so, too, was Baconian empiricism.

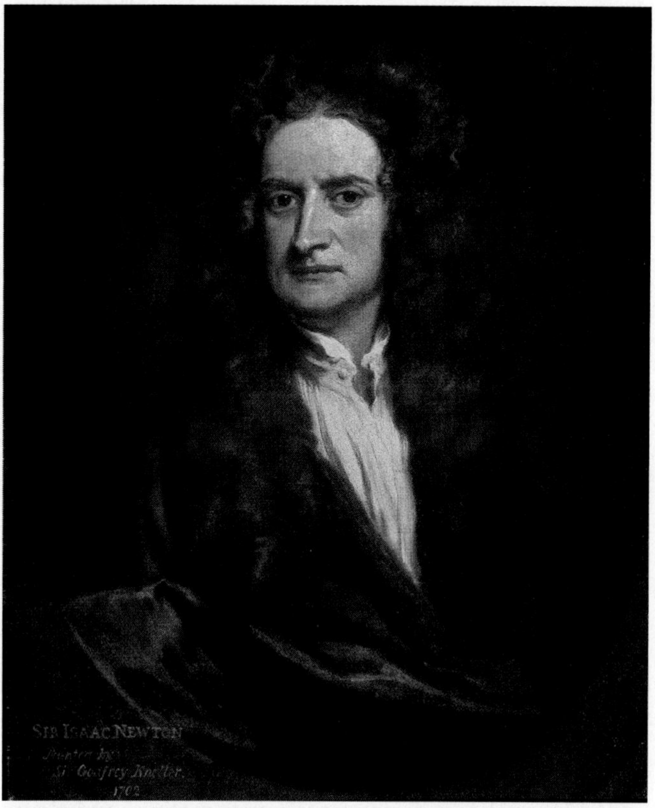

Sir Isaac Newton discovered the mathematical and physical laws governing the force of gravity. Newton believed that religion and science were compatible and mutually supportive, and that the study of nature gave one a better understanding of the Creator. This portrait of Newton is by Sir Godfrey Kneller. Sir Godfrey Kneller, *Sir Isaac Newton.* Bildarchiv Preussischer Kulturbesitz

Women in the World of the Scientific Revolution

The absence of women in the emergence of the new science of the seventeenth century has been a matter of much historical speculation. What characteristics of early modern European intellectual and cultural life worked against extensive contributions by women? Why have we heard so little of the activity by women that did actually occur in regard to the new science?

The same factors that had long excluded women from participating in most intellectual life continued to exclude them from working in the emerging natural philosophy. Traditionally, the institutions of European intellectual life had all but excluded women. Both monasteries and universities had been institutions associated with celibate male clerical culture. Except for a few exceptions in Italy, women had not been admitted to either medieval or early modern European universities; they would continue to be excluded from them until the end of the nineteenth century. Women could and did exercise much influence over princely courts where natural philosophers, such as Galileo, sought patronage, but they usually did not determine those patronage decisions or benefit from them. Queen Christina of Sweden was an exception by engaging René Descartes to provide the regulations for a new science academy. When various scientific societies were founded, women were not admitted to membership. In that regard, there were virtually no social spaces that might have permitted women easily to pursue science.

[4] Quoted in A. Rupert Hall, *From Galileo to Newton, 1630–1720* (London: Fontana, 1970), p. 300.

Yet a few isolated women from two different social settings did manage to engage in the new scientific activity—noblewomen and women from the artisan class. In both cases, they could do so only through their husbands or other men in their families.

The social standing of certain noblewomen allowed them to command the attention of ambitious natural philosophers who were part of their husband's social circle. Margaret Cavendish (1623–1673) actually made significant contributions to the scientific literature of the day. After she had been privately tutored and become widely read, her marriage to the duke of Newcastle introduced her into a circle of natural philosophers. She understood the new science, quarreled with the ideas of Descartes and Hobbes, and criticized the Royal Society for being more interested in novel scientific instruments than in solving practical problems. Her most important works were *Observations upon Experimental Philosophy* (1666) and *Grounds of Natural Philosophy* (1668). She was the only woman in the seventeenth century to be allowed to visit a meeting of the Royal Society of London.

Women associated with artisan crafts actually achieved greater freedom in pursuing the new sciences than did noblewomen. Traditionally, women had worked in artisan workshops, often with their husbands; and might take over the business when their spouse died. In Germany, much astronomy occurred in these settings, with women assisting their fathers or husbands. One such German female astronomer, Maria Cunitz, published a book on astronomy that many people thought her husband had written until he added a preface supporting her sole authorship. Elisabetha and Johannes Hevelius constituted a wife-and-husband astronomical team, as did Maria Winkelmann and her husband Gottfried Kirch. In each case, the wife served as the assistant to an artisan astronomer. Although Winkelmann discovered a comet in 1702, not until 1930 was the discovery ascribed to her rather than to her husband. Nonetheless, contemporary philosophers did recognize her abilities and understanding of astronomy. Winkelmann had worked jointly with her husband who was the official astronomer of the Berlin Academy of Sciences and was responsible for establishing an official calendar published by the Academy. When her husband died in 1710, Winkelmann applied for permission to continue the work, basing her application for the post on the guild's tradition of allowing women to continue their husband's work, in this case the completion of observations required for creating an accurate calendar. After much debate, the Academy formally rejected her application on the grounds of her gender, although its members knew of her ability and previous accomplishments. Years later, she returned to the Berlin Academy as an assistant to her son, who had been appointed astronomer. Again, the Academy insisted that she leave, forcing her to abandon astronomy. She died in 1720.

Such policies of exclusion, however, did not altogether prevent women from acquiring knowledge about the scientific endeavors of the age. Margaret Cavendish had composed a *Description of a New World, Called the Blazing World* (1666) to introduce women to the new science. Other examples of scientific writings for a female audience were Bernard de Fontenelle's *Conversations on the Plurality of Worlds* and Francesco Algarotti's *Newtonianism for Ladies* (1737). During the 1730s, Emilie du Châtelet aided Voltaire in his composition of an important French popularization of Newton's science. Her knowledge of mathematics was more extensive than his and crucial to his completing his book.

Still, with only a few exceptions, women were barred from science and medicine until the late nineteenth century, and not until the twentieth century did they enter these fields in any significant numbers. Not only did the institutions of science exclude them, but also, the ideas associated with medical practice, philosophy, and biology suggested that women and their minds were essentially different from, and inferior to, men and theirs. By the early eighteenth century, despite isolated precedents of women pursuing natural knowledge, reading scientific literature, and engaging socially with natural philosophers, it had become a fundamental assumption of European intellectual life that the pursuit of natural knowledge was a male vocation.

JOHN LOCKE

John Locke (1632–1704) attempted to achieve for philosophy a lawful picture of the human mind similar to that which Newton had presented of nature. Locke's three most famous works were the *Essay Concerning Human Understanding* (1690), *Two Treatises of Government*, and his *Letter Concerning Toleration* (1689). Each of them sounded philosophical themes that later writers of the Enlightenment found welcome. No other philosopher had so profound an impact on European and American thought during the eighteenth century.

In the *Essay Concerning Human Understanding*, Locke envisioned the human mind as being blank at the time of an individual's birth. In Locke's view, contrary to that of much medieval philosophy, there are no innate ideas (i.e., ideas people are born with); all knowledge is derived from actual sense experience. Each individual mind grows through experience as it confronts the world of sensation. Human ideas are either simple (that is, passive receptions from daily experience) or complex (that is, products of sustained mental exercise). What people know is not the external world in itself but the results of the interaction of their minds with the outside world. Locke's thinking thus represented an early form of behaviorism. Human nature is changeable and can be molded by modifying the surrounding physical and social environment. Locke also, in effect, rejected the Christian view that human beings were creatures permanently flawed by original sin. Human beings do not need to wait for the grace of God or other divine aid to better their lives. They can take charge of their own destiny.

Art and the World

JOSEPH WRIGHT, "AN EXPERIMENT ON A BIRD IN THE AIR-PUMP":

SCIENCE IN THE DRAWING ROOM

The air-pump, devised by the pioneering English natural philosopher Robert Boyle in the 1650s, stood for over a century as a major symbol of the new experimental science championed by the Royal Society of London. The instrument permitted air to be pumped out of a spherical glass jar to create a vacuum for the purpose of demonstrating the qualities of air and air pressure. The early air-pumps often functioned quite poorly because air would seep in through leaky seals, invading the vacuum. By the middle of the eighteenth century, however, many provincial English scientific societies possessed effective models such as the one portrayed in Joseph Wright's *An Experiment on a Bird in the Air-Pump* (1768).

Wright, who lived near Derby in an early industrial region of England, was a close friend of manufacturers and other persons interested in science several of whom be-

Joseph Wright of Derby, *An Experiment on a Bird in the Air-Pump* (1768).
National Gallery, London, Great Britain. The Bridgeman Art Library.

longed to the Lunar Society. In this dramatically lit painting, Wright portrays the excited interest of fashionable upper-class audiences in experimental science. At the same time, though, he suggests genuine apprehension about the practice of science.

Wright presents the central figure, who is operating the pump, as a natural philosopher about to demonstrate his superior knowledge and scientific skill through an experiment meant to indicate the necessity of air for the life of an animal. The experimenter holds the life and death of the bird in his hands as he moves to turn the switch that will create the vacuum. One figure observes the experiment with a sense of amazement, while another looks on with an expression of stoic acceptance. The man speaking to the young women, one of whom appears fearful and the other cautiously curious, may be explaining the need to place rationality above feelings in the pursuit of knowledge. Sacrificing the bird would advance the progress of science.

In his depiction of women (including one more interested in her male companion than in the experiment), Wright seems to be suggesting the commonly held view of the day that women may approach science and experiments as observers, but may lack the intellectual qualities required for active participation in the experimental method.

In art historical terms, Wright, an English artist, has taken a genre of painting known as the *conversation piece* and made a scientific experiment the center of attention. Wright has also made another important substitution of a scientific subject for a more traditional one. The painting dramatically contrasts light and dark, a technique originally devised to highlight elements in paintings of religious scenes. Here the drama of the light highlights a secular scientific experiment on a natural subject that, especially in England, many people believed might lead to a new understanding of the divine. Thus, Wright could see the reverence once reserved for religious subjects now being evoked by a scientific one.

His painting, though coming a century after the first air-pump experiments, demonstrates the manner in which, by the mid–eighteenth century, experimental science had established its cultural presence within polite society and its ability to foster civil conversation in place of political and religious disputes. Rather than discussing the Bible or politics, this group is observing a scientific experiment that will provide them with the opportunity for polite and presumably noncontroversial conversation, or at least conversation that will not lead to destructive quarrels.

Although, as an artist, Wright explored the challenges of painting light, the setting of this experiment would also seem to suggest that even in the eighteenth century he and others saw science as an uncertain and possibly temporary light surrounded by darkness and potential superstition.

Sources: David H. Solkin, *Painting for Money: The Visual Arts and the Public Sphere in Eighteenth-Century England* (New Haven, CT: Yale University Press, 1993); Steven Shapin and Simon Schaffer, *Leviathan and the Air-Pump: Hobbes, Boyle, and the Experimental Life* (Princeton, NJ: Princeton University Press, 1985).

John Locke (1632–1704), defender of the rights of the people against rulers who think their power absolute. By courtesy of the National Portrait Gallery, London

Locke wrote *Two Treatises of Government* during the reign of Charles II (r.1660–1685). Locke argued that rulers are not absolute in their power. They remain bound to the law of nature. That law is the voice of reason, teaching that human beings are equal and independent and that they should not harm one another or disturb one another's property because all persons are the images and property of God. According to Locke, people enter political contracts, empowering legislatures and monarchs to judge their disputes in order to preserve their natural rights (which include the possession of property) but not to give rulers an absolute power over them. Locke also contended that a monarch who violated the trust that had been placed in him could be overthrown. This argument reappeared in the American Declaration of Independence in 1776. But in eighteenth-century Europe it was Locke's argument against absolutism and in favor of limited government that was most influential. Like his philosophy, it opened a wider arena for individual action.

Locke's *Letter Concerning Toleration* contended that each person was responsible for his own religious salvation. Governments existed to protect property and the civil order. Matters only became confused when governments undertook to legislate on religion and require conformity to a single church. Yet Locke himself drew the line in England against toleration of Roman Catholics and Unitarians. During the eighteenth century, however, the logic of his argument was extended to advocate toleration for those faiths as well.

The Enlightenment

The movement that came to be known as the Enlightenment included a number of writers living at different times in various countries. Its early exponents, known as the *philosophes*, popularized the rationalism and scientific ideas of the seventeenth century. They worked to expose contemporary social and political abuses and argued that reform was necessary and possible. The advancement of their cause and ideas was anything but steady. They confronted vested interests, political oppression, and religious condemnation. Yet by midcentury they had brought enlightened ideas to the European public in a variety of formats.

By the second half of the century the *philosophes* were sufficiently safe from persecution to quarrel among themselves. They had stopped talking in generalities, and their major advocates were addressing themselves to specific abuses. Their books and articles had become more specialized and more practical. They were more concerned with politics than with religion. Having convinced Europeans that change was a good idea, they began to suggest exactly which changes were most desirable. They had become honored figures.

Voltaire

One of the earliest and by far the most influential of the *philosophes* was François Marie Arouet, known to posterity as Voltaire (1694–1778). During the 1720s Voltaire had offended the French authorities by certain of his writings. He was arrested and briefly imprisoned. Later he went to England, visiting its best literary circles, observing its tolerant intellectual and religious climate, relishing the freedom he felt in its moderate political atmosphere, and admiring its science and economic prosperity. In 1733 he published *Letters on the English*, which appeared in French the next year. The book praised the virtues of the English and indirectly criticized the abuses of French society. In 1738 he published *Elements of the Philosophy of Newton*, which popularized the thought of the great scientist. Both works enhanced his reputation.

Thereafter, Voltaire lived part of the time in France and part near Geneva, just across the French border, where the royal authorities could not bother him. His essays, history, plays, stories, and letters made him the literary dictator of Europe. He turned the bitter venom of his satire and sarcasm against one evil after another in French and European life. His most famous satire is *Candide* (1759), in which he attacked war, religious persecution, and what he regarded as unwarranted optimism about the human condi-

Philosopher, dramatist, poet, historian, and popularizer of scientific ideas, Voltaire (1694–1778) was the most famous and influential of the 18th-century philosophers. His sharp satire and criticism of religious institutions opened the way for a more general critique of the European political and social status quo.
Bildarchiv Preussischer Kulturbesitz

tion. Like most *philosophes*, Voltaire believed that human society could and should be improved. But he was never certain that reform, if achieved, would be permanent. The optimism of the Enlightenment constituted a tempered hopefulness rather than a glib certainty. Pessimism was an undercurrent in most of the works of the period.

The Encyclopedia

The midcentury witnessed the publication of the *Encyclopedia*, one of the greatest monuments of the Enlightenment. Under the heroic leadership of Denis Diderot (1713–1784) and Jean le Rond d'Alembert (1717–1783), the first volume appeared in 1751. When completed in 1772, it numbered seventeen volumes of text and eleven of plates. The *Encyclopedia* was the product of the collective effort of more than one hundred authors, and its editors had solicited articles from all the major French *philosophes*. The project reached fruition only after numerous attempts to censor it and to halt its publication. The *Encyclopedia* set forth the most advanced critical ideas in religion, government, and philosophy. This criticism often had to be hidden in obscure articles or under the cover of irony. The articles represented a collective plea for freedom of expression. However, the large volumes also provided important information on manufacturing, canal building, ship construction, and improved agriculture.

Between 14,000 and 16,000 copies of various editions of the *Encyclopedia* were sold before 1789. The project had been designed to secularize learning and to undermine the intellectual assumptions remaining from the Middle Ages and the Reformation. The articles on politics, ethics, and society ignored concerns about divine law and concentrated on humanity and its immediate well-being. The encyclopedists looked to antiquity rather than to the Christian centuries for their intellectual and ethical models. The future welfare of humankind lay not in pleasing God or following divine commandments, but rather in harnessing the power of the earth and its resources and in living at peace with one's fellow human beings. The good life was to be achieved through the application of reason to human relationships.

With the publication of the *Encyclopedia*, enlightened thought became more fully diffused over the Continent. Enlightened ideas penetrated German and Russian intellectual and political circles.

The Enlightenment and Religion

Throughout the century, in the eyes of the *philosophes*, the chief enemy of the improvement of humankind and the enjoyment of happiness was the church. The hatred of the *philosophes* for the church and Christianity was summed up in Voltaire's cry of "Crush the Infamous Thing." Almost all varieties of Christianity, but especially Roman Catholicism, invited the criticism of the *philosophes*. Intellectually, the churches perpetuated a religious rather than a scientific view of humankind and physical nature. The clergy taught that human beings were basically sinful and that they required divine grace to become worthy creatures. The doctrine of original sin in either its Catholic or its Protestant formulation suggested that meaningful improvement in human nature was impossible. Religious concerns turned human interest away from this world to the world to come. For the *philosophes*, the concept of predestination suggested that the fate of the human soul after death bore little or no relationship to virtuous living. Through their disagreements over obscure doctrines, the various churches favored the politics of intolerance and bigotry that in the past had caused human suffering, torture, and war.

Printing shops were the productive center for the book trade and newspaper publishing which spread the ideas of the Enlightenment.
The Granger Collection

Deism

The *philosophes* believed that religion should be reasonable and lead to moral behavior. The Newtonian worldview had convinced many writers that nature was rational. Therefore, the God who had created nature must also be rational, and the religion through which that God was worshiped should be rational. Moreover, Lockean philosophy, which limited human knowledge to empirical experience, cast doubt on whether divine revelation was possible. These considerations gave rise to a movement for enlightened religion known as *deism.*

The title of one of its earliest expositions, *Christianity Not Mysterious* (1696) by John Toland, indicates the general tenor of this religious outlook. Toland and later writers wished to consider religion a natural and rational, rather than a supernatural and mystical, phenomenon. In this respect the deists differed from Newton and Locke, who had regarded themselves as distinctly Christian. Newton had believed that God might interfere with the natural order, whereas the deists regarded God as resembling a divine watchmaker who had set the mechanism of nature to work and then let them operate without intervention.

There were two major points in the deists' creed. The first was a belief in the existence of God, which they thought could be empirically deduced from the contemplation of nature.

Because nature provided evidence of a rational God, that Deity must also favor rational morality. Consequently, the second point in the deists' creed was a belief in life after death, when rewards and punishments would be meted out according to the virtue of the life a person led on this earth.

Deism was empirical, tolerant, reasonable, and capable of encouraging virtuous living. It was the major positive religious component of the Enlightenment. Voltaire declared:

> The great name of Deist, which is not sufficiently revered, is the only name one ought to take. The only gospel one ought to read is the great book of Nature, written by the hand of God and sealed with his seal. The only religion that ought to be professed is the religion of worshiping God and being a good man.[5]

[5] Quoted in J. H. Randall, *The Making of the Modern Mind*, rev. ed. (New York: Houghton Mifflin, 1940), p. 292.

Chronology

Major Publication Dates of the Enlightenment

1687	Newton's *Principia Mathematica*
1690	Locke's *Essay Concerning Human Understanding*
1696	Toland's *Christianity Not Mysterious*
1733	Voltaire's *Letters on the English*
1738	Voltaire's *Elements of the Philosophy of Newton*
1748	Montesquieu's *Spirit of the Laws*
1750	Rousseau's *Discourse on the Moral Effects of the Arts and Sciences*
1751	First volume of the *Encyclopedia* edited by Diderot and d'Alembert
1755	Rousseau's *Discourse on the Origin of Inequality*
1762	Rousseau's *Social Contract*
1763	Voltaire's *Treatise on Tolerance*
1776	Smith's *Wealth of Nations*
1779	Lessing's *Nathan the Wise*
1792	Wollstonecraft's *A Vindication of the Rights of Woman*

If such a faith became widely accepted, it would overcome the fanaticism and rivalry of the various Christian sects. Religious conflict and persecutions would end. There would also be little or no necessity for a priestly class to foment fanaticism, denominational hatred, and bigotry.

TOLERATION

A primary social condition for such a life was the establishment of religious toleration. Voltaire took the lead in championing this cause. In 1762 the political authorities in Toulouse ordered the execution of a Huguenot named Jean Calas (1698–1762). He stood accused of having murdered his son to prevent him from converting to Roman Catholicism. Calas had been viciously tortured and publicly strangled without ever having confessed his guilt. The confession would not have saved his life, but it would have given the Catholics good propaganda to use against Protestants.

Voltaire learned of the case only after Calas's death. He made the dead man's cause his own. In 1763 he published a *Treatise on Tolerance* and hounded the authorities for a new investigation. Finally, in 1765 the judicial decision against the unfortunate man was reversed. For Voltaire, the case illustrated the fruits of religious fanaticism and the need for rational reform of judicial processes. Somewhat later in the century the German playwright and critic Gotthold Lessing (1729–1781) wrote *Nathan the Wise* (1779) as a plea for toleration not only of different Christian sects but also of religious faiths other than Christianity. All of these calls for toleration stated, in effect, that human life should not be subordinated to religion. Secular values and considerations were more important than religious ones.

THE ENLIGHTENMENT AND SOCIETY

Although the *philosophes* wrote much about religion, humanity was the center of their interest. As one writer in the *Encyclopedia* observed, "Man is the unique point to which we must refer everything, if we wish to interest and please amongst considerations the most arid and details the most dry."[6] The *philosophes* believed that the application of human reason to society would reveal laws in human relationships similar to those found in physical nature. Although the term did not appear until later, the idea of social science originated with the Enlightenment. The purpose of discovering social laws was to remove the inhumanity that existed through ignorance of them.

[6] Quoted in F. L. Baumer, *Main Currents of Western Thought*, 4th ed. (New Haven, CT: Yale University Press, 1978), p. 374.

MONTESQUIEU AND "THE SPIRIT OF THE LAWS"

Charles Louis de Secondat, Baron de Montesquieu (1689–1755), was a French noble of the robe and a magistrate. His work *The Spirit of the Laws* (1748), perhaps the single most influential book of the century, exhibits the internal tensions of the Enlightenment. Montesquieu pursued an empirical method, taking illustrative examples from the political experience of both ancient and modern nations. From them he concluded that no single set of political laws could apply to all peoples at all times and in all places. Rather, the good political life depended on the relationship of many political variables. Whether a monarchy or a republic was the best form of government depended on the size of the political unit and its population, its social and religious customs, economic structure, traditions, and climate. Only a careful examination and evaluation of these elements could reveal what mode of government would prove most beneficial to a particular people. A century later such speculations would have been classified as sociology.

So far as France was concerned, Montesquieu believed in a monarchy whose power was tempered and limited by various intermediary institutions, including the aristocracy, the

Charles de Secondat, Baron de Montesquieu (1689–1755) was the author of *The Spirit of the Laws*, possibly the most influential work of political thought of the 18th century. Hulton/UPI/Corbis-Bettmann

towns, and the other corporate bodies that enjoyed particular liberties that the monarch must respect. These corporate bodies might be said to represent various segments of the general population and thus of public opinion. In France he regarded the *parlements*, judicial courts dominated by aristocrats like himself, as the major example of an intermediary association. Their role was to limit the power of the monarchy and thus to preserve the liberty of the subjects. In championing these aristocratic bodies and the general role of the aristocracy, Montesquieu was a political conservative. He adopted that stance, however, in the hope of achieving reform, for he considered the oppressive and inefficient absolutism of the monarchy responsible for the degradation of French life.

One of Montesquieu's most influential ideas was that of division of power. He took Great Britain for his model of a government with power wisely separated among different branches. There he believed he had found a system in which executive power resided in the king, legislative power in the Parliament, and judicial power in the courts. He thought any two branches could check and balance the power of the other. His perception of the eighteenth-century British constitution was incorrect, because he failed to see how patronage and electoral corruption allowed a handful of aristocrats to dominate the government. Moreover, he was also unaware of the emerging cabinet system, which meant that the executive power was slowly becoming a creature of the Parliament. Nevertheless, the analysis illustrated Montesquieu's strong sense of the need to limit the exercise of power through a constitution and for legislatures, not monarchs, to make laws. Although Montesquieu set out to defend the political privileges of the French aristocracy, his ideas had a profound and enduring effect on the liberal democracies of the next two centuries.

Adam Smith on Economic Growth and Social Progress

The most important economic work of the Enlightenment was Adam Smith's (1723–1790) *Inquiry into the Nature and Causes of the Wealth of Nations* (1776). Smith, who was for a time a professor at Glasgow, believed that economic liberty was the foundation of a natural economic system. As a result, he urged that the mercantile system of England—including the navigation acts, the bounties, most tariffs, special trading monopolies, and the domestic regulation of labor and manufacture—be abolished. These regulations were intended to preserve the wealth of the nation, to capture wealth from other nations, and to maximize the work available for the nation's laborers. Smith argued, however, that they hindered the expansion of wealth and production. The best way to encourage economic growth, he maintained, was to unleash individuals to pursue their own selfish economic interests. As self-interested individuals sought to enrich themselves by meeting the needs of others in the marketplace, the economy would expand. Consumers would find their wants met as manufacturers and merchants competed for their business.

It was a basic assumption of mercantilism that the earth's resources are limited and scarce, so that one nation can acquire wealth only at the expense of others. Smith's book challenged this assumption. He saw the resources of nature—water, air, soil, and minerals—as boundless. To him, they demanded exploitation for the enrichment and comfort of humankind. In effect, Smith was saying that the nations and peoples of Europe need not be poor.

Smith is usually regarded as the founder of *laissez-faire* economic thought and policy, which favors a limited role for the government in economic life. *The Wealth of Nations* was, however, a complex book. Smith was no simple dogmatist. For example, he did not oppose all government activity touching the economy. The state, he argued, should provide schools, armies, navies, and roads. It should also undertake certain commercial ventures, such as the opening of dangerous new trade routes that were economically desirable, but too expensive or risky for private enterprise.

Within *The Wealth of Nations*, Smith, like other Scottish thinkers of the day, embraced an important theory of human social and economic development, known as the *four-stage theory*. According to this theory, human societies can be classified as hunting and gathering, pastoral or herding, agricultural, and commercial. The hunters and gatherers have little or no settled life. Pastoral societies are groups of nomads who tend their herds and develop some private property. Agricultural or farming societies are settled and have clear-cut property arrangements. Finally, in the commercial state there exist advanced cities, the manufacture of numerous items for wide consumption, extensive trade between cities and the countryside, as well as elaborate forms of property and financial arrangements. Smith and other Scottish writers described the passage of human society through these stages as a movement from barbarism to civilization.

The four-stage theory implicitly evaluated the later stages of economic development and the people dwelling in them as higher, more progressive, and more civilized than the earlier ones. A social theorist using this theory could thus very quickly look at a society and, on the basis of the state of its economic development and organizations, rank it in terms of the stage it had achieved. In point of fact, the commercial stage, the highest rank in the theory, described society as it appeared in northwestern Europe. Thus, Smith's theory allowed Europeans to look about the world and always find themselves dwelling at the highest level of human achievement. This outlook served as one of the major justifications in the minds of Europeans for their economic and imperial domination of the world during the next century. They repeatedly portrayed themselves as bringing a higher level of civilization to people elsewhere who, according to the four-stage theory, lived in lower stages of human social and economic development. Europeans thus imbued with the spirit of the Enlightenment presented themselves as carrying out a civilizing mission to the rest of the world.

ROUSSEAU

Jean-Jacques Rousseau (1712–1778) held a different view of political power. Rousseau was a strange, isolated genius who never felt comfortable with the other *philosophes.* Yet perhaps more than any other writer of the mid–eighteenth century, he transcended the thought and values of his own time. Rousseau had a deep antipathy toward the world and the society in which he lived. It seemed impossible for human beings living according to contemporary commercial values to achieve moral, virtuous, or sincere lives. In 1750, in his *Discourse on the Moral Effects of the Arts and Sciences,* he contended that civilization and enlightenment had corrupted human nature. Human beings in the state of nature had been more dignified. In 1755, in a *Discourse on the Origin of Inequality,* Rousseau blamed much of the evil in the world on maldistribution of property.

In both works, Rousseau directly challenged the social fabric of the day. He questioned the concepts of material and intellectual progress and the morality of a society in which commerce and industry were regarded as the most important human activities. He felt that the real purpose of society was to nurture better people. Rousseau's vision of reform was much more radical than that of other contemporary writers.

The writings of Jean-Jacques Rousseau (1712–1778) raised some of the most profound social and ethical questions of the Enlightenment. This portrait by Maurice Quentin was made ca. 1740 Bildarchiv Preussischer Kulturbesitz

Rousseau carried these same concerns into his political thought. His most extensive discussion of politics appeared in *The Social Contract* (1762). Compared to Montesquieu's *The Spirit of the Laws, The Social Contract* is an abstract book. It does not propose specific reforms but outlines the kind of political structure that Rousseau believed would overcome the evils of contemporary politics and society.

In the tradition of John Locke, most eighteenth-century political thinkers regarded society as a collection of independent individuals pursuing personal, selfish goals. These writers wished to liberate these individuals from the undue bonds of government. Rousseau picked up the stick from the other end. His book opens with the declaration, "All men are born free, but everywhere they are in chains."[7] The rest of the volume constitutes a defense of the chains of a properly organized society over its members. Rousseau suggested that society is more important than its individual members, because they are what they are only as a result of their relationship to the larger community. Independent human beings living alone can achieve little. Through their relationship to the larger community, they become moral creatures capable of significant action. The question then becomes what kind of community allows people to behave morally. Rousseau sought to project the vision of a society in which each person could maintain personal freedom while also behaving as a loyal member of the larger community. He drew on the traditions of Plato and Calvin to define freedom as obedience to law. In his case, the law to be obeyed was that created by the general will. This concept normally indicated the will of the majority of voting citizens who acted with adequate information and under the influence of virtuous customs and morals. Such democratic participation in decision making would bind the individual citizen to the community. Rousseau believed that the general will must always be right and that to obey the general will was to be free. This argument led him to the notorious conclusion that some people must be forced to be free. His politics thus constituted a justification for radical direct democracy and for collective action against individual citizens.

Rousseau had, in effect, assaulted the eighteenth-century cult of the individual and the fruits of selfishness. He stood at odds with the commercial spirit that was transforming society. Adam Smith wanted people to be prosperous; Rousseau wanted them to be good even if it meant they might remain poor. He saw human beings not as independent individuals but as creatures enmeshed in necessary social relationships. He believed that loyalty to the community should be encouraged. As one device to that end, he suggested a civic re-

[7] Jean-Jacques Rousseau, *The Social Contract and Discourses,* trans. by G. D. H. Cole (New York: Dutton, 1950), p. 3.

DOCUMENT: ROUSSEAU ARGUES FOR SEPARATE SPHERES FOR MEN AND WOMEN

Rousseau published Émile, *a novel about education, in 1762. In it he made one of the strongest and most influential arguments of the eighteenth century for distinct social roles for men and women. Furthermore, he portrayed women as fundamentally subordinate to men.* *See page 646 for a contemporary rebuttal.*

How does Rousseau move from the physical differences between men and women to an argument for distinct social roles and social spheres? What would be the proper kinds of social activities for women in Rousseau's vision? What kind of education would he think appropriate for women?

There is no parity between the two sexes in regard to the consequences of sex. The male is male only at certain moments. The female is female her whole life or at least during her whole youth. Everything constantly recalls her sex to her; and, to fulfill its functions well, she needs a constitution which corresponds to it. She needs care during her pregnancy; she needs rest at the time of childbirth; she needs a soft and sedentary life to suckle her children; she needs patience and gentleness, a zeal and an affection that nothing can rebuff in order to raise her children. She serves as the link between them and their father; she alone makes him love them and gives him the confidence to call them his own. How much tenderness and care is required to maintain the union of the whole family! And, finally, all this must come not from virtues but from tastes, or else the human species would soon be extinguished.

The strictness of the relative duties of the two sexes is not and cannot be the same. When woman complains on this score about unjust man-made inequality, she is wrong. This inequality is not a human institution—or, at least, it is the work not of prejudice but of reason. It is up to the sex that nature has charged with the bearing of children to be responsible for them to the other sex. Doubtless it is not permitted to any one to violate his faith, and every unfaithful husband who deprives his wife of the only reward of the austere duties of her sex is an unjust and barbarous man. But the unfaithful woman does more; she dissolves the family and breaks all the bonds of nature. . . .

Once it is demonstrated that man and woman are not and ought not be constituted in the same way in either character or temperament, it follows that they ought not to have the same education. In following nature's directions, man and woman ought to act in concert, but they ought not to do the same things. The goal of their labors is common, but their labors themselves are different, and consequently so are the tastes directing them. . . .

The good constitution of children initially depends on that of their mothers. The first education of men depends on the care of women. Men's morals, their passions, their tastes, their pleasures, their very happiness also depend on women. Thus the whole education of women ought to relate to men. To please men, to be useful to them, to make herself loved and honored by them, to raise them when young, to care for them when grown, to counsel them, to console them, to make their lives agreeable and sweet—these are the duties of women at all times, and they ought to be taught from childhood. So long as one does not return to this principle, one will deviate from the goal, and all the precepts taught to women will be of no use for their happiness or for ours.

From *Émile; or, On Education, by Jean-Jacques Rousseau,* by Allan Bloom, trans. Copyright © 1979 by Basic Books, a member of Perseus Books L.L.C.

ligion based on deism. Such a shared tolerant religious faith would unify society. Rousseau's chief intellectual inspiration arose from his study of Plato and the ancient Greek *polis.* Especially in Sparta, he thought he had discovered human beings dwelling in a moral society inspired by a common purpose. He hoped that modern human beings might also create such a moral commonwealth in which virtuous living would not become subordinate to commercial profit.

WOMEN IN THE THOUGHT AND PRACTICE OF THE ENLIGHTENMENT

Women, especially in France, helped significantly to promote the careers of the *philosophes.* In Paris the salons of women such as Marie-Thérèse Geoffrin (1699–1777), Julie de Lespinasse (1733–1776), and Claudine de Tencin (1689–1749) gave the *philosophes* access to useful social and political contacts and a receptive environment for their ideas. These women were well connected to major political figures who could help protect the *philosophes* and secure them pensions. The marquise de Pompadour (1721–1764), the mistress of Louis XV, for example, played a key role in overcoming efforts to censor the *Encyclopedia.* She also helped block the circulation of works attacking the *philosophes.*

Nonetheless, the *philosophes* were on the whole not strong feminists. Although many criticized the education women received as overly religious and tended to reject ascetic views of sexual relations, the *philosophes* advocated no radical changes in the social condition of women.

Montesquieu, for example, maintained in general that the status of women in a society was the result of climate, the political regime, culture, and women's physiological nature. He

The salon of Mme. Marie-Thérèse Geoffrin (1699–1777) was one of the most important gathering spots for Enlightenment writers during the middle of the 18th century. Well-connected women such as Mme. Geoffrin were instrumental in helping the *philosophes* they patronized to bring their ideas to the attention of influential people in French society and politics. Giraudon/Art Resource, N.Y.

believed women were not naturally inferior to men and should have a wider role in society. He was well aware of the personal, emotional, and sexual repression women endured in his day. Yet there were limits to his willingness to consider change in women's social role. He retained a traditional view of marriage and family and expected men to dominate those institutions. Furthermore, although he supported the right of women to divorce and opposed laws that directly oppressed them, he upheld the ideal of female chastity.

The views about women expressed in the *Encyclopedia* were less generous. The editors, Diderot and d'Alembert, recruited men almost exclusively as contributors and saw no need to include many articles by women. Most of the articles that dealt with women specifically or that discussed women in connection with other subjects often emphasized their physical weakness and inferiority, usually attributed to menstruation or childbearing. Contributors disagreed on the social equality of women. Some favored it, others opposed it, and still others were indifferent. The articles conveyed a general sense that women were reared to be frivolous and unconcerned with important issues. The encyclopedists discussed women primarily in a family context—as daughters, wives, and mothers—and considered motherhood their most important occupation. On sexual behavior, the encyclopedists upheld an unquestioned double standard.

In contrast to the articles, however, illustrations in the *Encyclopedia* showed women deeply involved in the economic activities of the day. The illustrations also showed the activities of lower- and working-class women, about whom the articles have little to say.

Rousseau urged a traditional role for women. In his novel *Émile* (1762) he declared that women should be educated for a position subordinate to men, emphasizing especially women's function in bearing and rearing children. He portrayed them as weaker and inferior to men in virtually all respects except perhaps for their capacity for feeling and giving love. He excluded them from political life. Women were assigned the domestic sphere alone. Many of these attitudes were not new—some have roots as ancient as Roman law—but Rousseau's powerful presentation and the influence of his other writings gave them new life, including in the legislation of the French Revolution.

Paradoxically, despite these views and his own ill treatment of the many women who bore his many children, Rousseau achieved a vast following among women in the eighteenth century. He is credited with persuading thousands of upper-class women to breast-feed their own children rather than putting them out to wet nurses. One explanation for this influence is that his writings, although they did not advocate liberating women or expanding their social or economic roles, did stress the importance of their emotions and subjective feelings. He portrayed the domestic life and the role of wife and mother as a noble and fulfilling vocation, giving middle- and upper-class women a sense that their daily occupations had purpose. He assigned them a degree of influence in the domestic sphere that they could not have competing with men outside it.

In 1792 in *A Vindication of the Rights of Woman*, Mary Wollstonecraft (1759–1797) brought Rousseau before the judgment of the rational Enlightenment ideal of progressive knowledge. Wollstonecraft (who, like so many women of her day, died shortly after childbirth of puerperal fever) accused Rousseau and others after him who upheld traditional roles for women of attempting to narrow women's vision and limit their experience. She argued

DOCUMENT MARY WOLLSTONECRAFT CRITICIZES ROUSSEAU'S VIEW OF WOMEN

Mary Wollstonecraft published A Vindication of the Rights of Woman *in 1792, thirty years after Rousseau's* Émile *had appeared. She criticized and rejected Rousseau's argument for distinct and separate spheres for men and women as defending the continued bondage of women to men and as hindering the wider education of the entire human race.*

What specific criticisms does Wollstonecraft direct against Rousseau's views? Why does Wollstonecraft put so much emphasis on a new kind of education for women?

The most perfect education . . . is such an exercise of the understanding as is best calculated to strengthen the body and form the heart. Or, in other words, to enable the individual to attain such habits of virtue as will render it independent. In fact, it is a farce to call any being virtuous whose virtues do not result from the exercise of its own reason. This was Rousseau's opinion respecting men: I extend it to women. . . .

I may be accused of arrogance; still I must declare what I firmly believe, that all the writers who have written on the subject of female education and manners from Rousseau to Dr. Gregory [a Scottish physician], have contributed to render women more artificial, weak characters, than they would other wise have been; and, consequently, more useless members of society. . . .

. . . Strengthen the female mind by enlarging it, and there will be an end to blind obedience; but, as blind obedience is ever sought for by power, tyrants and sensualists are in the right when they endeavour to keep women in the dark, because the former only wants slaves, and the latter a play-thing. The sensualist, indeed, has been the most dangerous of tyrants, and women have been duped by their lovers, as princes by their ministers, whilst dreaming that they reigned over them.

. . . Rousseau declares that a woman should never, for a moment, feel herself independent, that she should be governed by fear to exercise her natural cunning, and made a coquettish slave in order to render her a more alluring object of desire, a sweeter companion to man, whenever he chooses to relax himself. He carries the arguments, which he pretends to draw from the indications of nature, still further, and insinuates that truth and fortitude, the corner stones of all human virtue, should be cultivated with certain restrictions, because, with respect to the female character, obedience is the grand lesson which ought to be impressed with unrelenting rigour.

What nonsense! When will a great man arise with sufficient strength of mind to put away the fumes which pride and sensuality have thus spread over the subject! If women are by nature inferior to men, their virtues must be the same in quality, if not in degree, or virtue is a relative idea; consequently, their conduct should be founded on the same principles, and have the same aim.

Connected with man as daughters, wives, and mothers, their moral character may be estimated by their manner of fulfilling those simple duties; but the end, the grand end of their exertions should be to unfold their own faculties and acquire the dignity of conscious virtue. . . .

But avoiding . . . any direct comparison of the two sexes collectively, or frankly acknowledging the inferiority of women, according to the present appearance of things, I shall only insist that men have increased that inferiority till women are almost sunk below the standard of rational creatures. Let their faculties have room to unfold, and their virtues to gain strength, and then determine where the whole sex must stand in the intellectual scale. . . .

. . . I . . . will venture to assert, that till women are more rationally educated, the progress of human virtue and improvement in knowledge must receive continual checks. . . .

The mother, who wishes to give true dignity of character to her daughter, must regardless of the sneers of ignorance, proceed on a plan diametrically opposite to that which Rousseau has recommended with all the deluding charms of eloquence and philosophical sophistry: for his eloquence renders absurdities plausible, and his dogmatic conclusions puzzle, without convincing, those who have not ability to refute them.

From Mary Wollstonecraft, *A Vindication of the Rights of Woman*, ed. by Carol H. Poston. Copyright © 1975 W. W. Norton & Co., Inc., pp. 21, 22, 24–26, 35, 40, 41.

that to confine women to the separate domestic sphere because of their supposed physiological limitations was to make them the sensual slaves of men. Confined in this separate sphere, as the victims of male tyranny, they could never achieve their own moral or intellectual identity. Denying good education to women would impede the progress of all humanity. Wollstonecraft was demanding for women the kind of intellectual liberty that male writers of the Enlightenment had been championing for men for more than a century.

ENLIGHTENED ABSOLUTISM

During the last third of the century it seemed that several European rulers had embraced many of the reforms set forth by the *philosophes. Enlightened absolutism* is the term used to describe this phenomenon. The phrase indicates monarchical government dedicated to the rational strengthening of the central absolutist administration at the cost of lesser centers of political power. The monarchs most closely associated with it—Frederick II of Prussia, Joseph II of Austria, and Catherine

II of Russia—often found that the political and social realities of their realms caused them to moderate both their enlightenment and their absolutism. Frederick II corresponded with the *philosophes,* invited Voltaire to his court, and even wrote history and political tracts. Catherine II, who was a master of what would later be called public relations, consciously sought to create the image of being enlightened. She read the works of the *philosophes,* became a friend of Diderot and Voltaire, and made frequent references to their ideas, all in the hope that her nation might seem more modern and Western. Joseph II continued numerous initiatives begun by his mother, Maria Theresa, and imposed a series of religious, legal, and social reforms that contemporaries believed he had derived from suggestions of the *philosophes.*

Despite such appearances, the relationship between these rulers and the writers of the Enlightenment was more complicated. The rulers did wish to see their subjects enjoy better health, more accessible education, a more rational political administration, and economic prosperity. In many of these policies, they were more advanced than the rulers of western Europe. However, the humanitarian and liberating zeal of the Enlightenment directed only part of their policies. Frederick II, Joseph II, and Catherine II were also determined to play major diplomatic and military roles in Europe. In no small measure they sought the rational economic and social integration of their realms, so they could achieve military strength. After the Seven Years' War all the states of Europe understood that they would require stronger armed forces, which meant they needed new revenues. The search for new revenues and for more political support for their rule led these monarchs to make "enlightened" reforms. Consequently, they and their advisers used rationality to pursue many goals admired by the *philosophes* but also to further what the *philosophes* considered irrational militarism.

JOSEPH II OF AUSTRIA

No eighteenth-century ruler so embodied rational, impersonal force as the emperor Joseph II of Austria. He was the son of Maria Theresa (r. 1740–1780) and co-ruler with her from 1765 to 1780. During the next ten years he ruled alone. He has been aptly described as "an imperial puritan and a good deal of a prig."[8] He slept on straw and ate little but beef. He prided himself on a narrow, passionless rationality, which he sought to impose by his own will on the various Habsburg domains. Despite his eccentricities and cold personality, Joseph II genuinely and sincerely wished to improve the lot of his peoples. His well-intentioned efforts led to a series of aristocratic and peasant rebellions from Hungary to the Austrian Netherlands.

Of all the rising states of the eighteenth century, Austria was the most diverse in its people and problems. The Habsburgs never succeeded in creating either a unified administrative structure or a strong aristocratic loyalty. The price of preserving the monarchy during the War of the Austrian Succession (1740–1748) had been guarantees of considerable aristocratic independence, especially in Hungary.

During and after the conflict, however, Maria Theresa had strengthened her powers in Austria and Bohemia. Through major administrative reorganization she imposed a much more efficient system of tax collection that extracted funds even from the clergy and the nobles, and she established several central councils to deal with governmental problems. She was particularly concerned about bringing all educational institutions into the service of the crown so that she could have enough educated officials, and she expanded primary education on the local level.

Maria Theresa was also concerned about the welfare of the peasants and serfs. The extension of the authority of the royal bureaucracy over that of the local nobilities helped the peasants, as did the empress's decrees limiting the services that landowners could demand from them. This concern arose from her desire to assure a good military recruitment pool. In all these policies and in her general desire to stimulate prosperity and military strength by royal initiative, Maria Theresa anticipated the policies of her son.

Joseph II, however, was more determined, and his projected reforms were more wide ranging than his mother's. He was ambitious to expand at the expense of Poland, Bavaria, and the Ottoman Empire. But his greatest ambition was to change the authority of the Habsburg emperor over his various realms. He sought to overcome the pluralism of the Habsburg holdings by increasing the power of the central monarchy in areas of political and social life that Maria Theresa had wisely not disturbed. In particular, Joseph sought to lessen Hungarian autonomy. He refused to have himself crowned king of Hungary and even had the Crown of Saint Stephen sent to Vienna. He thus avoided having to guarantee existing or new Hungarian privileges in a coronation oath. He reorganized local government in Hungary to increase the authority of his own officials, and he required the use of the German language in all governmental matters. But the Magyar nobility resisted, and in 1790 Joseph had to rescind most of his centralizing measures.

Another target of Joseph's assertion of royal absolutism was religion. In October 1781 Joseph extended freedom of worship to Lutherans, Calvinists, and the Greek Orthodox. They were permitted to have their own churches, to sponsor schools, to enter skilled trades, and to hold academic appointments and positions in the public service. From 1781 through 1789 Joseph relieved the Jews of certain taxes and signs of personal degradation and gave them the right of private worship. Despite these benefits the Jews still did not enjoy general legal rights equal to those of other Habsburg subjects.

Above all, Joseph sought to bring the various institutions of the Roman Catholic Church directly under his control. He forbade direct communication between the bishops of his realms and the pope. He regarded most orders of monks and nuns as unproductive. Consequently, he dissolved over

[8] R. J. White, *Europe in the Eighteenth Century* (New York: St. Martin's, 1965), p. 214.

DOCUMENT MARIA THERESA AND JOSEPH II OF AUSTRIA DEBATE TOLERATION

In 1765 Joseph, the eldest son of the Empress Maria Theresa, had become co-regent with his mother. He began to believe that some measures of religious toleration should be introduced into the Habsburg realms. Maria Theresa, whose opinions on many political issues were quite advanced, adamantly refused to consider adopting a policy of toleration. This exchange of letters sets forth their sharply differing positions. The toleration of Protestants in dispute related only to Lutherans and Calvinists. Maria Theresa died in 1780; the next year Joseph issued an edict of toleration.

How does Joseph define toleration, and why does Maria Theresa believe it is the same as religious indifference? Why does Maria Theresa fear that toleration will bring about political as well as religious turmoil? Why does Maria Theresa think the belief in toleration has come from Joseph's acquaintance with wicked books? Compare the positions for and against religious toleration expressed in this correspondence to the actions of previous European rulers.

Joseph to Maria Theresa, July 20, 1777

. . . [I]t is only the word "toleration" which has caused the misunderstanding. You have taken it in quite a different meaning [from mine expressed in an earlier letter]. God preserve me from thinking it a matter of indifference whether the citizens turn Protestant or remain Catholic, still less, whether they cleave to, or at least observe, the cult which they have inherited from their fathers! I would give all I possess if all the Protestants of your states would go over to Catholicism.

The word "toleration," as I understand it, means only that I would employ any persons, without distinction of religion, in purely temporal matters, allow them to own property, practice trades, be citizens, if they were qualified and if this would be of advantage to the State and its industry. Those who, unfortunately, adhere to a false faith, are far further from being converted if they remain in their own country than if they migrate into another, in which they can hear and see the convincing truths of the Catholic faith. Similarly, the undisturbed practice of their religion makes them far better subjects and causes them to avoid irreligion, which is a far greater danger to our Catholics than if one lets them see others practice their religion unimpeded. . . .

Maria Theresa to Joseph, Late July, 1777

Without a dominant religion? Toleration, indifference are precisely the true means of undermining everything, taking away every foundation; we others will then be the greatest losers. . . . He is no friend of humanity, as the popular phrase is, who allows everyone his own thoughts. I am speaking only in the political sense, not as a Christian; nothing is so necessary and salutary as religion. Will you allow everyone to fashion his own religion as he pleases? No fixed cult, no subordination to the Church—what will then become of us? The result will not be quiet and contentment; its outcome will be the rule of the stronger and more unhappy times like those which we have already seen. A manifesto by you to this effect can produce the utmost distress and make you responsible for many thousands of souls. And what are my own sufferings, when I see you entangled in opinions so erroneous? What is at stake is not only the welfare of the State but your own salvation. . . . Turning your eyes and ears everywhere, mingling your spirit of contradiction with the simultaneous desire to create something, you are ruining yourself and dragging the Monarchy down with you into the abyss. . . . I only wish to live so long as I can hope to descend to my ancestors with the consolation that my son will be as great, as religious as his forebears, that he will return from his erroneous views, from those wicked books whose authors parade their cleverness at the expense of all that is most holy and most worthy of respect in the world, who want to introduce an imaginary freedom which can never exist and which degenerates into license and into complete revolution.

From *The Habsburg and Hohenzollern Dynasties in the Seventeenth and Eighteenth Centuries.* C. A. Macartney, ed., Copyright © 1980, Walker and Company, pp. 151–153. Reprinted by permission.

600 monasteries and confiscated their lands, although he excepted certain orders that ran schools or hospitals. He also dissolved the traditional Roman Catholic seminaries, which he believed taught priests too great a loyalty to the papacy and too little concern for their future parishioners. In their place he sponsored eight general seminaries that emphasized parish duties. In effect, Joseph's policies made Roman Catholic priests the employees of the state and ended the influence of the church as an independent institution in Habsburg lands. In many respects, the ecclesiastical policies of Joseph II, known as *Josephinism,* prefigured those of the French Revolution.

Toward serfdom and the land, Joseph II again pursued policies initiated by Maria Theresa to more far-reaching ends. During his reign he introduced reforms that touched the heart of rural society. He abolished the legal status of serfdom defined in terms of servitude to another person. He gave peasants much more personal freedom. They could marry, engage in skilled work, or have their children trained in such skills without permission of the landlord. The procedures of the manorial courts were reformed, and avenues of appeal to royal officials were opened. Joseph also encouraged landlords to change land leases, so that it would be easier for peasants to inherit them or to transfer them to another peasant without

Catherine the Great, here portrayed as a young princess, ascended to the Russian throne after the murder of her husband. She tried initially to enact major reforms but she never intended to abandon absolutism. She assured the nobility of their rights and by the end of her reign had imposed press censorship Corbis-Bettmann

bringing into doubt the landlord's title of ownership. Joseph believed that reducing traditional burdens would make the peasant tillers of the land more productive and industrious.

In 1789 Joseph proposed a new and daring system of land taxation. All proprietors were to be taxed, regardless of social status. No longer were the peasants alone to bear the burden of taxation. He commuted compulsory service into a monetary tax, split between the landlord and the state. The decree was drawn up, but resistance from the nobles delayed its implementation. Then in 1790 Joseph died, and the decree never went into effect. However, his measures had stirred up turmoil throughout the Habsburg realms. Peasants revolted over disagreements about the interpretation of their newly granted rights. The nobles of the various realms protested the taxation scheme.

On Joseph's death, the crown went to his brother Leopold II (r. 1790–1792). Although sympathetic to Joseph's goals, Leopold had to repeal many of the most controversial decrees, such as that changing taxation.

CATHERINE THE GREAT OF RUSSIA

Joseph II never grasped the practical necessity of cultivating political support for his policies. Catherine II (r. 1762–1796), who had been born a German princess, understood only too well the fragility of the Romanov dynasty's power base.

After the death of Peter the Great in 1725, the court nobles and the army had determined the Russian succession. As a result, the crown fell into the hands of people with little talent until 1741, when Peter's daughter Elizabeth came to the throne. At her death in 1762 Elizabeth was succeeded by Peter III, one of her nephews. He was a weak and possibly insane ruler who had been married in 1745 to a young German princess, the future Catherine the Great. Catherine had neither love nor loyalty for her demented husband. After a few months of rule Peter III was deposed and murdered with Catherine's approval, if not aid. On his deposition she was immediately proclaimed empress.

Catherine's familiarity with the Enlightenment and the general culture of western Europe convinced her that Russia must make major reforms if it were to remain a great power Since she had come to the throne through a palace coup, she understood that any major reform must enjoy wide political and social support.

Consequently, in 1767 Catherine summoned a Legislative Commission to advise her on revising the law and government of Russia. There were over 500 delegates drawn from all sectors of Russian life. Before the commission con-

CHRONOLOGY

RUSSIA FROM PETER THE GREAT THROUGH CATHERINE THE GREAT

1725	Death of Peter the Great
1741–1762	Elizabeth
1762	Peter III
1762	Catherine II (the Great) becomes empress
1767	Legislative Commission summoned
1768	War with Turkey
1771–1774	Pugachev's Rebellion
1772	First Partition of Poland
1774	Treaty of Kuchuk-Kainardji ends war with Turkey
1775	Reorganization of local government
1783	Russia annexes the Crimea
1785	Catherine issues the Charter of the Nobility
1793	Second Partition of Poland
1795	Third Partition of Poland
1796	Death of Catherine the Great

vened, Catherine wrote a set of *Instructions*, containing ideas drawn from the political writings of the *philosophes*. The revision of Russian law, however, did not occur for more than half a century. In 1768 Catherine dismissed the commission before several of its key committees had reported. Yet the commission had gathered a vast amount of information about the conditions of local administration and economic life throughout Russia. The inconclusive debates and the absence of programs from the delegates themselves suggested that most Russians saw no alternative to an autocratic monarchy. Catherine herself had no intention of departing from absolutism.

Catherine proceeded to carry out limited reforms on her own authority. She supported the rights and local power of the nobility. In 1775 she reorganized local government to solve problems brought to light by the Legislative Commission. She put most local offices into the hands of nobles rather than creating a royal bureaucracy. In 1785 Catherine issued the Charter of the Nobility, which guaranteed many noble rights and privileges. She issued a similar charter to the towns of her realms. In part, the empress had to favor the nobles. There were too few educated subjects in her realm to establish an independent bureaucracy, and the treasury could not afford an army strictly loyal to the crown. So Catherine wisely made a virtue of necessity. She strengthened the stability of her crown by a convenient alliance with her nobles and urban leaders.

MAP EXPLORATION

Interactive map: To explore this map further, go to http://www.prenhall.com/craig_map23.1

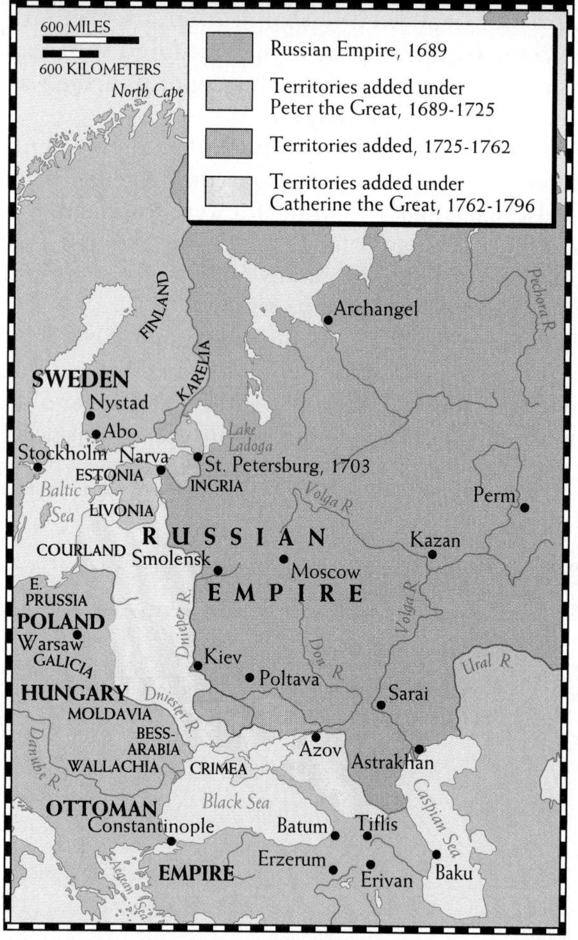

Map 23–1 Expansion of Russia, 1689–1796. The overriding territorial aim of the two most powerful Russian monarchs of the 18th century, Peter the Great (in the first quarter of the century) and Catherine the Great (in the last half of the century) was to secure navigable outlets to the sea in both the north and the south for Russia's vast empire; hence Peter's push to the Baltic Sea and Catherine's to the Black Sea. Catherine also managed to acquire much of Poland through the partitions of that country.

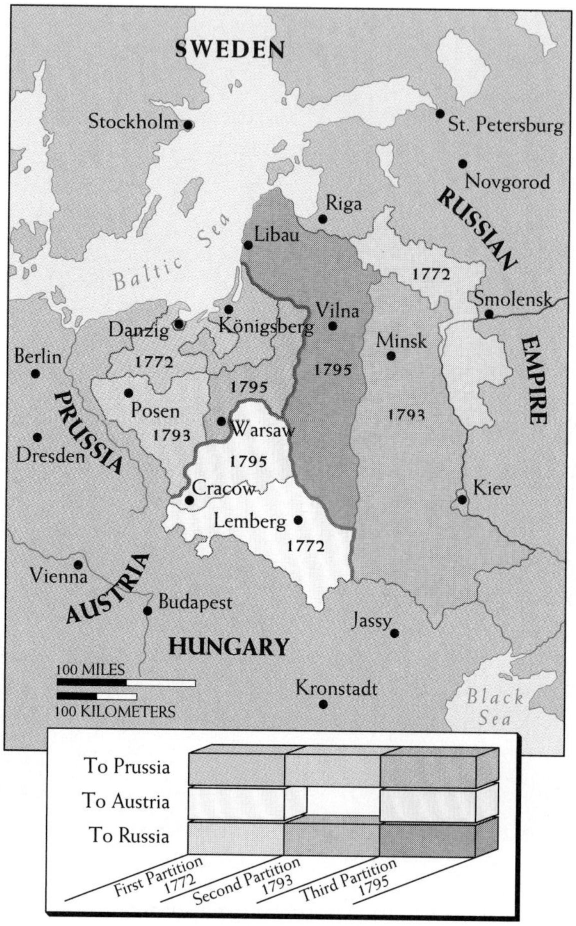

Map 23–2 Partitions of Poland, 1772, 1793, and 1795. The callous eradication of Poland from the map displayed 18th-century power politics at its most extreme. Poland, without a strong central government, fell victim to the strong absolute monarchies of central and eastern Europe.

Catherine continued the Russian drive for warm-water ports (see Map 23–1). This led to warfare with the Turks between 1768 and 1774, when the Treaty of Kuchuk-Kainardji gave Russia a direct outlet on the Black Sea, free navigation rights in its waters, and free access through the Bosphorus. Moreover, the Crimea became an independent state, which Catherine painlessly annexed in 1783.

THE PARTITION OF POLAND

These Russian military successes made the other states of eastern Europe uneasy. Their anxieties were allayed by the First Partition of Poland (see Map 23–2). The Russian victories along the Danube River in what is today Romania were most unwelcome to Austria, which had its own ambitions there. At the same time, the Ottoman Empire was pressing Prussia for aid against Russia. Frederick the Great made a proposal to Russia and Austria that would give each something it wanted, prevent conflict among them, and save appearances. After long, complicated, secret negotiations, the three powers agreed that Russia would abandon the Danubian provinces in return for a large chunk of Polish territory with almost 2 million inhabitants. As a reward for remaining neutral, Prussia annexed most of the Polish territory between East Prussia and Prussia proper, which allowed Frederick to unite two previously separate sections of his realm. Finally, Austria took Galicia, with its important salt mines, and other Polish territory with over 2.5 million inhabitants. The Polish state had lost approximately one third of its territory.

There were two additional partitions of Poland by Russia and Prussia, and one more by Austria. They occurred in 1793 and 1795 and removed Poland from the map of Europe until 1919. The great powers contended that they were saving themselves, and by implication the rest of Europe, from Polish anarchy. The argument was plausible to some contemporaries because of the fears spurred by the French Revolution. However, the truth was that the political weakness of Poland made the country and its resources a rich field for plunderous aggression.

In World Perspective

THE ENLIGHTENMENT HERITAGE

No other movements of European thought have remained as influential as the Scientific Revolution and the Enlightenment. A direct line of intellectual descent exists from those movements to the science and social criticism of the present day. Wherever modern science and technology are pursued and their effects felt, the spirit of the Enlightenment persists. From the eighteenth century to the present the *philosophes* provided a pattern for intellectuals who wished to make their societies more rational, scientific, and secular.

The Enlightenment *philosophes* believed in the emotions and passions as well as reason. But they used reason as a weapon for reform and the basis for a more productive economic life. In the two centuries since the Enlightenment, such a use of critical reason has become a mark of reforming and progressive social and intellectual movements. The *philosophes* first used reason against Christianity, but reason came to be used against other world religions as well.

The heritage of the Enlightenment has been more complex than was its political impact in the eighteenth century. One strand of Enlightenment political thought contributed to constitutionalism and modes of government in which the power and authority of the central government stand sharply circumscribed. Montesquieu, for example, influenced the Constitution of the United States and the numerous constitutions that document itself later influenced.

Another strand of Enlightenment political thought, found in Voltaire, contributed to the growth of strong central governments, as was the case with enlightened absolutism. Advocates of this method of government believed that a monarch or strong central bureaucracy could formulate and impose rational solutions to political or social problems.

Still another strand of political thought, arising from Rousseau, led to the socialist concern with inequality of wealth. In the modern world, liberal, socialist, and authoritarian governments all partake of the Enlightenment heritage.

Review Questions

1. Discuss the contributions of Copernicus, Brahe, Kepler, Galileo, and Newton to the Scientific Revolution. Which do you think made the most important contributions and why? How would you define the term *Scientific Revolution*? In what ways was it truly revolutionary? Which is more enduring, a political revolution or an intellectual one?
2. How did the Enlightenment change basic Western attitudes toward reform, faith, and reason? What were the major formative influences on the *philosophes*? How important were Voltaire and the *Encyclopedia* in the success of the Enlightenment?
3. Why did the *philosophes* consider organized religion to be their greatest enemy? Discuss the basic tenets of deism. What criticism might a deist direct at traditional Christianity, and how might he or she improve it?
4. What were the attitudes of the *philosophes* toward women? What was Rousseau's view of women? What were the separate spheres he imagined men and women occupying? What were Mary Wollstonecraft's criticisms of Rousseau's view?
5. Discuss the political views of Montesquieu and Rousseau. Was Montesquieu's view of England accurate? Was Rousseau a child of the Enlightenment or its enemy? Which did Rousseau value more, the individual or society? On what issues might Rousseau and Adam Smith have agreed and differed?
6. Were the enlightened monarchs true believers in the ideal of the *philosophes* or was their enlightenment a mere veneer? Were they really absolute in power? What motivated their reforms? What does the partition of Poland indicate about the spirit of enlightened absolutism?

Suggested Readings

R. Ashcraft, *Revolutionary Politics and Locke's Two Treatises of Government* (1986). Relates Locke to the political radicals of his day.

R. P. Bartlett, *Human Capital: The Settlement of Foreigners in Russia 1762–1804* (1979). Examines Catherine's policy of attracting farmers and skilled workers to Russia.

D. Beales, *Joseph II: In the Shadow of Maria Theresa, 1741–1780* (1987). The best treatment in English of the early political life of Joseph II.

C. Becker, *The Heavenly City of the Eighteenth Century Philosophers* (1932). An influential but very controversial discussion.

T. Bestermann, *Voltaire* (1969). A biography by the editor of Voltaire's letters.

M. Biagioli, *Galileo Courtier: The Practice of Science in the Culture of Absolutism* (1993). A major revisionist work that emphasizes the role of the political setting on Galileo's career and thought.

D. D. Bien, *The Calas Affair: Persecution, Toleration, and Heresy in Eighteenth-Century Toulouse* (1960). The standard treatment of the famous case.

R. Chartier, *The Cultural Origins of the French Revolution* (1991). A wide-ranging discussion of the emergence of the public sphere and the role of books and the book trade during the Enlightenment.

H. Chisick, *The Limits of Reform in the Enlightenment: Attitudes Toward the Education of the Lower Classes in Eighteenth-Century France* (1981). An attempt to examine the impact of the Enlightenment on nonelite classes.

I. B. Cohen, *Revolution in Science* (1985). A general consideration of the concept and of historical examples of change in scientific thought.

R. Darnton, *The Literary Underground of the Old Regime* (1982). Essays on the world of printers, publishers, and booksellers.

I. De Madariaga, *Catherine the Great: A Short History* (1990). A good brief biography.

J. Dunn, *The Political Thought of John Locke: An Historical Account of the "Two Treatises of Government"* (1969). An excellent introduction.

M. A. Finocchiaro, *The Galileo Affair: A Documentary History* (1989). A collection of all the relevant documents with an introductory commentary.

J. Gagliardo, *Enlightened Despotism* (1967). Remains a useful discussion.

P. Gay, *The Enlightenment: An Interpretation*, 2 vols. (1966, 1969). The most important and far-reaching treatment.

A. Goldgar, *Impolite Learning: Conduct and Community in the Republic of Letters, 1680–1750* (1995). A lively survey of the structure of the European intellectual community.

D. Goodman, *The Republic of Letters: A Cultural History of the French Enlightenment* (1994). Concentrates on the role of salons.

I. Harris, *The Mind of John Locke: A Study of Political Theory in Its Intellectual Setting* (1994). The most comprehensive recent treatment.

M. C. Jacob, *Living the Enlightenment: Freemasonry and Politics in Eighteenth-Century Europe* (1991). The best treatment in English of Freemasonry.

R. Kreiser, *Miracles, Convulsions, and Ecclesiastical Politics in Early Eighteenth-Century Paris* (1978). An important study of the kind of religious life that the *philosophes* opposed.

T. S. Kuhn, *The Copernican Revolution* (1957). Remains the most influential treatment.

D. LINDBERG AND R. L. NUMBERS, EDS., *Good and Nature: Historical Essays on the Encounter Between Christianity and Science* (1986). The best collection of essays on the subject.

C. A. MACARTNEY, *The Habsburg Empire, 1790–1918* (1971). Provides useful coverage of major mid-eighteenth-century developments.

F. MANUEL, *The Eighteenth Century Confronts the Gods* (1959). A broad examination of the *philosophes*' treatment of Christian and pagan religion.

R. R. PALMER, *Catholics and Unbelievers in Eighteenth-Century France* (1939). A discussion of the opponents of the *philosophes.*

G. RITTER, *Frederick the Great* (trans. 1968). A useful biography.

R. O. ROCKWOOD, ED., *Carl Becker's Heavenly City Revisited* (1958). Important essays qualifying Becker's thesis.

H. M. SCOTT, ED., *Enlightened Absolutism: Reform and Reformers in Later Eighteenth-Century Europe* (1990). A useful collection that incorporates recent scholarship.

S. SHAPIN, *The Scientific Revolution* (1996). An important revisionist survey emphasizing social factors.

J. N. SHKLAR, *Men and Citizens, a Study of Rousseau's Social Theory* (1969). A thoughtful and provocative overview of Rousseau's political thought.

D. SPADAFORA, *The Idea of Progress in Eighteenth Century Britain* (1990). A recent major study that covers many aspects of the Enlightenment in Britain.

L. STEINBRÜGGE, *The Moral Sex: Woman's Nature in the French Enlightenment* (1995). Emphasizes the conservative nature of Enlightenment thought on women.

L. STEWART, *The Rise of Public Science: Rhetoric, Technology, and Natural Philosophy in Newtonian Britain, 1660–1750* (1992). Examines how science became related to public life and economic development.

R. S. WESTFALL, *Never at Rest: A Biography of Isaac Newton* (1981). A very important major study.

A. M. WILSON, *Diderot* (1972). A splendid biography of the person behind the project for the *Encyclopedia* and other major Enlightenment publications.

L. WOLFF, *Inventing Eastern Europe: The Map of Civilization on the Mind of the Enlightenment* (1994). A remarkable study of the manner in which Enlightenment writers recast the understanding of this part of the continent.

N. WOLTERSTORFF, *John Locke and the Ethics of Belief* (1996). The best work on Locke's religious thought.

DOCUMENTS CD-ROM

1. John Locke, *The Second Treatise of Civil Government*
2. Jean-Jacques Rousseau, *The Social Contract*
3. Adam Smith: from *The Theory of Moral Sentiments*
4. Charles Montesquieu: Book 4 from *The Spirit of the Laws*
5. Catherine the Great, *The Instruction to the Commissioners for Composing a New Code of Laws*

WORLD AND THE WEB

Eighteenth-Century Resources

http://andromeda.rutgers.edu/~jlynch/18th/

This site covers all the significant Internet resources that focus on the eighteenth century, including the home pages of societies and people who work on eighteenth-century topics.

The Galileo Project

http://es.rice.edu/ES/humsoc/Galileo/

The Galileo Project is a hypertext source of information on the life and work of Galileo Galilei (1564-1642) and the science of his time.

The Jefferson Bible

http://www.angelfire.com/co/JeffersonBible/

In compiling what has come to be called "The Jefferson Bible," Thomas Jefferson sought to separate Jesus's ethical teachings from the religious dogma and other supernatural elements that are intermixed in the account provided by the four Gospels.

Voltaire: The Philosophical Dictionary (Hanover Historical Texts Project)

http://history.hanover.edu/texts/voltaire/volindex.htm

This link will take you to Voltaire's original texts commenting on everything from the Arts to Virtue, from Joan of Arc to Kissing.

The European Enlightenment

http://www.wsu.edu/~dee/ENLIGHT/ENLIGHT.HTM

The European Enlightenment is designed as a learning module in the form of a "research textbook."

Please go to http://www.prenhall.com/craig for the Technology and Civilization essay for this chapter, "The Shifting Balance of East and West."

24 Revolutions in the Transatlantic World

To symbolize the beginning of a new era in human history, French revolutionary legislators established a new calendar. This calendar for Year Two (1794) proclaims the indivisible unity of the revolution and the goals of Liberty, Equality, and Fraternity. Bildarchiv Preussischer Kulturbesitz

Chapter topics

- Revolution in the British Colonies in North America
- Revolution in France
- Wars of Independence in Latin America
- Toward the Abolition of Slavery in the Transatlantic Economy

IN WORLD PERSPECTIVE
The Transatlantic Revolutions

BETWEEN 1776 AND 1824 A WORLD-TRANSFORMING series of revolutions occurred in France and the Americas. In half a century the peoples of the two American continents established their independence of European political control. In Europe the French monarchy collapsed from the forces of aristocratic resistance and popular revolution. All the revolutionary leaders sought to establish new governments based largely, though never entirely, on Enlightenment principles.

From start to finish these revolutions were connected. The financial pressures from the Seven Years' War (1756–1763) had led Britain, Spain, and France to undertake a search for revenue that politically destabilized the Americas and France itself. Once the American Revolution began, France aided the colonists, thus exacerbating its own financial problem. In turn the French Revolution and the ensuing Napoleonic Wars created situations in Spain and Portugal to which the colonial elites in Latin America responded by seeking independence. Thus the transatlantic revolutions, despite their individual characters and developments, were interconnected events in world history. Furthermore, the era witnessed the commencement of a vast international crusade, first to abolish the slave trade and then to abolish slavery in the transatlantic world. The same ideas from the Enlightenment which inspired many of the revolutionaries also inspired the opponents of slavery as did religious convictions. The political and economic dislocations of the revolutionary era helped the antislavery forces achieve their goals. The political, social, and economic life of the transatlantic world would never be the same again.

REVOLUTION IN THE BRITISH COLONIES IN NORTH AMERICA

RESISTANCE TO THE IMPERIAL SEARCH FOR REVENUE

After the Treaty of Paris in 1763 ended the Seven Years' War, the British government faced two imperial problems (Map 24-1). The first was the sheer cost of empire, which the British felt they could no longer carry alone. The second was that the defeat of the French required the British to organize a vast expanse of new territory: all of North America east of the Mississippi, with its French settlers and, more important, its Indian possessors.

The British drive for revenue began in 1764 with the Sugar Act, which attempted to produce more revenue from imports into the colonies by the rigorous collection of what was actually a reduced tax on sugar. Smugglers were to be tried in admiralty courts without juries. The next year, Parliament passed the Stamp Act, which put a tax on legal documents and certain other items such as newspapers. The British considered these taxes legal and just because they had been approved by Parliament and because the revenue was to be spent in the colonies. The Americans responded that they alone through their assemblies had the right to tax themselves and that they were not represented in Parliament. Furthermore, the Americans feared that if colonial government were financed from Britain, they would cease to control it.

MAP EXPLORATION

Interactive map: To explore this map further, go to http://www.prenhall.com/craig_map24.1

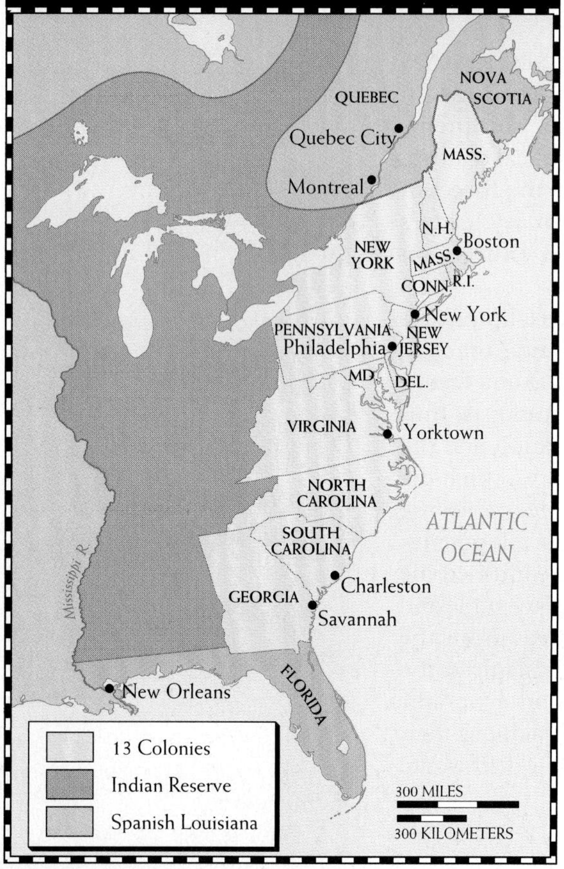

Map 24–1 North America in 1763. In the year of the victory over France, the English colonies lay along the Atlantic seaboard. The difficulties of organizing authority over the previous French territory in Canada and west of the Appalachian Mountains would contribute to the coming of the American Revolution.

In October 1765 the Stamp Act Congress met in America and drew up a protest to the Crown. There was much disorder in the colonies, particularly in Massachusetts, led by groups known as the Sons of Liberty. The colonists agreed to boycott British goods. In 1766 Parliament repealed the Stamp Act but, through the Declaratory Act, claimed the power to legislate for the colonies.

AMERICAN POLITICAL IDEAS

The political ideas of the American colonists had largely arisen from the struggle of seventeenth-century English aristocrats and gentry against the absolutism of the Stuart monarchs. The American colonists believed that the English Revolution of 1688 had established many of their own fundamental political liberties. The colonists claimed that, through the measures imposed from 1763 to 1776, George III (r. 1760–1820) and the British Parliament were attacking those liberties and dissolving the bonds of moral and political allegiance that had formerly united the two peoples. Consequently, the colonists employed a theory that had originally been developed to justify an aristocratic rebellion in England to support their own popular revolution.

These Whig political ideas, largely derived from John Locke (1632–1704), were only a part of the English ideological heritage that affected the Americans. Throughout the eighteenth century they had become familiar with a series of British political writers called the *Commonwealthmen.* These writers held republican political ideas that had their intellectual roots in the most radical thought of the Puritan revolution. They had relentlessly criticized the government patronage and parliamentary management of Robert Walpole (1676–1745) and his successors. They argued that such government was corrupt and that it undermined liberty. They regarded much parliamentary taxation as simply a means of financing political corruption. They also attacked standing armies as instruments of tyranny. In Great Britain this republican political tradition had only a marginal impact. Most Britons regarded themselves as the freest people in the world. In the colonies, however, these radical books and pamphlets were read widely and were often accepted at face value. The policy of Great Britain toward America after the Treaty of Paris made many colonists believe that the worst fears of the Commonwealthmen were coming true.

CRISIS AND INDEPENDENCE

In 1767 Charles Townshend (1725–1767) led Parliament to regulate and tax colonial imports. The colonists again resisted. The ministry sent over its own customs agents to administer the laws. To protect these new officers, the British sent troops to Boston in 1768. The obvious tensions resulted, and in March 1770 British troops killed five citizens in the Boston Massacre. In that same year Parliament repealed the Townshend duties except for the one on tea.

In May 1773 Parliament allowed the East India Company to import tea directly into the American colonies. Although the law lowered the price of tea, it retained the tax without the colonists' consent. In some cities the colonists refused to permit the tea to be unloaded; in Boston, a shipload of tea was thrown into the harbor, known since as the Boston Tea Party.

The British ministry of Lord North (1732–1792) was determined to assert the authority of Parliament over the resistant colonies. In 1774 Parliament passed a series of laws known in American history as the Intolerable Acts. These measures closed the port of Boston, reorganized the government of Massachusetts, allowed troops to be quartered in private homes, and removed the trials of royal customs

DOCUMENT THE STAMP ACT CONGRESS ADDRESSES GEORGE III

In 1765 the Stamp Act Congress met to protest the British imposition of taxes on the colonies. American leaders believed Great Britain had no right to impose such taxation. Their argument was that they were not and could not be represented in Parliament and that they were subject to the taxation only of their own assemblies. Later clauses implied that the taxation would prevent the colonists from purchasing manufactured goods from Britain and demanded the repeal of the act.

Why does the Congress insist on the same rights for subjects born in the colonies as those born in England? On what grounds does the Congress declare that Parliament may not levy taxes in the colonies? Why is the Congress so concerned about what courts may try cases arising from the Stamp Act?

The Members of this Congress, sincerely devoted, with the warmest sentiments of affection and duty to His Majesty's person and government . . . and with minds deeply impressed by a sense of the present and impending misfortunes of the British colonies on this continent; having considered as maturely as time will permit, the circumstances of the said colonies, esteem it our indispensable duty to make the following declarations of our humble opinion, respecting the most essential rights and liberties of the colonists, and of the grievances under which they labor, by reason of several late acts of Parliament.

1. That His Majesty's subjects in these colonies, owe the same allegiance to the crown of Great Britain, that is owing from his subjects born within the realm, and all due subordination to that august body the Parliament of Great Britain.
2. That His Majesty's liege subjects in these colonies are entitled to all the inherent rights and liberties of his natural born subjects, within the kingdom of Great Britain.
3. That it is inseparably essential to the freedom of a people, and the undoubted right of Englishmen, that no taxes be imposed on them but with their own consent, given personally, or by their representatives.
4. That the people of these colonies are not, and cannot, be represented in the House of Commons in Great Britain.
5. That the only representatives of the people of these colonies are persons chosen therein by themselves, and that no taxes ever have been, or can be constitutionally imposed on them, but by their respective legislatures.
6. That all supplies to the crown being free gifts of the people, it is unreasonable and inconsistent with the principles and spirit of the British constitution, for the people of Great Britain to grant to His Majesty the property of the colonists.
7. That trial by jury, is the inherent and invaluable right of every British subject in these colonies.
8. That the late act of Parliament entitled, *An act for granting and supplying certain stamp duties, and other duties, in the British colonies and plantations, in America, etc.* by imposing taxes on the inhabitants of these colonies, and the said act, and several other acts, by extending the jurisdiction of the courts of admiralty beyond its ancient limits, have a manifest tendency to subvert the rights and liberties of the colonists.

From *Journal of the First Congress of the American Colonies*. . . 1765 (New York, 1845), pp. 27–29, as quoted in Oscar Handlin, ed., *Readings in American History*. Copyright ©1957 Alfred A. Knopf, pp. 116–117.

officials to England. In the same year Parliament approved the Quebec Act, which extended the boundaries of Quebec to include the Ohio river valley. The Americans regarded the Quebec Act as an attempt to prevent the extension of their mode of self-government westward beyond the Appalachian Mountains.

During these years committees of correspondence, composed of citizens critical of Britain, had been established throughout the colonies. In September 1774 these committees organized the First Continental Congress in Philadelphia. This body hoped to persuade Parliament to restore self-government in the colonies and to abandon its attempt at direct supervision of colonial affairs. Conciliation, however, was not forthcoming. By April 1775 the battles of Lexington and Concord had been fought. In June the colonists were defeated at the Battle of Bunker Hill.

The Second Continental Congress gathered in May 1775. It still sought conciliation with Britain, but soon undertook the government of the colonies. By August 1775 George III had declared the colonies in rebellion. During the winter Thomas Paine's (1737–1809) pamphlet *Common Sense* galvanized public opinion in favor of separation from Great Britain. A colonial army and navy were organized. In April 1776 the Continental Congress opened American ports to the trade of all nations. Finally, on July 4, 1776, the Continental Congress adopted the Declaration of Independence.

This view of the "Boston Massacre" of March 5, 1770, by Paul Revere owes more to propaganda than fact. There was no order to fire and the innocent citizens portrayed here were really an angry, violent mob. Collection of New York Historical Society/The Granger Collection, N.Y.

CHRONOLOGY

THE AMERICAN REVOLUTION

1760	George III becomes king
1763	Treaty of Paris concludes the Seven Years' War
1764	Sugar Act
1765	Stamp Act
1766	Sugar Act repealed and Declaratory Act passed
1767	Townshend Acts
1770	Lord North becomes George III's chief minister
1770	Boston Massacre
1773	Boston Tea Party
1774	Intolerable Acts
1774	First Continental Congress
1775	Second Continental Congress
1776	Declaration of Independence
1778	France enters the war on the side of America
1781	British forces surrender at Yorktown
1783	Treaty of Paris concludes War of the American Revolution

Thereafter, the War of the American Revolution continued until 1781, when the forces of George Washington (1732–1799) defeated those of Lord Cornwallis (1738–1805) at Yorktown. Early in 1778, however, the war had widened into a European conflict when Benjamin Franklin (1706–1790) persuaded the French government to support the rebellion. In 1779 the Spanish also came to the aid of the colonies. The 1783 Treaty of Paris concluded the conflict, and the thirteen American colonies had established their independence.

As the crisis with Britain unfolded during the 1760s and 1770s, the American colonists came to see themselves as first preserving traditional English liberties against a tyrannical Crown and corrupt Parliament and then as developing a new sense of liberty. By the mid-1770s the colonists had embraced republican political ideals. They would govern themselves through elected assemblies without any monarchical authority. The Constitutional Convention met in 1787. After the constitution was adopted in 1788, Americans would insist on a bill of rights specifically protecting civil liberties. The Americans would reject the aristocratic social hierarchy that had existed in the colonies. They would embrace democratic ideals, even if the franchise remained limited. They would assert the equality of white male citizens not only before the law but also in ordinary social relations. They would reject social status based on birth and inheritance and assert the necessity of liberty for all citizens to improve their social standing and economic lot by engaging in free commercial activity. They did not free their slaves, nor did they address the rights of women or Native Americans, but the American Revolution produced a society freer than any the world had seen, one that would expand the circle of political and social liberty. The American Revolution was a genuinely radical movement, the influence of which would increase as Americans moved across the continent and as other peoples began to question traditional European government. The political and social values of the American Revolution would inspire the Wars of Independence in Latin America and, to a lesser extent, both liberal and radical political movements in Europe.

REVOLUTION IN FRANCE

The French monarchy emerged from the Seven Years' War both defeated and deeply in debt. The later French support for the American Revolution exacerbated the financial difficulties. Given the economic vitality of France, the government debt was neither overly large nor disproportionate to the debts of other European powers. The problem was the government's inability to collect sufficient taxes to service and repay the debt.

Between 1786 and 1788 Louis XVI (r. 1774–1792) appointed several different ministers to deal with the financial crisis. All failed to persuade the aristocracy and the church to pay more taxes. As these negotiations dragged on, the parlement of Paris declared that only the Estates General could institute new taxes. The Estates General had not met since 1614. Consequently, in July 1788, Louis XVI agreed to convene the Estates General the next year.

REVOLUTIONS OF 1789

THE ESTATES GENERAL BECOMES THE NATIONAL ASSEMBLY The Estates General had three divisions: the First Estate of the clergy, the Second Estate of the nobility, and the Third Estate, representing everyone else in the kingdom. Before the Estates General met at Versailles in May 1789, there had been much public debate over its organization. The monarchy had agreed that the Third Estate should have twice as many members as either the nobility or the clergy. Then there arose the question of how voting should be organized. The nobility wanted all votes to be taken by Estate, which would have allowed the nobles and clergy to outvote the Third Estate. The Third Estate wanted each member to vote individually so that, with its larger membership, it would dominate.

From the beginning the Third Estate, composed largely of local officials, professional men, and lawyers, refused to sit as a separate order as the king desired. For several weeks there was a standoff. Then, on June 1 the Third Estate invited the clergy and the nobles to join it in organizing a new legislative body. A few of the lower clergy did so. On June 17 that body declared itself the National Assembly.

Three days later, finding themselves accidentally locked out of their usual meeting place, the National Assembly moved to a nearby tennis court, where its members took

On July 14, 1789, crowds stormed the Bastille, a prison in Paris. This event, whose only practical effect was to free a few prisoners, marked the first time the populace of Paris redirected the course of the revolution.

Musee de la Ville de Paris, Musee Carnavalet/Giraudon/Art Resource, N.Y.

the famous Tennis Court Oath to continue to sit until they had given France a constitution. Louis XVI ordered the National Assembly to desist, but shortly afterward most of the clergy and many nobles joined the assembly. On June 27 the king capitulated and formally requested the First and Second Estates to meet with the National Assembly, where voting would occur by head rather than by order. Government by the privileged orders thus ended, and the National Assembly became the National Constituent Assembly.

FALL OF THE BASTILLE Two new factors soon intruded. First, Louis XVI attempted to regain the initiative by mustering troops near Versailles and Paris. This was the beginning of a steady, and consistently poorly executed, royal attempt to halt the revolution. Most of the National Constituent Assembly wished to create some form of constitutional monarchy, but from the start Louis's refusal to cooperate thwarted that effort.

The second new factor was the populace of Paris. The mustering of royal troops created anxiety in the city, where there had been several bread riots. By June the Parisians were organizing a citizen militia and collecting arms.

On July 14 around 800 people, mostly small shopkeepers, tradespeople, artisans, and wage earners, marched to the Bastille in search of weapons for the militia. This great fortress had once held political prisoners. Through miscalculations and ineptitude by the governor of the fortress, the troops in the Bastille fired into the crowd, killing ninety-eight people and wounding many others. The crowd then stormed the fortress, released its seven prisoners, none of whom was there for political reasons, and killed several soldiers and the governor. They found no weapons.

This was the first of many crucial *journées*, or days when the populace of Paris would redirect the course of the revolution. The fall of the Bastille signaled that the political future of the nation would not be decided solely by the National Constituent Assembly. As the news spread, similar disturbances took place in the provincial cities. A few days later Louis XVI, again bowing to events, came to Paris and recognized both the new elected government of the city and its National Guard. The citizens of Paris were, for the time being, satisfied.

THE GREAT FEAR AND SURRENDER OF FEUDAL PRIVILEGES As popular urban disturbances erupted in various cities, a movement known as the *Great Fear* swept across much of the French countryside. Peasants were reclaiming rights and property that they had lost through the aristocratic resurgence of the last quarter century, as well as venting their anger against the injustices of rural life. The Great Fear, which was an intensification of peasant disturbances that had begun during the spring, witnessed the burning of châteaux, the destruction of records and documents, and the refusal by peasants to pay feudal dues.

On the night of August 4, 1789, aristocrats in the National Constituent Assembly attempted to halt the disorder in the countryside. By prearrangement, liberal nobles and churchmen rose in the assembly and surrendered hunting and fishing rights, judicial authority, tithes, and special exemptions. In a sense, these nobles gave up what they had already lost and what they could not have regained without civil war. Later, many would also be compensated for their losses. Nonetheless, after August 4 all French citizens were subject to the same and equal laws.

The women of Paris marched to Versailles on October 5, 1789. The following day the royal family was forced to return to Paris with them. Henceforth, the French government would function under the constant threat of mob violence. Musee de la Ville de Paris, Musee Carnavalet/Giraudon/Art Resource, N.Y.

DOCUMENT FRENCH WOMEN PETITION TO BEAR ARMS

The issue of women serving in the revolutionary French military appeared early in the revolution. In March 1792 Pauline Léon presented a petition to the National Assembly on behalf of more than 300 Parisian women asking the right to bear arms and train for military service for the revolution. Similar requests were made during the next two years. Some women did serve in the military, but in 1793 legislation specifically forbade it on the grounds that women belonged in the domestic sphere and that military service would lead them to abandon family duties.

Citoyenne is the feminine form of the French word for citizen. How does this petition seek to challenge the concept of citizenship in the *French Declaration of the Rights of Man and Citizen*? How do these petitioners relate their demand to bear arms to their role as women in French society? How do the petitioners relate their demands to the use of all national resources against the enemies of the revolution?

Patriotic women come before you to claim the right which any individual has to defend his life and liberty.

. . . We are *citoyennes* [female citizens], and we cannot be indifferent to the fate of the fatherland.

. . . Yes, Gentlemen, we need arms, and we come to ask your permission to procure them. May our weakness be no obstacle; courage and intrepidity will supplant it, and the love of the fatherland and hatred of tyrants will allow us to brave all dangers with ease. . . .

No, Gentlemen, We will [use arms] only to defend ourselves the same as you; you cannot refuse us, and society cannot deny the right nature gives us, unless you pretend the *Declaration of Rights* does not apply to women and that they should let their throats be cut like lambs, without the right to defend themselves. For can you believe the tyrants would spare us? . . . Why then not terrorize aristocracy and tyranny with all the resources of civic effort and the pure zeal, zeal which cold men can well call fanaticism and exaggeration, but which is only the natural result of a heart burning with love for the public weal? . . .

. . . If, for reasons we cannot guess, you refuse our just demands, these women you have raised to the ranks of *citoyennes* by granting that title to their husbands, these women who have sampled the promises of liberty, who have conceived the hope of placing free men in the world, and who have sworn to live free or die—such women, I say, will never consent to concede the day to slaves; they will die first. They will uphold their oath, and a dagger aimed at their breasts will deliver them from the misfortunes of slavery! They will die, regretting not life, but the uselessness of their death; regretting moreover, not having been able to drench their hands in the impure blood of the enemies of the fatherland and to avenge some of their own!

But, Gentlemen, let us cast our eyes away from these cruel extremes. Whatever the rages and plots of aristocrats, they will not succeed in vanquishing a whole people of united brothers armed to defend their rights. We also demand only the honor of sharing their exhaustion and glorious labors and of making tyrants see that women also have blood to shed for the service of the fatherland in danger.

Gentlemen, here is what we hope to obtain from your justice and equity:

1. Permission to procure pikes, pistols, and sabres (even muskets for those who are strong enough to use them), within police regulations.
2. Permission to assemble on festival days and Sundays on the Champ de la Fédération, or in other suitable places, to practice maneuvers with these arms.
3. Permission to name the former French Guards to command us, always in conformity with the rules which the mayor's wisdom prescribes for good order and public calm.

From "French Women Petition to Bear Arms" in *Women in Revolutionary Paris 1789–1795*, trans. by Darline Gay Levy, Harriet Branson Applewhite, and Mary Durham Johnson. ©1979 by the Board of Trustees of the University of Illinois. Used with permission of the authors and the University of Illinois Press.

DECLARATION OF THE RIGHTS OF MAN AND CITIZEN On August 27, 1789, the assembly issued the *Declaration of the Rights of Man and Citizen.* This declaration drew together much of the political language of the Enlightenment and was also influenced by the Declaration of Rights adopted by Virginia in America in June 1776. The French declaration proclaimed that all men were "born and remain free and equal in rights." Their natural rights were "liberty, property, security, and resistance to oppression." Governments existed to protect those rights. All political sovereignty resided in the nation and its representatives. All citizens were to be equal before the law and were to be "equally admissible to all public dignities, offices and employments, according to their capacity, and with no other distinction than that of their virtues and talents." There were to be due process of law and presumption of innocence until proof of guilt. Freedom of religion was affirmed. Taxation was to be apportioned equally according to capacity to pay. Property constituted "an inviolable and sacred right."[1]

[1] Quoted in Georges Lefebvre, *The Coming of the French Revolution*, trans. by R. R. Palmer (Princeton, NJ: Princeton University Press, 1967), pp. 221–223.

Louis XVI stalled before ratifying both the declaration and the aristocratic renunciation of feudalism. His hesitations fanned suspicions that he might try to resort to force. Moreover, bread shortages continued. On October 5 several thousand Parisian women marched to Versailles, demanding more bread. This was one of several occasions when women played a major role in the actions of the Parisian crowd. On this day they milled about the palace, and many stayed the night. Under this pressure the king agreed to sanction the decrees of the assembly. The Parisians believed that the king had to be kept under the watchful eye of the people. Consequently they demanded that Louis and his family return to Paris. The monarch had no real choice. On October 6, 1789, his carriage followed the crowd into the city, where he and his family settled in the palace of the Tuileries. The National Constituent Assembly soon followed. Thereafter, both Paris and France remained relatively stable and peaceful until the summer of 1792.

RECONSTRUCTION OF FRANCE

Once established in Paris, the National Constituent Assembly set about reorganizing France. Throughout its proceedings the Assembly was determined to protect property and to limit the impact on national life of small-property owners as well as of the unpropertied elements of the nation. While championing civic equality before the law, the Assembly spurned social equality and extensive democracy. The Assembly thus charted a general course that, to a greater or lesser degree, nineteenth-century liberals across Europe and in other areas of the world would follow.

POLITICAL REORGANIZATION The Constitution of 1791, the product of the National Constituent Assembly's deliberations, established a constitutional monarchy. There was a unicameral Legislative Assembly vested with powers of war and peace. The monarch could delay but not halt legislation. The system of voting was complex and restricted. Only about 50,000 citizens of the French nation of 26 million could actually elect or serve in the Legislative Assembly.

The exclusion of women from both voting and holding office did not pass unnoticed. In 1791 Olympe de Gouges (d. 1793), a butcher's daughter who became a major radical in Paris, composed a *Declaration of the Rights of Woman*, which she ironically addressed to Queen Marie Antoinette (1755–1793). Much of the document reprinted the *Declaration of the Rights of Man and Citizen*, adding the word *woman* to the various original clauses. That strategy demanded that women be regarded as citizens and not merely as daughters, sisters, wives, and mothers of citizens. Olympe de Gouges further outlined rights that would permit women to own property and require men to recognize the paternity of their children. She called for equality of the sexes in marriage and improved education for women. She declared, "Women, wake up; the tocsin of reason is being heard throughout the whole universe; discover your rights."[2] Her demands illustrated how the public listing of rights in the *Declaration of the Rights of Man and Citizen* created universal civic expectations even among those it did not cover.

The National Constituent Assembly abolished the ancient French Provinces, such as Burgundy, and replaced them with eighty-three departments (*départements*) of generally equal size named after rivers, mountains, and other geographical features. The ancient judicial courts, including the seigneurial courts and the *parlements*, were suppressed and replaced by established uniform courts with elected judges and prosecutors. Legal procedures were simplified, and the most degrading punishments abolished.

ECONOMIC POLICY In economic matters the National Constituent Assembly suppressed the guilds and liberated the grain trade. The assembly established the metric system to provide the nation with uniform weights and measures. These policies of economic freedom and uniformity disappointed both peasants and urban workers caught in the cycle of inflation. By the decrees of 1790 the Assembly placed the burden of proof on the peasants to rid themselves of the residual feudal dues for which compensation was to be paid. On June 14, 1791, the Assembly enacted the Chapelier Law forbidding worker associations, thereby crushing the attempts of urban workers to protect their wages. Peasants and workers were to be left to the mercy of the free marketplace.

The National Constituent Assembly decided to pay the troublesome royal debt by confiscating and then selling the lands of the Roman Catholic Church in France. The Assembly then authorized the issuance of *assignats*, or government bonds, the value of which was guaranteed by the revenue to be generated from the sale of church property. When the *assignats* began to circulate as currency, the Assembly issued even larger quantities of them to liquidate the national debt. However, within a few months the value of *assignats* began to fall. Inflation increased and put new stress on the lives of the urban poor.

CIVIL CONSTITUTION OF THE CLERGY In July 1790 the National Constituent Assembly issued the Civil Constitution of the Clergy, which transformed the Roman Catholic Church in France into a branch of the secular state. This measure reduced the number of bishoprics, made borders of dioceses conform to those of the new departments, and provided for the election of priests and bishops, who henceforth became salaried employees of the state. The Assembly consulted neither the pope nor the French clergy about these broad changes. The king approved the measure only with the greatest reluctance.

[2] Quoted in Sara E. Melzer and Leslie W. Rabine, eds., *Rebel Daughters: Women and the French Revolution* (New York: Oxford University Press, 1992), p. 88.

The Civil Constitution of the Clergy was the major blunder of the National Constituent Assembly. The measure roused immense opposition within the French church, even from bishops who had long championed Gallican liberties over papal domination. Faced with this resistance, the Assembly unwisely ruled that all clergy must take an oath to support the Civil Constitution. Only seven bishops and about half the clergy did so. In reprisal, the assembly designated the clergy who had not taken the oath as "refractory" and removed them from their clerical functions. Refractory priests immediately attempted to celebrate Mass.

In February 1791 the pope condemned not only the Civil Constitution of the Clergy but also the *Declaration of the Rights of Man and Citizen.* That condemnation marked the opening of a Roman Catholic offensive against liberalism in Europe and revolution throughout the world that continued for over a century. Within France itself, the pope's action meant that religious devotion and revolutionary loyalty became incompatible for many people. French citizens quickly divided between those who supported the constitutional priests and those who resorted to the refractory clergy. Louis XVI and his family favored the latter.

COUNTERREVOLUTIONARY ACTIVITY In the summer of 1791 the queen and some nobles who had already left the country persuaded Louis XVI also to flee. The escape failed when Louis, along with his family, was recognized and stopped in the town of Varennes. On June 24 soldiers escorted the royal family back to Paris. Thereafter, the leaders of the National Constituent Assembly knew that the chief counterrevolutionary sat on the French throne.

Two months later, on August 27, 1791, Emperor Leopold II of Austria (r. 1790–1792), who was the brother of Marie Antoinette, and Frederick William II (r. 1786–1797), the king of Prussia, issued the Declaration of Pillnitz. The two monarchs promised to intervene in France to protect the royal family and to preserve the monarchy if the other major European powers agreed. The latter provision rendered the statement meaningless because Great Britain would not have given its consent. In France, however, the revolutionaries felt surrounded by aristocratic and monarchical foes.

Near its close in September 1791 the National Constituent Assembly forbade any of its own members to sit in the Legislative Assembly then being elected. This new body met on October 1 to confront immense problems.

A SECOND REVOLUTION

Since the earliest days of the revolution, various clubs of politically like-minded persons had organized themselves in Paris. The best organized were the *Jacobins,* whose name derived from the fact that the group met in a former Dominican (Jacobin) monastery located in the Rue St. Jacques. The Paris club was linked to other local clubs in the provinces. In the Legislative Assembly a group of Jacobins known as the *Girondists* (because many of them came from

One of the key events of the French Revolution was the unsuccessful attempt by Louis XVI and his family to escape the country in June 1791. They were recognized and captured in the French city of Varennes and then returned to Paris under armed escort. Corbis-Bettmann

DOCUMENT A PAMPHLETEER DESCRIBES A SANS-CULOTTE

This document from 1793 describes a sans-culotte as a hardworking, useful, patriotic citizen who sacrifices himself to the war effort. It contrasts those virtues with the lazy and unproductive luxury of the noble and the self-interested plottings of the politician.

What social resentments appear in this description? How could these resentments create solidarity among the *sans-culottes* to defend the revolution? How does this document relate civic virtue to work? Where does this document suggest that the *sans-culotte* may need to confront enemies of the republic?

A *sans-culotte* you rogues? He is someone who always goes on foot, who has no millions as you would all like to have, no chateaux, no valets to serve him, and who lives simply with his wife and children, if he has any, on a fourth or fifth story.

He is useful, because he knows how to work in the field, to forge iron, to use a saw, to use a file, to roof a house, to make shoes, and to shed his last drop of blood for the safety of the Republic.

And because he works, you are sure not to meet his person in the Café de Chartres, or in the gaming houses where others conspire and game; nor at the National theatre . . . nor in the literary clubs.. . .

In the evening he goes to his section, not powdered or perfumed, or smartly booted in the hope of catching the eye of the citizenesses in the galleries, but ready to support good proposals with all his might, and to crush those which come from the abominable faction of politicians.

Finally, a *sans-culotte* always has his sabre sharp, to cut off the ears of all enemies of the Revolution; sometimes he even goes out with his pike; but at the first sound of the drum he is ready to leave for the Vendée, for the army of the Alps or for the army of the North.. . .

From "Reply to an Impertinent Question: What Is a Sans-culotte?" April 1793. Reprinted in Walter Markov and Albert Soboul, eds., *Die Sansculotten von Paris*, and republished trans. by Clive Emsley in Merryn Williams, ed., *Revolutions: 1775–1830* (Baltimore: Penguin Books, in association with the Open University, 1971), pp. 100–101.

the department of the Gironde) assumed leadership.[3] They led the Legislative Assembly on April 20, 1792, to declare war on Austria, by this time governed by Francis II (r. 1792–1835) and allied to Prussia.

END OF THE MONARCHY The war radicalized the revolution and led to what is usually called the *second revolution*, which overthrew the constitutional monarchy and established a republic. The war initially went poorly, and the revolution seemed in danger. Late in July, under radical working-class pressure, the government of Paris passed from the elected council to a committee, or commune, of representatives from the sections (municipal wards) of Paris. On August 10, 1792, a large crowd invaded the Tuileries and forced Louis XVI and Marie Antoinette to take refuge in the Legislative Assembly itself. During the disturbance several hundred of the royal Swiss guards and many Parisians died. Thereafter, the royal family was imprisoned in comfortable quarters, but the king was suspended from his political functions.

THE CONVENTION AND THE ROLE OF SANS-CULOTTES During the first week of September, in what are known as the September Massacres, the Paris Commune summarily killed about 1,200 people in the city jails. Many were aristocrats or priests, but most were simply common criminals. The crowd had assumed that the prisoners were all counterrevolutionaries. The Paris Commune then compelled the Legislative Assembly to call for the election, by universal manhood suffrage, of a new assembly to write a democratic constitution. That body, called the Convention after its American counterpart of 1787, met on September 21, 1792.

As its first act the Convention declared France a republic, that is, a nation governed by an elected assembly without a king. The second revolution had been the work of Jacobins more radical than the Girondists and of the people of Paris known as the *sans-culottes*. The name of the latter means "without breeches," and was derived from the long trousers that, as working people, they wore instead of aristocratic knee breeches. The *sans-culottes* were shopkeepers, artisans, wage earners, and a few factory workers. The politics of the Old Regime had ignored them, and the policies of the National Constituent Assembly had left them victims of unregulated economic liberty.

The *sans-culottes*, whose labor and military service were needed for the war effort, generally knew what they wanted. They sought immediate price controls for relief from food shortages and rising prices. They believed that all people had a right to subsistence and profoundly resented most forms of social inequality. They felt intense hostility toward the aristocracy and the original leaders of the revolution, whom they believed simply wanted to take over the social privileges of the aristocracy. They did not demand the abolition of property, but advocated a community of relatively small-property owners. They were antimonarchical, strongly republican, and suspicious even of representative government.

[3] The Girondists are also frequently called the *Brissotins* after Jacques-Pierre Brissot (1754–1793), who was their chief representative in early 1792.

Louis XVI was executed on January 21, 1793. Execution of Louis XVI. Aquatint. French, 18th century. Musée de la Ville de Paris, Musée Carnavalet, Paris. France. Giraudon/Art Resource, NY

In contrast, the Jacobins were republicans who sought representative government. Their hatred of the aristocracy did not extend to a general suspicion of wealth. Basically, the Jacobins favored an unregulated economy. However, from Louis XVI's flight to Varennes onward, the more extreme Jacobins began to cooperate with leaders of the Parisian *sans-culottes* and the Paris Commune to overthrow the monarchy. Once the Convention began its deliberations, these advanced Jacobins, known as the Mountain because of their seats high in the assembly hall, worked with *sans-culottes* to carry the revolution forward and win the war.

In December 1792 Louis XVI was put on trial as mere "Citizen Capet." (Capet was the family name of medieval forebears of the royal family.) The Girondists sought to spare his life, but the Mountain defeated the effort. By a narrow majority, Louis was convicted of conspiring against the liberty of the people and the security of the state. Condemned to death, he was beheaded on January 21, 1793.

The next month, the Convention declared war on Great Britain, Holland, and Spain. France was now at war with virtually all Europe. Civil war soon followed. In March 1793 aristocratic officers and priests commenced a royalist revolt in the Vendée in western France and roused much local popular support. The Girondists had led the country into the war but had proved themselves incapable either of winning it or of suppressing the enemies of the revolution at home. The Mountain stood ready to take up the task.

The Reign of Terror and Its Aftermath

The Reign of Terror is the name given to the months of quasi-judicial executions and murders stretching from the autumn of 1793 to the midsummer of 1794. The Terror can be understood only in the context of the internal and external wars, on the one hand, and the revolutionary expectations of the Convention and the *sans-culottes*, on the other.

Committee of Public Safety In April 1793 the Convention established a Committee of General Security and a Committee of Public Safety to perform the executive

Chronology

The French Revolution

1789	
May 5	Estates General opens at Versailles
June 17	Third Estate declares itself the National Assembly
June 20	National Assembly takes the Tennis Court Oath
July 14	Fall of the Bastille
July	Great Fear spreads in the countryside
August 4	Nobles surrender their feudal rights in a meeting of the National Constituent Assembly
August 27	*Declaration of the Rights of Man and Citizen*
October 5–6	Parisian women march to Versailles and force Louis XVI and his family to return to Paris
1790	
July 12	Civil Constitution of the Clergy adopted
July 14	New constitution accepted by the king
1791	
June 20–24	Louis XVI and his family attempt to flee France and are stopped at Varennes
August 27	Declaration of Pillnitz
October 1	Legislative Assembly meets
1792	
April 20	France declares war on Austria
August 10	Tuileries palace stormed, and Louis XVI takes refuge in the Legislative Assembly
September 2–7	September Massacres
September 21	Convention meets, and monarchy abolished
1793	
January 21	Louis XVI executed
February 1	France declares war on Great Britain
March	Counterrevolution breaks out in the Vendée
April 6	Committee of Public Safety formed
June 22	Constitution of 1793 adopted but not put into operation
July	Robespierre enters Committee of Public Safety
August 23	*Levée en masse* proclaimed
September 29	Maximum prices set on food and other commodities
October 16	Queen Marie Antoinette executed
November 10	Cult of Reason proclaimed; revolutionary calendar beginning in September
1794	
May 7	Cult of the Supreme Being proclaimed
June 8	Robespierre leads the celebration of Festival of the Supreme Being
July 27	Ninth of Thermidor and fall of Robespierre
July 28	Robespierre executed
1795	
August 22	Constitution of the Year III adopted, establishing the Directory

duties of the government. The latter committee eventually enjoyed almost dictatorial power. The committee conceived of their task as saving the revolution from mortal enemies at home and abroad. They generally enjoyed a working political relationship with the *sans-culottes* of Paris, but it was an alliance of expediency for the committee.

The major problem was to secure domestic support for the war. In early June 1793 the Parisian *sans-culottes* invaded the Convention and secured the expulsion of the Girondist members. That gave the Mountain complete control. On June 22 the Convention approved a fully democratic constitution but suspended its operation until after the war emergency. August 23 saw a *levée en masse*, or general military requisition of population, which conscripted males into the army and directed economic production for military purposes. On September 29 a maximum on prices was established in accord with *sans-culottes*' demands. During these same months the armies of the revolution also crushed many of the counterrevolutionary disturbances in the provinces.

The Society of Revolutionary Republican Women Revolutionary women established their own distinct institutions to fight the internal enemies of the revolution. In May 1793 Pauline Léon and Claire Lacombe founded the Society of Revolutionary Republican Women. Its members and other women filled the galleries of the Convention to hear the debates and cheer their favorite speakers. The Society became increasingly radical, however. Its members sought stricter controls on the price of food and other commodities, worked to ferret out food hoarders, and brawled with working market women thought to be insufficiently revolutionary. The women of the Society also demanded the right to wear the revolutionary cap or cockade usually worn only by male citizens. By October 1793 the Jacobins in the Convention had begun to fear the turmoil the Society was causing and banned all women's clubs and societies.

There were other examples of repression of women in 1793. Olympe de Gouges, author of the *Declaration of the Rights of Woman*, opposed the Terror and accused certain Jacobins of corruption. She was tried and guillotined in November 1793. In the same year women were formally excluded from the French army and from attending the galleries of the Convention.

The Republic of Virtue The pressures of war made it relatively easy to dispense with legal due process. However, the people in the Convention and the Committee of Public Safety also believed they had made a new departure in world history. They had established a republic in which civic virtue rather than aristocratic and monarchical corruption might flourish.

Dechristianization The most dramatic departure of the republic of virtue was an attempt to dechristianize France. In October 1793 the Convention proclaimed a new calendar dating from the first day of the French Republic. There were twelve months of thirty days with names associated with the seasons and climate. Every tenth day, rather than every seventh, was a holiday. Many of the most important events of the next few years became known by their dates on the revolutionary calendar.[4]

In November 1793 the convention decreed the Cathedral of Notre Dame to be a Temple of Reason. The legislature then sent trusted members, known as deputies on mission, into the provinces to enforce dechristianization by closing churches, persecuting clergy and believers, and occasionally forcing priests to marry. This religious policy roused much opposition and deeply separated the French provinces from the revolutionary government in Paris.

PROGRESS OF THE TERROR During late 1793 and early 1794 Maximilien Robespierre (1758–1794) emerged as the chief figure on the Committee of Public Safety. The Jacobin Club provided his primary forum and base of power. A shrewd and sensitive politician, he had opposed the war in 1792, believing it to be a measure that might aid the monarchy. He largely depended on the support of the *sans-culottes* of Paris, but continued to dress as he had before the revolution and opposed dechristianization as a political blunder. For him, the republic of virtue meant wholehearted support of republican government and the renunciation of selfish gains from political life. He once told the Convention:

> If the mainspring of popular government in peacetime is virtue, amid revolution it is at the same time virtue and terror: virtue, without which terror is fatal; terror, without which virtue is impotent. Terror is nothing but prompt, severe, inflexible justice; it is therefore an emanation of virtue."[5]

The Reign of Terror manifested itself through a series of revolutionary tribunals established by the Convention during the summer of 1793. The tribunals were to try the enemies of the Republic, but the definition of enemy remained uncertain and shifted as the months passed. The first victims were Marie Antoinette, other members of the royal family, and aristocrats, who were executed in October 1793. They were followed by Girondist politicians who had been prominent in the Legislative Assembly.

By early 1794 the Terror had moved to the provinces, where the deputies-on-mission presided over the summary execution of thousands of people who had allegedly supported internal opposition to the revolution. In Paris during the late winter of 1794 Robespierre turned the Terror against republican political figures of the left and right. On March 24 he secured the execution of certain

On the way to her execution in 1793, Marie Antoinette was sketched from life by Jacques-Louis David as she passed his window. Bibliotheque Nationale, Paris, France/Giraudon/Art Resource, N.Y.

extreme *sans-culottes* leaders. Shortly thereafter he moved against more conservative republicans. Robespierre thus exterminated the leadership from both groups that might have threatened his own position. Finally, on June 10 he secured passage of a law that permitted the revolutionary tribunal to convict suspects without hearing substantial evidence.

In May 1794, at the height of his power, Robespierre, considering the worship of reason too abstract for most citizens, abolished it and established the Cult of the Supreme Being. He did not long preside over this new religion. On June 26 he made an ill-tempered speech in the Convention, declaring the existence of a conspiracy among other leaders of the government against him and the revolution. Such accusations against unnamed persons had usually preceded his earlier attacks. On July 27 (the Ninth of Thermidor) members of the Convention, by prearrangement, shouted him down when he rose to speak. Robespierre was arrested that night and executed the next day.

The Reign of Terror soon ended, having claimed as many as 40,000 victims. Most were peasants and *sans-culottes* who had rebelled against the revolutionary government. By the late summer of 1794 those provincial uprisings had been

[4] From summer to spring, the months on the revolutionary calendar were *Messidor, Thermidor, Fructidor, Vendémiaire, Brumaire, Frimaire, Nivose, Pluviose, Ventose, Germinal, Floréal,* and *Prairial.*

[5] Quoted in Richard T. Bienvenu, *The Ninth of Thermidor: The Fall of Robespierre* (New York: Oxford University Press, 1968), p. 38.

crushed, and the war against foreign enemies was also going well. Those factors, combined with the feeling in Paris that the revolution had consumed enough of its own children, brought the Terror to an end.

The Thermidorian Reaction: End of the Terror and Establishment of the Directory

The tempering of the revolution, called the Thermidorian Reaction, began in July 1794. It destroyed the machinery of terror and set up a new constitutional regime. The influence of generally wealthy middle-class and professional people replaced that of the *sans-culottes.* Many of the people responsible for the Terror were removed from public life. The Paris Jacobin Club was closed, and provincial Jacobin clubs were forbidden to correspond with each other.

The Thermidorian Reaction also involved still further political reconstruction. In place of the fully democratic constitution of 1793, which had never gone into effect, the Convention issued the Constitution of the Year III. It was a conservative document that provided for a bicameral legislative government heavily favoring property owners. The executive body, consisting of a five-person Directory, was elected by the upper legislative house, known as the Council of Elders.

By the Treaty of Basel of March 1795, the Convention concluded peace with Prussia and Spain. With the war effort succeeding, the Convention severed its ties with the *sans-culottes.* True to their belief in an unregulated economy, the Thermidorians repealed the ceiling on prices. When food riots resulted during the winter of 1794–1795, the Convention put them down to prove that the era of the *sans-culottes journées* had ended. On October 5, 1795 (13 Vendémiaire) the sections (municipal units, each with its own assembly) of Paris rebelled against the Convention. For the first time in the history of the revolution, artillery was turned against the people of Paris. A general named Napoleon Bonaparte (1769–1821) commanded the cannon, and with what he termed a "whiff of grapeshot" dispersed the crowd. Other enemies of the Directory would be more difficult to disperse.

The Napoleonic Era

Napoleon Bonaparte was born in 1769 to a poor family of lesser nobles in Corsica. Because France had annexed Corsica in 1768, he went to French schools, pursued a military career, and in 1785 obtained a commission as a French artillery officer. He strongly favored the revolution and was a fiery Jacobin. In 1793 he played a leading role in recovering the port of Toulon from the British. As a reward the government appointed him a brigadier general. His defense of the new regime on 13 Vendémiaire won him another promotion and a command in Italy. By October 1797 he had crushed the Austrian army in Italy and concluded on his own initiative the Treaty of Campo Formio which took Austria out of the war. Soon all of Italy and Switzerland lay under French domination.

In November 1797 the triumphant Bonaparte returned to Paris to be hailed as a hero and to confront France's only remaining enemy, Britain. Judging it impossible to cross the Channel and invade England at that time, he chose to capture Egypt from the Ottoman Empire. He thus hoped to drive the British fleet from the Mediterranean, cut off British communication with India, damage British trade, and threaten the British Empire. But the invasion of Egypt was a failure. Admiral Horatio Nelson (1758–1805) destroyed the French fleet at Aboukir on August 1, 1798. The French army could then neither accomplish anything of importance in the Near East nor get home. The French invasion of Egypt had alarmed Russia, which had its own ambitions in the Near East. The Russians, the Austrians, and the Ottomans joined Britain to form the Second Coalition. In 1799 the Russian and Austrian armies defeated the French in Italy and Switzerland and threatened to invade France.

Having heard of these misfortunes, Napoleon abandoned his army in Egypt and returned to France in October 1799. On November 10, 1799 (19 Brumaire) his troops overthrew the Directory. Bonaparte issued the Constitution of the Year VII in December 1799, establishing himself as the First Consul. The constitution received overwhelming approval from the electorate in a largely rigged plebiscite. The establishment of the Consulate, in effect, closed the revolution in France.

The Consulate in France (1799–1804)

Bonaparte quickly justified the public's confidence by achieving peace with France's enemies. Russia had already left the Second Coalition. A campaign in Italy brought another victory over Austria at Marengo in 1800. The Treaty of Lunéville early in 1801 took Austria out of the war and confirmed the earlier settlement of Campo Formio. Britain was now alone and, in 1802, concluded the Treaty of Amiens, which temporarily brought peace to Europe.

Bonaparte also restored peace and order at home. Although he used generosity, flattery, and bribery to win over some of his enemies, issued a general amnesty, and employed persons from all political factions, Bonaparte was ruthless and efficient in suppressing political opposition. He established a highly centralized administration in which all departments were managed by prefects directly responsible to the central government in Paris. He employed secret police. He stamped out, once and for all, the royalist rebellion in the west and moved against other royalist plots.

Napoleon also alleviated the hostility of French Catholics. In 1801 he concluded a concordat with Pope Pius VII (r. 1800–1823), to the shock and dismay of his

DOCUMENT NAPOLEON DESCRIBES CONDITIONS LEADING TO THE CONSULATE

In late 1799 various political groups in France became convinced that the constitution that had established the Directory could not allow France to achieve military victory. They also feared domestic unrest and new outbreaks of the radicalism that had characterized the French Revolution during the mid-1790s. With the aid of such groups Napoleon Bonaparte seized power in Paris in November 1799. Thereafter, under various political arrangements, he governed France until 1814. He later gave his own version of the situation that brought him to power.

What are the factors that Napoleon outlines as having created a situation in which the government of France required change? In his narration how does he justify the use of military force? How does he portray himself as a savior of political order and liberty?

On my return to Paris I found division among all authorities, and agreement upon only one point, namely, that the Constitution was half destroyed and was unable to save liberty.

All parties came to me, confided to me their designs, disclosed their secrets, and requested my support; I refused to be the man of a party.

The Council of Elders summoned me; I answered its appeal. A plan of general restoration had been devised by men whom the nation has been accustomed to regard as defenders of liberty, equality, and property; this plan required an examination, calm, free, exempt from all influence and all fear. Accordingly, the Council of Elders resolved upon the removal of the Legislative Body to Saint-Cloud; it gave me the responsibility of disposing the force necessary for its independence. I believe it my duty to my fellow citizens, to the soldiers perishing in our armies, to the national glory acquired at the cost of their blood, to accept the command. . . .

I presented myself to the Council of Five Hundred, alone, unarmed, my head uncovered, just as the Elders had received and applauded me; I came to remind the majority of its wishes, and to assure it of its power.

The stilettos which menaced the deputies were instantly raised against their liberator; twenty assassins threw themselves upon me and aimed at my breast. The grenadiers of the Legislative Body whom I had left at the door of the hall ran forward, placed themselves between the assassins and myself. One of these brave grenadiers had his clothes pieced by a stiletto. They bore me out.

At the same moment cries of "Outlaw" were raised against the defender of the law. It was the fierce cry of assassins against the power destined to repress them.

They crowded around the president, uttering threats, arms in their hands; they commanded him to outlaw me. I was informed of this; I ordered him to be rescued from their fury, and six grenadiers of the Legislative Body secured him. Immediately afterwards some grenadiers of the Legislative Body charged into the hall and cleared it.

The factions, intimidated, dispersed and fled. . . .

Frenchmen, you will doubtless recognize in this conduct the zeal of a soldier of liberty, a citizen devoted to the Republic. Conservative, tutelary, and liberal ideas have been restored to their rights through the dispersal of the rebels who oppressed the Councils. . . .

From J. H. Stuart, *A Documentary Survey of the French Revolution* (New York: Macmillan, 1951), pp. 763–765.

anticlerical supporters. The concordat declared that "Roman Catholicism is the religion of the great majority of French citizens." This was merely a statement of fact and fell far short of what the pope had wanted—religious dominance for the Roman Catholic Church. Both refractory and constitutional clergy were forced to resign. Their replacements received their spiritual investiture from the pope, but the state named the bishops and paid their salaries and the salary of one priest in each parish. In return, the church gave up its claims to its confiscated property. The clergy had to swear an oath of loyalty to the state, and the Organic Articles of 1802, which were actually distinct from the concordat, established the supremacy of state over church. Similar laws were applied to the Protestant and Jewish religious communities as well, reducing still further the privileged position of the Catholic Church.

In 1802 another plebiscite appointed Napoleon consul for life, and he soon produced still another new constitution, which granted him what amounted to full power. He transformed the basic laws and institutions of France on the basis of both liberal principles derived from the Enlightenment and the early years of the revolution and conservative principles going back to the Old Regime, on the one hand, and the spirit that had triumphed at Thermidor, on the other. This was especially true of the Civil Code of 1804, usually called the Napoleonic Code. However, these laws stopped far short of the full equality advocated by liberal rationalists. Fathers were granted extensive control over their children and men over their wives. Labor unions were still forbidden, and the rights of workers were inferior to those of their employers.

In 1804 Bonaparte seized on a bomb attack on his life to make himself emperor. He argued that the establishment of a dynasty would make the new regime secure

Francisco Goya Memorializes a Night of Executions: "The Third of May, 1808"

Napoleon had begun to send troops into Spain in 1807 after the king of Spain had agreed to aid France against Portugal, which was assisting Britain. By early 1808 Spain had essentially become an occupied nation. On May 2 riots took place in Madrid between French troops, including many soldiers whom Napoleon had recruited in Egypt, and Spanish civilians. The Spaniards were attempting to prevent the departure of members of the Spanish royal family whom they considered to be French prisoners. In response to the riots, the French marshall Joachim Murat ordered numerous executions, especially of artisans and clergy, during the night of May 2 and 3. The events of these two days marked the opening of five years of the Spanish effort to free their country from French rule.

After the restoration of the Spanish monarchy, Francisco Goya (1745–1828) depicted the savagery of those executions in the most memorable war painting of the Napoleonic era, *The Third of May, 1808.* Because the executions had taken place at night, and the French chose their victims at random, Goya portrays a mechanical process of execution. One group has already been shot; another is being killed; and a third group, some of whom are covering their eyes, will be next. None of these people were necessarily heroes of the insurgency of the previous day. They were ordinary people being executed by troops of a nation that considered itself the champion of popular sovereignty. Goya's painting is one of the first works of art to illustrate victims of modern ideological wars.

In portraying these modern political executions, Goya recalled the traditional portrayal of Christian martyrdom—the pose of the central figure suggests a crucifixion. But more important, he drew on popular political prints of military firing squads, such as Paul Revere's famous print of the Boston Massacre. The painting thus presents the French as both infidels violating Christian Spaniards, and as a mechanical killing force picking out hapless civilians, as if in prophecy of the summary executions of civilians in modern warfare.

Goya's painting also illustrates two forces of modern warfare confronting each other: the professional solider and the guerilla (a term coined during this era). The guerilla is a civilian who must fight with what he finds. By contrast, the soldiers in this painting appear well disciplined and have modern rifles. They carry out the executions by the light of the large technologically advanced gas or oil lanterns with which Napoleon equipped his troops.

The Napoleonic conquest of Europe awakened the force of nationalism as ordinary people in the conquered nations resisted French domination. In *The Third of May*, Goya succeeds in making ordinary people, rather than elite officers, the symbolic heroes of the national war of liberation. But once the French were defeated and the royal family restored to the Spanish throne, the interpretation of the May 1808 events became more complicated.

In fact, Goya prepared this painting to please the royal family upon its return to Madrid in 1815. The conservative monarchy could not tolerate the insurgency as a popular uprising. It had to be seen as loyal humble citizens protecting the monarchy and the church against Napoleon and an infidel France. The victims portrayed in his painting thus appeared in 1815 to be less martyrs for liberty than defenders of the evicted royal family

Sources: Alfonso E. Perez Sanchez and Eleanor A. Sayre, *Goya and the Spirit of Enlightenment* (Boston: Museum of Fine Arts, 1989); Albert Boime, *Art in an Age of Bonapartism 1800–1815* (Chicago: University of Chicago Press, 1990), pp. 210–212, 297–300; Janis A. Tomlinson, *Goya in the Twilight of Enlightenment* (New Haven: Yale University Press, 1992), pp. 131–149; Robet Rosenblum and H. W. Janson, *19th-Century Art* (Englewood Cliffs, NJ: Prentice Hall Inc. and New York: Harry N. Abrams, Inc, Publishers, 1984, pp. 55–56.

Goya y Lucientes, Francisco de Goya. ***The Third of May, 1808.*** 1814–1815 Oil painting on canvas. Museo del Prado, Madrid, Spain. Scala/Art Resource, N.Y.

and make further attempts on his life useless. Still another new constitution, ratified by a plebiscite, was promulgated, designating Napoleon Emperor of the French instead of First Consul of the Republic. Napoleon summoned the pope to Notre Dame to take part in the coronation. But at the last minute the pope agreed that Napoleon should actually crown himself. The emperor had no intention of allowing anyone to think that his power and authority depended on the approval of the church. Henceforth he was called Napoleon I.

NAPOLEON'S EMPIRE (1804–1814) Between his coronation as emperor and his final defeat at Waterloo (1815), Napoleon conquered most of Europe in military campaigns that astonished the world. France's victories changed the map of Europe, ended the Old Regime and its feudal trappings in western Europe, and forced the eastern European states to reorganize themselves to resist Napoleon's armies. Everywhere, Napoleon's advance unleashed the powerful force of nationalism.

The Treaty of Amiens with Britain (1802) could not last. Napoleon intervened militarily to extend French influence in Europe. The British issued an ultimatum. When Napoleon ignored it, Britain declared war, in May 1803. William Pitt the Younger (1759–1806) returned to office as prime minister in 1804 and began to construct the Third Coalition. By August 1805 he had persuaded Russia and Austria to move once again against French aggression. On October 21, 1805, Lord Nelson destroyed the combined French and Spanish fleets at the Battle of Trafalgar just off the Spanish coast. Nelson was killed, but the British lost no ships. Trafalgar put an end to the French hope of invading Britain and guaranteed British control of the sea.

On land, however, the story was different. Between mid-October 1805 and July 1807 Napoleon had defeated the armies of Austria, Prussia, and Russia in stunning victories. The most famous of the victories was that of Austerlitz on December 2, 1805. Through these campaigns he forced Austria to withdraw from northern Italy, where Napoleon himself was recognized as king. He replaced the ancient Holy Roman Empire with the Confederation of the Rhine. On July 7, 1807, Napoleon and Emperor Alexander I (r. 1800–1825) of Russia concluded the Treaty of Tilsit, which confirmed France's gains in central and eastern Europe. Prussia and Russia became allies of Napoleon.

Napoleon knew that he could not be genuinely secure until he had defeated Britain. Unable to compete with the British navy, he adopted economic warfare to cut off all British trade with the European continent. He thus hoped to cripple British commercial and financial power, cause domestic unrest and revolution, and drive the British from the war. On November 21, 1806, he had issued the Berlin Decrees forbidding his allies to import British goods. The Milan Decree of 1807 attempted to halt neutral nations, such as the United States, from trading with Britain. Nonetheless, the British economy survived because of its access to the growing markets of North and South America and the eastern Mediterranean. Known as the Continental System, Napoleon's policies harmed the European economies and roused resentment against France.

In this early 19th century cartoon England, personified by a caricature of William Pitt, and France, personified by a caricature of Napoleon, are carving out their areas of interest around the globe.
Cartoon by Gillray/Corbis-Bettmann

DOCUMENT A COMMANDER RECALLS AN INCIDENT IN SPAIN

William Napier was a British officer during the Napoleonic Wars. In this passage, he describes his experiences in a battle that took place in 1811 in Spain.

What were Napier's expectations of his men? of his officers? How does he explain the difficulties that his troops had in responding to his orders? How does he indicate his contempt for bad officers and yet a certain understanding that in war a person's character may display different faces?

I arrived [with two companies] just in time to save Captain Dobbs, 52nd, and two men who were cut off from their regiment. The French were gathering fast about us, we could scarcely retreat, and Dobbs agreed with me that boldness would be our best chance; so we called upon the men to follow, and, jumping over a wall which had given us cover, charged the enemy with a shout which sent the nearest back.. . .

Only the two men of the 52nd followed us, and we four arrived unsupported at a second wall, close to a considerable body of French, who rallied and began to close upon us. Their fire was very violent, but the wall gave cover. I was, however, stung by the backwardness of my men, and told Dobbs I would save him or lose my life by bringing up the two companies; he entreated me not, saying I could not make two paces from the wall and live. Yet I did go back to the first wall, escaped the fire, and, reproaching the men gave them the word again, and returned to Dobbs, who was now upon the point of being taken; but again I returned alone! The soldiers had indeed crossed the wall in their front, but kept edging away to the right to avoid the heavy fire. Being now maddened by this second failure, I made another attempt, but I had not made ten paces when a shot struck my spine, and the enemy very ungenerously continued to fire at me when I was down. I escaped death by dragging myself by my hands—for my lower extremities were paralyzed—towards a small heap of stones which was in the midst of the field, and thus covering my head and shoulders.. . . However, Captain Lloyd and my company, and some of the 52nd, came up at that moment, and the French were driven away.

The excuses for the soldiers were—1st That I had not made allowance for their exertions in climbing from the ravine up the hill-side with their heavy packs, and they were very much blown. 2nd Their own captains had not been with them for a long time, and they were commanded by two lieutenants, remarkable for their harsh, vulgar, tyrannical dispositions, and very dull bad officers withall; and one of them exhibited on this occasion such miserable cowardice as would be incredible if I had not witnessed it. I am sure he ordered the men not to advance; and I saw him leading them the second time to the right. This man was lying down with his face on the ground; I called to him, reproached him, bad him remember his uniform; nothing would stir him; until losing all patience I threw a large stone at his head. This made him get up, but when he got over the wall he was wild, his eyes staring and his hand spread out. He was a duellist, and had wounded one of the officers some time before. I would have broken him, but before I recovered my wound sufficiently to join, he had received a cannon-shot in the leg, and died at the old, desolate, melancholy mill below Sabugal. Everything combined to render death appalling, yet he showed no signs of weakness. Such is human nature, and so hard it is to form correct opinions of character!

Quoted in H. A. Bruce, *Life of Sir William Napier* (London: John Murray, 1864), 1:55–57.

THE WARS OF LIBERATION In 1807, as part of the strategy of crippling the British economy, a French army invaded the Iberian Peninsula to force Portugal to abandon its traditional alliance with Britain. The army stayed in Spain to protect lines of supply and communication. When a revolt broke out in Madrid in 1808, Napoleon deposed the Bourbons and placed his brother Joseph (1768–1844) on the Spanish throne. Attacks on the privileges of the church increased public outrage.

In Spain Napoleon faced a kind of warfare not vulnerable to his usual tactics. Guerrilla bands cut communications, killed stragglers, destroyed isolated units, and then disappeared. The British landed an army under Sir Arthur Wellesley (1769–1852), later the Duke of Wellington, to support the Spanish insurgents. Thus began the long peninsular campaign that would drain French strength and play a critical role in Napoleon's eventual defeat.

Encouraged by the French troubles in Spain, the Austrians renewed the war in 1809. The French army nonetheless marched swiftly into Austria and won the battle of Wagram. The resulting peace deprived Austria of much territory and 3.5 million subjects. Another spoil of victory was the Archduchess Marie Louise (1791–1847), Francis I's eighteen-year-old daughter, whom Napoleon married for dynastic purposes after divorcing his wife Josephine de Beauharnais (1763–1814), who had borne him no children.

The Franco-Russian alliance concluded at Tilsit was faltering. The Continental System had harmed the Russian economy. Napoleon's organization of a Polish state, the Grand Duchy of Warsaw, on the Russian doorstep and its enlargement in 1809 after the battle of Wagram angered Alexander I. Napoleon's annexation of Holland in violation of the Treaty of Tilsit, his recognition of the

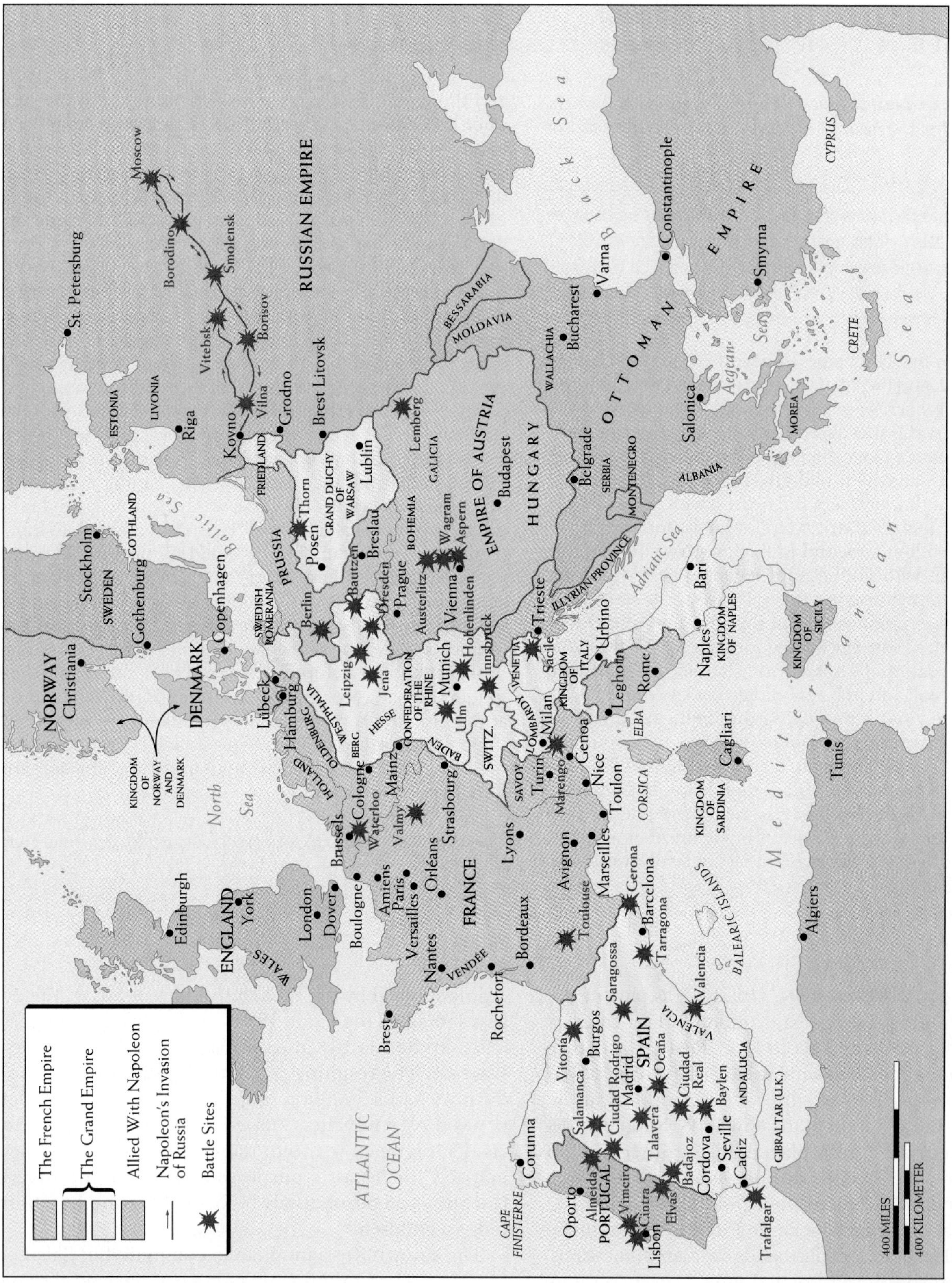

Map 24–2 Napoleonic Europe in late 1812. By mid-1812 the areas shown in peach were incorporated into France, and most of the rest of Europe was directly controlled by or allied with Napoleon. But Russia had withdrawn from the failing Continental System, and the decline of Napoleon was about to begin.

French Marshal Bernadotte as the future king of Sweden (r. 1818–1844), and his marriage to an Austrian princess further disturbed the tsar. At the end of 1810 Russia withdrew from the Continental System and began to prepare for war (see Map 24–2).

Determined to stifle the Russian military threat, Napoleon amassed an army of over 600,000 men, including over 400,000 non-French soldiers drawn from his empire and allies. He intended the usual short campaign crowned by a decisive battle, but the Russians retreated before his advance. His vast superiority in numbers—the Russians had only about 160,000 troops—made it foolish for them to risk a battle. Instead, they destroyed all food and supplies as they retreated. The so-called Grand Army of Napoleon could not live off the country, and Russia was too vast for supply lines. Terrible rains, fierce heat, shortages of food and water, and the courage of the Russian rear guard eroded the morale of Napoleon's army.

In September 1812 Russian public opinion forced the army to stand and fight. At Borodino, not far west of Moscow, the bloodiest battle of the Napoleonic era cost the French 30,000 casualties and the Russians almost twice as many. Yet the Russian army was not destroyed. Napoleon had won nothing substantial. By October, after occupying Moscow, the Grand Army was forced to retreat. By December Napoleon realized that the Russian fiasco would encourage plots against him at home. He returned to Paris, leaving the remnants of his army to struggle westward. Perhaps only as many as 100,000 lived to tell the tale of their terrible ordeal. Even as the news of the disaster reached the west, the total defeat of Napoleon was far from certain. He was able to suppress his opponents in Paris and raise another 350,000 men.

In 1813 patriotic pressure and national ambition brought together the last and most powerful coalition against Napoleon. Financed by the British, the Russians drove westward to be joined by Prussia and then Austria. From the west Wellington marched his peninsular army into France. Napoleon waged a skillful campaign in central Europe and defeated the allies at Dresden. In October, however, he met decisive defeat at Leipzig from the combined armies of his enemies, in what the Germans called the Battle of the Nations. At the end of March 1814 the allied army marched into Paris. Napoleon abdicated and went into exile on the island of Elba off the coast of northern Italy.

The Congress of Vienna and the European Settlement

Once Napoleon was removed, the allies began to pursue their own separate ambitions. The key person in achieving eventual agreement among the allies was Robert Stewart, Viscount Castlereagh (1769–1822), the British foreign secretary. Even before the victorious armies had entered Paris, he achieved the Treaty of Chaumont on March 9, 1814, providing for the restoration of the Bourbons to the French throne and the contraction of France to its 1792 frontiers. Even more important, Britain, Austria, Russia, and Prussia formed a Quadruple Alliance for twenty years to preserve whatever settlement they later agreed on. Remaining problems—and there were many—and final details were left for a conference to be held at Vienna.

The Congress of Vienna assembled in September 1814 but did not conclude its work until November 1815. The four great powers conducted the important work of the conference. The victors agreed that no single state should be allowed to dominate Europe. They constructed a series of states to serve as barriers to any new French expansion (see Map 24–3). Thus, they established the kingdom of the Netherlands, including Belgium in the north, and added Genoa to Piedmont in the south. Prussia, whose power was increased by acquisitions in eastern Europe, was given important new territories in the west to deter French aggression along the Rhine River. Austria was given full control of northern Italy to prevent a repetition of Napoleon's conquests there. Most of Napoleon's arrangements in the rest of Germany were left untouched. The Holy Roman Empire was not revived. The Congress established the rule of legitimate monarchs and

Chronology

Napoleonic Europe

1797	Napoleon concludes Treaty of Campo Formio
1798	Nelson defeats French navy at Aboukir
1799	Consulate established
1801	Concordat between France and papacy
1802	Treaty of Amiens
1803	War renewed between France and Britain
1804	Execution of Duke of Enghien; Napoleonic Civil Code issued; Napoleon crowned emperor
1805	Nelson defeats French fleet at Trafalgar (October 21); Austerlitz (December 2)
1806	Continental System established by Berlin Decrees
1807	Treaty of Tilsit
1808	Beginning of Spanish resistance to Napoleonic domination
1809	Wagram; Napoleon marries Archduchess Marie Louise of Austria
1812	Invasion of Russia
1813	Leipzig (Battle of the Nations)
1814	Treaty of Chaumont (March) establishes Quadruple Alliance; Congress of Vienna convenes (September)
1815	Napoleon returns from Elba (March 1); Waterloo (June 18); Holy Alliance formed (September 26); Quadruple Alliance renewed (November 20)
1821	Napoleon dies on Saint Helena

In this political cartoon of the Congress of Vienna, Talleyrand simply watches which way the wind is blowing, Castlereagh hesitates, while the monarchs of Russia, Prussia, and Austria form the dance of the Holy Alliance. The King of Saxony holds onto his crown and the republic of Geneva pays homage to the Kingdom of Sardinia.
Bildarchiv Preussischer Kulturbesitz

rejected any hint of the republican and democratic politics that had flowed from the French Revolution.

However, the settlement of eastern Europe sharply divided the victors. Alexander I wanted Russia to govern all of Poland. Prussia was willing if it received all of Saxony. Austria, however, refused to surrender its share of Poland or to see Prussian power grow and Russia penetrate deeper into central Europe. The Polish-Saxon question enabled France to rejoin the great powers. The French Foreign Minister Talleyrand (1754–1838) suggested that the weight of France, added to that of Britain and Austria, might bring Alexander to his senses. When news of a secret treaty among the three leaked out, the tsar agreed to become ruler of a smaller Poland, and Frederick William III of Prussia (r. 1797–1840) agreed to settle for part of Saxony. Thereafter, France was included as a fifth great power in all deliberations.

Napoleon's escape from Elba on March 1, 1815, further restored unity among the victors. He promised a liberal constitution and a peaceful foreign policy, but the allies declared him an outlaw (a new device under international law) and sent their armies to crush him. Wellington, with the crucial help of the Prussians, defeated Napoleon at Waterloo in Belgium on June 18, 1815. Napoleon again abdicated and was exiled to Saint Helena, a tiny Atlantic island off the coast of Africa, where he died in 1821.

The Hundred Days, as the period of Napoleons' return is called, made the peace settlement somewhat harsher for France, but the other main outlines of the Vienna Settlement remained in place. The Quadruple Alliance between England, Austria, Prussia, and Russia was renewed on November 20, 1815. Henceforth, it was as much a coalition for the maintenance of peace as for the pursuit of victory over France. A coalition with such a purpose had not previously existed in European international relations. Its existence and later operation represented an important new departure in European affairs. Unlike the situation in the eighteenth century, certain European powers were determined to prevent the outbreak of future war. The statesmen at Vienna, unlike their eighteenth-century counterparts, had seen the armies of the French Revolution change major

MAP EXPLORATION

Interactive map: To explore this map further, go to http://www.prenhall.com/craig_map24.3

Map 24–3 Europe 1815, after the Congress of Vienna. The Congress of Vienna achieved the post-Napoleonic territorial adjustments shown on the map. The most notable arrangements dealt with areas along France's borders (the Netherlands, Prussia, Switzerland, and Piedmont) and in Poland and northern Italy.

frontiers of the European states and overturn the political and social order of much of the Continent. They had seen unprecedented military destruction. They were determined to prevent a recurrence of those upheavals. The shared purpose of the diplomats was to establish a framework for future stability, not to punish a defeated France. The great powers through the Vienna Settlement framed international relations in such a manner that the major powers would respect that settlement and not as in the eighteenth century use military force to change it.

The Congress of Vienna succeeded in preventing future French aggression and in arranging an acceptable settlement for Europe that produced a long-lasting peace. Its work has been criticized for failing to recognize and provide for the great forces that would stir the nineteenth century—nationalism and democracy—but such criticism is inappropriate. The settlement, like all such agreements, was aimed at solving past ills, and in that it succeeded. The Vienna Settlement remained essentially intact for almost half a century and spared Europe a general war until 1914.

Wars of Independence in Latin America

The wars of the French Revolution, particularly those of Napoleon, sparked movements for independence throughout Latin America. Between 1804 and 1824 France was driven from Haiti, Portugal lost control of Brazil, and Spain was forced to withdraw from all of its American empire except for Cuba and Puerto Rico. Three centuries of Iberian colonial government over the South American continent ended.

Eighteenth-Century Developments

Spain was one of the defeated powers in 1763. Charles III (r. 1759–1788) and the government circles in Spain were convinced that the American colonial system had to be changed. After 1765 the monarch abolished the monopolies of Seville and Cádiz and permitted other Spanish commercial centers to trade with America. He also opened more South American and Caribbean ports to trade and authorized commerce between American ports. In 1776 he organized a fourth viceroyalty in the region of the Río de la Plata, which included much of present-day Argentina, Uruguay, Paraguay, and Bolivia. Charles III also attempted to make tax collection more efficient and to eliminate bureaucratic corruption. To achieve those ends, he introduced into the empire *intendents*, who were royal bureaucrats loyal only to the Crown.

These reforms, which took place during the same years as the unsuccessful British effort to reorganize its authority in its North American colonies, largely succeeded in returning the empire to direct Spanish control. Many *peninsulares*, whites born in Spain, went to the New World to fill new posts at the expense of Creoles, whites born in America. Expanding trade likewise brought more Spanish merchants to Latin America. The economy retained its export orientation, and economic life continued to be organized for the benefit of Spain. There matters stood until the early nineteenth century.

First Movements Toward Independence

Haiti achieved independence from France in 1804, following a slave revolt that commenced in 1794 led by Toussaint L'Ouverture (1744–1803) and Jean-Jacques Dessalines (ca. 1756–1806). Haiti's revolution involved the popular uprising of a repressed social group, which proved to be the great exception in the Latin American drive for liberty from European masters. Generally speaking, on the South American continent it was the Creole elite—merchants, landowners, and professional people—who led the movements against Spain and Portugal. Few Indians, blacks,

Toussaint L'Ouverture (1744–1803) began the revolt that led to Haitian independence in 1804 Historical Pictures Collection/Stock Montage, Inc.

mestizos, mulattos, or slaves became involved or benefited from the end of Iberian rule. Indeed, the Haitian slave revolt haunted the Creoles, as did an Indian revolt in the Andes in 1780 and 1781. The Creoles were determined that political independence from Spain and Portugal should not cause social disruption or the loss of their social and economic privileges. In this respect the Creole revolutionaries were not unlike American revolutionaries in the Southern colonies who wanted to reject British rule but keep their slaves, or French revolutionaries who wanted to depose the king but not extend liberty to the French working class.

Creole complaints resembled those of the American colonists against Great Britain. Latin American merchants wanted to trade more freely within the region and with North American and European markets. They wanted commercial regulations that would benefit them rather than Spain.

Creoles also feared that Spanish imperial regulations might affect landholdings, access to commissions in the army, local government policy, and the treatment of slaves and Indians in ways that would harm their interests. They also deeply resented Spanish policies favoring *peninsulares* for political patronage, including appointments in the colonial government, church, and army. They believed the *peninsulares* improperly secured all the best positions. Seen in this light, the royal patronage system represented another device with which Spain extracted wealth and income from America for its own people rather than its colonial subjects.

From the 1790s onward Spain suffered military reverses in the wars associated with the French Revolution and Napoleon, and the commercial situation turned sharply against the inhabitants of the Spanish Empire. The military pressures led the Spanish monarchy into a desperate search for new revenues, including increased taxation and the confiscation of property in the American Empire. The policies harmed the economic life of the Creole elite.

Creole leaders had read the Enlightenment *philosophes* and regarded their reforms as potentially beneficial to the region. They were also well aware of the events and the political philosophy of the American Revolution. But something more than reform programs and revolutionary example was required to transform Creole discontent into revolt against the Spanish government. That transforming event occurred in Europe when Napoleon toppled the Portuguese monarchy in 1807 and the Spanish government in 1808 and then placed his own brother on the thrones of both countries. The Portuguese royal family fled to Brazil and established its government there. But the Bourbon monarchy of Spain seemed wholly vanquished.

The Creole elite feared that a liberal Napoleonic monarchy in Spain would impose reforms in Latin America harmful to their economic and social interests and would drain the region of the wealth and resources needed for Napoleon's wars. To protect their interests, various Creole juntas, or political committees, between 1808 and 1810 claimed the right to govern different regions of Latin America. After the establishment of these local juntas, the Spanish would not again directly govern the continent and after ten years of politically and economically exhausting warfare were to recognize the permanence of Latin American independence.

SAN MARTÍN IN RÍO DE LA PLATA

The first region to assert its independence was the Río de la Plata, or modern Argentina. As early as 1806 the citizens of Buenos Aires had fought off a British invasion and thus had learned that they could look to themselves rather than Spain for effective political and military action. In 1810 the junta in Buenos Aires not only thrust off Spanish authority but also sent liberation forces against Paraguay and Uruguay. The armies were defeated, but Spain nonetheless soon lost control in the two areas. Paraguay asserted its own independence. Uruguay was eventually absorbed by Brazil.

Undiscouraged by these early defeats, the Buenos Aires government remained determined to liberate Peru, the greatest stronghold of royalist power and loyalty on the continent. By 1814 José de San Martín (1778–1850), the leading general of the Río de la Plata forces, had organized and led a disciplined army in a daring march over the Andes Mountains. By early 1817 he had occupied Santiago in Chile, and established the Chilean independence leader Bernardo O'Higgins (1778–1842) as supreme dictator. San Martín then constructed a naval force that in 1820 transported his army to Peru. The next year, he drove royalist forces from Lima and assumed the title of Protector of Peru (Map 24–4).

SIMÓN BOLÍVAR'S LIBERATION OF VENEZUELA

While San Martín had been liberating the southern portion of the Continent, Simón Bolívar (1783–1830) had been pursuing a similar task in the north. In 1810, as a

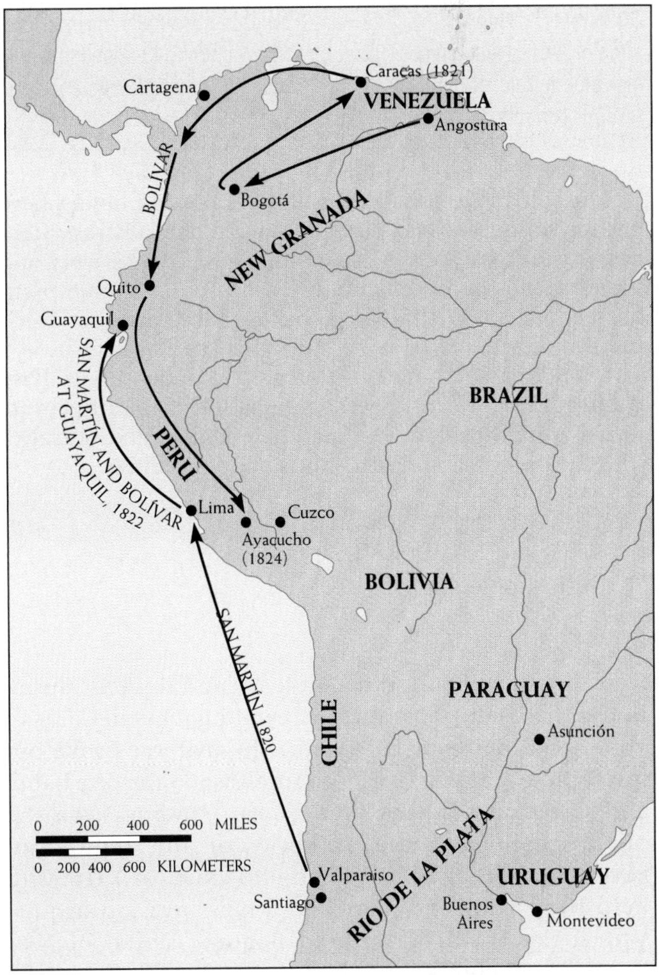

Map 24–4 The Independence campaigns of San Martín and Bolívar.

DOCUMENT BOLÍVAR DENOUNCES SPANISH RULE IN LATIN AMERICA

In September 1815 Simón Bolívar published a long statement, often called The Jamaica Letter, in which he explained the political and economic difficulties under which the Creole elite of the Spanish Empire had lived. He defined Americans as referring to those persons in Latin America who were neither Indian nor European by birth. He also implicitly excluded black slaves. Consequently his attack on Spain was voiced on behalf of the white population of the South American continent who had been born there and who demanded rights of political participation and economic freedom.

Why does Bolívar describe the Creole elite as having lived in a permanent political infancy? What are the economic disadvantages that he describes, and why had those become more burdensome in the half century before he wrote this letter? How had Spanish economic regulation prevented the Creole elite from achieving positions of responsibility in Latin America? How does this document compare with others concerned with movements of independence and nationalism? See "The Stamp Act Congress Addresses George III" (earlier in this chapter), "Mazzini Defines Nationality" (Chapter 25), "The Pan-Slavic Congress Calls for the Liberation of Slavic Nationalities" (Chapter 25), "William Gladstone Pleads for Irish Home Rule" (Chapter 26), and "Gandhi on Passive Resistance and Swaraj" (Chapter 28).

The role of the inhabitants of the American hemisphere has for centuries been purely passive. Politically they were non-existent. We are still in a position lower than slavery, and therefore it is more difficult for us to rise to the enjoyment of freedom. . . . We have been harassed by a conduct which has not only deprived us of our rights but has kept us in a sort of permanent infancy with regard to public affairs. If we could at least have managed our domestic affairs and our internal administration, we could have acquainted ourselves with the processes and mechanics of public affairs. . . .

Americans today, and perhaps to a greater extent than ever before, who live within the Spanish system occupy a position in society no better than that of serfs destined for labor, or at best they have no more status than that of mere consumers. Yet even this status is surrounded with galling restrictions, such as being forbidden to grow European crops, or to store products which are royal monopolies, or to establish factories of a type the [Spanish] Peninsula itself does not possess. To this add the exclusive trading privileges, even in articles of prime necessity, and the barriers between American provinces, designed to prevent all exchange of trade, traffic, and understanding. In short, do you wish to know what our future held?—simply the cultivation of the fields of indigo, grain, coffee, sugar cane, cacao, and cotton; cattle raising on the broad plains; hunting wild game in the jungles; digging in the earth to mine its gold—but even these limitations could never satisfy the greed of Spain.

So negative was our existence that I can find nothing comparable in any other civilized society, examine as I may the entire history of time and the politics of all nations. Is it not an outrage and a violation of human rights to expect a land so splendidly endowed, so vast, rich, and populous, to remain merely passive?

As I have just explained, we were cut off and, as it were, removed from the world in relation to the science of government and administration of the state. We were never viceroys or governors, save in the rarest of instances; seldom archbishops and bishops; diplomats never; as military men, only subordinates; as nobles, without royal privileges. In brief, we were neither magistrates nor financiers and seldom merchants. . . .

From Harold A. Bierck, Jr., ed., *Selected Writings of Bolívar*, Vol. 1. Copyright ©1951 The Colonial Press, pp. 110–112.

firm advocate of both independence and republicanism, Bolívar had helped organize a liberating junta in Caracas, Venezuela. Between 1811 and 1814 civil war broke out throughout Venezuela as both royalists, on the one hand, and slaves and *llaneros* (Venezuelan cowboys), on the other, challenged the authority of the republican government. Bolívar had to go into exile. In 1816, with help from Haiti, he launched a new invasion against Venezuela. He first captured Bogotá, capital of New Granada (including modern Colombia, Bolivia, and Ecuador), as a base for attacking Venezuela. By the summer of 1821 his forces had captured Caracas, and he had been named president.

A year later, in July 1822, the armies of Bolívar and San Martín joined to liberate Quito. At a famous meeting in Guayaquil the two leaders sharply disagreed about the future political structure of Latin America. San Martín believed that monarchies were required; Bolívar maintained his republicanism. Not long thereafter San Martín quietly retired from public life and went into exile in Europe. Meanwhile, Bolívar purposefully allowed the political situation in Peru to fall into confusion, and in 1823 he sent troops to establish his control. On December 9, 1824, at the Battle of Ayacucho, the Spanish royalist forces suffered a major defeat at the hands of the liberating army. The battle marked the conclusion of Spain's effort to retain its American empire.

Simón Bolívar was the liberator of much of Latin America. He inclined toward a policy of political liberalism.
Hulton/Corbis-Bettmann

INDEPENDENCE IN NEW SPAIN

The drive for independence in New Spain, which included present-day Mexico as well as Texas, California, and the rest of the southwestern United States, clearly illustrates the socially conservative outcome of the Latin American colonial revolutions. As elsewhere, a local governing junta was organized. But before it had undertaken any significant measures, a Creole priest, Miguel Hidalgo y Costilla (1753–1811), issued a call for rebellion to the Indians in his parish. They and other repressed groups of black and mestizo urban and rural workers responded. Father Hidalgo set forth a program of social change, including hints of land reform. Soon he stood at the head of a rather unorganized group of 80,000 followers and marched on Mexico City. Both Hidalgo's forces and the royalist army that opposed them committed numerous atrocities. In July 1811 he was captured and executed. Leadership of his movement then fell to José María Morelos y Pavón (1765–1815), a mestizo priest. Far more radical than Hidalgo, he called for an end to forced labor and for substantial land reforms. He was executed in 1815, ending five years of popular uprising.

In 1820, however, the conservative political groups in Mexico, both Creole and Spanish, found their recently achieved security challenged from an unexpected source. A revolution in Spain had forced Ferdinand VII (r. 1813–1833) to accept a liberal constitution. Conservative Mexicans feared that the new liberal monarchy would attempt to impose liberal reforms on Mexico. Therefore, for the most conservative of reasons, they rallied to a former royalist general, Agustín de Iturbide (1783–1824), who in 1821 declared Mexico independent of Spain. Shortly thereafter, Iturbide was declared emperor. His own regime did not last long, but an independent Mexico, governed by persons determined to resist any significant social reform, had been created.

Great Britain was highly sympathetic to the independence movements in the different regions of Latin America. By breaking the hold of the Spanish empire the movement toward independence opened the markets of the continent to British trade and investment. Consequently in 1823 Great Britain supported the American Monroe Doctrine that prohibited further colonization and intervention by European powers in America. Britain soon recognized the Spanish colonies as independent states. Through the rest of the century, British commercial interests dominated Latin America.

BRAZILIAN INDEPENDENCE

Brazilian independence, in contrast to that of Spanish Latin America, came relatively simply and peacefully. As already noted, the Portuguese royal family, along with several thousand government officials and members of the court, took refuge in Brazil in 1807. Their arrival immediately transformed Rio de Janeiro into a court city. The prince regent Joao (r. 1816–1826) addressed many of the local complaints, equivalent to those of the Spanish Creoles. In 1815 he made Brazil a kingdom, which meant that it was no longer to be regarded merely as a colony of Portugal. This transformation was in many respects long overdue because Brazil was far larger and more prosperous than Portugal itself. Then in 1820 a revolution occurred in Portugal, and its leaders demanded Joao's return to Lisbon. They also demanded the return of Brazil to colonial status. Joao, who had become Joao VI in 1816, returned to Portugal but left his son Pedro (r. 1822–1831) as regent in Brazil, encouraging him to be sympathetic to the political aspirations of the Brazilians. In September 1822 Pedro embraced Brazilian independence against the recolonializing efforts of Portugal. By the end of the year he had become emperor of an independent Brazil, which remained a monarchy until 1889. Thus in contrast to virtually all other nations of Latin America, Brazil achieved independence in a way that left no real dispute as to where the center of political authority lay.

Another factor aided the peaceful transition to independence in Brazil. The political and social elite there were determined to preserve slavery against the forces (to be discussed in the next section) that were challenging that institution. The Wars of Independence elsewhere had led to the abolition of slavery or moved the independent states closer to abolition. Any attempt to gain independence from Portugal through warfare might have caused social as well as political turmoil that would open the slavery question.

Toward the Abolition of Slavery in the Transatlantic Economy

In 1750 almost no one seriously questioned the institution of slavery; by 1888 slavery no longer existed in the transatlantic economy. This vast transformation of economic and social life occurred as the result of an international effort, first to abolish the slave trade and then to abolish the institution of slavery itself. At no previous time in world history had a society actually attempted to abolish slavery. Its eventual abolition in the transatlantic world stands as one of the most permanent achievements of the forces unleashed by the eighteenth-century Enlightenment and Revolutions.

The eighteenth-century crusade against slavery in the plantation economy that stretched from Maryland south to Brazil (see Chapter 18) originated among writers of the Enlightenment and religious critics of slavery. Although some authors associated with the Enlightenment, including John Locke, were reluctant to question slavery or even defended it, the general Enlightenment rhetoric of equality stood in sharp contrast to the radical inequality of slavery. Montesquieu satirized slavery in *The Spirit of the Laws*. Adam Smith's emphasis in *The Wealth of Nations* on free labor and the efficiency of free markets undermined economic defenses of slavery. Much eighteenth-century literature idealized primitive peoples living in cultures very different from those of Europe and portrayed them as embodying a lost human virtue. This literature allowed some Europeans to look upon African slaves in the Americas as having been betrayed and robbed of an original innocence. In such a climate, slavery, once considered the natural and deserved result of some deficiency in slaves themselves, grew to be regarded as undeserved and unacceptable. Other Enlightenment ethical thinking led reformers to believe that by working against slavery, for virtually the first time defined as an unmitigated evil, they would realize their own highest moral character.

The initial religious protest against slavery originated among English Quakers, a radical Protestant religious group founded by George Fox in the seventeenth century. By the early eighteenth century it had solidified itself into a small but relatively wealthy sect in England. Members of Quaker congregations at that time actually owned slaves in the West Indies and participated in the transatlantic slave trade. During the Seven Years' War (1756–1763), however, many Quakers experienced economic hardship. Furthermore, the war created other difficulties for the English population as a whole. Certain Quakers decided that the presence of the evil of slavery in the world explained these troubles. They then sought to remove this evil from their own lives and from the lives of their congregations by taking action against the whole system of slavery that characterized the transatlantic economy.

Just as the slave system was a transatlantic affair, so was the crusade against it. There were Quaker communities in America, and soon Quakers in both Philadelphia and England wrote and organized against the institution. By the earliest stages of the American Revolution small groups of reformers, usually spearheaded by Quakers, had established an antislavery network. The turmoil of the American Revolution and the founding of the American republic gave these groups the occasion for some of their earliest successes. Emancipation gradually, but nonetheless steadily, spread among the northern states. In 1787 the Continental Congress forbade slavery in the newly organized Northwest Territory north of the Ohio River.

Chronology

The Wars of Latin American Independence

1759–1788	Charles III of Spain carries out imperial reforms
1776	Organization of Viceroyalty of Río de la Plata
1780–1781	Revolt of Indians in the Andes
1794	Toussaint L'Ouverture leads slave revolt in Haiti
1804	Independence of Haiti
1807	Portuguese royal family flees to Brazil
1808	Spanish monarchy falls to Napoleon
1808–1810	Creole Committees organized to govern much of Latin America
1810	Buenos Aires junta sends forces to liberate Paraguay and Uruguay
1811	Miguel Hidalgo y Costilla leads rebellion in New Spain and is executed
1811–1815	José María Morelos y Pavón leads rebellion in New Spain and is executed
1814	San Martín organizes army
1815	Brazil declared a kingdom
1816	Bolívar invades Venezuela
1817	San Martín occupies Santiago, Chile
1820	Revolution in Spain
1821	
February 24	New Spain declares independence
June 29	Bolívar captures Caracas, Venezuela
July 28	San Martín liberates Peru
1822	
July 26–27	San Martín and Bolívar quarrel at Guayaquil; San Martín goes into exile in Europe
September 7	Dom Pedro declares Brazilian independence
1824	Battle of Ayacucho—final Spanish defeat

Despite these American developments, Great Britain became and remained the center for the antislavery movement. In 1772 a decision by the chief justice affirmed that slaves brought into Great Britain could not forcibly be removed. During the early 1780s the antislavery reformers in Great Britain decided to work toward ending the slave trade rather than the institution of slavery itself. The horrors of the slave trade caught the public's attention in 1783 when the captain of the slave ship *Zong* threw more than 130 slaves overboard in order to collect insurance. Soon after, groups from the Church of England and the English Quakers formed the Society for the Abolition of the Slave Trade. The most famous of the new leaders was William Wilberforce, who, each year for the rest of his life, introduced a bill to end the slave trade.

For the reformers, attacking the trade rather than the institution appeared a less radical and more achievable reform. To many, the slave trade appeared a more obvious crime than the holding of slaves, which seemed a more passive act. Furthermore, attacking slavery itself involved serious issues of property rights, which might alienate potential supporters of the abolition of the slave trade. The antislavery groups also believed that if the trade were ended, planters would have to treat their remaining slaves more humanely.

While the British reformers worked for the abolition of the slave trade, slaves themselves in certain areas took matters into their own hands. Indeed, the largest emancipation of slaves to occur in the eighteenth century came on the island of Saint Domingue (Haiti), France's wealthiest colony, as a result of the slave revolt of 1794 led by Toussaint L'Ouverture and Jean-Jacques Dessalines (see p. 678). The revolt in Haiti and Haiti's eventual independence in 1804 stood as a warning to slave owners throughout the West Indies. Other slave revolts occurred, such as those in Virginia led by Gabriel Prosser in 1800 and by Nat Turner in 1831, in South Carolina led by Denmark Vesey in 1822, in British-controlled Demarra in 1823 and 1824, and in Jamaica in 1831. Each of these was brutally suppressed.

For complicated economic reasons some British West Indies planters began to consider abolition of the slave trade useful to their interests. Within the West Indies themselves the planters were experiencing soil exhaustion and competition from newly tilled islands opened for sugar cultivation. Some older plantations were being abandoned while others operated with low profitability. With the new islands there was a glut of sugar on the market, and as a consequence the price was falling. Under these conditions some British West Indies planters, for reasons that had nothing to do with religion or enlightened humanitarianism, began to favor curtailing the slave trade. Without new slaves competing French planters would lack the labor they needed to exploit their islands.

Then, during the Napoleonic Wars, the British captured a number of the valuable French islands. In 1805 to protect the planters of the older British West Indies islands, the British Cabinet forbade the importation of slaves into the newly acquired French islands. By 1807 the abolition sentiment was strong enough for Parliament to pass Wilberforce's often proposed measure prohibiting slave trading from any British port.

After 1807 the British Royal Navy patrolled the West African coast attempting to intercept slave-trading ships. In 1846 the British ship HMS *Albatross* captured a Spanish slave ship, the *Albanoz*, and freed the slaves. A British officer depicted the appalling conditions in the slavehold in this watercolor.
The Granger Collection, N.Y.

Thereafter the suppression of this trade became one of the fundamental pillars of nineteenth-century British foreign policy. The British navy maintained a squadron of ships around the coast of West Africa to halt slave traders. Although the French and Americans also patrolled the West African coast, neither was deeply committed to ending the slave trade. Nonetheless, in 1824 the American Congress had made slave trading a capital offense.

Leaders of the Latin American wars of independence, disposed by Enlightenment ideas to disapprove of slavery, had sought the support of slaves by promises of emancipation. Once free of Spanish domination, the newly independent nations slowly freed their slave populations in order to maintain good relations with Great Britain from whom they needed economic support. Despite the gradual nature of this abolition, slavery would disappear from all nations of Latin America by the middle of the century, with the important exception of Brazil.

Having slowly recognized that the abolition of the slave trade had not actually improved the lot of slaves, British reformers in 1823 adopted as a new goal the gradual emancipation of slaves and founded the Abolition Society. The savagery with which West Indian planters put down slave revolts in 1823 and 1824 and again in 1831 strengthened the resolve of the antislavery reformers. By 1830 the reformers abandoned the goal of gradual abolition and demanded immediate complete abolition of slavery. In 1833, following the passage of the Reform Bill in Great Britain, they achieved that goal when Parliament abolished the right of British subjects to hold slaves. In the British West Indies, 750,000 slaves were freed within a few years.

The other old colonial powers in the New World tended to be much slower in their abolition of slavery. Portugal did little or nothing about slavery in Brazil, and when that nation became independent, its new government continued slavery. Portugal ended slavery elsewhere in its American possessions in 1836; the Swedes, in 1847; the Danes, in 1848, but the Dutch not until 1863. France had witnessed a significant antislavery movement throughout the first half of the century, but did not abolish slavery in its West Indian possessions until the revolutions of 1848.

Despite all of these considerable achievements of the antislavery movement, during the first thirty years of the nineteenth century the institution of slavery actually revived and achieved new footholds in the transatlantic world. These areas included the lower south of the United States for the cultivation of cotton, Brazil for the cultivation of coffee, and Cuba for the cultivation of sugar. World demand for those products made the slave system economically viable in those regions. Slavery would end in the United States only after American abolitionists brought it to the center of American politics in the 1850s and the Civil War was fought during the next decade. In Cuba it would persist until 1886, and full emancipation would occur in Brazil only in 1888. (See Chapters 25, 26, and 27.)

The emancipation crusade, like slave trading itself, drew Europeans into African affairs. In 1787 the British established a colony for poor free blacks from Britain in Sierra Leone, which actually succeeded only after the British navy began to settle Africans rescued from captured slave-trading ships. The French established a smaller experiment at Libreville in Gabon. The most famous and lasting attempt to settle former black slaves in Africa was the establishment of Liberia through the efforts of the American Colonization Society after 1817. Liberia became an independent republic in 1847. All of these efforts to move former slaves back to Africa had only modest success, but they did affect the future of West Africa itself.

Other antislavery reformers were less interested in establishing outposts for settlement of former slaves than in transforming the African economy itself. These reformers attempted to spread both Christianity and free trade to Africa, hoping to exchange British manufactured goods, particularly textiles, for tropical goods produced by Africans. These commercial efforts of the antislavery movement marked the first serious intrusions of European powers well beyond the coast of West Africa into the heart of the continent.

After the American Civil War finally halted any large-scale demand for slaves from Africa, the antislavery reformers began to focus on ending the slave trade in East Africa and the Indian Ocean. This new drive against slavery and the slave trade in Africa itself became one of the rationales for European interference in Africa during the second half of the century and served as one of the foundations for the establishment of the late-century colonial empires.

In World Perspective

THE TRANSATLANTIC REVOLUTIONS

The revolutions and the crusade against slavery that occurred throughout the transatlantic world between 1776 and 1824 transformed the political, social, and economic life of three continents. In North America, in France and other parts of Europe, and in South America bold political experiments challenged government by both monarchy and aristocracy. The foundations of modern liberal democracy were laid. The largest republic since ancient times had been established in North America. In France, despite the ongoing political turmoil after 1789, written constitutions and elected legislatures remained essential parts of the government. In Latin America republicanism triumphed soon after independence everywhere except Brazil. Never again could government be undertaken in these regions without some form of participation by and consultation with the governed.

The expanding forms of political liberty found their counterparts in an economic life freed from the constraints of the old colonial empires and the slavery that marked their plantations. The new American republic constituted a vast free trade zone. Its commerce and ports were open to the whole world. And for the first time since the encounter with Europe, all of Latin America could trade freely among its own peoples and those of the rest of the world. In France and across much of Europe, where the Napoleonic armies had carried the doctrines of the rights of man, economic life had been rationalized and freed from the domination of local authorities and local weights and measures. National law formed the framework for economic activity. The movement to abolish slavery fostered a wage economy of free laborers. That kind of economy would generate its own set of problems and social dislocation, but it was nonetheless an economy of free human beings who were the chattel of no other human being.

Finally, the age of transatlantic revolutions saw the emergence of nationalism as a political force. All of the revolutions, because of their popular political base, had given power to the idea of nations defined by their own character and historical past rather than by dynastic rulers. The Americans saw themselves as forming a new kind of nation. The French had demonstrated the power of a nation fully mobilized for military purposes. In turn the aggression of France had aroused national sentiment, especially in Great Britain, Spain, and Germany. The new nations of Latin America also sought to define themselves by their heritage and historical experience rather than by their past in the Spanish and Portuguese empires.

These various revolutions, their political doctrines, and their social and economic departures provided examples to peoples elsewhere in the world. But even more important, the transformations of the transatlantic revolutions and eventual abolition of slavery meant that new political classes and newly organized independent nations would become actors on the world scene. Europeans would have to deal with a score of new nations in the Americas. The rest of the world confronted new nations freed from the direction and authority of European powers. In turn the political changes in Europe meant that those nations and their relationships with the rest of the world would be directed by a broader range of political groups and forces than in the past.

Review Questions

1. Discuss the American Revolution in the context of transatlantic history. To what extent were the colonists influenced by their position in the transatlantic economy? To what extent were they influenced by European ideas and political developments? How did their demands for liberty compare and contrast with the ideas of liberty championed during the French Revolution?
2. How was the Estates General transformed into the National Assembly? How does the *Declaration of the Rights of Man and Citizen* reflect the social and political values of the eighteenth-century Enlightenment? What were the chief ways in which France and its government were reorganized in the early years of the revolution? Why has the Civil Constitution of the Clergy been called the greatest blunder of the National Assembly?
3. Why were some political factions dissatisfied with the constitutional settlement of 1791 in France? What was the revolution of 1792 and why did it occur? What were the causes of the Reign of Terror and what political coalitions made it possible?
4. How did Napoleon rise to power? What were his major domestic achievements? Did his rule more nearly fulfill or betray the ideals of the French Revolution? Why did Napoleon decide to invade Russia? Why did he fail? What were the major outlines of the peace settlement achieved by the Congress of Vienna?
5. What political changes took place in Latin America in the twenty years between 1804 and 1824? What were the main reasons for Creole discontent with Spanish rule? Who were some of the primary leaders of Latin American independence and why were they successful? How were the movements to Latin American independence influenced by the American and French Revolutions? What were the factors that made the Latin American Wars of Independence different from those two revolutions?
6. A motto of the French Revolution was "liberty, equality, and fraternity." How might one compare the American Revolution, the French Revolution, and the Latin American Wars of Independence in regard to the achievement of these goals? Which groups in each country or region benefited from the revolution and which gained little or nothing from the changes?
7. What intellectual and religious factors contributed to the rise of the antislavery movement? To what extent did nonhumanitarian forces contribute to it? What opposition did it meet? Why did slavery receive a new lease on life during the same years that the antislavery movement emerged?

Suggested Readings

R. ANSTEY, *The Atlantic Slave Trade and British Abolition, 1760–1810* (1975). A standard overview that emphasizes the role of religious factors.

B. BAILYN, *The Ideological Origins of the American Revolution* (1967). An important work illustrating the role of English radical thought in the perceptions of the American colonists.

K. M. BAKER, *Inventing the French Revolution: Essays on French Political Culture in the Eighteenth Century* (1990). Important essays on political thought before and during the revolution.

K. M. BAKER AND C. LUCAS, EDS., *The French Revolution and the Creation of Modern Political Culture*, 3 vols. (1987). A splendid collection of important original articles on all aspects of politics during the revolution.

R. J. Barman, *Brazil: The Forging of a Nation, 1798–1852* (1988). The best coverage of this period.

C. Becker, *The Declaration of Independence: A Study in the History of Political Ideas* (1922). Remains an important examination of the political and imperial theory of the Declaration.

J. F. Bernard, *Talleyrand: A Biography* (1973). A useful account.

L. Bethell, *The Cambridge History of Latin America*, Vol. 3 (1985). Contains an extensive treatment of independence.

R. Blackburn, *The Overthrow of Colonial Slavery, 1776–1848* (1988). A major discussion quite skeptical of the humanitarian interpretation.

T. C. W. Blanning, ed., *The Rise and Fall of the French Revolution* (1996). A wide-ranging collection of essays illustrating the debates over the French Revolution.

J. Brooke, *King George III* (1972). The best biography.

R. Cobb, *The People's Armies* (1987). The major treatment in English of the revolutionary army.

O. Connelly, *Napoleon's Satellite Kingdoms* (1965). The rule of Napoleon and his family in Europe.

E. V. da Costa, *The Brazilian Empire* (1985). Excellent coverage of the entire nineteenth-century experience of Brazil.

D. B. Davis, *The Problem of Slavery in the Age of Revolution, 1770–1823* (1975). A transatlantic perspective on the issue.

F. Fehér, *The French Revolution and the Birth of Modernity* (1990). A wide-ranging collection of essays on political and cultural facets of the revolution.

A. Forrest, *The French Revolution and the Poor* (1981). A study that expands consideration of the revolution beyond the standard social boundaries.

M. Glover, *The Peninsular War, 1807–1814: A Concise Military History* (1974). An interesting account of the military campaign that so drained Napoleon's resources in western Europe.

J. Godechot, *The Counter-Revolution: Doctrine and Action, 1789–1804* (1971). An examination of opposition to the revolution.

A. Goodwin, *The Friends of Liberty: The English Democratic Movement in the Age of the French Revolution* (1979). A major work that explores the impact of the French Revolution on English radicalism.

L. Hunt, *Politics, Culture, and Class in the French Revolution* (1986). A series of essays that focus on the modes of expression of the revolutionary values and political ideas.

W. W. Kaufmann, *British Policy and the Independence of Latin America, 1802–1828* (1951). A standard discussion of an important relationship.

E. Kennedy, *A Cultural History of the French Revolution* (1989). An important examination of the role of the arts, schools, clubs, and intellectual institutions.

M. Kennedy, *The Jacobin Clubs in the French Revolution: The First Years* (1982). A careful scrutiny of the organizations chiefly responsible for the radicalizing of the revolution.

M. Kennedy, *The Jacobin Clubs in the French Revolution: The Middle Years* (1988). A continuation of the previously listed study.

H. Kissinger, *A World Restored: Metternich, Castlereagh and the Problems of Peace, 1812–1822* (1957). A provocative study by an author who became an American secretary of state.

G. Lefebvre, *The Coming of the French Revolution* (trans. 1947). A classic examination of the crisis of the French monarchy and the events of 1789.

G. Lefebvre, *Napoleon*, 2 vols., trans. by H. Stockhold (1969). The fullest and finest biography.

J. Lynch, *The Spanish American Revolutions, 1808–1826* (1986). An excellent one-volume treatment.

P. Maier, *American Scripture: Making the Declaration of Independence* (1997). Stands as a major revision of our understanding of the Declaration.

G. Masur, *Simón Bolívar* (1969). The standard biography in English.

S. E. Melzer and L. W. Rabine, eds., *Rebel Daughters: Women and the French Revolution* (1992). A collection of essays exploring various aspects of the role and image of women in the French Revolution.

M. Morris, *The British Monarchy and the French Revolution* (1998). Explores the manner in which the British monarchy saved itself from possible revolution.

R. Muir, *Tactics and the Experience of Battle in the Age of Napoleon* (1998). Examines the wars from the standpoint of the soldiers in combat.

H. Nicolson, *The Congress of Vienna* (1946). A good, readable account.

T. O. Ott, *The Haitian Revolution, 1789–1804* (1973). An account that clearly relates the events in Haiti to those in France.

R. R. Palmer, *Twelve Who Ruled: The Committee of Public Safety During the Terror* (1941). A clear narrative and analysis of the policies and problems of the committee.

R. R. Palmer, *The Age of the Democratic Revolution: A Political History of Europe and America, 1760–1800*, 2 vols. (1959, 1964). An impressive survey of the political turmoil in the transatlantic world.

C. Proctor, *Women, Equality, and the French Revolution* (1990). An examination of how the ideas of the Enlightenment and the attitudes of revolutionaries affected the legal status of women.

A. J. Russell-Wood, ed., *From Colony to Nation: Essays on the Independence of Brazil* (1975). A series of important essays.

P. Schroeder, *The Transformation of European Politics, 1763–1848* (1994). A fundamental treatment of the diplomacy of the era.

T. E. Skidmore and P. H. Smith, *Modern Latin America*, 4th ed. (1997). A very useful survey.

A. SOBOUL, *The Parisian Sans-Culottes and the French Revolution, 1793–94* (1964). The best work on the subject.

A. SOBOUL, *The French Revolution* (trans. 1975). An important work by a Marxist scholar.

D. G. SUTHERLAND, *France, 1789–1825: Revolution and Counterrevolution* (1986). A major synthesis based on recent scholarship in social history.

T. TACKETT, *Religion, Revolution, and Regional Culture in Eighteenth-Century France: The Ecclesiastical Oath of 1791* (1986). The most important study of this topic.

T. TACKETT, *Becoming a Revolutionary: The Deputies of the French National Assembly and the Emergence of a Revolutionary Culture* (1789–1790) (1996). The best study of the early months of the revolution.

J. M. THOMPSON, *Robespierre*, 2 vols. (1935). The best biography.

D. K. VAN KEY, *The Religious Origins of the French Revolution: From Calvin to the Civil Constitution, 1560–1791* (1996). Examines the manner in which debates within French Catholicism influenced the coming of the revolution.

M. WALZER, ED., *Regicide and Revolution: Speeches at the Trial of Louis XVI* (1974). An important and exceedingly interesting collection of documents with a useful introduction.

I. WOLOCH, *The New Regime: Transformations of the French Civic Order, 1789–1820s* (1994). An important overview of just what had and had not changed in France after the quarter century of revolution and war.

G. WOOD, *The Radicalism of the American Revolution* (1991). A major interpretation.

DOCUMENTS CD-ROM

1. Edmund Burke: from Speech on Conciliation with America
2. Thomas Paine: from *Common Sense*
3. John Adams: *Thoughts on Government*
4. The Declaration of the Rights of Man and Citizen, 1789
5. Robespierre's Theory of Revolutionary Government, 1793
6. Edmund Burke: *The Moral Imagination*

WORLD AND THE WEB

The American Revolution

http://revolution.h-net.msu.edu/

This site was created by H-Net, Humanities & Social Sciences OnLine. It is supported by the National Endowment for the Humanities and serves as a complement to the official companion site to PBS's Liberty! documentary series.

Liberty, Equality, Fraternity: Exploring the French Revolution

http://chnm.gmu.edu/revolution/

Provides an accessible and lively introduction to the French Revolution as well as an extraordinary archive of some of the most important documentary evidence from the Revolution, including 338 texts, 245 images, and a number of maps and songs. The site is a collaboration between the Center for History and New Media (George Mason University) and the American Social History Project (City University of New York), supported by grants from the Florence Gould Foundation and the National Endowment for the Humanities.

Napoleon Bonaparte Internet Guide

http://www.napoleonbonaparte.nl/

Within this site you will find some of the finest Napoleonic links on the Internet.

Colonial Latin America

http://www.emory.edu/COLLEGE/CULPEPER/BAKEWELL/index.html

This site lists the important dates and events of Colonial Latin America from 1450 to 1800. It also includes a collection of images, sounds, and text, ThinkSheets©, a collection of pages designed to illustrate a specific topic, historical point, or period.

Africa Centre

http://www.africacentre.org.uk/Unfinishedbusinesspapers.htm

The Africa Centre, a charity established in 1961, has been the heart of Africa in the heart of London, a unique and dynamic centre. Conscious of the historical and personal links between Africa and Europe, the Africa Centre, as an independent charity, was developed to create greater awareness among British and other European people about developments in Africa and its diaspora.

Index

Italic page numbers refer to illustrations.

Abbas I, 611, *612,* 613
Abbas II, 614
Abd al-Rahman I, 340
Abd al-Rahman III, 340
Abolition Society, 683
Acheh, 621
Act of Settlement (1701), 563
Act of Succession (1534), 434
Act of Supremacy (1534), 434
Act of Uniformity (1549), 434
Address to the Christian Nobility of the German Nation (Luther), 428
Admonitions for Women (Pan Chao), 428
Advancement of Learning, The (Bacon), 633
Affonso I, Kongo ruler, 474, 475
Africa
  See also specific country and range
  events/dates, major, 419, 627
  transatlantic slave trade and, 500–501, 504–508
Afrikaans, 480, 481
Agriculture/farming
  in the Americas, 360, 365, 378, 497
  Black Death and, 397, 400
  eighteenth-century revolution in, 592–594
  in Japan (Tokugawa), 533–534
  manors and serfdom in Middle Ages, 328, 329
  Ming-Ch'ing, 514
  open-field method replaced by enclosure, 593
Ah Cacau, 367
Ahmad Shah Durrani, 614–615
Aix-la-Chapelle, treaty of (1668), 567
Aix-la-Chapelle, treaty of (1748), 576
Akbar, 613
Alawma, Idris, 470
Alba, duke of, 443
Albrecht of Mainz, 427
Aleksei I, 570
Alembert, Jean le Rond d', 639
Aleppo, 347
Alexander I, tsar of Russia, 672, 676
Alexander VI, pope, 407
Alexius I Comnenus, 387
Algarotti, Francesco, 635
Alhambra castle, 340, *341,* 344–345, *344, 345*
Ali, 467
Ali, Kinalizade, 609
Ali, Mustafa, 609
All Men Are Brothers, 525
Almagest (Ptolemy), 630
Almohads, 340, 341
Almoravids, 340–341, 463
Alwa, 470
America, colonial
  crisis and independence, 656–658
  political ideas, 656
  resistance to British government, 655–656
American Colonization Society, 684
American Revolution, events/dates for, 658
Americas
  See also Andean civilization; Mesoamerica; *specific country*
  discovery of, 422–424
  events/dates, major, 361, 419, 627
  exploitation of, 488–508
  gold and spices, 422–423
  impact on Europe and America, 424
  Neolithic societies, 359
  problems in reconstructing history of, 359–360
  slavery in, 498–508, 682–684
  voyages of Columbus, 423–424, 488, 492
Amiens, treaty of (1802), 668
Anabaptists, 429–431
Anatolia, 347
Andean civilization
  Chavín de Huantar, 375
  Chimu, 378–379
  early intermediate, 375, 378
  Huari, 378
  Incas, 379–381, 488–489
  middle through late intermediate, 378
  Moche, *358,* 375, 378
  Nazca, 375
  periods in, 374
  preceramic and initial, 374–375
  range of, 373–374
  Tiwanaku, 378
Angevin empire, 395
Anglican Church, 562, 563
Anglo-Saxons (Angles), 395
Angola, 475
Animals, domestication of, 374
Anna, empress, 583
Anne, daughter of James II, queen of England, 563
Apartheid, 481
Aquinas, Thomas, 395
Arawak, 423
Architecture
  Baroque, 448–449, *448, 449*
  Gothic, *396*
  Islamic, *339, 341,* 344–345, *344, 345, 350*
  Japanese (Tokugawa), *528, 534,* 539
  Mesoamerica, 376–377, *377*
  Mughal, 613–614
  Ottoman, 609
  Peru (ancient), 374
  pyramids, 361, 363, 364, *364,* 375
  Safavid, 612
  Teotihuacán, 363–364, *364*
Argentina, Río de la Plata, 678, 679
Aristocracy
  See also Social classes/society
  eighteenth century, 582–584
Aristotle, 391
Arjun, 616
Arkwright, Richard, 595
Armenia, 347
Arouet, François Marie. *See* Voltaire
Art
  Benin, *460,* 471, 472–473, *472, 473*
  Buddhist, *355*
  genre painting, 590–591, *590, 591*
  history painting, 502–503, *503*
  Inca, 381
  Islamic, *336, 342, 346, 348, 352*
  mannerism, 406
  Middle Ages, late, 402–403, *402, 403*
  Ming-Ch'ing, *512, 515,* 525, *527*
  Moche, *358,* 378
  Nazca, 375
  Olmec, 361, *362,* 363
  Ottoman, 609
  Paracas, 375, 376–377, *377*
  Renaissance, 405–406, *405–406, 408*

Safavid, 612
still life, 558–559, *558*
Teotihuacán, 364
Tokugawa, 535, *535*, *537*, 538, 539, 540, *540*
Artisans, as a social class, 599
Asam, Cosmas Damian, *448*
Asam, Egid Quirin, *448*
Ashikaga, 527–528, 529
Ashoka, 613
Aski dynasty, 467–468
Astronomy
Brahe, *628*, 631, *631*
Copernicus, 630–631
Galileo, 632–633
Kepler, 631
women in, 635
Atahualpa, 488
Augsburg, league of, 568
Augsburg, Peace of (1555), 432, 440, 443, 446
Austria
aristocracy, 583
Congress of Vienna and, 675–677
Habsburg Empire, 572–573
peasant/serfs in, 584–585
Seven Years' War (1756–1763), 576–577
War of the Austrian Succession (1740–1748), 576
Averroës (ibn-Rushd), 341
Avignon, papal court at, 400–401
Awdaghast, 462, 463
Awrangzeb, 614
Aybak, 343
Ayutthaya, 547
Ayyubid dynasty, 342
Azcazpotzalco, 369
Aztecs, 368
art, 376
extractive empire, 369, 371
human sacrifice, 371
religion, 371, 372
society, 371–373
Spanish conquest of, 368, 488–489
Tenochtitlán, 368, 371

Babur, 613
Babylonian Captivity of the Church (Luther), 428
Bacon, Francis, 633
Baghdad, 346, 347
Bahmanids in the Deccan, 351
Bakri, al-, 463, 465
Bakufu, Tokugawa, 532–533, 537
Baroque architecture, 448–449, *448*, *449*
Basel, Council of (1431–1449), 435
Basel, treaty of (1795), 668
Bashō, 541
Bastille, fall of, *659*, 660
Bavaria, 385
Baybars, 346
Behaim, Martin, 423, *423*
Benin, *460*, 470–471, 472–473, *472*, *473*
Berbers, 340
Berke, 347
Bernard of Clairvaux, Saint, 387
Bernini, Gianlorenzo, 448
Bhakti, 352, 354, 615
Bible
Erasmus' translation of, 425
Jiménez de Cisneros' translation, 425–426
Luther's translation of, 425, 428
Bihzad, 612
Birth control, eighteenth-century, 587, 589
Biruni, al-, 346, 354
Black Death
in Arab Middle East, 346
causes of, 397, 400
social and economic consequences, 400
spread of, 399
Black Legend, 491
Boccaccio, Giovanni, 404
Bohemia, 573
Boleyn, Anne, 433, 434
Bolívar, Simón, 679–680, *681*
Bologna
Concordat of (1516), 408
universities in, *384*, 391
Boniface VIII, pope, 400, *400*
Book of Common Prayer (Cranmer), 434
Borgia family, 407
Bossuet, Jacques-Bénigne, 566
Boston Tea Party, 656, *658*
Boucher, F., 590, *590*
Boulton, Matthew, 596
Bourbons, 440
Bouvines, 395
Brahe, Tycho, *628*, 631, *631*
Brandenburg-Prussia, 573–574
Brazil, independence for, 681–682
Breakfast, The, 590, *590*
Brothers of the Common Life, 425
Bucer, Martin, 431
Buenos Aires, 679
Bunker Hill, battle of, 657
Burgundians, 397, 410
Buyids, 339–340, 346
Byzantine/Byzantine Empire, Middle Ages and, 316–317, 320, 387

Cahuachi, 375
Cairo, 341
Calas, Jean, 641
Calendar
Mayan, 365, 366
Mesoamerican, 363, 365
Calixtus II, pope, 386
Calvin, John, 431–432, *431*, 438, 439
Calvinism, 431–432, 439–440
Calvinist Reformed Church, 556
Campo Formio, treaty of, (1797), 668
Canada, 497, 576
Candide (Voltaire), 638–639
Cape Colony, 480–481
Capetian dynasty, 395
Carnal Prayer Mat, The, 525
Casa de Contratación (House of Trade), 493
Castiglione, Baldassare, *406*
Castlereagh, Viscount, 675
Cathedral of St. Basil, *410*
Catherine of Aragon, 411, 432, 433
Catherine the Great, 583, 584, 599, 649–651, *649*
Catholic Emancipation Act (1829), 696
Catholicism
See also Roman Catholic church
Reformation, 435–436
Catholic League, 440–441, 446
Cavaliers, 561
Cavendish, Margaret, 635
Central Africa
Angola, 474
events/dates, major, 474
Kongo kingdom, 474–475
Cerro Blanco, 375
Cervantes Saavedra, Miguel de, 450–451, *450*
Chaghatays, 616
Chaitanya, 615
Champlain, Samuel de, *498*
Chams, 550
Chanca, 380
Chan Chan, 379
Changamire, 479
Chan Muan, 365
Chardin, Jean Baptiste, 590–591, *591*
Charles I, king of England, 560–561, *560*
Charles I, king of Spain, 411, 427
Charles II, king of England, 562
Charles II, king of Spain, 568
Charles III, king of Spain, 678
Charles V, emperor, 408, 411, 427–428, 432
Charles V, king of France, 400–401
Charles VI, Habsburg emperor, 573
Charles VIII, king of France, 407
Charles IX, king of France, 440
Charles XII, king of Sweden, 571
Charles the Bold, 410
Châtelet, Emilie du, 635
Chaumont, treaty of (1814), 675
Chavín de Huantar, 375
Chelebi, Evliya, 609

Chelebi, Katib, 609
Cheng Ho, 522
Chichén Itzá, 368
Ch'ien Lung, 521, *520,* 523, 524
Chikamatsu Monzaemon, 538, 541–542
Childbirth, dangers of, 588, 589
Children
abandoned, 592
eighteenth-century, 586, 587, 588–589, *589,* 592
wet nursing, 587
Chile,independence for, 679
Chimu, 378–379
China, dynasties
Ch'ing, 514–527
Ming, 514–527
China, late imperial
civil service examinations, 518, 519
commercial revolution, 514–517
contacts with the West, 523–525
culture, 525–527
emperor, role of, 517–518
events/dates, major, 520
foreign relations, 521–525
land and people, 514
Manchu rule, pattern of, 519–521
political system, 517–521
women in, 516–517
Ch'ing dynasty, 514–527
Chitam, 367
Cholas, 354
Choson culture, 546–547
Christian II, 432
Christian III, 432
Christianity
See also Catholicism; Roman Catholic church
in China, 523–524
in Japan, 530–531
overview of, 458–459
Christianity Not Mysterious (Toland), 640
Christine de Pisan, 405
Churchill, John, 568
Church of England, 497
City of Ladies, The (Christine de Pisan), 405
City-states
Italian, 401, 404
Mesoamerica, 363
Civil Constitution of the Clergy, 662–663
Clarendon Code, 562
Clement III, pope, *387*
Clement V, pope, 400
Clement VII, pope, 401, 408, 433
Clergy
in the Middle Ages, 392
witch hunts and role of, 447
Clericis Laicos, 400
Clermont, Council of (1095), 387
Clive, Robert, 576
Cluny reform movement, 386
Coligny, Gaspard de, 440
Columbus, Christopher, 411, 422, 423–424, 488, 492
Commerce
British East India Company in China, 524
China's third commercial revolution, 514–517
Crusades and, 388
in Japan (seventeenth-century), 534–535
medieval trade routes, 390
mercantilism, 486–487
merchants, rise of in Middle Ages, 389
regulation and flota system in the Americas, 492–495
slave trade, abolition of, 682–684
Warring States of Japan and, 529–531
Common Sense (Paine), 657
Commonwealthmen, 656
Concordat of Bologna (1516), 408
Concordat of Worms (1122), 386
Confederation of the Rhine, 672
Confucius (Confucianism)
in China (late imperial), 517
Japanese Tokugawa, 542–543
Congregationalists, 444
Congress of Vienna (1814), 675–677
Conquistadores, 491
Constance, Council of (1414–1417), 401, 435
Constantinople, 606
Conversations on the Plurality of Worlds (Fontenelle), 635
Copernicus, Nicolaus, 630–631
Copley, John Singleton, 502–503, *503*
Córdoba, 340
Cornwallis, Lord, 658
Cort, Henry, 596–597
Cortés, Hernán, 369, 488
Council of Basel (1431–1449), 435
Council of Blood, 443
Council of Clermont (1095), 387
Council of Constance (1414–1417), 401, 435
Council of the Indies, 492
Council of Trent (1545–1563), 435–436
Council of Troubles, 443
Counter-Reformation, 435–436
Courtesan's Jewel Box, The, 525
Court of Star Chamber, 411
Cranmer, Thomas, 433, 434
Creoles, 678–679
Croatia/Croats, 573
Cromwell, Oliver, 561–562, *563*
Cromwell, Thomas, 425, 433
Crusades
events/dates, major, 388
First, 387, 388
Fourth, 388
Second, 387
Third, 388
Cuauhtemoc, 488
Cuicuilco, 363
Cuintz, Maria, 635
Cuzco, 379
Czechoslovakia, 573

Dadu, 615
Damian, Asam Cosmas, *448*
Dante Alighieri, 404, 630
David (Michelangelo), 406
Dawud, 468
Death, images of, 402–403, *402, 403*
Decameron (Boccaccio), 404
Deccan, 351
Decembrist Revolt (1825), 693, *694*
Declaration of Independence (U.S.), 657
Declaration of Indulgence, 562
Declaration of Pillnitz, 663
Declaration of the Rights of Man and Citizen, 661–662, 663
Declaration of the Rights of Woman, 662, 666
Deism, 640
Denmark, Reformation in, 432
Descartes, René, 634
Dessalines, Jean-Jacques, 678, 683
Dialogues on the Two Chief Systems of the World (Galileo), 632
Dias, Bartholomew, 422
Díaz del Castillo, Bernal, 369
Dibbalemi, Mai Dunama, 469
Diderot, Denis, 639
Diet of Speyer (1526), 428
Diet of Vesteras (1527), 432
Diet of Worms (1521), 427–428
Dimitri of Moscow, Grand Duke, 410
Discourse on the Moral Effects of the Arts and Sciences (Rousseau), 643
Discourse on the Origin of Inequality(Rousseau), 643
Diseases/illnesses
Black Death, 397, 399, 400
childbirth, dangers of, 588, 589
Divine Comedy (Dante), 404
Divorce, impact of Reformation on, 438
Dominicans, *391,* 392, 524
Don Quixote (Cervantes), 451
Dover, treaty of (1670), 562, 567
Drake, Francis, 444
Dream of the Red Chamber, 526
Druze, 342
Dutch
in China, 524

in South Africa, 480–481
Dutch East India Co., 480, 556
Dutch Studies, 543–544

East Africa
events/dates, major, 479
Swahili culture and commerce, 475–476
Zanzibar, 476–478
East Asia
See also specific country
events/dates, major, 419, 627
East India Company, 524, 576, 615, 656
Eck, John, 427
Economy
Black Death, affects of, 400
Enlightenment and, 642
exploitation in Spanish Empire, 491–492
family eighteenth-century, 585–589, 592
French Revolution and issues of, 662
in Japan (Tokugawa), 533–535, 538
laissez-faire, 642
mercantilism, 486–487
in the Netherlands, 556
Ottoman, 608
plantation, 498–499
Smith, 642
Edict of Nantes (1598), 441, 568
Edo (culture of Benin), 470
Edo, Japan, 532, 534–535, 536
Education
in Ming and Ch'ing dynasties, 518, 519
reforms of Renaissance, 404–405
schools and universities in the Middle Ages, 391
Sunni *Madrasa,* 337–338, 342, 347
of women, impact of Reformation, 438
of women (Middle Ages), 394–395
Education Act (1870), 697
Edward III, king of England, 397
Edward IV, king of England, 411
Edward VI, king of England, *433,* 434–435
Edward the Confessor, 395
Egypt
Fatimids, 341–342
Mamluks, 343, 346
Napoleon's invasion of, 668
power struggles in, 461
El Cid, 341
Eleanor of Aquitaine, 395
Elements of the Philosophy of Newton (Voltaire), 638
Elizabeth I, queen of England, 411, *433,* 435, 443–446, *443*
Elizabeth of Russia, 576
Elizabeth of York, 411
Embossed Tea Kettle, The (Hakuin), 539
Émile (Rousseau), 644, 645
Encomienda, 492
Encyclopedia, 639, 641, 644, 645
England
aristocracy, 582
Charles I, 560–561, *560*
Charles II and restoration of the monarchy, 562
colonies in North America, 497–498, 655
Congress of Vienna and, 675–677
Cromwell and Puritan Republic, 561–562
events/dates, major, 563
Glorious Revolution, 563
Hundred Years' War, 397
Industrial Revolution, 594–595
James I, 557, 560
James II, 562–563
Long Parliament and Civil War, 560–561
medieval, 395, 396
Reformation in, 432–435
relations with Spain (1558–1603), 443–446, 557
revival of monarchy, 411
Seven Years' War (1756–1763), 576–577
Walpole, age of, 563–565
War of Spanish Succession (1701–1714), 568–569
Enlightened absolutism, 646–651
Enlightenment
absolutism, 646–651
Deism, 640–641
Encyclopedia, 639
Montesquieu, 641–642, *641*
publication dates of major works, 640
religion and, 639
Rousseau, 643–644, *643*
Smith, 642
society and, 641
use of term, 638
Voltaire, 638–639, *639*
women and, 644–646
Entertainment
Kabuki, *541,* 542
Mayan ball game, 366
Mesoamerica ball game, 361, 366
Nō plays, 539, 542
puppet theater, 542
Erasmus, Desiderius, 425
Essay Concerning Human Understanding (Locke), 453, 635
Estates General, 557, 658–660
Ethics (Spinoza), 452
Euclid, 391
Eugenius IV, pope, 401
Europe
See also specific country
after the Congress of Vienna, 675–677
contacts with Ming-Ch'ing China, 523–525
events/dates, major, 418, 626
Ewuare, king, 471
Experiment on a Bird in the Air-Pump, An, 636–637, *637*

Faqihs, 338
Family
eighteenth-century, 585–589, 592
impact of Reformation on, 437–438
in Ming and Ch'ing dynasties, 516
Farming. *See* Agriculture/farming
Fatima, 341
Fatimids, 341–342
Feltre, Vittorino da, 404–405
Ferdinand VII, king of Spain, 681
Ferdinand of Aragon, 407, 411
Firdawsi, 346, 618–619
First Continental Congress, 657
First Crusade, 387, 388
Fleury, Cardinal, 569, 576
Florence, 401, 404, 407
Flower Still Life, 558–559, *558*
Fontenelle, Bernard de, 635
Footbinding, 516
Forbidden Palace (Peking), 517
Foreign relations
See also under specific country
Ming–Ch'ing, 521–525
Warring States of Japan and, 529–531
Fourth Crusade, 388
Four Treasures, 521
Fox, George, 682
France
See also French Revolution
aristocracy, 582–583
colonies in North America, 497–498
Consulate (1799–1804), 668–669, 672
events/dates, major, 568
Hundred Years' War, 397
invasion of Italy (1494–1527), 407–408
Louis XIV, 441, 532, *554,* 555, 557, 565–568
Louis XVI, 658–660, 662, 663, 664, 665
Marie Antoinette, 662, 663, 664, 667, *667*
medieval, 395, 396
Napoleon Bonaparte, 668–669, 672–677
Paris Commune, 664
religious wars (1562–1598), 440–441
revival of monarchy, 410–411
Seven Years' War (1756–1763), 576–577
War of Spanish Succession (1701–1714), 568–569
Francis I, king of France, 408, 427

Francis II, king of France, 440
Franciscans, *391*, 392, 524, 530
Franconia, 385
Franklin, Benjamin, 658
Frederick I (Barbarossa), emperor, 388, 397
Frederick I, king of Prussia, 575
Frederick II, emperor, 397
Frederick II, king of Prussia, 573, 575, 576
Frederick III, of Palatine, 446
Frederick IV, of Palatine, 446
Frederick the Wise, 428
Frederick William, The Great Elector, 574–575, 583
Frederick William I, king of Prussia, 575
Frederick William II, king of Prussia, 663
Frederick William III, king of Prussia, 676
Freedom of a Christian (Luther), 428
French and Indian War, 576
French Revolution
 Bastille, fall of, *659*, 660
 Civil Constitution of the Clergy, 662–663
 Convention and role of sans-culottes, 664–665
 counterrevolutionary activity, 663
 dechristianization, 666–667
 Declaration of the Rights of Man and Citizen, 661–662, 663
 Declaration of the Rights of Woman, 662, 666
 Directory, establishment of, 668
 economic policy, 662
 end of monarchy, 664
 Estates General becomes the National Assembly, 659–660
 events/dates, major, 666
 Great Fear and surrender of feudal privileges, 660
 Jacobins and Girondists, 663–664
 reconstruction of France, 662–663
 Reign of Terror, 665–668
 Robespierre, 667
 Thermidorian Reaction, 668
Fukuzawa Yukichi, 544
Fulbe/Fulani, 195, 462
Funji state, 470

Galileo Galilei, 632–633
Gama, Vasco da, 422
Gao, 422, 462, 468
Geneva
 Calvinism, 431–432
 political revolt and religious reform in, 431
Genghis Khan, 347, *348*
Geoffrin, Marie-Thérèse, 644
George I, king of England, 563
George III, king of England, 524, 576, 656, 657
Germany
 Hohenstaufen Empire, 397
 medieval, 385, 397, 398
 Reformation in, 426–428
 Thirty Years' War (1618–1648), 446
Ghana, 462, 463, 465
Ghaznavids, 346
Ghazzali, Muhammad al-, 347
Ghent, 443
Girondists, 663–664
Gita Govinda (Jayadeva), 354
Glorious Revolution, 563
Gobind Singh, 614
Godwinsson, Harold, 395
Gold Coast, 471, 474
Golden Horde, 347, 410, 523
Golden Lotus, 525–526
Gouges, Olmype de, 662, 666
Government
 absolute monarchy in France, 556, 557, 565–568
 enlightened absolutism, 646–651
 Long Parliament, 560–561
 in Ming and Ch'ing dynasties, 517–521
 Montesquieu on, 641–642, 644–645
 new models of, during Middle Ages, 389–390
 parliamentary monarchy in England, 556–557, 560–561
Goya, Francisco, 670, *671*
Grand Alliance, 568
Grand Canal (China), 514, 521
Great Britain, formation of, 562
Great Mosque, Cordoba, Spain, 340
Great Northern War (1700–1721), 571
Great Pyramid (La Venta), 361
Great Schism (1378–1417), 400–401
Gregory VII, pope, 386, *387*
Gregory XI, pope, 400
Gregory XII, pope, 401
Grounds of Natural Philosophy (Cavendish), 635
Gruenwald, Mathias, *402*
Guises, 440
Gur-i-mir, *350*
Gutenberg, Johann, 425, *425*

Habsburg Empire, 572–573
Hacienda, 492
Hai Jui, 517
Haiti
 emancipation of slaves, 683
 independence from France, 678–679
Hakka, 516
Hakuin, 539
Hanbalites, 338
Hargreaves, James, 595
Hastings, battle of (1066), 395
Hawkins, John, 444
Henrietta Marie, 557
Henry I, the Fowler, 385
Henry II, king of England, 395
Henry II, king of France, 440
Henry III, king of France (Henry of Navarre), 440–441
Henry IV, emperor, 386, *387*
Henry IV, king of France, 441, 557
Henry V, emperor, 386
Henry VI, emperor, 397
Henry VI, king of England and France, 411
Henry VII, king of England, 411
Henry VIII, king of England, 411, 432–434, *433*
Henry the Navigator, 422
Herat, 348
Hevelius, Elisabetha, 635
Hevelius, Johannes, 635
Hidalgo y Costilla, Miguel, 681
Hideyoshi, Toyotomi, 528, 530, 531–532, 546
Hindi, 351–352
Hinduism
 historical development of, 352–354
 relations with Muslims, 349–350
Hiroshige, 535
Hobbes, Thomas, 452–453
Hohenstaufen Empire, 397
Hohenzollerns, 574–585
Holy Land, 387–388
Holy League (1511), 408
Holy League of Spain, 441
Holy Roman Empire
 medieval, 397, 398
 Thirty Years' War (1618–1648), 446
House of Lancaster, 411
House of York, 411
Huari, 378
Hubertusburg, treaty of (1763), 576
Hughes, Besançon, 440
Huguenots, 440, 568
Huitzilopochtli, 368, 369, 371, *373*
Hulagu Khan, 347
Humanism, 404–405, 425–426
Human sacrifice
 Andean civilizations, 378
 Aztec, 371
 Benin, 471
 Mayan, 365–366
 in Mesoamerica, 363, 365–366, 368, 371
 Teotihuacán, 365
 Toltecs, 368
Hundred Years' War, 397
Hungary, 573

aristocracy, 583
Hus, Jan, 428
Husayn I, 611

Ibn al-Arabi, 341
Ibn al-Athir, 349
Ibn Battuta, 476, 477
Ibn Hanibal, 338
Ibn Khaldun, 346
Ibn Maymum (Maimonides), 341, 343
Ibn Rushd (Averroës), 341
Ieyasu, Tokugawa, 528, 529, 530, 532
Igbo-Ukwu, 471
Ignatius of Loyola, 434, 435
Ihara Saikaku, 541
Ilkhanids, 347
Iltutmish, 350
Incas, 379–381, 488–489
India
British colonial rule, 575
events/dates, 354, 418, 617, 626
Islam in, 349
India, Mughals (Timurids)
Akbar's reign, 613
events/dates, major, 617
last great, 614
origins, 613
political decline, 614–615
Sikhs and Marathas, 614
Indulgences, attack on, 426–427
Industrial Revolution
eighteenth-century, 594–597
iron production, 596–597
major inventions, 597
steam engine, 596
textile industry, 595–596
Innocent III, pope, 397
Inquiry into the Nature and Causes of the Wealth of Nations, An (Smith), 642
Inquisition, 411
Institutes of the Christian Religion (Calvin), 431
Intolerable Acts, 656–657
Investiture struggle, 386
Iron production, 596–597
Isabella of Castile, 411, 492
Ishraqi school, 612
Islam (1000–1500)
in Egypt, 341–343
events/dates, major, 342
Ghaznavids, 346
in India, 349
in North Africa, 340–341
Saljuqs, 347
Shi'ite, consolidation of, 339–340
south of the Sahara, 462
in Spain, 340–341
states and dynasties, 350–351
Sufi piety and organization, 338–339
Sunni, consolidation of, 337–338
Islam/Islamic empires
in Asia, 616–617, 620
Ottoman Empire, 605–610
Safavid Shi'ite Empire, 610–612
Shari'a, 607, 609
Shi'ite-Sunni political rift, 616–617, 620
in the southern seas, 620–621
south of the Sahara, 462
Timurids/Mughals, 613–616
Ulama, 607, 608
Uzbeks and Chaghatays, 616
Isma'ilis, 339, 341
Assassins, 342
Istanbul, 606
Italy
city-state, 401, 404
French invasion of (1494–1527), 407–408
medieval, 398
political decline of, 407–408
Renaissance in, 401–409
Iturbide, Agustín de, 681
Itzcoatl, 369
Ivan III (Ivan the Great), 410
Ivan IV (Ivan the Terrible), 523, 570
Ivan V, 570

Jacobins/Jacobin Club, 663–664
Jaguar Paw line, 367
Jahan, 614
Jahangir, 614, *615*
Jains, 352
James I, king of England, 557, 560
James II, king of England, 562–563
James VI of Scotland, 557
James Edward Stuart, 563
Jamestown, Virginia, 497
Janissaries, 608
Japan
events/dates, major, 530
Warring States Era, 527–531
Japan, Tokugawa era
bureaucratization, 537–538
culture, 538–545
cycles of reform, 537
economy, 533–535, 538
establishment of, 532–533
events/dates, major, 545
Hideyoshi's rule, 531–532
loyalty, 536–537
overthrow of, 439
Jaunpur, 351
Jayadeva, 354
Jenkins, Robert, 575–576
Jenne, 466, *466*
Jerusalem, 387
Jesuits, 435, 446
in China, 523–524
in Japan, 530
Jews
eighteenth-century ghettos, 599–600, *599*
First Crusades and, 387
during the Middle Ages, 391
Ottoman, 610
in Spain, 411
Jiménez de Cisneros, Francisco, 425–426
Joanna the Mad, 411
Joan of Arc, 397
Joao VI, 681
John I, king of England, 395, 396
John XII, pope, 386
Johnson, Ben, 451
Joseph, brother of Napoleon, 673
Joseph I, Habsburg emperor, 573
Joseph II, of Austria, 647–649
Josephine de Beauharnais, 673
Julius II, pope, 406, 407, 427
Junkers (German noble landlords), 574–575, 583

Kabir, 352
Kabuki, *541,* 542
Kaibara Ekken, 539
Kanal Ikal, 367
Kanem, 468–470
K'ang Hsi, 521, 523, 524
Kay, James, 595
Keita dynasty, 465–466
Kepler, Johannes, 631
Khaljis, 350
Khamsa, 352
Khoikhoi, 480–481
Khorasan, 347
Khwarizm, 347
Kiev, medieval, 410
Kilwa, 476, 477
King Sejong, 546
Kirch, Gottfried, 635
Kitagawa Utamaro, 540, *540*
Kongo kingdom, 474–475
Koprülüs rulers, 608
Korea, early history of, 545–547
Koryo, 546
Kotosh, 374
Krishna, *355*
Kuchuk-Kainardji, treaty of (1774), 651
Kulikov Meadow, battle of, 410
Kumbi/Kumbi Saleh, 462, 463
Kunisada, *537*
Ku Yen-wu, 525

Lacombe, Claire, 666
Las Casas, Bartolomé de, *489,* 490–491

Las Navas de Tolosa, *342*
Latin America
See also Americas; *specific country*
eighteenth-century developments, 678
first movements toward independence, 678–679
wars for independence in, 682
Laud, William, 560–561
La Venta, 361
Law
Magna Carta (1215), 395, 396
Montesquieu on, 641–642, 644–645
League of Augsburg, 568
League of Venice, 407, 408
Lechfeld, 385
Leo X, pope, 408, 427
Léon, Pauline, 661, 666
Leonardo da Vinci, 405–406
Leopold I, Habsburg emperor, 568, 573
Leopold II, Habsburg emperor, 649, 663
Lepanto, 441, 444
Lespinasse, Julie de, 644
Lessing, Gotthold, 641
Le Thanh Tong, 550
Letter Concerning Toleration (Locke), 635, 638
Letters on the English (Voltaire), 638
Leviathan (Hobbes), 452
Liberia, 684
Libreville, 684
Literature
See also under name of work or author
humanism, 404–405, 425–426
Mayan, 366
Ming-Ch'ing dynasty, 525–527
Ottoman, 609
sixteenth century, 450–453
Tokugawa, 541–542
Locke, John, 453, 635, 638, *638*, 656, 682
Lodis, 350
London Foundling Hospital, 592
Long Parliament and Civil War, 560–561
Lorenzo the Magnificent, 404
Louis I, king of France, 440
Louis IX, king of France, 395
Louis XI, king of France, 410–411
Louis XII, king of France, 407
Louis XIII, king of France, 565
Louis XIV, king of France, 441, 532, *554*, 555, 557, 565–568
Louis XV, king of France, 569
Louis XVI, king of France, 658–660, 662, 663, 664, 665
L'Ouverture, Toussaint, 678, 683
Luba, 474
Ludovico il Moro, 407
Lunda, 474
Luther, Martin, *420*, 425, 426–428, 429, 438
Lutheranism, political consolidation of the reformation, 432

Macartney, Lord, 524–525
Machiavelli, Niccolò, 408, *408*, 409
Machu Picchu, *380*
Madrasa, 337–338, 342, 347, 466
Magellan, Ferdinand, 424
Magna Carta (1215), 395, 396
Mahmud of Ghazna, 346
Maimonides (ibn Maymun), 321, 341, 343
Mali, 182, 464–466
Malinke, 465
Mamakuna, 380
Mamluks, 343, 346
Manchu dynasty
rule, pattern of, 519–521
women, 516
Mande, 464
Mannerism, 406
Mansa Musa, 466
Marathas, 614
Marburg Colloquy, 429
Marco Polo, 423
Maria Theresa of Austria, *572*, 573, 576, 647–648
Marie Antoinette, Queen of France, 662, 663, 664, 667, *667*
Marie Louise, Archduchess, 673
Marie Thérèse, 566
Marriage(s)
eighteenth-century, 585, 587
impact of Reformation on, 438
Martin V, pope, 401
Mary II, 563
Mary Stuart, 443, 445, 557
Mary Tudor, 432, *433*, 434–435, 443
Mathematical Principles of Natural Philosophy (Newton), 634
Mathematics, Mayan, 366
Maximilian, duke of Bavaria, 446
Maximilian I, emperor, 407, 411, 427
Mayapan, 368
Mayas/Mayans, 359, 365–368
Mazarin, Cardinal, 557, 565
Medici, Cosimo de', 404, *405*
Medici family, 408
Médicis, Catherine de, 440
Mehmed II, 606, 607
Melanchthon, Philip, 432
Mercantilism, 486–487
Merchants, rise of, 389
Merian, Anna Maria Sibylla, 559
Mesoamerica
Aztecs, 368–373, 488–489
classic, 363–368
events/dates, major, 361
formative (pre-classic), 361–363
human sacrifice, 363, 365–366, 368, 371
Mayas/Mayans, 359, 365–368
meaning of name, 360
Monte Alban, 363
Neolithic societies, 359
Olmec, 361, *362*, 363
periods of, 360
post-classic, 368–373
range of, 360
Teotihuacán, 363–365
Toltecs, 368
Valley of Oaxaca, 363
writing and use of a calendar in, 363, 365
Mesta, 411
Mexico (New Spain), independence for, 678–679
Miao Wars, 514
Michelangelo, 406, *406*
Middle Ages, High
Crusades, 387–388
government, 389–390
Jews in Christian society, 391
merchants, rise of, 389
Otto I and revival of the empire, 385–386
peasants/serfs, 394
revival of Roman Catholic church, 386
schools and universities, 391
society, 391–395
towns, 388–389, 390–391
women in, 394–395
Middle Ages, Late
Black Death, 397, 399, 400
breakdown and revival of the church, 400–401
growth of monarchies, 395–397
Hundred Years' War, 397
revival of monarchies, 409–411
Milan, 401, 407, 408
Military/weaponry
Aztec, 372–373
foot soldiers of the Warring States era, 528–529
French women petition to bear arms, 661
Grand Army of Napoleon, 675
slave soldiers *(devshirme)*, 608, *610*
Ming dynasty, 514–527
Missionaries
in China, 523–524
in Japan, 530–531
Mita, 380
Mitimaqs, 380
Moche, *358*, 375, 378
Moctezuma II, 488

Mogadishu, 476, 477
Mona Lisa (Leonardo da Vinci), 406
Monarchies
absolute, in France, 556, 557, 565–568
growth of national, 395–397
revival of, 409–411
Monastic culture
See also under name of order
in the fifteenth-century, 437
in Japan, 530
Ming-Ch'ing dynasties and, 523–524
Mongols, 515, 517, 522
Genghis Khan, 347
Ilkhanids and, 347
in Russia, 410
Monroe Doctrine, 681
Montague, Mary Wortley, 564
Monte Alban, 363
Montesquieu, 641–642, *641*, 644–645, 682
Montmorency-Châtillons, 440
Moorish culture, 340–341
Moravia, 573
More, Thomas, 425
Morelos y Pavón, José María, 681
Morocco, power struggles in, 461
Mossi, 468
Motoori Norinaga, 543
Mughals (Timurids)
Akbar's reign, 613
events/dates, major, 617
last great, 614
origins, 613
political decline, 614–615
Sikhs and Marathas, 614
Muhammad V, 344
Muhammad Shaybani, 616
Mumtaz Mahal, 614
Murad IV, 608
Muslims, relations with Hindus, 349–350

Nadir Shah, 611–612, 614
Nagashino, battle of (1575), 529
Na'ima, 609
Nakae Tōju, 542
Nanak, Guru, 614, 615
Nantes, Edict of (1598), 441, 568
Napier, William, 673
Naples, 401, 407, 408
Napoleon Bonaparte, 668–669, 672–677
Narrow Road of Oku, The (Bashō), 541
Nasir, al-, 347
Nathan the Wise (Lessing), 641
National Studies, 543
Native Americans, decline in population of, 488–489, 492
Nazca, 375
Near East
See also specific country
events/dates, major, 418, 626
Nedim, 609
Nelson, Horatio, 668, 672
Neolocalism, 585
Nerchinsk, treaty of (1689), 523
Netherlands
Congress of Vienna and, 675–677
revolt against Spain, 442–443
United Provinces, 555–556
New Atlantis (Bacon), 633
Newburn, battle of (1640), 560
Newcomen, Thomas, 596
New Spain, independence for, 681
Newton, Isaac, 634, *634*
Newtonianism for Ladies (Algarotti), 635
New World. *See* Americas
Nezahualcoyotl, 372
Nguyen dynasty, 549, 550
Niani, 466
Nijmwegen, peace of (1678, 1679), 568
Nine Years' War, 568
Nizam al-Mulk, 347
Nizami, 352
Nobility
eighteenth century, 582–584
Junkers (German noble landlords), 574–575, 583
in the Middle Ages, 389, 392
Nobunaga, Oda, 528, 529
Nō plays, 539, 542
North, Lord, 656
North Africa
See also under name of country
Islam in, 340–341
power struggles in, 461
North America
See also America; Canada
French and British colonies in, 497–498
slavery in, 498–508
Novuum Organum (Bacon), 633
Nunneries, 437, 438
Nur al-Din, 342
Nystad, Peace of (1721), 571

Oaxaca, 363
Observations upon Experimental Philosophy (Cavendish), 635
Ogata Kōrin, 539
O'Higgins, Bernardo, 679
Ôishi Kuranosuke, 536
Olmec, 361, *362*, 363
Oman/Omanis, 476–478
On the Morals That Befit a Free Man (Vergerio), 404–405
On the Motion of Mars (Kepler), 631
On the Revolutions of the Heavenly Spheres (Copernicus), 630, 631
Oppenheimer, Samuel, 600
Otto I, emperor, 385–386
Ottoman Empire
classical, 607–609
culture and society, 608–610
decline of, 610
economic development, 608
events/dates, major, 611
origins and development of, before 1600, 605–607
political and military developments, 608
slave soldiers *(devshirme)*, 608, *610*
Ottoman Turks, 347, 461

Pacal, Lord, 367
Pachacuti, 380
Pacification of Ghent, 443
Pain, Thomas, 657
Palenque, 367
Papacy. *See* Popes/papacy
Papal States, 325, 401, 408
Paracas, 375, 376–377, *377*
Paraguay, independence for, 679
Paris, treaty of (1763), 576, 655
Paris, treaty of (1783), 658
Paris Commune, 664
Paris Foundling Hospital, 592
Parleying, 395
Pascal, Blaise, 451–452
Paul III, pope, 435–436
Peace of Augsburg (1555), 432, 440, 443, 446
Peace of Nijmwegen (1678, 1679), 568
Peace of Nystad (1721), 571
Peace of Ryswick (1697), 568
Peaceof Westphalia (1648), 443, 446, 574
Peasants' Revolt (1524–1525), 428, 430
Peasants/serfs
of the eighteenth century, 584–585, 648
in the Middle Ages, 328, 393, 394
Pedro, regent in Brazil, 681
Persian, language, 351
Peru
See also Andean civilization
independence for, 679
Peter III (tsar of Russia), 576, 583, 649
Peter the Great, 523, 570–572, 583, 584, 649
Petition of Right, 560, 561
Petrarch, Francesco, 404
Philip, Archduke, 411
Philip II, king of Spain, *433*, 441–443
Philip II Augustus, king of France, 388, 395
Philip IV (the Fair), king of France, 397, 400
Philip V, king of Spain, 568–569
Philip of Hesse, 429
Phillips, Thomas, 505
Philosophy

Bacon, 633
Hobbes, 452–453
Locke, 453
Montesquieu, 641–642, *641*
Newton, 634
Rousseau, 643–644, *643*
sixteenth century, 452–453
Spinoza, 452
Tokugawa (Japan), 542–543
Voltaire, 638–639, *639*
Pico della Mirandola, 407
Pietà (Michelangelo), *406*
Pitt the Elder, William, 576
Pitt the Younger, William, 672
Pius VII, pope, 668
Pizarro, Francisco, 379, 488
Plantations, slavery on, 499–500
Plassey, battle of (1757), 576, 615
Podesta, 404
Poland
aristocracy, 583
partition of (1772, 1793, and 1795), 651
Reformation in, 432
Polo, Marco, 423
Pompadour, Marquise de, 644
Popes/papacy
See also name of pope
Avignon, papal court at, 400–401
Boniface VIII and Philip the Fair, 400
Council of Constance (1414–1417), 401
Great Schism (1378–1417), 400–401
investiture struggle, 386
Papal States, 401, 408
Popol Vuh, 366
Population explosion, eighteenth-century, 594
Portebello fair, 495
Portugal
exploration by, 422–423, 474–475, 476–478, 480, 524
Southeast Asian trade and, 530
Potosí, 490, *491*
Pragmatic Sanction, 573, 575
Praise of Folly, The (More), 425
Presbyterians, 560, 561
Prince of the World, 403, 403
Principia Mathematica (Newton), 634
Printing, invention of, 425
Prosser, Gabriel, 683
Protestant Ethic and the Spirit of Capitalism (Weber), 431
Protestantism, in North America, 497
Protestant Reformation. *See* Reformation
Prussia
aristocracy, 583
Congress of Vienna and, 675–677
Hohenzollerns and, 574–575
Seven Years' War (1756–1763), 576–577
War of Austrian Succession (1740–1748), 576
Ptolemy, 391, 630, 631
Pugachev, Emelyan, *584,* 585
Puppet theater, 542
Puritans, 443–444, 557, 560–562
Pyramid of the Sun, 363, 364, *364,* 375
Pyramids, 361, 363, 364, *364,* 375

Quadruple Alliance, 675, 676
Quakers, 682
Quebec, 497, 576
Quebec Act (1774), 657
Quechua, 380

Rajputs, 350
Ramananda, 352
Ramanuja, 352
Ramayana, 615
Raphael, 406, *406*
Rastadt, treaty of (1714), 573
Raziyya, 350
Reformation
Anabaptists, 429–431
Augsburg, peace of, 432
Calvinism, 431–432
Catholic reform and Counter-, 435–436
election of Charles V and the Diet of Worms, 427–428
in England, 432–435
events/dates, major, 432, 433
expansion of, 432
factors leading to, 424–426
indulgences, attack on, 426–427
Luther, *420,* 425, 426–428
Peasants' Revolt (1524–1525), 428
political consolidation of the Lutheran reformation, 432
social significance of, 437
in Switzerland, 428–429
women and, 437–438
Reign of Terror, 665–668
Reims Cathedral, *396*
Religion
See also specific type
Aztec, 371, 372
Deism, 640–641
Enlightenment and, 639
Mayan, 365–366
in North America, 497
Teotihuacán, 364–365
toleration, 641, 648
Religious wars
Crusades, 387–388
in England, 443–446
in France, 440–441
in Germany/Holy Roman Empire, 446
in Spain, 441–446
Rembrandt van Rijn, 448
Renaissance
art, 405–407
humanism, 404–405
in Italy, 401–409
Repartimiento, 492
Resurrection, The, (Gruenwald), 402, *402*
Return from the Market, The, 590–591, *591*
Richard I (the Lion-Hearted), king of England, 388, 395
Richard III, king of England, 411
Richelieu, Cardinal, 557, 565
Río de la Plata, 678, 679
Roanoke Island, *499*
Robespierre, Maximilien, 667–668
Romagna, 408
Roman Catholic church
See also Catholicism; Christianity; Popes/papacy
Avignon, papal court at, 400–401
Boniface VIII and Philip the Fair, 400
Civil Constitution of the Clergy, 662–663
Cluny reform movement, 386
Great Schism (1378–1417), 400–401
investiture struggle, 386
Napoleon and, 668–669, 672
reform and Counter-Reformation, 435–436
revival of, during high Middle Ages, 386
in Spanish America, 489–491
Romance of the Three Kingdoms, 525
Romanov, Michael, 570
Rorbach, Jacob, *428*
Roundheads, 561
Rousseau, Jean-Jacques, 643–644, *643,* 645
Ruba'iyat (Umar Khayyam), 347, 348
Rubens, Peter Paul, 448
Rumi, 340
Russia
Alexander I, 672, 676
aristocracy, 583–584
Catherine the Great, 583, 584, 599, 649–651, *649*
Ch'ing dynasty and, 522–523
Congress of Vienna and, 675–677
events/dates, major, 573, 649
medieval, 410
Peter the Great, 570–572, 583, 584, 649
serfdom in eighteenth-century, 584–585
Time of Troubles, 570
Ruysch, Rachel, 558–559, *558*
Ryswick, peace of (1697), 568

Sa'dis, 461
Sadra, Mulla, 612
Safavid Shi'ite Empire, 340, 348
culture, 612–613

decline of, 611–612
events/dates, major, 612
origins, 610–611
Shah Abbas I, 611
Sahel, 463
Saikaku, Ihara, 538
St. Bartholomew's Day massacre, *439,* 440
St. Lawrence River, 497
St. Petersburg (Leningrad), 571
Saladin, 342, 387
Saljuqs, 347
Samanids, 346
Samarkand, 348
Samarra, 339
San José Mogote, 363
San Lorenzo, 361
San Martín, José de, 679
San Salvador, 423
Sans-culottes, 664–665
Sanskrit, 351
Saxony, Congress of Vienna and, 676
Sayyids, 350
Schmalkaldic League, 432
Scholars, The, 526, 527
Scholasticism, 391, 395
School of Athens (Raphael), 406
Scientific Revolution, 629–630
Second Continental Congress, 657
Second Crusade, 387
Sekigahara, battle of (1600), 528
Selim I, 606, 607
Selim II, 608
Seljuk sultans/Turks, 387
Seljuqs of Rum, 605
Senclaes, Jean't, 446
Senegambia, 471
Serfs,Middle Ages, 328, 393, 394
Seveners, 339
Seven Years' War (1756–1763), 576–577
Seymour, Jane, 434
Shah-nameh (Firdawsi), 346, 618
Shahrukh, 348, *350, 352*
Shakespeare, William, 451
Shari'a, 607, 609, 811
Sharifian dynasty, 461
Shi'ites, 304, 339–340, 341
See also Safavids Shi'ite Empire
-Sunni political rift, 616–617, 620
Shivaji, 614
Shona, 478, 479
Short Parliament, 560
Sican, 378
Sicily
Hohenstaufens and, 397
Islamic conquest of, 341
Sigismund, emperor, 401
Sikhs, 614
Silesia, 573, 575, 576
Silla, 546
Sinan, 609
Sirhindi, Ahmad, 615
Slaves/slave trade, soldiers *(devshirme),* 608, *610*
Slaves/slave trade in the Americas
Atlantic passage, description of, 502–503, 505
background of, 501
in Brazil, 495–496
consequences of, for Africa, 505–508
economic issues, 498–499
establishment of, 498
events/dates, major, 507
extent of, 501, 504–505, 506
on plantations, 499–500
statistics, 501
transatlantic trade, 498–499, 500–506
Smith, Adam, 642, 682
Social classes/society
See also Peasants; Serfs
aristocracy of the eighteenth century, 582–584
artisans, 599
Aztec, 371–373
conflict in Florence, 404
gentry (Chinese), 518–519
Junkers (German noble landlords), 574–575, 583
Korean yangban, 546
middle class, 598
in Ming and Ch'ing dynasties, 518–519
Olmec, 361
Tokugawa, 531
upper classes, 597–598
urban, 597–599
Social classes/society, in the Middle Ages
clergy, 392
merchants, 389
nobility, 389, 392
peasants/serfs, 393, 394
women, 394–395
Social Contract (Rousseau), 643
Society for the Abolition of the Slave Trade, 683
Society of Jesus, 435, 530
Society of Revolutionary Republican Women, 666
Solomon, Job ben, *506*
Songhai, 466–468, 469
Sons of Liberty, 656
Sophia, 570
Soso, 463, 465
South Africa
Cape Colony, 480–481
events/dates, major, 479, 480
Zimbabwe, 478–479
South America
See also under name of country
exploration of, 424
Southern seas, Islamic traders in, 620–621
Spain
exploration by, 422–424, 488–496
Islam in, 340–341
Philip II, reign of, 441–443
relations with England (1558–1603), 444–446, 557
religious wars (1556–1598) in, 441–443
revival of monarchy, 411
War of Spanish Succession (1701–1714), 568–569
Spanish America, independence from Spanish rule, 678–679
Spanish Armada, 445
Spinoza, Baruch, 452
Spirit of the Laws (Montesquieu), 641–642, 682
Stamp Act (1765), 655–656, 657
Steam engine, 596
Stewart, Robert, 675
Still life, 558–559, *558*
Stories from a Ming Collection, 525
Story of the Stone, 526
Subuktigin, 346
Sudan
central and western, 463–470
eastern, 470
events/dates, major, 468, 470
Ghana, 463, 465
Kanem/Kanuri, 468–470
Mali, 464–466
Songhai, 466–468, 469
Sufi, 615
piety and organization, 338–339, 340
Sugar Act (1764), 655
Sukhothai, 547
Süleyman, 606–607, *607*
Sultan Hasan Madrasa and Tomb-Mosque, *339*
Sundiata (Sunjaata), 466
Sunni
consolidation of, 337–338
political rift with Shi'ite, 616–617, 620
Sunni (Sonni), 466–468
Swabia, 385
Swahili culture and commerce, 475–476
Sweden, Reformation in, 432
Swiss Reformation, 428–429

Tai Ch'in, *515*
Taino, 423
Taj Mahal, *604,* 614
Takrur, 464
Talleyrand, 676
Tamil, 351
Tarascan Empire, 369

Technology
eighteenth-century industrial revolution, 594–597
Scientific Revolution, 629–635
Teg Bahadur, 614
Temple Mayor (Great Temple), 376
Tencin, Claudine de, 644
Tenochtitlán, 368, 371, 488
Teotihuacán, 363–365
Test Act, 562
Tetzel, John, 427
Texcoco, lake, 368, 369
Textile industry, 595–596
Tezcatlipoca, 371
Theodore III, 570
Thermidorian Reaction, 668
Third Crusade, 388
Third of May, 670, *671*
Thirty Years' War (1618–1648), 446
Tibet, 523
Tikal, 365, 366–367, *367*
Tilsit, treaty of (1807), 672
Timbuktu, 466
Timurids, 347–348
See also Mughals
Timur-i Lang, 347–348, *350*
Tiwanaku, 378
Tlacopan, 369
Tlaloc, 371
Tlatelolco, 371, 372
Tlatoani, 371
Tlaxcala, 369, 371, 488
Toland, John, 640
Toleration Act (1689), 563
Toltecs, 368
Tomás de Torquemada, 411
Tordesillas, treaty of (1494), 495
Towns, in the Middle Ages, 388
chartering of, 389
relationships with kings, 390–391
Townshend, Charles, 656
Tran dynasty, 549
Transoxiana, 347, 348
Transylvania, 573
Treaties
of Aix-la-Chapelle (1668), 567
of Aix-la-Chapelle (1748), 576
of Amiens (1802), 668
of Basel (1795), 668
of Campo Formio (1797), 668
of Chaumont (1814), 675
of Dover (1670), 562, 567
of Hubertusburg (1763), 576
of Kuchuk-Kainardji (1774), 651
of Nerchinsk (1689), 523
of Paris (1763), 576, 655
of Paris (1783), 658
of Rastadt (1714), 573
of Tilsit (1807), 672
of Tordesillas (1494), 495
of Utrecht, 575
of Westphalia (1648), 443, 446, 574
Treatise on Tolerance (Voltaire), 641
Trekboers, 481
Trent, Council of (1545–1563), 435–436
Triple Alliance (Aztec), 369
Triple Alliance (England, Sweden and United Provinces), 567
Tughlugs, 350
Tughril Beg, 347
Tula, 368
Tulasidas, 615
Tunisia
power struggles in, 461
Turi, Muhammad al-, 467–468
Turkomans, 346, 347–348
Turks
Ottoman, 347, 461
Seljuk, 387
Turner, J.M.W., 698–699, *698*
Turner, Nat, 683
Twelvers, 339–340
Two Treatises of Government (Locke), 453

Ulama, 607, 608
Ulug Beg, *350*
Umar Khayyam, 347, 348
Umayyads, 340
Unam Sanctam, 400
Union of Arras, 443
Union of Utrecht, 443
Universities in the Middle Ages, 391
University of Bologna, *384,* 391
Urban II, pope, 387, 388
Urban VI, pope, 401
Urban classes, 597–599
Urban settlements/urbanization, eighteenth-century, 597
Urdu-Hindi, 351–352
Uruguay, independence for, 679
Utamaro, 538
Utopia (More), 425
Utrecht, treaty of, 575
Uzbeks, 616

Vaishnavas, 352
Valley of Oaxaca, 363
Vasa, Gustavus, 432
Venezuela, independence for, 679–680
Venice, 401, 407, 408
Vergerio, Pietro Paolo, 404–405
Versailles, 565–566
Vesey, Denmark, 683
Vespucci, Amerigo, 424
Vesteras, diet of (1527), 432
Viceroyalties, 492–495
Vietnam, early history of, 547–550
Vijayanagar, 351, 354
Vindication of the Rights of Woman, A (Wollstonecraft), 645–646
Vita Nuova (Dante), 404
Vladimir of Kiev, prince, 410
Voltaire, 638–639, *639,* 641

Wakefield, Priscilla, 588
Walpole, Robert, 563–565, 576, 656
Wang Yang-ming, 525
War of the Austrian Succession (1740–1748), 576
War of the Roses, 411
War of the Spanish Succession (1701–1714), 568–569
Warring States Era, 527–530
Washington, George, 658
Waterloo, 672, 676
Watson and the Shark (Copley), 502–503, *503*
Watt, James, 596
Wealth of Nations (Smith), 642, 682
Weber, Max, 431
Wellesley, Arthur. *See* Wellington, Duke of
Wellington, Duke of, 673, 676, 695–696
Wentworth, Thomas (earl of Strafford), 560
West Africa
Benin, *460,* 470–471, 472–473, *472, 473*
Gold Coast, 471, 474
Senegambia, 471
West Indies, 683–684
Westphalia, peace/treaty of (1648), 443, 446, 574
Wheatley, Francis, *587*
White, John, *499*
White Lotus Rebellion (1796–1804), 514, 521
Wilberforce, William, 683
Wilkinson, John, 596
William I, Prince of Orange (William the Silent), 442, 443
William III, king of England and Prince of Orange, 555, 556, 563
William of Normandy, 395
William Pitt the Elder, 576
William Pitt the Younger, 672
Winkelmann, Maria, 635
Witchcraft/witch hunts, 447, 450
Wollstonecraft, Mary, 645–646
Wolsey, Cardinal, 433
Women
Aztec, 373
Christine de Pisan (writer), 405
Declaration of the Rights of Woman, 662, 666
eighteenth-century, 586–588

Enlightenment and, 644–646
footbinding of Chinese, 516
French Revolution and role of, *660,* 661, 662, 666
medieval, 394–395
in Ming and Ch'ing dynasties, 516–517
Reformation and changing role of, 437–438
Rousseau's views of, 644, 645
Scientific Revolution and, 634–635
Vindication of the Rights of Woman, 645–646
witch hunts and, 447, 450
Women, as rulers
Catherine the Great, 583, 584, 599, 649–651, *649*
Eleanor of Aquitaine, 395
Elizabeth I, queen of England, 411, *433,* 435, 443–446, *443*
Isabella of Castile, 411
Kanal Ikal, 367
Marie Antoinette, Queen of France, 662, 663, 664, 667, *667*
Mary II, 563
Zac Kuk, 367
Worms
Concordat of, 386
Diet of (1521), 427–428
Wren, Christopher, 448
Wright, Joseph, *596,* 636–637, *636*
Writing
Mayan, 365
in Mesoamerica, 363, 365
Wu Ti, 545–546, 548
Wu Wei, *527*

Xavier, Francis, 530

Yamagata Bantō, 544–545
Yaroslav the Wise, 410
Yax Kin, 367
Yi Songgye, 546
Yoshimune, Tokugawa, 544
Yusuf I, 344

Zac Kuk, 367
Zaghawah, 468–469
Zanzibar, 476–478
Zimbabwe, 478–479
Zurich, reformation in, 429
Zwingli, Ulrich, 428–429

SINGLE PC LICENSE AGREEMENT AND LIMITED WARRANTY

READ THIS LICENSE CAREFULLY BEFORE OPENING THIS PACKAGE. BY OPENING THIS PACKAGE, YOU ARE AGREEING TO THE TERMS AND CONDITIONS OF THIS LICENSE. IF YOU DO NOT AGREE, DO NOT OPEN THE PACKAGE. PROMPTLY RETURN THE UNOPENED PACKAGE AND ALL ACCOMPANYING ITEMS TO THE PLACE YOU OBTAINED THEM [[FOR A FULL REFUND OF ANY SUMS YOU HAVE PAID FOR THE SOFTWARE]]. ***THESE TERMS APPLY TO ALL LICENSED SOFTWARE ON THE DISK EXCEPT THAT THE TERMS FOR USE OF ANY SHAREWARE OR FREEWARE ON THE DISKETTES ARE AS SET FORTH IN THE ELECTRONIC LICENSE LOCATED ON THE DISK:***

1. GRANT OF LICENSE and OWNERSHIP: The enclosed computer programs and data ("Software") are licensed, not sold, to you by Prentice-Hall, Inc. ("We" or the "Company") and in consideration of your purchase or adoption of the accompanying Company textbooks and/or other materials, and your agreement to these terms. We reserve any rights not granted to you. You own only the disk(s) but we and/or our licensors own the Software itself. This license allows you to use and display your copy of the Software on a single computer (i.e., with a single CPU) at a single location for academic use only, so long as you comply with the terms of this Agreement. You may make one copy for back up, or transfer your copy to another CPU, provided that the Software is usable on only one computer.

2. RESTRICTIONS: You may not transfer or distribute the Software or documentation to anyone else. Except for backup, you may not copy the documentation or the Software. You may not network the Software or otherwise use it on more than one computer or computer terminal at the same time. You may not reverse engineer, disassemble, decompile, modify, adapt, translate, or create derivative works based on the Software or the Documentation. You may be held legally responsible for any copying or copyright infringement which is caused by your failure to abide by the terms of these restrictions.

3. TERMINATION: This license is effective until terminated. This license will terminate automatically without notice from the Company if you fail to comply with any provisions or limitations of this license. Upon termination, you shall destroy the Documentation and all copies of the Software. All provisions of this Agreement as to limitation and disclaimer of warranties, limitation of liability, remedies or damages, and our ownership rights shall survive termination.

4. LIMITED WARRANTY AND DISCLAIMER OF WARRANTY: Company warrants that for a period of 60 days from the date you purchase or adopt the accompanying textbook, the Software, when properly installed and used in accordance with the Documentation, will operate in substantial conformity with the description of the Software set forth in the Documentation, and that for a period of 30 days the disk(s) on which the Software is delivered shall be free from defects in materials and workmanship under normal use. The Company does not warrant that the Software will meet your requirements or that the operation of the Software will be uninterrupted or error-free. Your only remedy and the Company's only obligation under these limited warranties is, at the Company's option, return of the disk for a refund of any amounts paid for it by you or replacement of the disk. THIS LIMITED WARRANTY IS THE ONLY WARRANTY PROVIDED BY THE COMPANY AND ITS LICENSORS, AND THE COMPANY AND ITS LICENSORS DISCLAIM ALL OTHER WARRANTIES, EXPRESS OR IMPLIED, INCLUDING WITHOUT LIMITATION, THE IMPLIED WARRANTIES OF MERCHANTABILITY AND FITNESS FOR A PARTICULAR PURPOSE. THE COMPANY DOES NOT WARRANT, GUARANTEE OR MAKE ANY REPRESENTATION REGARDING THE ACCURACY, RELIABILITY, CURRENTNESS, USE, OR RESULTS OF USE, OF THE SOFTWARE.

5. LIMITATION OF REMEDIES AND DAMAGES: IN NO EVENT, SHALL THE COMPANY OR ITS EMPLOYEES, AGENTS, LICENSORS, OR CONTRACTORS BE LIABLE FOR ANY INCIDENTAL, INDIRECT, SPECIAL, OR CONSEQUENTIAL DAMAGES ARISING OUT OF OR IN CONNECTION WITH THIS LICENSE OR THE SOFTWARE, INCLUDING FOR LOSS OF USE, LOSS OF DATA, LOSS OF INCOME OR PROFIT, OR OTHER LOSSES, SUSTAINED AS A RESULT OF INJURY TO ANY PERSON, OR LOSS OF OR DAMAGE TO PROPERTY, OR CLAIMS OF THIRD PARTIES, EVEN IF THE COMPANY OR AN AUTHORIZED REPRESENTATIVE OF THE COMPANY HAS BEEN ADVISED OF THE POSSIBILITY OF SUCH DAMAGES. IN NO EVENT SHALL THE LIABILITY OF THE COMPANY FOR DAMAGES WITH RESPECT TO THE SOFTWARE EXCEED THE AMOUNTS ACTUALLY PAID BY YOU, IF ANY, FOR THE SOFTWARE OR THE ACCOMPANYING TEXTBOOK. BECAUSE SOME JURISDICTIONS DO NOT ALLOW THE LIMITATION OF LIABILITY IN CERTAIN CIRCUMSTANCES, THE ABOVE LIMITATIONS MAY NOT ALWAYS APPLY TO YOU.

6. GENERAL: THIS AGREEMENT SHALL BE CONSTRUED IN ACCORDANCE WITH THE LAWS OF THE UNITED STATES OF AMERICA AND THE STATE OF NEW YORK, APPLICABLE TO CONTRACTS MADE IN NEW YORK, AND SHALL BENEFIT THE COMPANY, ITS AFFILIATES AND ASSIGNEES. THIS AGREEMENT IS THE COMPLETE AND EXCLUSIVE STATEMENT OF THE AGREEMENT BETWEEN YOU AND THE COMPANY AND SUPERSEDES ALL PROPOSALS OR PRIOR AGREEMENTS, ORAL, OR WRITTEN, AND ANY OTHER COMMUNICATIONS BETWEEN YOU AND THE COMPANY OR ANY REPRESENTATIVE OF THE COMPANY RELATING TO THE SUBJECT MATTER OF THIS AGREEMENT. If you are a U.S. Government user, this Software is licensed with "restricted rights" as set forth in subparagraphs (a)-(d) of the Commercial Computer-Restricted Rights clause at FAR 52.227-19 or in subparagraphs (c)(1)(ii) of the Rights in Technical Data and Computer Software clause at DFARS 252.227-7013, and similar clauses, as applicable.

Should you have any questions concerning this agreement or if you wish to contact the Company for any reason, please contact in writing: Legal Department, Prentice Hall, One Lake Street, Upper Saddle River, NJ 07458. If you need assistance with technical difficulties, call: 1-800-677-6337.